The Crystal Connection

The Crystal Connection

A Guidebook for Personal and Planetary Ascension

Randall N. Baer
and
Vicki Vittitow Baer

1817
Harper & Row, Publishers,
San Francisco

Cambridge, Hagerstown, New York, Philadelphia, Washington
London, Mexico City, São Paulo, Singapore, Sydney

THE CRYSTAL CONNECTION.

Printed in the United States of America.

For information address
Harper & Row, Publishers, Inc.,
10 East 53rd Street, New York, N.Y. 10022.
Published simultaneously in Canada
by Fitzhenry & Whiteside Limited, Toronto.

FIRST EDITION

Artist: Steve Swanson,
Paper Architecture,
Santa Fe, New Mexico
Designer: Brad Greene

Library of Congress Cataloging-in-Publication Data

Baer, Randall N.
The crystal connection.

Bibliography: p.
1. Crystal-gazing. I. Baer, Vicki Vittitow.
II. Title.
BF1331.B33 1986 133 86-45011
ISBN 0-06-250033-3

---

86 87 88 89 90 MPC 10 9 8 7 6 5 4 3 2 1

To the Merkabah of the Heavenly Host
and to H. W. A.

Seek ye first the Kingdom of God
and all these things
shall be added unto you.
—Matthew 6:33

Table of Contents

Acknowledgements xi

Preface xiii

Introduction xv

The Book of Knowledge: The Keys of Enoch Introduced by J. J. Hurtak xvii

Part I: Spiritual-Scientific Syntheses 1

Introduction to Part I 3

Chapter 1 Crystalline Wholeness: Facets of Infinitude 4

Chapter 2 The Universal Energy Network: A Threefold Intelligence Matrix 16

Chapter 3 Interdimensional Communication: Evolutionary Imperative 36

Chapter 4 Crystalline Essence: Axis and Form 55

Chapter 5 Unifying Spirit and Science: A New World Paradigm of Interdimensional Science... 66

Part II: Ascension-oriented Concepts, Tools, and Techniques ... 73

Introduction to Part II 75

Chapter 6 Crystal Basics 76

Chapter 7 Crystal Foundation 81

Chapter 8 Programming 119

Chapter 9 Reprogramming for the Ascension 141

Chapter 10 Mind-Center Activation 158

Chapter 11 Form Energy and Crystals.................................. 181

Chapter 12 The Pyramid-Crystal Synergy............................ 200

Chapter 13 Light-Tools: Wands, Breastplates, Pendants, Templates, and Discs 224

Chapter 14 Crystal Gridworks... 251

Chapter 15 Advanced Unified Energy Field Concepts 302

Chapter 16 Radionics and Crystals 327

Chapter 17 Healing with Crystals... 331

Chapter 18 The Human Biocrystalline Energy System 342

Chapter 19 Interdimensional Communication: Further Perspectives 351

Part III: Visions and Vistas **363**

Introduction to Part III 365

Chapter 20 Crystalline Windows: Visions of a New World.......... 366

Chapter 21 Vistas of Tomorrow 378

Notes.. 384

Bibliography.. 392

About the Authors 396

Acknowledgments

The authors wish to express their deepest gratitude to the Universal Intelligence that bestowed great blessings toward the creation of *The Crystal Connection.* It is hoped that this book will serve its purpose in helping to prepare the way for personal and planetary ascension.

Considerable acknowledgment is also due to *The Book of Knowledge: The Keys of Enoch,* by J.J. Hurtak, Ph.D., for the "keys" in that text catalyzed the opening of consciousness access channels necessary to the writing of this book. Though not exclusively so, *The Keys of Enoch* is foundational to significant portions of *The Crystal Connection*'s conceptual material.

In addition, Bruce Conway assisted in the design of several Light-tools, grid-works, and advanced unified energy fields.

We would also like to express our appreciation to our respective sets of parents for their abiding support.

Randall N. and Vicki V. Baer
Los Alamos, New Mexico

Preface

As the time quickens toward a monumental recrystallization of personal and planetary consciousness, higher Light stirs unto awakening as transcendence into a New World beckons. The crystalline codes of the greater Light-dimensions are becoming increasingly one with the crystallinity of the earth and receptive consciousness therein. As this unification sequence unfolds, acceleratory processes impel exponential paradigm transformations, both spiritual and scientific, of unparalleled proportions. The culmination of a megaevolutionary cycle draws to completion as the human biocrystalline energy system and the planetary energy network are to be transposed to higher dimensional octaves of Light within the Universal Mind. Herein lies humankind's divine heritage, the opportunity to ascend into vistas of grandeur undreamed, thereupon to evolve through the succeeding eon cycles as multidimensional consciousness expanding through the realms of freedom-in-Spirit.

The dramatic rise of popular awareness regarding the higher Light-properties of quartz crystals and other rarefied crystalline matrices is a catalyzing precursor to the accelerated development of new, more encompassing paradigms of both spiritual and scientific thought. Verging upon the precipice of awakening is a sweeping revolution of consciousness activation and spiritual-scientific synthesis. Crystals serve for many as keys to unlocking the access-windows of awareness to horizons of Light previously unimagined. Old boundaries dissolve as a new era of individual and collective en-Light-ening emerges through stage after quantum stage of metamorphic unfoldment. Crystal matrices amplify and transform the crystalline codes of consciousness, thereby serving to interconnect the personal and planetary spheres with the encoded crystallinity of the greater domains of Universal Light—this is the "crystal connection."

Introduction

Reality is crystalline in nature. Herein abides creation's most essential ordering principle. For all Light, all Life, all Intelligence is coded crystallinity. The overriding importance of the "crystal connection" is its universal interconnecting properties. The systematic coherence of all energy interactions throughout the cosmos depends upon the highly ordered communicative interlinkage of coded crystalline matrices. Fundamentally, this is how creation works. For Universal Intelligence functions upon code principles; like-code selectively interacts with like-code. This is how the Universal Mind creates and maintains its differentiated integrity as well as its holographic wholeness. Every part is selectively linked with other parts and the whole via the crystallinity principle. This preeminent principle functions as the codified multidimensional media through which Universal Intelligence operates.

Quartz crystals and other precious stones are matrixed means by which the crystalline codes of personal and planetary consciousness are connectively interlinked with the higher Light-dimensions in an amplified, coherent manner. Physical-plane crystals can be viewed as the materialized end of a broad interdimensional spectrum of crystalline matrices, originating on the higher planes of Thought and extending through the many celestial and cosmic octaves into the realms of materiality. Not only can quartz and other crystals function as energy amplifiers, transformers, capacitors, modifiers, and focusers within the boundaries of the earth's energy field, but also, more important, they serve as physical-plane link-up points with the next higher dimensional octave of universal crystallinity. And by so linking, selective access can be gained to the rest of the interdimensional spectrum-network of coded crystalline energy patterns, thereby establishing communicative interrelationality. This is the singular importance of the "crystal connection"—the megadimensionally spanning spectrum of interrelated, highly ordered, crystallinity to which access can be gained via crystalline code principles. Physical crystals are exceedingly helpful tools that assist the codes of individual consciousness to amplifiably interconnect with selective aspects of Universal Intelligence; they are, as well, central components of the Light-based tools and technologies integral to the manifestation of a multidimensionally oriented New World era.

The Crystal Connection is divided into three parts. Part I is a spiritual-scientific treatise concerning the Universal Energy Network (UEN), its origin, structure, and dynamics. Perspectives are shown regarding the nature of macroevolutionary soul growth sequences enacted in and through Alpha–Omega threshold zones of the UEN. Chapter 5, in particular, is a discourse regarding the unification of Spirit and science into a spiritually-oriented interdimensional science. As a whole, Part I is philosophical in nature, setting the overarching parameters from which Parts II and III flow. In Part II an integrated array of major topics are presented relating primarily to individual and collective preparation for the ascension and the further development and practical applications of interdimensional science. From mind-center activation and healing to crystal gridworks and advanced unified energy fields, a broad range of key subjects are covered in which multitudinous practical techniques, tools, designs, seed-ideas, and procedures are presented. Part II is primarily practical in nature, spanning from what can easily be done by any interested individual to sophisticated blueprint outlines for professional applications. Finally, Part III is visionary in scope, exploring expansive possibilities of a New World of unlimited, undreamed horizons. In all, *The Crystal Connection* helps lay the philosophical, conceptual, and practical foundations of a ground-breaking paradigm of interdimensional science, with special focus upon its key roles in preparing for the personal and planetary ascension process. The higher Light-properties and usages of quartz crystals are the centrally recurrent theme pervading the book. Material of considerable depth, sometimes quite technical in nature, is presented in this subject area as an integral function of laying the groundwork for the extensive and complex field of crystallographic sacred science.

The Crystal Connection is not based upon or limited to the domain of orthodox science. This will be clear after reading Chapter 5, where the marked distinctions between interdimensional science and orthodox science are explicated. Although various fundamentally universal scientific principles common to both domains are part of the book, their distinct divergences will be illustrated, both explicitly and implicitly, throughout the entire text.

The reader should be aware that numerous techniques, tools, designs, and procedures presented in Part II need to be approached with caution. Many of them, particularly those involving magnetics, lasers, advanced gridworks, and unified energy fields, are of such potential power that they should be engaged in only with knowledgeable discernment and personal responsibility.

Finally, *The Crystal Connection* is offered both as an integrated, holistic paradigm of knowledge and derived applications and as a seed-bed of ideas that may be selectively culled and integrated into other belief patterns as felt appropriate by each individual. The contents of this book may be taken as a whole or in discerned parts as it resonates truthfully within the reader. The authors sincerely hope that *The Crystal Connection* will serve to stimulate a new wave of the increasing of knowledge as well as innovative practical developments. May this text be a springboard from which each individual receives those "sparks of Light" that will catalyze his or her fullest Light-potential. In these times approaching the Omega point of personal and planetary ascension, may the People of Light shine like the brightness of the firmament.

The Book of Knowledge: The Keys of Enoch Introduced by J. J. Hurtak

The Book of Knowledge: The Keys of Enoch is a document of future science "in coded form." The Keys affirm that it is everyone's birthright to coevolve and cocreate within the laws that govern the universe and human development. They challenge the assumptions of orthodox spiritual and scientific thought by working through a nonlinear process of "metalanguage" and presenting a cosmic view that emphasizes process over structure, and consciousness evolution over material evolution.

Each Key, written on several levels of inner mental attunement—requiring musical and vibratory correspondences—is intended to provide some logistical and conceptual correlations pertinent to precise levels of cosmic oscillations that can be experienced in the material and nonmaterial realms. Human beings are functioning—at all times—simultaneously in the physical and the paraphysical.

The inner reaches of the human mind are endowed with powers and a versatile memory system that can break down sounds and thought-forms in their fundamental frequencies and then amplify them with speeds and tones via hundreds of microfrequency generating oscillators operating together. The wave forms are given new and powerful manifestations, all of which can be stored in human memory. In effect, the modern orchestra is obsolete when compared with the sound reaches of the human mind as biosynthesizer. Thus, the *Keys of Enoch* give us the understanding that there are radiations of thought-forms through which critical levels of information can be sent and received.

Some scholars felt when Clerk Maxwell brought together in a unified mathematical treatment the relationship between matter-forces and immaterial light waves (experiments confirmed by Heinrich Hertz and Nicola Tesla in the early 1880s), it seemed there was nothing left to argue about in the realm of science. However, in the vast breakthroughs in understanding the microstructure of intelligence in the latter part of the twentieth century, we are beginning to witness a mutation of the human race that can evolve our scientific consciousness beyond "space-binding" and "time-binding."

The "Keys" work to open the conceptual doors to the greater evolutionary design, from the biophysical to the astrophysical and spiritual frontiers of life.

Remember that analogies with the prevailing concepts of classical science were disregarded and even attacked in the first attempts to model atomic structure, the matter-energy postulates of de Broglie, and the quantum-corpuscular hypothesis of Planck and Einstein. It was only after such approachs had established their unity in representing the phenomena that the more earthshaking and self-consis-tant formalisms of Dirac, Schroedinger, and Heisenberg began to evolve.

The Keys were first experienced in real science (that is, external space) as multidimensional superluminal realities. The Keys were not channeled but were witnessed in the concreteness of their own respective dimensions and multileveled systems. The fire letters were given in pictographic forms of superluminal light so they could be seen and precisely written down.

The Keys are to function as ciphers for 64 areas of knowledge in the evolution of the human experience. For example, they reveal "specific areas," as well as whole "systems of correspondence" in such subjects as the language of the genetic code, archeological zones of earlier evolution on the planet earth, the artifacts of Mars, and the use of superluminal energy sources, and others. Much of this revealed blueprint was not understood by the scientific community in the early 1970s when the Keys were given. Now, however, we have witnessed the evolution of these concepts and seen the confirmation of much of this unique information within a larger picture of consciousness and physics.

The emphasis of *The Keys of Enoch* is on the new direction of humankind's innovations through which the new sciences, research, and development of con-sciousness can unify humankind with other parts of creation of which it is not always conscious, yet are within it and surrounding it. In coevolution with other physical, mental, and spiritual potentials, the veils of ignorance are lifted by higher consciousness, which leads to interaction with greater families of intelligence in the universe who share the same higher evolution.

No longer will there be triumphs of materialistic science at the expense of consciousness and spiritual domains; there will be, instead, a unique interconnec-tion with the continuous transformation of form. We must realize that humankind is no longer of the old nature—subspecies *aeternitatis*—but already participating in supernature, recognizing that creation by pure thought is God and, as creation expands, this pure thought cascades and models itself on the metadesign of the universe. In effect, there is a "blueprint" given of how the discovery and re-creative power of pure thought ultimately comes into being by Ultimate Human.

As we work together, let us realize that our destiny depends on faith growing in the integrity and indwelling power of the Human–God partnership and the Spirit of creativity which rules over it. Let an active faith in a positive future bring forth creativity of the divine within the human and may the Keys open the door to a new human community—in the Spirit of the Highest—and show us that we as its representatives have an active role in the redesign of the universe.

J. J. Hurtak, Ph.D.
Academy for Future Science
Los Gatos, California

PART I
Spiritual-Scientific Syntheses

This book deals with the experimental nature of quartz crystals and the sacred sciences, but it is in no way intended to replace medical care. Please consult your physician or health care professional before trying any of the recommendations in this book.

INTRODUCTION TO PART I

Crystallinity is the code of creation. The foundational essence and structure of all manifestation is its crystalline ordering, which spans all of existence, from the subatomic microcosmic levels to the megadimensional macrocosmic levels of reality. The precise exactitude of essence and form inherent in each energetic unit throughout the Universal Mind derives from, and is sustained by, causal code-patterns of Light. These code patterns of Intelligence precipitate as crystallization structures as they are extended into the expanses of creation, therein functioning as templates of highly ordered stability through which their imprinted Light-blueprint is enacted in manifestation. The entire omniverse is founded and sustained by a network of interdimensionally interrconnected crystalline code-patterns that function as the fundamental coordinating blueprints for all vibrational interactions throughout the Universal Mind. This all-encompassing network is termed the Universal Energy Network (UEN)

Part I of *The Crystal Connection* is an in-depth exploration of the elegantly complex structure and inner workings of the UEN. From the heights of Number-based Abstract Light to the depths of material-plane crystallization, Universal Intelligence functions within the highly ordered principles of divine Law. This Law is the keystone of Light-in-creation and the spiritual-scientific understanding of creation's many-dimensioned dynamics. Part I approaches spiritual knowledge from a scientific-philosophic orientation. The realms of Spirit and science unite within the revolutionary paradigm of interdimensional science, the ramifications of which open new horizons of research and development, many of which are explored in Part II. The sacred principles intrinsic to all reality are the basis for every facet of interdimensional science. Therein, the crystalline codes of the cosmos are decoded and established as the "indices and measures" of a New World science, and the boundaries that have kept the earth plane limited to a minute spectrum of universal realities for so long are breached and illimitable multidimensional potentialities are activated as ascension into the Kingdom of Light is fulfilled.

The reader may find the material in Part I (and in some sections of Part II) to be quite complex, for it is written on many levels of spiritual-intellectual understanding and assumes a base of knowledge concerning fundamental energy dynamics principles. A book recommended as a complementary source of knowledge is Itzhak Bentov's *Stalking the Wild Pendulum: On the Mechanics of Consciousness.* Further, repeated readings of Part I at various intervals of time may facilitate the assimilation of progressively deeper levels of comprehension. Certain phrases and key ideas may function as coded seed-thoughts and catalysts for activating higher Light thought processes and energy processes in consciousness; therefore, read between the lines also, using the intuitive-mental planes of awareness to perceive the greater Light-realities that the text depicts within the somewhat limitingly linear confines of an earth-based language system.

Enjoy the rarefied reaches of the Universal Mind's multifaceted complexity and elegant grandeur. . . .

CHAPTER 1

Crystalline Wholeness: Facets of Infinitude

Wholeness infuses the infinite facets of creation with crystalline perfection. The Creative Word encompasses the supraholographic diversification of manifestation; the One is the source of All and All mirrors the wholeness of the One. Oscillatory reality bears the imprint of the metaoscillatory Absolute within the core blueprint of each and every vibratory unit throughout the expanses of infinitude. The crystal connection is the Oneness transformed into the numerological-geometrical differentiation of the Word made manifest.

ONENESS: A TREATISE

Beyond the awesome complexities of infinitely diversified Oneness lies the paradoxical simplicity of the Absolute One. Within the Creative Breath of the One is the all-encompassing blueprint of wholeness—the supraholographic unity of one Breath, one Energy . . . One. There is naught but One—one Electron is all electrons, one Human is all humans, one Galaxy is all galaxies, one God is All That Is . . . I AM THAT I AM.

One made unifiedly polar is Two. Harmonious "opposition" is the necessary prerequisite for the Word to be made manifest. The principle of opposition creates a polar tension for vibration to occur. For vibration requires polar opposites to set the parameters of oscillation. Without such parameters, singularity remains single; creation remains *in potentia.* One becomes Two, thereby setting the metaoscillatory waters of the Infinite Void in motion. An omnipresent singularity point divides into infinite poles of unified opposition. Polarization yields separation of unified potential into equal and opposite poles that must maintain that force of oscillatory opposition in order to remain manifest.

At the same time, Oneness is immanent in polarity and works in and through this diversification as the driving ontological factor intrinsic to the principium of manifest creation. Twoness is a necessary vehicle through which Oneness must flow; it is the gateway for the metaoscillatory to become oscillatory. Should the oscillatory state cease, resumption of metaoscillatory status inevitably occurs, for the opposition necessary for the manifest condition dissolves back into the unmanifest potentiality. Therefore, the unified state of Oneness, while being the ultimately superseding unmanifest Source of All, manifests itself into a unified state of Twoness as an integral and necessary expression of creative wholeness.

Wholeness-of-Two is no less real or consequential than Wholeness-in-One, for the former is the requisite pathway of creative physics that is no less than the first numerological Image of the One. One begets Two in the Image of the One; thereupon the Two mirrors the Image of the Absolute throughout the numberless polarized facets of infinitude.

Twoness begets Threeness in the Image of the One. The physics of dual polarization undergoes a matrix transformation into a physics of trinitized polarization. Trinity rests upon the *mater* of duality, bringing forth countless diversification potentials that were previously nonexistent. The coordinates of creation now become numerologically outlined as omni-trinitization crystallization principles "map" the deeps of the Void. Three in the Image of One is matrixed wholeness in the Image of Three; potential becomes "faceted" coalescence.

One and Two and Three beget Four. From the combined radical matrix transformation of One-Two-Three (and Three-Two-One) springs the principle of unlimited differentiation throughout all possible dimensional matrix vectors—Fourness. As stated in the *Tao te Ching,* "From the Four springs the 10,000 things." The One-Two-Three-Four matrix union is the foundational keystone transformation of all potential angular dimensional vectors. The Creative Breath flows through this abstract Number matrix, thus imparting the foundational physics Law-codes of Intelligence interrelationships with infinite possible multidimensional combinations and permutations. This echoes the ancient Pythagorean principle: "Everything is arranged according to Number." Interestingly, *rhythmos* and *arithmos* have the same root—*rhein*—meaning "to flow." And so it is that the Divine Breath flowing through this Fourfold matrix imparts coded oscillatory rhythmic vectors that then determine the numeric-geometric matrices of faceted infinitude.

Beyond Fourness lies the primary numerological spectrum of crystallization principles—Fiveness, Sixness, Sevenness, and so on—that establish the myriad intricacies of One-in-Creation and Creation-in-One.

Thus, Number constitutes the apexial font and eternally dynamizing matrix principiums of the Absolute creatively crystallized. The Image of the One creates endless diversification patterns of Intelligence development through selective alignment of numerological matrix spectrums, thereby transforming One Image into Infinite Images, all mirroring absolute wholeness. The crystallization patterning principles and axis avenues of limitless intercommunication of the crystal connection maintain the Absolute Image of Wholeness-in-All and the Wholeness of all Images in the Eye of the One.

The Universal Energy Network: Crystalline Ordering

The creative Logic of Universal Intelligence is inscribed within the codes of crystallinity. From the microcosmic to the macrocosmic levels of universal energy patterns, crystalline principles pervade the causal codes that serve to originate, maintain, and transform creation's blueprints with mathematical exactitude. With numerological-geometrical efficiency, the Light is processed through countless multidimensional planes, each with precise energy spectrum indexes requiring that divine order be maintained with exacting accuracy. Throughout the vast complexities of this universal "engineering" process, the principles and forms of crystallinity enact a wide variety of key functions, from blueprints and code-matrices to templates and timepieces.

The concept of crystallinity must be clarified into two overlapping but significantly different domains. The first involves abstract numerological perspectives and the second concerns geometrized Number and its relationship to universal energy flow.

Abstract crystallinity encompasses rarefied principles of the highest order. In the most exalted realms of the Universal Mind, abstracted Intelligence principles are the sole reality. Pure Number interacts as formless matrices of ordered qualitative principles. Oneness begets Twoness, Twoness transforms into Threeness, Threeness steps down to Fourness . . . this is the supernal fabric of the highest of celestial crystalline domains. The abstract architectural blueprints of manifestation are formulated herein, containing in their formless numerological matrices the seed-vectors of wholeness that are transduced into the forms and patterns of the realms below.

These abstract crystalline domains are the forebears and ongoing archetypal blueprints of the myriad interdimensional levels of *crystalline form.* As the abstract crystalline matrix-codes are transduced into the thresholds of rarefied form, Abstract Light precipitates into energy patterns of more defined characteristics. From these first dimensional planes of Number-based geometric crystallization, there are then innumerable transformations through the interdimensional spectrums via matrix symmetry transpositions, each spectrum level crystallization code corresponding to predetermined dimension parameters. That is, the geometric code-pattern is sequentially crystallized through layer after multi-dimensional layer of reality. At each layer the geometric code-pattern crystallizes in a manner that corresponds to both the originating Number-based code and the specific dimensional parameters of a given level. In each dimensional plane the archetypal energy pattern is an interdimensional variation of the primary, originating Theme.

Throughout the process of multidimensional crystalline transformations, the crucial factors of interdimensional coherence and symmetrical connectedness are established. One of the key characteristics of crystallinity is the stable mathematical-geometrical orderliness that is maintained with extreme precision. The capacity to form and hold steady a matrix within which intradimensional and interdimensional energy dynamics can interact is one of the most fundamental aspects of the crystal connection. Sequential series of crystallization patterns form interdimensionally connected energy pathways that span the expanse of the depths and heights of manifestation. Indeed, it is the resultant Universal Energy Network (UEN) that serves as ordered pathways for all spectrums of universal energy flow.

Universally, energy follows exact laws of interdimensional physics. These laws are based upon quantum harmonic theory which, in the present context, exemplifies that all energy exists on quantum levels at harmonically interrelated energetic domains. The UEN, in this way, crystallizes its symmetrically corresponding energy-code matrices at quantum harmonic domain levels. This concept parallels and encompasses the well-known atomic quantum orbital shell paradigm. On the more macrocosmic as well as microcosmic levels, the UEN forms exceptionally stable interrelated quantum matrix transformation patterns. This state of affairs lends itself, with exquisite elegance, to innumerable applications relating to intradimensional and interdimensional code-formulating, code-transforming, code-stabilizing, and code-storing functions.

Viewing the UEN as a whole, then, it can be seen that Oneness undergoes abstract Number matrix formulations at the highest levels of Abstract Light. Then Number-based geometries precipitate and the energy transformation process continues throughout the vast harmonically sequential levels of multidimensional reality. Crystallization patterns form abiding, symmetrically related, interdimensional matrix transformation pathways. These pathways then form a primary crystalline-coded Intelligence matrix that spans the heights and depths of creation and functions primarily as megamatrix code stabilizer-transformers and intercommunication effectors.

Herein lies the monumental importance of the UEN. The task of maintaining, monitoring, modifying, and transforming every unit of Intelligence throughout manifestation is indeed a massive one. From a higher perspective, all of reality can be seen to be a code process: *All is code.* Each unit and domain level of Intelligence originates as, is maintained by, and evolves through interdimensionally interconnected code processing. The human level of Intelligence, for example, utilizes the DNA-RNA complex, and the higher dimensional correlates thereof, as one of the most fundamental interdimensional coordinative intercommunicative blueprints of divine Image extension and modifiable interlinkage.

The primary aspects of this concept are the vision and understanding of every unit and form of Intelligence throughout the omniverse as an interdimensionally interconnected Thought-form originating on the highest levels of Light and transformed through innumerable vibratory domains. This originating Thought-form has a directly corresponding code-pattern that is precisely and harmonically transduced within the full extent of the UEN. The resultant interlinked blueprint crystallization codes are, then, the very core media of communication of all universal energy interactions.

Such an omnifold Universal Intelligence is indeed awesome to behold. Universal Law manifests as mathematical majesty and geometric glory. Mind within mind, Membrane within membrane, Geometry within geometry, the One facets into Infinity. Endlessly, effortlessly, the Creative Breath spirals into grander, more glorious spheres and fields of diversification encompassed within one ever-expanding omnipresent, omnipotent, omniscient Universal Mind.

The Crystal Connection: Thought-architecture of the Eternal

The Universal Mind imprints functions of the Eternal Image into the UEN. *The Keys of Enoch* states: "He is beyond all universes, and yet all universes function collective as the brain diagram of the higher order of Creation."[1] It is the function of the UEN to form the parameters of Image crystallizing into creation. It forms the axes of creative differentiation and maintains them continuously so that the Images originating from the Eternal may be sustained and modifiably ordered amidst the flux of oscillatory reality.

A hierarchical systemization transduces Light from dimension to dimension through the Thought-circuitry of myriad dimensional levels. A basic outline of these levels is thus: (1) Numeric Abstract Light ultramatrices crystallize to (2) the Merkabah of the Heavenly Host that code to (3) Light-templates of the higher celestial planes that transduce to (4) celestial template recorder cells of the lower celestial planes that transpose to (5) template recorder cells of the greater cosmic domains that further differentiate into (6) etheric crystals, that then precipitate into (7) crystals of rarefied matter (that is, physical plane crystals).

Fundamentally, levels one through seven of the UEN are progressive energy code step-down transformations. The ultimately foundational Abstract Light-codes of level one are systematically extended into the multidimensional differentiation of the UEN, levels two though seven functioning as transduction enacters of crystallization codes to discrete domain levels.* Essentially, all Light-functions enacted within the Infinite Mind are variously phased synaptic interactions of the Universal Thought-circuitry.

> Seen from the perspective of the Higher Evolution, life upon this planetary orb is a radiated series of biological events primarily lattice-like in nature. Through the crystalline lattice, the Higher Evolution controls the various biological kingdoms by organizing inter-gravitational and interradiational effects of lattice merging with lattice.[2]

Images of the Eternal (level one), when extended throughout levels two through seven evolve via Alpha-Omega code program sequences. Abstract Images lie in the eternity domains of Light wherein blueprints of wholeness are formulated. An entire evolutionary cycle-sequence is immanent within such Images, similar to the acorn containing the entire life cycle sequence coding in seed form. An Image of wholeness uses the medium of supradimensional unfoldment on the higher levels of Light and the medium of dimensionalized time-space in the lower realms as the fundamental polarized infrastructure through which an Image *in potentia* becomes an actualized image unfolding in creation. When projected into multidimensional crystallization, the Image remains at the Abstract Light level while simultaneously enacting myriad dimension-specific Alpha-Omega cycles in the UEN; each Image is a vast scenario abstract of a Light-cycle sequencing pattern. Through predetermined facets of the UEN, each primary Image is dispatched into the depths of creation, there to undergo multidimensional teleological unfoldments via Alpha–Omega cycles.

Looking further into this process, each Abstract level one Image differentiates into myriad Parent Images that abide within level two—the Merkabah Light-Unity Level. Parent Images are yet of the grandest of orders of hierarchical ordering and contain scenario abstraction-coding sequences for numberless facets of Infinite Intelligence. These Parent Images further crystallize and diversify down to the next major domainship level—the Light-templates of the higher celestial planes (level three) wherein the Parent Image starts to form a "family grouping" of resonantly related scenario abstracts of Light-functions. These family groupings continue to differentiate according to predetermined codings (derived from level one) in and through each of the fourth to seventh levels of the UEN. One Image becomes myriad resonantly ordered images, and the numerological-geometrical faceting of creation provides the omniopposition necessary to diversify endlessly through family groupings within family grouping within family grouping.

Mind within mind, Image within image, Matrix within matrix, Geometry within

*Each of the seven levels will be further explicated in Chapter 2.

geometry, Consciousness Cell within consciousness cell, Universe within universe, Membrane within membrane . . . *Ehyeh Asher Ehyeh.*

Infinity Within Singularity: Omniholographic Harmony

> We live in a Many and One universe . . . And when you see the many as well as the one, you recognize that the most perfect plurality is also the most perfect unity.[3]

Energy flow throughout the UEN is not simply a linear transduction process from higher dimensions to lower dimensions: rather, the energy flow is diametrically regenerative. This is to say that universal vibrations emanate from the One to the Many and the Many flow back to the One, thereby being sustained and regenerated from micromoment to micromoment, millenia to millenia, Breath to Breath. Energy flow is cyclic in nature (from micro- to macrolevels), and when an antipodal point is reached, a singular "still point" expands to encompass the All with infinite speed.

In *Space-Time and Beyond,* physicists Bob Toben and Fred Alan Wolf assert in this regard that:

> Information transmits through the wormholes at ordinary speeds (which appear to be faster than the speed of light for observers outside the wormholes), connecting all points in space with all others in an indefinite number of possible patterns, constantly changing, and turning on and off at incredible frequencies up to 10^{43} times per second!"[4]

From micromoment to micromoment the Many flash through an infinity asymptote to One; and then with the same flash of omnipresent speed the One is the Many. This is the grand paradox of the mystics and sages—an essence with an infinitely fast velocity infuses into an infinite number of infinitely small points throughout an infinite amount of space in an infinitely short period of time. An omnipresent One enfolds into all singularity points in creation such that it is at any given point and simultaneously in every other point in zero time. The One is Many and the Many are One at the same time . . . zero time. A dimensionless One is immanently mirrored within infinite dimensions—omnipresently, omnisciently, omnipotently.

The eternal instantaneous alteration between singularity and infinity enfolds the facets of infinitude with synchrosimilar similitude. It provides a model for understanding the omniholographic mirroring of One Image within many images. At the "zero moment" of singularity-infinity interconversion, all images unify into One Image. At the converse zero moment, One Image crystallizes all images, stepping the images down through the UEN through image family after image family into infinitude. This step-down process cannot be viewed strictly as a linearly sequential procedure (that is, level one steps down to level two, two to three, three to four, and so on.) More precisely, this process can be viewed as being an instantaneous omniholographic synchrosimilar mirroring throughout the harmonically resonant facets of the UEN.

Understanding the omniholographic nature of Universal Intelligence is essential in comprehending the immanent hierarchical matrix structure of reality. In present-day holographic theory, theoretically every single point in a hologram contains the information of the whole. By breaking a hologram into pieces and then shining a laser beam through any given piece, the entire holographic image is reconstructed. Omniholographic theory supersedes the relatively linear orthodox holographic theory by incorporating multidimensional hierarchical matrix perspectives. It would be possible to break a theoretical multidimensionally encoded hologram into pieces and reconstruct any single dimensional hologram via a reconstruction beam of a specifically corresponding universal constant (that is, the lowest/highest common denominator frequency for a given dimensional plane). The entire hologram could be reconstructed via the universal constant of the highest dimensional level of the hologram, a universal constant that encompasses the constants of all the lower corresponding dimensions.

Omniholographic theory rests upon the foundation of multidimensional matrix theory. This concept is one in which a series of dimensional domainship levels establish a hierarchical symmetry transformation relationship. Each domainship level is inclusive of the others below it in the hierarchical spectrum *and* exists on a higher, more encompassing dimensional level of order. For instance, matrix one (say, a cell domain) is encompassed and exceeded in domainship complexity by matrix two (say, a tissue of which the cell is a part), and so too is matrix three (for example, an organ of which the matrix two tissue is a part) in relationship to matrix two; this progression continues with matrix four (for example, a body system—say, the circulatory system), matrix five (for example, physical body functions as a whole), matrix six (etheric body functions), continuing via quantum domain levels to the highest levels of Light. From this example it can be seen that each matrix level has an integral, orderly relationship with all other matrices; they all function as coordinating parts of the synergistic whole (the synergistic whole being the highest possible matrix level). In addition, a higher matrix level *includes* all lower matrix levels *and* encompasses a more highly evolved level of universal order.

This matrix transform theory is integral to omniholographic theory. Each dimensional/domainship stratum throughout creation exists within a spectrum of hierarchical matrix levels, each higher dimensional zone being inclusive of and more encompassing of Universal Intelligence than the dimensions below. Also in keeping with matrix theory, the various coded crystallization levels throughout the UEN have directly symmetrical intra- and interdimensional correspondence relationships. In fact, these coded crystallization zones *are* supraholographic matrix-code transform zones. It is in and through these matrix zones that Light is supraholographically encoded for precise parameters of hierarchical manifestation and interdimensional interconnectedness.

Omniholographic theory requires explication as to the nature of the "reconstruction beam" that serves as the constant with which the "working beam" intermeshes to form a "hologram." The key here lies with foundational universal constants that are as quantum fundamental harmonics for the myriad vibrational intervals and octaves that crystallize within dimensional parameters. These universal "common denominators" are equationally specific to any given dimensional zone and also have hierarchical matrix interrelationships between themselves. Simply put, to manifest the holographic energy field whose codes are held steady in a given UEN matrix zone, the corresponding universal constant frequency is "shone" through the coded crystalline matrix, which then produces the multidimensional hologram code-pattern. Many variations on this theme may be precisely actuated by modulating various combinations and permutations of the numberless harmonic intervals and octaves of the fundamental universal constant. To actuate the fundamental universal constant on the highest matrix levels of Abstract Light is to set in motion an interdimensional harmonic resonance effect reverberating through the matrixed facets of the UEN's infinitude. The universal constant of each dimensional level vibrates in resonant response to the "sounding" of the fundamental harmonic constant of the Abstract Light-matrix. From matrix to matrix, the supraholographic codes of each octave of the UEN resound with universal symphonics as synchrosimilar Image groupings reverberate in synergistic omniholographic concord.

Here is yet another facet of the Oneness of creation—the supraholographic harmonics of the Heavens is transformed through the UEN into countless facetings of wholeness in which Image within image consists of matrix-transform holograms, each enfolded within the other, each a minutely sensitive harmonic whole within a whole.

Omniholographic omnipresence, infusing singularity throughout infinite plurality at each and every zero moment of manifest creation, *is* the verity that: one Electron is all electrons, one Human is all humans, one Galaxy is all galaxies, one omniholographic God is All That Is . . . I AM THAT I AM.

THE WHOLENESS OF HUMANKIND: ALPHA–OMEGA CYCLES OF ETERNITY

> So God created man in his own image, in the image of God he created him. (Genesis 1:27)

Humankind interfaces with the UEN in great Glory. Throughout the cycles of eternity, the archetypal human genetic Image has been seeded within innumerable facets of the Universal Mind, thereby enriching the myriad creative facetings of this divine Image-form. The archetypal Human originated and is seated within the causal realms of the Heavens. This primary Image-form of the One serves as the "weights and measures" for creatively diversifying this archetypal Thought-pattern within the many mansion worlds and galaxies. The Mind of the archetypal Human projects untold blueprint Thought-Images to be processed through the UEN to their appointed universal spectrum worlds, thereafter enacting Alpha–Omega cycles of creative service and evolutionary enrichment.

> Adamic Man was created simultaneously in the heavens and transposed along energy grids into physical embodiment from a divine form which he is to return to after this exploration of consciousness.[5]

The primary Face-form (Image) and genetic Light-codes of the archetypal Human are utilized as a type of grand celestial template through which Abstract Light flows, thereby imprinting the codes of the Human in a conjoining with the blueprints of Alpha–Omega evolutionary cycles, to then be dispatched into creative enfoldment. The Human originates as Light crystallized from the Abstract realms and created as a Light-form Intelligence-matrix that goes forth from the higher Heavens and further diversifies the seed codes of the Human in countlessly creative ways to en-Light-en manifestation, thereby glorifying the One. The Human is a Light-vehicle through which the Eternal is made host unto the endless evolutionary pathways of enrichment.

The supreme archetypal Image of the Human diversifies into a next level of primary Images, also seen as Face-forms serving as varied and related Image-patterns that function as further step-down templates. This process further differentiates in other celestial realms. Vast fields of Human Intelligence domains are as grand stars emitting awesome fields of genetic-Image patterns, all being dispatched along proper astrophysics templates and grids of the UEN. The genetic-Image patterns are in-built with the entire blueprint of evolutionary unfoldment for a grand Alpha–Omega cycle. These patterns are processed through the appropriate interdimensional energy meridians and threshold matrix zones with great mathematical-geometrical precision, matching the matrix-code patterning of a given genetic-Image pattern to its assigned matrix domain of development. As the Light-code Image enters its assigned matrix domain it is processed through various threshold levels as the human Self is synchronized with unique rhythm codes of the domain and then further processed to the individual-specific evolutionary circumstances. Some of the threshold levels to which the Self is synchronized include corresponding star seed-fields, galactic threshold rhythm patterns, universe-specific code membranes, planetary gridwork timepieces and incarnation grids, and genetic patterning tables specific to body-vehicle incarnation spectrums. The heavenly Code is seeded into celestial and star fields of growth, there to enact scenarios that partake of and advance the overall Light-indexes of that threshold's Intelligence-field.

This process of Human Image creation-seeding manifests a network of multidimensionally interrelated Image-bodies or Light-Bodies. As the primary Face-forms of the Human are dispatched through the celestial schematic Mind-circuitry into the mansion worlds and cosmic domains, an interdimensionally continuous network of Light-bodies is created and sustained. At primary threshold domains along the matrix-meridians of incarnation through the UEN, an Image is encoded into the specific spectrum boundaries, and an Alpha–Omega program is set in motion while further projections of the primary Image continue to the next major threshold matrix. There the same process occurs, except the spectrum parameter codings will correspond to a different matrix zone. One can envision endless projections of the original Face-form creating a vast multidimensional network of Light-bodies, all forming a grand interdimensional Intelligence-matrix of Light-transformations. Thus: "Man is a thinking membrane between star fields."[6] Like a branching tree, the Higher Self of individual and soul-group consciousness extends into the far reaches of celestial and intergalactic star fields, manifesting a spectrum-continuous interdimensionally interconnected "thinking membrane" spanning unimaginable expanses. Each individual Light-body is omniholographically linked to the entire multidimensional network of Light-bodies and functions as a single cell to a whole body, a brain cell within an encompassing Mind. The enactment of abstract scenario events within this multidimensional Intelligence-matrix takes on new light as synchrosimilarly related facets of a primary scenario unfold as a vast interdimensionally connected panorama of Light-transformations.

The primary functions of the Human-in-creation are twofold: first, to be a vehicle through which Light is infused to higher degrees into star systems, galactic-universal systems, planetary systems, biome systems, and so on. In this way more advanced Light-functions are infused into sectors of creation. Thus one can see that: "The people of Light are the vessels of Light in which the galactic intelligence programs itself into every biochemical unit in the human body."[7] From this perspective, Light-bodies are vehicles through which manifestation is enriched and brought to higher planes of Glory. The People of Light serve as Light-bearers of the One. The second function of the Human-in-creation is that the multidimensional Light-body matrix is evolutionarily enriched by incarnating within threshold sectors of the Universal Mind in which the abiding Light-codes and enacting Alpha–Omega program help to transform the Light-body matrix to higher levels of soul growth. Threshold matrix codes flow through the Light-body matrix, facilitating an ingathering of higher Light-energies into the Light-body(ies). From another perspective, the matrix "weave" (that is, crystallographic axes-codes) of the threshold zone interfaces in and through the matrix weave (that is, consciousness codes) of the multidimensional Light-body, transforming the latter to a higher degree of evolutionary encompassment and associated soul growth.

> Man was made to grow into the image of the Living Light, to become the Adam Kadmon who is capable of chemically generating an infinite number of spatial forms.
>
> The key stresses the human creation as one of the repeating units in a state of being purified between star fields.[8]

The principle "Serve the Light and in serving, be served" is one of the most essential, abiding universal foundational Laws. Encoded within the very highest celestial Tablets of Light, it forms a fundamental Law of interdimensional physics.

ALPHA–OMEGA CYCLE COMPLETION: PROGRAM ASCENSION IS ACTIVATED

Grand evolutionary cycles have a beginning—Alpha—and an end—Omega. Each is a seed-blueprint of wholeness. The Alpha point is the seed of wholeness containing the blueprint of unfoldment for an entire megaevolutionary cycle. The Alpha, until activated into polarized unfoldment, remains *in potentia.* When actuated, Alpha serves as the central coded timepiece that activates the progressive enactment of the evolutionary blueprint in proper form, energy, and time sequencing. The Omega, on the other hand, is the seed of wholeness containing the blueprint for the ending of an evolutionary cycle as Intelligence of all orders is prepared for an ascension into a new Alpha program on a higher Light-dimension or other levels of soul reapportionment in other commensurate Alpha programs.

For millennia upon millennia, Alpha–Omega Intelligence-programs manifest their coded scenarios in grand synchronized synergy. Upon approaching an Omega point of consciousness reprogramming, a process of Intelligence acceleration takes place in which final stages of evolutionary advancement opportunities are made available in preparation for the Omega weighing and measuring of individual and collective indexes of consciousness progression. As Omega is reached, a radical transformation-reapportionment procedure is activated. In direct correlation to the degree of evolutionary advancement, stasis, or regression, consciousness is processed through the UEN to an appropriately corresponding new Alpha–Omega cycle in direct accordance with divine Law.

Each atom of energy-matter and unit of Intelligence, from micro- to macrolevels, within a given cosmic or celestial threshold zone flows through this reapportionment sequence. Entire universes are reprogrammed and relocated within new astrophysical and celestial threshold zones. Entire civilizations and planetary systems as well as each individual entity experience this quantum transformational process with chosen degrees of cooperation. Even matter itself as well as the myriad spectrums of energy-matter and pure-energy emissions receive a grand ingathering of Light thereupon transposing to a higher orbital level of the Universal Mind.

> During the present space-time overlap, there will be the passing of one energy universe within another as our planetary mind crosses the present electromagnetic density threshold and is raised to the next electromagnetic orbit of the Universal Mind. At this point, we as sons of Man become the Sons of Light and transplant our consciousness Light into other regions of our local universe.[9]

During the time of Omega reprogramming, a higher order of Light is infused throughout the entire threshold zone's matrix, causing qualifying intelligence indexes to ingather Light to such a degree that consciousness "leaps" to the next orbital valence of Light. This is the ascension—the quantum consciousness exodus from one dimensional domain to another domain of higher Light-matrix codings—providing more exalted evolutionary growth opportunities in a newly set Alpha–Omega threshold zone.

For humankind, the ascension provides a pathway to a multitude of greater cosmic and celestial mansion worlds in the Kingdom of Heaven. Receptive consciousness activates and aligns into higher spheres of unified interconnectedness with the Higher Self. An individual entitity on earth is but one single projection of Light within a manifold multidimensional Light-body network. Such an entity, upon ascending, unifies on a higher "orbital shell level" of the Light-body within a given Alpha–Omega threshold and ascends to higher Light-fields of evolutionary advancement. The individual entity rises from the earthbound dimensions of lower, constrictive energy-matter spectrums as the earthly self transmutes into a greater ultrastructure of Light-wholeness, a grander freedom-in-Light.

> Thus, those who believe in the Father's Will and desire to work with the Brotherhood are those who will feel tremendous energy changes in their bodies, for they are being chemically respatialized to live in a more active Light environment.
>
> No longer will it be said "The spirit is willing but the flesh is weak" for the flesh and the spirit will be in one highly charged body of Light.[10]

It is the Merkabah vehicle of Higher Evolutionary Intelligence that monitors and enacts the ascension scenario-program with cyclic megadimensional precision.

> Merkabah is a sovereignty of Light moving over the waters of creation in oneness with the Eternal God; it is the image of holiness formed in the air and the Light materialization of the spoken word.
>
> . . . Merkabah is the vehicle of communication used by the Command of the Hosts.
>
> . . . We can see how Merkabah can spiral through the inner chemical lattice of planetary programming so as to attune the species to central growth cycles, or speed through star systems and connect a lattice of stellar growth with parent

> universes or super-universes in different dimensions which can aid the evolutionary intelligence.[11]

The all-encompassing overfunctioning of the Merkabah Host Intelligence provides the "capstone" of Higher Evolutionary Light interfacing with the "cornerstone" of an Alpha–Omega program of wholeness, therein enacting the fusion of Light into light, Mind into mind, Wholeness into wholeness.

> At that time, the People of God will rise to the heavens and shine like the brightness of the firmament; this is the Glory, the Love, and the Message for the People of God.[12]

CHAPTER 2

The Universal Energy Network: A Threefold Intelligence Matrix

The illimitable vastness of the Universal Energy Network (UEN) is the megamatrix for enacting the functions of the Eternal's Thought patterns into multidimensional supraholographically synchrosimilar unfoldments through Alpha–Omega cycles. Thought is circuited throughout the synapses of the Universal Mind. The UEN is that circuitry, serving to form dimensions and domains of intelligence-functions coalescing, interacting, and glorifying in exact accordance with inter- and intradimensional equational parameters. Intelligence crystallizes at dimension-specific universal levels, units of Thought of a resonantly like nature pooling together in a highly ordered manner to enact the blueprints of their Abstract Light-origin. The UEN has three primary functions in this regard. The first function is to form the dimensionally differentiated latticework in which discrete Intelligence-patterns may enact their functions within bounded parameters, therefore enabling them to interact within zones of energetic integrity and nonharmonic interference. The second function is to maintain dimensional interrelatedness within their predetermined patterns of supraholographic ordering, thereby keeping every level of the UEN aligned with their originating Abstract Blueprint and, therefore, with each other. The third function is to provide a network of interactions that not only acts as a universal communications medium but also as the coded matrix through which such interactions are continuously maintained, modulated, and accessed. In all, the UEN is the all-encompassing Intelligence-matrix in which and through which the Eternal "breathes" the One and Many.

The foundation of the UEN is threefold in nature, consisting of DNA Light-Life codes, a pictographic Language of Light, and the crystallographic component. Their complementary interweaving forms the multi-faceted crystalline codes of creation. Each one interacts with the other with complex and symmetrical synchronization. Each has principles and properties distinct from the others, yet there is also a fundamental core of harmonic commonality. Together they function as the core-code of creation, the primary patterning agent for Abstract Intelligence transposed into the multifold intelligence-codings of manifestation.

THE PICTOGRAPHIC UNIVERSAL LANGUAGE OF LIGHT

The *pictographic Universal Language of Light* bears the imprint of Abstract Thought transduced into abstract geometric interference patterns. This type of universal coding is highly active in nature, serving as a primary medium by which Thought is "fired" into the UEN and remains therein as a membrane-formulating, -maintaining, and -modifying intelligence-modality. Its conjunctive aspect is as a fundamental universal "alphabet" of singular and integratable constants of intercommunication. The highly active quality of these pictographic hieroglyphs makes them particularly predisposed to thought-pattern exchange and interaction via telethought communication (in all its many forms and functions).

Each pictograph, also called a flame letter, encapsulates vast orders of Thought in its elegantly simple form. Pictographs are marvelous examples of great complexity crystallized into singular conciseness. As such, singly and in myriad combinations, they act as archetypal constants of interconnection and as seed-crystal templates of encodement. Their high degree of synchrosimilar interactiveness is utilized throughout the UEN as a primary means by which continuous multidimensional interconnectedness is maintained via their fiery nature. That is, these flame letters harmonically interact within the UEN latticework, maintaining and modifying their apportioned interdimensional standing wave patterning by highly active energetic interreactivity. Put more simply, these physics hieroglyphics utilize the crystallographic UEN component as a highly stable matrix that helps sustain their dimensional continuity and interconnection. Without the crystallographic element, it would be as if there were no underlying foundational framework in and through which the pictographs could either be fired into manifestation and the resultant code-patternings could not be continuously sustained. This may be likened to a lightning bolt, which quickly dissipates once its force has been spent; within the UEN the pictographic "lightning bolts" have the crystallographic matrix that harnesses the flaming force into stabilized continuity and designated encodement. On virtually all levels of the UEN the crystallographic element stands as a cornerstone that spans the cosmos through which the Universal Language of Light is keyed into encodement and continuously sustained in the flux of manifestation.

Five of the "facets" of the Universal Language of Light known to the earth plane are Hebrew, Tibetan, Chinese, Sanskrit, and Egyptian.[1] Figure 1 demonstrates one example of the ideographic nature of Hebrew specifically, and all five languages in general. These pictographs are a step-down transformation of archetypal Family-Image groupings that perform many levels of universal functioning. Stepped down to the level of human language systems, they are intended within the divine plan as a communication medium by which humanity bases its thought- and expression-matrix upon the foundation of universal order. Thereby humanity partakes of universal order as it is intended to be by the Eternal.

Furthermore, these languages also form one of the keystones of a sacred scientific "language." The archetypal numeric-geometric interference patterns that the flame letters are serve as fundamental code-templates of a wide spectrum of Light-interactions. These codes provide sacred science with a major "alphabet" of universal Light that provides seed-patterns of scientific knowledge and technological application.

Figure 1: Pictographic Flame Letter

In all, the pictographic component of the UEN functions as the physics hieroglyphics of manifestation, firing Thoughts into designated dimensional threshold and domain membrane code-patterns. In conjunction with the DNA Light-Life codes, they complement the intricate dynamics of consciousness Life. In association with the crystallographic UEN element, the flame letters complement the stable foundational structuralization of manifestation with their interweaving high-energy coding factors. As a fiery circuitry matrix for universal Thought-patterns, the Universal Language of Light provides one of the primary mediums of intercommunication throughout creation.

THE DNA LIGHT-LIFE CODES

DNA Light-Life codes set primary "weights and measures" for consciousness in manifestation. This spirally latticed code complex is symmetrically counterpoised and synergistically complementary to the two other components of the UEN. The resultant triangulation collectively serves as the infinitely creative universal latticework Language.

The primary purpose of the Light-Life codes is to provide a blueprinted interdimensional matrix through which the Living Light of consciousness is formulated, projected to myriad evolutionary domains, and connectively maintained within a modifiable multidimensional network. This divine Language of Life is the core coding for the enactment of all consciousness evolution as it functions to form a matrixed Light-vehicle of Life through which Intelligence is "breathed" into manifest evolutionary unfoldment.

The DNA of the physical body is but one step-down transformation of a vast network of interconnected Life codes. The pattern and content of the physical DNA originates on the level of the Higher Self, which serves to transcribe the Eternal's Blueprint-Thoughts of archetypal Humanity into a multidimensional consciousness network through the medium of the Life coding. At each harmonic matrix level of this network is a DNA template that functions as a wave-guide through which the Life codes are transduced and maintained from dimension to dimension. Therefore, the domain-specific codes of Life abide at every level of the UEN.

The DNA templates are woven of precisely triangulated relationships between the pictographic flame letters, numerological matrix indexes, and mathematically coded color-sound indexes. Within the boundless creative possibilities that such inter-combined spectrums afford, living multidimensional DNA templates form the building block alphabet of Life for the Thought-patterns of Universal Intelligence.

The crystallographic cornerstone of the UEN interfaces with the Light-Life codes in perfect complementarity. Like a key fitting into a lock, these two Languages of Light are intricately interwoven. The crystallographic component functions as a latticework of high stability and receptive codability in which DNA may imprint its template functions. In addition, the DNA templates are provided with an interdimensional gridwork through which projection, transduction, and modifiable continuity is possible with exceptionally stable exactitude. In this way the genetic-crystal interaction carries out the most enduring and centrally causal aspects of the consciousness-crystallographic relationships. Far beyond humankind's evolutionary need to utilize crystals and crystal-based Light-technologies, the genetic-crystallographic connection will abide as the keystone of consciousness coded into creation.

The spiral form of physical DNA is a mirrored reflection of the principal importance of the helical wave-form in coherently maintaining the interdimensional interconnectedness of the Life-codes. The spiral is a fundamental archetypal wave-form of universal energy flow. It is a perfectly balanced intersecting resultant of combined linear and rotational motion. The resulting spiraling wave is the primary means by which the myriad multidimensional planes are interconnected and by which the Life-codes are infused and maintained in manifestation. Its unique properties of angular momentum create an efficiently direct penetration action through interdimensional layers. As an archetypal fundamental of Thought-form physics, the spiraling motion of the DNA-code Language forms a matrix of limitless intercommunication throughout the depths and heights of creation.

Through the helix, information transfer and energy-code continuity occurs with optimal effectiveness. Just as the physical-plane DNA is able to retain and duplicate awesome amounts of code information, so too the higher dimensional DNA helical wave-forms are able to perform parallel functions of even grander macrodimensional scope. The Higher Mind infuses Life-codes throughout the UEN by powerfully projected superhelix pulses.[2] The superhelix is the archetypal Helix through which vastly complex "helixes within helixes within helixes" are formulated and projected into manifestation. Higher matrix level DNA grids containing innumerable lower DNA matrix levels pulse into the UEN, and branch out down the dimensional spectrum, allotting each DNA coding level to its exact place in the overall Blueprint. This matrix step-down process of the superhelix is a pulse action that is rhythmically repeated (at extremely high rates of speed) that continuously energizes and modifies the full spectrum of Life-codes with Higher Light. Precisely fluctuated proportional balances between the linear and rotational vectors of the spiraling wave-form is one primary means for the encoding and transfering of information. The interdimensional physics factors that enact this entire exacting process on the micro to macro levels would fill countless volumes of text. The superhelix utilizes the crystallographic gridwork through which it pulses for three primary purposes: 1) as a means of maintaining DNA template code sequences steady within the matrix thresholds of the UEN network, 2) as a wave guide that provides a stable interdimensional gridwork through which the helix waves are aligned and directed, and 3) as an interconnective network wherein the coding of the DNA templates may be continuously interlinked and modified.

The Light-Life genetic coding is the *interdimensional intercommunication linkage* connecting consciousness with the cycles and rhythms of the Higher Self, the Heavens, and the surrounding cosmos. On a most fundamental level, evolutionary unfoldment, as seen from a Higher Evolution perspective, is the assimilation of consciousness learning scenarios that, in turn, are directly mirrored in a negentropic upgrading of the DNA coding-grid. This is a process that facilitates the transfer of more evolved genetic coding patterns from the higher planes of the Universal Mind into the DNA patterning of evolving consciousness. The genetic Images of Universal Intelligence are assimilated in the genetic image of individual consciousness, thus producing corresponding evolutionary progress. The infusion of heavenly "genes" is an infusion of higher dimension Light-frequencies via the genetic Language. When an individual's DNA grid reflects a certain threshold of advancement, this grid acts as a key that unlocks the access corridors to the next octave of Light-development.

As an interdimensional communication medium, the genetic Language of Light is an essential means by which intelligence is eternally linked with the heavenly domains, and through which the Heavens transpose Images of Light to evolving consciousness. Through the DNA Life-Light coding, Code is linked to code, Consciousness is connected with consciousness, Mind is infused into mind.

THE CRYSTALLOGRAPHIC STATE

The crystallographic state is characterized by its *highly ordered stability, supraholographic harmonics,* and *full-spectrum interdimensional transparency.* The synergy of these key attributes makes this state a quintessential medium of energy interactions throughout the UEN.

Whether physical or higher dimensional, like-vibration crystallographic units are spaced at regular intervals, thus creating a multi-directional latticework. Row upon row, layer upon layer, grid upon grid of periodic ordering manifests the logical end result of one primary geometric building block (for example, in quartz, a tetrahedron) duplicated billions of times. The spacing between these primary building blocks and their method of bonding with one another is determined primarily by their magneto-gravitational and electromagnetic properties. Like BBs filling a box, each vibrational unit finds the most natural manner to pack together and repeats this pattern indefinitely; this is called the close packing of vibrational units, and different types of building blocks close pack in different geometric arrays (see a mineralogy text for information on this subject). Such methodical regularity on the microscopic levels manifests with parallel logic on the macroscopic levels. The result is a mathematically ordered crystallographic energy field bounded by precisely angled plane surfaces. In fact, the external characteristics are a symmetrical reflection of the internal patternings, a perfect example of the Hermetic axiom, "As above, so below."

Such all-inclusive symmetrical uniformity is held steady in a latticework of exceptional stability. While this characteristic is more widely known as a property of physical-plane crystals, parallel (and superior) stability quotients are also a primary quality of higher dimensional crystallographic correspondents. The combined attributes of coherent order and steadiness make the crystallographic state an ultimate medium for predictable, orderly energy interactions. Energy input can be encoded, amplified, stored, precisely transformed, and transmitted with great systematization. It is no wonder, then, that the crystallographic state is the perfect foundational matrix for the UEN. Specifically, it is the computerlike efficiency, programmability, and stabilization that make the crystallographic component the infrastructural cornerstone through which the pictographic and DNA Light-Life codes enact their own particular functions.

The next major aspect of crystallographic attributes is that of *supraholographic harmonics* or *holo-harmonics,* for short. This trait is characterized by quantum matrix theory in conjunction with multidimensional holographic perspectives. Stated in short, *matrix theory* involves a set of dimensionally discrete, holographically interrelated quantum "orbital shell levels." Figure 2 shows a simplified depiction of five different matrix levels. The higher the level the greater the dimensional complexity and consciousness expansion encompassment. Higher levels interpenetrate all lower levels and are more causal (as the etheric body is causal to the physical body); the higher the level the more hierarchically causal it is. Each lower level functions according to a stepped-down blueprint from the next higher matrix level and operates at its own discrete dimensional level. A quantum threshold gap exists between the various matrix layers, much like the quantum nature of electron orbital shells. Each matrix level tends to remain dimensionally discrete because of this threshold gap, similar to different radio wavelengths not crossing over into one another, thereby maintaining their wavelength integrity. Interactive energy exchange occurs via *interdimensional harmonic resonance* as governed by the parameters and dynamics of *interdimensional transparency,* both of which are discussed in the text that follows.

Supraholography (also referred to as omniholography) adds a multidimensional perspective to the concept of holography by combining it with matrix theory. Here, each matrix layer is holographic in nature (that is, each part contains the whole, and the whole is the synergistic sum of the parts). At each ascending level of the hierarchical matrix structure, the corresponding holograms are of greater holographic complexity and dimensional encompassment. The result is an interpenetrating spectrum of lesser to greater matrix holograms; lesser being less causal, greater being more causal. As an energetic hologram is stepped down from a higher layer to a lower layer, the hologram must necessarily undergo a transformation process. The more dimensionally complex hologram is transformed into its exactly corresponding correlate of lesser dimensional complexity. This is a *matrix transformation process;* through a holographically coded grid (that is, matrix) one level of energy patterning passes through a type of lattice-filtering that serves to convert one type of supraholographic coding into its corresponding stepped-down version. At every matrix level there is a supraholographically encoded threshold zone that is the membrane of intermatrix transformation. This forms the blueprint for the matrix transform process. This generalized explanation is a key to greater comprehension of such concepts as Mind within mind, Membrane within Membrance, Lattice within lattice, and so on. Greater multidimensional

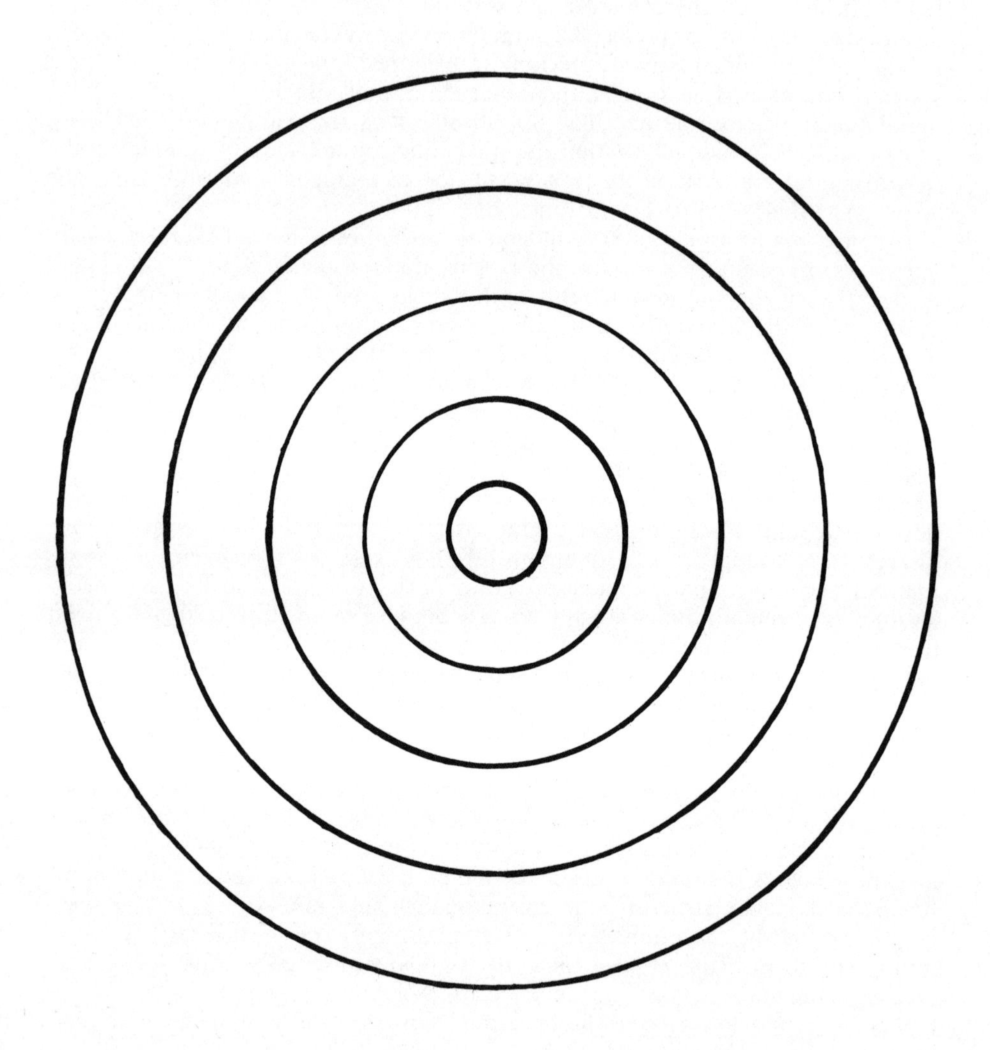

Figure 2: Matrix Theory Representation

holographic codings encompass, interpenetrate, and form the blueprint of crystallization of each successively lower dimensional holographic manifestation.

In creation, matrix levels from micro- to megadimensions crystallize at intra- and interdimensionally harmonic vibrational levels. Just as striking a middle C on a piano stimulates the oscillation of a distinct and repeatable set of intervals and octaves through harmonic sympathetic resonance, so too does reality organize itself in harmonically interrelating dimensional matrix layers. Bode's Law is an excellent illustration of this principle operating intradimensionally. This law is the observed fact that a harmonic distance relationship exists between the planets in our universe. The mean orbital distances from the innermost planet, Mercury, become progessively greater by a ratio of 2:1, a perfect octave, as the planets increase in distance from the sun. This harmonic spatial organization reflects a parallel organizing principle occuring interdimensionally as well, as shall be scientifically verified later in the evolutionary sequence.

Energy interactions between each quantum harmonic level occurs through *interdimensional harmonic resonance.* The harmonic resonance principle is simply extended to encompass multidimensional energetic interchanges. That is, to sound a note of C, for example, is to stimulate not only the intervals and octaves of the physical plane note but also correlating multidimensional intervals and octaves (in esoteric music, called the unheard strains). These dynamics apply not only to sonics but also to all universal energy modalities.

Further, interdimensional harmonic resonance occurs via *holo-harmonic synchrosimilarity*. All energy patterning originates as a Thought form in the highest matrix levels of the Universal Mind. As this energy code undergoes matrix transformation after supraholographic matrix transformation, the same fundamental archetypal pattern is tranduced to an infinite number of hierarchically decreasing matrix levels throughout creation. This is known as synchrosimilarity. Bob Toben and Fred Alan Wolf define this concept in *Space-Time and Beyond*: "Basic energy relations manifest concurrently throughout an indefinite number of levels of perception. The same energy relations wear different clothes in different levels of perception.[3] The concurrent supraholographic stepping down of higher matrix energy patterns is the manner in which universally synchronized interrelatedness occurs. Thought patterns of Universal Intelligence holoharmonically become matrix-discrete synchrosimilar energy patterns; Mind imprints into mind, thus infusing the divine Image into a distinct layer of reality to enact the stepped-down image in concordance with the originating Thought. Thus the Universal Mind, the supermatrix of all universal matrices, synchrosimilarly transforms One Thought into the far reaches of the UEN, therein to branch into innumerable variations on the originating Theme.

The *transparency quotient* is the third of the major crystallographic traits covered in this section. The attribute of crystal transparency is founded upon the awareness that the crystallographic component of the UEN, on the most essential levels, is composed of universal numerological common denominators, energy code constants, and fundamental carrier frequencies. Because of this verity, an all-inclusive energy spectrum range can work in and through this aspect of the UEN, including its lower octave correlates, physical-plane crystals. This is to say that the common denominator and energy-constant vibrations function as universal fundamentals from which virtually infinite series of harmonics can be generated and worked with. A fundamental is the first and lowest frequency of a given vibration. Doubling the frequency of the fundamental (the first harmonic) yields the second harmonic, which is a stepped-up reflection of the fundamental. The frequencies of all succeeding harmonics are all integral multiples of the fundamental frequency. Theoretically, an infinite series of harmonics can thus be generated from a given fundamental. Such numerological entities are similar (at more causal dimensional levels) to present-day quantum physics' Planck's constant and de Broglie wavelength. From this, it is clear that these entities are foundationally integral to broad spectrums of universal physics equations. Knowing that the crystallographic aspect of the UEN must necessarily work with all vibrational spectrums, it makes elegant sense to see the constituency of this crystallographic gridwork as being composed of keynote universal fundamental constants and common denominators. This is to understand that the UEN's crystallographic component is transparent to the totality of the universal energy spectrum.

Transparency is a function of the interdimensional interchange of energy flow. The quotient, or defined degree, of transparency is directly related to the dimensional parameters as delineated by matrix theory. Shortly, the higher the dimensional level (that is, the matrix level), the greater the transparency quotient; that is, the crystallographic correspondent is functionally responsive to a broader universal spectrum range. Lesser degrees of transparency delineate functional nonresponsiveness to higher dimensional vibrational ranges; transparency quotients decrease as the dimensional spectrum decreases. Therefore, for example, celestial template recorder cells* work with a significantly broader spectrum range than do cosmic recorder cells.*

The interdimensional physics of transparency now goes to a deeper level of explication. Between all matrix levels, from micro to macro, exist *threshold barriers* that maintain the discreteness of the dimensional layers. These threshold barriers are interdimensional membranes or "spark gaps" that keep different matrix levels discretely separate; without such insulating gaps, reality would be a homogeneous mix. To cross the spark gap from one level to another requires an *overlap gradient zone* through which interdimensional matrix transformations occur. An example of such zones are the primary and secondary vortexes of the Earth's planetary gridwork. Energy interchange between the Earth and the surrounding cosmos and throughout the planet itself does not occur randomly, homogeneously; rather it occurs in and through a highly organized, interconnected gridwork that serves as a gradient-overlap area through which multidimensional energy exchange and processing can occur. Outside of the primary gridwork vortexes the interdimensional threshold barrier potential is much higher and greater degrees of applied energy are required to bridge the insulating gap between matrix-dimensional levels.

The overlap-gradient zones occur in harmonically interrelated gridwork patterns at every dimensional threshold. In accordance with the principles of sacred geometry, the gridwork patterns are principally composed of Platonic solid geometrics (and their hypersolid correlates) and their primary derivatives (as well as crystal axes system parameters). Interdimensionally, the various matrix levels appear as coherently interrelated geometric nesting patterns, analogous in nature

*Refer to Chapters 1 and 2.

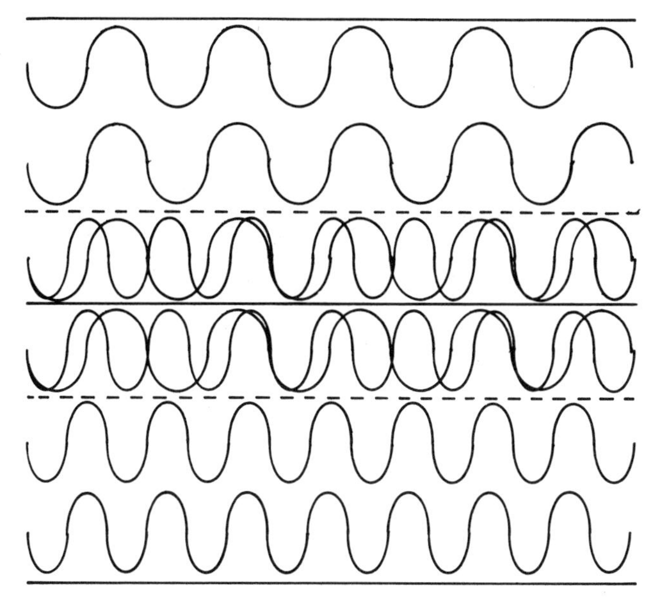

Figure 3: Overlap Gradient Zone Representation

to nested Platonic solids (see Figure 4). Geometry within harmonically coherent geometry forms the intermatrix lattice of energy transformations. For example, *The Book of Knowledge: The Keys of Enoch* states that the primary energy gridwork of the Earth is composed of superimposed icosahedral and pentagonal dodecahedral geometries surrounded by a hexahedron.[4] As stated previously, outside of these intermatrix lattices, energy interactions between matrixes have a high degree of threshold barrier potential, and therefore primary intermatrix interactions do not normally occur in these areas. The manner in which the primary *inter*matrix exchanges are processed and distributed within any given *intra*matrix level is through a hierarchically branching system of secondary and tertiary gridworks that "nest" within the primary gridwork (that is, other Platonic solids or crystal axes patterns nested within the primary geometries). Therefore, it can be seen that *inter*matrix interactions occur through the *primary threshold barrier zones,* and *intra*matrix interactions occur through the *secondary and tertiary gridworks* that process energy within the boundaries of a given primary threshold zone.

Understanding the nature of the energy dynamics that occur within intermatrix overlap gradient zones is crucial to understanding the transparent nature of the crystallographic aspect of the UEN. At each of these zones, two or more dimensional matrices overlap into one another at an extreme end of their respective spectrums. That is, common ground is created wherein dimensional spectrums extend into one another within precise parameters, thus creating a step-down/step-up gradient zone for intermatrix transformations. Figure 3 shows a simplified perspective of this overlap gradient to assist visualization; however, a more accurate conception is a phase locking of supraholographic, mathematically-geometrically coded standing wave patterns interpenetrating (or nested) within one another.

It is at the *nodal points* of geometrical-mathematical intersection that the matrix levels primarily interchange. The nodal points reflect the extremely complex patterns of a supraholographically coded matrix transform, a crystallographically encoded pathway of intermatrix energy transformation. Within this complex overlap gradient zone the nodal points serve as energy sinks, or holo-harmonic conductivity points, that establish the gradient of least energetic resistance and highest conductivity. As a whole, this manifests primary flow lines of force that energy naturally follows, the nodal geometries acting as coherency wave guides in this regard.

William Tiller, Ph.D., a professor in the department of materials science and engineering at Stanford University, adds an overlapping perspective here. First, he proposes an agent by which intermatrix interactions occur. The *deltron* is a five dimensional substance (in his six-dimensional matrix theory).

> ''*Deltrons* which are a higher dimensional bridging substance and which have no spin and no charge. (They do have mass but they are very light.) They are like a fluid that can go faster than light or slower than light, so they can couple with substances in both the positive and negative space/time frames and allow an energy transfer between the two.[5]

Dr. Tiller proposes a six-dimensional model of matrix lattices (the positive and negative space/time frames being the two lowest of them) in which causal energy patterns are transferred via transformation symmetries through the various matrix levels.

> A second important conclusion of this model (for the case of a perfect lattice) relates to the diffraction of waves between the sublattices. Since each sublattice is a reciprocal of the others, when waves traveling in the mind sublattice are diffracted from the nodal points at that level, the constructive interference beams pass through the nodal points of the negative and positive space/time sublattices. Thus, correlative patterns of the mind level information are imprinted onto the −ve S-T (negative space/time) and +ve S-T (positive space-time) sublattices and vice versa; i.e., there is a connectivity and integration of patterns from all levels. The patterns stored at the Mind level of the universe are automatically projected onto a duplex screen—the negative and positive space-time gridpoint. Substance interacts with these grid points via deltron coupling. The information potential patterns on these grids are transferred to the physical and etheric domains of substance; i.e., when we make an action at the physical level, we do so because our physical and etheric substances are trying to conform to the changing patterns stored in the positive and negative space-time grids.[6]

In addition to some apparent parallels between Dr. Tiller's model and the authors', the concept of the deltron as a higher dimension bridging substance bears further examination in the authors' context, for the deltron concept is an integral aspect of the crystallographic transparency quotient. Viewing its activity in relationship to *threshold coherency theory* sheds more light on its nature and manner of functioning.

As stated earlier, the crystallographic state is one characterized by periodic repetition of identical vibrational building blocks into a multidirectional lattice of oscillating symmetrical uniformity. From fundamental vibrational theory it is known that oscillators of like or near-like vibration have a strong tendency to phase lock with one another, becoming a system of tuned oscillators in a state of rhythm entrainment. The vibrational units oscillate in unison like pendulum wall clocks that, over time, fall into a rhythmic unison. In *Stalking the Wild Pendulum,* Itzhak Bentov notes several characteristics that accrue to a system of tuned oscillators: 1) The larger the number of oscillators the more stable the system is and the more difficult it is to disturb. It will force a wayward oscillator back into line very quickly. 2) The system requires a minimum amount of energy to drive the system and to perpetuate its individual and collective vibratory rate. This is the universe's most economical, efficient vibratory mode and there is a tendency to draw like-vibrational systems into such a state. 3) Whenever there is a state of resonance, there is a transfer of energy. And in systems of tuned oscillators, energy transfer is optimal.[7]

Within a crystallographic matrix, these three characteristics are especially strong because of the singularity of the oscillating building blocks and their symmetrical orientation in relationship to one another. In one manner of viewing, the crystallographic state is creation's most strikingly simple, most coherently resonant system. The identical building blocks are of like vibration and are easily able to phase entrain within the symmetrical close packing arrangement, thus yielding one whole crystallographic unit with a unified coherency of collective oscillations. The exterior plane surfaces—the macroscopic reflection of the collective microscopic state—serve not only to help maintain the overall vibratory integrity but also adds a nonlinear element of synergy that amplifies the coherency quotient even further.

Together, all these aspects of the crystallographic state create a condition of tuned oscillatory coherency that is predisposed to potential states of nonlinear, synergic coherency. An analogy for the concept of synergic coherence is the threshold at which electromagnetic light waves convert into a higher state of coherency to actuate a laser beam. Below a certain defined threshold, light waves are generally out of phase with another; there is relative randomness in this regard. If, however, light waves are oriented so that they are all in phase, then at what is termed the *laser threshold,* a completely new state is engaged. All the light waves suddenly lock into phase and become technically coherent. With coherency, a quantum increase in the intensity of light is produced. In *The Global Brain,* physicist Peter Russell states:

> A hundred out-of-phase waves, for example, are only ten times as strong as a single wave. Thus a small number of units acting coherently can easily outshine a much greater number acting incoherently. The larger the number of units, the more dramatic the effect. Out of one million units, only one thousand (one-tenth of one percent) would need to act coherently for their effect to dominate.[8]

The crystallographic state, because of its singular oscillatory coherence, is an unparalleled medium in which certain types of parallely similar laserlike synergistic coherency may occur. Within the dynamics of intermatrix energy interactions through the threshold overlap gradient zone, the crystallographic medium's ability to assume synergistic coherency is another key to understanding. In terms of overlap gradient dynamics, Light-energies reaching certain critical levels of oscillatory dynamics (which is different for each matrix level) induce a state of synergistic coherency within the crystallographic matrix. This state functions as: 1) a high-speed on/off coding mechanism of intermatrix transformations, and 2) a principal means of bridging the interdimensional overlap gradient.

The first function involves ultrarapid coded pulsations of energy being projected into the nodal points of interdimensional matrix transduction. Simply put, employing an on/off, pulse/no-pulse type of coding transfer, the energy pulsations going through any given nodal point will convey a "message", a code parallel to computer binary information processing of today. Collectively, the myriad nodal points can be activated/not-activated in numberless combinations and permutations within the parameters of the preexisting matrix transformation coding inscribed within the crystallographic matrix at that particular overlap zone. In actuality, even this level of sophistication does not encompass the greater complexities. The coding mechanism is not actually of a linear binary nature; rather, it involves a spectrum gradation of supraholographic mathematical-geometrical coding that yields complexities beyond the scope of this text.

The second function overlaps with the first in that it is in conjunction with the dynamics of the coding mechanism that the interdimensional spark gap is actually bridged. In order for the coding mechanism to function a state of synergistic coherency must exist; it is in this state that the on (versus off), pulse (versus no-pulse) is enacted, and the intermatrix transduction occurs. Further, in the supercoherent state several nonlinear energy states are stimulated. Just as laser light is many times more intense than normal light, so too are certain critical levels of Light passing through the crystallographic matrix made much more intense than before. In this supercoherent, amplified state the stimulation of *hyper-Light emissions* manifests. This spectrum-type of Light is one that expands and transcends the magneto-gravitational parameters and, in most cases, the universal frequency constants of the given matrix level in which this effect occurs. Succinctly explained, it expands the dimensional Light-cone to a more all-inclusive state. The amplified stimulation of deltrons is one aspect among others of the hyper-Light emissions spectrum. Overall, the effect is that of an extremely rarefied spectrum of pure energy opening the dimensional gateway for the intermatrix transformations. This concept is simply a more technical understanding of the mechanisms involved in overlap gradient zone energy transduction. Hyper-Light is the linking agent between matrix-dimensions, making intermatrix transformations possible as the antipodal key that unlocks the dimensional gateways. As emissions go, those of the hyper-Light spectrum are not long-lived; however, through activating the crystallographic medium constantly with Light-codes flowing through the threshold zone, the hyper-Light effect is ongoing; that is, as some emissions transform to a lower energy state, others are being generated. There is a spectrum of hyper-Light that accords with each different dimension's parameters. This particular spectrum of Light is integral to the crystallographic transparency quotient. Hyper-Light makes dimensions transparent to one another; where there was potential opacity of interdimensional threshold energy interactions, there is now selective, coded transparency. The transparency quotient is a measure of interdimensional physics that indicates which dimensions can engage in energy exchange and to what degree. The crystallographic state is the primary medium through which transparency occurs.

With regard to physical-plane crystals, the trait of physical transparency in high-quality quartz and other precious gems is a visual analog and vibrational mirroring of their interdimensional transparency quotient. Such precious minerals are stepped-down materializations of different "facets" of the universal crystallographic state. In this way they serve as physical-plane extensions of the UEN.

Quartz, in particular, is the stepped-down crystallization of the White Light spectrum. Silicon dioxide is that specific molecular-vibratory medium that is the physical-plane substance having a primary resonant affinity with White Light. As White Light steps it crystallization patterns down through the UEN, by principles of harmonic attraction it is magnetically drawn to the appropriately corresponding medium of crystallization in any given matrix-dimension level. On the physical plane, this medium is pure silicon dioxide. Other more specialized universal crystallographic ranges also enact the same type of process as that of White Light-transduced precipitating into quartz. A particular spectrum profile of the Green ray, for example, crystallizes within the physical matrix of the emerald; so too a spectrum profile of the Red ray within the ruby; and so on. Each type of precious stone serves as the crystallization medium for a specific portion and intermixture of one or more Light-color-sound indexes.

Each precious stone, then, becomes a "window of Light"with different quotients of transparency. Because these gems are step-down crystallizations of higher dimensional matrix correspondents, there is a strong interdimensional harmonic resonance potential. Precious stones are the physical-plane correspondence of their originating crystallographic component of the UEN; they are, simply put, this component materialized. This verity is reflected in the high degree of order, physical transparency, and purity of these gems—they are, in fact, rarefied matter. And just as two hierarchically adjacent levels of the UEN undergo mutual overlap gradient interactions, physical crystals serve as link-up matrices to the next highest level of the UEN—the etheric crystals of the planetary gridwork. This is to say that physical crystals are highly predisposed to engaging etheric crystals through an interlinking overlap gradient zone for amplified, direct energy interractions. This also means that through the etheric crystals there is access to the next highest level, and the next, and so on up the UEN matrix spectrum. Via this network, the Higher Evolution also uses the physical gems as a primary medium through which to infuse Light to the earth plane. These gems serve as the mathematical-geometrical correspondents of higher plane vibratory patterns, supraholographic standing-wave patterns of rarefied energy-matter that hold the access lines of interdimensional energy exchange open and steady for receiving higher Light and for gaining amplified, coherent access to the UEN. The same intermatrix overlap gradient dynamics described earlier in this chapter section hold true for the threshold barrier between the physical gem matrix and etheric crystal matrix. These concepts have tremendous ramifications in many areas, from interdimensional communication to Light-based technologies, which will be explored in later chapters.

White Light is the synergistic union of all universal spectrums of vibration. Therefore, quartz as a step-down materialization of White Light, is able to work with the full spectrum of White Light as it manifests within the Earth's energy spectrum. The Infinite White Light as it manifests on the highest dimensions of creation is infinitely more powerful than White Light stepped down to the earthly octave equivalency of Light. Therefore is is an oversimplification to state that quartz is White Light crystallized; this concept must be clarified within a more universal context. Quartz crystal is a matrix by which higher dimension octaves of White Light and discrete vibrational ranges encompassed by this spectrum can be directly accessed through the UEN. This same concept holds true regarding other gem varieties; that is, a specific Green ray profile stepped down to its earthly energy spectrum is emerald. So too with ruby as an example of a Red ray spectrum profile correlate; and so on with all precious gem matrices.

Different gems have differing degrees of interdimensional transparency. It can been seen, then, that quartz has a broad range of transparency because of its ability to work with the full spectrum of earth-correlate White Light and its access to the higher octaves of White Light. All other known gems on earth have a much more specific, limited range of transparency. The emerald, for instance, is transparent only to a specific profile of the Green spectrum; the topaz only to a specific profile of the Blue spectrum, and so on. Therefore, all precious minerals save quartz are highly specialized in their vibrational capacities, while quartz is generalized in its functional range. There are a very few crystal matrices that have a vibrational range that exceeds the upper limits of quartz, but only in a defined and limited range of the universal energy spectrum. Gold and diamond are two of these substances that are transparent to extremely rarefied, range-specific vibrational ultra-frequencies. Quartz is the single most broad-range capacity crystallographic matrix known, that is, it has the widest spectrum of interdimensional and intradimensional transparency. This singular ability makes it and its higher octave correspondents the exceptionally versatile foundational workhorse of the UEN.

In all, the highly ordered stability, supra-holographic harmonics, and interdimensional transparency are the synergistically interacting principles that together constitute three major characteristics that make the crystallographic state uniquely important to every energetic function throughout the infinite expanses of the UEN.

CRYSTALLINE CORRESPONDENCES

Intercommunication among crystalline aspects of the UEN occurs by interdimensional harmonic resonance induced via *crystalline correspondences*. Crystallinity is the code of creation; for each level and type of Intelligence there is a corresponding crystallization code-pattern that is a mirrored reflection of its abstract essence translated into manifestation. Intelligence, as it is encoded into the crystalline reaches of the UEN, therein precipitates into its specifically corresponding crystallization patterning. Viewing the UEN as a vast gridwork of countless interweavings of oscillating crystallization lattices, energetic intercommunication occurs through like-crystalline patterns harmonically resonating with like-crystalline patterns. Spatio-temporal differences are merely secondary beat cycles in this regard; it is the quotient of the "order, phase, and grid" of an energy patterning that is the primary determiner of interdimensional energetic interactions. Stated another way, it is the mathematical-geometrical *lattice-coding orientation* that determines the degree of energy interaction among vibrational units, dimensional level differences notwithstanding. Corresponding crystalline energy patterns throughout all levels of the UEN establish harmonically resonant lattice-code coherence that induce selective energetic interactions among them.

Axes systems, geometric forms, numerological code-patterns, latticework "weaves", crystallized lines of force—this is the language of crystallinity. When any given crystallization code-pattern vibrates, all like-crystalline codes on all intra- and interdimensional harmonic intervals and octaves vibrate in resonant unison with the original code-pattern and with each other. This occurs through the principle of interdimensional harmonic resonance. To illustrate, when, for instance, the note of middle C is struck on a piano, all harmonic intervals and octaves of that C note also start to vibrate; this is harmonic resonance. The principle of interdimensional harmonic resonance simply adds a multidimensional element; a given vibration creates a condition of harmonic resonance not only in its own octave-dimension, but also in higher octave-dimensions.

When a state of multidimensional harmonic resonance occurs, the oscillating intervals and octaves also phase-lock with one another. Phase-locking is a coherent bonding action in which vibrations oscillate in periodic unison with each other, and thereby exchange energy. Within the vast interwoven crystalline latticeworks of the UEN, harmonically related lattice-codes phase-lock, establish interrelated orientations, and exchange energy.

The degree of harmonic interaction between any two or more lattice-codings determines the degree to which energy is exchanged. Like Platonic solid nesting patterns wherein harmonically coherent interrelationships are established (see Figure 4), so too in parallel manner do the crystalline lattices of the UEN establish nesting pattern relationships. Unlike the Platonic solids, the nesting patterns of the UEN can be created both interdimensionally and with secondary regard to spatio-temporal differences. If, as in the Platonic solids illustration, there is a high degree of mutual harmonic lattice coherence, then there is a correspondingly high degree of energetic exchange. But if, say, the nested Platonic solids are out of kilter in relation to one another, then a correspondingly low degree of energy interaction occurs. Put more simply, harmonically like interacts very strongly with harmonically like; harmonically unlike interacts very little with harmonically unlike; degrees between totally alike versus unalike establish a spectrum of correlating degrees of energy exchange.

Crystallinity is inextricably woven into the fabric of creation. From fundamental abstract crystalline patterns derive infinite complexities of lattices within lattices, axes systems within axes systems, geometries within geometries. Crystalline correspondence theory shows how this awesome complexity sorts itself out into multidimensionally harmonic coherency. Reduced to the essence of universal physics, the UEN is simply a harmonic relationship between crystalline lattice-code orientations. Like-orientation establishes a communicative harmonization with like-orientation. This leads to a greater understanding of how the many crystalline subsystems within the UEN create and maintain intradimensional and interdimensional space-time-energy coherence.

From this information the principle that is arrived at is this: when there is a crystalline system of any sort, of any code, through interdimensional harmonic resonance a crystalline correspondence is created between the original crystalline system and all other like-crystalline systems throughout the UEN. One crystalline unit can be potentially utilized to interconnect with a vast gridwork of corresponding units, spanning subatomic to supragalactic levels of reality; microunit connects with macrounit (and vice versa). To hold a gemstone in one's hands, for instance, is to have a key to unlock correlating codes of creation.

And, as shall be explained later in this book, this principle also has farreaching ramifications in terms of evolutionary transformation of the human biocrystalline

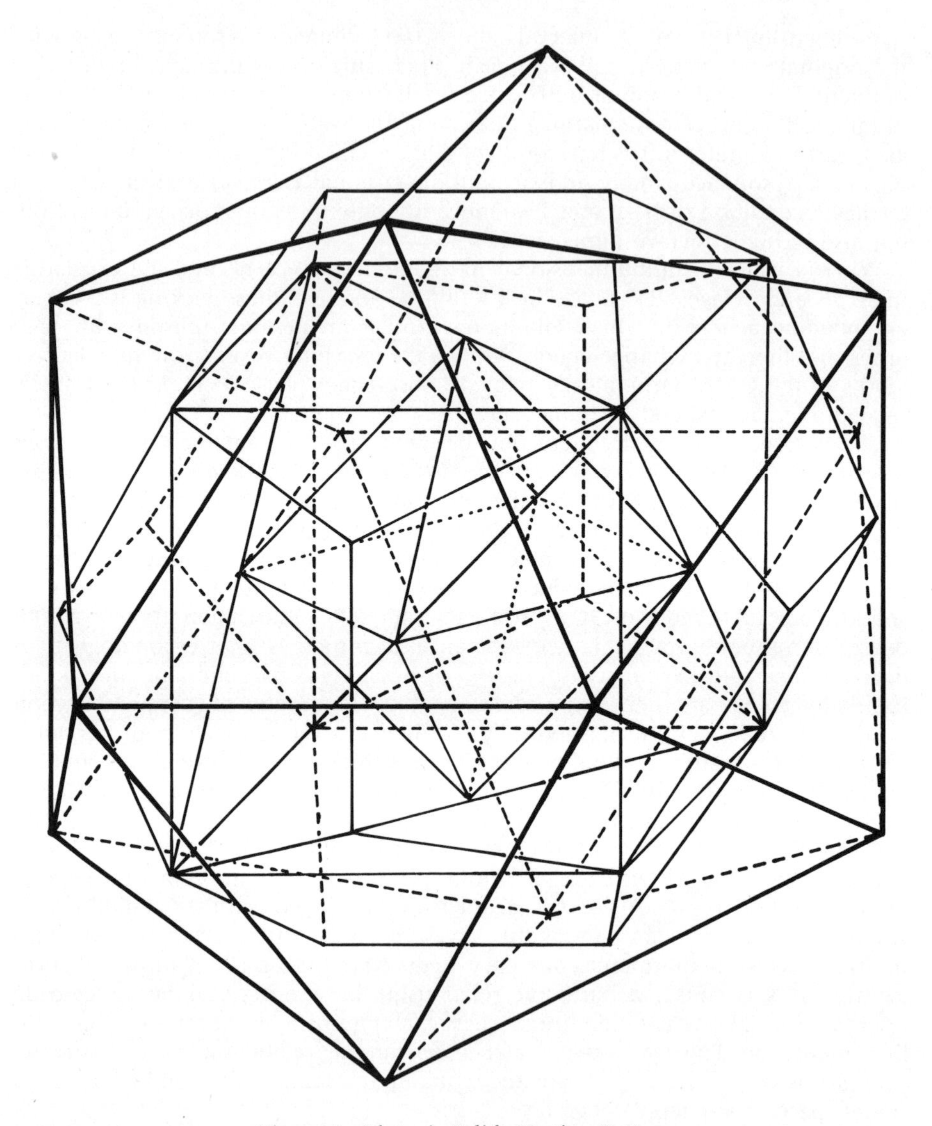

Figure 4: Platonic Solids Nesting Pattern

system. To foreshadow, how the biocrystalline structures of the human system create crystalline correspondences with correlating higher dimension Light-codings is the essence of consciousness transformation and ascension.

SEVEN LEVELS OF THE UEN: BASIC PERSPECTIVES

Within the myriad complexity of the innumerable dimensions and domains spanning the heights and depths of the UEN, there may be discerned a generalized outline of the seven major hierarchical levels of ordering, as introduced in chapter

1. These seven levels are: 1) Abstract Light, 2) the Merkabah of the Heavenly Host, 3) celestial Light-templates, 4) celestial template recorder cells, 5) cosmic template recorder cells, 6) etheric crystals, and 7) physical-plane crystals. Each level encompasses vast expanses of universal ordering, from the most causal and rarefied of celestial planes to the lower cosmic domains. In the text that follows is a discussion of highlighted characteristics of each UEN level. The purpose here is to provide fundamental properties and distinctions in the hierarchical scheme. This material is of a very general nature, for the UEN is infinitely complex: only the most basic of paradigms is presented here.

Abstract Light

This most causal of dimensional levels is inclusive of the entire universal sector wherein the Absolute Void crosses into the most abstract levels of pure numerological realities, as discussed in Chapter 1—Oneness, Twoness, Threeness, and so on. These most rarefied of planes step down to primary axis codes and fundamental seed-code geometrics, wherein supraarchetypal numeric-geometric ultramatrices formulate, yet in high abstraction. These matrices are the blueprints of crystallization for all other levels of the UEN.

The Merkabah of the Heavenly Host

Below the abstract Light-realms is yet another most exalted multidimensional spectrum of Light-interactions. The Merkabah is the capstone Higher Intelligence of the entire Kingdom of God and Spiritual Hierarchy of Light. It is the collective consciousness of the Elohim God-Family, the supreme Lords of Light. This is a vast realm of the Universal Mind, one in which abides the Image-blueprints for a million myriad levels of creation and all the infinitely intricate details therein. In addition to this being the seat of the Government of Light, there are Merkabah vehicles that are formulated and dispatched to key threshold zones above the celestial Light-templates whereby the higher level Image-blueprints are translated from these master threshold control regions into the rest of the UEN, and controlled and modified with exacting precision throughout the unfoldments of every Alpha–Omega cycle throughout the eternity domains and the realms of space-time.

Celestial Light-Templates

The celestial realms are universal regions of pure energy emissions, highly rarefied dimensional levels beyond any spectrum of matter-energy, no matter how subtle such spectrums might be. The Light-templates abide within the higher reaches of the celestial planes, functioning as tremendously complex ultracomputers capable of an awesome range of multidimensionally multiplexed Light-interactions. They serve as primary circuit-gating mechanisms for the translation (that is, matrix transformation) of Merkabah into celestial domains of towering transcendence. Also, a direct interconnection is continuously maintained with the celestial template recorder cells such that step-down blueprints that correspond to that level and all those below are transmitted and appropriately transformed.

Celestial Template Recorder Cells

Spanning the countless celestial mansion worlds, and all the dimensions and domains therein, are celestial template recorder cells receiving Thought-Image blueprints as received from the celestial Light-templates. Each celestial template recorder cell is the repository for the entirety of Alpha–Omega code-parameters for the manifestation and unfoldment of whole celestial sectors. A subnetwork carries out subfunctions of these more causal celestial template recorder cells.

Cosmic Template Recorder Cells

The cosmic realms are defined here as inclusive of any dimension of energy-matter, including quite rarefied spectrums within this range. This is a realm spanning inconceivable reaches of intergalactic realities, of which earth is as a lower-end microcosmic dot. Carrying out the primary threshold control functions, stationed at key vortex junctures, are the cosmic template recorder cells. These receive tremendously complex Light-codings from the celestial template recorder cells, transduce them into threshold-specific parameters, and then transmit these controlling and monitoring parameters along corresponding energy lines of force. They are "living" supercomputers of a form of crystalline ultraintelligence that works in conjunctive harmony with associated Light-beings assigned to specific complementary tasks. Again, a subnetwork carries out secondary and tertiary Light-functions as directed by the cosmic template recorder cells.

Etheric Crystals

In relationship to earth, the etheric crystals are integrally associated with the planetary energy network. Existing on one major quantum dimension level higher than the physical plane, these etheric crystals are located at the 12 major vortex areas around the earth plane. These vortex zones are the primary areas of earth's interdimensional interconnection and the threshold control areas for the regulation of the planet's entire energy field. The etheric crystals work in conjunction with the pyramidal form and associated Light-technologies and Light-beings. This network receives its appropriate Image-blueprint functions as transformed throughout all of the previously stated UEN levels, the earth receiving those complex Light-codes specifically formulated in the highest Abstract Light levels particularly for earth. Such is the incredible orderly precision of the UEN.

Physical-Plane Crystals

Light-codes as transformed through the etheric crystal network are superimposed upon crystalline mediums as they grow out of solution into solid form, thereby translating these codes into crystalline form. Within this process, not only are the Light-codes infused into physical form, but also the gem matrix itself undergoes an "alchemical" process of rarefication; that is, it undergoes a transmutation from lower quantum levels of energy-matter to higher levels. Rarefied physical-plane crystals are the earthly access link-up matrices to the etheric planetary network. Once linked with this network, consciousness intention is processed through the appropriate aspects of the UEN according to the nature of the intention in addition to access factors (discussed in Chapter 3). Therefore, the crystal-to-etheric crystal network connection is the main gateway to access the rest of the UEN. It is also the means by which the appropriate aspects of the UEN and the Light-entities of the Higher Evolution may transmit appropriate energy-patterns to the earth in general and the individual and collective consciousness therein. Quartz in particular is the crystallization of White Light transduced to a rarefied earthly dimension; because of its White Light nature, it functions as the centrally important wide-spectrum ultrahigh-frequency range crystal matrix for both personal and planetary evolutionary unfoldment and interdimensional interconnection.

THE ASCENSION

The New World ascension process is the quantum recrystallization of every atom of energy-matter and (qualifying) unit of consciousness within the earth's entire galactic threshold zone to a higher Light-dimension. As an Alpha–Omega program cycle is completed, a new evolutionary cycle is born; a grand recrystallization code-sequence is enacted into a new code-sequence.

The recrystallization process is key here. When an energy pattern or physical crystal *de*-crystallizes it is dissolved back into a state of amorphous disorder. *Re*crystallization, on the other hand, is the process of transforming one crystalline structuring pattern into another. One example of this occurs when quartz is heated to 576° C. At that heat threshold point the usually extremely stable lattice structure (called the alpha state) then expands, establishing a different lattice patterning (called the beta state). Another example is the conversion of graphite under intense heat and pressure into diamond. Here, there is no change in the chemical elements themselves; it is the recrystallization of the latticework that produces a pristine gem from common, unrefined substance. In similar manner, the ascension involves bringing the present galactic crystalline structure to a conversion threshold wherein a radical restructurization occurs, resulting in the creation of a new, more "gem-like" galactic lattice-coding. Unlike the quartz and diamond analogies, the newly recrystallized galactic "crystal" is *restationed* in a cosmic threshold zone that harmonizes with the more elevated Light-lattice structure.

On the individual level, the human bioenergetic system undergoes a parallel recrystallization process. Of importance is the fact that in the Omega conversion threshold restructuralization sequence, the weights and measures of consciousness determine the level of recrystallization that is to occur. In accordance with the laws of universal physics, the crystalline correspondences of the individual—that is, the blood crystals, DNA, brain cells, auric geometry patterns, and so on—are measured, and the individual's evolutionary status is delineated by the Higher Evolution. The recrystallization that then occurs apportions consciousness along specific vector-angles of crystallization that accord with evolutionary status. An extensive spectrum of such vector-angles directs consciousness into sectors of universal learning for which each individual has prepared himself or herself.

Toward the higher end of this spectrum of recrystallization, the individual experiences a transformation similar to that of graphite's into a more highly ordered, jewellike state—the multidimensional Light-body. This process is a quantum leap of the earthbound self into union with the rarefied crystalline lattice-coding of the Higher Self in conjunction with the Kingdom of Light. Higher octaves of Light-energy are infused into the causal crystalline aspects of the human bioenergetic system, catalyzing a conversion of the earthly energy-matter spectrums into higher octaves of consciousness Light. Multidimensional freedom-in-Spirit is then enjoyed as the opacity of the earthly self has been recrystallized into latticed transparency-in-Light.

CHAPTER 3

Interdimensional Communication: Evolutionary Imperative

COMMUNICATION THEORY

The capacity to have access to and assimilate increasing degrees of Universal Intelligence is the essence of consciousness development. The necessity to be actively receptive to the higher octaves of Light-communication now opening to personal and planetary awareness is the evolutionary imperative of our current epoch. Increasing awareness of the multidimensional nature and scope of universal realities and the concurrent interlinkage of consciousness within this multifaceted Light-spectrum provide the keys to having access to greater degrees of the Universal Energy Network (UEN). And as the gateways are cleared for the Light of the grander celestial realms to be shone upon the earth plane, the "ascension imperative" is activated and the time comes to realize the interdimensional Light-beings we truly are.

Communication is creation. Existence necessarily implies a state of communicatory interrelatedness, for nothing in all of manifest reality exists in isolation. Some form, some degree of energetic interchange exists, whether it be the most minute of subatomic particle interactions or the grandest of supragalactic gravitational attraction. Oneness is the inextricable unity of all that is throughout manifestation; this is the overarching divine Law that is omnipresently immanent in every vibratory unit in existence. This unity factor translates into the blueprint of creation as the foundational seed-crystal form in which all has its origin and in which all has its existence. Therefore, creation bears this unity-imprint within the causal laws of every vibrational interaction. Unitive intercommunication is the core code of existence.

Communication, in the broadest sense of the word, is unified interactions of the One Energy in creatively differentiated manifestation. Communicative interaction is the polarized "weave" that is One Energy in perpetual unfoldment. The element of communication is the supraholographic unifying interrelatedness inherent to the existence of consciousness and the increasing of consciousness. Without this element, the synergic organized coherence of reality would not be; reality would

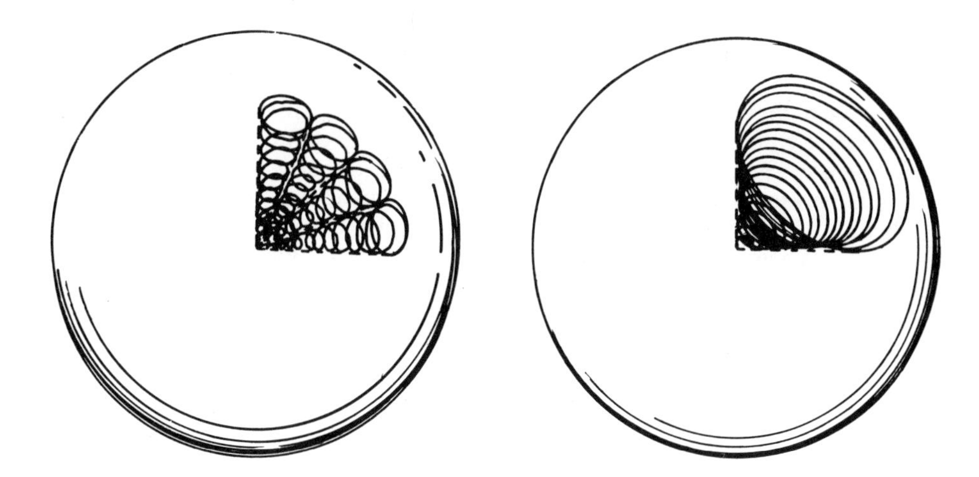

Figure 5: Spiral Cone of Perception Representation

be happenstance randomness. *Consciousness* is a domain of organized intra- and intercommunicative coherence of abiding coded vibratory patterns. With an increase of the communication quotient, the consciousness domain expands into a more evolved set of coded consistency relationships. The process of communication is fundamentally one of "matching" intelligence codes to corresponding code-levels of the UEN, thus inducing correlative interactions. Consciousness can access only those UEN code-levels with which there is a code correspondence; if communication abilities are not of a comparable evolutionary status, access is not yet possible within the intricate hierarchical workings of divine order. With increasing spiritual advancement, progressively higher UEN matrix-code levels can be engaged. The Universal Mind serves in this regard as the hierarchically organized field of Infinite Intelligence in which and through which consciousness expands into greater communicative access. As access to a more evolved state of Intelligence is achieved, consciousness then evolves through this Light-field, thereby incorporating the crystalline code-patterns of that specific field into the codes of consciousness. And so the evolutionary rhythms go, intelligence cyclically flowing through the crystalline "weave-patterns" of the Universal Mind, assimilating these Light-field codes into its own consciousness-patterns, thus creating the matrixed means to gain access in even greater heights of universal communications.

Another way to view evolutionary communication dynamics is with *spiral-cone of perception* principles. All information, all communication within the Universal Mind is essentially whole. A supraholographic principle relates directly to this: every unit of a whole mirrors the whole, and the two are ultimately one and the same. Universal Intelligence is omniscient and omnipresent, and therefore every individual unit of manifestation mirrors all knowledge, and ultimately *is* the whole. All universal Gnosis, all Intelligence is always available, always immanent within every unit of creation. Visualizing this wholeness as a sphere, the communication quotient of consciousness can be seen as a conical section of a sphere, delineating the outline of a spiral (see figure 5-1). The spiral-cone section depicts the degree of Universal Intelligence with which this consciousness has the capacity to communicate. That which is beyond intelligence's communicatory capacity to encompass (that is, outside the spiral-cone) is simply not received into awareness. The degree of the informational context of the whole that can be reached is defined by the spiral-cone. The larger the spiral-cone of the perceptual field of consciousness, the greater the degree of universal omniscience that is incorporated within individual awareness. Infinite communication encompassment yields at-one-ment, a spherical perceptual field (composed of infinite potential spiral-cones) resonating within the Whole and every unified facet of the Whole; or put differently, a sphere with center everywhere, circumference nowhere.

Viewed from the perspective of supraholographic matrix principles, spiral-cone perception concepts are brought to greater clarity. The degree of Universal Intelligence that the perceptual field encompasses correlates directly with the hierarchical matrix level of UEN that consciousness encompasses; that is, the higher the matrix level the more expanded the spiral-cone of perception. The Whole is mirrored throughout each matrix level; yet when it is supraholographically transformed, or stepped down to the next lower matrix level, a dimensional aspect of the UEN communication complexity is not transferred. This lower level operates within its own discrete dimensional parameters. And with each successively decreasing level, another Intelligence matrix layer is "filtered" out. Consciousness access to, say, matrix level four (of ten levels) provides perception of the Whole as it is stepped down at that specific dimension level. It is the stepped-down dimensional mirroring of the whole that is perceived. Should consciousness expand its perceptual field to be inclusive of level five, the whole will be perceived with greater dimensional completeness than when only up to level four was perceived, but it will be less than when levels six through ten are perceived. The difference between the two matrix levels is like the disparity between a two-dimensional flat plane versus a three-dimensional solid. What is seen as square from a two-dimensional point of view is a cube or rectangular solid seen from a three-dimensional point of view. The same reality is being perceived, but a higher matrix level of perception (that is, an expanded spiral-cone of perception) encompasses a much more inclusive degree of the whole. Put more simply, consciousness having access to, say, level four may perceive this dimension with clarity, but it is still a limited perspective. From level five, level four appears less encompassing, more linear and limited, just as a two-dimensional perspective appears to someone with a three-dimensional point of view.

This concept applies to consciousness access abilities within the UEN, what may be called channeling or interdimensional communication. Reaching a certain dimension of the UEN and perceiving it correctly does not necessarily mean that the perception is totally accurate, because from higher dimension levels the lower levels are *relatively* true. What is true from a two-dimensional point of view is indeed truth, but from a three-dimensional viewpoint it appears simplistic and limited in its scope and accuracy, and even more so from four-dimensional, five-dimensional, and so on perspectives. So too in interdimensional communication—it is wise to realize that channeling is dimensionally relative; one may perceive a stepped-down mirroring of a higher reality that is relative truth in relation to a much more encompassing higher reality. As the spiral-cone of perception progressively increases, what was channeled truth before is then viewed as a simplified foundation from which more encompassing perspectives are to be achieved.

Also, in reaching any given dimension level, what is perceived by consciousness can be distorted by imbalanced ego-personality traits, expectation patterns, and fantasy. The interdimensional communicator is the filter through which the higher dimensions are perceived. If the filter is out of focus, so are the perceptions.

There are also transitional states of integration into new communication zones. When first breaking through into a new level, the "rush" of powerful energy is many times overvalued. This is a transitional breakthrough, and in order for effective communication to take place in the future, a time of integration and adjustment is necessary. As repeated communications within this new access area occur, consciousness becomes able to focus, integrate, and assimilate more efficiently and clearly. The individual is then able to put the new informational context into a more balanced, accurate perspective.

For all these reasons, there is an abundance of limited and mischanneled information on the earth plane today. It is imperative that each person exercise astute judgment as to what channeled information to choose to believe, regardless of the form that it takes. It is the inalienable right of each individual to accept or reject any or all aspects of any given interdimensionally-derived information.

In judging the accuracy of one's own or others' channelings, then, it is wise to realize that: 1) perceived truths are many times limited in relation to the more encompassing higher dimension octaves of these truths; 2) there are margins of error related to the imperfections of consciousness; 3) balanced integration into higher communication levels is necessary before the information is received in a clear context; and 4) all paradigms of knowledge are open-ended and so is all information received from interdimensional communication. (Further perspectives in this regard are explored in Chapter 19, "Interdimensional Communication.")

THE BIOCRYSTALLINE HUMAN ENERGY SYSTEM AS AN INTERDIMENSIONAL MATRIX OF EVOLUTION

The human bioenergetic system is a living crystal communication system. The multitude of biocrystalline components composing it create a multifaceted biocosmic resonating matrix. This essential crystallinity plays a crucial role in creating and maintaining resonant interdimensional interconnectedness within the UEN. Like a jewel floating in deep space, the biocrystalline human energy system is "suspended" within the universal latticework between star systems. In this way, the crystallinity of the individual is in synchronized rhythm entrainment with the multitudinous levels of the Higher Self and with the Universal Mind as a whole. All of evolutionary development occurs in and through this human lattice superimposed within the UEN lattice.

The crystalline aspects of the human bioenergetic system are manifold. In fact, the entirety of this system can be viewed as a living biocrystalline matrix. Blood, cerebrospinal fluid, and cholesterol esters, for example, are bodily liquid crystal mediums. A liquid crystal has characteristics that lie between those of a true liquid and a true solid crystal. Their orderly behavior is illustrated in such technologies as liquid crystal displays (LCDs). Bone, cell salts, DNA, proteins, and microtubules, for example, are inorganically and organically based biocrystalline substances. Specifics about these substances will be explored in Part II; the points that are pertinent here are: 1) biocrystalline substances are directly involved with all of the most causal aspects of the human energy system (as well as being primary health maintainers and regulators); 2) there are numerous different types of biocrystal mediums, each having particular vibrational patternings and corresponding functions; and 3) many of them serve as primary interdimensional linkage matrices. As shall be shown later, the crystalline correspondences between these biocrystalline substances and the far reaches of the multidimensional Light-body network in relation to the UEN create a unified matrix for universal orientation, interconnection, and evolutionary progression.

In order to set the framework in which to understand the full scope of the human–UEN crystalline correspondence and their far-reaching ramifications, it is first necessary to see that humankind functions as a thinking membrane between star systems.[1] Each individual originates as a multidimensional Though-form on the levels of the Higher Self. Also called the Overself, this level exists within the greater celestial causal levels wherein the divine Image differentiates into numerous Family-group Images and these further diversify into groups of interrelated Higher Selves. Each Overself is able to formulate many Though-code Images, each to be dispatched into a predetermined sector of the UEN. The precise incarnation codes are inscribed within this Image-form and are thereby projected along the appropriate pathways of the UEN. As the Image-form or Light-body is transposed through dimension after dimension, level after level, coded membrane after coded membrane, a Light-body level remains at each UEN matrix zone through which it is projected. This is parallel to the crystalline code-patterns of the UEN that form a full spectrum of different step-down levels of a primary Thought-code pattern that remain at each dimension layer of this network. In this way a multidimensional latticework extending throughout creation is formed and sustained. So too with the primary Image-form—it branches out through the UEN's latticework and leaves a Light-body that corresponds to each dimension level, thus forming a spectrum of step-down crystallizations; this is called the *multidimensional Light-body network.* Thus an interdimensionally continuous network-spectrum of symmetrically corresponding Light-body codes extends into manifestation, all of which maintains a direct linkage with the originating Thought-Image of the Higher Self. This interdimensional encodement process forms a hierarchical grid-work of primary Light-bodies that branch into secondary systems of Light-bodies, and these diversify even further down through virtually numberless dimension levels.

Figure 6 demonstrates this hierarchically branching network in a simplified manner. Here it is seen that numerous Higher Self step-down levels serve as primary coordinators for a subsystem of Light-bodies that emanate from that particular strata of the Higher Self. These sub-higher selves are stationed at primary threshold dimension zones in the UEN; many times, in the cosmic dimensions, these are star system threshold areas. They then function as a master control blueprint for the Light-body spectrum enacting evolutionary functions in that particular star system (or in the higher domains, celestial threshold zones). Additionally, they serve to receive code-patterns from the next highest level of Higher Self (which receives Light-codes from the next level up, and so on to the Overself) and project them into enactment within its subsidiary Light-body network. This entire Higher Self network is a vast spectrum of hierarchically interrelated, interdimensionally interconnected subsystems whereby the Overself projects coded Light-body patterns into creation to enact evolutionary Light-functions.

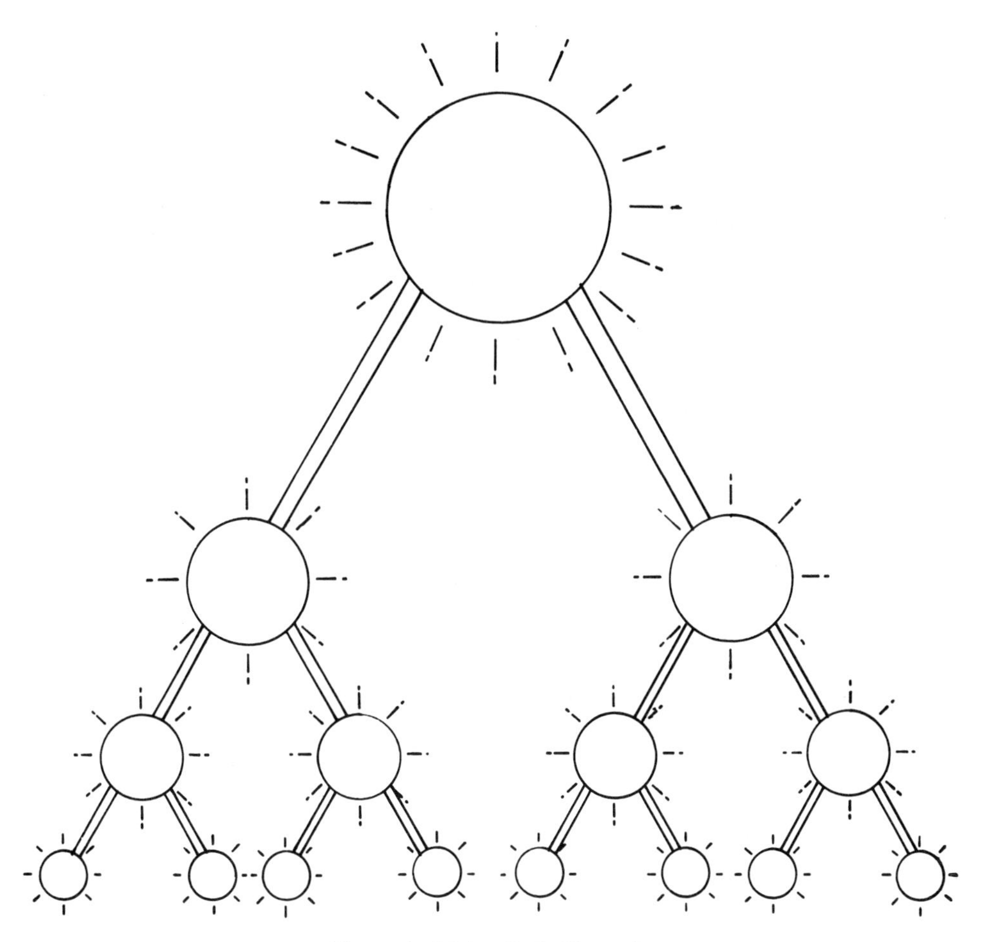

Figure 6: Light–Body Network

A Light-body network within a specific dimension's domain coordinated by a sub-higher self level enacts a program of Light-functions as a collective group. Within certain multidimensional parameters determined by the specific cosmic or celestial threshold zone, the Light-body network "fans out" into myriad dimensions, domains, galactic zones, and planetary systems within a threshold zone. Each projection of this network has a particular function to enact that relates to the overall purpose of the entire Light-body network. This process is formulated and enacted with synchronized synchrosimilarity. The unfoldment of this multidimensional gridwork can be viewed as facets of Light mirroring diverse aspects of an overall plan, each Light-body projection enacting its function in interdimensional harmony with other such projections, all enacting different facets of the blueprint of the coordinating Higher Self sublevel. The Light-body network establishes a field of Light within a threshold zone's field of Light therein to effect individual and collectivized programs of evolutionary development and spiritual service.

The dynamics of this Overself network constitute the framework for all evolutionary unfoldment enacted in the Light. Within these dynamics there are two fundamental evolutionary purposes. One involves the projection of a more advanced Light-body network into a less evolved threshold zone for purposes of service. The other is the stationing of a Light-body network within a threshold area containing Light-coding patterns that facilitate evolutionary progression.

The infusion of more advanced individual and collective networks of Higher Intelligence into lower evolutionary domains is a function of the *star seed* and *celestial seed*. The star seed consists of these Light-body Intelligence networks whose primary evolutionary domains are the advanced cosmic, intergalactic species of greater spiritual advancement. The celestial seed originates from beyond the intergalactic energy-matter Light-spectrums—the celestial realms of pure energy emissions—inclusive of the domains of higher angelic orders and a spectrum of levels of mastership. These star and celestial Intelligence networks are projected into lower evolutionary kingdoms for the purpose of providing various levels and types of service in assisting the entities in that threshold zone to evolve in the most optimal manner within divine Law. The individual and collective Light-body networks of this Light-seed are infused throughout the myriad dimensions, domains, and membrane-levels of an entire evolutionary threshold kingdom. This Light-network serves to: 1) create an interlinkage with the higher levels of Universal Intelligence, 2) teach and maintain divine Law, 3) monitor and assist lower evolutionary intelligence in spiritual growth cycles, both individually and collectively, and 4) infuse higher Light-code energy patterns throughout the evolutionary kingdom in preparing it for the Omega point of ascension and reprogramming into the next major cycle of spiritual growth. Note that the primary function of the star and celestial seed is service through the employment of already highly developed spiritual abilities. This service is analogous to a college graduate teaching second graders material that is on the second grade level. The second graders would learn from the college graduate, but the college graduate's knowledge of the material would not be significantly furthered by the second graders. So also with the Light-seed; spiritual growth that may occur is a by-product of serving the Light with advanced consciousness capabilities.

The second evolutionary process is that in which a Light-body spectrum is encoded into a particular evolutionary kingdom to partake of the spiritual growth opportunities intrinsic to that zone. It is said that in the Father's House there are many mansions; there are countless fields and "pastures" of Intelligence spanning the heights and depths of creation, each threshold-field manifested within specifically coded parameters. Within this hierarchically arranged, access-controlled expanse of Infinite Intelligence, each major threshold zone is like a vast sphere with a semipermeable membrane. This membrane is part of the UEN and the primary areas through which it is semipermeable are called *threshold control zones.* These zones are encoded with the blueprint of evolutionary unfoldment for the entire threshold and with the parameters of Light-code patterns that are to be maintained within the zone. The semipermeable membrane around each sphere also maintains the integrity of that threshold's encodement. Similar to the way that matrix theory is carried out, the threshold sphere is contained within an even greater sphere that is of a higher evolutionary program status and has its own threshold spectrum parameters of Light to maintain. And this larger sphere is encompassed by an even greater sphere, and so on beyond the possibilities of earthly imagination.

Within this scheme, individual and collective Light-body networks are projected to a specific threshold zone that is best suited to its evolutionary growth. As the Light-body network passes through the threshold control entrance, it is encoded with the Alpha–Omega evolutionary program-cycle of that particular threshold. Then, according to its predetermined blueprint, the Light-bodies are established within the framework-lattice of that threshold's field of Intelligence. Each threshold has a distinct spectrum of crystalline Light-codes that *is* that threshold. And as the Alpha–Omega cycle unfolds in conjunction with the blueprint of unfoldment of the Light-body network, the threshold's crystalline energy-code patterns flow through the biocrystalline matrix of the Light-body network. As this occurs, crystalline patterns interact with biocrystalline patterns, and the latter assimilate the weave-patterns into their own Light-body coded matrix. In this way, consciousness is evolutionarily enriched as it incorporates the vibratory patterns that are maintained within a specific threshold.

Another aspect of this process is that the blueprint-program of the coordinating Higher Self also has more individual-specific evolutionary scenarios for the Light-body network to execute. Such scenarios of spiritual development can be enacted only within the Light-spectrum parameters of the threshold zone. That is, within any given threshold, a large, defined spectrum of creative evolutionary programs may be enacted by the Higher Self, utilizing the threshold as the fundamental spectrum-specific substratum that serves as "fertile ground" for evolutionary development.

In all, then, it can be seen that innumerable threshold-fields of Intelligence throughout creation serve as "mansions" and testing zones in which certain patterns of evolutionary growth can be realized. The particular field of Intelligence, itself, is a specific spectrum-pattern of Light in which consciousness is encoded and through which the crystalline threshold Light-codes flow, thereby enriching the crystalline codes of consciousness. And, too, the Light-body spectrum may enact creative spiritual learning-growth sequences within the parameters of the specific threshold. It should be noted also that much of the star and celestial seed, when not in lower evolutionary kingdoms performing service functions, may also partake of spiritual growth cycles in the countless rarefied threshold-fields of Universal Intelligence in the higher cosmic and celestial realms.

Each Alpha–Omega sequence is a grand macrocycle of evolutionary development. The Alpha is the seed-blueprint of wholeness containing the evolutionary program of the entire cycle, just as a seed contains the blueprint of unfoldment of a plant through its complete growth cycle. The Alpha-program unfolds in direct accordance to the original blueprint over eons of time. When the ending of this sequence draws nigh, the Omega point of evolutionary completion and reprogramming arrives. At this time, an accelerated series of spiritual growth opportunities are unveiled in preparation for the Omega "graduation." When Omega is reached, all consciousness is individually weighed and measured to ascertain its evolutionary status and then reapportioned according to divine Law to other evolutionary threshold kingdoms, therein to undergo another complete Alpha–Omega cycle.

Through millions of such evolutionary growth cycles, consciousness experiences grand coded pattern-sequences of progressively spiralling spiritual ascension into higher octaves of spiritual communication capacities. By abiding within myriad threshold fields of Intelligence, the crystalline weave-patterns of each threshold are interwoven within consciousness. And as the cycles progress, the sphere of communicatory encompassment increases in quantum growth progressions with each Alpha–Omega sequence. The more complex and evolved the crystalline codes of consciousness are, the greater the spectrum of communication access throughout the UEN that is gained—each individual's spiral-cone of perception progressively unfolding toward a complete spherical perceptual field of omnipresent communicatory access.

From an earth-plane point of view, the crystalline nature of the earthly self (DNA, blood crystals, and so on) plays a central role in creating a living communication interlinkage with the evolutionary process, from micro- to macrodimensions. The various biocrystalline structures of the human energy system serve as the fundamental interdimensional interconnection points wherein synchronization is maintained with the higher aspects of its Light-body network. Through the crystalline correspondence between biocrystals and their higher octave correlates in the Light-body network, an integrality of multidimensional functions is created and maintained. The physical-plane biocrystals function as interdimensional antenna-receiver-processors that are tuned via interdimensional harmonic resonance to a specific portion of the Light-body spectrum. They selectively receive and absorb higher Light-frequencies and transduce them into the bioenergetic system in addition to transmitting these vibration-specific codes, thus continuously interconnecting the earthly self with the multidimensional Light-body. Christopher Hills shares a perspective in this regard.

> The whole human biological structure can be viewed as an aggregate of liquid crystals and much of the human body is made of such liquid crystals like cholesterol, these crystal structures receiving the radiations of nature peculiar to each crystal form. . . . when these crystals are squeezed or pressured by electrical charges or excited by radiation of any form from an external source, they themselves begin to oscillate and begin to produce electro-magnetic radiomagnetic wave-fields from the nucleus of their atoms. The first radio sets were crystal oscillators and perhaps the human being will be the ultimate radio set when he can . . . excite his own molecular crystal structure through the induction of cosmic rays.[2]

Two of the more important biocrystalline mediums of interdimensional communication are the blood system and the DNA. Although material that is more in depth will cover these two biocrystals and the others in Part II, it is important here to see the primary principles of their higher functioning. The blood system is a water-based liquid crystal medium in which other biocrystalline substances such as cell salts, mineral crystalloids, and hemoglobin function. Water itself is a liquid crystal and, in conjunction with the other biocrystalline substances in the blood, functions as an interdimensional receiver-transducer-distributor of the life essence. The blood system is a stepped-down crystallization of the life-force codes of the multidimensional Light-body and because of the strong interdimensional harmonic resonance between the various dimension levels of the life-essence blood codes, the earthly self is able to set up a communicatory interlinkage with these higher levels. Ruth Drown, D.C., a well-known pioneer of radionics shares a similar perspective.

Ruth Drown, D.C. . . . referred to the blood specimen accordingly as "crystallized light." "It acts," she noted, "as light from the actual living tissues in the body." She noted further that this light is the "Life Force of the body," explaining that "each small atom is the precipitated crystallized end of an invisible line which reached into the ethers" . . . and that this invisible line constitutes an invisible white ray just above white light in the spectrum.[3]

Earlyne Chaney, noted mystic and author, amplifies this perspective.

"The life is in the blood," states the Bible, conveying a secret mystery. The pranic life force in our ethers constantly penetrates the blood stream of mankind. So does the Christ Substance, a divine life stream downflowing from the very heart of the Godhead.[4]

This Mind Level is charged with cosmic crystalline force, flowing down into man's mundane awareness if such awareness opens itself to receive it. For those who do, the bloodstream is gradually becoming a river of light—charged with the love of God.[5]

As a primary crystalline interface between the earthly self and higher Light-vibrations pervading our evolutionary kingdom, the blood is a source of Life-increasing Light.

The DNA, too, is integral to the intercommunication of causal Life-Light codes. The double helix form of DNA falls under the category of a biocrystalline substance primarily because of its highly ordered and complex helical blueprint information storage and duplication abilities (technically, it is classed as a quasi-periodic crystal.) From a more encompassing perspective, the DNA codes of the earthly self are interlinked with the more causal DNA Light-Life codes of the multidimensional Light-body. The physical DNA serves as a harmonic wave-guide/antenna-receiver that is selectively attuned to the higher dimensional DNA codes, thereby linking the earthly self to these causal levels and also serving as the means through which more evolved DNA patterns can be transmitted to and assimilated within the earthly DNA.

The DNA-RNA can then work with higher Light irradiation factors which allow for new changes to take place enabling the body to be ultimately a body of Light. Hence, the recoding DNA-RNA will give forth a new physical form for the body of Light. Man will see how the body of the physical flesh, the physical DNA-RNA, is simply the biochemical preparation necessary for the infusing of the Christ Body of Light.[6]

In sum, then, the crystalline correspondences between the biocrystalline components of the human energy system and their higher-octave vibrational correlates of the multidimensional Light-body create an interdimensional communication network that links the Higher Self with the earthly self both in maintaining the continuous integrity of multidimensional synchronous interlinkage as well as functioning as the matrix through which more advanced Light-code patterns are transmitted to the earthly self to enact spiritual growth cycles. Thus, the human energy system can be viewed as a crystalline body-vehicle of multidimensional Light-communication.

The surging wave of interest in the higher Light-properties of quartz crystals and other gemstones in recent years is an integral aspect of the accelerating crystalline interlinkage between the earthly self and Light-body. It is becoming increasingly common to hear reports that sometimes even the simple act of looking at, holding, or carrying a crystal changes lives in dramatic ways, and that regular wearing or carrying of a crystal, or meditation with it provoke longer term quickenings of consciousness. This would seem to be a somewhat mysterious happenstance, given that the crystal "phenomenon" has only very recently gained a more widespread awareness and intense interest.

Only a few years ago, knowledge and use of the higher properties of crystals was but a small fraction of what it is currently. This mystery clears if one sees the workings of the divine Plan in reactivating ancient knowledge and infusing new thought-forms and vibrational codes at a predetermined time in the earth's Alpha–Omega evolutionary sequence. The accelerating of spiritual growth opportunities in preparation for the Omega point of evolutionary completion and relocation includes the rapid awakening of crystal knowledge. Much of the usefulness of crystals in this regard lies on their consciousness-catalyzing properties. Their energy amplification properties are subtly but profoundly significant in assisting the breakthrough of bioenergetic and consciousness evolutionary thresholds into more accelerated states of awareness in those who are receptive and energetically prepared. In the act of the human energy system interacting with a quartz crystal especially, the crystal's energies establish a resonant rapport with the biocrystalline matrices and stimulate not only an energetic amplification in the biocrystals but also greater states of vibrational coherency and actual changes in the biocrystalline lattice structures on the auric and microscopic levels (that is, recrystallization of bond angles, lattice-code reorientations, and the like). In receptive, prepared consciousness, the effect is one of catalyzing the biocrystalline structures into greater resonant correspondence with the higher Light-codes of the multidimensional Light-body; the earthly self becomes more connected with higher Light. It must be emphasized, also, that it is wise not to be too enamored with the "rush" of extremely potent energies that may accompany the breaking through to a new level of Light. The glittery glamour of such experiences can sometimes blind spiritual perception. Each breakthrough is simply the first transitional step toward incorporating a higher quantum level of Light in an integrated, balanced manner. The period of balanced integration takes time, grounded spiritual practices, and common sense.

Increasingly greater quantum degrees of higher Light are being activated and infused into personal and planetary consciousness, the crystal being a premier catalyst in this regard. Like the swift upsweep of the exponential curve, these Light-energies are accelerating with ever-quickening momentum. Old paradigms are surpassed, the new paradigms then bow to even more encompassing paradigms, and so on through numerous cycles with a pace not ever before experienced on earth. Let us continually keep the spiral-cone of perception open to ever-increasing levels of interdimensional communication.

DIVINE LAW: KEYSTONE OF INTERDIMENSIONAL COMMUNICATION

Divine Law sets the foundations of creation. It is the Law that governs the righteous peoplehood of Light. Whoever lives within this Law becomes the Law; and in so becoming, a living Pillar of Light connecting the individual to the very Source of creation is the verity of one's existence. This Law is the ultimate code for interdimensional communication, for it is inscribed into the quintessential core coding of every vibratory unit throughout the realms of Light. And in incorporating this master code within the codes of consciousness, the key to unlimited communicatory access and absolute communion with the One is activated.

Divine Law is universally all-encompassing in its scope and power. It is like a microscopic seed-crystal, which when placed in a growth medium serves as the blueprint for the growth of the entire crystalline structure; every molecular unit throughout the crystal is duplicated and based upon the original seed-crystal patterning and principle and duplicated accordingly. As the One differentiates into the Many, the seed-crystal ordering principle of divine Law governs the diversification process with great exactitude; thus every vibration inevitably, inexorably bears the supremely causal imprint of the Law.

The laws of universal physics are synonymous with divine Law. As the grids of manifestation are formulated in the highest aspects of the Universal Mind, the abstract numerological-geometrical code-patterns crystallize in direct accordance with divine Law as physics formulations. These abstract code-grids being causal to all derivative formulations as transcribed throughout the UEN, the physics hieroglyphics of the Law are transposed into every subatomic recess throughout Light-creation. In terms of the Law relating to the physics of human manifestation, *The Keys of Enoch* state: "The Ten Commandments are ten pyramidal grids of astroharmonics used to code man, as a space-filling substance, on the Magnetic grids which shape the embryonic lines of growth into perfect mathematical units of living membrane tissue and cellular form."[7] This is another perspective on the truth that humans are made in the Image and Likeness of God. Translated into the physics of humankind's Image-formulation and manifestation throughout the Overself network, the Law is the governing mathematical-geometrical values of grid-code formulation and resultant interdimensional matrix transformation. Herein lies the ruling standard of the weights and measures of the One crystallizing into the Many.

The key here for relating the Law to personal evolvement processes is that this ruling standard is a matrix-code of limitless intercommunication. It is a master matrix that is the true measure of evolutionary development. That is, the greater the degree that consciousness incorporates and activates this code into the matrix of its being, the higher the degree of spiritual advancement. Consciousness codes in relationship to the Law's matrix-codes determine the level of access within the UEN. It is the ultimate access code that first and foremost provides direct access to the One. To "walk in the Light" is to activate the Living Pillar of Light between consciousness and the Eternal, through which the highest power and glory of the Light is shone. Then and only then are the greatest attributes and gifts of Light added to consciousness. Divine Law is a Ten-plus-One dynamic. The Ten Commandments are the foundational framework of the Law. Yahweh inscribed them into stone, then gave them to Moses so that all would know the ruling standards of human conduct and, on higher levels, consciousness evolution and sacred science. These Ten Commandments are the requirements for living in the Light and ascending within optimal spirals of evolutionary development. With the Ten founded within consciousness the matrix is then activated and aligned for the One final fulfilling commandment to be infused; the Ten sets the foundation for the infusion of the One, setting in motion a Ten-plus-One dynamic. The final commandment is the Christ commandment: "A new commandment I give to you, that you love one another; even as I have loved you, that you also love one another (John 1:34)." "This is my commandment, that you love one another as I have loved you (John 16:12)." Visualizing the Living Pillar of Light of the Ten Commandments as a vertical shaft of White Light extending infinitely upward, the action of the Christ commandment is like a thin laser beam of even grander degrees of White Light infused through the central core of the Pillar. This Christ Light pulses downward with instantaneous force and at the bottom converts into an ascension ray going back upward into infinity. The downward-to-upward pulsing action is so fast as to be instantaneous. The Christ Ray synergizes the Ten Commandments into a higher relationship as the final commandment fulfills the wholeness of the Law. It is the "eleventh commandment" that is the Christ Ray of ascension and limitless intercommunication—the Ray in which the earthly self is infused with the Christ Body of Light at the time of personal and planetary ascension.

Notice that the Ten-plus-One commandments are not requests or optional petitions; they are, quite plainly commandments that must be incorporated in one's being in order to live in union with the Light. For individual consciousness, this requires humble acceptance that there are certain Laws that must be adhered to as fundamental facts of existence simply because that is the way that the Kingdom of Light works. The Eternal created each individual in His Image and Likeness; therefore, there are ruling standards that govern how each individual image and likeness must relate to the founding Image in order to be in right relation with the originating Code-Image of existence. To step outside the Ten-plus-One commandments is to step into a state of spiritual ignorance, into darkness-without-Light; it is as simple as that. No amount or degree of spiritual practice, self-transformation and self-healing methods, crystal expertise, interpersonal sensitivity skills, pure and strict dietary and exercise regimes, or anything else outside of these commandments can replace them as the keystone of living a life in the Light. The Ten Commandments are the foundation of the Living Pillar of Light and the Eleventh Commandment activates the Christ Body of Light. Outside of this central reality all other spiritual practices and orientations are secondarily complementary. The truth of the Law is that straightforward.

Humankind was not made for the sake of the Law, but rather the Law was made for the sake of Humankind. Divine Law is conceived in the Eternal's Love for His creation, given as the way in which all consciousness can rejoice in the infinite Love-Light of manifestation in direct union with YHWH. This supreme ordering principle can be viewed as the ultimate access code for freedom-in-Spirit. It is not meant to be a restrictive constraint upon the individual; instead, it is the Way of Living Light, the path that opens the doors to boundless glorification and expanding evolutionary creativity. Humankind was given the sacrosanct gift of free will, to be applied in union with divine Law or outside of it. The choice to follow the path of Light is to abide within the matrix-codes that have access to the illimitable fields of luminous Light. Those that have not chosen to abide within the Law of Light do not have access to the Kingdom of God because their matrix-codes of consciousness do not fulfill the requirements to interact in and through the thresholds of Light. Fulfilling these requirements is not a mere matter of observing the exterior letter of the Law but *being the Spirit of the Law.* That is to say, the innermost attitudes of consciousness are the determining factor, not the outer motions of observance alone. The matrix of the Law becomes imprinted within the deepest levels of beingness; and as they do, they become the foundational evolutionary blueprint of consciousness*.

This process of Law-assimilation is the most essential basis of all spiritual growth, for the Ten-plus-One commandments are not linear statements to be taken at face value alone; they are, in fact, the megamatrix of Light-creation. Each one is an infinitely multidimensional seed-crystal coding of expansive complexity; together, all levels of Light-reality, from microscopic minutiae to macrocosmic immensity, are woven of the crystalline fabric derived from the innumerable energetic combinations and permutations that are possible within the awesome creative potential of the Law-matrix. The crystalline codes of Universal Intelligence are the Law itself differentiated within a universal hierarchical spectrum of evolutionary domains. Eternal Law is like a Jacob's Ladder of ascending freedom-in-Spirit spiraling into perpetually expanding infinitude. The degree to which consciousness has assimilated the hierarchical matrix-code levels of divine Law is the exact degree of evolutionary development, and is the determining factor in the setting of spiritual Alpha–Omega growth cycles and communication access within the UEN. The crystalline human bioenergetic system, resonating within the latticework of the Universal Mind, is "magnetically" attracted to and sustained within those sectors of the UEN with which its own codes match. The lattice of consciousness interacts with a universal lattice level of like-vibration. And as spiritual growth unfolds so, correspondingly, do the codes of consciousness, thereby activating and aligning it to ascend to higher dimensional levels of Jacob's Ladder-Lattice. In this way, an exact congruence is maintained between the hierarchical access levels of divine Law and the relative evolutionary standing of individual consciousness. By providing an all-encompassing latticework in which and through which all consciousness may evolve in union with God, the Eternal Law acts as the supreme matrix of ascending freedom-in-Light.

COMMUNICATIONS ACCESS PRINCIPLES

The principles of communication access throughout the UEN are founded upon laws of code correlation that operate in a manner of access/access-denied. The UEN can be likened to a vast multidimensional supercomputer system that works within precise code-patterns of threshold integrity. Each evolutionary threshold control zone is composed of template code-patterns that determine which spectrums of Light-energies and consciousness codes may pass into that zone. These code patterns are like selective filters that are permeable to specific spectrum profiles of Light and impermeable to others. The same is true within the countless dimensional levels within a given Alpha–Omega threshold zone. Like cells within membranes, membranes within tissues, tissues within organs, and so on, each sublevel within a threshold zone is nested within the others in a hierarchically coded, orderly manner. The codes of consciousness, which have been assimilated through processes of spiritual evolvement, are the determiners of communication access by either passing or not passing through the code-matrix entrance zones to any given dimensional level. Because of this, consciousness gains entrance only

*See in Chapter 14 a specialized Ten-plus-One Commandments gridwork technique.

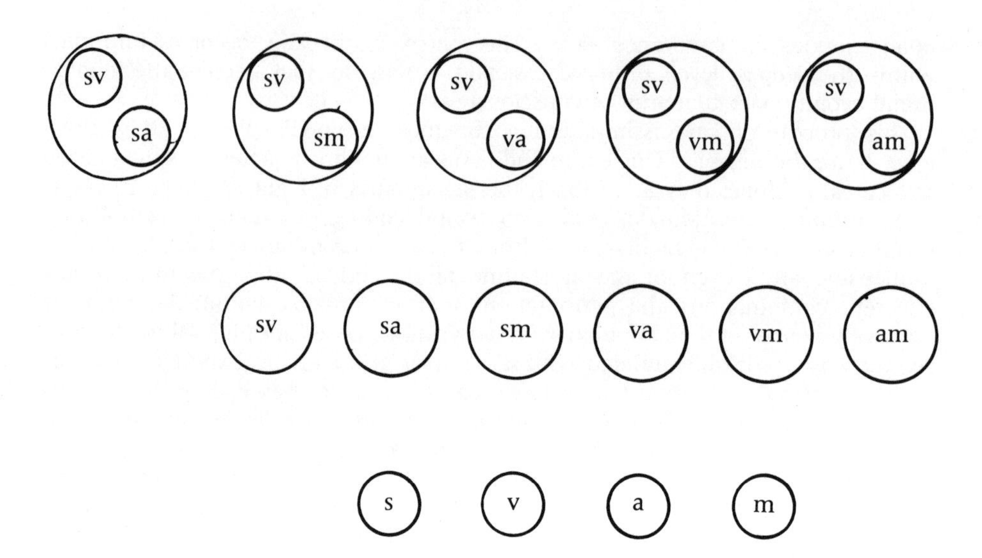

Figure 7: Interdimensional Code-Access Representation

to those communication levels for which it is appropriate to interact within the parameters of divine Law.

To illustrate this concept further, Level I, seen in Figure 7, shows simplified evolutionary threshold codes that consciousness incorporates into its own code-matrix through successfully completing a spiritual growth cycle within that threshold. After completing an Alpha–Omega cycle within an *s* zone, for instance, consciousness has fully assimilated that coding within its matrix. Should consciousness go through *s, v,* and *a* zones, its matrix coding would be an integrated composite of these codes—consciousness would be encoded *sva*. The same is true for any other level I code-zones. Access to the more hierarchically evolved level II zones is determined by which level I codes the individual has assimilated. On the most basic level of understanding, a consciousness matrix with, for example, a level I $a+m$ coding cannot have access to *sv, sa, sm, va,* or *vm* zones. The level I $a+m$ can enter only the level II *am* zone, because it is the only Level II area where the codes match. Further, if an individual has an $s+v+a$ level I coding, the second level areas that can be entered are *sv, sa,* and *va;* those to which access is impossible are the other three—*sm, vm,* and *am*—because the $s+v+a$ consciousness code does not include the level I *m* matrix, and therefore there is not a correlating code-matching in these three no-access areas. When consciousness assimilates all Level I zones—$s+v+a+m$—then all level II zones will be accessible for interdimensional communication and spiritual evolvement. The same principles hold true for gaining access to level III—only where consciousness codes include all the codes of the access template zone will entrance into that zone occur. An individual's gaining or being denied access does not mean that the individual has been judged "good" or "bad;" this process is simply one of code correlation determining communication access according to the physics principles of divine Law.

To go a step beyond these basic concepts just presented, the idea of *fractional access* comes into play. It is not necessary to have total code correlation in order to gain access to another code-zone *in part.* Any consciousness coding will gain access to some degree to the same codings in higher levels (via principles of interdimensional harmonic resonance), even if the matrix codes of consciousness do not fully include all the codings of the matrix to which access has been gained. To illustrate: a level I *s* will indeed gain access to level II *sv, sa,* and *sm* areas because of the inclusion of the *s* element in their coding. Access to these three zones, however, will be only fractional. Consciousness spiral-cone of perception will perceive the *s* portions of *sv, sa,* and *sm,* but will *not* perceive the *v, a,* and *m* portions or the interrelationships between *s* and other associated codes in any given level. Also, there will be fractional access to even those Level III areas that include an *s* coding, but the same principle applies—neither the associated codes nor the complex interactions between *s* and other codings will be perceivable. Basically then, in this example, an *s* coded consciousness has access to an infinite number of higher matrix levels that include the *s* component, but the perception of these higher levels is vague and linear in comparison with the multifaceted complexity that these zones encompass. The effect is analogous to consciousness wearing blinders that limit vision to only a single facet of a much more encompassing reality.

This concept of fractional access applies in practice to a deeper understanding of interdimensional communication (or channeling) and its ramifications. The spiral-cone of perception of an interdimensional communicator is limited to those consciousness codes that have been assimilated via successful spiritual growth cycles through various evolutionary thresholds. Each individual has his or her own profile of assimilated consciousness access codes. Therefore, the specific UEN zones to which a person has access and the wholeness of access are determined by this consciousness profile. Two points must be emphasized here. First, every individual on earth has access codes that are more fully developed in some areas that in others. Spiritual growth patterns over many Alpha–Omega cycles tend to concentrate within certain spectrums of the Universal Mind that correlate to the individual's chosen avenues of evolvement. That is, some individuals have much greater access to aspects of the UEN that contain scientific code-patterns; others have more well-developed lines of communication with, for instance, artistic code-patterns; and so on. There are myriad possible areas of specialization in this regard. Interdimensional communication outside the boundaries of specialization becomes progressively more fractionally accessed.

Where an individual's delineated lines of communicatory access lie is directly related to the specific area in which the person has divine authority to perform certain functions of Light-work. A person's area of specialized interdimensional access usually has direct correlation with his or her Spirit-derived authority to act. This authority does not necessarily correlate with societal authority and its diplomas, certifications, positions of earthly authority, and the like. For example, an individual may have divine authority in an area of healing, but may or may not have undergone corresponding earthly schooling and accreditation processes. An interdimensional scientist may have divine authority to research, develop and teach the sacred sciences but may or may not have university scientific degrees. Spirit-derived authority, within Universal Law, is the foundation for performing

Light-work on earth. Determination of one's exact area of divine authority and enactment of such authority within divinely prescribed bounds is one of the most critical issues that an individual faces. For, to either not actively enact one's area of authority or to perform Light-work outside the bounds of divine authority is to be less within divine Law. This is a personal issue, one that can be assessed only in humble communication with one's own Higher Self and the Eternal.

The second point concerning fractional access complements the concept discussed earlier in this chapter of the interdimensional communicator discerning only partial perceptions in the communication process and the limitations therein. Recall the idea of a higher truth being stepped down to lower dimensional levels so that the whole picture is mirrored in only a relative way within these lower levels. The principle of fractional access adds yet another perspective in comprehending how interdimensional communication many times does not encompass the whole picture. Not only is a higher truth stepped down through the UEN but there is also the possibility of having only fractional access to this stepped-down truth. Hence, here is another reason to use astute judgment concerning any interdimensionally derived information.

This applies to every form of channeling, including the type in which the channel leaves the body and a higher dimension entity talks through the channel's consciousness-vehicle (many times called trance channeling). The channel is the filter through which communication occurs, and the spiritual advancement and limitations of the channel determines how much of the higher truths can come through, regardless of how advanced the higher dimension entity is. The channel can be seen as a consciousness matrix whose access codes determine the area of specialization in which the clearest channeling will occur and the degree of depth of access to higher truths. All principles described here concerning communication access pertain to *all* types of channeling. Again, every individual must decide whether to accept or reject channeling and interdimensional communication that occurs in any form.

Crystals play an important role in clarifying, extending, and amplifying interdimensional communication abilities. As discussed in chapters 1 and 2, physical-plane crystals are the earthly materializations of the crystallographic aspect of the UEN. They function as primary interdimensional linkage mediums through which access to the next higher level of the UEN—the planetary etheric crystals—is facilitated; and through the etheric crystals communication access to successively higher levels of the UEN is possible. Crystals help establish a harmonic interconnection with the UEN in which the access code-patterns are held in place with great stability and through which consciousness is amplified to higher quotients of communication capabilities. As consciousness interacts with an appropriate crystal, the vibratory pattern of the individual start to oscillate in synchronized harmony with the vibrating crystal latticework. A resonant feedback loop between the crystal and consciousness progressively builds up the overall energy charge. As the individual decides what aspect of the Universal Mind he or she wishes to gain access to, this specific energy-pattern also intermixes with the building charge within the crystal-consciousness interaction. When this energy reaches a certain threshold, interlinkage occurs that connects consciousness to the etheric crystal network. As this happens, the etheric level of the UEN automatically processes consciousness through the appropriate pathways of the UEN to the desired zone. Throughout this entire process the principles of communication access are in operation, and if the individual has code clearance to the desired realms, it occurs without interruption. If there is only partial clearance, then the consciousness signal is processed according to the principles of fractional access described earlier. The UEN works in an automatic fashion in processing consciousness codes along the desired lines of intention, in much the same way as a phone is picked up, the telephone number is punched in, and the phone company processes the signals automatically to connect with the desired communication region. Once connected with the appropriate realm the person is able to establish two-way communication for receiving desired information vibratory frequencies. The physical-plane crystal assists consciousness in focusing applied energies, amplifying them for stronger interdimensional linkage, and holding the access lines of communication steady during the entire process. Crystals both clarify an individual's spiral-cone of perception and extend it to the next higher quantum level, thus affording consciousness with magnified communication abilities.

THE ASCENSION: PROGRAM VICTORY

> Rejoice Children of Uprighteousness and Light, the crystalline fields of Light upon your doorposts of the body temple have been activated, for you are part of the greater star seed.[8]

> The transformation of the specie occurs through the infusion of light crystals which generate a field of Light around the body and a feeding of Light to the body for the next stage of creation.[9]

> Those who will be delivered directly from the face of the Earth will be taken through the crystalline staircase that corresponds to the Christ crystal within their body of physical form.[10]

The ascension is *the* spiritual imperative of our time. All other issues, from attempting planetary peace to alleviating world hunger, pale beside this trumpet Call to all nations, all peoples, all individuals. For nothing else can come to fruition until the ascension is fully completed. The Omega point of evolutionary completion fast approaches. Like the dawn that breaks through the deepest dark, the Omega point of renewal, regeneration, and reestablishment of divine Law inevitably unfolds as the foundations of darkness upon this planet crumble into dust only to be wholly remade into the crystalline Light-particles of a New World ascended.

The planetary timepieces approach the twelfth hour. A deep undercurrent of Light swells to a world oblivious. Causal crises quicken, perhaps to awaken some. Deception then to many, and a false peace slumbers. Children of Light, empty, cry out. The Hand of God delivers the righteous seed. Two more callings to all the world. The swiftness of deliverance eludes many unborn. Darkness closes within itself—void black hole to banishment. Earth to Heavens, ascended. Children of Light born in Spirit unto eternity. Christ and the Lords of Light govern the Kingdom of God on Earth. *Ehyeh Asher Ehyeh*—I Am That I Am.

The People of Light are to be activated into their higher calling. Indeed, the crystalline fields of Light within the human network are being infused with increasing gradients of Higher Intelligence toward activating the star and celestial seed to their seats of knowledge and authority. With the coming of new Light never before seen on earth, even in ancient times, this call includes the need to release a new age-become-old, the vestiges of one metamorphic cycle leading to others far grander and greater. Esoterica collapses unto its very foundations, as do the priesthoods of modern science, as Light suffuses the matrices of earthly knowledge with a matrix anew. Middling new age phenomena dissolve into a polarity of opposites—one crystallizing into rigid attachment, the other releasing into new, quantumly increasing paradigms of Light. And not the least, this call requires an end to the games of children playing out dramas of inaction and false action as well as egocentric strutting of false personas. The Light calls for righteous action in a time of rampant flailing at shadows. To respond to the Higher Intelligence overseeing Program Victory is to humbly bow one's head to a crucifixion of all remaining egocentric pride and attachment. There is no middle ground; there is either total commitment to Light and corresponding action, or there is a holding on to comfort that is no comfort, money that is no money, truths that are no truths. All falseness that blinds must be purged completely, else the falseness will not only blind, but bind to earthbound dust and corruption. Know that an accounting is due upon arrival of the Christ and the Lords of Light on earth, for all are indeed held accountable for actions and attitudes accruing to the Light or denying of the Light.

Where to start? Start with the blade of the Ten-plus-One Commandments. Look not only to their surface meaning but to their higher correspondences. Cannot one steal not only physically but also emotionally, mentally, and spiritually? Does not having no other gods before YHWH include the "gods" of attachments, attitudes, and actions that do not put divine Will above all else? Sear the misaligned codes of consciousness with the sword-imprint of these most holy of universal codes. Then and only then will the Christ crystal within the body of physical form be activated as a seal of ascending Light-consciousness.

The Scriptures of Light state that a miraculous outpouring of the gifts of the Holy Spirit will break forth as the end times near. The treasures of the Heavens will rain upon those of abiding determination to manifest Light in the face of increasing adversity. It is written: "And the ones having insight will shine like the brightness of the expanse; and those who are bringing the many to righteousness, like the stars to time indefinite, even forever."[12] As the bonds of the foundations of earth are unleashed and the earthbound shells of materialism crack and crumble, those who abide in Light in defiance of external appearances shall shine with radiance dimly remembered and spiritual authority recently rekindled. Know this as the Call is given through yet another means that though temporary adversity falls upon the world in clouds of darkness, the Light shines with piercing power and glory as the appointed times unswervingly draw nigh. Rejoice, for the tables are set in the Heavens for the People of Light to unite with the Elohim God-Family. Yet to be in countless millenia to come, the fields and pastures of Yahweh's Kingdom will be as unimagined dreams of freedom-in-Spirit, even unto forever.

The Kingdom of YHWH is the birthright of all. The Family of God is open to all the peoples of the world. The gateways to the higher mansion worlds are laid clear to those who would "choose to be chosen." The Higher Evolution who administer Program Victory serve all who humbly ask. Lay bare the soul to the Eternal and be filled to overflowing, even unto forever. . . .

CHAPTER 4

Crystalline Essence: Axis and Form

The essence of crystallinity is its axis interrelationship coding. From the highest realms of Abstract Light wherein purely numerological matrix formulations crystallize as abstract seed axis-codes, all else throughout creation derives and is interconnected. Axes within axes, lattices within lattices, universal crystallinity unfolds its supraholographic matrices through level after quantum level, each aspect inextricably interconnected with all other via axis-code and form energy affinity harmonics. All is Number-based angle; all interrelates via angular correspondences; the UEN *is* axis interconnections.

Number is the *ontos* of creation. *Abstract Light* on the highest dimensions is Number-without-Form; Numerological principiums engage in objectless abstractions of unity-imaging. Oneness, Twoness, Threeness . . . the awesome substratum-foundation of the deeps as well as the majestic heights of glorification-in-wholeness . . . the All in All . . . Creation's Blueprint in Crystalline Wholeness.

Omnivector-coded Abstract Light transduces into the lattice-axes of *Abstract Form-Life-Light.* Grand omniholographic numerological vector-codes crystallize as ultrararefied seed-code axes-interrelationships. The master codes of manifestation are thus set, for these axis abstractions are the essence of Consciousness encoded into creation. All potential consciousness interactions derive from these supreme blueprints of universal order, these vector templates of universal Law. Axes-code abstractions establish the founding orientational and interactional indexes for all Light in every mode of manifestation and interrelation. Far from being just the crystal-mineral kingdoms' formational parameters, they apply to every module of Intelligence. Figure 8 illustrates the seven known primary crystal axes systems; these are the "fundamentals" from which innumerable primary, secondary, and tertiary axis-code "harmonics" derive. The 32 crystal classes* are the primary derived formulations (or "harmonics") of the seven axes systems. These 7 crystal systems and 32 classes are the supracausal "alphabet" of axes interrelation codes for every unit of crystallinity in creation. These axes formulations are the seed-core dictums of universal order; from them, all the innumerable universal spectrums of form and energy pattern derivations and variations are possible. They are

*These can be viewed in comprehensive mineralogy and crystallography texts.

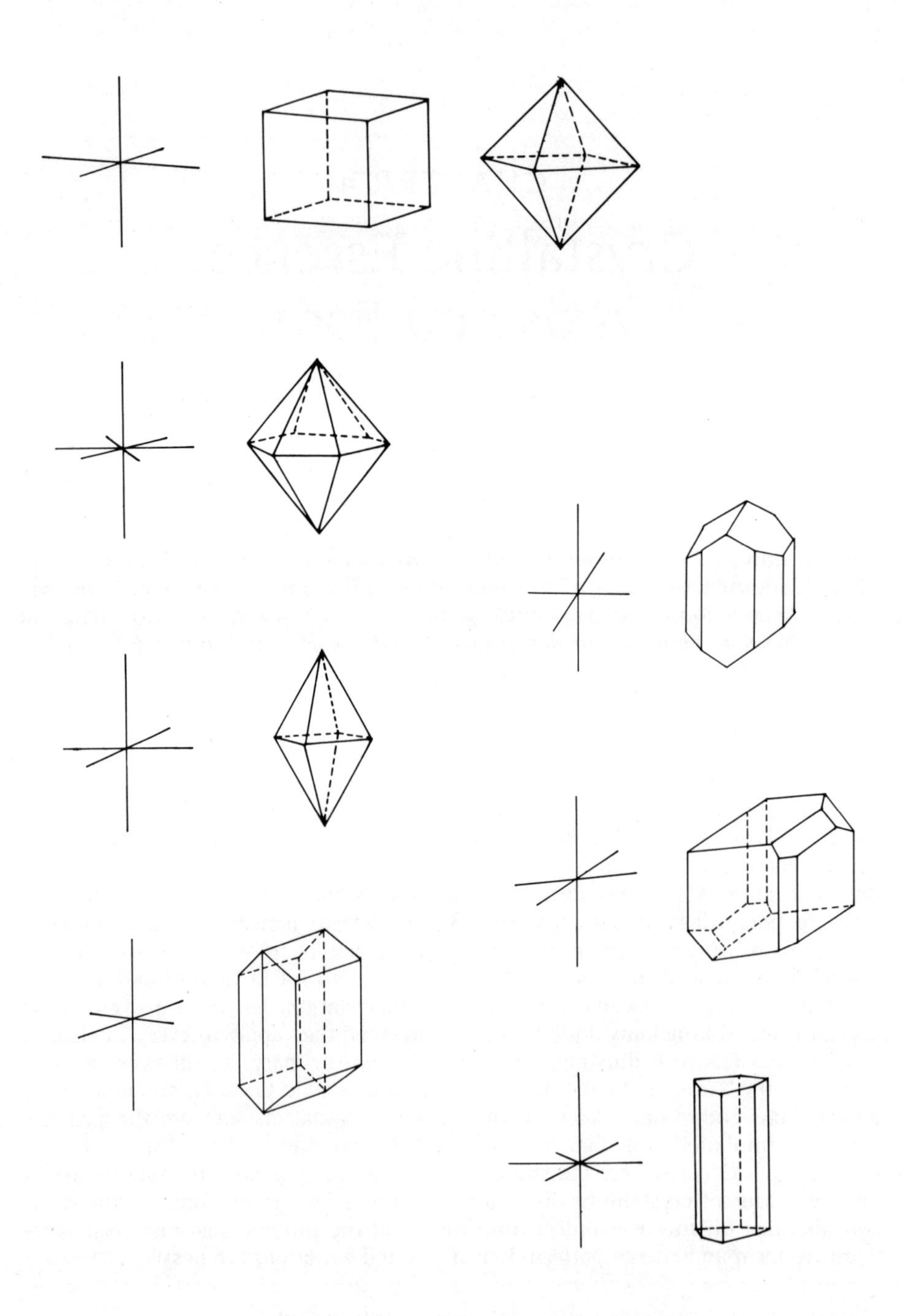

Figure 8 (a, b, & c): The Seven Crystal Systems

seed-crystals, acting as the keystones that provide the essential blueprint dictums of Universal Intelligence. From each different axis-pattern, countless variations of the fundamental theme are possible, each variation unfolding within the indexed multidimensional ordering of a single axis-code spectrum. The 32 crystal systems and 7 classes are the veritable code-keys of the universe. Their unvarying dictums form the parameters of the divine Law within which infinite creative differentiation is then possible. (Note that these crystal systems and classes as they are presented in the three-dimensional form are derivations from more causally inclusive hypergeometries of the hierarchical quantum dimensional matrix spectrum. These axis-codes would appear quite different within the higher realms of Light than they do on the earth plane.)

The singularly supreme axis-code that encompasses and originates these 7 and 32 seed axis-patterns is that of the Pyramid of Light. At this level of reality—Abstract Form-Light-Life—the actual geometric form of the Pyramid is not yet actualized; its abstract causal parameters herein abide. The Pyramid of Light abstract is the Code for all codes, the Root of axis-pattern derivations, the ultra-Seed from which all axis-seeds originate. The Pyramid, then, at this level, is the preeminent source whose axis-codes create the core from which the full spectrum of the 7 and 32 axis patterns originate and from whose foundational parameters they derive. The Pyramid's abstract coding cannot be envisioned within three-dimensional coordinates, for all-inclusive, multidimensional axes parameters go far beyond into the most complex of hypergeometric and hypernumeric levels of scientific understanding. (The Pyramid of Light steps down to the Great Pyramid geometrics on the physical plane of reality.) The essence of the matter is that this single axis-code forms the root from whence the entire spectrum of universal axes interrelationships originates, and is the master paradigm encompassing every level of Light-interactions throughout the UEN.

As the axis-codes of Abstract Form-Life-Light step down to the next major quantum dimensional stage of crystallization into manifestation, the level of *Primary Form* develops. At this level axis patterns "precipitate" into their corresponding primary geometric forms; the planar correspondence to numeric-angular abstractions formulate into geometric actualization. At the higher levels of Primary Form, only the primary geometries that accord with each of the 7 and 32 axis-codes crystallize. At succeeding levels, the secondary and tertiary derivations of each primary geometry "branch out" in a wide array of interrelated crystallization patterns. Each of the geometries throughout the realm of Primary Form (and, indeed, throughout creation) has a corresponding numerological-axis code equation that describes its unique configuration and abiding Light-activity principles. It is important to understand that these geometric crystallization patterns are code-constructs of Light-activity principles in their most rarefied of seed-formats. Rather than being static figures, they are the lattice-templates through which higher Light flows into creative diversification. They are a universal "alphabet" that singly, and in limitless combinations, forms the causal matrix relationships of Light that are then transferred into corresponding sectors of the UEN and transduced to their appropriate multidimensional settings. Therein they function as the nucleus coding from which manifold derivative Light-codings formulate and interact in a given dimensional or domain sector. This universal geometric alphabet is the governing principle of Light-in-creation.

Also occurring in the Primary Form level are the higher octave correspondents of the five Platonic solids (that is, Platonic hyper-solids)—the tetrahedron, octahedron, cube, pentagonal dodecahedron, and icosahedron (see Figure 9). These are the only five forms possible (in three-dimensional geometry) that are bounded by plane surfaces having exactly the same size and shape. In each of these five regular polyhedrons, and in no others, the angles between the edges are the same, the angles between the faces are the same, the length of the edges and the distance between adjacent vertexes is the same, and the size and area of each of the faces is the same. Their origin is unique. They formulate during the transition from Abstract Form-Life-Light to Primary Form as a result of harmonic interreactivity between the Pyramid of Light and the different harmonic interactions of the 7 and 32 axis-codes. The Platonic solids are the results of complex interconjunctions, being the nodal points of interaxis-code harmonics. The unique symmetry relationships of the Platonic solids are direct mirrored reflections of the elegance intrinisic to the complexity of universal order at these rarefied levels and, reflectively, throughout manifestation. The Platonic solids, then, can be viewed as key standing wave form results of the harmonic union of the 7 and 32 axis-codes (overpatterned by the Pyramid). As such, they exemplify in miniature "seed" form the interpatterning relationships of these primary axis-codes. Because of their unique centrally unitive positions, the Platonic solids exemplify the master codes regarding the interrelationships between the axis-codes of the entire realm of Abstract Light as it transduces into Primary Form.

The Platonic solids have a nesting pattern wherein each form is harmonically superimposed within another (see Figure 4). There are also numerous ways by which they can be generated from each other, thus showing their integral collective relationship. For example, by connecting both diagonals of all six faces of a cube, the edges of two interlocking tetrahedrons are generated. The other such numerous geometric relationships are well explicated in the literature of sacred geometry. The main idea here is that it is the nesting pattern itself and all the associated intergeometric relationships between the Platonic solids that form the harmonic nodal points of the Abstract Light axis-codes combine, interreact, and transduce to succeeding dimensional levels. This same type of relationship between Platonic solids and axis-codes is mirrored in numerous ways throughout the energy dynamics of the UEN.

Within the Primary Form level as a whole, a full universal spectrum of numeric-geometric potentialities is generated. Variation upon variation, derivation upon derivation originate from the more primary axis-code geometries unfolding in a highly ordered, dimensionally differentiated, indexed manner. The geometry of Universal Intelligence in all its infinite combinations and permutations herein abide.

From the higher levels of pure *potentia*, the Universal Mind formulates specific Thought-scenarios as to the blueprinted manifestation of grand threshold zones. The geometrics of Primary Form crystallize about these Thought-scenarios such that geometric patterns are "magnetically" attracted to those facets of the scenario-blueprint with which they have resonant correspondence. This is a most complex process, one in which geometry within geometry within geometry couples together in intricate multidimensionally multiplexed code arrangements. Unimaginable centillions of such geometrically coded arrays formulate with

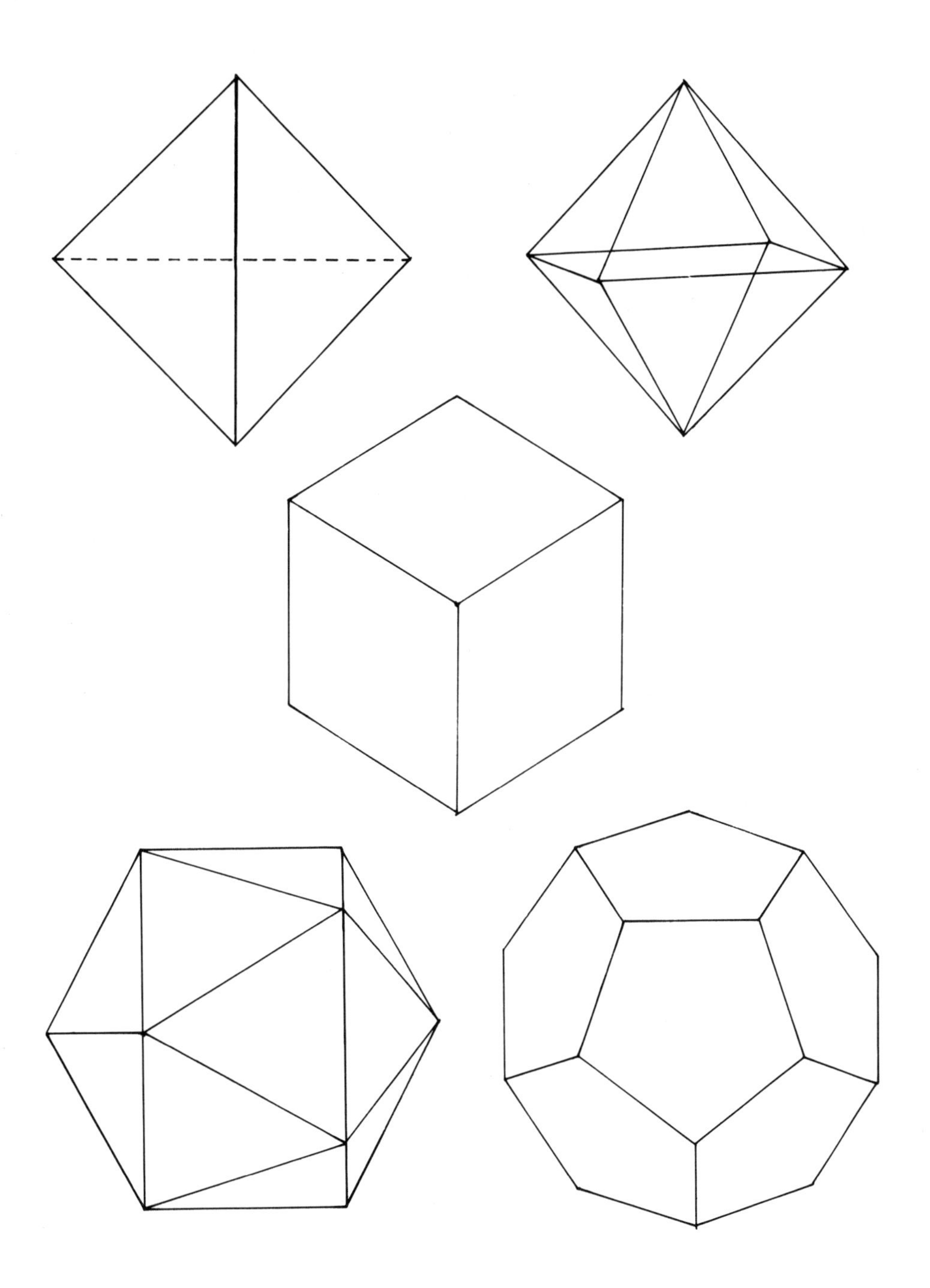

Figure 9: The Five Platonic Solids

mathematical exactitude within code-patterns that correspond directly to the abstract Thought-form transduced into the level of Primary Form. In this manner the architectural schematic of every Alpha–Omega Light-function within grand threshold zones of the UEN are crystallized. During this incredible megacrystallization process, the DNA Light-Life codes and pictographic Language of Light aspects are held in abstract *potentia* until the geometric axis "framework" has precipitated, into which these two complementary elements are predeterminatively "nested." That is, an integral part of a geometrically based crystallographic component's coding contains parameters that provide the complementary "supportive" receiver-matrix in which which appropriate corresponding DNA and pictographic codes interlink like keys fitting into a lock. Thereby the Abstract Thought-scenario transduction into correlating crystallization codes is holistically completed.

Toward the lower levels of Primary Form as the megacrystallization comes unto completion, different Thought-scenarios are "magnetically" drawn to various orientations with regard to the rest of the vast UEN network. Different threshold zones have zone-specific angular orientations relative to each other and the levels of Primary Form. That is to say, each threshold zone has its relative place within the wholeness of the UEN, parallel to an organ's or body system's ordered orientation in relation to the whole of the bioenergetic system. Each Thought-scenario is processed along multidimensional lines of orientation to which its particular macrocoding corresponds. This occurs as part of the natural flow of interdimensional physics; effortlessly, each Thought-scenario follows those particular lines of force that harmonically mesh with the scenario-specific overall UEN code orientation.

At the point of reaching the membrane between the lower levels of Primary Form and the upper reaches of the celestial Light-realms, each coded aspect of the Thought-scenario is in perfect synchronous alignment with the UEN at large and those multidimensional realms into which the Thought-patterns are to be infused. An interesting phenomena occurs within that aspect of the Crystalline Sea into which the Thought-scenario is to be projected, reflecting instantaneity and unity-imaging factors intrinsic to the Universal Mind. What occurs is that the Crystalline Sea of relatively undifferentiated Light coalesces into a more coherent patterning reflective of the future Thought-scenario to be infused. This occurs as an anticipatory response of the relatively undifferentiated Light so that it forms an associative, complementary matrix of receivership into which the Thought-scenario is processed with effortless efficiency.

The nature of the Thought-scenario coding is that of multidimensional supra-holographic matrix symmetry relationships. There are codes within codes within codes on myriad dimensional levels, all interrelated via matrix symmetry principles. That is, a single Code in accordance with its overall code complex blueprint, has numerous dimensions, levels, and layers of networklike numeric-geometric codes and code derivations. A branching network of a complexly interrelated, differentiated coding structure fills in the outlined details, structuring, and Light-dynamics of a single Code. A Code projected into manifestation has the complete blueprint of wholeness for its vastly diversified multidimensional unfoldment. As it processes through the UEN it leaves a code-pattern that correlates to a specific dimension level. The remainder of the code-structure that has yet to reach its predetermined destination of crystallization into manifest reality remains "dormant" within the overall Code. When each matrix level of the Code reaches its specific positional orientation, it is activated into actualization and thereby apportioned within its corresponding dimensional layer according to its code-patterns. What was previously a receptive but uncoded Sea-matrix now crystallizes from relative homogeneity into intricately encoded heterogeneity. The code-patterns unfold within the Crystalline Sea, precipitating it into precisely crystallized supra-holographic axial constellations. The Sea matrix is latticed unto Light-bearing-Life of scenario-specific Alpha–Omega cycles and patterns. The seed code unfolds into manifold structuralization, enacting Thought-functions of the Universal Mind.

As a multidimensional whole the Code is quantumly transposed into countless symmetrically interrelated matrix levels. Viewed as a single Code extended into multifold dimensions of unfoldment, each dimension thereof is angularly-geometrically synchronized. Dimensional differences notwithstanding, the full spectrum of code-patterned-into-creation is symmetrically interconnected via *axis-code affinity harmonics.* Within the dynamics of interdimensional harmonic resonance, angular affinity relationships govern the access parameters of universal energetic interconnection and intercommunication.

In essence, like-angle harmonically resonants with like-angle. Angles combine into axis patterns and associated geometries create an angular quotient that describes the specific combinatory relationships that compose them as a numerological-geometric equation. That is, every different geometric form (with its intrinsic axis-coding) is a specific universal equation; with the full spectrum of such forms there is corresponding spectrum of correlating equations. Within this spectrum are harmonic relationships, roughly analogous to the harmonics of a piano keyboard, except infinitely more intricate and multidimensionally complex. In terms of intercommunication, access factors regulating communicative exchange are governed by angular quotient harmonics. This is to say that harmonically related crystallization codes have an inherent universal interactive affinity. Where there is harmonic affinity, there is interrelation potential; lack of such affinity neutralizes this potential. If the interrelation potential is stimulated into activity, there is a mutually coherent orientation and, thereby, a resonant transfer of energy. The nature of this energy exchange accords with the angular quotients involved and their mutual interactions. The intensity of the resonant energy exchange correlates with orientational harmonic phase relationships and threshold overlap gradient zone parameters. Numeric-geometric equations and their axis-code affinity harmonics are the essential governing modality establishing the indexes and measures for all Light-dynamics within the entirety of the UEN.

Every unit of consciousness, energy, and matter has a particular crystalline code that it *is.* Collectivities of harmonically-like units coalesce to form crystalline entities. From the microcosm to the macrocosm, such organized unities constitute the full spectrum of Intelligence-functions within a given threshold zone. From DNA and blood crystals to planetoids and galaxial unities, spectrum profile-specific crystalline entities of defined axis-code grouping function as the ordering principle through which holistically diversified Alpha–Omega Intelligence-functions are manifested and enacted. The specifications of the numeric-geometric equation for each type of crystalline entity defines the parameters of Intelligence for which it serves as a matrix of receivership. The specifications of DNA, for example, make it a highly selective antenna-receiver-processor of universal DNA Light-Life-codes. Each individual's unique DNA coding is not only selective to the

DNA Light-life code spectrum in general, but also exceptionally specific in interconnecting that individual to his or her own uniquely corresponding Higher Self network. So it is too with every type of crystalline entity.

There are two primary aspects to any crystalline entity that constitutes its specific vibrational identity and its selective, harmonically synergistic interrelation with the holistic collectivity of its originating Thought-scenario. These two aspects are *axis-code* and *geometric form*. The fundamental axis-code is the core determiner of crystallinity in manifestation. In the crystal kingdom, for example, in each of the 7 and 32 crystal axis codes, only certain crystallographic substances may crystallize in any given class. Pure silicon dioxide—that is, quartz—will formulate only within one particular system without deviation. So too with not only all other minerals, but with all universal crystalline entities as well. Viewing this same phenomenon from a more causal perspective, White Light transduced into a physical crystallographic substance will formulate only within a particular axis system that corresponds with its originating Abstract Light axis-code. In this instance, silicon dioxide is the specific physical medium within the correlating axis class that has the strongest harmonic affinity with transduced White Light. In like manner, all crystalline entities have a preexistent causal axis-code that determines which axis-code system it will crystallize into and the medium (whether pure energy or of the energy-matter spectrums) that will be "magnetically" attracted to coalesce about this axis-coding. Blood crystals, as another example, have a defined axis-code that the primary Light-force principle utilizes as the physical medium in which it crystallizes and through which it flows. This overall principle is the supreme ordering function of axis-codes in creation.

Further, individualization processes within a crystalline entity's domain occur such that within its unvarying axis-code dictums there are many possibilities within those dictums for wide-ranging diversity. A simple example of this is the infinite diversity of snowflake forms within strict hexagonal dictums. In accordance with the universal principle of crystallinity that the exterior macroscopic form is a direct reflection of the internal microscopic form, the outer geometric form of a crystalline entity will demonstrate both its fundamental axis-code system and its unique code-variation. Quartz crystals provide an exemplary illustration of this concept; their exterior planar form is a visible reflection of their internal molecular patternings. The code-variation that each quartz crystal *is* in conjunction with its unvarying axis system crystallizes into physical form as a crystal of unique geometrical form. This preeminent principle applies to all crystalline entities under ideal growth conditions. Universally, all crystallizations' external forms are necessarily directly reflective of the collectivity of the entity's entire code-patterning. For numerous reasons relating to inhibiting energy parameter factors, on the earth plane many crystalline entities do not materialize in their ideal external geometry. For example, most emeralds to not grow as planar, faceted crystalline forms. However, this does not detract from the previously stated universal crystallinity principle; for under ideal, noninhibiting growth conditions, emeralds and all other earth-plane crystalline entities will indeed materialize in their perfect external forms. It is this externalization of the causal axis-coding in addition to the constituent molecular "building blocks" that compose the entity itself that is the complementary aspect to axis-code affinity harmonics. This principle is termed *form energy.*

Form energy is a twofold phenomenon that functions as a universal code affinity harmonic. First, the angular quotient of the external geometrics is a direct indicator of the crystal's entire coding-pattern. This is because the outer form is an externalized logical end result of the interior ordering pattern of harmonically-like units. Second, the matrix substance of which the form is composed contributes associated angular and harmonic aspects. As discussed previously, the substance into which an aspect of Intelligence crystallizes corresponds directly in terms of fundamental vibratory frequency pattern and its atomic-molecular angularity; White Light, for example, transduces into silicon dioxide, the physical medium whose intrinsic vibratory and axis-coding correlates to the blueprint parameters of White Light. Therefore, the physical medium itself is a step-down symmetry reflection of its originating causal blueprint; it is an externalization of both the unvarying and variational axis coding factors.

These two factors of form energy—the external geometric equation and the interior substance qualities and patterning—create a condition of selective harmonic resonant affinity with other like-form entities. Intra- and interdimensionally, the interactional form dynamics occurring between harmonically-like crystalline entities are fundamentally the same as those previously described for axis-code affinity harmonics. The main differences are twofold. One is that form energy is inclusive not only of the ever constant axis-code pattern but also the individual-specific variations upon that fundamental axis constant. Axis-code affinity harmonics include the former, but not the latter. The other is that the form itself externalizes the causal code-patterns into a manifest dimensional setting. It is the "grounded" extension of its originating Thought-pattern within a particular plane. Such dimension-specific crystallization is a necessary aspect of the Thought-pattern being operative within a given dimensional plane.

Form energy, then, is the necessary "outer" complement to the "inner" axis-code. In parallel manner, as with axis-code affinity harmonics, harmonically-like form-equations have a strong interaction potential, both intra- and interdimensionally. The form itself serves as an antenna-receiver-processor of a highly selective energy-profile of the universal Light-spectrum. The external geometry plus the constituent substance is an access formula that predetermines the exact parameters of the universal Light-spectrum with which a particular form has interactive access potential. Blood crystals, DNA, quartz, and so on, have highly specialized *form-code affinity harmonics* with crystalline entities of like-nature. Energetic inter-reactivity and intercommunication throughout the UEN are exceptionally form-code specific. Orientational integrity and ordered interactiveness are created and maintained within the dynamics of form-code affinity harmonics.

The axis-code of a given form determines the unvarying parameter outline of form-code affinity harmonics. The variational coding of a form determines the specific energy profile of affinity harmonics within the invariable parameter outlines set by the axis-code. For instance, blood crystals per se are energetically responsive to the Life-force principle as it relates to the blood in general. On the other hand, each individual has a unique blood-coding that interconnects him or her with a particular Light-body network. So too with DNA in terms of the interdimensional Life-Light codes of a person's Light-body network. With quartz crystals, the selective affinity harmonic attunement is with the crystallographic White Light-principle. The variation-coding of a particular quartz determines the specific access parameters of that single crystal within the White Light spectrum. The angular quotient of a crystal's external form is the specialized access formula; a difference of angular conformation between crystals is a prime indicator of their differences in energetic harmonic affinity, that is, intra- and interdimensional vibrational access. Therefore, each form-code is an angular access formula determinant of both the specific entity-type (that is, as blood is to the Life Force) and individual entity-specific (that is, as the highly specialized blood-coding of a particular individual is to his or her unique Light-body network) parameters. In this way, each crystalline entity is created as and functions as a precise antenna–receiver–processor of highly specific energy-profiles of Intelligence Light-functions.

Furthermore, when humankind creates a particular form—say, the popular pyramidal form—with the exact geometrical proportions and angularity as an archetypal Thought-code (in this case, the physical plane step-down symmetry pattern of the Pyramid of Light), that form is the access formula for creating a resonant receiver for tapping into the spectrum profile and corresponding energy dynamics of the Thought-code. As experiments have shown, the pyramid energy phenomenon will occur to some degree as long as the primary angular outline of the form is present and oriented correctly. Even an open frame pyramid works as well as one with full exterior siding. As with pyramids, so too with all crystalline forms: the angular proportions are the key to creating a form energy resonator that selectively receives a desired aspect of the universal energy spectrum.

Also, the substance of which a form is composed is an important factor for amplifying and focalizing the form energy effect. With pyramids, for example, those made with gold, platinum, or silver will generate optimal results, in large part because their ideal crystalline forms are octahedral; the form-code of these substances has a primary harmonic affinity with the pyramidal form-code, therefore amplifying the overall form-code affinity dynamics to maximal degrees. Further, a form could be made exactly duplicating the exterior geometry of a quartz crystal and that shape would have only the most generalized of form energy access. It is the fundamental frequency and axis-coding parameters of the substance silicon dioxide that maximize the specificity and overall power of the form energy effect. This applies to all other crystalline entities: the angular proportionality of the external geometry in addition to the axis code and fundamental vibrational parameters of the constituent substance are the two major aspects of form energy dynamics. (See Chapters 11 and 12 for further information in this field.)

Thus, Number-based Geometry codes creation. Every aspect of crystallographic, pictographic, and DNA Light-Life codes is numerologically geometrized into manifestation as the quintessential principle of universal order. The axis-code and form-code of every unit of Universal Intelligence is the "language" of universal orientation, vibrational spectrum profile, and access interdynamics. Master Thought-codes extend into multilevel dimensional symmetrical unfoldment, precipitating corresponding axis- and form-codes into actualization. In this way, a vast interdimensional network of symmetrically interrelated crystalline codings are interconnected with each other and the originating Abstract Code-blueprint via axis- and form-code affinity harmonics. The structuralization and interdynamics of the heights and depths of the UEN are thereby established. Thus, the primary mode of intra- and interdimensional interconnection and intercommunication is founded upon exacting principles of numerological and geometrical ordering. Number and Geometry are, then, the inextricable essence of the crystallinity of All, forming the illimitably diverse and ultimately exacting coding of universal existence.

CHAPTER 5

Unifying Spirit and Science: A New World Paradigm of Interdimensional Science

The true spirit of science is illuminated in its root word, *scire,* meaning "to know," and in the Greek root of *physics,* meaning "the endeavor of seeing the essential nature of all things." What has been for so long separated into two dichotomized, nonoverlapping domains—the spiritual quest for universal Truth and the scientific pursuit of the universal truths—are actually two aspects of one unified province of soul evolvement in unison with the Eternal. The Universal Mind *is* Truth and all the infinite truths therein. All knowledge is already known; there are no real "discoveries," only the en-Lightening of consciousness with what has been in existence since the dawning of creation. Soul growth involves the progressive consciousness encompassment of greater and greater degrees of Universal Intelligence. Inextricably linked with this process is the increasing of knowledge concerning the nature and functioning dynamics of the Universal Mind. This knowledge, if it is accurately perceived and assimilated, is necessarily sacred in nature, for it necessarily derives from the manifest Light and universal Law of the Eternal. Such knowledge applied bears consciousness abilities and technologies that reflect the imprint of their divine origin. Interdimensional science is the "crystallization" of universal knowledge into holistic scientific paradigms and Light-based technologies that are in perfect concord with divine order.

Science and technology are fundamentally a direct reflection of consciousness. This is easy to see, for scientific paradigms are necessarily operant in the mind of humankind and thereby implemented via technological tools. Given that the Universal Mind contains preexisting divine Law and all potential intelligence paradigms, if consciousness is aligned in harmony with divine Law then the corresponding science and technology will also be aligned. If, on the other hand, consciousness is out of alignment with divine Law, its scientific-technological conceptions and fruits will then be discordant.

The cornerstone of interdimensional science (also known as sacred science) is an exact congruence with divine Law. Each axiom, tenet, and detail is based upon the elegantly complex Truth and truths of universal order. Light translates into knowledge; therefore the indexes and tables of sacred science are a reflection of the differentiated synergistic holism of Light-in-creation. These indexes and tables are the very scientific Scriptures of Light forming the core blueprint of all scientific wisdom, knowledge, and applications dispensed by the Higher Evolution to a specific level of the UEN. Consciousness aligned with the principles of sacred science will naturally transpose these scientific Scriptures into technologies bearing fruits of wholeness and service to soul growth. In this way, consciousness serves as a scientific vehicle of Intelligence reception, assimilation, and applicative enactment. As this occurs within the parameters of divine Law, Light is glorified and soul growth is served in perfection, abundance, and Love.

The overall function of interdimensional science is as an integrated matrix that both provides the foundational infrastructure supporting individual and collective existence and facilitates soul evolvement opportunities. Each evolutionary level of existence throughout the omniverse has a corresponding blueprint of science and Light-based technologies. Here sacred science is seen as a many-faceted, multilevel phenomenon that can be appropriately modified to suit unique evolutionary parameters as blueprinted by the divine plan. In this way, the highest interests of souls in a UEN domain are served in an optimal manner. In myriad ways, sacred science assists individuals, civilizations, and planetary systems to create a systematized technological matrix that fulfills fundamental survival needs as well as providing accoutrements to individual and collective ways of life appropriate to a given domain. The harmony, abundance, and ordered efficiency of the Universal Mind translates through the scientific-technological matrix such that these qualities are mirrored within a civilization's design. In great part, extraneous tasks and procedures not an intrinsic component of soul growth are minimized, thereby providing maximal time and efficiency for engaging in evolvement-oriented Lightwork and growth exploration. Light-based technologies extend consciousness to a greater scope and magnitude of capabilities through the use of externalized tools that perform a broad spectrum of desired functions. In essence, technology is an externalization of consciousness formulated to support soul existence in ways that synergistically complement a particular stage of consciousness evolvement.

Furthermore, sacred science serves as a matrix bridge that provides multifold means of spiritual advancement. Technology, in this context, does not replace the inimitably essential role of divine grace; rather it serves as an ordered matrix by which consciousness is focused, amplified, and extended through evolutionary pathways in accelerated ways not as readily available without assisting tools. Since the technologies involved ultimately derive from the highest levels of Universal Intelligence and are manifested in accordance with their Light-blueprint, sacred science can be seen as an expression of divine grace given as a gift of Love through which consciousness comes into greater unity with the Eternal. While evolvement-oriented technologies are not absolutely necessary to soul growth, they are exceedingly helpful in facilitating its most efficient and accelerated unfoldment. Some souls within the divine plan opt not to directly partake of Light-based technologies in their chosen path; this is a viable option. On the universal scale, however, the overwhelming majority of souls choose among the vast array of spiritual-scientific spectrums of evolvement-facilitating technologies.

It is emphasized that Light-based technologies are not valued as the goal or "be-all-and-end-all" of evolution. On the contrary, they are simply tools that perform a designated function, and once that function is fulfilled, they are laid aside as consciousness proceeds to higher endeavors. There is no attachment to the tool; it is something that provides complementary assistance. Beyond this, there is no intrinsic worth or valuation of the tool. It is not for consciousness to glorify the tool but for the tool to help glorify consciousness. And ultimately, consciousness surpasses the need for the use of any tool for growth processes in the realms of pure Spirit and thought-form technology.

As a civilization evolves spiritually so, correspondingly, does its science. Within the parameters of interdimensional science, spiritual growth necessarily precedes quantum scientific-technological advancement. Within the illimitable vastness of the Universal Mind are countless levels of scientific knowledge and correlating stages of technological sophistication. Each civilization, according to its blueprint within the divine plan in conjunction with individual and collective interdimensional access capabilities, has a specific level of universal scientific knowledge paradigms that is divinely appropriate for its unique evolutionary status and needs. As a civilization unfolds on the spiritual level so does its access to higher levels of universal knowledge. As consciousness is able to reach greater quantum plateaus of Universal Intelligence, it receives spiritual-scientific truths that imbue consciousness with advanced wisdom and knowledge paradigms. When translated into technological application, a correlating upgrading of sophistication and capabilities accrues. With this, the civilization as a whole advances to a higher level of soul growth support and growth potential. Throughout the eons, a civilization advances through level after level of scientific-technological growth in perfect concordance with the highest interests of its constituent souls, the Universal Mind serving as the font from which all concepts, inventions, and paradigm upgrading flows in accordance with divine Law. Sacred science thereby serves as a Jacob's Ladder of progressive ascendance, an individual and collective matrixed means by which consciousness spans the heights of Universal Intelligence.

The pristine purity and perfection of interdimensional science as just presented is not a utopian dream. It already exists! Within the countless mansion worlds and dimensional domains within the Kingdom of Light, a full spectrum of levels of sacred scientific manifestations are in fully developed operation, and have been for time untold. In these dimensions and worlds, the magnificent abundance, sophisticated harmonization with universal energies, and unimaginable growth potentials of sacred science are an everyday reality; this is a verity of cosmic and celestial existence, for it is the abiding natural condition of all that is within the Kingdom of Light.

This is the divine heritage of planet earth and all those who choose to ascend along with it into the Light-realms. It only appears to be a utopian dream now because in the present epoch humankind has not known interdimensional science save for transient, fleeting glimpses that have had not abiding impact on the orthodox science of today due to orthodox non-receptivity and vested interest manipulation. With the dawning of the climactic Omega point of evolutionary culmination and reapportionment, the knowledge and Light-based technologies of sacred science are to be inexorably activated, supplanting a profane science with one founded upon divine Law.

Current-day science and technology are founded upon aspiritual, human-derived philosophical axioms and "laws." Though an entire book would be required to fully delineate a critique of orthodox science vis-à-vis sacred science, the essence of the matter is this: the former is based upon "objective" human-derived truths and the latter originates from universal Truth, divine Law. From the perspective of the Higher Evolution, humanity divorces itself from the very source of its beingness by denying the truly objective, eternally abiding, universally operative spiritual-scientific principles of divine Law. This Law, far transcending religious belief-systems, is the code-keystone from which all Light-dynamics derive and receive their lawful principles of interaction. This applies to all consciousness activity and quantum physics as well as intergalactic astrophysics and Higher Evolution interdimensional thought-form engineering; in short, divine Law and its correlative derivations are scientific laws that apply to every aspect of Light-in-creation. Unless a science is based upon this Law, it is highly relativistic in nature and acts as a separative force, divorcing humankind from the Eternal, thereby binding it to gross limitation.

No example is more potently illustrative of orthodox science's core defects than its continued use today in the military-industrial complex as a technology of death and destruction. Sacred science glorifies creation and consciousness therein; profane, human-derived science desecrates the holy ground upon which humankind walks and defiles human consciousness thereupon. In the eyes of the Eternal, though humankind may give erudite and prolifically "logical" justifications for such misqualification of science and technology, all such rationalizations are hollow shells of humankind's illusions. Atomic terror, humanity's violence to humanity, and so on, are fueled and increasingly amplified by advanced technological toys conceived and developed in humankind's scientific laboratories. Scientists arrogantly, unthinkingly, unLawfully impregnate the world with the seeds of destruction, both through dramatic means such as atomic and conventional weapons and through more insidious means such as psychotronic weaponry, bacterial warfare, genetic code manipulation, and, sad to say, multitudinous others. Science, rather than being a wondrous matrix of Light-glorification and service to soul growth, is today a pestilence battering humankind into submission to earthbound magistrates.

Even what could be regarded as the brighter scientific side of this portrait of darkness is inevitably affected by the fundamental falseness of the philosophical axioms of orthodoxy. Higher standards of life, quantum advancements in medicine, communications, transportation, and information technology, and all the "positive" benefits of the exponential progress of science and technology suffer from a false premise—human law. A science founded upon divine Law, as opposed to human law, has intrinsic to it principles of harmonization, balance, and regeneration, mirroring the elegant holistic perfection of Universal Intelligence. Light-based technologies are based upon superior knowledge paradigms that provide blueprints of wholeness, harmony, and ordered efficiency. Such technologies have an elegant balance that harmonizes with the universe, and every by-product is harmonic with divine Law. Consider, on the other hand, the price that humankind pays for its "positive benefits." Planet earth has been pillaged and polluted with savage relentlessness and sophisticated systematization. *This* is the foundation upon which rests virtually all modern civilizations' technological progress.

Consider, for example, the inelegance and disharmony of the car (and, implicitly, all petroleum powered devices). The fuel upon which it operates depends upon the massive, systematic draining of the life-fluids of the planetary body: living, breathing Gaia is given no quarter: economic–political–technological concerns are given the highest, and only, priority. Not only this, but the petroleum products are processed through highly inefficient car-machines that spew out pollutants harmful to all life and the planet as a whole. Sacred science, conversely, utilizes such modalities as antigravity technologies, the burning of hydrogen (the most common element in the universe, whose only by-product in this context is heat and water), highly efficient crystal-based technologies with no harmful by-products, and others. Here Light-based technology harmonizes with universal energies. Congruence with divine order yields only balanced and ultraefficient fruits.

Much more could be stated in this regard. Suffice it to say, however, that a penetrating analysis of orthodox science and its apparently advanced knowledge and technological fruits show it be, at core, seriously flawed. While some aspects reflect such non-Law-based flaws more than others, even the more positive aspects are a product of lesser knowledge paradigms dramatically surpassed in superiority of Spirit-derived intelligence by interdimensional science. At base, the error of orthodoxy is a flaw of consciousness. As stated at the beginning of this chapter, consciousness in alignment with the Eternal bears Light-filled fruits, but misaligned consciousness inevitably results in discord. This is exactly what has happened to bring this planet to its current lamentable state of affairs. It is provocative to contemplate what incredible worldwide impact would occur if major laboratory research centers, such as the Los Alamos and Lawrence Livermore laboratories, now predominantly dealing with technologies of death and destruction were turned to receiving and manifesting sacred science. The awesome facilities, brilliant minds, and ample funding could revolutionize the world within a decade with the work of key sacred scientists activated into higher knowledge. What cost, human and otherwise, in pain, suffering, inefficiency, and desecration is the world now paying that it need not?

Earlyne Chaney, in her book entitled *Revelations of Things to Come,* extrapolates to a verity of the coming years with eloquence:

> No longer will visions be relegated to visionaries alone. The entire scientific spectrum will gradually be indrawn into the world of the mystic. Scientists will stand en masse at the threshold of the world of matter and realize, aghast, there is nowhere else to go. Matter will disappear before their advancing technologies leaving only the shining substance of mind, soul, spirit.
>
> Scientists will at first retreat as a body, too bewildered to believe that their sacred laws, their treasured concepts, are anchored on quicksand, paradoxes and contradictions. Then one by one the bolder researchers will brave the abyss, and step cautiously over the gaping chasm that has held them apart from the visionary, the mystic, the prophet, the meta-scientist.[1]

Esoteric science, province of the many Mystery religions, Hermetic thought, yogic traditions, and numerous others has provided humankind for centuries with valuable knowledge regarding the inner dimensions of the cosmos and the human being as well as the keys to unlock the pathways therein. This tradition, in its many forms, has functioned over time as a principal force counterbalancing its historical antagonist, the rationalist school of thought (versus the empiricist esoteric school). Now, at this period of time when we approach the Omega point of ascension, new and surpassingly unitive Light-knowledge is being activated within the Earth's planetary field. Although the higher echelons of esoteric science are indeed valuable sources of wisdom, as the gateways of the heavens open and radiate octaves of information and vibrations never before shone to the earth-plane, the resulting major paradigm transformations will shed new Light upon esoteric science and thereby lift it to new heights of encompassing vision and knowledge. A unique synthesis will occur during this process. Interdimensional science will serve, metaphorically, as the upper apex of a triangle with esoteric science and orthodox science at the lower two corners. With its emphasis on "high" technology, sacred science with illuminate ways in which selective aspects of orthodox science's technology may conjoin with the subtle dimensional knowledge of esoteric science so that they are integrated and then elevated to higher levels of unification via the capstone paradigm of sacred science. In this way, the tools and knowledge of both esoteric and orthodox sciences will coalesce within the integrative, more all-inclusive model of interdimensional science.

It is no coincidence that as consciousness acceleration is being experienced at an increasingly stepped-up pace in these latter days that there is also an incredible acceleration of the orthodox sciences as well as activation of interdimensional science. In fact, all three phenomena are interlinked in significant ways that are key to preparing for the New World ascension. The quickening of sacred science and its first few generations of Light-based technologies is one of the major catalytic means for preparing individual and collective consciousness for the ascension process. One of its primary functions in this regard is to facilitate the controlled transmutation of the human bioenergetic system into higher octaves of Light-receivership and the catalyzation of key brain-mind centers for expanding interdimensional access abilities. An integral part of this process is the activation of the star- and celestial-seeds' Light-knowledge and capabilities. In this way, an astounding rise of sacred science as well as other sectors of spiritual knowledge and abilities will come to pass in a remarkably short period of time, all in unison with the accelerating cycles of the divine plan. In the area of sacred science, ancient and celestial knowledge will arise with startling rapidity, stimulating a revolutionary sequence of scientific events, the magnitude of which will greatly surpass even the Einsteinian sequence of the early 1900s. Select tools already developed in the orthodox high-technology sector will be utilized in ingeniously innovative, integrative modalities. In addition, orthodox tools will be modified in key ways that will upgrade their capacities in quite unexpected, nonlinear ways. In all, the inexorable spiritual metamorphosis of personal and planetary consciousness is integrally interlinked with a remarkable spiritual-scientific synthesis that will quicken evolutionary unfoldment manyfold in preparation for the final sequence of ascensional events.

The fullness of interdimensional science will not occur until the Omega and post-Omega periods. In great part, this science has already been prepared, for the Higher Evolution will descend upon planet earth with the "pyramidal capstone of Light-based technology" in the last stages of the end times. Further, scientific scriptures of Light and Light-based technologies will be unearthed in both expected and unexpected ways. These scriptures have been left from previous ancient civilizations of Light to be revealed and utilized once again in synchrony with the divine plan. At this time, the Higher Evolution will culminate in the completion of a grand cycle of evolvement, and through its Light-messengers and revealed sacred science, will offer an olive branch of Light to the world for those who will receive it. As the pyramidal capstone of Light-based technologies descends, the Omega sequence will be activated, and a world made anew will be borne into the new heavens.

Part II
Ascension-oriented Concepts, Tools, and Techniques

INTRODUCTION TO PART II

Crystal-based sacred science is one of the primary catalytic means by which personal and planetary consciousness will prepare for and receive the ascension into the New World. Yet in its beginning stages of earthly remanifestation, the advent of increasingly advanced crystal knowledge is being actualized in direct accordance with the divine plan, each stage being activated from the higher levels of Light as the cycles of evolvement unfold. For each stage of spiritual growth, correspondingly appropriate knowledge and tools will be made available through many sources for individual and collective consciousness to receive and take responsibility for its earthly realization in the highest Light.

Part II of *The Crystal Connection* is based upon the theoretical-philosophical foundation of Part I, and from this, explicates key fields of knowledge in greater detail and translates it into practical techniques and modalities by which such knowledge may be manifested and utilized. The primary orientation of Part II is to provide a step-down translation of more rarefied octaves of philosophy into its correlating practicality. Not only is there a vision of personal and planetary ascension, but also means by which this vision may be catalyzed and actualized.

It is crucial that responsibility and caution be exercised with the knowledge and techniques presented herein. Some of the following material, if manifested and utilized, involves magnitudes of power and energetic potential heretofore dormant, now being activated once again. Though certainly there will be further cycles of progressive advancement, the knowledge contained in Part II unleashes a new era of crystal-based sacred science that bears correspondingly increased levels of individual and collective responsibility. Let the memory of latter-day Atlantis temper enthusiasm with a balanced caution and a waiting for receivership of Spirit-derived authority. The authors urge special care and caution in approaching the more advanced sections of the ensuing chapters, particularly concerning the use of magnetism, lasers, sonics, unified energy fields, and the nonlinear energetic potentials of crystals in general. Without the use of good judgment, greater harm than good can result. Therefore it is the responsibility of each individual to exercise caution in experimenting with and utilizing any concept and technique presented in *The Crystal Connection*.

The knowledge, techniques, and tools presented in Part II are a foundation for exploration, utilization, and further development. The reader should take that which resonates as being in his or her highest interest, work with it in conjunction with inner spiritual guidance, and allow the results to unfold within divine order. The material contained herein is extensive, encompassing a broad range of interrelated fields. Each section contains numerous levels of understanding and application, and therefore each rereading will avail the reader of new insights, fresh perspectives, and further seed-ideas. In this way, Part II can serve as a reference text that will facilitate the growth of the reader's knowledge of crystal science through many cycles of evolvement.

May the blessings of the higher realms of Light shine through with ever increasing brilliance as crystal-based interdimensional science matures and helps open the gateways of personal and planetary ascension.

CHAPTER 6
Crystal Basics

The basics of crystal use—choosing, clearing and cleansing, charging, activating, and determining crystal categories—are quite important in laying a solid foundation for everyday applications as well as advanced modalities. The material in this chapter is an extension of information presented on the same subject matter in *Windows of Light* (Baer & Baer, pp. 53–66). In this text, additional information and key perspectives will be shared in an effort to provide a more comprehensive array of knowledge concerning these fundamentals.

CHOOSING CRYSTALS

The principal idea here is to match the individual's vibratory blueprint with that of a crystal. Just as every person's energy patterns are unique, so too are all crystals' vibrational patterning different from the others. When there is an energetic similarity between an individual and a particular crystal, a harmonic resonance is stimulated between the two, and a strong interlinkage occurs along with an intuitive feeling of rightness.

Currently, the predominant way by which an optimal crystal for an individual is chosen is through intuitive means. For the most part, it is best if a person chooses his or her own crystals, though this should not discourage the giving of them as gifts, for this can be a most Light-filled act. Usually the "right" crystals are discerned by some sort of interaction that happens between the person and a crystal that stands out in a positive way. This might be a strong tingling sensation when holding one, a particular angle that pleases the eye, a feeling that the crystal is "calling," or anything else that sparks a recognition of affinity. Pendulums, too, are quite useful in this regard for those who utilize this tool. Whatever the means, this process can be a very enjoyable, intuitive adventure.

Those crystals that are to be used as personal tools should be the most carefully chosen of crystals. Other crystals used in less direct interaction with the individual, such as gridwork crystals, environmental harmonizing crystals, and so on, need only a more basic and less highly specific affinity. It is the personal tools that most strongly affect the person in direct, and many times deeply interpenetrative ways. Therefore, a harmonic mutuality is quite important here. Sometimes an individual will "outgrow" a crystal when the person's vibratory patterns have evolved to a different state and the crystal no longer has a strong interactive effect.

The crystal has not lost any inherent effectiveness; it just no longer matches with the individual. In such cases, the crystal can either be put to use in a more generalized, less direct manner or it can be transferred to another person who feels a harmonic attraction.

Should a crystal with specific energetic qualities be desired, in addition to intuitive methods for finding one, the exterior form characteristics can sometimes provide a guideline as to the specific crystal's properties. For more information on this subject along with illustrations of some of the fundamental crystal form-types, see Chapter 11.

In the future, as a crystal-based sacred science unfolds, there will be technological devices that can exactly determine an optimal match-up between crystals and individuals. But for now, the process is fundamentally an intuitive one that can be a most exciting journey of exploring the subtle aspects and nuances of the crystal kingdom.

CLEARING AND CLEANSING CRYSTALS

Because of crystals' propensity for accumulating ambient "static" energies in addition to various individual and environmental imbalanced vibrations, they need to be cleared and cleansed on a regular basis.

Windows of Light (Baer & Baer) describes a host of techniques for accomplishing this purpose, all of which have proven to be effective. Especially effective are salt-based clearing methods either involving the covering of crystals completely with table salt or sea salt or the placing of crystals in a supersaturated salt water solution. Both these techniques, when done over a 24-hour period, have proven to be among the most effective and easily done of the more deep-acting clearing modalities. Though orthodox scientific perspectives have been used to state a case against the efficacy of salt-based clearing methods, long-term experience by many people has proven that there are subtle-energy characteristics of salt that make it a most effective absorption medium for clearing crystals.

Some guidelines regarding how often to clear and cleanse crystals are as follows:

Personal crystals that are worn and carried, and those used regularly as special tools in a personal spiritual regime, need to undergo this process most often. In general, once per week is a good guideline for these crystals, more often if considerable personal releasing processes are occurring or if the crystals are exposed to strong imbalanced energies, either personal or otherwise. A sticky crystal exterior is many times an indication that cleansing processes are needed.

All other crystals should be put through a clearing and cleansing cycle at least once every one to three months, depending upon how often they are actively used and the nature of the environment in which they are usually positioned. The more often crystals are utilized by the individual and the greater the occurrence of imbalanced energetics in the crystals' environment, the more often they need to be cleared and cleansed. Should an occurrence of potent disharmonious vibrations occur within the close vicinity of crystals, they will need to be cleared as soon as possible. Otherwise, simply be aware of any diminishment of the crystals' overall energy output; they will tend to become less potent as well as sometimes physically cloudy when in need of clearing. Intuitive feeling will be the best guideline, though it is a good practice to clear and cleanse all crystals at least once every one to three months.

When cleansing a crystal with running water, be careful that the water's temperature is not extremely hot or cold, because a rapid change in the crystal's temperature may cause it to crack in some cases. Keeping the water temperature between cool and lukewarm is a practice that will ensure safety in this regard.

It is recommended that only nonmetallic containers be used in these techniques. For clearing large numbers of crystals, a simple low-cut cardboard box or plastic basin works well. For a single large crystal, a plastic bucket filled with salt is an inexpensive, effective mode of clearing.

CHARGING CRYSTALS

Crystals accumulate, hold steady, and emit energy charges. In general, the larger the mass, the greater the clarity, and the lesser the degree of internal and external fracturing and chipping of a crystal, the more energy charge capacity it has. Especially when a crystal is actively used or kept within an individual's bioenergetic field on a regular basis, the crystal tends to discharge its accumulated energy charge into the recipient's field. Although in a basically harmonious environment crystals tend to be self-charging over time without additional assistance, there are techniques that facilitate the recharging process, helping it to occur more quickly and with heightened overall effectiveness.

Techniques for charging include:

1. Placing the crystal inside a crystal gridwork, either large- or small-diameter, yields good results. The Star of David and double Star of David grid patterns work well here. With the addition of magnets to the gridwork crystals as described in Chapter 14, the charging process is considerably amplified.
2. Laser light directed into a crystal for approximately 10–15 minutes imparts a high intensity charge.
3. Placing crystals inside a pyramid overnight or for approximately 12 hours (time will vary according to crystal size and depletion of charge) is an excellent charging mode, one of the best.
4. A good quality geode cut in two provides a hollow space in which a crystal may be set. Close the two geode sections together and leave for 24 hours or so to recharge the crystal.
5. When possible, crystals can be left within the boundaries of a vortex area, holy place, or other place of positive energy abundance for 24 hours, energizing them extremely well.
6. Various combinations of these modalities will further magnify the results.

ACTIVATING CRYSTALS

Activation is distinctly different from charging. While charging concerns the renewal of the vibrational charge capacities of a crystal, activation concerns the expansion of a crystal's overall energy charge capacities and Light-spectrum access capabilities. Most crystals have yet to be activated into their full energetic potential, and are presently in a state of relative dormancy. When a crystal becomes more highly activated it is able to work with a more encompassing degree of the universal energy spectrum than before. Therefore, the range and intensity of energies that flow through the crystal are correspondingly increased. As crystal science unfolds further, the means to stimulate increasingly higher levels of crystal activation will be actualized. Crystals undergoing such processes will "hum" so powerfully that even skeptics will not be able to deny the energetic flow of such crystals.

For now, there are a few basic means to catalyze the activation process:

1. Subjecting crystals to very high and very low temperatures is one effective activation technique. It needs to be emphasized that any temperature changes during this process must be *gradual*, otherwise it is very likely that the crystals will crack.
2. Expose crystals to extreme weather conditions, such as blizzards, lightning storms, heavy rains, and the like.
3. Significant activation can be effected by exposing crystals to focal energy zones of such devices as Tesla coils, Jacob's Ladder plasma generators, and electrostatic generators.
4. Set up a small crystal gridwork in a Star of David or double Star of David pattern in an out of the way place. The location needs to be in a harmoniously balanced setting that will be minimally disturbed during the activation process. Set a pyramid over the central gridwork region—a 12-inch-base pyramid will work fine. Optimally, the pyramid will have a ⅜-inch-base pyramid-faceted crystal attached to the apex and the other crystals will have magnets placed on opposite sides of their bases. (See Chapter 14 for instructions.) Place the crystal to be activated in the center of the gridwork, if possible with its lengthwise axis standing vertically upright in direct alignment with the pyramidal apex. The base can be put into a putty or clay substance. Leave this set-up undisturbed for seven to ten days. Each day one asks a sector of the Spiritual Hierarchy of Light with which one has an affinity to activate the crystal to the highest degree within divine order. Results from this procedure are sometimes quite dramatic.

DETERMINING CRYSTAL CATEGORIES

Each crystal has an inherent optimal pattern of usage deriving from its originating Light-blueprint. Pages 54–59 in *Windows of Light* (Baer &Baer) delineate 16 categories along with basic perspectives regarding the properties and uses of each one.

Discerning which category a specific crystal is a part of must, at the present time, be done intuitively. Sometimes it will be quite obvious what a crystal's highest pattern of usage is; othertimes it will take focused intuitive guidance and experimentation. It is important to know that even if a crystal is not used in its highest category of usage, it will still be an effective tool. When a crystal is utilized within the parameters of its category, however, the energetic effects are the most powerful and effective. For the most part, intuit how a particular crystal would best be utilized, use it in this way for a time, and as increasing rapport with it develops its true category will become clearer.

Another method is done through through the use of a pendulum in conjunction with a crystal category chart.[1] To make such a chart, draw a half-circle and connect the two ends together with a line. Then from the center of this line, draw lines from this point to the half-circle, such that 16 pie sections are created within the entire half-circle. Now write the name of one of each of the 16 crystal categories presented in *Windows of Light* in each pie section. The chart is then complete. To discern the category of a particular crystal, hold it in the left hand and the pendulum in the right hand so that it is aligned directly over the midpoint of the half-circle's base. Formulate a question in the mind concerning the discernment of what category the crystal in the left hand is. Allow the pendulum to swing freely. After a time, the pendulum will likely swing in alignment with one of the 16 half-circle sections. The name of the category in this section is the category of the crystal.

CRYSTAL CARE PERSPECTIVES

Protecting crystals from physical damage is an integral part of individual responsibility in the caretaking of crystals. Even though quartz is a very hard substance (7 on the Moh's scale of hardness), it is still quite susceptible to chipping and cracking from collisions and impacts with other objects. To prevent such damage, a few simple guidelines can be followed. First, keep crystals away from areas where there is a lot of physical activity. Put them in areas where they will be undisturbed and out of the flow of daily activities as much as possible. Second, do not allow crystals to hit or grind against one another. When transporting, wrap them in protective cloth or in separate pouches and make sure that they are situated so that they will not abruptly hit against one another. In this regard, the most attention should be placed upon protecting the crystal's termination, as this is by far the most energy-sensitive part of the crystal anatomy. Third, handle carefully, picking them up and putting them down with conscientious awareness. The handiwork of nature and the Light-realms that has taken hundreds and quite possible thousands of years must be protected.

Further, it is highly recommended that crystals not be associated in any way with leather or any other animal-derived substances. The lower vibrational nature of this subtly but significantly downgrades the more refined, rarefied crystalline energies. Much preferred for pouches, pendants, protective wrapping, and the like are natural fabrics such as cotton or silk.

In sum, crystal basics set an optimal groundwork from which crystal usages and applications in all their diversity will actualize the highest and most efficient results.

CHAPTER 7
Crystal Foundation

Crystallography is one of the most comprehensively complex fields of knowledge and application within the entire domain of sacred science. The tremendous tomes and annals that fill the crystallography sections in the libraries of orthodox science today portend even greater magnitudes of voluminous technicality in the crystal library-computers of the interdimensional science of tomorrow. For this is a discipline that encompasses not only the vast complexities inherent to quartz and other gems but also all crystallographic substances, including metals, magnetic materials, and other mineral matrices, inclusive of much of the realm of today's materials science. In this more encompassing understanding of crystallography's domain, it can be seen that it forms the foundation and matrixed means for the establishment of Light-based technologies in the great majority of their multitudinous manifestations.

Distinct differences exist between crystallography as it is understood and applied in the realms of orthodox science versus interdimensional science. The overriding philosophical differences have been more generally discussed in Chapter 5. The primary theoretical foundations of both view crystals in diametrically opposing ways. Orthodox crystallography sees crystalline substances as lifeless, consciousnessless, linear, neutral material objects confined to earthbound energetic interactions. On the other hand, sacred crystallography views crystals as celestially derived intelligence matrices having multidimensional interlinking and interacting capacities. These two viewpoints see the same physical crystal with opposite paradigmatic visions. As consciousness' vision and comprehension of the higher nature of reality grows, so does its realization of the universal thought-forms that embody the keys to spiritual growth and technological evolvement. To confine the vision of crystals' nature and potential to the linear limitations of mainstream science is to be unreceptive to awesome vistas of universal crystal knowledge, well developed by numerous ancient civilizations and to be inexorably reactivated by the Light-scientists of the present and future. For, within the ordering of the divine plan for Earth, this knowledge is reawakened at precise intervals of individual and collective evolvement to serve as one of the major catalysts and technological means to prepare receptive sectors of the planetary population for the New World ascension.

The most centrally useful and versatile crystalline substance throughout the domain of sacred crystal science is the clear quartz. It is this particular mineral matrix that holds the keys to the progressive maturation of a great portion of future crystallographic knowledge. The higher crystal science of today is yet embryonic, awaiting fuller cyclic stages of maturation in increasingly accelerated quantum leaps as the Omega point of evolutionary renewal quickly approaches. The quartz crystal is the starting point, the "philosopher's stone" that, when progressively decoded, activates paradigms of knowledge that function as seed-catalysts and a fundamental foundation for the entire expanse of the crystallographic domain. Therefore, in this book in general and this chapter in particular, the primary focus is upon mastering the mysteries of the quartz crystal. Throughout this chapter, and those following, quartz is seen time and again as a central core matrix of coded multidimensional energetic focalization, transformation, and unification. Let us explore the profound depths of crystalline suprarealities wherein the heights of celestial ascendancy may be be illuminated.

CELESTIAL ORIGINS, PLANETARY RELATIONSHIPS

Crystals derive from Thought-form blueprints of the Abstract Light levels of the Universal Mind. As described in detail in chapters 1 and 5, the abstract numerological-geometrical blueprints of all manifestation abide on the highest causal dimensions of Light. From these prototypal templates the vast expanses of the Universal Energy Network (UEN) crystallize into actualization, thus forming a gridwork interconnecting an infinitude of dimensions and domains in which and through which the Thoughts of the Eternal are enacted. A cornerstone of the UEN is its crystallographic component. Spanning each dimension plane are crystallographic templates coded in accordance with the dictates of its originating blueprint. Through level after dimensional level of the UEN a primary Thought-form is systematically transduced via an interdimensionally continuous series of crystallographic templates, each succeeding template being a reflection of its abstract blueprint as it crystallizes at a specific dimension level. Therefore, it can be envisioned as a sequential series of templates forming a vast network in which each template is a harmonic variation of the originating Thought. This network extends through creation in a quantumly continuous succession of interdimensionally interconnected, harmonically symmetrical crystallographic templates. These templates form the encoded megamatrix that provides the highly stabilized code-patterns through which universal energy flow is patterned in direct accordance with the parameters of divine order.

Physical-plane quartz crystals derive their codified geometrics from specifically correlating Thought-patterns translated through the UEN and superimposed within a silicon dioxide growth medium. As the silicon dioxide crystallizes from a superheated, highly pressured liquid state to solid crystal form, the superimposed Light-field translates its coding into the molecular and macroscopic patterns of crystallization. In other words, as quartz solidifies, the last quantum level of the UEN Thought-pattern transference takes place. Thereby, every aspect of the resulting crystals mirrors their Abstract Light blueprints transduced to physical materialization.

The nature of the Light-field that is imbued into quartz is unique. It is White Light stepped down to earth-plane dimensional parameters. It would be an oversimplification to say that quartz is solidified White Light; rather, quartz is a matrix in which an earth-plane correlate of White Light is infused. On the highest of celestial dimensional levels, White Light in its fullest nature abides. If one could imagine the radiant intensity of a billion or more of this universe's suns combined, only a small fraction of the effulgence of White Light would be encompassed. As dimensional levels of the UEN progressively step down from planes of the highest celestial refinement to the the lowest levels of materiality, so too is White Light correspondingly stepped down. Each dimensional plane of the UEN has a correlatingly appropriate spectrum profile of White Light-transduced. The earth plane, too, has a lower dimensional White Light spectrum corresponding to its particular place in universal order. Therefore, the spectral parameters of White Light that are transferred to quartz will necessarily conform to those of the planetary energy field. Quartz, then, embodies a particular octave-spectrum UEN transduction of White Light.

Because of its White Light-correlate nature, quartz crystals have one of the highest frequency capacities in the entire mineral kingdom. In addition, quartz is the single most versatile spectrum-range capacity crystal native to the earth plane. Chromatically, white is the synergistic unity of all chromatic vibrations. The term *White Light* is much more inclusive, for it signifies the synergistic collectivity of all universal energetic modalities, such as Sound, Color, gravitics, electromagetism, form energy, and so on. Quartz crystals, as a lower octave correlate, have the full spectrum capacities of the White Light spectrum that they embody. This capability is unique in the mineral kingdom. All other crystallographic substances are notably more specialized in the energy spectrum profile that they embody and their corresponding range capacities are thereby quite specific. To give a brief, simplified example, the emerald is a Green ray step-down correlate, materializing a specific spectrum profile of the Green ray. (The emerald is only one type of crystal among other Green ray derivative crystals, each one having a different spectrum profile within the Green range.) Emerald does not have full energy range capabilities like quartz does, but rather has a very defined spectrum profile of universal energies with which it may actively interact. Any vibration outside of its strict energetic boundaries will simply not interact with the emerald.* As with emerald, so also with every other known mineral matrix-type. Quartz is unique in its versatile, full range capability potential. This quality is one of the central reasons why quartz crystals are so important in so many domains of consciousness and technological applications. They are energetic "mixing chambers" in which a broad range of vibrational parameter combinations and permutations can be selectively actualized. Thus quartz crystals are highly versatile tools of Light (with an exceptionally high frequency to low frequency range) and are key to unlocking limitless vibrational potentials.

Silicon dioxide is the unique physical medium that has a harmonic affinity with the spectrum parameters of White Light-transduced. No other physical substance has this singular profile of resonant concordance. During the crystal growth process, because of their cross-matched interdimensional resonant affinity, as Thought-patterned White Light is transformed through the UEN to the planetary energy field, there is a strong "magnetic" attraction to regions within the earth where receptive silicon dioxide deposits exist. The Light-field is processed through the planetary energy network to the appropriate silicon dioxide solution deposits

---

*Under forced conditions, the effects would not be harmonically balanced.

and interacts with the growth medium on subtle energy levels. An interdimensional cross-linkage is made wherein the Light-field patterns form a predetermined causal blueprint of quartz crystallization. Therefore as quartz solidifies molecule by molecule, the microscopic patterning symmetrically mirrors the superimposed Light-field. The end product—the macroscopic crystal—thereby becomes a physical-plane reflection image of its archetypal Image.

Silicon dioxide has certain nonlinear properties by which it is "alchemically" transformed into a more rarefied chemico-energetic medium when a Light-field interacts with it. Specific magneto-gravitic quantum energy levels are shifted to higher phase orientations as the interdimensional cross-linkage between the Light-field and quartz occurs. Because of this interactivity, the quartz becomes quite sensitively responsive to being imprinted with the Light-field in general and extremely subtle multilevel coding patterns in particular. This rarefication is the process whereby sentience—crystalline intelligence—is infused into previously lifeless, densified matter. Without this process, quartz remains inert, lifeless, and totally unactivated on subtle dimensional levels. This is the primary difference between "natural" quartz and the laboratory-gorwn quartz of today.

Quartz constitutes an amazingly high percentage of the earth's crust. The single elements silicon and oxygen together constitute approximately 75 percent of the outer planetary shell. Out of this, 13 percent is quartz. Other precious stones and metals have far less incidence percentages. In addition to quartz having the greatest sheer quantity of all refined crystallographic substances, it is also the most widespread. Mostly regarded in rock-collecting circles as a common mineral of lesser import, quartz is occurrent in all sectors of the globe in one form or another, in greater quantities and qualities in some sectors than others. It has a broad range of ways in which it manifests itself, from the unrefined levels—for instance, as included in the tripartite structure of granite—to the most refined of modes—clear rock crystal.

Because of these basic minerological facts in combination with quartz's higher level properties, it may be seen that this "living" mineral plays a major role in the planetary energy network. In fact, naturally occurring quartz plus Higher Evolution "seeded" crystals form the capstone-controlling matrix for the entire planet.

Rudolf Hauschka, in his insightful book *The Nature of Substance,* provides a valuable perspective:

> We must widen our search beyond physico-chemical limits and observe silica in the entire range of its activity. It is not just an earthly substance; it is a macrocosmic force or process that has shaped the whole earth-globe as a sculptor's hands create form on the surface of some plastic medium. The silicon process is a form-giving process. . . .
>
> This shaping with the cosmic dynamics of infinity is the silica process, which manifests in a fixed form as the substance, silica. It is the force active wherever surfaces come into being: the surfaces of ocean waves and mountains, the epidermis of plants, the skins of man and animals, the membranes enclosing their internal organs. . . .
>
> The silica process is by no means bound to the substance silica. Only where its activity has been intense, does material silica come into being. Substances are the final stages of processes.[1]

The overriding form-giving nature of the generalized substance of silica, from microcosmic to macrocosmic levels, shows it to be physically, energetically, and dimensionally the controlling blueprint-patterning component.

Where the most intense activity of the silica process occurs, therein quartz crystallizes into physical form. Quartz crystal is the epitome of the silica essence and is its most centrally powerful regulator. Within planetary consciousness (also known as Gaia) this fundamental quality is exemplified. Quartz crystals, both grown in nature and those "seeded" by the Higher Evolution, constitute the primary intelligence matrix of the entire planetary energy network. It is in and through this transparent matrix structure that the main energetic pathways of the earth-field are established, sustained, and modulated. Occurrent physically or etherically at all primary and secondary vortex zones and other key harmonic energy regions, the collective quartz matrix pervades the centrally controlling energetic zones, providing its broad-range spectrum capacities for the fullness of vibrational flow that constitutes planetary metabolism. Gaia utilizes quartz as a locus medium of consciousness superimposition and regulatory enactment, parallel to the way that the higher levels of human consciousness employ the physical brain medium. Therefore, it can be seen that quartz crystal is the apexal "brain" structure of the planetary energy network, the central command control of earth-plane homeostasis and cyclic evolvement, other types of gems functioning in associative aspects of the planet's brain-mind.

Furthermore, the collective quartz matrix, in conjunction with pyramidal structures (both physical and higher plane) situated as primary vortex zones, form the earth's primary interdimensional interconnection pathways. Within the overall stratified structuring of the UEN, each different domainship establishes and maintains its necessary universal interrelatedness through multidimensional linkage pathways. This is parallel to the way that each cell within the human body maintains its individual functioning integrity through interlinking with the collective wholeness of the bioenergetic system's metabolic pathways. So the earth, too, as a single cell in the Universal Mind, receives its individual orientation to the whole and resultant mutual interelatedness through the crystal-pyramid planetary complexes (the Great Pyramid being a prime example). This is necessary to the synchronizing of earth with the more encompassing celestial-cosmic evolvement sequences, thereby keying the planet with the measured unfoldment of this entire threshold control zone's Alpha–Omega cycle. And through the timepiece crystals seeded within the planetary vortex zones by the Higher Evolution, the earth's unique individual evolvement sequences unfold according to its blueprint-program. The *Keys of Enoch* amplify this concept: "In earlier aeons, our seed crystals of light were transmitted by the Lords of Light when they came to evolve life in the galaxy through memory codes which were then recorded within the pyramids, seven aeons ago, twelve aeons ago, thirty-six aeons ago, and ages past."[2] Such seed crystals are complexly coded crystalline computer-timepieces serving to regulate the earth's blueprint-program in all its completeness. In synchrony with associated higher dimensional regulatory timepieces (that is, celestial and cosmic recorder cells), the planetary program is precisely enacted.

The earth's energy network has 12 primary vortex zones that are positioned roughly in a pentagonal dodecahedral geometry. Altogether, with the Great Pyramid as the apex control, the 12 vortexes sustain the earth's multidimensional energetic gridwork structure. The overall patterning of the grid structure is composed of three interpenetrating geometric standing wave patterns—the icosahedron, pentagonal dodecahedron, and hexahedron (that is, cube).[3] It is this collectivity that forms the primary pathways of the planetary energy network. In understanding the nature and function of quartz as it occurs around the world in natural deposits and the relationship of crystals to the UEN in general, it is the world's vortex gridwork sustaining the central control of interlinkage between earth and the rest of the cosmos that will be seen to be a primary causal focal factor.

All natural quartz deposits receive their controlling blueprint through the planetary energy network. The location, quantity, quality, and programming of crystals is predetermined by the earth's Alpha–Omega blueprint and enacted through the vortex control timepieces in conjunction with Higher Evolution coparticipatory activity.

The distribution of quartz fields around the world shows that there is a generalized, widespread incidence of less refined quartz, both as lesser quality crystals and as a matrix component of other rock structures (for example, granite). There are only a few select regions where high quality clear crystals occur. From an overall perspective, the great diversity of quality-types and rock-intermixture-types form a spectrum of quartz matrices that function as different mediums for various functional levels of the planetary energy field in general and the higher energetic aspects of the crystal kingdom in particular. Each matrix-type, according to its specific vibrational profile, serves as a medium in which particular quantum crystalline energy levels may function. One may view these quantum energy levels as being similar to the different electron orbital shell levels of an atom, in terms of their discrete quantum shells of energy. From the least to the most refined quartz matrix-types, corresponding energetic parameters, from lesser to greater vibrational frequency refinement, function through the different quantum quartz energy "shells" as an integral part of planetary energetic metabolism. The main point here is the differentiation between the various levels of crystal quality and the type of correlating vibrational function that they carry out. Basically, the less refined quartz mediums act to maintain a generalized planetary distribution of basic, lower-to-middle range energies. The more refined crystals are the climax communities of the quartz kingdom, serving to focalize, modulate, and distribute the highest ranges of Light within planetary consciousness. It is this latter rarefied type of clear quartz that is of greatest causal effect, and therefore also of the most interest in the context of this book.

There are only a few climax communities of quartz throughout the the world. Three of the most prominent ones in the Western hemisphere are in Brazil, in Hot Springs, Arkansas, and in Herkimer County, New York. These are regions that were predetermined within the earth's blueprint to receive the highest influx of Light into the quartz kingdom. Crystals from these areas, as a whole, have a relatively high percentage of good-to-excellent quality clear quartz. No other known places in the Western hemisphere come close to rivaling the overall quality and quantity of more rarefied crystals found in these locations. Such mineral climax communities are therefore the seat of the most valuable natural crystal tools for consciousness and sacred science applications.

At certain predetermined points in the Earth's evolutionary cycles, the planetary matrix became predisposed to receiving a transference of White Light-transduced into prepared silicon dioxide deposits. These deposits were located not at the primary vortex zones, but at key harmonic energy regions within the overall planetary gridwork that were delineated within the earth's blueprint-patterns. Therefore all necessary preconditions to receiving the Light-infusion were prepared. Gaia, in conjunction with the master control timepieces and authorized sectors of the Higher Evolution, set in motion all the necessary preparations as the earth's divine plan unfolded over many thousands of years. When the time was right, the final stages of Light-infusion were enacted.

Each climax community received an overall encompassing Light-field that was processed through the pathways of the planetary energy network as it was received from the higher levels of the UEN. Within this overall energy field were "fields within fields within fields." That is, Light-code patterns on many different levels were infused into specific sectors of the silicon dioxide deposits, specific deposits within each sector, and specific individual crystals within each deposit. The complex multidimensional, multi-code Light-field was superimposed over a vast area, deep within the crust, transferring its Thought-derived blueprint into earthly crystalline manifestation.

Therefore, just as it is observed in the quartz mining profession, innumerable deposits, veins, and pockets are spread throughout an entire region. These various deposits, veins, and pockets have widely differing characteristics, both physically and energetically. In some areas, the crystals are of good quality but relatively common in their characteristics; in other areas, the crystals mined have exceptional properties. Some individual crystals contain important coding patterns; others are much more generalized. All of this variance is a reflection of the original multilevel, multicode transference of the Light-field blueprint into crystal form.

The role of the Higher Evolution in the enactment of this formative process is both complex and varied. In general, assigned sectors of the Spiritual Hierarchy of Light include overseeing Light-scientists, certain angelic beings with an affinity for crystal-work, devas and elementals, Light-beings working in association with vortex timepieces, and universal crystalline intelligence factors.* Virtually all such work is performed from the higher dimensional causal planes. During the formative processes there is a great concentration of effort by these intercooperative Light-beings to enact every micronuance of the Light-field's patterning. After the crystals have solidified and receive finalized coding, many of the Higher Evolution sectors disengage from the project, their assigned tasks fulfilled, while a host of others stay and perform continuous tasks in the caretaking of the crystal region.

The period of time during which each climax community of quartz is formulated occurs at different cyclic sequences of planetary unfoldment. The actual formative process in each case takes hundreds, thousands, and perhaps tens of thousands of years. Each major quartz region goes through a unique sequence of crystallization, depending upon many variable factors. The fact that it is probable that most crystal deposits undergo two or more periods of decrystallization and subsequent recrystallization deep within the earth's crust at various cycles of time does not mean that they lose the properties and coding of the original causal Light-field. The Light-field does not dissipate; rather, it is continuously maintained at higher dimensional planes. Therefore, if a crystal deposit decrystallizes back into a superheated, highly pressured solution, it will regain the original characteristics as it recrystallizes back into solid form. Also, periods of decrystallization sometimes

*See the next section, entitled "The Nature of Crystalline Intelligence."

synchronize with major planetary evolutionary cycle transformations. The decrystallization allows for an efficient modification of the causal Light-field to match corresponding changes of earth's cyclic unfoldment. Then, when recrystallized, the resulting crystal deposits are synchronized with the shift in the planetary energy network.

Further, it is an integral mechanism of the Higher Evolution for modulating individual, collective, and planetary evolutionary processes to modify and activate quartz and other crystalline deposits at predetermined intervals while they remain in solid form. The energy parameters and coding-patterns of crystalline regions can be altered in order to institute changes in the planetary field. Over time, these changes cause corresponding modifications of the earth's evolutionary growth cycles as well as those of individual and collective consciousness. In fact, this very process is occurring in ever-accelerating ways as the Omega point of ascension approaches. Quartz and other mineral matrices can be activated, or quickened, into higher vibratory states, thereby having a much more profound effect upon consciousness. This is happening within the earth's crust, causing a greater alignment of the crystals with higher Light-frequencies and correspondingly transferring these vibrations into the collective planetary network. "The activation of these crystals by the Merkabah creates a proton spin coupling so that our body becomes sensitized to their Light and can be remade into a more perfect form cell by cell."[4] This is also occurring on a more individual level. Specially activated and programmed crystals are gravitating to appropriate individuals with greater and greater frequency. Also, using activation technique number 3 presented in Chapter 6, opportunities for Higher Evolution activation of personal crystals can be realized. As a whole, then, the integral role of quartz as a powerful facilitative medium for personal and planetary transformative processes is seen.

THE NATURE OF CRYSTALLINE INTELLIGENCE

There is a type of consciousness that is necessarily intrinsic to all rarified crystalline matrices. Crystal literature through the centuries has numerous references to quartz in particular as a "live" mineral, and indeed this is so. For Light-derived, "natural" quartz is not simply a neutral, mechanistic object, void of any form of consciousness. This is a quite linear perspective, one of orthodox crystallography but definitely not of sacred crystal science. The latter discipline is fully cognizant of the specialized intelligence principles inherent in all crystalline matrices, both physical and higher dimensional. This intelligence activity is most versatile and most strongly active on all universal levels in and through the quartz matrix and its UEN correlates.

Crystalline intelligence is as alien to that of humankind's as humankind's is to that of the plant kingdom's. As with all universal forms of consciousness, that of the crystalline type originates at the highest causal levels of the Universal Mind. And as presented in detail in Chapter 2, it is seen that the entirety of the UEN has a fundamentally tripartite structure, the crystallographic component being the computerlike, highly stabilizing cornerstone element. It is on the higher levels of the UEN that the nature of the crystallographic aspect can best illuminate the essence of its intelligence-type. Though difficult to exemplify in linear language, a suggestive description of crystalline intelligence is as follows. It is rather like a tremendously potent electrical force, potentially highly active while also being extremely "magnetically cool." There is a built-in, constantly active momentum toward stabilization within exceedingly refined degrees of order. It is also exceptionally responsive to receiving and integrating program-codes that cause the crystalline intelligence to structure itself with corresponding mirrored symmetry, thus being programmed. Once so programmed, it will maintain these code-patterns with abiding endurance. In this way, it can serve as a fixed template through which other energy modalities, no matter how intense, flow through and are patterned according to the coding of the template.

Crystalline intelligence can be imbued with virtually infinite complexities of programmed decision-making options of a degree of sophistication requiring active intelligence. This concept is exemplified well in the functioning of astrochronomic computers. As discussed in *Windows of Light:*

> It is both a repository and computation mechanism for every possible combination and permutation of Divine Intelligence. As a sophisticated and distinct level of consciousness—a living computer—it is the pinnacle of the interface between "artificial intelligence" and "living Intelligence." Indeed, it is a higher-octave example of the "living geometric forms" on which Pythagoras expounded in ancient history. Such a computer can receive and process instructions from various Light-beings and can also monitor and adjust a wide spectrum of intra- and interdimensional functions according to its basic programming. The nature of its "thoughts" are such that it can intelligently reprogram itself within certain parameters and can creatively modify projected instructions within its overall programming. Unlike any computer on Earth today, these living computers are composed of spherical units of consciousness that operate in a supraholographic manner and are able to receive and process billions of multiplexed "thoughts" instantaneously.[5]

Therefore, qualities of infinite versatility within an ultimately stable intelligence matrix are illustrated.

In addition, the "language" of crystalline intelligence is a mathematically-geometrically based supraholographic mode. From a certain point of view, crystalline language is seen as a purely scientific-technical one that processes all energy flow within equational parameters. A correlate of this understanding is the realization that crystalline consciousness is void of emotions as human beings relate to them. The Love-Joy factor of creation is implicit within this modality as the necessary underlying framework of all equational interactions. The collectivity of crystalline intelligence is countless differentiations of numerological-geometrical derivations of Love-Joy; however, it is not experienced on a personal level as humankind comprehends it. Rather, crystalline consciousness *is;* without attachment, without ego, without personality, in a parallel mode in which electricity simply is.

Thus, this unique form of intelligence is a multidimensionally supraholographic mode of consciousness that functions within extreme patterns of stable, numerological-geometrical order. Highly programmable, yet surpassingly undeviating, crystalline intelligence is a keystone *modus operandi* of every facet of the UEN. Upon its singular properties the very building blocks of manifestation rest, and are infinitely modifiable with exact precision.

It is through understanding crystalline intelligence as an overarching collectivity in which inextricably interdependent functioning occurs that greater comprehension of the role of physical-plane crystals is further illuminated.

> Crystals are to be used as cyberg devices to amplify and filter communication signals.
> They are used by the Higher Evolution as fundamental building blocks to set up a measurable grid of a larger harmonic system which allows for different combinations of wave structures to unite and form myriads of gravitational wave combinations which, in turn, react with one another to transmit thought-forms to physical planetary realities.[6]

In their highest levels of utilization, no crystal exists or functions save in relation to other harmonically related crystals and associated network of crystalline intelligence. One has only to recall the derivation of any and all physical-plane crystals as an alchemical transfer of a crystallographic Light-field that originates on the highest levels of Abstract Light. All crystallographic intelligence is inherently interconnected and operates in its highest applications as interdimensionally interlinked gridworks. On the physical plane, the same principle applies. Yes, there are many applications whereby crystals will work quite effectively in relative isolation from other physical crystals and the crystallographic component of the UEN; this is perfectly fine. The point here is that the most powerfully effective crystal-based modalities occur when a direct harmonic interlinkage is established between one or more physical crystals and correlative higher octaves of the UEN. It is this multidimensional relationality that provides an extended interdimensional matrix into those sectors of the Universal Mind that have corresponding Light-spectrums to bring to bear for specific purposes on the earth plane. When crystals are understood and applied as *interdimensional interlinkage matrices* to gain access to particular sectors of Universal Intelligence, then the boundless reaches and infinite blessings of the Kingdom of Light are opened.

Physical crystals can, in this regard, function as "windows" through which access is gained in an amplified and clarified manner to the planetary energy network. Once this network is engaged, access lines through sectors of successively higher octaves of the UEN are enacted according to the universal laws of access and consciousness intention. When the desired sector is engaged the intercommunication pathways are open and the physical crystal magnifies the ability of consciousness to receive and transmit thought-patterns and vibrational fields accordingly. Here, then, the crystal is utilized as an interdimensional interlinkage matrix. Further, the sacred science of creating and operating crystal-based Unified Energy Fields* is the most advanced means by which personal and planetary consciousness is able to become more integrally interlinked with the expanses of Universal Intelligence. The fundamental concept of the interdimensional interlinkage matrix will prove to be the key to the opening of universal windows, unlocking many facets of humankind's divine heritage.

CRYSTAL FUNDAMENTALS

This section of the chapter is devoted to presenting an outline of basic facts of crystallography, especially as they relate to quartz, in order to provide the reader

*Refer to Chapter 14.

with fundamental concepts that will help in understanding the higher principles and applications of crystals presented in the rest of this book. For those who wish to delve more deeply into the disciplines of orthodox crystallography and mineralogy, many texts are available for further reading.

A crystal can be defined as a solid composed of atoms arranged in an orderly, repetitive array.[7] All crystals are composed of fundamental molecular building blocks that combine together in a periodic, regular manner throughout the entire crystal structure. Each type of crystal—quartz and others—is built from one primary geometric molecular pattern, repeated over and over again. In quartz the shape of the molecular building block is a tetrahedron—a four-sided figure of equilateral triangles. Each tetrahedron is composed of four oxygen atoms, one each at the four corners of the tetrahedron, plus one silicon atom nested in the center of the oxygen atoms. This is one molecular unit cell. Each of the four oxygen atoms shares some of its outer orbit shell electrons with an oxygen atom of other molecular building blocks. Tetrahedral unit cells, or building blocks, in quartz are interlinked so that they form spiral patterns. Therefore, one can envision millions upon millions of microscopic spiraling tetrahedrons arranged in highly organized, regularly repeated patterns throughout the entire quartz crystal matrix.

The end result of quartz's internal microscopic patterning is mirrored by its external planar geometry. That is, the exterior is an exact reflection of the interior, and vice versa. It can be easily observed that each quartz crystal is uniquely different in its overall external shape. These differences provide valuable indicators in more advanced crystal science as to the unique internal molecular patterning and a crystal's specific energetic properties.*

Even amid virtually infinite crystal form diversity there are exact, undeviating laws of uniformity. Due to certain fundamental laws of electromagnetic repulsion and attraction, quartz always crystallizes in certain axis and angular relationships. The archetypal axis patterning is the hexagonal axis system, one of the seven axis systems into which all minerals form.** Figure 10 shows the fundamental axis relationships that define the hexagonal system of crystals, of which quartz is a member. There are four axes, three of which are arranged in one plane at 120° angles to each other (a1, a2, a3). The vertical axis, also referred to as the c axis, is perpendicular to the other three. Within the strict parameters of the hexagonal system, quartz crystals unfailingly form six prism (or body) faces and six major pyramidal (or termination) faces (see Figure 11). Also, alternating *r* and *z* pyramidal faces constitute the termination, the former being generally smaller and the latter being generally larger. A basic mineralogical law, called the Law of Constancy of Interfacial Angles, states that the angles between adjacent corresponding faces in any given crystal are the same for every crystal of its mineral-type and are a characteristic trait of that mineral. In quartz, this law is embodied in the fact that the angle between any two adjacent body faces is always exactly 120°, no matter how distorted or normal a given quartz crystal is. Notice that because of this opposite sides are unfailingly parallel. Also, the angle between each body face and its corresponding termination face is always 141°. A note of interest here

*See Chapter 11 for further development of this subject. Also, refer to "Low Relief Termination Patterns" later in this chapter.

**Recent crystallography research indicates the possible addition of an eighth axis system, icosahedral in nature.

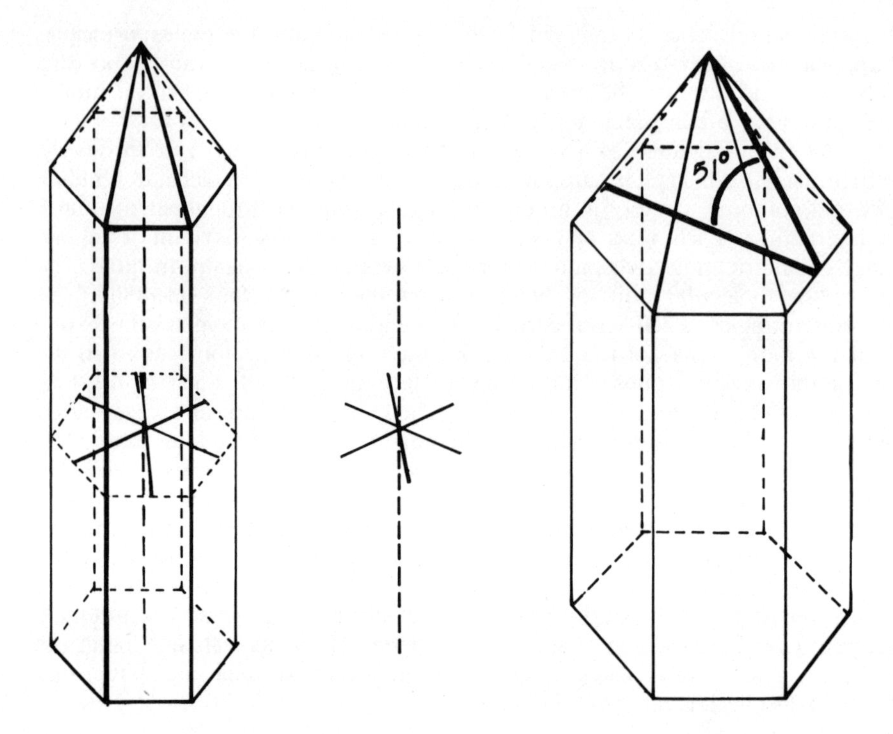

Figure 10: Quartz and the Hexagonal Crystal System

Figure 11: The 51° Angle of Quartz Terminations

is that if a right angle is subtracted from the body-to-termination angle (starting at the body), the angle that is left is 51°, which is almost exactly the same as the Great Pyramid's corner angles. Here the crystal has as an invariable aspect of its fundamental structure one of the central angles of a key pyramidal conformation. This interrelationship will be explored in later chapters.* Thus, like the snowflake that always has six sides yet manifests in infinite diversity, so too the quartz crystal has unyielding strict axis and angular dictates yet crystallizes in countless patterns of differentiation.

This short overview has presented basic perspectives of crystal structural order, from the microscopic to the macroscopic levels. From these fundamentals much concerning quartz crystal dynamics derives.

QUARTZ CRYSTAL ENERGY DYNAMICS

One would be hard pressed to find a technological tool whose energy dynamics have greater multilevel complexity than quartz crystals, even the most sophisticated of present-day supercomputers. In other chapters throughout this text many aspects of quartz's energetic functioning are explored. This particular section

*See Chapter 11 and Chapter 12.

provides fundamental facts and perspectives but, for the most part, leaves further information to be explained in its appropriate contexts at other locations in this book.

Each tetrahedral molecular unit of quartz oscillates at the same fundamental frequency. Therefore, under equalized conditions, in a single crystal there are millions of identically vibrating units arranged in helical, coherently interlinked conformation patterns. Like-vibrational oscillating systems have an inherent momentum toward vibrating in unison, like wall clocks whose pendulum motion will rhythm entrain over time, thus creating a resonant system. This rhythm entrainment dynamic has a strong tendency to occur in quartz because of the uniform identicalness of each of the oscillating tetrahedral building blocks. This is one of the great energetic advantages that crystals have over less uniformly repeated matrices. The more intermixed and irregular the matrix, the greater the nonresonant interactions, in addition to a decreased degree of entrainment potential and efficiency thereof. With crystals in general and quartz in particular, the phase-locking coherency conditions are maximized, for there is a minimal nonresonant interference throughout the matrix. There are a number of energetic benefits from such a condition that make crystals exceptionally efficient and responsive mediums. Once in motion, phase-locked resonant systems require a minimum input of energy to sustain their motion. And the larger the number of oscillators within any given system, the more stable it is and the more difficult it is to disturb the individual and collective resonantly coherent state. Thus the crystal can be seen as a matrix of singular oscillating unison, a tuned resonant system of stable, coherent concord.

Because of this, there is a very high degree of coherent interreactivity among the crystal's molecular units. A harmonic change in one molecule or group of molecules will be systematically mirrored through the crystal's matrix in a resonant, wavelike motion. Each single oscillating molecule is sensitively coupled with all others (especially those in close proximity) such that a change in one molecule is resonantly transferred through the crystal matrix like ripples in a pond. Interactive resonant affinity among the latticed molecules occurs with harmonic musicality. Intermolecular coherence is the keynote; interlattice proportions are the harmonic "scales."

When in a state of oscillatory resonance, the crystal molecules vibrate and pulse energy waves in rhythmic periodicity through the latticed helical framework. A harmonically related energetic input interacts with this dynamic standing wave matrix through the principles of sympathetic and (interdimensional) harmonic resonance. Multi-interval, multioctave vibrational coupling generates a state of matrix excitation and interreactivity. The fundamental frequency harmonics intrinsic to the crystal matrix set the stable pattern for the interreactions between the crystal and the energy input. The incoming energy processes through the latticed interior, becoming phase locked on multiple harmonic levels with the crystal's oscillatory harmonic patterning. Thereby the energy input flowing through the crystal becomes imprinted with the harmonic patterns of the crystalline matrix, its energy profile symmetrically reflecting that of the crystal's. The crystal serves as a stable oscillatory template through which incoming vibrations become patterned and then pulse-emitted from the crystal.

The crystal body and termination have distinctly different functions in the overall dynamics of the quartz matrix. Basically, the body serves as a preparatory mixing chamber for inputting and formulating energy flow. The termination is where the focused finalization processes occur. The relationship between the body and termination is roughly analogous to that between the body and the brain, respectively. For the termination performs the most vitally causal focusing and angular qualification of the crystal's energetic functioning. The inward sloping of the six facets toward the tip region sensitively and powerfully patterns the energy flow in direct accordance with the geometric interrelationships of the facets, both singularly and collectively. In effect, the crystal body prepares and predisposes energetic flow for the final stages of specificity and focusing. One of its primary dynamics in this regard is the establishment of a helical columnar standing wave pattern along the c axis. The main directional orientation of the spiraling molecular lattices throughout the crystal is along the c axis. Energetic input coming into the crystal through its base and body faces is processed into the fundamental vertical standing wave pattern dynamics. Within this helical wave-guide, it is "templated" according to the crystal's energy profile and thereby prepared for precision finalization processes in the termination. In addition, there are significant amplification factors mainly occurring in the body, the specifics of which will be presented later in this section. As a general rule, the larger the total mass and the greater the overall clarity and integrity of the body, the higher the amplification quotient.

As the vibrational flow completes its processing through the termination, a large percentage of it comes to a focus at and near the termination tip and is emitted in a coherent, intense, laserlike energy beam. These pulsations occur at extremely high frequency rates and are spirally micromodulated in a very "compressed" fashion with the complex code-patternings of the internal latticework and the external termination facets. The beam is quite forcefully directional, emitting in orientation with the c axis. This energy dynamic is termed the *primary* vibrational flow (see Figure 12).

Other subsidiary types of energy dynamics also occur. They can be grouped into two generalized categories, termed *secondary* and *tertiary.* The secondary dynamics also occur in conjunction with the termination's functioning. The primary energy flow occurs mainly at the very top of the termination. Adjunctive energetics from the primary dynamics plus additional input from vibrations reflecting at different angles from the inner termination face surfaces create wavelike patterns emanating at different angles from the six primary termination facets. The angles are all upwardly directed, and are significantly less focused, directional, and coherent than the primary dynamics. Nonetheless they do play a significant role. Because of the many angular reflection patterns that occur in the termination,* a wide spectrum of partial combinations and permutations of the crystal's energy dynamics formulate and are emitted; this activity defines what constitutes secondary energetics. Taken as a whole group, these partial combinatory patterns describe a broad differentiated spectrum of energetics; the technical term for this type of vibrational activity is *spectral emissions.* Each facet will emanate a different set (or profile) of spectral emissions.

Tertiary dynamics are a subsidiary by-product of the interactions occurring

*See the definition of *critical angle of reflection,* which follows.

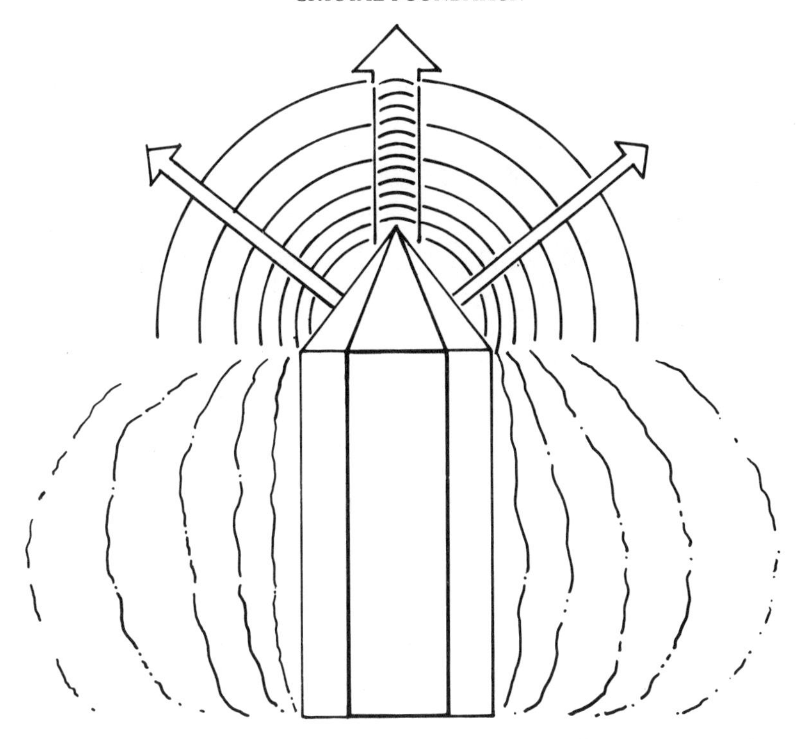

Figure 12: Primary, Secondary, and Tertiary Crystal Energy Dynamics

within the crystal body. They are the least significant of the quartz's emissions. There is relatively little focus, directionality, strength, or applicatory modes for these vibrational dynamics. In advanced sacred crystal science under extremely controlled conditions, tertiary energetics do play a distinct, though tributary role. In practical terms today, however, they are insignificant. The crystal body plays a much more important function for the inputting of energies rather than for its emissions.

The highlighting of a select few additional specific energy dynamics will assist in visualizing and comprehending the primary, secondary, and tertiary energetics just described.

The *refractive index* is the bending of light at a specific angle immediately upon entering and leaving the crystal. This is exactly the same phenomenon that occurs when a straight stick appears disjointed when part of it is put into a pool of water. Figure 13 illustrates how light bends as a result of slowing down when entering the crystal and then again when leaving the crystal as it quickens back to its original speed.

The *critical angle of reflection* is a threshold angle at which light will reflect off the inner surface of a crystal's body face or termination facet. Figure 14 shows that if the angle of light in relation to the inner crystal is above the critical angle, it will not be reflected and will exit the crystal (refracting as it does so). If the angle of light is at the critical angle or below, it will be reflected in accordance with the laws of optics.

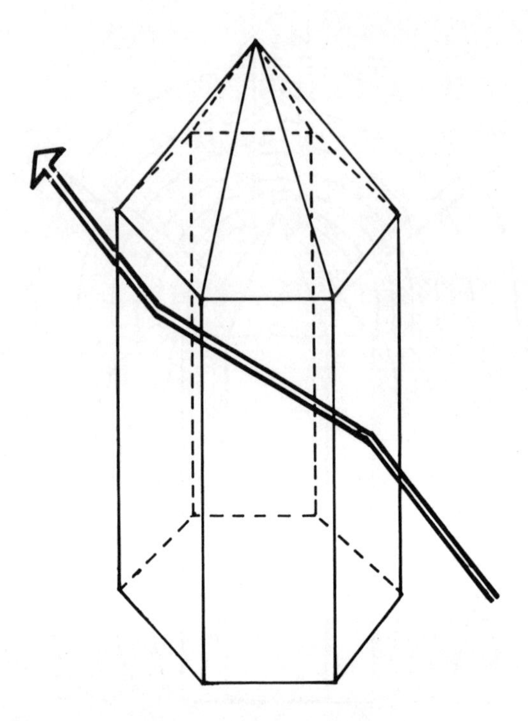

Figure 13: The Refractive Index

The *rotation of the plane of polarized light along the c axis* is an unusual trait. Figure 15 demonstrates this dynamic, showing that the plane of the polarized light is helically twisted as it proceeds along the c axis. This particular trait will not occur along any other axis or angle of the quartz crystal. Its occurrence is not restricted to the vertical midline of the crystal; rather, it may happen along all vertical portions of the crystal parallel to the c axis. Also, the amount of helical twist is proportional to the length within the crystal that it has traversed.

A brief commentary on these three traits will help give a better perspective regarding their roles in crystal dynamics. The discussions of the first two—the refractive index and critical angle of reflection—help the reader to visualize some aspects of the primary, secondary, and tertiary energetics. The tertiary energetics mainly occur as a result of their not being internally reflected and therefore emitting out of the crystal. Much of the secondary dynamics occurs as a result of zero, one, or more internal reflections and eventual exiting refraction. On the other hand, it should also be pointed out that these two traits do not describe the dynamics of the processing of all energy-types within a crystal. Instead, they apply to some aspects of the universal energy spectrums. There are many more dynamics traits than these that apply to crystal energetics.

Further, the rotation of the plane of polarized light along the c axis provides insight into the preparatory dynamics of the crystal body in addition to the primary energetics. In short, this property implements the body's spiraling molecular lattices in establishing micro-helical standing wave patterns extending through

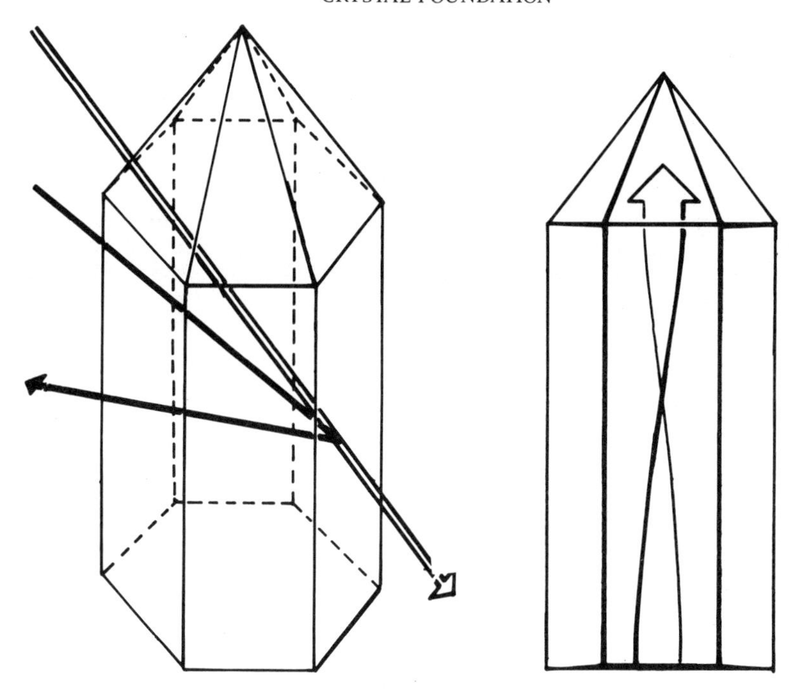

Figure 14: The Critical Angle of Reflection
Figure 15: Rotation of the Plane of Polarized Light Along the C Axis

the vertical axis. It is also a catalytic-amplifying mechanism under certain energetic conditions, helping to spark the crystal's vibrational flow to higher threshold levels of nonlinear characteristics. The vertical axis is the only direction through the crystal where the refractive index does not occur. Therefore, not only does this property help spark the primary energetics but it also contributes to the vertical directionality by not bending energy flow and keeping it in vertical alignment through the crystal matrix. In addition, though the technicalities will not be discussed here, the rotation of the polarized plane is responsible for certain important aspects of multidimensional orientation phase shifts that facilitate nonlinear interdimensional threshold interreactivity within the crystalline matrix.

It is well known that quartz crystals amplify energy. The technicalities as to how this occurs, however, are not so well known. There are four main pathways by which crystal amplification occurs. These pathways involve dimension-specific acceleration, laser/maser dynamics, spiraling amplification, and angular reflective factors. The information in this subject area is presented in the text that follows in an outlined, seed-thought format; the tremendous technical complexities will be explicated in the authors' next book to come.

In *Windows of Light* (Baer & Baer, p. 38) the *moment of refraction* illustrates one means by which amplification occurs. The moment of refraction is an acceleratory shift that happens on certain dimensional planes at the exact moment when energy enters a crystal. This many seem to contradict the concept just presented with the refractive index that light slows and bends when it enters a crystal. Both, in fact, are true. The crucial point of understanding here is that whether energy slows or quickens when interacting with a crystal depends upon the dimensional nature of that energy. Electromagnetic light slows; magneto-electric energy, as William Tiller, Ph.D., explains, accelerates.

> If we consider the behavior of magnetoelectric light versus electromagnetic light on passing through lenses, an interesting prediction can be made. Because of the mirror relationship . . . ME (magnetoelectric) light should speed up in passing from air to glass whereas EM (electromagnetic) light slows down. Thus, the index of refraction . . . for ME light should be less than unity in contrast to the case for EM light where the index of refraction . . . is greater than unity.[8]

What will hold true for glass in this case will hold true for the behavior of ME light in quartz. ME light is a dimensional mirroring of EM light, which travels 10^{10} times faster than ordinary EM light. In addition, there are numerous other dimensional planes beyond the EM and ME spectrums that accelerate to different degrees within crystalline matrices.

The second amplification factor involves the internal reflection of energy at specific angles in both the body faces and termination facets. In the book entitled *Gems, Stones, and Metals,* an illuminating quotation is found concerning Atlantean crystal science. "It is known that a beam of light directed intensely and focused specifically on a certain series of facets in a gem will, when it exists from the reflective plane of the gem, be amplified rather than diminished."[10] The keys to actualizing this dynamic are the use of intense, focused, coherent energy beams (such as lasers, for instance) and directing such a beam at angles that satisfy specific numerological-geometrical equational parameters specific to amplification.

A third amplification factor concerns the nonlinear energetic dynamic stimulated by quartz's helical latticework. The spiraling crystal latticework acts as a wave-guide, holding a particular matrix structuring steady through which energy is patterned as it flows through the crystal. The helical matrix phase locks with the energy flow, causing the latter to oscillate at specific phase orientations that stimulate a cross-dimensional periodic vibrational exchange, thereby "alchemically" transforming the energy flow into an amplified, nonlinear quantum state. Integral to many aspects of this process is the rotation of polarized light along the c axis. An example of this dynamic is the crystal's integral role in controlled matter-antimatter reactions.

> Atlantis. Their technology was based upon crystalline attunement of the matter and anti-matter cycles of the physical and non-physical worlds. By stepping up or slowing down the frequency of energy between the two cycles, they could cause a shift in time-space to occur.[10]

A fourth amplification factor involves laser/maser dynamics. The word *laser* is an acronym for *light amplification by stimulated emission of radiation* (*maser* simply substitutes *microwave* for *light*). It is well known that certain types of lasers and masers utilize crystals as the matrices in which the light or microwave amplification occurs.

> Along lines previously laid out by N. Bloembergen of Harvard University, H.E.D. Jcovil, G. Feher and H. Seidel of the Bell Telephone laboratories succeeded in constructing and operating a "MASER." . . . The amplification is achieved by

> storing up energy in a small insulating crystal of special magnetic properties. The release of energy is triggered off by an incident signal, so that the crystal passes on more energy than it receives.[11]

When intense, focused, coherent energy is introduced into quartz crystal—higher consciousness energies, laser light, sonics, and others—a population inversion process occurs not only physically but on higher dimensional quantum levels, and the subsequent stimulated return to a ground energy state generates an amplification of the energy flow in addition to crystal matrix-induced coherency factors.*

The *piezoelectric effect* is another centrally significant energetic property of quartz. Simply stated, when oscillating electrical impulses interact with quartz, corresponding mechanical oscillations occur in the quartz; the mechanical vibrations cause correlating emissions of sound. Conversely, when pressure waves (for instance, sound or mechanical pressure) interact with the crystal matrix, corresponding electric impulses are stimulated. To condense: applied electricity stimulates sound, and applied sound stimulates electricity.

This fundamental attribute of quartz is the primary reason for its widespread use in today's technology. Its high degree of both vibrational stability and predictability combined with its piezoelectric transduction abilities make it an integral component in a broad array of applications, from frequency stabilizing in telecommunications and timing elements to vibrational transduction in ultrasonic generators, pressure gauges, and sensitive measurement devices.

Though much more could be presented on the technicalities of quartz's piezoelectric technological applications, it is the bioenergetic and higher consciousness interactions that are most significant in this context.

On a basic level, it is easy to see that quartz does indeed have a subtle piezoelectric interactive responsiveness to the sonic and electric aspects of the human bioenergetic system. The bioelectric nature of the human energy system is well established. For example, the researchers Albert Roy Davis and Walter Rawls conclude in their book entitled *Magnetism and Its Effects on the Living System:*

> In this . . . outline of the bioelectrical potential found to exist in man there is evidence of human electrical and electromagnetic aura. The entire body of man is a field of continuing flowing electromagnetic energy, and the space emissions of this form of energy have been recorded.[12]

Furthermore, subtle sonic vibrations are also an integral aspect of the bioenergy field. The heartbeat, breathing, and myriad metabolic processes generate microsonic emissions that have been recorded. For instance, from Victor Beasley's *Your Electro-Vibratory Body:*

> It was . . . discovered that some aspect of man's somatic vibrations translates as audible sound frequencies. Dr. Von H. Rohracher of the Psychological Institute of Vienna University has recorded sonic micro-vibrations emitted by the skin of humans and animals. These emissions are complex sound waves which differ with each individual, as indicated on recorded graphs made by Rohracher.[13]

Given that a piezoelectrically based sports biomechanic device has been shown

*A population inversion involves the energetic pumping of a large percentage of atoms into a higher quantum state. This is a necessary precondition to the stimulated emission process.

capable of measuring the heartbeat pulses of a person standing next to it,[14] the simple act of holding a crystal in hand can be seen to stimulate the piezoelectric effect, both from sound to electric voltage and electricity to sound. The crystal's matrix is thereby stimulated into heightened reactivity and interactive rapport with the bioenergetic system.

The effects of this dynamic are fascinating to explore. In effect, the emissions of the bioenergetic system carrying modulated information (that is, vibrational patternings) about that system are systematically processed into the crystalline matrix via piezoelectric transduction. This transduction process maintains the bioenergetic informational coding, for it is converted into a different energetic modality by which it interacts with the crystal. The transduced bioenergetic information-patterns process through the crystalline matrix, and as this occurs the overall vibrational quality of the quartz plus its specific lattice patterning-codes conjoin with the bioenergetic patterns. The resultant energetic combination then is piezoelectrically transduced out of the crystal into the bioenergetic system. The auric system receives the subtle modulated vibrations and assimilates them. In addition, if the crystal is in contact with the skin, the pacinian corpuscles (that is, mechanoreceptors) are capable of transducing sonic input into modulated bioelectric frequencies. The bioelectric signals are then processed through the biosystem, causing correlating results.

Thus a mutually interactive feedback process occurs in the crystal-bioenergy system interaction. Pattern interacts with pattern, the crystal functioning as a vibrational tool that adds both its overall vibrational stabilizing and heightening properties as well as its specific matrix codings. The conjoined bioenergy and crystal vibrational patterns are also amplified by the crystal as they then emit into the auric and body systems, to be processed and integrated accordingly.

The intricate technicalities and application potentials of this interaction are both wide-ranging and complex, and when fully developed in the future, will occupy numerous volumes of information. Following are some brief quotations and thoughts on this subject.

It is known that many components of the body function piezoelectrically. These include bone, keratin, collagen, the brain as a whole,[15] nucleic acids,[16] tendon, dentin, aorta, trachea, intestine, elastin, and skin. The scientist-philosopher Guy Murchie summarizes and adds a further perspective in his book entitled *The Seven Mysteries of Life:*

> In sum, it now appears almost certain that piezoelectricity is a common attribute of tissues, working unobtrusively not only in much of the mineral kingdom but in virtually all of the vegetable and animal kingdoms. And accumulating evidence strongly hints that senses in every kingdom operate more or less piezoelectrically, probably including still undeveloped ones.[19]

Thus quartz crystal can be viewed as one piezoelectric matrix among others. The key to understanding quartz' role in interacting with one or more of these biomatrices lies in the following traits of quartz: 1) full-spectrum energy range, 2) sensitive interreactivity with subtle bioenergies and micromodulated patterns thereof, 3) coherently rarefied overall vibratory nature, 4) specifically programmable matrix, 5) multidimensional transduction potential, and 6) energy amplification attributes. The crystal, then, functions as a programmable mixing chamber through which bioenergy patterns are modified in both general and specific ways. Resultant energy pattern modification is amplifiably emitted back into the body or auric system. The reception and integration of this vibratory field can be quite specifically applicable to the balancing or reprogramming of any components of any level of the bioenergetic system.

Current progress in this regard is already being enacted. Though in its beginning stages, the implications, especially in light of quartz' potential applications, are quite thought-provoking.

> New York researchers Robert O. Becker and Andrew Marino have shown that the piezoelectric effect in bone and other tissues is not due to mineral content, but to an organic compound: the structural protein collagen. They are especially interested in the possibility that piezoelectricity may be a biological transducer, capable, as they put it, of converting environmental stimuli into biologically recognizable signals capable of controlling growth. In other words, outside forces can perhaps be converted into signals inside the body.[18]

Further,

> The Medical Tribune quoted Dr. Bassett as saying, "We're learning to talk the electrical language of the cell. By choosing the proper pulse width and frequency distribution for the electromagnetic waveform we can communicate some very subtle bits of information to the cell. . . . It is entirely possible that, in the future, many other functional disorders of the human body can be rectified by changing the electrical environment of cells and organs with specific external messages communicated through an electromagnetic field that is very specific in its pulse characteristics. . . . The cells don't care if the potential they experience is from an electrical source or is piezoelectric in origin—they respond with activity in either case."[19]

When contemplating such possibilities, include the potentials for consciousness modulated input into programmed crystals for subsequent pieozoelectric stimulation of specific bioenergetic regions. Also, laser or sonic-induced stimulation of a programmed crystal for particular applications is a modality of the future in healing and reprogramming. Possibilities for higher mind/higher consciousness energy code modulations have great potential.

Multidimensional piezoelectric reactivity (MPR) is the cross-dimensional vibrational activation of the crystalline matrix stimulated by the piezoelectric effect. When the piezoelectric effect is set in motion on the physical plane, this activity in and of itself provides a spark impetus toward stimulating an oscillating interdimensional crosslinkage transfer-transduction of energetics on numerous quantum dimensional planes. In Chapter 2, the nature of the semipermeable membrane barrier occurring between dimensional planes is explained regarding the need to generate certain predetermined thresholds of vibrational frequency and intensity in order to break through from one dimension to another. Without attaining these vibrational breakthrough thresholds, energy exchange between dimensional planes is basically at a minimum ground level. Herein lies the greatest significance of the piezoelectric effect. For it provides an activator impetus that induces interdimensional interchange by crossing the dimensional membrane threshold barrier quotient. This action effects interreactivity through numerous dimensional planes, depending primarily upon the intensity and overall coherence of the piezoelectric effect in combination with energy input into the crystal.

Overall, MPR activates an interdimensional staircase of interconnection and resultant transference of energetics both up and down the dimensional spectrum. This trait illuminates one of the keys as to why quartz is such a supreme multidimensional interlinkage matrix, and how these dynamics occur.

In addition to the generalized interlinkage dynamics, the crossdimensional vibrational transfer-transduction occurs with a great deal of specificity. The crystalline matrix sets the stable, generalized parameters of selectively permeable multidimensional interconnection. Within this outline the specific patterns of the crystal/energy input dynamics are selectively activated into cross-dimensional transduction during MPR. To use a simple illustration, if the sonic note of C is input into the crystal, in addition to the abiding crystalline matrix interlinkage patterns, the specific note of C is selectively induced to interconnect with higher dimensional octaves (and intervals) of C. This principle, then, operates in like manner with complex energy code-patterns. The effects of this dynamic are twofold. First, there is a multidimensional alignment effect wherein higher octave correlates of a given energy pattern are connected, thereby aligning the latter with the more causal former. For example, in healing, the interconnection of an imbalanced energy pattern with its more causal higher plane blueprint of perfection would induce the imbalanced patterns to be aligned with balanced codes, and healing would thereby occur. Second, there is an infusion of higher dimensional Light into the lower octave energy patterns. Parallel to the alchemical way by which raw silicon dioxide becomes rarefied as a higher Light-field is infused into it during crystal growth processes, so also this type of effect occurs with other kinds of physical substances and energy patterns through MPR. Higher Light is sparked into lower dimensional planes and integrated accordingly therein. This helps to explain the catalytic effect that quartz has with so many individuals and how it functions over the long term to quicken the Light within consciousness and reprogram the bioenergetic system.

Furthermore, the MPR shows the way to activating the highest potentials of quartz as an interdimensional linkage matrix. The more intensely and coherently the piezoelectric effect is stimulated, the greater the *m*ultidimensional *p*iezoelectric *r*eactivity. The higher the degree of MPR the higher the dimensional planes to which access is gained and the greater the strength and efficiency of energetic transfer-transduction. Thus, herein lies the reason why crystals work much more effectively when consciousness energies are focused therein. And here is the key concept for activating the MPR to heretofore unattained magnitudes via input of intense, coherent energy modalities such as lasers, sonics, magnetics, and others.*

The *Star of David energy dynamics* are central to crystal energetics. These dynamics are "written" into the very archetypal pattern of the quartz's axis system. Figure 16 shows the three horizontal axes of the hexagonal system—a1, a2, and a3—that lie at 120° angles to each other. Superimposed upon these axes is a Star of David figure, in perfect alignment. It is also possible to create Stars of David with any number of diameters within this axis relationship because each line describes the angular relation of opposite vertexes of this symbol. Now, if Figure

*See later in this chapter for more information in this regard.

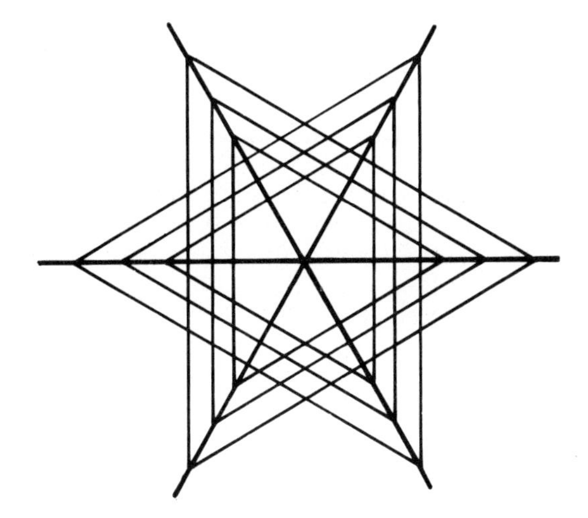

Figure 16: The Star of David Geometry Superimposed within the Horizontal Cross-Section Plane

16 can be envisioned as one horizontal cross-section out of innumerable possible cross-sections throughout a crystal form (see Figure 17), it can be seen that the Star of David symbol and energy pattern is active throughout the entire length and width of the crystal. Further, the Star of David is not a static energy pattern;

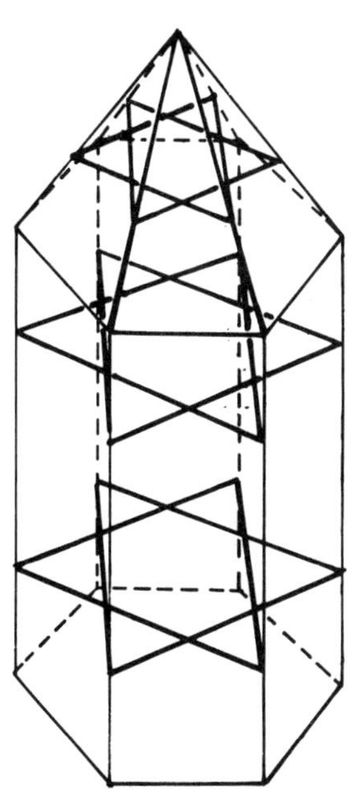

Figure 17:
The Star of David Geometry at Different Horizontal Cross-Sections

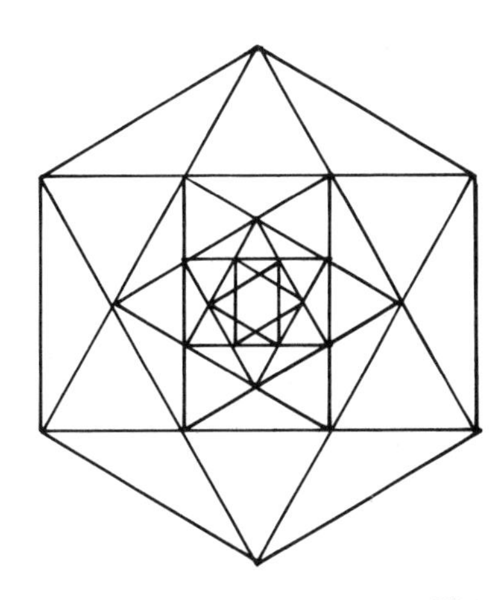

Figure 18:
Counterpoised Star of David Geometries Within a Horizontal Cross-Section

in activity, the two equilateral triangles are counterrotating at equal or harmonically interrelated rates such that the Star of David is actually a *standing wave pattern*. To go one step further, Figure 18 demonstrates the fact that within the hexagon contained within the outer Star of David is another such figure on a smaller scale and perfectly counterpoised within the hexagon; and within the second Star of David is yet another one; and so on, *ad infinitum*.

The total effect, then, of the outermost Star of David in conjunction with all the other implicitly potential counterrotating figures contained within it is essentially one of dynamizing the spiralling energetics of the crystal. The counterrotating motion generates a double helical wave-pulse action perpendicular to the horizontal plane of the Star of David. With such activity intrinsic to every horizontal level of the crystal, the causal root of quartz's spiralling dynamics is seen. This also further illuminates the predominantly vertical energy flow dynamics of the crystal body plus the formulation of primary crystal energetics (that is, the intense, coherent emanations that project out of the termination tip).

Therefore, to sum up this chapter section, the fundamental principles of quartz crystal energy dynamics have been highlighted. The surpassing complexities of crystal energetics have been glimpsed amid the primary outline of basic concepts and seed-perspectives presented. From this core knowledge, the remainder of this chapter and other sections of this book will further explicate the multifaceted aspects of crystal dynamics.

THE MIND–CRYSTAL INTERACTION

The human mind interacts in synergetic complementarity with the quartz matrix. Like a lock and key, the mind matrix interlinks with harmonic exactitude with the tetrahedron-spiral crystal latticework, thus unlocking the fuller potentials of both. On the atomic and subatomic levels of the crystal there is mostly pure space, atomic particles whirling in their orbits and harmonic interactions on a microcosmic scaling level parallel to the macrocosmic universe of suns, planets, asteroids, and so on. Contrary to what human senses indicate, instead of the crystal being composed of purely compacted solid matter, rather it is mostly holding patterns of highly organized spatial harmonics. This gives considerable latitude for the mind matrix to interact with it. As one of the many perfect synchronicities of the divine plan, the fundamental harmonics of the human mind interlock with those of quartz with elegant concord.

There are numerous characteristics of the quartz crystal that make it such a remarkable tool for extending and amplifying consciousness capabilities. Herein the major aspects of this relationship will be delineated.

First, one of the greatest strengths of crystals in general and quartz specifically is the matrix stability and the latticed resonant coherence of the oscillating molecules. The fluctuating, many times less than steady dynamics of the mind are well noted in spiritual and psychological literature, being vividly metaphorized in yogic traditions as a drunken monkey bitten by a scorpion. When the mind is superimposed within the stabilized harmonic order of the crystal, there is a strong tendency for the mind to start to oscillate in resonance with the matrix, thus aiding the mind to be more steadily focused and coherent.

Second, there is a primary resonant affinity between quartz crystal and the third eye chakra/pineal gland complex. Through interacting with one another strongly, the third eye center is stimulated to a higher state of functioning and therefore the operations associated with it step up into greater quantum levels of operative activity. The functions of the third eye that are so affected include telethought communication abilities, inner dimensional sight, and higher mental faculties. Overall, the spiral-cone of perception is able to expand to higher degrees than otherwise usually accessible.

Third, in addition to third eye activation specifically, clear quartz is a general consciousness catalyst. Because of its interdimensional interlinkage capacities and White Light-transduced nature, whenever the mind interconnects with quartz higher quantum levels of interdimensional Light-energies are stimulated into interaction with the mind.

Fourth, though consciousness has full potential to gain access to the UEN, quartz crystals clarify and amplify this potential. In addition to the three reasons just cited, the quartz matrix holds steady the access lines through which access to the UEN may be gained more efficiently. Not only does it hold these access lines steady, but it also amplifies consciousness along these lines when the mind resonantly interlinks with the crystal. Further, a crystal can be programmed with specifically desired areas or sectors of the UEN to which access is desired; thereafter, that crystal will serve as a tool that holds particular access lines steady for facilitative alignment of consciousness with those specific sectors.

And fifth, through *m*ultidimensional *p*iezoelectric *r*eactivity, the crystal matrix helps consciousness to break through dimensional membrane areas with significantly greater amplified effectiveness. Because of this property, higher reaches of interdimensional communication are opened and the subsequent interlinkage has increased clarity and efficiency.

Therefore, the mind-crystal synergy is one particularly helpful to humankind. For although crystals are not necessary to consciousness growth, they are indeed exceptionally useful tools for facilitating a much heightened, many times catalyzed interconnection with the Light that each individual truly is.

SUBSTANCES AND ENERGIES WITH A PRIMARY RESONANT AFFINITY WITH QUARTZ

Primary resonant affinity is a state in which there is a mutual harmonic correspondence between two (or more) substances or energetic modalities. In this state there is a direct interrelationality that is usually complementary and always resonantly interactive. Between two substances/energies in primary resonant affinity a mutual harmonic phase locking and a strong, efficient interchange of energetics occurs, many times in a synergistic manner. Those substances and energies having this type of relationship with quartz have the strongest interactions with it and are the most central to its highest applications.

A simple list of those substances and energies with a primary resonant affinity with quartz will suffice here. Further explication may be found in other sections of this text.

1. DNA.
2. Spiral form energy/spiral energy flow.
3. Water and its higher octave correlates composing the universal aqueous element.

4. Blood crystals.
5. Third eye chakra and higher mental human consciousness.
6. Pyramidal and tetrahedral form energy.
7. Planetary vortex etheric crystals.
8. Gravitational and magnetic energy modalities (specific critical thresholds).
9. Refined gem matrices.

DOUBLE-TERMINATION QUARTZ CRYSTALS

Double-terminated crystals are the most complete and whole form of the quartz kingdom. It is the form that all quartz will grow into if there are no growth restrictions. The majority of quartz is single-terminated because there is a chemical affinity between the crystal and the rock matrix upon which it is growing. When the first seed-crystals crystallize out of solution into solidity they attach to the underlying matrix rock. Therefore as the crystal grows it can form but one termination because the other end is blocked from doing so by the rock matrix. Most double-terminations grow attached to single-terminations so that both terminations are free to grow without restriction. An exceptionally high percentage of double-terminations are found in the "Herkimer diamonds," or quartz that is mined in Herkimer County, New York. In Herkimer County there is often no chemical affinity between the matrix rock and the quartz, and therefore there is little primary attachment between the two. Few restrictions to both terminations' growth have resulted in Herkimer County having the highest percentage of double-terminations found in the world.[20]

As a group, good quality double-terminations are the most powerful, efficient, and useful crystals in the quartz kingdom. These qualities mainly derive from the uninterrupted c axis plus their "holistic polarity." Single-terminations have a more linear polarization; that is, there is a definite difference in vibrational orientation between the base and the termination. While it would not be correct to assign negative or positive polarity designations to the base and termination, there is a predominance of energy flow in the direction from the base to the termination and distinct differences in the qualities of their respective energies. With double-terminations there is a greater holistic balance of polarization between the two ends. Figure 19 shows a way of denoting this holistic polarity. In all double-terminations, corresponding faces on opposite terminations are always *r* and *z* faces; that is, the two terminations that are connected on either end of a single body face will always be a *z* and *r* or *r* and *z*; this is a mineralogical fact. What this signifies in terms of energy dynamics is that there is an opposite polarity potential between both sets of termination facets (because *r* and *z* faces have opposite charges because of the piezoelectric effect). From Figure 19 it is seen that there is a counterbalance between the two terminations and that there is an attraction set up between each opposite pair of facets. This establishes energetic parameters such that there is a balanced dual directionality, that is, energy flows in both directions. In addition, in a well-formed, high quality double-termination there is a crucial phase conversion zone in the middle horizontal section of the body, similar in nature to magnetism's Bloch Wall, that in this case involves Spirit polarity dynamics as seen in Figure 20 (refer below in chapter for further explication). Because of these dynamics, which occur to a significantly lesser degree

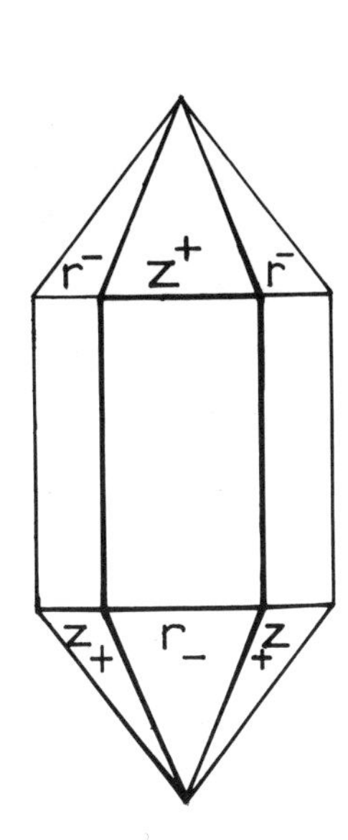

Figure 19:
Counter-balancing Factors in Double-Terminations

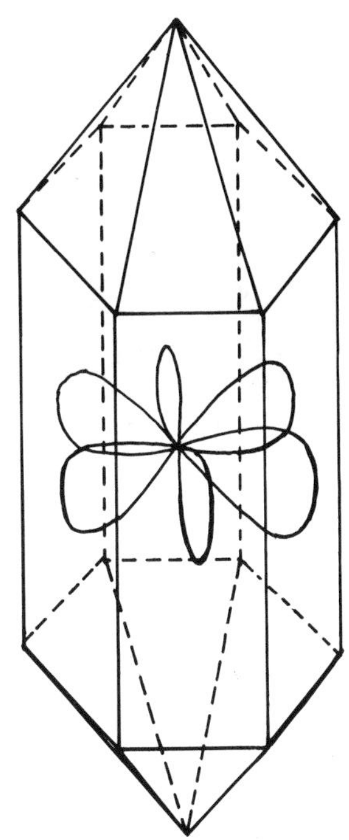

Figure 20:
"Spirit Polarity," or Unipolar Energy Dynamic in Double-Terminations

in single-terminations, there is a tremendously heightened capacity for inter-dimensional interlinkage and Light-processing. In many advanced crystal-based technologies of the future, the use of double-terminations is imperative because of their holographically whole, Spirit polarity properties. For today, though single-terminations are extremely useful, good quality double-terminations with an uninterrupted c axis (that is, no heavy inclusions) should be highly valued and put to special use.

LOW RELIEF TERMINATION PATTERNS

Visible on many crystals' terminations are subtle patternings on the outer surface. Some are more readily visible than others because of differences in subtlety; most viewers will have to experiment with catching the light reflecting off the facets' surfaces. When the correct angle is found, the observer will see slightly raised patternings, some of which look like those in Figure 21. No two low relief motifs are alike, and there is a virtually infinite spectrum of possibilities.

What these motifs signify is quite important. Recall the mineralogical fact that the exterior form of the crystal is a reflection of its internal molecular patterns. The low relief designs are indicators of these molecular patterns to a much more specific degree than is the crystal's overall outline-geometry. In effect, they "fill in" the geometry outline as they bring to the surface the more intricate details of the molecular patterning.

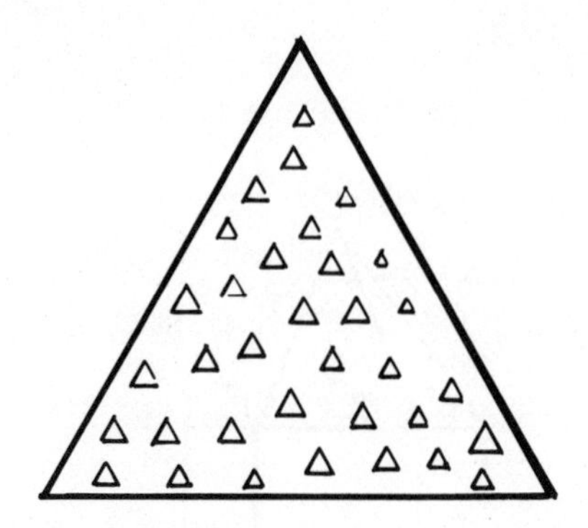

Figure 21: Low Relief Termination Patterns

On the microscale, these termination motifs are where the outermost interactions between the crystal and the environment take place. They act as templates through which incoming energy is subtly imprinted and then processed through the corresponding pathways as they unfold from the surface into the crystal interior. Conversely, they are templates that complete the molecular patterns as energy is processed from the interior to the exterior and out through the low relief patterns. Thus this specific region acts as a sensitive membrane region of subtle energy imprinting and processing between the crystal and its surrounding.

Sometimes, by observing the low relief motifs, better intuitive (and sometimes analytical) comprehension of the individual energy "personality" of a crystal is gained. Particularly intuitively attractive patterns can sometimes indicate specific facets with which it would be beneficial to transfer crystal codes into consciousness. One way to do this is to place the facet in direct skin contact over the third eye region while focusing awareness on the crystal. Also, while holding the crystal for periods of time, have the thumb in contact with the specifically desired facet-code region for assimilation of the coded energy patterns.

Because of the important role that low relief patterns play in crystal energetics, it is crucial not to polish or otherwise alter the crystal's termination. Only in specific cases (as discussed in Chapter 11) is it appropriate to modify this area. The low relief patterns may thus be seen as the microwindows of the crystal.

GEM AND REFINED METALS PERSPECTIVES

Though this text does not expand into this domain of knowledge extensively, it is certainly an important one in the field of sacred crystallography. As discussed more thoroughly in other sections of this book, quartz is the broad spectrum-range crystal, and all other refined mineralic matrices, such as emerald, diamond, and gold, are specialized in their energetic parameters.

Each of the refined mineralic matrices is a unique formulaic spectral variation. Different refined crystallographic substances are mediums in which rarefied universal energetics may be patterned into the physical plane. As with quartz, there is a "raw" crystallographic solution medium into which higher dimensional vibrational patterns are superimposed, thereby causing an alchemical rarefication of the medium itself plus the crystallization of the causal Light-codes into physicality.

The main idea with nonquartz mineralic matrices is that they are specialized formulations of vibrational codes and characteristics. Altogether, they manifest an extensive spectrum of energy tools with which to selectively work.

Different matrices in this realm have different colorations. Although the specific color is one indicator (among others) as to the main spectral range of which it is a part, for example, ruby with the Red ray, it is an oversimplification to state that it *is* that part of the spectrum. Ruby, for instance, is an aspect of the Red ray-*transduced* (as with quartz being White Light-transduced, and not White Light itself in solidified form). Also, ruby is one highly specialized formulation of the Red ray, transduced. There are numerous other gem and precious stone matrices (as well as metallic matrices) that are yet other specific spectrum-profile formulations of the Red ray-transduced. As with ruby, so with all other refined crystallographic matrices. Each type of substance has a characteristic profile of the energy that it absorbs and releases. Therefore, a gem or refined metal matrix will have a delineated characteristic range of absorption and release. In the future, especially when subtle and higher dimensional energetics can be objectively measured and analyzed, a laboratory (or scientific higher consciousness) procedure will be utilized to create specific indexings of properties and parameters of the entire crystal domain.*

Colored quartz variations fit into the general category of specialized crystalline matrices because of the specificity that the color "impurity" creates. Physically, what makes quartz a specific color is a substance in addition to silicon dioxide that intermixes with it, causing perceptible color. For example, the violet coloration of amethyst is due to the minute addition of iron molecules. What happens in this case is that when light goes through the amethyst every color frequency except violet is absorbed and dispersed while the violet is released, thus showing color to the eye. The same is true of the other colored quartz variations (except smoky quartz, whose coloration is due to radiation activity). In effect, the colored quartz is a specific tool that relates to the correlating color ray in the same manner that gems relate to theirs. In this case, there is also a background fundamental vibration of quartz itself but it is qualified into the keynote vibration of the particular color frequency. Basically, then, colored quartz can be thought of as being in league with all the other refined crystallographic matrices, separate from the clear quartz category.

PRIMARY UNIVERSAL ENERGETIC MODALITIES AND THEIR INTERRELATION WITH QUARTZ CRYSTALS

Throughout the far reaches of the UEN, the crystallographic component forms a keystone of Light-interactions. Through this centrally abiding focus-matrix, all other universal energetic modalities receive their templated parameters of formulation, differentiation, sustainment, and continuous modulative interlinkage. The multidimensionally spanning crystallographic component forms the framework-code of manifestation's crystallization by which all energetics are metrically indexed. The Light-synthesis interactions occurrent in and through universal crystallographic matrices are the most fundamentally essential to all of divine order.

*Two currently available books in this field that are recommended are *The Secrets of Metals* by Wilhelm Pelikan, and *The Nature of Substance*, by Rudolf Hauschka.

By examining the causal outlining concerning the universal energetics/crystallographic interaction, key perspectives are illuminated in the reactivation of sacred crystal science, long lost and now being regained.

Light, the Color-Crystal-Sound Trinity, and Spirit Polarity

Light is the all-inclusive totality of manifest creation. The Eternal's edict "Let there be Light" is the ultimate creative sounding whereby the quintessence of All That Is is dynamized from the Absolute Void into omnimanifestation. From the overarching Whole-Light Synthesis derives all the infinite differentiation that constitutes the polarized fabric of creation. White Light, transduced, refracts into the fundamental universal energy modalities constituting the core forces causal to the countless Light-spectrums that set the measured boundaries of each dimensional domain. Such primary forces integratively synthesize octave after dimensional octave through the heights and depths of the UEN. Sound and Color, mathematically modulated through the indexed crystallographic templates, refract and harmonically interfuse to set the parameters of Light transduced into ordered unfoldment.

White Light, therefore, is seen as the apex quintessence inclusive of all, from which all derives. Light-interactions induce Sound and Color into multifaceted, infinitely mirrored index-sets of diversification. Each index-set is a formulaic combinatory spectrum-code functioning as the constant measure of an assigned dimensional domainship. At the highest levels of Abstract Light the creation of Sound-Color spectrum indexes is inextricably interlinked with the numerological equivalencies of the crystallographic element. The fusionary processes therein crystallize about the numerical-axial crystallographic code-framework. This trinitization, in all its illimitable creative potential, is the keystone transduced into multifold dimensional layers of symmetrically equivalent derivational template codings, dispatched to their corresponding relational positionings within the UEN.

Sound and Color should not be confused with their perceived earthly derivations, rather they are universal principiums of the highest order. In a general sense, Sound may be likened to the formative organizational principle. The Sounding of the universal "deeps" causes coalescence into boundaried ordering—the "magnetic" parameters of dynamically unfolding systematized organization are set. In fundamental counterpoint, Color is the radiative, "electric" principle that infuses animating luminosity into the primeval substratum, enlivening it with Ultraluminescence. Together, Color and Sound are the antipodal polarities of Light, interactively combined to form the polyphonic weavework of the myriad Light-spectrums through the cross-combinatory crystallographic intermediary.

The crystallographic intermediatory property confers the Sound-Crystal-Color trinitization with a supracoherency principle of the utmost centrality in divine order, termed in this context *Spirit polarity*. As Light is the apexial font of the Sound-Crystal-Color trinity, so is Spirit polarity the supracausal core dynamic of the myriad *polarity orientation-sets* that establish the different dimensional cross-combinatory indexing. Polarity relationships span a wide spectrum of potential orientations. The earth plane abides in but one subset of this spectral range. Each dimensional domain is founded upon the "phase, order, and matrix" orientation template factors that establish its polarity parameters. All functions—time-space, harmonics, gravitometrics, Color-Sound indexing phases, and so on—depend upon the particular code settings of the polarity orientation sets. Spirit polarity is the foundational derivation root of all polarity orientation sets. Such sets are like beat cycle variations of one singular unipolar infinity-core that *is* Spirit polarity. Not to be confused with such a concept as a magnetic monopole (which is merely separated from its necessary antipodal complement), unipolarity constitutes an absolute wholeness in and of itself inclusive of all potential polarity orientation sets, the very seed-core of unity.

Light is the "fundamental harmonic" of unipolarity (that is, Spirit polarity). Light transduced into Color-Crystal-Sound utilizes the crystallographic component to maintain unipolar harmonics as the various trinitized index sets extend into the countless dimensional levels of the UEN. It is the Crystal element that has the unique properties by which Spirit polarity is able to be established and sustained in the midst of the polarity flux and the varied orientation sets thereof throughout creation. This provides understanding of important interdimensional linkage and intermediary functions of the "crystal connection." For it is by the crystallographic aspect of the UEN that the various "orbital shell levels" or "wave harmonics" of a single unipolar centrality may be extended into manifestation and still be integrally linked in a state of interconnected wholeness. In short, the Crystal element is a primary designated means by which the One and the Many are one. This is a key of keys for all advanced crystal-based science.

Quartz and its higher-octave correlates are the central matrices in which this unipolar harmonic dynamic occurs in its most encompassing degree. This is true because it is the crystallographic extension of Light-transduced. It thereby partakes of the primary unipolarity of Light, for as Light steps down into the successive dimensions of the UEN it does not lose its originating unipolar essence but rather extends it into creation via its corresponding Crystal element. Color and Sound necessarily originate from the Spirit polarity of Light, but they do not have the unique high stability quotient intrinsic to Crystal. Without the crystallographic aspect, Color and Sound could not maintain ordered integrity amid the energetic flux of the cosmos. This is why, for example, Crystal is utilized as a timepiece in the planetary vortex gridwork. It is this element that provides undeviating stability within the parameters of its templated coding by which all other energetic modalities receive and maintain their appropriate ordering on the micro to macro scales.

Therefore, in the context of crystal science, the quartz crystal is a master crucible in which and through which unipolarity can be activated into higher quantum states of functioning. This is achieved in great part by interacting with other energetic modalities so as to induce specific types and levels of supracoherency states within the crystal matrix. In so doing, the unipolar potential within the crystal is stimulated from a state of relative dormancy to higher states of activation. In this way interdimensional interconnection quotients in addition to overall power and spectrum-modulation potentials are vastly increased. Thus the gateways are opened into a new era of consciousness and technological advancement.

Sonics

Sonics affects quartz especially powerfully for three reasons: 1) the higher essence of sonics and crystallographic matrices are closely paralleling in some aspects and intersecting and complementary in others; 2) sonics being by definition pressure waves, the piezoelectric effect is stimulated, thereby also strongly inducing the MPR; and 3) sonics induces nonlinear magnetic and gravitic responses in quartz.

> The science of harmony in music is, in these terms, practically identical with the science of symmetry in crystals. Indeed the crystals can now literally be seen to be the philosopher's stone, frozen music which presents to the eye . . . the dynamism of the molecules, atoms, particles, and standing waves of which they are composed.[21]

Rhythm is in time what symmetry is in space. The periodicity and proportion of a crystalline latticework can be seen as "solidified" standing wave patterns. The reverberating resonance of millions of identical, co-oriented molecular oscillators creates a condition of harmonic coherency throughout the crystal structure. A highly tuned resonating system such as this is exquisitely responsive to harmonically related applied input. The crystalline matrix-patterns function as millions of microhelical "tuning forks" processing spiraling pulses of harmonically tuned energy flow. The proportionality of the latticwork symmetry provides a stable geometric standard by which vibrations are qualified into correlating wave harmonics.

The quartz crystal, and crystals in general, are not densified Sound per se but do indeed partake of high degrees of Sound's abstract numeric-geometric principles, especially regarding proportionality of structuring. Sound and Crystal remain related but harmonically diverge from each other as Numerologically–based Abstract Light transduces into levels where Geometry crystallizes as archetypal Form. Sound closely interweaves with Crystal because of its formative, form-giving activity orientation. Crystal specializes into modes of stablization, template activities, and unipolar dynamics. Crystal serves as an interresonant "framework" through which Sound interweaves via magneto-gravitically oriented wave harmonics. Multilevel modulation, coherency wave-guide dynamics, and interdimensional linkage synergy all describe Crystal's functionality in relation to its close counterpart, Sound.

On the physical level, the pressure waves of sonics efficiently stimulate quartz's piezoelectric effect, something that neither magnetics nor chromatics does. Because the modulation of the pressure waves is the sonics' patterning, the impingement of these waves occurs against the crystal surface with according rhythmic periodicity. Therefore, the piezoelectric conversion from pressure to correlating electrical charges creates a microscopic symphonics of electrical charge oscillation, reflecting the sonics' patterns. The piezoelectric effect is not simply a surface phenomenon, for the oscillating flow of electrons throughout the matrix causes associative changes throughout the crystal.

Too, the low relief patterns of the outer surface create a sensitive membrane of interreactivity with the sonic input. Depending upon the sonics' intensity and harmonic affinity with the crystal, the low relief-sonics interaction generates an outer magnetic membrane shell co-associative with the crystal's exterior surface. This creates a strong outer form energy dynamic, adds significantly to the crystal's dimensional interlinkage properties, and functions as a sensitively responsive outer energetic membrane.

Further, at specific indexed sonic frequency thresholds, intensely focused sonic input induces a state of hypercoherency within the crystal matrix. Normal molecular and lattice coherency orientations undergo a quantum matrix transposition to a higher level of energetic order in which the magneto-gravitic profile induces a major dimensional threshold level breakthrough. In this state, the crystal's "windows" of multidimensional interconnectedness open to greater degrees. Multidimensional piezoelectric reactivity (MPR) adds considerably to this dynamic. As a result, a Jacob's Ladder of higher dimensional access is amplified manyfold, and the way is clear for spectrum profiles of vibrational interreactivity not previously available.

There are also modalities by which sonics are intermixed in desired ways, utilizing the crystalline matrix as an alchemical mixing chamber. Two of the more powerful means of allowing sonics to interact with quartz are to position the sound so it is in direct contact with the crystal's surface or to use highly focused, directional sonic speakers (or acoustic lasers) directly adjacent to the crystal. The main idea is to infuse continuous streams or rhythmic injections of intense, focused sonics so that the entire crystal matrix is permeated by this input. A potent piezoelectric and MPR effect is so generated, thereby inducing a higher degree of interdimensional harmonic resonance, overall crystal activation, and amplified harmonic coherence in both the crystal and sonics. Fundamental and harmonic standing wave patterns may be established in a wide array of modulated possibilities. The focusing action of the termination angles sonics waves (especially with a c axis orientation) together according to the facets' geometric relationality. A great deal of energy accumulates at the termination tip. This energy bears considerable investigation, for it is anomalous and of importance as a fusionary zone in crystal-sonic science.

Further, the primary and secondary crystal energetics may be exactly calculated for any given crystal in conjunction with known sonic input. Because of the coherently focused amplification and correlating interdimensional sonic interlinkage, the primary energy flow is an extremely potent standing wave stream of micromodulated code-patterns of a nonlinear magneto-gravitic nature. The secondary energy flow is composed of wave harmonics of diverse modulated codings according to internal angular reflection patterns in addition to the patterning of the outer magnetic membrane-facet from which it exits. Overall, the crystal-sonic interaction is a dynamically synergistic one that provides ordered, calculable spectrums of interdimensionally entrained, coherently micromodulated, resonantly amplified energetics for application in a very broad range.

When sonics is discussed here, it is viewed in the context of a scientific discipline encompassing both technological and consciousness-derived applications. In today's context the magnitude of the sonic-crystal unity as just presented relies mainly upon technologically applied sonics, though in the years to come, as higher consciousness abilities of specialists in sonics are activated, consciousness applications will come to be of equal importance. The effects just described optimally will occur within a sophisticated Unified Energy Field (UEF) custom designed for sonic-crystal modalities.

Additional thoughts:

> Mankind is destined to recognize and use "magic music" whereby the blind shall see, the lame shall walk, and the veils of materialism will be drawn aside as communion with invisible Hosts is re-established.[22]

> Music, particularly ultrasonic music in the presence of heat, has been found

capable of changing the chemical structure and the strength of crystals by spreading imperfections at grain boundaries in the lattice.[23]

Mathematically, harmonics or overtones are not a mystery in the sense that the mathematical equation for figuring out overtones is a basic geometrical formula.[24]

On Dr. Hans Jenny's tonoscope experiments:

Complex and meaningful patterns are even more apparent in Jenny's sound-affected substances when viewed at the *microscopic* level. Then are revealed beautiful and mathematically-precise mandala-structures looking like groupings of microscopically-viewed snowflakes. The stress-interactions created in substances by their exposure to sound frequencies always result in formations replete with meaningful numerological, proportional and symmetrical qualities.[25]

Now let us define substance: Substance is that state in the universe similar to the condition in solution just before the point of precipitation and matter is the precipitate.

In the larger picture of the universe, sound moving in orderly sequence causes substance to precipitate and it becomes matter with the stamp of orderly sequence upon it and a perfect pattern which we call different elements.[26]

The point of view of modern force-field theory and wave mechanics corresponds to the ancient geometric-harmonic vision of universal order as being an interwoven configuration of wave patterns. Bertrand Russell . . . also supported this view in *The Analysis of Matter*: "What we perceive as various qualities of matter," he said, "are actually differences in periodicity."[27]

There may be ways of infusing various sound frequencies into specific crystals, that when placed together, would work harmonically to produce visions of celestial worlds. These special groupings would be "keys" to conscious coparticipation in other-dimensional realms.[28]

MAGNETICS

Though crystals are not ferro-magnetic on the physical level (being paramagnetic), the highly ordered latticed coherence of the crystalline matrix is indeed a powerfully magnetic medium on the etheric and other prescribed quantum dimensional levels. Universally, crystals and the crystallographic mediums in general are known for their exceptional magnetic cohesiveness and coherence, for it is these qualities in addition to gravitic factors that create such high stability quotients in the crystalline matrix. As focal points in the UEN of extremely high magnetic flux and magneto-gravitic code-patterning of energetics, quartz and its higher octave correlates are inextricably central to universal magnetic order.

Ferro-magnetism, whose knowledge has been developed by orthodox science and is well known by all from commercially available magnets, is but one octave of universal magnetics. The conjunction of physical plane magnetics with the higher octave magnetics of crystals is key in completing the interdimensional circuit of interconnection between earth and the more causal reaches of the cosmos. Each octave of the universal magnetic spectrum has a specific symmetry relationship with those octaves above and below. This is parallel to the well-known perpendicular symmetry relationships between electricity and magnetism.

The nature of interoctave magnetic relationships is one of interdimensional phase orientation; interoctave magnetic coupling factors occur when certain dimensional membrane orientations harmonically overlap, thus stimulating a crossover linkage among magnetic octaves. The specific conditions required to facilitate this crossover linkage occur to optimal degrees in the quartz crystal matrix (and higher octave correlates). The proper application of physical-plane ferro-magnetics to the quartz crystal creates a heightened crossover linkage potential. The physical-magnetic lines of force applied perpendicular to the crystal's c axis create a focused counterflow intersection with higher octave magnetics intrinsic to the crystal. A crossover linkage manifests, thus opening the gateway for much-heightened coupling of the physical crystal matrix with its higher energetic levels. That is, a threshold that was previously insulated from fuller levels of interdimensional interreactions is now activated. With the addition of ferro-magnetics the multidimensional "circuits" within the crystal are completed to a much greater degree.

This magnetic activation potential will occur to widely varying degrees according to many variables. The strength of the magnets applied will make a large difference. It will be found that increasing gauss levels will stimulate increasing interdimensional magnetic potential until certain threshold levels are reached, above which much more sophisticated knowledge is required to stimulate the limitless higher magnetic thresholds. Also, the substance of which the magnets are made make a significant difference in the results. In particular, magnets with a high aluminum content and certain rare earth magnets have properties optimal to the physics of crossover linkage. In addition, the manner of application will also vary the results considerably. Perspectives in this regard are described and illustrated in Chapter 14. In general, two magnets attracting one another are placed on opposite crystal body faces. With single-terminations, they are positioned at the middle of the most energetically active sector of the crystal's body. With double-terminations, the middle of the magnets are placed at the body's midsection. With such placements, the crystal body is utilized as the mixing chamber for the crossover dynamics, which then feed into the vertical axis crystal energetics moving toward finalization in the termination. On more advanced levels, electromagnet and rotating magnet configurations will prove to be fruitful.

Additional perspectives:

> Crystals . . . contain the code patterns of the electromagnetic (and gravitic) coordinates of Light-frequencies as they crystallize into the form of quartz. The molecular latticework holds this information code steady and functions as a "seed of wholeness" that can be stimulated in order to activate powerful force fields of specific parameters. This is basically a matter of activating the code patterns and extending them through the environment, thus recrystallizing the electromagnetic fields. The Oraxians and Atlanteans, for example, created energy domes that covered thousands of square miles.[29]

> Electricity manufactures all the qualities and attributes of light in wave motion which we think of as substance. All qualities and even appearance is given to waves of light by the two electrical workers which build up the universe and tear it apart in polarized fields measured out by the two magnetic surveyors which keep all electric actions in balance with their reactions.[30]

> It seems appropriate, to cite the increasing evidence that, in magnetically

ordered crystals, the spins of the atoms periodically do something that could be called a flip, reversing their direction and polarity, just as happens much more slowly to the magnetic polarity of the Earth, the sun and stars and probably the galaxies. And this change actually advances from atom to atom like a row of falling dominoes in a microprogression physicists call a spin wave that sweeps through the material like swells on the ocean. Indeed it is a vital factor in the melodic reality behind the wave nature of all matter.[31]

Crystals are orderly arranged molecularly and magnets have an orderly arrangement of molecules also which makes possible the magnetic lines of force. By correspondence: a) the magnet is the Matter polarity and b) crystals are the Spirit polarity. The orderly arrangement of molecules in crystals produces an etheric field. The etheric field is similar to the magnetic field of force. Just as the magnetic field is a key to electricity, so the etheric field of crystals is the key to di-electric energy.[32]

The magnet represents the most orderly focus of what we may call the matter polarity. The crystal represents the most orderly focus of what we may call the spirit polarity. Creativity takes place always between two polarities. Therefore, the right combination of magnets and crystals will produce the creative effect of energy. . . . Light on the crystal and magnet, that is, lines of force from the magnet, are the components of a new energy system. Future lighting will be glowing crystals.[33]

CHROMATICS/LASERS

In the context of chromatics, the earthly equivalency of Color, it is laser light whose coherency, intensity, directionality, and monochromaticity produces the most significant interaction with quartz crystal. The coherency of laser light closely parallels the uniform periodicity of the crystal latticework. Their conjoinment is as crystalline light coherently interweaving with standing wave crystallographic Light. Because they both have the qualities of high order, singularity of vibrational structure, and oscillatory coherence, the crystal and laser interact in remarkable ways.

As laser light flows through quartz, its frequency (that is, color) has a strong tendency to harmonically phase lock with the crystal's oscillating molecular latticework. This phase-locking occurs at numerous harmonic octave and interval quantum levels. The interaction between the two is predominantly governed by the stable vibrational fundamental frequency of the crystal matrix; this is the steady ground level that abides through all the various interactions. The various harmonic quantum levels above and below the quartz fundamental, however, are increasingly subject to laser modification the farther away from the fundamental they are. Depending upon the laser's frequency, certain quartz harmonic levels will selectively be the primary ones that establish a resonant phase-locking with the laser; the profile of this interaction dynamic will differ for each laser frequency (both in the visible color spectrum and otherwise).

The coherence of the laser induces a higher state of oscillatory coherence in the quartz matrix. What occurs within the crystal is similar to what happens at the laser threshold when out of phase light wave bundles suddenly lock into phase coherence with an associated quantum leap of intensity. In its normal physical state quartz has some degree of vibrational coherence but there are numerous higher thresholds possible. Laser light stimulates a threshold breakthrough to a higher quantum supra-coherency level in the crystal latticework. And just as laser light assumes distinctly different properties of a higher order (versus normal light), so too does quartz in this more activated state.

A primary aspect of this activated state is exemplified in the phenomenon of laser harmonics.

> The enormous intensities of laser beams make it possible to observe nonlinear effects with light too, and here there is more than just a quantitative difference from ordinary light. The response to small disturbances in most physical systems follows a linear law: doubling the disturbance doubles the effect. If an ordinary beam of light shines onto certain types of crystals, some of the light is reflected and some goes straight through. If the intensity of the beam is doubled, the only result will be a doubling of the intensities of the reflected and transmitted beam. But if the intensity is increased many millions of times, rather than just two or three times, quite new effects—such as the generation of harmonics—begin to be observed.
>
> This kind of nonlinear response to light waves occurs because the dielectric constant of a material, which is a measure of its insulating ability, is not really a constant at all. At the very high field-strengths encountered in focused laser beams it depends on the value of the electric field intensity. The material will therefore distort any laser beam passing through it, and when analyzed this distortion is found to be the result of the addition of one or more harmonics to the original laser beam.[34]

University of Michigan researchers have demonstrated this principle with quartz. They focused a red laser beam into a block of quartz. On the other side they detected not only the red beam but also a faint but measurable blue beam, blue being the second harmonic of red. In later experiments the blue beam was as much as 20 percent the intensity of the red beam.[35] This experiment is illuminating in and of itself, but is also an indicator of more encompassing laser-crystal properties. It is an indicator of the interdimensional harmonic resonance effect that lasers induce to much higher degrees in quartz. It will be found in the future that the dielectric constant—a form of threshold membrane—is by far the strongest on the physical plane, being considerably less on the higher dimensions. The point of importance here is that the harmonic potentials of quartz are activated by lasers, not only on the physical plane but also multidimensionally. The upward reaches of the universal energy spectrum are stimulated through the principle of interdimensional harmonic resonance. Interplane vibrational interreactivity and exchange is made possible to greatly heightened degrees.

The coherency activation of quartz by lasers also stimulates the overall crystal energetics, amplifying the output intensity in general and the lattice code-patterns in particular. The resulting emanations also have laser-induced nonlinear gravitic parameters that make them quite causally penetrative in respatializaing the dimensional parameters of the medium into which they are directed. Varying the color-frequency of the laser used will cause fundamentally related but different effects for each. The most effective way to introduce laser light into a crystal in most applications is through the c axis, from base to termination in single-terminations. Further, a large variety of laser scanner-produced sacred geometric patterns shone into the base or through one of the crystal's major termination facets will induce selective coherency activation within the matrix corresponding to the input pattern. Emanative output will have the qualities and energy patterning of the specific geometric pattern, activated through the quartz medium. Consciousness projected into the crystal while laser light is also being input will experience amplified interdimensional access. Further, the programming of a crystal is effected much more deeply with laser dynamics occurring through the matrix as it is exposed to the desired programming influence.

In all, the laser, in parallel complementary ways as with sonics and magnetics, helps activate the inherent higher dimensional potentials of quartz. Lasers in particular are especially valuable in their radiative intensity, focused directionality, and coherence properties. Sonics complements these attributes with its potent piezoelectric stimulation along with associated multidimensional piezoelectric reactivity (MPR); its proportionally intervaled nature interacts in elegant concord with the crystal matrix toward mutually synergistic effects. And last, magnetics is the interdimensional cross–linkage key to grounding higher octave magnetics to the crystal's physical-plane level, thus generating a powerful key to a door of universal access.

As these three keys are further developed in the years to come, they will be the foundation from which other keys are found and through which advanced sacred crystal science will be reborn.

CHAPTER 8
Programming

Quartz has few peers in its renowned capacity to receptively imprint vibrational energy patterns and to maintain such informational coding steady within its latticework with virtual permanence. Throughout the eons of time, the crystallographic stability and superholographic computerlike qualities of quartz crystals and their higher dimensional correlates have played an integral role in the coded interdimensional communication throughout the Universal Energy Network (UEN). In programming crystals, the individual utilizes quartz as a sentient tool that functions as an extension of personal consciousness, an intelligence-template that holds desired energy patterns stable for amplified duplication. The human-crystal interaction has always been a marvelous cosmic synergy, each component fulfilling its own divinely chosen function in serving and expanding the Light of creation.

As modern-day civilization's technologies have grown increasingly more sophisticated, the cornerstone role of crystalline substances has come increasingly to the fore. Solid-state physics and materials science play foundational roles in such crucial fields as computer and communication technologies. Natural crystals and laboratory produced variations form the crux of many of today's most far-reaching technological advancements. From the solid-state laser in the fiber optics revolution to the quantum leaps of progress in the microchip field, crystalline substances serve as predictably responsive, highly regulatable energy processing matrices. The scope and magnitude of current and near-future developments in such crystal-based fields promise a near-unimaginable technological revolution by the end of this century. As supercomputers' speed increases by quantum leaps and bounds, the capacity of silicon chips to hold extensive amounts of coded information continues at an unabated, almost exponential rise. Some state-of-the-art microchips are able to hold 1 million bits of information within a fingernail-size space (the equivalent of 100 double-spaced typewritten pages). Bubble memory can now hold 4 million bits of information on a device the size of a tack's head. And some video disks are able to encode approximately 2 million typewritten pages of data![1]

The horizons of micro-sophisticated crystal technology are being expanded into the very atomic and sub-atomic scales of reality. At the National Research and Resource Facility for Submicron Structures in upstate New York, researchers have performed some astounding crystallographic deeds. For instance, they have inscribed letters small enough to reproduce the entire Encyclopaedia Britannica on a space the size of a postage stamp. In another demonstration, they etched a billion angels on the head of a straight pin, each one wearing a microhalo filled with atoms of gold![2] In molecular beam epitaxy, crystals are grown two to three atomic layers at a time to create custom-grown superlattices. In addition, glimpses of the crystal supercomputers of the future can be caught in one of IBM's research projects. A laser-crystal computer system is currently being developed that can now store 100 million bits—the equivalent of the information in one and a half volumes of the Encyclopaedia Britannica—in a square centimeter. Scientists predict that a single laser-crystal unit about the size of a refrigerator will eventually be able to store all the books in the Library of Congress. This gives it the ability to replace 100 to 1000 of today's biggest disk drives.[3]

Yet today's silicon chips and other laboratory crystalline substances are only linear forerunners of the interdimensional holographic supercomputers of today and tomorrow. The Universal Mind as it works through the UEN is the ultimate omniscient "supercomputer." Naturally formed quartz, as an integral crystallographic extension of the UEN, mirrors this ultra-Intelligence in its operative characteristics. The holographic wholeness, multidimensional capacities, and interdimensional interconnectedness of quartz are the primary traits that surpass today's more unidimensional crystal application and growth techniques.

Quartz functions as an interlinkage device that provides stabilized, encoded access to the innumerable domains and dimensions throughout the UEN. A programmed crystal, in its highest applications, serves as a primary access tool through which communicative interconnection is established to specific "facets" of the Universal Mind. A crystal is not actually a computer in and of itself; it is rather an intelligence matrix in which and through which access to the ultimate "supercomputer"—the Universal Mind—is facilitated.

The crystal applications of the ancient past and the future defy the imagination. It is not always easy to discern the verity of information on this subject, but the underlying concepts are true. For example, in *Secret of the Andes*, it states that one of the many ancient superadvanced civilizations—that of the Els—left "great libraries in their deep, underground empire of enormous cities. In these libraries tiny crystal records contain the history of the Universe, and are enclosed in a magnetic field which, at times, finds an affinity with some 'sensitive' person living on Earth today."[4]

In *The Treasure of El Dorado*, Joseph Whitfield experiences a remarkable demonstration.

> What you are about to see, Joseph, is how the Great Pyramid was constructed, and why. . . . I sat spellbound as the room darkened and the space in front of our chairs became alive with three-dimensional activity. The machine turned out to be a laser holographic projector. The holographic images were somehow stored in the crystal, and the laser projector was able to register the stored images and show them as a perfect three-dimensional movie.[5]

The Light-code imprinting and maintaining properties of quartz and other crystalline matrices are suggested in the *Keys of Enoch*:

> . . . the secrets of the heavenly temples of YHWH coded into stone models and

> left behind in 'holy dwelling places' of the Sons of Light as a beacon to higher Wisdom.[6]
>
> At the end of this time cycle, there shall be scriptures of crystal found in the oceans and scriptures of stone found in the land of Yucatan, and scriptures of Light found throughout the world.[7]

Speculation abounds concerning the famous Mitchell-Hedges crystal skull found in British Honduras in 1922 underneath a Mayan altar. Many think that this enigma was utilized as a computerlike storage device in which some ancient civilizations imprinted the entirety of their knowledge. Hewlett-Packard crystallographers, upon examining this anomaly, concluded that:

> It is the product of a civilization which possessed a crystallographic ability equivalent to ours today. As a crystallographer from Hewlett-Packard said, "The damn thing shouldn't even be."[8]
>
> And we are left with a beautiful quartz crystal eye to the elsewhere, carved in the form of a human skull and very possibly a time bomb in the history of science.[9]

The libraries of the future may very well be collections of crystals and crystal tablets and templates, both natural and laboratory grown, each encoded with vast volumes of holographically recorded information that the individual need only mentally scan to obtain exceptionally accelerated knowledge. Access to the supercomputers of tomorrow may be through specifically designed "windows" or facets of specially prepared crystal systems through which consciousness may selectively engage different memory banks and universal access domains with a swiftness that will make present-day computer keyboards seem positively cumbersome. In such futuristic libraries and computers, more highly evolved consciousness and crystalline intelligence may synergize—mind with mind, lattice with lattice—with such lightning-swift instantaneity that what now takes years to learn may take mere hours. Such is the promise of tomorrow as interdimensional science helps activate the potential of the human-crystal interface.

The essence of programming lies in formulating a thought-form or other energy pattern and superimposing it within the crystalline latticework in a focused and coherent manner. Holographic energy patterns juxtapose within the stable, holographically operating crystal matrix. The conformation of the energy pattern, held steady and focused for a sufficient period of time, causes the crystal matrix to respond with sensitive receptivity as it subtly alters its own patterning structure to enfold an imprint of the energy field's configuration. Thus a holographic transference-imprinting process takes place in which the crystal becomes encoded with a vibratory inscription.

Every thought has a corresponding holographic geometry of motion. It is this standing wave geometry of motion that assumes a specific paterning for each different thought-vibration that is the causal factor in the programming process. The concept of cymatics, developed by Dr. Hans Jenny is his books entitled *Cymatics I* and *Cymatics II*, illustrates a primary aspect of this fundamental principle. In cymatics, it is demonstrated that every sound tone has a corresponding mandala-like ordering pattern when it is transduced into a horizontal vibrating plate containing such responsive substances as iron filings, sand, and others. The device, called a tonoscope, consists of a microphone that transduces sound input into mechanical vibrations applied to the horizontal plate. The results are often astounding.

> Complex and meaningful patterns are even more apparent in Jenny's sound-affected substances when viewed at the *microscopic* level. They are revealed as beautiful and mathematically-precise mandala-like structures looking like groupings of microscopically-viewed snowflakes. The stress-interactions created in substances by their exposure to sound frequencies always result in formations replete with meaningful numerological, proportional and symmetrical qualities.[10]

So too with thought-forms and other superholographic types of energy fields—when coherently focused, a multidimensional standing wave pattern is created, each different thought manifests a distinct energy field, mathematically-geometrically latticed even into the atomic and subatomic ranges. This basic concept was exhibited by Charles Littlefield, M.D., author of *Man, Minerals and Masters*, concerning the influence of thought upon crystallizing cell salts. By formulating a thought-pattern of precise sacred number, letter, and word correlations, and projecting it into a cell salt solution crystallizing into solid form, he found that the resulting crystallized structures varied with each distinct thought-pattern. Not only this, but the same thought-vibration produced identical crystalline patterns repeatedly. Applying Cabala based thought-formulations, a thoroughly amazing series of hieroglyphics, symbolic shapes, and even face-forms of higher Light-beings precipitated into form.

> "A mental image" is the beginning of every created thing. This "mental image" has the power to group the twelve mineral salts normally found in organic nature, in the exact proportion necessary to build the form, and all the tissues and organs necessary to express all the functions, faculties and qualities with which the "mind image" may be endowed.[11]

Thus an illustrative display of the mind's power to imprint subtle-plane energy formulations into the matrices of a mineral-crystallographic structure is remarkably demonstrated.

The programming process, on the slightly more technical levels, is an interdimensional matrix transduction in which a higher dimensional causal energy-coding structure is superimposed within a receptive crystalline structure that enfolds it within the latticework supraholographically. To make a long and technical story shorter and simpler, the higher dimensional thought-pattern forms dimensional membrane "stress" patterns that produce a matrix-pattern of interdimensional hyperLight/deltron firing patterns that transpose a holographic standing wave pattern into an ordered latticework. The responsive latticework enfolds the conformation of the causal energy pattern within the atomic-subatomic magneto-gravitational quantum valence levels that serve then to hold the pattern steady. The imprinting process is then complete as the gravitic element, especially, holds the code-pattern with a high degree of stability. William Tiller, Ph.D., professor of materials science and engineering at Stanford University, amplifies the dynamics of interdimensional transduction processes:

> The potentials existing at the nonspace/nontime levels are thought to act as force fields which directly influence every coincidence in space/time. Through human intention changes, the nonspace/nontime potentials are altered which, in

> turn, alter the imposed boundary conditions on space/time, thus shifting the pattern of wave flow and the details or form of events in space/time; i.e., space/time is clearly a domain of appearance rather than reality.[12]

Quartz, being operative within the full spectrum of universal energies and a matrix of high stability and imprintability, is the medium par excellence for programming functions.

In programming a crystal, a tool is created that is essentially an extension of the self. The intricacies of each individual's consciousness blueprint are also sensitively encoded along with the intended program. And especially after continued use by an individual, the crystal becomes well keyed to that person's unique bioenergetic energy codes. A strong harmonic resonance is thereby established between crystal and consciousness. Coded energetic interchange between the two will, therefore, occur quite efficiently. In effect, the crystal's program serves as a template of sorts that patterns incoming energies according to the energy patterning of the program and emits that coherent supra-holographic coding into the surrounding environment. Add to this the fact that the crystal also amplifies the emitting energy patterns and it becomes clear that the crystal-consciousness interaction is most powerful. Fundamentally, whatever is programmed into the crystal will duplicate its programming and, over time, infuse-imprint it into the consciousness matrix of the programmer, thus effecting corresponding changes. The crystal is an amplified extension of the self.

The intention of the programmer, therefore, becomes the crucial factor as to the nature of the crystal programming and the results that will accrue. Through the universal laws of cause and effect, any energy field set in motion inevitably causes a directly corresponding effect that feeds back to its origin. Therefore, especially because of the crystal's continuously amplified emission of a specifically programmed cause, the programmer's state of consciousness and the particular nature of the program is the single most important issue in programming crystals. In this regard, two types of programming can be seen, called *Higher Self programming* and *personality programming*. The former is a thought-field formulated in unified conjunction with the higher levels of the programmer's multidimensional Light-body wherein grander perspectives of divine Wisdom abide. Because all influences from any aspect of the Higher Evolution reach the individual through his or her Light-body network, Higher Self programming also includes authorized input from interdimensional Light-beings. This form of programming involves both the crucial element of asking the higher realms of Light for assistance in creating a program that is in the programmer's highest interest and accurately receiving such a program. In this Light, Higher Self programming can be seen as a form of interdimensional communication in which consciousness gains access to specific realms of the UEN and receives an appropriately formulated energy field, which is then transposed to the earth plane for interacting with a crystal.

Personality programming, on the other hand, is the forming of a thought-pattern that reflects the desires and perceived needs of the earthly self with little or no input asked for or received from the Higher Self. What the Higher Self knows to be the individual's highest interest is often different from the expectations and desire-patterns of the earthly self. Although crystals programmed with personality-derived energy patterns will work within the impartial universal laws of cause and effect, any such cause put into motion and coupled with quartz actually blocks the unfoldment of the highest aspects of the soul's chosen blueprint of spiritual growth. Personality-centered desires for such things as money, adventure, jobs, prestige, power, sex, and the like can so blind the individual's spiritual perception that soul-growth will abate. With the amplifying powers of quartz, such patterns can become even more powerfully entrenched. Therefore, crystals are double-edged swords, the use of which calls for careful spiritual discernment and interior reflection before they are utilized. For just as they can be potent tools of spiritual expansion, they can also be devices that enmesh the individual further in the realms of illusion.

The first step of programming is, therefore, careful contemplation of the nature and content of the energy patterns that are to be formulated. Second, a crystal that best suits the program needs to be found. In *Windows of Light*, it is shown that each crystal, reflecting its origin as a Thought-form in the Universal Mind, has an inherent blueprint-program that sets its patterns of optimal usage.

> According to the different vibrational qualities that are infused into a particular crystal at the time of its formation or at various times thereafter, most crystals can be placed into categories of specialized functions. Each category has a characteristic manner of receiving, processing, and transmitting energy, therefore making each group more suitable for a specific kind of use. This is not to say that some overlapping of categories does not happen or that those of a particular grouping cannot perform other functions. Indeed, the majority of these tools have the capacity to serve a wide spectrum of purposes. However, many of them are *better* suited to operate in specific ways than others. And it is in using them as specialized tools that their highest potential is realized.[13]

These crystal categories include: power rods, devic crystals, attunement crystals, energy crystals, healing crystals, energy rods, archetype crystals, library crystals, numerological crystals, abominological crystals, transmitting crystals, modulatory crystals, vision crystals, toning crystals, "surgery" crystals, and open-ended crystals. (See *Windows of Light*, Baer & Baer, pp. 54–59, for more information.) Keep in mind that quartz crystals are versatile tools; each crystal will work for any given program. The point here is that the closer a crystal is programmed and utilized in accordance with its inherent category-programming, the more powerful and efficient its effects will be. Put another way, each crystal has an optimal usage pattern; although it will work effectively with all programs, it will work better with programs closer in nature to its innate category, and best with programs directly correlating with its category. Sometimes an individual will program a crystal and use it for that purpose for a time and then intuit that it would be better employed for a different purpose. The program is then changed and the crystal utilized in a more effective way. This type of process may go through several stages of programming changes as an intuitive journey of becoming more attuned to the highest nature of a given crystal. Such a process is quite natural and beneficial, for as consciousness becomes more attuned to the crystal's highest nature, a heightened awareness of the nature of the crystal kingdom in general and the specific crystal in particular is gained as part of an ongoing growth process. For more information on discerning crystal categories, see Chapter 6.

Not all crystals need to be or should be programmed by the individual. Certain quartz and other refined gemstones contain highly specialized information and vibratory code-patterns programmed into them during their formation process through higher dimensional channels. Such special crystals are in the minority and generally gravitate to individuals who recognize their unique value.

But if it is stated that all crystals have an innate category, what is the difference between the special crystals and the rest? Both types indeed have an innate category. The difference is one of degree. The specialized crystals have received an additional infusion of Light-codes from higher dimensional sources. The rest of the crystals still contain/are the codes of their origin, but have not had the extra attention that the others have received. In addition, the less specialized crystals' inherent category programming is quite generalized. By programming these crystals within the broad parameters of their category, they are made more effective and specific tools. On the other hand, the highly specialized crystals are already functioning at a peak level and therefore need no further programming input. The act of programming in harmony with the innate category is one of instructing the crystal as to the specifics of the desired effect and also of keying the crystal to the individual.

Another primary aspect of the programming process is learning how consciousness can interact with the crystalline matrix effectively. Gaining efficient entrance to the inner-dimensional levels of the crystal's latticework is a skill developed to greater degrees over time and repeated application. An excellent way to become familiar with the subtle nature of the sights, sounds, touch-sensations, smells, and tastes within crystals is to experience the "Sensing the Crystal Meditation" in *Windows of Light* (Baer & Baer, pp. 149-150).

Many programming and meditating techniques with crystals involve holding the quartz in front of the third eye region. A simple method for holding it there for a length of time with minimal fatique is to fold the right arm comfortably across the solar plexus region; then, with the crystal pointed upward in the left hand, rest the back of the upper arm (or elbow) directly on top of the right arm. Let the weight of the left arm rest totally on the right arm so that it is quite relaxed and comfortable. This method enables the individual to hold a crystal in this position for a considerable length of time.

Next, determine which facet of the crystal's termination seems to be the best "window" with which to gain access into the interior. Many times the largest facet serves this purpose optimally. Position this facet so it is parallel to the vertical plane of the forehead at the third eye region. Then slowly move the crystal (maintaining the parallel position) away from the forehead about six to ten inches and then bring it gradually back toward the forehead until it is touching the skin. Many individuals notice a distinct difference in the strength of the energy sensation perceived at different distances from the third eye. In effect, there are various harmonic octaves and intervals of greater resonance established between the third eye energies and the crystal. Find the distance at which the strongest resonant interaction occurs. From here, fine tuning can be done by very slightly varying the angle between the third eye and the access facet. Experiment with this until a point of optimal resonance is felt.

Consciously project focused awareness through the facet and into the crystal. If it is difficult to perceive the subtle energies, imagine what they might be like (many times this is needed as a growth step toward heightened perception of subtle energies). A way to amplify the crystal–mind interaction is to take long, slow, deep breaths, with carefully controlled inhalations and exhalations. The resonant interaction between crystal and consciousness is progressively charged to higher degrees in this way.

The preceding guidelines, then, are an outline to help the individual in learning how to develop an effective interaction with crystals. As further rapport is developed with personal crystals and the crystal kingdom in general, each person develops his or her own creative patterns for interacting with the quartz matrix.

The following is a step-by-step procedure for optimal programming of thought-forms and energy fields into crystals:

1. Hold the crystal in your left hand and allow your hand to rest on your lap. Take a few minutes to relax and center consciousness in the manner most comfortable to you. Then consciously align awareness with the higher realms of Light, the Higher Self, and any appropriate Light-beings. Ask for guidance, protection, and assistance with the programming process. Open consciousness to a receptive mode.
2. With the crystal still in hand, ascend to the highest possible levels of consciousness-in-Light. There, formulate the thought-pattern of the program. For this there are two suggested methods. For instances when you know what program you desire to work with, formulate a concise seed-phrase that accurately depicts the nature of the program, for example, "angelic communication," "reprogramming of the heart chakra," "harmony and balance," and so on. Repeat this short, concise seed-phrase in conjunction with visualizing or feeling the desired effect of the program. Repeat 20 to 30 times in succession while in a heightened state of awareness. As this is done, an energy field will progressively build up that is the holographic energy pattern of the program. Be open to higher assistance during this process. The second method for formulating a program is for when you do not consciously know what type of program you want to work with, or when you want to receive an appropriate program energy-field from the higher realms of Light. While in spiritual attunement, ask to receive the program that is in your highest spiritual interest. A seed-phrase to repeat in order to help the receiving process is "I ask to receive the highest Light in divine order . . . highest Light in divine order. . . . " Repeat 20 to 30 times and feel the energy field being generated.
3. While maintaining full awareness of the program's energy field, bring the focus of consciousness to the third eye.
4. Position the crystal in front of the forehead and establish the strongest possible resonant interconnection with it, as just described.
5. Project consciousness inside the crystalline matrix. Hold the program's energy field as steady and as focused as possible within the latticework for 30 to 60 seconds. Allow the program to be sensitively imprinted within the crystal. (A feeling, a knowing as to how deeply the program is being imprinted and when the cycle is complete comes with experience.)
6. Detach consciousness from the crystal.

With time and practice, this straightforward and logical procedure will become a comfortable programming pattern. As with all things, increasing levels of skill unfold as consciousness utilizes this type of skill. Allow individual creativity to flourish as spiritual pathways expand.

In order to ensure that the desired program has been imprinted with sufficient depth and stability within the crystal latticework, it is a good practice to go through the preceding step-by-step procedure once a day for seven days. In doing this with each crystal being programmed, not only is the crystal imprinted sufficiently with the desired energy patterns, but also consciousness itself undergoes a clarifying process in which the program is also imprinted more deeply within the mind matrix. To program the crystal is also to program the self.

Once programmed, the crystal is a specialized extension of the individual. There is an energetic bond created between the person's consciousness and the crystal, regardless of distance. Because of this, the condition of the crystal must be carefully maintained so that imbalanced influences do not strongly affect the crystal and, thereby, the individual. Try to keep crystals in as ordered and balanced an environment as possible. Strong imbalanced thoughts and emotions are particularly prone to upsetting the energetic balance within a crystal. Should they be exposed to such influences, either from being in the general surroundings of potent imbalanced energies or from personal mental-emotional fluctuations, clear and cleanse them as soon as possible. Also, simply during the course of normal everyday events, crystals tend to accumulate ambient static and imbalanced energies. For this reason, it is wise to put personal programmed crystals through a regular maintenance schedule of clearing and cleansing. (See Chapter 6 for clearing and cleansing information.)

The energetic interlinkage between a programmed crystal and the programmer exists to varying degrees depending primarily upon the nature, intensity, and coherence of energy that is flowing through the crystal. A basic tenet of crystal energy flow is simply that the more energy goes in, the more energy goes out. Outside a person's auric field, whether it be 20 yards or halfway around the world, a crystal still has a subtle energetic influence upon the individual's subconsciuous and superconscious levels of being. The effect is faint and is the least powerful of programmed crystal–person interactions. If, on the other hand, a crystal at a distance is exposed to strong energetic influences, the effect on the individual is correspondingly greater. This is one reason why using crystals as radionics witnesses is especially useful for healing at a distance with precision and effectiveness. Another scenario involves the crystal being within the person's auric field, but without any focused attention being placed upon it. Since the auric field is constantly flowing through the crystal in this case, the effects are that much amplified. This scenario is much more potent than the crystal at a distance without additional energy input. The most effective means of utilizing programmed crystals for personal use is having the crystal within the auric field and placing focused awareness upon it. Not only does the auric field flow through the crystal but also conscious attention, which adds considerable focused energy input. Especially if consciousness is in a centered, Light-attuned state, the crystal will have optimal effect in sensitively but powerfully amplifying the program patterns, imprinting them into multidimensional levels of awareness.

Two other scenarios of this nature are possible. This first involves utilizing crystal energies at a distance. By visualizing the three-dimensional exterior and interior form of a crystal in a balanced, centered state of mind, the crystal's energies can be engaged regardless of distance. This is particularly useful for tapping into generator crystals (which are usually very large and heavy) and special personal crystals that cannot always be carried. The key elements here are focused consciousness and clearly defined visualization of the crystal. The crystal energies are then available for desired purposes. The other scenario of programmed crystal usage is having the crystal inside the auric field with focused attention plus additional energy input factors. Such factors can include crystal gridworks around the programmed crystal, applied pyramidal energy fields, sonics, chromatics, lasers being directed through the crystal, and other energetic influences. With such additional vibrations a most powerful effect can be realized. And by modifying which additional energies and combinations thereof are directed into the crystal, a spectrum of consciousness modulating possibilities arises.

During the course of everyday affairs there are a number of easy ways to keep programmed crystals within the auric field over extended periods of time. The more time a person spends around programmed crystals the greater the effect that the accelerative energy patterns have upon the codes of consciousness. First, wearing and carrying crystals is a classic way of keeping crystals within the aura over long periods. In addition to the program-codes themselves, the aura in general is amplified for greater strength and protection during daily events. Jewelry, especially pendants worn over the heart chakra, are excellent in this regard. The carrying of a crystal in a pocket or purse works well, too. Second, crystals can be kept in areas of the home where one spends a lot of time, for example, where one watches TV or reads. The crystals can simply sit within the auric field's range or can be held. Third, programmed crystals may be situated in the work area; in fact, the crystals may be programmed to assist in various aspects of work. Last, and most important, crystals kept in the bedroom are exceptionally helpful in facilitating the great degrees of higher spiritual attunement and education that occur during sleep. A gridwork underneath or around the sleep space is helpful, as well as putting a crystal in the pillowcase. Most optimal is a crystal kept taped onto the third eye area (hypoallergenic first aid tape is best) during sleep. These crystals can be programmed to assist in gaining access to desired areas of the Universal Mind at night, for whatever purposes of spiritual growth, healing, or education are desired. It is especially effective to focus awareness within the taped-on third eye crystal while moving from the waking to the dream state. Dream recall and, in some cases, lucid dreams of higher realities are facilitated by this method.

In all, a long-term, everyday interconnected continuity with programmed crystals in order to best absorb and reinforce desired positive growth patterns is easily maintained. Over time, the subtly powerful effects of crystals make an increasingly noticeable difference in one's life, from the cellular to subconscious to superconscious levels of being.

Any type of energy influence can be programmed into a crystal. This means that the types of programming are limited only by the imagination. In this section, numerous creative programming ideas will be presented as seed-ideas to experiment with and from which other ideas may follow.

One procedure that cannot be overemphasized when programming "external" energetic influences (such as color, sound, and so on) is that the matrix must be prepared to selectively receive and imprint the desired energies. To be anthropomorphic, the crystal needs to be told what one wants it to do. Otherwise, it does not know to selectively imprint one specific type of vibratory influence in the midst of many others. Without such instructions, the crystal will not imprint the desired energy patterns deeply, rather only superficially along with the rest of the energy spectrum to which it is exposed. Preparing the matrix simply involves using the step-by-step programming procedure presented, formulating the thought of the type of energy one wants to be programmed. For example, if the color vibration of blue is the program-to-be, formulate the seed-phase of "preparing the crystal matrix for programming with the blue vibration" while in a heightened state of consciousness, repeating it 20 to 30 times as the procedure states. The programming procedure remains the same, the only difference being in the nature of the formulated thought-pattern. In effect, by preparing the matrix the crystal's latticework reapportions itself so that when exposed to the desired energetic field, the crystal will selectively sort out from all other ambient energies that one specific vibrational influence to receive and imprint. These energy patterns are processed along receptively oriented latticed pathways, created by the preparation procedure, guiding them into deep infusion and imprinting. Therefore, the procedure is fundamentally this: prepare the matrix and then expose the crystal to that particular energy field to be programmed. The crystal then becomes a specialized tool keyed within the coding patterns of the programmed vibratory influence.

DIFFERENT TYPES OF CREATIVE PROGRAMMING

1. Reprogramming patterns:* Programs concerning the repatterning to higher Light-states of the blood crystals, the DNA Light-Life codes, and the brain-mind matrix. A suggested seed-phrase for each is: a) blood crystals—"activation of the living crystals of Light in the physical body"; b) DNA Light-Life codes—"infusion of DNA Light-Life codes of the Light body into the DNA system of the earthly self in divine order"; c) brain-mind matrix—"activation of crystalline Light-channels within the brain-mind matrix."
2. Healing energies: An individual can program appropriate healing energies required for a specific condition into a crystal for himself or herself or another. An affirmation, visualization, or pure energy patterns can be used to program healing energies. By keeping such crystals within the auric field and with focused application, the cells, tissues, etheric energy field, and so on are continually exposed to energy field "instructions" emitting from the crystal. Health-care practitioners (with spiritual authority to do so) can program crystals (or have individuals program them for themselves) with the optimal patterns of wholeness regarding those areas that are being worked with in the sessions. The treatment recipients can then carry this crystal between sessions and perform additional self-healing exercises with it so that the treatment momentum is optimalized.

Additionally, appropriate crystals can be programmed with energy patterns that correlate with the healthy state of specific bodily organs, body systems, individual chakras, and so on. Radionic rate charts show that each distinct aspect of the human bioenergetic system has a different corresponding vibratory rate of health. Crystals can be programmed in a general fashion for a specific aspect of the bioenergies and then subprogrammed with the individual's unique blueprint subpatterns.
3. Affirmations, visualizations, spiritual symbols, mandalas, and pictographic flame

*See Chapter 9.

letters:† Affirmations can be either spoken aloud or repeated internally, or both, during the act of programming. The remainder of these program-types require the visualization of a specific image to be projected into the crystal matrix for program-imprinting.

4. Color: Colored gels, plastic, and glass are useful for programming crystals with one or more color vibrations. After preparing the matrix, expose the crystal to the color. One method is to place the crystal in direct sunlight and moonlight for 24 to 48 hours with the gel, plastic, or glass placed or taped over one or more of the termination's facets. Pin spotlights and projectors can also be used in conjunction with color gels. With this method, expose the crystals to the color for 45 to 60 minutes in a dimly lit room.

Theatrical color gels are the best medium for color programming. They are not only more available in a wide array of precise color frequencies, but also they are actually crystallized color pigment. Results obtained with the gels are clearly superior to plastic and all but the best colored glass.

Multiple colors can be programmed into a single crystal to create a custom-programming to suit the multicolor chromatic spectrum profile that best suits an individual's needs.

5. Sound: Tuning forks, musical instruments, musical compositions, and mantras. Crystals are especially responsive to sound vibrations.

With tuning forks, place the vibrating handle on the body of the crystal, allowing the sonic frequency to be infused throughout the crystal. Repeat this procedure for five to seven minutes once a day for seven days, preparing the matrix each day before sonic exposure. Maintain crystals in the process of being programmed inside a Star of David gridwork within a 12 inch × 12 inch-base pyramid (or larger) during the seven day period.

A similar procedure holds for applying single tones or chords played by musical instruments. Use the same gridwork-pyramid set-up and play the desired sonics seven to ten minutes per day for seven days.

To imprint an entire musical composition, it is best to place the crystal within the gridwork-pyramid arrangement with the speakers on opposite sides of the gridwork focused toward the crystal being programmed. Play the full composition one to two times each day for five to seven days.

With mantras, intone the vocal sonics directly into the crystal five to ten minutes each day for seven days. Utilize the grid-pyramid set-up.

6. Environmental influences: Similar to the notion of the Bach Flower essences, any environmental influence can be encoded within crystals. Energy essence patterns such as those of pine trees, oak trees, flowers, a flowing stream, and others can be programmed. Prepare the matrix, then leave the crystal in the area where the energy abides for seven to ten days. Ask for assistance from the angelic and devic kingdoms associated with the workings of the particular energetic influence.

7. Vortex and holy areas: Certain areas are blessed with powerful cosmic energy currents and an abundance of Light. By programming a crystal with these vibrations, a direct energetic link-up is created with the blessed area even if it is distant. Prepare the matrix, then, if possible, leave it in the area undisturbed for

---

†See Chapter 2.

seven to ten days. If this is not possible, do a focused meditation for 15 to 30 minutes asking the Light-beings who work with that area to assist in the effective programming of the crystal.

8. Energies of particular star systems, specific Light-beings, Spirit guides, angelic domains, and space vehicle computer systems: For those who would like to create an amplified, continuous link-up with some of these higher realities, excellent results can be obtained. The need is especially strong here to find an out-of-the-way location that is harmonious and undisturbed. Make a small-diameter Star of David or double Star of David gridwork (that is, one to two feet) within or around a 12 inch × 12 inch-base or larger pyramid. Prepare the matrix with the intention and place it in the middle of the gridwork, standing upright directly below the pyramid's apex at ground level, if possible.* Communicate with the desired Light-realm and ask for assistance and protection in the programming process. Leave this arrangement undisturbed for seven to ten days. Each day communicate to the specific Light-realms and again call upon their help.

9. Other possibilities: Here are some seed-ideas for programming possibilities: Interdimensional communication, high space command communication, angelic communication, activation and alignment into the Light-body, catalyzing spiritual energies, dream state enhancement, emotional healing, harmony and balance, opening of channeling abilities with protection, contact and communication with the Elohim levels of Light, mental clarity, enhancement of the physical healing process, activation and purification of the chakras, communication with the devic realms (general), communication with the crystal devas, divine order on the physical plane, interdimensional traveling with protection, contact and communication with planetary etheric crystals, self-transformation catalyst, and activation of chakras of the Light-body.

ADDITIONAL PROGRAMMING PERSPECTIVES

With a well-programmed crystal, clearing and cleansing procedures do not erase the programming. Such procedures clear out the static within the crystal's latticework (physical and higher dimensional) and do not disturb the gravitationally held holographic program codes.

To erase a program, simply go through the step-by-step programming process, formulate the seed-phrase "erase the existing program," and proceed with the remaining steps. This need only be done once (not once a day for seven days), but needs to be a very focused effort. Then put the crystal through a standard clearing and cleansing cycle. It is then ready to receive another program.

Multiple programming is the imprinting of two or more programs in the same crystal. Theoretically, any crystal can hold ten to hundreds, and perhaps thousands, of programs. (If humankind can store 100 pages of typewritten material on a single microchip a centimeter square, think how much more can be done with a product of the Universal Mind.) The primary requisite for effective multiple programming is that the different programs be harmonically interrelated, that is, within similar spheres of energy activity. For example, an interdimensional communication-type program is working with a distinctly different aspect of the

---

*Sticking the base of a single-terminated crystal in a small amount of clay or putty works well.

Universal Mind than, say, a healing program; mixing two different types such as these would tend to neutralize the effectiveness of both programs. To imprint multiple programs, take each program and proceed through the step-by-step programming procedure separately for each program. During the seven day programming cycle, it is fine to multiple program a crystal (rather than taking a week for each program). To erase only one program without erasing the others, perform the programming procedure and for the seed-phrase, use "erase (name of program)." To erase all programs at once, state this intention in the seed-phrase.

Subprogramming is a variation of multiple programming. This occurs when a crystal has a general programming within whose parameters subprogramming is possible. For example, a general programming would be healing of the physical body; this is broad in scope, outlining an entire spectrum of activity. Within this general outline, numerous subprograms can also be imprinted within the crystal to help specify which areas of the physical body are the focus points of healing; for example, subprograms might include healing of the liver, healing of the lymphatic system, and so on. The same concept can be applied to a general programming such as interdimensional communication; subprograms might include different access areas of communication, such as angelic communication, devic communication, and so on.

It is recommended that two primary subprograms be imprinted in every programmed crystal. One is the *Divine Order subprogram.* This is another way of stating "Not my will, but Thy Will be done, O Lord." It involves deliberately opening up consciousness during the act of programming and asking for divine Will to be the overriding factor in the formulation and enactment of the crystal's programming. Divine order must be asked for, and once asked for receptively, it is then incorporated within the programming structure. The second subprogram is *protection in the Light.* In the inner planes, crystals "stick out like a sore thumb" because of their rarefied Light-properties. Therefore, when engaging a crystal during meditation or various forms of Light-work and interdimensional communication, it is important to enact certain protective measures so that entities of spiritual ignorance have less opportunity to negatively influence multidimensional energetic interactions. Also, with the protection in the Light subprogram within the crystal, such lesser entities cannot tamper with the overall programming itself, this thereby being transferred to the individual over time. When programming this vibration, it also works well to visualize a pillar of White Light being infused into the crystal and to call upon the Order of Michael for assistance in this process.

Programmed sets are gradated series of crystals, each being programmed with one aspect of an entire spectrum of energies. A prime example of this would be a color crystal set consisting of eight crystals, each programmed with one of the seven major rays of the rainbow plus one of White Light. Sonic and chakra sets are two possibilities among others in this regard. Such sets are quite valuable because the individual or practitioner has a full spectrum of vibrations with which to work as the need arises. These may be some of the primary practitioner's toolsets of the future! Many creative potentials are possible in this area.

PROGRAMMING CLUSTERS

Crystal clusters are groups of three or more crystals joined to a common matrix. Each distinct crystal is vibrationally joined to the fundamental inherent programming of the whole. Every single crystal in the cluster can be programmed with different, though harmonically related, programs. For example, numerous color vibrations and sonic tones can be programmed into the cluster, one color or one sonic tone in each crystal. Together, such a cluster would be a symphony of vibrations for such applications as reprogramming, healing, self-transformation, and environmental harmonizing. Each of these purposes would require a distinct harmonic array of color–sound programs to suit each different energetic situation.

TWO OTHER PROGRAMMING TECHNIQUES

1. Hold the crystal between the hands (hands touching each other). Formulate the thought-form as discussed in the programming process previously described. Then say the seed-phrase aloud 20 to 30 times, concentrating the attention within the crystal. The sonic vibrations plus the brain-hand nervous feedback loop assist in the imprinting process.[14]
2. For those who desire to program with a chakra other than the third eye, for example, the heart or throat chakra, apply the technique just described, but hold the crystal between the hands in front of the chakra. Focus the consciousness along with the program in and through that chakra into the crystal. Saying the seed-phrase aloud is helpful but optional here.

CREATING A COMPUTER CRYSTAL

After gaining more advanced expertise with programming in particular and utilizing crystals in general, more sophisticated applications become possible. Some of the quartz crystals of today are the computers of tomorrow. As consciousness evolution progresses, the use of quartz computers becomes more and more a part of daily life. The procedure described herein is one quantum step in this direction.

The crystal chosen for this task must be well suited for the purpose of computer-type information interactions, information storage and retrieval, and strong inter-dimensional access to certain computerlike realms of crystalline intelligence within the UEN. There also needs to be a strong resonant relationship between the individual and the specific crystal. For seven to ten days prior to using the computer crystal for any computer functions, set aside 20 to 30 minutes for the consciousness to interact with the crystal in creative ways (see the programming exercises later in this chapter and also the advanced programming exercises and applications in *Windows of Light,* Baer & Baer, pp. 76–82). The idea is to facilitate the keying of the crystal to the mind and the mind to the crystal, so that each is quite sensitively responsive to the other. During this time of mutual attunement, it is best to maintain the crystal within a Star of David gridwork inside a 12 inch × 12 inch-base pyramid; in fact, it is optimal to keep the computer crystal in such an arrangement at all times unless in active use. Also, each day ask appropriate Light-realms to assist in the attunement process and ask for protection in the Light.

Once this preliminary process is completed, explore the many possibilities. Find one facet as the primary access window. While reading a book, for example, formulate a basic concept being learned in the mind and project it into the crystal and hold for three to five focused seconds. Continue with this through the entire reading. Then formulate the intention of gaining access to the encoded information on a particular subject and project awareness into the crystal. Maintain an actively receptive focused state of mind. Let the information crystallize on its own within the mind; be receptive and not actively seeking out the information. Later on, after a number of days or weeks have passed by, again gain access to this particular bank of information and see how much information crystallizes in the mind. With time and practice this computer crystal can become as valuable an information storage and retrieval system as present-day home computers. In the more advanced stages, for some, when gaining access to the computer banks the mind becomes like a read-out screen that recalls and works with information with great precision and versatility. Eventually all information becomes unfolding pictographic, equational, or image-oriented multilevel holograms of tremendous coded sophistication.

The computer crystal can also be utilized as an interdimensional attraction module,* a subcomputer system that is used to gain access to different levels of the UEN. As seen in Chaper 2, the UEN operates like a vast living supraholographic computer system and access to the different dimensions and domains therein can be gained in an orderly access/no-access manner, depending upon the codes of individual consciousness. The computer crystal may be linked to specific aspects of Universal Intelligence that contain desired information/vibrations to function as a downput mechanism that will receive and imprint such energy codes. The individual then interacts with the crystal and allows the universal knowledge to be imprinted/recalled into consciousness. Several points are important to note here. First, it is imperative when utilizing this advanced technique to request protective assistance from the higher Light-realms. Second, when gaining access to the specific sectors of the Universal Mind, consciously connect the computer crystal with the communications network of the UEN, as described in Chapter 19. It is best to maintain the crystal within a potent crystal gridwork with, optimally, a gold-plated 12 inch × 12 inch-base pyramid with a crystal pyramid capstone (a ¼ inch base works well). Progress in using this techinque will usually come in stages as consciousness becomes more and more multidimensionally proficient. It is recommended that the focus be turned to gaining access to a specific sector of universal knowledge (for example, an aspect of crystal knowledge) for a considerable period of time before moving on the other areas. Continue each day to reinforce the access to the particular sector of the Universal Mind and allow the mind to receptively interact with the crystal. Many times the knowledge so received will not at first read out consciously but will be subtly absorbed within the sub- and superconscious levels, and gradually filter into conscious awareness over time.

*See Chapter 14.

OTHER IDEAS FOR EXPERIMENTATION

One information bank in the middle of the crystal's termination may be set aside for being programmed for the synergistic integration of all stored information from all the other banks plus an access link to higher Light-realms. By projecting consciousness into the information bank, an overall synthesized integration of all fields of study plus new creative syntheses derived from such a coalescence of information can be gained. Also, each of the six termination facets may be used as access windows through which different types of subject matter can be imprinted and retrieved. Further, while learning new material it may assist in the programming process to have the fingertips resting lightly on the crystal's sides or facets.

A group of individuals can apply these same concepts for creating a crystal computer for collective use. Such a group needs to be exceptionally harmonized both in terms of interpersonal relations and spiritual orientation and intent. Use the same principles just cited for the seven to ten day matrix preparation, having each individual spend time keying the crystal to his or her mind-matrix and to the group intention. Because of the practical logistics considerations of making the crystal available to each group member for periods of time, the seven to ten day period may need to be extended. Each individual may be assigned a particular facet through which to conduct programming and gaining access. A sector in the middle of the faceted termination can be programmed for synthesis and integration of the group mind in connection with appropriate Light-realms with which the group has the strongest connection. It is most helpful to maintain the computer within a pyramid–crystal gridwork arrangement with photographs of each individual within the grid, especially when not in active use. Such a crystal computer can assist the group to fulfill its individual and collective Light-work and reprogramming processes with amplification and acceleration.

Crystal computers: farfetched? Not according to present-day research and experts' projections into the future. In an article called "Direct Brain-Computer Interfacing" in *Science Digest,* a description of current developments in the area of brainwave controlled computers is presented.

> The technique works as follows: A person is linked to the computer by electrodes attached to his head. A separate screen, also hooked to the computer, displays a matrix of flashing boxes. When the person focuses on one of the boxes, each of which flashes at a different rate, his brain emits a specific pattern of waves. The computer, programmed to recognize the various patterns, can tell which box the person is looking at. Each box contains a letter symbol that instructs the computer to perform a task. . . . It seems inevitable that someday—without speaking, touching or even looking at a computer—we could command it to do exactly what we want.[15]

In *The Omni Book of Computers and Robots,* G. Harry Stine writes in an article entitled "The Bionic Brain" concerning the future directions of the brain–computer interaction.

> Cy, a cybernetic interface device . . . responded directly to Lee's thoughts, calling up information and taking dictation as quickly as he could think. The work was

not interrupted by talking to the computer or by typing on a keyboard. In fact, when Lee had trouble thinking, Cy would often help organize his ideas into coherent paragraphs.

The executive settled back in the interface couch and donned the cap. It took only minor positioning to fit the sensors into place. Then he closed his eyes and pressed the switch built into the armrest. . . .

After what seemed like hours, Lee stopped the summary so he could tape his report. As he dictated, the computer image occasionally asked whether he wanted to rephrase something. Then Cy projected a series of graphs and color photos. . . . into Lee's visual cortex. Lee selected several, added captions, and ordered, Okay, put it on the net to the office, and let's call it a day.

He checked the clock. It told him he had been linked to Cy for 28 minutes. A good day's work![16]

Marcel Vogel, noted crystal authority and former IBM senior research scientist, adds additional perspectives on the crystal computer–mind interaction. In an interview in *Science of Mind,* he states:

The modern electronic computer breaks down complex concepts into on-and-off numerical patterns which are stored on magnetic media. But the ancients had a much more intriguing computer—the crystal. Like the human mind, it stores and retrieves knowledge as whole, intact images which don't need to be converted into constituent parts, as in the electronic computer. Thus, ancient seers could mentally project their knowledge, whole and complete, into the natural micro-computer field of a crystal. Whenever they needed to retrieve their knowledge, they attuned themselves to the crystal, and the stored images were reconverted into the original concepts. . . .

Imagine, then, how a student might learn mathematics, art, or science with his "crystal computer" in a school of the future. Just like an electronic computer with its program, the student's learning crystal will have a program of stored-image "subjects" he wishes to master. By making his mind at-one with the crystal, the student can easily process huge amounts of information instantaneously and holographically.[17]

The "first-generation" supercomputers of the future are here now. Technological advancements from the realm of sacred science will certainly add increased sophistication to the quartz-based interdimensional holographic computers of tomorrow, but it is now consciousness that needs to make the next quantum step into utilizing the computers of the future, today. The primary concepts in this regard are twofold. First, the crystal–mind interaction is a perfect holographic synergistic meld that goes far beyond present-day computers in both speed and multi-level holographic wholeness. And second, crystals that are able to gain access through the crystallographic UEN to specific sectors of the ultimate "supercomputer system"—the Universal Mind.

PROGRAMMING EXERCISES

Following are some exercises for developing holographic and supraholographic programming skills. Each increasing level of programming expertise is built upon the foundation of holographic visualization skills, for this is the fundamental language modality of the Universal Mind. Concurrent with increased programming skills, expanded interdimensional communication access abilities also accompany progress with these and related exercises. (See also sections on advanced programming exercises and application in *Windows of Light,* Baer & Baer, pp. 76–82.)

1. Take a crystal in hand. Hold it stationary and view its exterior and interior three-dimensionality. Then close the eyes and try to reconstruct this image within the mind. Open the eyes again and focus on those aspects of the crystal that were vague within the mind. Close the eyes again and visualize once more. Repeat this cycle until the mind's image of the crystal encompasses every detail with clarity and exactitude.

Then, rotate the crystal and go through the same process from a different perspective.[18]

Next, with the eyes open, rotate the crystal slowly about its vertical axis until a full revolution is completed. Then close the eyes and try to reconstruct how the crystal appeared as it was rotated. Repeat this process again and again until the mind's visualization is complete.

The next step is to imagine the crystal rotating 360° about its vertical axis within the central portion of the brain. Visualize the crystal, as it is rotating, becoming progressively smaller until it is microscopic. Then, gradually increase the size until the crystal encompasses first the entire head, and then the entire body. Experiment with varying the speed of rotation, from very slow to as fast as can be imagined. A significant shift in consciousness as the rotation speed varies is likely. Keys and clues gained from this can be most effectively utilized in advanced reprogramming modalities and amplified interdimensional communication access.

2. Visualizing the Platonic solids, ideal crystalline forms*, and other sacred geometric patterns is especially beneficial for advancing programming skills and interdimensional communication abilities. As discussed in Chapter 4, these are a primary geometric language of Light, the fundamental form and axis-code access keys to unlocking the codes of creation. By becoming more and more proficient in visualizing and modulating these forms within consciousness, multidimensional doors open for receiving more complexly coded universal Thought-forms.

There are numerous more advanced variations on this theme. They can be visualized as rotating at various speeds and shifting sizes as in the preceding exercise. Two or more forms can be superimposed within one another, rotating at the same rate, at different rates, and in opposite directions. By focusing consciousness within the central point of these rotating forms, a consciousness communication access module is created. Also, various key spiritual symbols, mandala patterns, flame letters, and the like can be projected into the center of the geometric forms along with consciousness. When engaging in such exercises, by linking consciousness with a Light-realm with which one feels an affinity and allowing these various combinations of forms within forms within forms to unfold in awareness, experiences may occur that before could have not been imagined.

3. The creating and receiving of thought-form crystals is not only good for increasing programming expertise but also for use as higher dimensional tools of Light.

*Refer to Chapter 11.

For creating a thought-form crystal, first quiet and balance consciousness and then let the imagination formulate various possible crystal forms. Try looking at a variety of physical-plane crystals beforehand to obtain some seed-ideas from which creative variations may unfold. Playing celestial music in the background is helpful when doing this exercies.

The receiving of thought-form crystals is significantly different from creating them. These crystals are actual higher dimensional crystalline forms that are given from the Light-realms at appropriate times to receptive individuals. Such crystalline forms are harmoniously incorporated into the subtle levels of the bioenergetic system as Light-tools that amplify consciousness in any of a number of ways. Such knowledge is given to the recipient at the appropriate time. In order to prepare to receive a thought-form crystal, cultivate a receptive state of consciousness, gain access to the Light-realm with which there is an affinity, state the intention, and then remain in a quiet, receptive, nonexpectant state of being. If it is appropriate that this should occur, it will, and information will be imparted for future use regarding the nature and function of the thought-crystals. It is emphasized here that the element of protection in the Light is most essential when opening the consciousness to such higher realities. It is also imperative to note that such higher dimensional crystals are part of the individual's chosen blueprint of consciousness; they are not an outside element that is implanted. In fact, the receiving of a thought-crystal is actually an activation of a heretofore dormant aspect of the individual's preexisting Light-blueprint of evolutionary unfoldment. "The transformation of the specie occurs through the infusion of light crystals which generate a field of Light around the body and a feeding of Light to the body for the next stage of creation."[19]

ADVANCED PERSPECTIVES AND SEED-THOUGHTS

The programming of the future will be a sophisticated and precise aspect of sacred science. It will be a science of intra- and interdimensional consciousness access and code transposition, one involving complex technological tools and advanced consciousness capabilities. It will include decoding the already existing knowledge and key vibrational codes now abiding within some crystals and imprinting program codes into large varieties of crystalline mediums with mathematical exactitude. Part of this aspect will include enlightened laboratory crystal growing methodologies. The present-day orthodox scientists who have such capacities as inscribing a billion angel figures on the head of a pin give just a glimpse into the multidimensional supraholographic scientific precision of future programming modalities. The keys to the crystallographic programming science of the New World are inscribed in the templates of the heavens and re-revealed in the scientific scriptures of Light.

Further concepts:

> The sacred scriptures contain the precise architectural progressions which gave the mapping for creation. They hold the keys to lay bare the secrets of the heavenly temples of YHWH coded into stone models and left behind in "holy dwelling places" of the Sons of Light as a beacon to higher Wisdom . . . we should understand that the sacred scriptures of Light are more than just the scriptures of parchment; they are scriptures also written on embellished stones,

and placed within crystal spheres that need to be decoded through the power of Light.[20]

It may be possible in the not-too-distant future to program computer microchips with information that is desired to be incorporated into consciousness. Then positioned between precisely coded and inscribed quartz templates, it would be placed on the third eye. Activated by a geometrically scanning white laser beam, the programmed information would be infused into consciousness as an accelerated learning modality.

Beware of any thought-crystal or microchip implantations. Anything that is not part of the individual's preexisting Light-image is not associated with the Image and Likeness of God that *is* the blueprint of the Human.

In an article from *The Omni Book of Computers and Robots* entitled "BioChip Revolution," the dangers of a non-Spirit-based crystal science are seen.

> Almost unnoticed, the ultimate biological computer has reached the drawing boards.
>
> The bioprocessor will be a molecular latticework that can grow and reproduce. Capable of logic, reason, perhaps even feeling, its three-dimensional organic circuitry will not process data in the rigid, linear style of earlier computers, but network-fashion, like the living brain. Small enough to mesh directly with the human nervous system, biochip implants may restore sight to the blind and hearing to the deaf, replace damaged spinal nerves, and give the human brain memory a number-crunching power to rival today's mightiest computers.
>
> The gemlike biocomputer. . . . implanted in the brain, will sprout nerve projections from its tiny protein facets. The host's neurons will link up with these spindly outgrowths, sending out electrochemical pulses in the brain's own language. . . . The biocomputer is not just another implant. . . . but a symbiote, living from the cells it inhabits and giving them, in turn, the chance to evolve into a higher intelligence.[21]

This is a most serious issue, one which every individual on the face of the earth will be confronted with before the time of the New World ascension.

Advanced technological programming methodologies involve the use of such tools as sonics, lasers, radionics, magnetics, and gravitics. There are certain critical energy thresholds wherein the bond angles of a crystal latticework expand or contract to various quantum phase levels. By modulating the crystal's matrix to a given threshold level, certain prescribed energy interactions may take place. By maintaining that threshold level for a time, coded energy patterns can be imprinted with exceptional depth. When the coding process is over, the crystal latticework is allowed to fold back into its original patterning, thereby enfolding the imprinted codes. These energy code-patterns will then be maintained with extreme stability, even when exposed to high energy frequencies and intensities.

These thresholds exist at distinct temperature, magnetic, gravitic, and Light-frequency levels. Different crystallographic mediums have different threshold profiles, and every medium has numerous thresholds, each one facilitating different energetic interactions.

What follows is an illustration of one type of programming scenario of the future. In a custom-designed unified energy field, a gridwork of vertically rotating quartz crystals in conjunction with magnetic fields create a gravitic threshold within the quartz crystal being programmed. The crystal is in the center of a two to three foot titanium frame Platonic solid. A powerfully focused sonic beam of precise frequency is infused through the crystal's c axis, causing the latticework to be excited within desired parameters. A circularly polarized white laser beam carrying modulated coded information is infused into the crystal by a computer system at many angles throughout the crystal's length and breadth. The codes now delicately imprinted in the matrix, the surrounding energy field gradually steps down out of the threshold zone, progressively modulating the field back to its original state by measured increments. Back at "ground zero" the laser-infused codes are enfolded in place and will serve as a template for patterning Light-interactions.

Another scenario of the future follows. Certain highly trained, spiritually authorized individuals utilize their consciousness to gain access to energy-code patterns from other dimensions and domains in the UEN that are needed for earth's evolutionary development. Consciousness is utilized as a medium of communicative interlinkage and transcription into appropriately prepared crystalline matrices and templates. These encoded crystals are then used in a wide array of consciousness evolvement and technological functions.

In sum, then, the computerlike quartz crystal is a multifaceted tool of versatile imprinting of energetic code-patterns. Programming is one of the most fundamental aspects of actualizing the potentials of quartz. From the most basic to the most advanced of skills and applications, programming is an abidingly central component of crystal usage.

CHAPTER 9

Reprogramming for the Ascension

The preparation of the human biocrystalline energy system for the ascension process is the preeminent spiritual imperative of current times. All else pales in view of this inexorable evolutionary reality. As the earth plane approaches the Omega point of an evolutionary megacycle of soul growth, accelerative Light-energies are activated within individual and collective consciousness matrices in preparation for soul reapportionment to other Alpha–Omega threshold-fields of spiritual growth. Far from being a linear "high" or "low," "heaven" or "hell," soul choice, there is instead a wide spectrum of possibilities for the soul's reapportionment throughout the Kingdom of Light and other universal realms, for there are indeed many mansions in the Father's House. In accordance with the individual's blueprint of Light-assimilation at the Omega point, a corresponding universal threshold-field for the next Alpha–Omega cycle will be determined by authorized sectors of the Light-Hierarchy and the soul will be therein relocated and encoded within the parameters of that particular threshold's Light-codes.

Presently the last stages of the cosmic timetable for the Earth's Alpha–Omega cycle are being completed. Integral to this is the infusion of higher gradients and spectrums of Light into the planetary matrix. This serves a twofold purpose in terms of human evolutoin. One is to activate the star- and celestial-seed Light-workers of the planet to fulfill their assigned tasks of assisting in the ascension process. The second purpose is to make available to human consciousness in general accelerated opportunities for soul advancement within a short time-matrix. The *reprogramming process* is the activation-assimilation of higher Light-codes and Light-matrices within the human energy system that, in turn, set the parameters of reapportionment into a new Alpha point of evolutionary development. As the templates and gateways of the heavens are opened to this planet to increasingly higher quantum degrees, the individual soul chooses to what extent this Light is incorporated into consciousness. The *ascension process* is the last phase of the reprogramming process. When the Omega point is reached, the individual has the opportunity to experience a quantum-octave consciousness "leap" into the Kingdom of Light. As this occurs, the earthly bioenergetic matrix is infused with the Christ Body of Light, thus effecting a transmutative ascension into a multidimensional Light-body. This is the divine promise and birthright of all (if one so chooses it), enacted within the parameters of Universal Law.

> During the present space-time overlap, there will be the passing of one energy universe within another as our planetary mind crosses the present electromagnetic density threshold and is raised to the next electromagnetic orbit of the Universal Mind. At this point, we as sons of Man become the Sons of Light.[1]

> The People of God will collectively put on new garments of Light as they ascend through the spheres and through the thresholds of the other worlds of creation.[2]

The ascension process is the quantum recrystallization of every atom of matter and (qualifying) unit of consciousness on the earth plane to a higher Light-dimensional level. Far from being merely a process of manifesting world peace and enlightened sociopolitical reforms within the earth's current energy parameters, it is rather the total restructuring of the entire planetary system through a radical Light-transformation process. Only then will world peace, enlightened government, and so on manifest; it will manifest as the by-product of the ascension itself. A couple of popular media images can be used as metaphors for the ascension. One such image in the movie *Dark Crystal* is the sweeping transformation process that occurs when the missing crystal shard is replaced into the massive Dark Crystal. This crystal is the energy focus of the civilization, and when activated according to the prophesied timetable, it is converted through a powerful transmutation process into a Light Crystal whose Light-matrix is then rapidly infused into the civilization's energy matrix, transforming it to a higher dimensional plane. Another media image helping to illustrate the ascension is the "Genesis effect" in the movie *Star Trek II.* Instilled into a previously lifeless matrix is a seed-catalyst that creates a chain reaction effect wherein the host matrix is transmuted into a new energy threshold in which life is generated from lifelessness, the new life-matrix transforming the previous matrix. In these two cases, science fiction is not far from interdimensional science fact. As Light is infused into the Earth's energy field, a new matrix is progressively formed that transforms the original planetary field. A new program, or blueprint, is superimposed within the earth's gridwork, thus causing an accelerated recrystallization process. This process proceeds in a progressive manner, transforming the earth-matrix step by quantum step until the final Omega threshold is reached, whereupon the ascension occurs. At this final threshold, the reprogrammed earth-matrix reaches a point of dimensional breakthrough, and a massive, completely encompassing transmutation process takes place in which the new program-blueprint is catalyzed through its final stages, and interdimensional translocation to a higher Light-dimension occurs. The earth as a planetary consciousness ascends into the higher cosmic domains of Light as part of its evolutionary heritage.

Receptive human consciousness, as well, is transformed into higher quantum levels of Light-body network as a new Christ garment of Light replaces the original earthbound bioenergetic garment. This consciousness transfiguration involves an exodus from the earthbound constraints and space-time dimensional location of the earth through to more multidimensionally expansive realms of freedom-in-Spirit within the Kingdom of YHWH. Each ascending individual receives a new Light-garment that correlates to his or her evolutionary growth status. This is to say that there is a broad spectrum of Light-body levels, and the degree of spiritual growth that the individual had attained at the Omega point determines which Light-body spectrum the soul then inhabits.

Individual reprogramming is the activation and alignment of higher Light-code matrices within the earthly bioenergetic system. On the individual level, it is a process in which the earthly self comes into greater interdimensional union with its corresponding Light-body network. As this unity increases, the earthly self receives and incorporates the crystalline codings of the Light-body into the self's bioenergetic system. Herein lower octaves of energy-matter are converted into higher energy octaves—earthbound human metamorphosizes into multidimensional Spirit-human.

It is important to note here that the term *reprogramming* relates to the assimilation of a blueprint-program of Light. The word should not be confused with brainwashing or religious indoctrination. Reprogramming, rather, is a universal evolutionary growth process in which a soul-chosen program of Light-energy code is assimilated into consciousness. Put another way, Blueprint activates and aligns with the earthly blueprint, causing a reprogramming to occur whereby the blueprint becomes Blueprint; Light reprograms light into Light.

Just as the acorn contains the species- and individual-specific blueprint-program of the oak's growth from the beginning to the end of its growth cycle, so too the individual self has a blueprint-program of evolvement chosen on the Higher Self levels, to be enacted within a given Alpha–Omega cycle. This program is the incorporation of increasing degrees of higher Light-codes into the codes of consciousness in ways that are prescribed by that soul-chosen program. In the "latter days" preceding the advent of an Omega point, the reprogramming process accelerates manyfold as the last phases of the individual's blueprint-program can be fully realized. Should there be less than a full realization of one's chosen program by not harmonizing with the reprogramming process, the program-codes of consciousness are incomplete, and access to higher levels of evolutionary development is incrementally less attained. In such cases, those aspects of the soul-program not assimilated are an integral aspect of the individual's new program that must be realized before greater growth can occur. Relocation to each soul's corresponding Alpha–Omega threshold zone is thereby manifested according to divine Law. Reprogramming, then, is a matter of the utmost significance for every individual.

To reprogram is to permanently ingather higher Light within the codes of consciousness. Every cell, every bioenergy system, every unit of consciousness within an individual vibrates within a spectrum of Light that corresponds to the person's level of evolutionary development. This is to say that the human bioenergetic system, as an interdimensional antenna-receiver-processing matrix, responds to and assimilates that spectrum-profile of Light that correlates with a given state of spiritual evolvement. With each increasing level of spiritual growth, higher gradients of Light-energy become coded, or ingathered, into the consciousness matrix, and thereby every part of that matrix undergoes corresponding vibrational changes that reflect the individual's higher quotients of Light-assimilation. Such differences in Light-assimilation are reflected, for example, in the aura—that is, the more spiritually realized a person becomes, the brighter and more radiantly Light-filled his or her aura becomes. This is reflective of the fact that higher degrees of Light are being received and processed through the individual. With less evolvement, the aura reflects a lesser degree of Light-assimilation, for the higher spectrums of Light are simply not received and processed through the system. The "frequency band" within which each individual vibrates is reflected on every level of beingness down to the molecular and sub-atomic structuring of the physical body.

The human biocrystalline energy system can be progressively transmuted by activating and aligning its biocrystalline components with their crystalline Light-body correspondents. In so doing, the higher code-matrices of the Light-body are infused within the biocrystalline system, causing metabolic and crystallographic orientation changes such that a greater degree of interdimensional interconnectedness is created. This is the essential nature of the reprogramming process—the progressive increasing of the unity between the Light-body and the earthly self; an interdimensional transfer of Light-codes is enacted into a receptive earthly energy-matter matrix. This process continues to occur to greater and greater degrees until the time of the ascension, wherein the earthly system may be completely transmuted into the Light-body as the earthbound energy-matter constraints are breached and realization of the multidimensional Light-body takes place.

From an orthodox scientific point of view, the earthly bioenergetic system is indeed a "light-body," for many of its normal metabolic reactions involve the emission of radiance and luminescence. Every cell in the human body emits light as part of its normal functioning, including such wavelengths as ultraviolet, visible red, infrared, radio waves, microwaves, and others.[3,4] Some scientists now feel that the DNA helix functions as a four-level biolaser capable of emitting coherent radiation.[5] Hiroshi Motoyama, Ph.D., has performed experiments utilizing photoelectric equipment able to detect light radiating from the chakras of his subjects. He found that some chakras (awakened chakras) emitted measurably more light than others (dormant chakras). Differences in the chakras of a single individual could also be detected, the energy radiating more brightly and strongly in the more active chakras. "By observing instabilities of chakra-related organs in the computer readout, Motoyama is able both to recognize psychic persons and to predict something of what their paranormal capacities may be!"[6]

Christopher Hills adds a perspective on other aspects of human radiance potential.

> In addition to the electronic/protonic electricity of the body there is the well-known ability of human tissues to floresce in states of high emotional excitement. This ability to create light from within the cell by the chemical combinations of certain proteins and nucleic acids has been reported most famously in the transfiguration of Christ, but also in the language itself when we say that a person is glowing (with love, health, etc.).[7]

In addition to Christ's transfiguration, luminescent radiance is also widely known as indicative of more en-Light-ened states in such phenomenon as the halos of the saints, the radiance witnessed at various well-known sightings of Light-beings (such as the famous Virgin Mary sightings), the sometimes overpowering Light-intensity associated with UFO encounters, as well as the Biblical reference to the brilliantly glowing face of Moses upon descending from Mt. Sinai. From physical cells to the higher auric levels of being, a state of life metabolism is indicated not only by luminescence but also by tremendous excitation of Spirit flowing through the individual. This latter state is exactly what the Light-body is—a highly rarefied state of pure energy emissions vibrating at a higher dimensional level of Light (within domainship parameters). The reprogramming process can be seen as making a stronger and more direct interdimensional connectedness between the Light-body and the earthly self, thus making the latter luminesce and radiate to increasingly higher levels as the two progressively unite. The chakras of the Light-body align with the chakras of the bioenergetic system; the crystalline blood codes, DNA Light-codes, and other crystalline correspondences are activated and aligned with each other so that there is decreasing impedance of energy between the two dimensional realms. The two start to become more and more at-one, and as they do, the Light-body becomes "grounded" to higher degrees on the earth plane, also thereby activating higher spiritual knowledge and abilities, sometimes quite dramatically and other times in more gradual increments. And as the Omega point arrives, the two finally complete their union as the earthly self enacts the last phases of matrix transformation and ascends from the physical dimensions into the higher Light-realms as a multidimensional Light-body.

The differences between reprogramming and healing are crucial to note here. Healing can be regarded as the reestablishment of harmonized balance within the earthly bioenergetic levels of being. This realm is primarily concerned with the rectification of abnormal and imbalanced bioenergetic patterns of the physical and emotional and mental aspects of the individual's health. Healing includes both preventive medicine and the active process of facilitating optimal harmonization. The primary distinction between reprogramming and healing is that the latter is not ascension-oriented; healing does not include the interdimensional activation of the earthly self with the Light-body. Reprogramming *is* the soul's blueprint-pattern of evolutionary development on the most causal dimensions and the infusion of the vibratory patterns of the Light-body into the bioenergetic system that determines the individual's growth patterns. In this light, reprogramming can be seen to be a more determinative process than healing, for as the higher Light-codes are assimilated within the individual, the inherent perfection of the Light-body becomes part of the earthly self and health imbalances are harmonized as a by-product of this process. Thus, reprogramming can be seen as the predominant motivating dynamic of soul growth, encompassing the more causal levels of being and the healing process.

The foundation of reprogramming is exemplified in the Biblical passage: "Seek ye first the Kingdom of God and all these things shall be added unto you (Matthew 6:33)." Without the enactment of this primary spiritual directive in thought, word, and deed, reprogramming will not manifest to any significant degree. As discussed in Chapter 3, the Ten-plus-One Commandments are the very core of a life lived within the Light; these Commandments are the blueprint for seeking first the Kingdom of God and, in fact, are the necessary prerequisite for higher thresholds of reprogramming. When these fundamental universal Light-codes are crystallized within consciousness, then and only then are "all these things" added unto the individual. Therefore, it is with this in mind that every aspect of reprogramming and healing must be approached.

The quest for both healing and reprogramming can be a spiritually fruitless exercise in self-absorption unless the overriding motivation of the individual is to serve the Light, and in so doing, serve others. When spiritual service is of the highest priority in life, then the emphasis is not on self-improvement, self-healing, and self-growth for the individual's own sake, but for the sake of harmonizing and balancing the self in order to facilitate the best possible fulfillment of the individual's chosen Light-work. For it is in serving the Light in every way possible and appropriate that the gateways of the Higher Evolution and the Light-body open to the individual and spiritual growth and appropriate healing thereby occur.

Though apparently paradoxical, there can be imbalance in the quest for and attainment of perfect earthly balance. For if the healing and enlightenment of the self are the primary focus, the fruits will accrue only to the self. For example, if the healing of an imbalanced condition becomes so absorbing that spiritual service is forgotten or given secondary importance, the healing of such a condition is not only less likely to occur at the causal levels of being but also the fruits of the balancing process will be empty. If, instead of placing primary emphasis on undergoing the healing process, the individual focuses on serving the Light in spite of such an imbalance, the healing that accrues will be a true healing. This is not to say that active, regular healing (and reprogramming) modalities do not have their place; certainly when done with balanced discernment this is a positive endeavor in generating momentum toward the harmonization of the self. It is when this process becomes such a focusing upon the self that spiritual service becomes less than the highest of priorities, then healing and reprogramming become shallow and, in the cosmic overview, ineffective. The quest for the perfecting of the body, emotions, or mind can so engulf an individual who does not place service to the Kingdom of God first that an entire lifetime or many lifetimes can pass without an iota of spiritual growth. Achieving the perfectly trained mind, the perfect physique and metabolism, or the immaculately cleansed aura and emotional state is secondary to the attainment of the Kingdom of Light. Whether a person is overweight, has chronic emotional problems, has imperfect body metabolism, or the like is of subordinate concern to the Higher Evolution. The all-important criterion in this regard is how well the soul enacts its chosen role of spiritual service and if the Kingdom of God is utmost in thought, word, and deed. If this criterion is observed, all imbalanced conditions that are in the individual's highest interest to be healed will be so as a by-product of such a life. So, too, with reprogramming in preparation for the ascension; no matter how intense and lengthy the performing of such techniques and modalities, reprogramming does not occur in proportion to effort exerted but in proportion to Light-focused attitude and active spiritual service.

From *The Keys of Enoch:*

> Man was made to grow into the image of the Living Light, to become the Adam Kadmon who is capable of chemically generating an infinite number of spatial forms.
>
> The key stresses the human creation as one of the repeating energy units in a state of being purified between star fields.
>
> This is why the overall blueprint of the physical form is used on the day of resurrection, for it is the physical form plus the entire energy model which is resurrected and used for transduction creation in other worlds of physical form.[8]

The earth-based bioenergetic matrix functions as a blueprint-pattern in which Light is ingathered and through which the Light-body is reactivated. The human is made in the image and likeness of God, and the human energy system is the earth-plane crystallization of this archetypal Thought-pattern. The bioenergetic matrix, then, serves as an interdimensional Thought-extension in which higher Light can be received and grounded within the earth's energy parameters. It can be viewed as an alchemical crucible through which the human self is transmuted from lower octaves of earthly energy-matter to increasingly higher octaves of consciousness Light. Via the biocrystalline matrices of the human energy system, the crystalline codes of the Light-body transpose into their earth-plane correspondents, thereby catalyzing lattice-membrane transformations on every level of the earthly self.

The great Master of Light, Yeshua (known colloquially as Jesus), laid the foundation for this process to occur on earth nearly 2000 years ago as the necessary blueprint for the reprogramming of today and ascension of tomorrow.

> The biochemical processes can rebuild the body, cell by cell, once the chemical elements are balanced within the projection of the Living Light.
>
> This was demonstrated by Jesus when he balanced the basic thirty-two chemical elements in his human body with the thirty-third transformation of Light known as the *Lak Boymer.* (This showed how his cellular chemical functions could be completely rebuilt into a Christ body of Light over a three and a half day cycle compared to seven years to replace the body cells.)
>
> . . . Jesus came to reactivate the chemical blueprint of Light in Man and allow him to use this as an enabling function for a higher ultrastructure of Light which is the Holy Spirit resonance of the Eternal Light.[9]

An entire branch of interdimensional science unto itself, the more technical perspectives of reprogramming will fill volumes in the years to come. In this text, the highlights will be noted. In essence, the bioenergetic codes of the earthly self engage in a matrix superimposition process that converts the dimensional parameters of the entire system into higher Light-indexes that then determine their meridian of reconstitution.

The most fundamental characteristics of this process are as follows:

1. The molecular density level becomes less dense and more transparent as it is respatialized onto a higher valence of Light of a less dense spectrum of energy-matter.

2. The entire human energy system is biomagnetically recoded to adapt to new biological environmental parameters. This occurs through the activation of an energy circulation system associated with the Light-body that superimposes over the bioenergetic matrix and realigns the blood, lymphatic, and nervous circulatory systems to function within higher biomagnetic coordinates.

3. The magneto-gravitational fields of the biosystem are transposed to higher-octave quantum energetic levels that accord with the new Alpha–Omega threshold vibrational parameters.

4. The blood crystals are infused with the blood-codes of the Christ body of Light, transforming its membrane matrix to be freed from the binding forces of the earth plane, thereby becoming an interdimensional membrane of Living Light.

5. There is an encoding of Light upon every brain cell and life cell.

6. The crystalline network of the brain-mind is activated. This Urim circuitry overrides the present neurocircuitry, accelerating consciousness time while also opening interdimensional thought- and communication-processes.

7. Centropy—the electrification of matter—occurs, converting the energy-matter spectrums into higher Light-spectrums.
8. The physical DNA matrix interconnects with the DNA codes of the Light-body, thus functioning as a primary interlinkage medium through which the Christ body of Light is infused. The gel of the DNA-RNA plasma is then reconstituted on a higher wavelength of Light.
9. The chakra system of the Light-body becomes activated within the chakra circuitry of the earthly self, causing a complete dimensional transformation onto a higher valency of Light. This includes the activation of the Alpha and Omega chakras.
10. The infusion of the Christ Body of Light into the earthly garment of Light lifts the soul through a spiritual birth into eternal co-union with Christ and YHWH within the Kingdom of Light.

Every cell, organ, body system, auric level, and aspect of consciousness undergoes a radical Light-transformation. This is evolutionary opportunity presented to humankind in these latter days. It is also an important branch of the interdimensional science to come.

REPROGRAMMING MODALITIES

In reprogramming for the ascension, the individual utilizes key aspects of the bioenergetic system as a matrix of receivership through which to facilitate and amplify activation and alignment with the Light-body. Through employing the following reprogramming techniques, certain bioenergetic reactions are set in motion that can: 1) cultivate a greater receptivity to receiving higher gradients of Light, 2) catalyze interdimensional Light-energy transposition in predisposed matrix-systems, and 3) facilitate an optimal Light-code transfer over time. The great value of these techniques lies in its giving the individual effective means for overcoming much of the pervasive inertial aspects of the earth's energy field that tend to inhibit reprogramming processes.

The primary areas for reprogramming modalities are the blood system, DNA, mind centers/brain cells, and the nine fundamental chakras (the seven chakras-in-polarity and the Alpha and Omega chakras). Quartz and other crystalline matrices are particularly valuable in working with these areas because of their multidimensionallly accelerative and programmable properties. Sensitive care and discernment needs to be exercised with the following techniques because of their potentially powerful effects within these most causal aspects of the human energy system. This is true especially when applying the more advanced modalities, for example, laser-crystal mind center activation, and when experiencing them in the more powerful gridworks, unified energy fields, and temple chambers.

BLOOD SYSTEM REPROGRAMMING TECHNIQUES

> The Light will probe the face of the Earth and will pick up the vibratory light crystal of the Christ blood coded upon the doorposts of the body temple.[10]

The life essence of consciousness flows through the "living crystals of Light" within the bloodstream. As the blood is transformed by the infusion of Light, these biocrystals both record this information code-pattern within their structure and absorb the energy charge. Then, as the blood flows in interactive contact with the cells of the body, it releases the energy charge into the cellular environment along with the Light-code pattern. The cells receive and demodulate these signals, then transduce them into the information "language" of the cellular level. The coded Light-charge is thereby modulated throughout the cell's matrix, affecting each subsystem in subtle but powerfully foundational ways. This affects even the DNA-RNA complex, whose profound recrystallization responses affect directly and indirectly every aspect of the bioenergy system. Through its capacities for continuous interdimensional transduction of Light-vibrations, the blood system provides one of the most important crystal connections within the human energy system. As the reprogramming process continues, the blood becomes a living crystalline stream of Life-increasing Light acting to ingather the Christ blood-codes within the progressively rarefying aqueous biocrystalline medium.

The use of *crystal water* is one of the most potent and easily accessible reprogramming techniques presently available. Water's strong resonant affinity with quartz, in addition to its receptively programmable structure, makes it an elegantly perfect synergistic counterpart of crystal. Interestingly, both mediums are transparent, chemically neutral, extremely impressionable, similar in their molecular space groupings, and symbols of purity and clarity.

> The formative boundary surfaces in flowing movement prove to be areas of sensitivity. They respond to the slightest changes in their surroundings by expanding, contracting or making rhythmical waves. . . . It is interwoven with countless sensitive membranes, which are prepared to perceive everything taking place in the surroundings. Water is not enclosed within its inner surfaces but open to its surroundings and to all the stimuli and formative impulses from without. It is the impressionable medium *par excellence.*[11]

Experiments demonstrate water's receptivity to a variety of energy influences. When exposed to such vibrations, the crystalline lattice structure of the elastic bond angles absorbs the influence and stores it with subtle sensitivity on both physical and subtle planes. It is then a programmed medium that will exert corresponding influence upon the environment as it releases the programmed energy pattern (along with its accompanying charge). Holy water has long been utilized in a variety of religious and spiritual traditions as a medium that can receive, hold steady, and transfer vibrations of a sacred nature. Scientific experiments have also demonstrated parallel capacities with other types of influences.

> The results of the experiment described in this paper indicate that a primary energy, different from the energies recognized by modern science, is emitted by magnets and by the hands of healers. The energies from both sources cause decreases in the surface tension of water, change the structure and color of crystals from cupric chloride solutions, change the hydrogen bonding of water, and accelerate the growth rate of rye grass.[12]

Patrick Flanagan, Ph.D., and Gael Flanagan have also observed in scientific experiements that magnets, crystals, and pyramids all decrease the measurable surface tension of water.[13]

Although other energy fields can influence water significantly, for purposes of reprogramming, quartz crystals are by far the best means for programming specifically desired energy-code programs into water. Because of their primary resonant affinity with one another and their versatile multidimensional responsiveness, more complexly supraholographic program patterns can be imprinted within the aqueous medium. Also the accelerative amplification of quartz adds considerable energy input that water can absorb and later release.

To Make Crystal Water

First obtain a clear glass container. Gallon-size sun tea jars work well and can be bought cheaply in variety stores. It is important for best results that the container used for crystal water be as clear and neutral as possible; plastic will not work as well as glass but is still acceptable. Next, at least eight crystals are required for best effects. One is used for placing in the water itself, six are for creating a Star of David gridwork around the jar, and the last one is for standing vertically atop the jar. The crystal to be put inside the water needs to be programmed for the type of effects that are desired. For working with the blood system, a seed-phrase (see Chaper 8) would be "activating the living crystals of Light in the physical body" or "interdimensional activation and alignment of the blood system with the Light-code patterns of the Higher Self." Other types of seed-phrases for reprogramming include "activation and alignment with the Light-body," "reprogramming of the mind-centers," and "reprogramming of the entire bioenergetic system in the Light in preparation for the ascension." Once programmed, place this crystal inside the jar. Then fill the container with high-quality water. Tap water will generally not yield the best results because of its plethora of chemical additives and other nonoptimal influences. Distilled, purified, or certain types of spring water are the best mediums with which to work. With spring water, experience has shown that those waters from Hot Springs, Arkansas, and Evian, France, yield superb results.

Once the jar is filled with water (with the crystal inside), place it in the center of a Star of David gridwork. Optimally, this gridwork is set up so that the crystals are as close as possible (say one to two inches) to the surrounding circunference of the container's base. If desired, program these crystals for "energy flow for activating and charging crystal water." Also, it is best if this grid arrangement is set up permanently in a quiet, undisturbed location. For peak effects, place two magnets on opposite sides of each of the six crystals (see Chapter 14, "Crystal Gridworks" for instructions).

Then take the last crystal and situate it on top of the jar's lid with the termination pointing vertically upward. This is to facilitate the Pillar of Light effect and is quite important to obtain optimal benefits. If possible, find a crystal whose base allows it to stand vertically upright without any additional support. Because these are not easy to find, another possibility is to obtain one with a small portion of the base sawed off so that a flat horizontal plane is created.* Or else take a small amount of putty or clay, put it in the middle of the jar's lid, and push the crystal's base into it so that the crystal can stay upright.

Other crystals, preferably double-terminations, are glued on the outside of the jar in four to six vertical lines. That is, a number of crystals are glued in vertical alignment with each other from top to bottom of the jar's sides (single-terminations would point downwards); this is repeated at four to six equidistant intervals all the way around the jar.

Then suspend a pyramid from the ceiling with thread so that the pyramid is

*See Chapter 11 for discretionary perspectives.

directly over the upright crystal on top of the container. The crystal's termination should be in alignment with the pyramid's apex along the vertical axis. This amplifies the Pillar of Light effect and also adds the pyramid–crystal synergy component for enhanced results.

When this entire arrangement is completely set up, take the jar and tap it firmly and rhythmically approximately 100 times (some find 108 repetitions a good numerological standard). Place it in the gridwork, then leave the water undisturbed for 24 to 48 hours, and ask the Higher Evolution for their assistance in this process. After this time period, the now-charged and programmed crystal water can be drunk. It is important to maintain the water inside the gridwork and the crystal inside the jar between uses because the water will gradually lose its effectiveness over time if not kept inside the energy field. It is not recommended to expose this water to direct sunlight because of the degenerative-destructive aspects of the sun's light spectrum. Also, even more powerful results may be obtained by exposing the water to laser light, advanced gridworks, or suitable unified energy fields.

Crystal water is best taken plain, without any additional substances added. Used for making tea and other hot beverages, the heating and boiling dissipates a significant portion of the water's charge and program. For optimal results, replace normal daily fluid intake with crystal water. It is through the constant day-by-day, month-by-month infusion of the amplified energy charge and programmed energy patterns into the body system that gradual and profoundly transforming effects manifest. The observed results are usually not dramatic, noticed for the most part in retrospect and seen as a constant influence adding continual positive momentum to the bioenergetic system, and predisposing it to optimal reprogramming processes.

The sequence by which crystal water is assimilated into the human energy system is: 1) the water is primarily absorbed into the blood system; 2) the energy charge and program of the crystal water release into the biocrystalline aspects of the blood system, modulating its crystalline structure and charge capacities; 3) the affected blood flows to virtually every cell in the body; 4) during interactive exchange with the cells the programmed energy charge is transferred to the cells; 5) this is then transduced into the vibrational language of the intracellular structure, which affects selective components by subtly transforming their structure and bioenergy metabolic cellular components; 6) subtle but profound effects are absorbed and integrated within the DNA nuclear complex, causing recrystallization processes corresponding to the original programming imprinted into the crystal placed inside the crystal water jar; and 7) the cells and DNA complex are progressively restructured so as to function on higher quantum levels of Light, thus also creating a stronger interdimensional linkage with the Light-body. Greater gradients of higher Light then can be effectively infused into the entire bioenergetic matrix. Over time, these effects facilitate profound Light-transmutation processes throughout every level of the individual's consciousness.

In all, the making and usage of crystal water is one of the most effective and generally accessible reprogramming modalities available. In deciding which crystal-based techniques to include in one's regime, it is recommended that crystal water be included as an integral, ongoing part of the reprogramming process.

OTHER BLOOD SYSTEM TECHNIQUES

1. One excellent means to interact with the blood system is through the wrist pulse areas, which are quite sensitive and powerful energy zones of the bioenergy system. Find a crystal that is well suited for blood system reprogramming purposes, and program it (for example, "activation of the living crystals of Light in the physical body"). Bring the left arm in toward the stomach/solar plexus region so that the palm is facing upward and the arm is positioned comfortably. Place the crystal directly on top of the wrist pulse area with the termination pointing in alignment with the elbow, that is, aligned with the receptive intake-flow of energy going up the arm. Then position the right wrist pulse area on top of the crystal directly over the left pulse area. Make sure that the crystal is secure and the arms are comfortable. Sit or lie down in a receptive state of consciousness. Ask the Light-realms to assist in this blood activation procedure and remain actively receptive and sensitive to the processes and sensations that may be perceived. Focus upon the area of the wrists and crystal; visualize and feel the amplified energy program of the crystals being infused into the bloodstream. Allow the breath to become slow, deep, and rhythmic, and continue the exercise for five to ten minutes.

This technique works via pathways similar to those described for crystal water, except that the crystalline energy patterns are directly infused into the blood system instead of the water medium being used. As preparation for other healing, self-transformation, and reprogramming exercises or for integration of the beneficial effects of such exercises, this technique (done for five to ten minutes immediately following other exercises) is a simple and quite effective blood activation modality.

2. Another primary blood flow access area is the temple region of the head. For this exercise, three crystals are needed. Two are programmed for reprogramming the blood crystals and one for third eye activation. Tape the third eye crystal (preferably a small double-termination) on the forehead region with first-aid tape, so that it is pointing up and down in alignment with the spinal axis of the body. Take the other two crystals, one in each hand, and gently hold them in place on the temple areas so that the terminations are pointing toward the third eye crystal. Quiet the consciousness and connect with the Higher Evolution. State the intention and ask for assistance. Then focus upon the triangulation of energy dynamics occurring between the three crystals and the concomitant infusion of the crystals' programmed energy patterns into the bloodstream flowing through the head. This technique works both to activate the blood system in general (as with the wrist procedure just described), as well as to apply energies through the medium of the blood to help activate the mind centers of the head. Done for five to seven minutes before or after other exercises, this procedure is excellent for preparatory or integration reprogramming functions.

3. In this procedure, two crystals programmed for blood system activation are used. Hold the arms in a comfortable position with palms turned upward, and place one crystal on each wrist pulse area with the terminations pointing up the arm and into the body. One individual shines a laser beam into each crystal in turn for three to five minutes each while the other receptively absorbs the crystal's

amplified output. As always, use caution and discretion when applying laser beams through crystals into the bioenergetic system.

THE ALPHA AND OMEGA CHAKRAS

Above and below the seven primary chakras-in-polarity lie the Alpha and Omega chakras of wholeness. As presented in greater detail in Chapter 4 of *Windows of Light* (Baer & Baer), these two chakras are primary keys to the enactment of the reprogramming process. Just as every universal cycle of unfoldment in polarity has a beginning—the Alpha—and an ending—the Omega—so, too, does the human energy system reflect this macrocosmic verity on the microcosmic level. To briefly review, the Alpha is the seed-blueprint of wholeness for an entire cycle of evolutionary unfoldment; the Omega is the seed-blueprint of completion of an evolutionary sequence leading into a new Alpha–Omega cycle. Both Alpha and Omega transcend the realms of dualized polarity; that is, they are in a state of wholeness that encompasses the all-inclusive pattern-sequences of polarized evolutionary development suspended beyond space-time, even while manifesting their polarized patterning codes in space-time. The beginning and the end are one and the same, and in being enacted within polarized creation their potential patterns become actualized. At the Omega point, these actualized patterns are completed and unite as an Alpha–Omega unity leading to new Alpha–Omega cycle formulation and manifestation.

This same dynamic occurs as the earthly self completes its Alpha–Omega program and ascends into the higher octave chakra system of the Light-body. The seven chakras in polarity are activated into full unity with the present Alpha–Omega patterns and are then reformulated within a higher octave cycle of manifestation. Figure 22 illustrates the concordance between the primary energy dynamics and structure of the Great Pyramid and the human energy system as explicated in *Windows of Light* (Baer & Baer). The essential idea is that the Great Pyramid is a master cipher containing the codes of creation. As part of it is deciphered, revealed is the fact that the inverted and upright apexes of the Great Pyramid encompass seven primary standing wave energy patterns as the Alpha and Omega, respectively, of the pyramid's blueprint of wholeness. So, too, with the human bioenergy system—the seven chakras are encompassed by an Alpha chakra four to six inches below the coccyx center and an Omega chakra four to six inches above the crown center. The primary energy dynamics of the pyramid are parallel to those of the human energy system.

The importance of this concept in terms of its role in the reprogramming process cannot be overemphasized. These two chakras of the Christ body of Light form the causal apexes of all reprogramming energy dynamics. When integrated into reprogramming energy modalities, this energy pattern becomes more highly activated toward catalyzing greater activation and alignment into the Light-body.

There are a number of ways that this energetic pattern can be applied in practice:

1. Focused visualization is one such means. For this, follow the energy pattern presented in Figure 22. Energy first comes into the upright apex and then spirals around the upright pyramid both clockwise and counterclockwise, expanding until it reaches the octahedral midline. At this level the spiraling patterns progressively

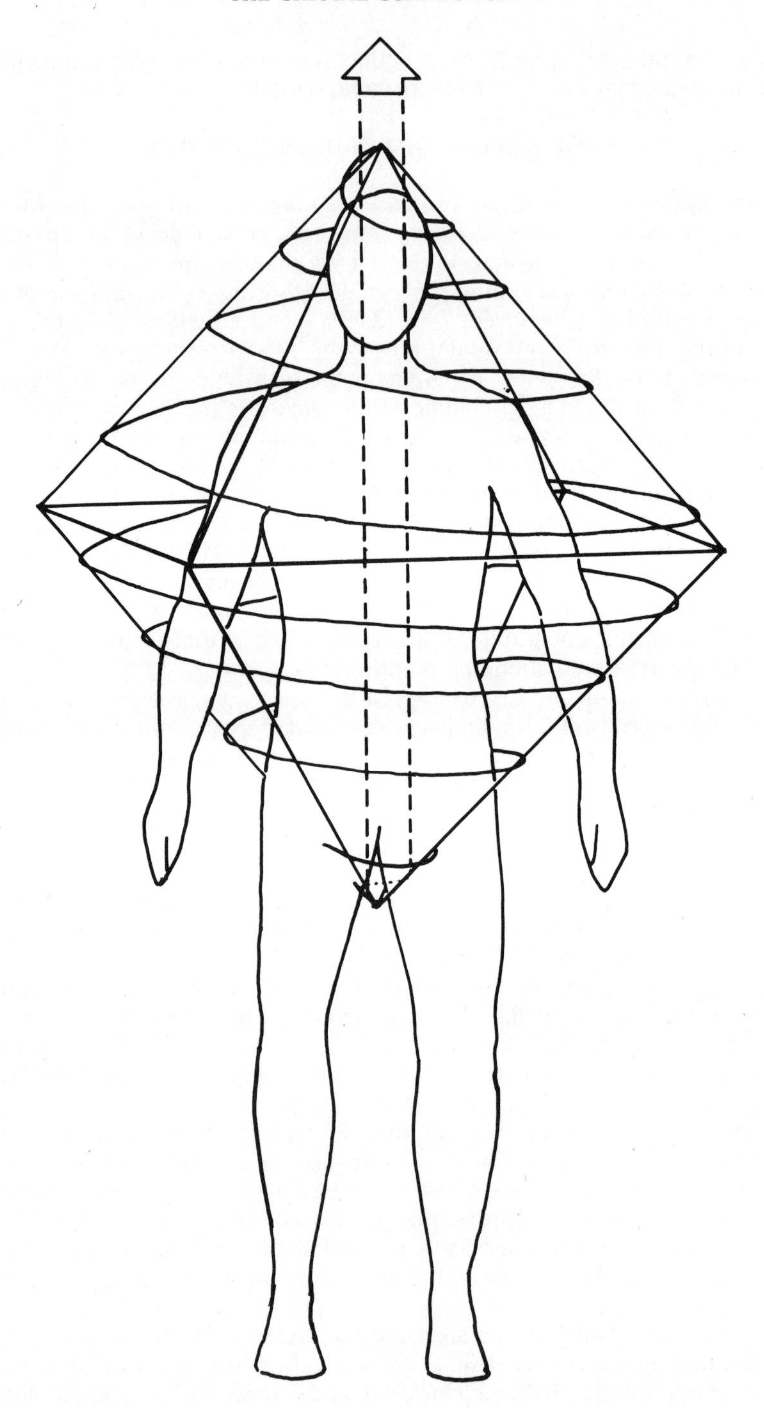

Figure 22: Alpha-Omega Pyramidal Energy Dynamics of the Human Energy System

converge down to the inverted apex. This apex—the Alpha—is a "zero point" of energy focus, amplification, and conversion into a laserlike beam of Light that shoots directly from inverted apex to upright apex. Then the main force of the Light is amplified through the upright apex and directed straight upward in a powerful, focused beam.

These energy dynamics simply superimpose themselves within the human bioenergetic system in the same proportions. The inverted and upright apexes are the Alpha and Omega chakras, respectively. Visualize and feel these energy lines of force as they spiral around the circumference of the body, converging powerfully at the Alpha chakra and shooting straight upward through the entire chakra system out through the crown into the Omega chakra, and then with even greater force projecting up out of the Omega chakra and into the Light-body chakra system. Visualize this sequence for five to ten minutes before or after engaging in other reprogramming, self–transformation, or healing exercises. Also, see *Windows of Light,* Baer & Baer, pp. 157–158 for a meditation designed to guide the individual through the Alpha–Omega energy dynamics.

2. Find two crystals, one suitable for use as an Alpha chakra crystal and one suitable for use as an Omega chakra crystal. Optimally, they will be double-terminations. Program each crystal to harmonize with the energy vibration-pattern of one of these chakras and to amplify the Alpha–Omega energy dynamics.

If a supine (face up) position is preferred, these crystals can be propped up with books, wood blocks, or other neutral objects so that they are aligned with the horizontal midsection of the body. That is, the crystals are at a horizontal level such that one termination points into the top middle of the head from four to six inches away (Omega), and the other lies four to six inches below the coccyx chakra in between the thighs, approximately 1½ to 2 inches from floor level pointing up the line of chakras (Alpha). This can be incorporated into both personal usage patterns as well as holistic health care settings. Optimally, double-terminations are also placed on each of the other seven primary chakras, with the points parallel to the spinal axis. If double-terminations are not available for any of the nine chakras, position the terminations pointing in the direction of the Alpha–Omega energy dynamic, and for the Omega chakra the crystal should point in the direction of the energy flow shooting out of the Omega point.

If an upright seated position is preferred, the Alpha crystal can be propped up to the appropriate horizontal level at which this chakra occurs (directly under the seat of the chair and pointing up into the line of chakras). The Omega crystal can be suspended by string from the ceiling over the head at the correct level. The primary termination of each crystal should point vertically upward.

3. In pyramids large enough for a person to be seated upright, either in a chair or sitting on the floor, the pyramidal energy dynamics can be aligned with the human energy system dynamics to assist reprogramming. Position the body so that the spine and head are in alignment with the midpoint of the pyramid base and with the upper apex. In this way the Alpha–Omega pyramidal energy flow shoots directly through the Alpha–Omega bioenergetic flow. Here, the pyramid is a tool that provides an energy matrix that superimposes over the human energy system, amplifying the latter.

4. Any of the preceding techniques in this list can be integrated into a self-transformation/reprogramming session. At the beginning of such a session as the

transition is being made into a relaxed state, the individual can spend two to five minutes consciously experiencing Alpha–Omega dynamics as a way to amplify the connection with the Light-body. Then the chosen modalities are enacted. For the last five to seven minutes of the session the person can integrate the benefits of this session by again consciously attuning to and amplifying this energy flow pattern. In this way not only is the effectiveness of the session magnified, but also the keynote of reprogrammed activation and alignment into the Light-body is integrated as the beginning and ending of these time periods.

OTHER REPROGRAMMING MODALITIES

1. *Gem tinctures* are excellent adjuncts to the reprogramming process. They are variations on the crystal water theme, working through the same energetic pathways and yielding similar effects. The primary difference is that each gem matrix has a distinct vibrational patterning and essense that is its program. Quartz crystals can be programmed with a wide array of thought-patterns and energy fields, but the gem matrices are quite specific in their energy spectrum parameters. As with the Bach Flower remedies, the essence and vibrational pattern of the gem is infused into a receptive programmable aqueous medium. The tincture preparation holds these vibrations steady so that they can be diluted with specified amounts of water and then taken internally. According to the essential qualities and energy patterns of the particular gem, corresponding effects will be caused within the bioenergy system.

Gen tinctures are particularly useful in reprogramming because of their strong affinity with the blood system. Bach Flower remedies are more effective in balancing emotional patterns; gem tinctures have their primary effect upon the gravito-magnetic crystallization patterns of the blood. Some of these tinctures have a strong magnetic reorientation effect opon the brain cells and brain-mind centers. (See the section entitled "Gem and Refined Metal Perspectives" in Chapter 7 for more information on the nature of gem matrices.)

2. *Silica cell salt* is many times a most helpful addition to a reprogramming regime. The silica element in the body is an integral part of the biocrystallinity of the human energy system. It has numerous parallels with its "cousin," quartz crystal, in its function as a receiving-amplifying agent for significant portions of the higher Light-frequencies that flow through the individual. If there is a deficiency of this element, the capacity for these higher Light-frequences to be received and processed through the person is correspondingly less. For those who do a great deal of Light-work and crystal work, the silica element appears to be metabolized quicker than normal in some cases, sometimes resulting over time in "silica burnout," a condition of high stress and metabolic imbalance caused by not being able to process Light-energies in a harmonious way through the biosystem. Regular replenishment of this element rectifies this condition over a period of time. During the reprogramming process, more and more higher octave Light is being assimilated within the individual, many times calling for additional nutritional silica to help facilitate the optimal receiving and integration of these energies. Please note: silica cell salt is not quartz dust; such dust should never be taken internally.

3. Creating a *DNA crystal* is the most direct means for reprogramming the DNA

complex. Find a high quality, preferably double-termination, crystal that harmonizes with this purpose and program it with the seed-phrase "transfer of the DNA Light-Life codes of the Light-body into the DNA complex of the earthly self in the highest Light in divine order." The programming procedure for this crystal needs to follow the process presented in number 8 under "Different Types of Creative Programming" in Chapter 8. For best results, keep this crystal within the auric field as much as possible, carrying it in a pocket, or wearing it as a pendant. The DNA crystal becomes synchronized with the unique and intricate DNA codes of the individual while also maintaining an interdimensional linkage with the DNA codes of the Light-body. As appropriate, the higher DNA patterns will be transposed into the earthly self, thereby progressively reprogramming one of the most causal aspects of the entire bioenergetic system. These effects will be subtle and will take place over week, months, and years.

4. Refer to Chapter 10. Every technique in this chapter is for reprogramming, with special focus on the brain cells and mind centers.

5. Refer to exercise number 3 under "Programming Exercises" in Chapter 8. This is also an excellent reprogramming modality.

6. The most effective reprogramming takes place in ascension-oriented gridworks, advanced unified energy fields, and temple chambers. As the power and sophistication of these energy fields increases, so does the depth of reprogramming. As these disciplines start to mature in the years to come, more and more professional unified energy fields and temple chambers will arise that will bring higher knowledge and advanced Light-tools and Light-technologies. For now, there are numerous advanced gridworks in Chaper 14 that are easy to make. And in Chapter 15, glimpses of the sophisticated reprogramming modalities of the future can be seen.

As a whole, the role and importance of reprogramming for the ascension is the capstone of the evolutionary imperative of the current times. Knowledge concerning this realm is reactivated at appropriate intervals as an integral aspect of offering theoretical and practical perspectives toward preparing for the ascension. May the information presented here be of assistance toward becoming the interdimensional Light-beings that all truly are.

CHAPTER 10

Mind-Center Activation

The brain of man is part of the Divine Mind, and by decoding the human brain's mechanisms of memory storage in relationship to the universal language process, a higher hierarchical memory is revealed and Man discovers that he is a pulsating geometry of a Divine Language system.[1]

The mind of the Human is a mind within a Mind, a membrane within a Membrane, a cell within a Cell. The functioning network of Universal Intelligence enfolds within itself mind-jewels superimposed throughout the latticework of manifestation. Light flows through this Intelligence-processing network step by dimensional step, lattice within universal lattice. The Universal Mind processes through infinite universal minds in a process of Light-distribution and glorification. Each mind-jewel is situated at harmonic nodal points of intra- and interdimensional grid-relatedness. Earth-human is a subextension of a vast individual and collective Intelligence network spanning the depths and heights of the Eternal. As an individual cell is to the entire physical body, so too, is the individual human entity to the Higher Self; cell to body/self to Self.

To extend this analogy, the level of cellular consciousness is encompassed by and expanded to the next higher quantum ordering level—tissue consciousness; and the tissue matrix is enfolded within the organ level of consciousness; and the organ within the body system; and the body system within the master control of individual consciousness. Each progressively higher level of bodily awareness is inclusive of all lower levels and encompasses those collective interrelationships within a higher quantum level of consciousness. As with the cells, tissues, and so on, so also with the individual self within the hierarchically enfolded Light-body network of the Higher Self. To activate the self's mind-centers is to awaken higher quotients of inclusive encompassment of Universal Intelligence in general and the Light-body network in particular. The spiral-cone of perception increases; the pathways to the Universal Mind are magnified.

The brain-mind of the individual human is the antennalike receiving-processing unit that is the primary connection zone between the individual and the rest of the Light-body network as well as the cosmos at large. Like an interstellar radar unit, the brain-mind is a sensitive reception center of Light-energy spectrums to which it is able to attune. Like a quartz crystal, it also amplifies incoming universal signals, processes them through correlating channels, and stores their imprint for further usage. The mind encompasses the brain and is that part of self which is considerably less constricted by the physical plane; it is the more causal supramatrix that functions as the interlinkage medium with higher levels of the Higher Self. The brain is the stepped-down physical-plane matrix within which the mind interpenetrates and through which it is grounded into earthly functioning. While not constricted to the physical plane, the mind is yet constrained within the boundaries of its spiral-cone of perception,which are reflected in the bioenergetic anatomy and physiology of the brain. This is to say, the state of the brain is bioenergetically reflective of the state of the mind; and as the mind's capacities grow there are associative transformational changes that occur in the brain's physical matrix that reflect the expansion of the spiral-cone of perception.

To sum up, the brain grounds the mind; it is a consciousness attraction module* whose bioenergetic matrix forms the receptivity parameters for the interdimensional functioning of the mind-matrix. The sacred science of mind-center activation is the application of accelerative Light-energy code-patterns within the brain-mind network to recrystallize its conjugate matrices toward greater levels of multidimensional access and encompassment.

The brain is a crystalline biocosmic resonating system. As the mind interpenetrates the brain, different anatomical sectors resonate with and ground particular aspects of the mind's multifaceted functioning. Itzhak Bentov, scientist and author of *Stalking the Wild Pendulum* and *A Cosmic Book: On the Mechanics of Creation*, cites four separate resonating systems in the human brain—the skull, the third and lateral ventricles, the sensory cortex, and in each hemisphere of the brain. These are areas "where pulsating magnetic fields of opposite polarities are set up, these being very sensitive to environmental fields and providing a possible mechanism by which the brain picks up information from the environment through 'resonant feedback.' "[2] Built into the brain, then, are four primary resonant subsystems by which communication occurs between the individual and the surrounding cosmic environment. Each area of the brain acts as a receptor-amplifier for particular aspects of the universal energy spectrum and as a processing center programmed for specific energetic interactions.

The skull is a masterpiece of integrated sacred geometric interrelationships that, as a whole, serves as a crystal-based form energy consciousness attraction module. As the chalice which nests the brain it forms the exterior wave-interference template that receives and "refracts" certain energy spectrum profiles into their assigned seat in the brain. The holographic interference pattern that is the skull is composed of complex sacred geometric proportions. In a sense, the skull is the exterior bony crystallization that, like quartz crystals, is a reflection of the interior vibrational patternings; the outer skull mirrors the interior brain anatomy and energetic physiology. The skull, then, can be seen as a solid-state crystalline receiver that functions according to the sophisticated principles of form energy.† It is the selectively permeable interface between what is outside and what is inside the individual; it thereby serves to filter and focus universal energies into brain-area specific energy profiles and pathways. Perhaps the discipline of phrenology has much to teach here. The human skull, as a chalice of living geometrical

---

*See Chapter 14.

†See Chapters 4 and 12.

interference patterns, enshrines the brain with a crystalline template of energetic encoding and refraction.

Furthermore, the skull can be likened to the exterior form and function of the great temples of this world (and worlds to come). The archetypal temple serves as a primary intermediary interconnection for humankind. The Universe-Temple-Human interrelationship is one in which the temple's structure and function is a macrocorrelate of the Human and a microcorrelate of the Universe; the temple mirrors both the heavens and the earthly human in every facet of its beingness. In his book entitled *The Temple in Man: Sacred Architecture and the Perfect Man*, the French scholar R. A. Schwaller de Lubicz demonstrates the interrelationship between the geometry of the architecture of the Temple of Luxor and the geometry of the human skull, as well as the major brain areas and the rest of the body form. From another perspective, the noted author and scholar Ashley Montagu writes in an article entitled "The Skull as Architecture" of the correspondences between the skull and the grand Middle Ages cathedrals.

> Your head and the Cathedral of Notre Dame have more in common than you might think.
>
> The human skull is one of the most structurally efficient pieces of architecture ever developed. . . .
>
> Architects and historians have long debated whether the ornate flying buttresses of Gothic cathedrals serve a purpose or exist merely as decoration. Recently, . . . Princeton structural engineers have shown that the buttresses indeed play a vital supporting role: apparently they were designed to absorb stresses caused by high winds.
>
> Since medieval architects were field trained and apparently build no models of their great cathedrals, how could they have known intuitively that their buttresses and pillars would work? Could it be that they literally used their heads? . . . Could architects of the Middle Ages have modeled their cathedrals after the vaulted, buttressed, pillared, beautifully designed human skull?[3]

The skull functions as a blueprint in yet another way. In Matila Ghyka's *The Geometry of Art and Life*, it is illustratively proven that the head's geometry expanded into a higher quantum of space is precisely duplicated in the geometry of the rest of the body structure.[4] This is the reasoning underlying the great historical significance placed upon the skull as a quintessential symbol of Higher Intelligence, crystal skulls being crystal-based working models of this principle.*

In many ways, the function of the skull in relation to the brain and body is the same as that of the temple's exterior form in relation to the form and function of its chambers, halls, pillars, domes, and so on. Every geometric detail of a temple's outer architecture relates directly to its twofold purpose of functioning as an interdimensional interconnection station as a whole and as a form energy collector and focuser for the interior architecture. All the great temples known—the Temple of Luxor, the Great Pyramid, Stonehenge, Chartres Cathedral, and others—are exteriorly "faceted" in correspondence to the spectrum-profile of Light received via form energy resonance and to the refractory parameters for internal energy

Note: The authors urge extreme care in discerning whether to interlock individual consciousness with the Mitchell-Hedges crystal skull, directly or via photographs, slides, and holograms, due to its known integral association in previous centuries with religious systems wherein human sacrifice was practiced. The same level of discernment should be applied also to all the various crystal skulls.

processing. So it can be seen analogously that the crystal-based human skull acts as the outer temple form for the internal temple functions of the different brain areas that serve as the master-control centers for the enactment of the Higher Self blueprint.

The other resonating systems of the head—the third and lateral ventricles, the sensory cortex, and each hemisphere—in conjunction with the primary glandular-chakra center areas perform the master-control functioning for the entirety of the earthly self's consciousness. They enact the brain-mind's differentiated functions. This situation can be likened to white light refracted into its rainbow differentiations, each rainbow ray being analogous to different aspects of the brain-mind's functioning. The liquid crystal-colloidal structure of the brain is a membrane sheeting within membrane sheeting that has a potentially infinitely sensitive interactive responsiveness with the full spectrum of Universal Intelligence. Being of the image and likeness of God-Mind, the brain areas serve as multifaceted crystalline interdimensional connection zones and intradimensional control centers. The supraholographic maser-type functioning of the brain is a step-down reflection of the greater macrostate Universal Mind.

> The brain of man is part of the Divine Mind . . . and Man discovers that he is a pulsating geometry of a Divine Language system.[5]

> Your mind forms the filament or template membrane for the direct encoding of the fire letters, the wisdom of Light upon membrane circuits. For you are a biotransducer subsystem for higher intelligence to indwell within you.[6]

This crystalline biocomputer operates by processing information signals through the magneto-gravitationally oriented liquid crystal-colloidal matrix. Magneto-gravitic domains orient in relationship to the causal mind-centers and their interrelating energy channels. Supraholographically coded energy patterns are focalized within the primary mind-centers and then mirrored within the brain matrix along various quantum holographic axial network branchings. Domain intersecting with mirrored domain form the additive (and synergistic) resultant standing wave interference patterns of information encoded into memory membranes. This process is based upon the concept of different geometries of unit cells orientated within crystallographic space groupings reacting with resonant responsiveness to incoming angled crystallographic information-coded space groupings, thus causing concomitant domain superimposition. The concept of the supraholographic resonant mirroring occurring with the brain-mind as its modus operandi is a key to a greater understanding of the crystalline biocomputer that the brain is.

The brain-mind, as a mind within a vast hierarchical Universal Mind, a cell within the body of Universal Intelligence, vibrates within spectrum-specific parameters of the universal energy spectrum. Each dimensional reality, depending upon its relative place within the Light-spectrum, will determine the vibrational valence upon which human brain-mind functions occur. This is to say that the energetic parameters of the earth's energy-matter spectrum determine the brain-mind's spectrum of functioning to a significant degree. To transcend certain interdimensional communication access thresholds, the mind must "sever" all but a few fine threads of attachment to the physical brain. When the transcending mind returns to being grounded within the earthly self's brain-mind matrix, higher dimensional thought-forms can be integrated within the biocomputer only to degrees that are described by earthly bioenergetic parameters. In the reprogramming process the physical self is progressively transmuted and, thereby, the bonds of the physical plane diminish and interdimensional communication capacities broaden beyond previous bounds. As energy-matter is transformed to higher octaves of Light, the brain itself is transmuted and the spiral-cone of perception expands in direct concordance. The science of mind-center activation is a specialization area of the reprogramming process. This specific science focuses on activating higher dimensional crystalline mind channels and aligning these channels with the selectively receptive biocrystalline matrix of the brain. As this occurs, the various components of the brain undergo quantum shifts in their energetic parameters of functioning. Physical modulations of brain structure and functioning also necessarily accompany this process. The baseline magneto-gravitic orientations of the liquid crystal medium and other biocrystalline structures are reoriented in alignment with higher spectrum energy fields of the Light-body. Brain cells expand, skull crystalline domain orientations shift, liquid crystals realign along new axes-orientation lines, the neurocircuitry pathways are gradually overridden into higher circuitry-pathways, and other important changes manifest as the brain matrix conforms with greater Light-energy matrices. The living crystalline blood, as it flows through the brain structure, receives higher coding signals and incorporates them into its schemata, thereafter transferring this higher energy patterning throughout the rest of the bioenergetic system. Concomitantly, the spiral-cone of perception expands and greater degrees of Universal Intelligence are encompassed within consciousness. A form of hyperintelligence progressively dawns in consciousness as the brain-mind enacts incremental shifts into higher energy octaves that operate with supraholographic hyperfunctioning.

The Keys of Enoch amplifies this understanding in its description of Urim circuitry.

> In order for the brain to accept new knowledge, to put a new bioengineering process to work, and to correct the retrogressive evolution, it is necessary that the brain goes through time acceleration.
>
> Presently, your brain works according to the consciousness plan of the specie which establishes the flow of ions through the membrane circuitry.
>
> In order for you to go beyond the increments of the chemical time scale requires the use of *Urim circuitry* which overrides the old flow time of the sodium ions and allows for immediate information transfer between the brain codes and new memory storage.
>
> Here, the Urim circuitry allows for the reception of information at rates faster than analytical comprehension. . . . Consciousness time actually speeds up.[7]

The Urim circuitry is now mostly dormant within humankind. As part of the reprogramming process, it is progressively activated within humankind's preexisting blueprint of consciousness. This Light-circuitry is a type of energy overlay originating from the levels of the Light-body and transferred to the earthly self at the appropriate time in an orderly sequence of transition. Now, in the reprogramming of the earth-individual in preparation for the ascension, various cosmic energy "locks" are being opened and an interdimensional garment emitting from the Light-body can be superimposed within a receptive earthly bioenergetic system, thus effecting quantum physical and consciousness transformations. This "garment of Light" is composed of a higher Light-network of energy flow that correlates with the preexisting physical structures of the brain-mind. Like a harmonic lattice coherently interlocking with a lower harmonic octave lattice, nodes and vertexes lock into phase with one another, acting as primary points of interlattice energy transduction. (There is also an interaction with the acupuncture meridian system on secondary levels.) The result of this process is ultra-intelligence, the birth of a new order of human Thought processing-accessing capabilities.

This process of activating the crystalline brain-mind channels is now available to the earth plane as an integral part of the reprogramming process. For the vast majority it is a step-by-step unfoldment of increment after increment of integration of the earthly mind with the Higher Self Mind. The primary purpose of this chapter is to set down a theoretical foundation of mind-center activation and to offer techniques and ideas to facilitate the activation process. Quartz crystals and other refined crystalline matrices are perfect tools to assist in mind-center activation. Their accelerative nature combined with their programmability, energetic stability, wide energy spectrum capacities, consciousness catalyzing properties, and form energy focusing make for a matrix uniquely qualified for this task.

PRIMARY MIND-CENTER AREAS

For purposes of mind-center activation there are certain key aspects of the brain-mind that are central to actualizing this process. Following is a summarization of each of these areas along with their primary functions, locations, and roles.

Brain

A few primary points are pertinent to this discussion. First, the brain as a whole is the seat of the individual's intelligence/consciousness; it is that physical zone that grounds the higher dimensional aspects of the mind's functions. Thought-forms do not originate in the physical brain; rather, they are received, processed, and stored from the more causal levels of the mind. The brain is an antennalike amplifying-receiving unit that functions as a biocrystalline computer system. It is the master control for all aspects of the individual self's bioenergetic functioning and the principal zone in which and through which continuous interdimensional interconnection with the Light-body network occurs. It houses the most hierarchically causal zones of all aspects of spiritual-mental-emotional-physical energy dynamics. In all, it is the temple-template of consciousness oriented within the universal latticework as a thinking membrane "floating" between star systems.

Brain-Mind Tensors

The template of the brain-mind selectively receives and transduces higher level input through a series of highly sensitive tensors. These tensors are like microscopic antennae, millions of which form energy-sensitive templates at various dimensional thresholds of brain-mind dynamics. Succinctly put, they are excitatory threshold membranes that process the firing-rate patterns of thought-forms and energy fields in a go/no-go fashion. The coded configuration of any given energy field has corresponding (supraholographic) stress/no-stress patterns. As the energy field passes through the brain-mind tensor threshold areas, the millions of individual tensors respond with great on-off rapidity to the coding patterns of the energy pattern input.* The tensor templates serve to selectively transduce input into the next lower dimensional energy modality. There are a series of such tensor templates ranging through the numerous brain-mind levels of consciousness at various thresholds of interlevel energetic exchange. At the level of the physical brain, these tensors manifest as microscopic villi, cilia, and spherical bodies lining the various brain ventricles. Christopher Hills elaborates upon their functioning in *Nuclear Evolution*:

> The chemical Ph of the (cerebrospinal) fluid is determined by ionisation of the villi and cilia which in turn control resonance with cosmic forces of light.
>
> The villi in the ventricles are constantly vibrating to cosmic radiations in the total environment.
>
> Man's brain is a tuner for his vibrating antenna. The tiny villi on the inside of the cerebral cavities act as cathode and anode and cause the brain to become a resonating radiating vehicle of an enhanced wave-field.[8]

> The ionisation of the tiny cilia of the inner membranes of the brain cavities and specifically in the third and fourth ventricles is achieved through atomic resonance. Like a whale whose head is full of sperm oil for sounding off signals and receiving them by sonar over thousands of miles, so can the human cerebrospinal fluids commune with world within worlds through ionisation of the liquid crystals in the brain.[9]

The fluctuating patterns of ionization of the villi, cilia, and spherical bodies of the brain are primarily determined by the fluctuating tensor code-patterns of the next higher level of brain-mind functioning. Therefore, it can be seen that the multilevel latticework of tensor-templates is the delicately responsive antenna-transduction pathways through which brain-mind functions occur.

As mind-center activation progresses, these tensor templates become more responsive to higher spectrums of Light-energies. Before mind-center activation occurs, these antennae are not excited by more refined Light-frequencies; they simply pass through the tensors without being received, because of the limited capacity of the tensors to pick up more rarefied energy spectrums. When mind-center activation occurs, the tensors are transformed into increasingly more Light-sensitive antennae. Frequency response to these more rarefied energies increases, and the spiral-cone of perception thereby expands.

Alpha and Omega Chakras

Situated four to six inches below the coccyx center and four to six inches above the crown chakra are, respectively, the Alpha and Omega chakras of wholeness, containing the blueprint of the beginning and the blueprint of the completion of individual consciousness. Their importance in the reprogramming process is presented both in Chapter 9 of this text and Chapter 4 of *Windows of Light* (Baer & Baer). To mention them in the context of mind-center activation is to affirm their significant role in this aspect of individual reprogramming. In fact, without due recognition of their causal nature, mind-center activation techniques yield only limited results.

---

*See Chapter 2: Overlap gradient zone dynamics are parallel to this process.

Pituitary Gland/Crown Chakra (Number 11 in Figure 23)

As the crown chakra is the master control of the chakra system (that is, the seven major chakras functioning in polarity), so correspondingly is the pituitary gland the master endocrine gland. The pituitary-crown chakra complex is two levels of one unified aspect of consciousness; the pituitary gland, situated in the third ventricle of the brain, is the physical matrix area in which the higher octave energy functions of the crown chakra interpenetrate the body's spatial-material dimensions. This complex is the chakra of dominion-receivership[10]—that area which is the first chakra of the earthly self to receive polarized Light-input and which processes these energy signals to their appropriate differentiated levels of functioning within the brain areas and the rest of the chakra system. This chakra can be viewed as a crystalline form (a diamond in the heart of the lotus) that works with the full spectrum of universal energies and refracts input into a "rainbow" of diversified frequencies that are processed to their corresponding levels of functioning throughout the bioenergetic system.

Pineal Gland/Third Eye Center (Number 10 in Figure 23)

The pineal gland can be seen as a physical-plane photoreceptor and neurochemical transducer that mirrors the higher level workings of the third eye center. John Ott, Ph.D., author of the acclaimed book *Health and Light*, states that:

> We are just beginning to find that light, *entering the eyes*, in addition to vision, stimulates activity in both the pituitary and pineal glands and possibly other areas in the mid-brain and hypothalamic regions. These control the endocrine system and the production of hormones. Thus, light energy exerts an influence on the (human) body chemistry.[11]

This oculo-endocrine connection reflects the more causal levels of third eye chakra functions. It is this center that controls all aspects of Light-synthesis in the cerebral cortex area,[12] the most highly evolved aspect of the brain-mind membrane.

> These crystalline channels can be seen as three jewel-crystals forming a pyramid. These three crystals in your third eye area allow resonance attunement to flow between the third eye and a spiritual template over your crown chakra which is necessary to project and receive the higher thought vibrations of Light.[13]

Thus, the threefold crystalline structure of the third eye couples with the Omega chakra in creating primary communication channels with the higher spectrums of Light. This telethought communication occurs primarily via modulation of gravitational waves through the interaction of consciousness with the third eye "crystals." It is also this dynamic that is the means by which inner vision occurs. As the crystalline nature of the third eye is increasingly activated, consciousness interactions through these jewels of Light are amplified manyfold and latent abilities associated with this region progressively unfold.

Cave of Brahma

The "Cave of Brahma," as Christopher Hills has named it, is the third ventricle of the brain that houses both the pituitary and pineal glands (as well as the hypothalamus). This is the holiest of holies within the temple of the Human, wherein direct communication access to the Eternal occurs. The unique configuration of the pituitary and pineal glands in conjunction with myriad microscopic cilia, villi, and spherical bodies in a resonant chamber creates the most causally receptive consciousness attraction module within the archetypal blueprint of the Human.

> "The Cave of Brahma" . . . referred to in the Sanskrit texts as the seat of resonance with the ONE ocean of cosmic vibrations. It manufactures the cerebrospinal fluid in IV (the fourth ventricle) which floats the whole brain and spinal nerves. The chemical Ph of the fluid is determined by ionization of the villi and cilia which in turn control resonance with cosmic forces of light.[14]

Within mind-center activation modalities, the Cave of Brahma, or the Absolute vector, is like the hub of a wheel about which all else revolves.

Front and Rear Cerebral Cortex Lobes

As seen in Figure 23, numbers 1–4, the front and rear cerebral cortex lobes are four areas on opposite sides of the top front and rear of the head. The cerebral cortex is known to be the seat of higher thought-processes; it is the most highly evolved strata of the brain. In this area, too, on the subtle planes, most complex and rarefied Light-interactions take place, being controlled primarily by the third eye chakra. The cerebral cortex as a whole also acts as a secondary but significant antenna-receiving area for higher spectrums of Light. The four areas noted in Figure 23 are primary input zones into this region.

Temples (Numbers 8 and 9 in Figure 23)

The temples on both sides of the head function, in terms of mind-center activation, as excellent input areas for the cave of Brahma and other primary areas within the central brain regions as well as primary access zones for infusing acceleratory crystal energies into the bloodstream flowing through the brain structure.

Right and Left Posterior Points

As illustrated in Figure 23, numbers 5–6, the right and left posterior points are approximately 1½ to 1¾ inches vertically upward from the occipital ridge on both sides of the head. These areas, similar to the four points over the front and rear cerebral cortex, are also "antenna-receiving" zones and act as important input-access regions to the innermost brain areas, including the Cave of Brahma.

Medulla Oblongatta

The medulla oblongatta is number 7 in Figure 23. This area is located directly above the middle of the occipital ridge; it forms a small indentation, easily perceivable by touch, in that part of the skull. As well as its numerous physical plane functions, it also has a polar relationship with the third eye region. The pulsating magnetic oscillation between the two areas makes this energy pathway a significant one both for activating the third eye and for coupling the third eye with energy flowing through the medulla oblongatta.

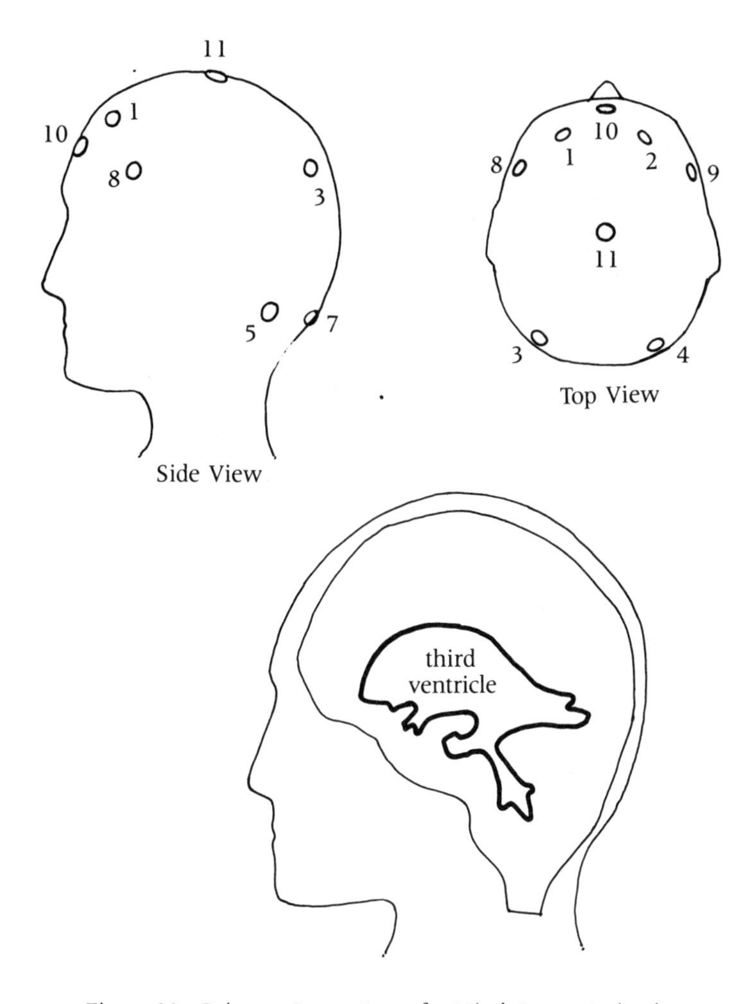

Figure 23: Primary Input Areas for Mind-Center Activation

Spinal Column

The spinal column is a helically based energy pathway acting not only as an effective antenna for the grounding of Light-energies, but also as a chakra interconnecting-coupling medium. Like a crystalline rod wrapped with helical coils, the spinal column is the foundational route of distribution, processing, and interconnection for the innumerable energetic dynamics occurring in bioenergetic metabolism. The lower five chakras-in-polarity, from the throat center to the coccyx center, are subvortexes within the causal vortexes of the third eye and crown chakras; they are refractory subcomponents that derive from the topmost control center chakras. The third eye has a strong oscillatory polarity relationship with the heart chakra; the throat is at a harmonic interval between the magnetic oscillations occurring between the third eye and heart, and derives a major degree of its power from the modulation of these oscillations focused through the throat area. From the heart derives the lower three chakras—solar plexus, spleen, and coccyx. These three centers form a triangulation of functional interrelationships that mirrors the triangulation of the heart, throat, and third eye on a lower dimensional plane.

Therefore, it can be seen that proper engagement of the spinal centers in conjunction with mind-center techniques associated more directly with the head region is an important aspect of these procedures.

Caudate Nucleus

Within brain anatomy the caudate nucleus is part of the basal ganglia, islands of gray matter deep inside each cerebral hemisphere. In *Through the Curtain*, by Viola Petitt Neal, Ph.D., and Shafica Karagulla, M.D., the authors propose a stimulating concept concerning the higher nature of the caudate nucleus. This original concept bears further examination because of the quality of the authors' work as well as their credentials.

> The caudate nucleus deals with the head antennae—millions of antennae which in the future will deal with the ability of all the extrasensory perception abilities, such as the ability to see events at a distance and the ability for telepathic contact.
>
> . . . the caudate nucleus is like a miniature brain for higher stages of development. The centers for higher sense perception were located in different points in this caudate nucleus and the antennae for these were focused at a point. There were certain foci which were pointed out in it that had to do with each higher sense development. In most people the circuits in the caudate nucleus are not connected. . . .
>
> When the esoteric teaching talked about antankarana, or the bridge in the brain, it was really referring to a connecting of the caudate nucleus with the rest of the brain.[15]

Crystal Recorder Cell

The crystal recorder cell, discussed in *The Keys of Enoch*, is another little-known and unique concept that bears further examination.

> . . . thought-forms of information which are continually active in space. Forms of advanced physical intelligence can directly tap into this information if they have a crystalline network within their brain cavity. For this reason the brains of advanced physicals will reveal the right and left hemispheres fused and a small crystal network in the right frontal lobe which acts as a crystal recorder cell or third brain transposing the language of the Higher Evolution into the vernacular.[16]

The primary brain-mind centers just presented give a basic outline of the most important areas in mind-center activation and their fundamental roles within these dynamics. This is but a general framework within which to work; greater technicalities are beyond the scope of this book. As this field becomes increasingly recognized as a professional discipline, more research will be undertaken.

STEP-BY-STEP MIND-CENTER ACTIVATION PROCEDURE

This procedure presents an outline for two people—a facilitator and a recipient—to enact an integrated process for mind-center activation. Logistically, it is best for the recipient to be seated in an upright position. Follow the outlined procedure, allowing intuitive rhythms, rather than the letter of the instructions, to be the guiding force. The recipient simply needs to maintain as receptive and open a state of awareness as possible. The facilitator needs to be in a very clear, focused, and spiritually attuned state; this is especially important because of the power of this exercise to affect the recipient's brain-mind channels and centers.

1. Quiet consciousness. Spend a few minutes relaxing and balancing individual bioenergies.

Align the consciousness with the Higher Self and any appropriate Light-realms or Light-beings with whom there is an affinity. State the intention—"activating and aligning the mind-centers with the highest Light in divine Order." Ask for protection and assistance.

2. If possible, have two crystals situated at the Alpha and Omega chakras, as described in number 2 under "The Alpha and Omega Chakras" in Chapter 9. This is important in order to obtain optimal results. The recipient visualizes and feels the crystal chakra dynamics pulsing down and around the body, fusing at the Alpha center, and then shooting straight upward through the spine and out the Omega chakra. Spend about two to three minutes with this. A slightly more advanced technique is to incorporate into this step the visualizing of spinning crystalline forms at the Alpha–Omega centers.

3. After resting for a moment after step no. 2, the recipient continues to maintain a receptive consciousness. The facilitator positions the hands with crystals pointing toward both sides of the head. Approximately 1 to 2 inches away from the skull, describe circles with the crystals that outline the entire circumference of the head on both sides in unison. The direction of the circles is forward and down over the eyes from the experiencer's perspective and the facilitator is situated in back of the recipient. Repeat this for about one to four minutes with slow, rhythmic motions while maintaining a focused and receptive state of awareness. Allow any appropriate channeled energies to flow through to the recipient.

Then describe small, faster circles at the temple regions. Gradually step up the speed of circular rotation until it peaks at the fastest possible rate. Take about one minute for this.

Now hold the crystals steady, pointing into the temple regions for 15 to 30 seconds. Rest the arms if needed, and focus awareness.

4. Position the hands with crystals pointing in toward the right and left frontal lobe areas (see Figure 23) about 1 to 2 inches away from the head. Describe circles that go in opposite directions; maintain a rhythmic unison between the right and left hands. Do this for one minute or so. Then reverse the rotational directions of the circles; the circles will still be going in opposite directions in relation to each other, but will now be going in a reverse direction from the first stage of this step. Do this for one minute. Now hold the crystals steady, pointing directly at the lobe areas. Then rest the arms and relax.

5. Repeat step 4, except direct the positions of the crystals to the right and left rear cortex areas. (See Figure 23.)

6. Next place the right hand at the medulla oblongatta with the crystal tilting slightly upward so that it is pointing at the third eye area. Also, have the left hand over the third eye zone with the crystal pointing toward the medulla oblongatta. Perform parallel rotations, both clockwise and counterclockwise, for a total of one to two minutes. Hold crystals steady for 15 to 30 seconds. Rest.

7. Place crystals on temple areas, cupping them gently on top of the skin. The crystal points are directed at the third eye center. Have the recipient focus attention on the third eye for one minute or so. Rest.
8. Working with the crystal recorder cell: The right hand is positioned over the right frontal lobe, crystal pointed in toward this region. The left hand is directly in back of the right hand, crystal pointing directly in line with the right-hand crystal. While the left hand remains stationary, the right hand rotates in two-inch to three-inch diameter circles over the right frontal lobe. Do this for 30 to 45 seconds counterclockwise and then 30 to 45 seconds clockwise. Hold crystals steady for 15 to 30 seconds. Rest.
9. Repeat step 3.
10. Repeat step 2.
11. Allow the recipient at least three to five minutes to absorb and integrate the effects of this session. When the individual opens the eyes, have them focus on the senses—sight, sound, and so on—and observe any differences compared to how they were at the beginning of the exercise. Many find an increase in clarity of perception.

After some practice with this procedure, it will flow more and more smoothly and individual rhythms will unfold. Use inner guidance to make any creative variations on the outlined exercise. This can be applied in a professional setting or between friends. In the latter case, it works well to trade off being the facilitator and recipient. This step-by-step process can be a session in and of itself, or can be a lead-in modality for other spiritual processes. This exercise infuses streams of accelerative crystal energies in conjunction with the facilitator's channeled vibrations into key brain-mind centers, thus exciting them into a higher state of energetic activity. The spiral-cone of perception is expanded to a higher quantum level so that multidimensional channels of communication are more accessible. Optimally, the two crystals used are well suited to the purpose of this procedure, are used solely for this and related techniques, and are programmed specifically for working with the mind-centers.

A few other techniques can be selectively incorporated into the step-by-step outline. One is to have the facilitator hold a crystal (preferably a double-termination) in the left hand at the recipient's Omega chakra; the right hand holds a crystal just above the top middle of the head. The left hand stays stationary and the right hand describes small circles over the head. The facilitator channels additional mind-reprogramming energies in conjunction with the technique. Another method is for the facilitator to place one crystal's largest facet over a mind-center of the recipient, one to five inches away from the skin parallel to the plane of the head. Focus channeled activation energies through the third eye region through the crystal and into the desired area. Repeat this process over each one of the mind centers. Finally, for specific work with the brain-mind tensors, the facilitator slowly and smoothly sweeps a crystal in the right hand one to six inches from the skin of the recipient in arcs, from front to back, and back to front of the head. Usually it is best to have the crystal's largest facet parallel to the plane of the skull. Start making sweeps on one side of the head, making each sweep slightly more toward the top of the head than the one before. Gradually progress to making arcs over the top of the skull and then on over to ear level of the other side.

Other Light-tools and modalities can be joined with the mind-activation techniques to excellent effect. Wands (the more directionally focused models) can be used in place of crystals alone. Select and use only the types of wands that would be suited for mind-catalyzing purposes. Many of the following helmet and crown applications, headband applications, and other techniques presented can, when used creatively and with discretion, amplify the results of the activation sessions. Also, if these procedures are done within appropriate gridworks or advanced unified energy fields, the effects will be enhanced.

CROWNS AND HELMETS

Crowns and helmets have, in various forms, been integrally linked with concepts of mind-center activation throughout the ages. Crowns of royalty and spiritual leaders, conical hats of wizards and dunces, helmets of extraterrestrials, and others all reflect the essential principles of amplifying brain-mind capacities with precise applications of sacred science. The primary idea is the creation of devices that interact in synergic union with the key mind-centers, exposing them to prescribed energy patterns and frequencies. In this way, the brain-mind can be tuned to a desired level and amplified for heightened interdimensional energy access. In *Magic of Precious Stones,* Mellie Ulydert gives a glimpse of the higher purposes of crowns. "The more precious stones one wears, the more strongly will they be charged with cosmic forces, which they will radiate out into their surroundings. That is why a monarch used to wear so many jewels, in order to turn himself into a living battery of power for the nation."[17]

Indeed, the form energy of a crown or helmet in conjunction with refined metals, precious stones, or other possible modalities can create a powerful effect in amplifying the capacities of consciousness. In the more enlightened times of the past, sacred scientists, alchemists, wizards, and the like knew the science of manifesting crowns and helmets in a wide array of variations that would "plug into" the brain-mind network, providing an amplifying intermediary between the individual and the Light-body and higher Light-realms. Today, this sacred science is being reborn toward the quickening the consciousness with precision and efficent acceleration as an integral aspect of reprogramming for the ascension.

Headbands

Headbands provide the individual with an easily accessible means to utilize crown and helmet principles in personal reprogramming, self-transformation, and interdimensional communication. Although more sophisticated headbands can be made of refined metals, the easiest way to utilize headbands is with stretchable cotton sports headbands. White is highly preferred as a color. Leather headbands are discouraged, because the animal vibration is not conducive to high-frequency brain-center work.

Crown, Helmet, and Headband Applications

1. With the headband covering the third eye, temples, and rear left and right points above the occipital ridge (see Figure 23), place the six double-terminated crystals horizontally in a circle grid so that the energy of each crystal's terminations are feeding into the next all the way around the head. Optimal placement of

the crystals is on the third eye, temples, two points above the occipital ridge, and medulla oblongatta.

2. Try a variation of the headband in number 1; position the crystals so that they are all pointing vertically up and down. A further variation is to attach 33 small, clear single-terminations at equidistant intervals around the exterior of the headband, with all terminations pointing upward.

3. Using the same placements as in numbers 1 and 2, use pyramid-faceted clear quartz in place of double-terminated crystals. For best results, the crystal pyramid need to be faceted according the Great Pyramid's angles and the size needs to be at least 1 inch at the base, with a 1½ inch base being optimal. To understand the effectiveness of using crystal pyramids in this way, refer to Chapter 12 regarding pyramidal energy dynamics. Because the pyramidal energy pulses are penetrating into the brain-mind area via the octahedral energy dynamic, a strong inductive pulse in initiated directly into the mind channels. The effect is considerable more directionally focused than with natural unfaceted quartz.

4. Experiment with different gridwork arrangements that would be logistically appropriate for use with a headband (See Chapter 14 for different grid patterns.)

5. Even if only one crystal pyramid or one unfaceted quartz crystal is available to work with for mind-center activation purposes, it is quite beneficial to position it over the third eye with a headband or first aid tape.

6. Specifically constructed crystal templates about 1½ to 1¾ inches in diameter are excellent for activation effects (see Chapter 13). If there is only one with which to work, it could be positioned at the third eye with a headband. The template could also be used on a series of mind-centers in conjunction with accompanying facilitator activation techniques. And if there were six templates, all could be placed in pertinent headband positions to great effect.

7. The "Chromatics-Lasers" section in Chapter 7 states that the laser-crystal synergy creates some highly significant coherency and amplification effects in a crystalline matrix. A majority of the most powerful and advanced mind-center activation modalities involve numerous creative variations of the laser-crystal synergy. In Figure 24, one of the more basic professional arrangements is shown. Six 1 inch base crystal pyramids are placed at the areas discussed in headband concept number 1, with the tops of the pyramids exposed through the headband so that direct laser light can be focused into them. Six frequency-tunable low power lasers are infused straight into the pyramids' apexes. A computer is programmed to project coded color sequences into each crystal pyramid. The inductive pulses and streaming crystalline energies infuse tremendous degrees of highly amplified and coherent vibratory patterns, producing profound mind-center reprogramming effeects. (Note: please use extreme caution and professional discernment in any laser-crystal-consciousness experiences—the effects are quite potent.)

If a computer-controlled six-laser set-up is not available, a variation of this concept is to use one (or more) lasers to shine the light into the crystals through fiber optics. The fiber optics can take the light from one laser, if necessary, to all six crystals.

The use of crystal templates in conjunction with professional laser set-ups is most effective. The laser excites not only the crystal matrix of the template in general but also energizes the inscribed codes so that these specialized patterns are infused into the mind-centers with considerable force and deep penetration into the brain-mind membranes.

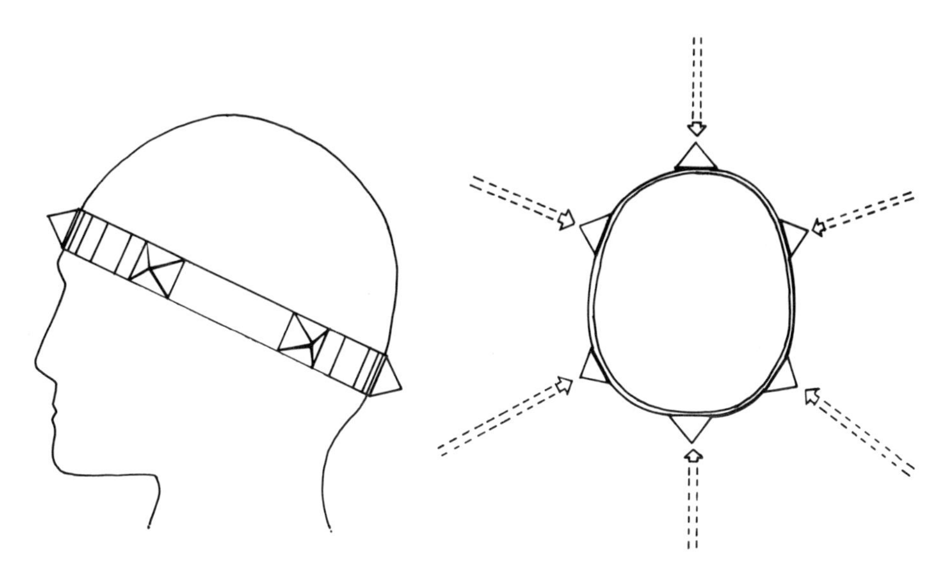

Figure 24a:
Crystal Pyramid Headband Concept

Figure 24b:
Multi-Laser Input (Top view)

For a more generally accessible variation of this theme, 1 inch base crystal pyramids can be obtained at a reasonable cost. Low-power lasers are also available for $250–$350. A regular white headband can be modified so that the pyramids stick out of the material enough to allow direct laser light to go into them. Then the facilitator spends two to five minutes focusing the laser into each crystal in turn all the way around the head. The facilitator can also focus reprogramming energies in and through the pyramids at the same time. If the laser is mounted on an adjustable framework (such as a camera stand), it can be focused onto a given area, leaving the facilitator free to perform other techniques at the same time the laser is shining into a crystal.

Even a laser focused into a single crystal pyramid or unfaceted, good-quality quartz on the third eye or crown works quite well as a step to take toward more advanced modalities.

The programmable laser scanner adds a new dimension to more advanced laser-crystal-consciousness activation techniques. Lasers can be used to create an enormous spectrum of multicolor geometric patterns, unfolding through space and time. Therefore, the laser scanner could be programmed to describe a host of mandala patterns, geometric forms, and flame letters. If such patterns were shone upon crystal templates and placed upon specific mind-centers, the effect would be one of activating a given code-pattern's structure within the crystal matrix, which would then transmit that selectively excited pattern into the mind center. If a coded template is available, the laser scanner could scan the inscription-code itself, thus reinforcing and amplifying it manyfold. Another idea: through a non-inscribed crystal template an unfolding series of mandala patterns, geometric forms, or flame letters could be programmed in a coded sequence.

It becomes clear, then, that an integral part of advanced mind-center activation modalities in basic to quite sophisticated applications of the laser-crystal synergy.

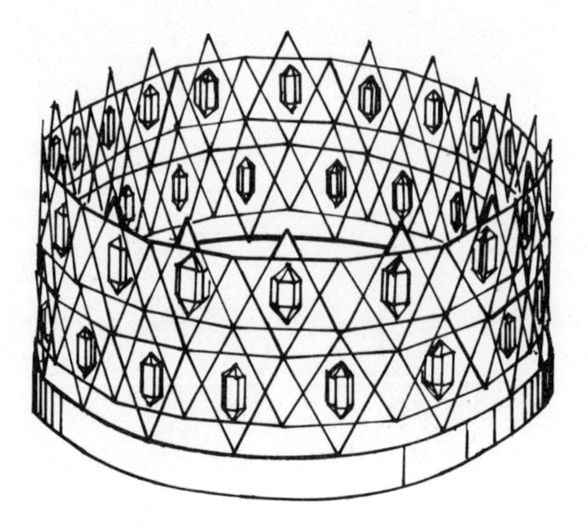

Figure 25: Star of David Crown

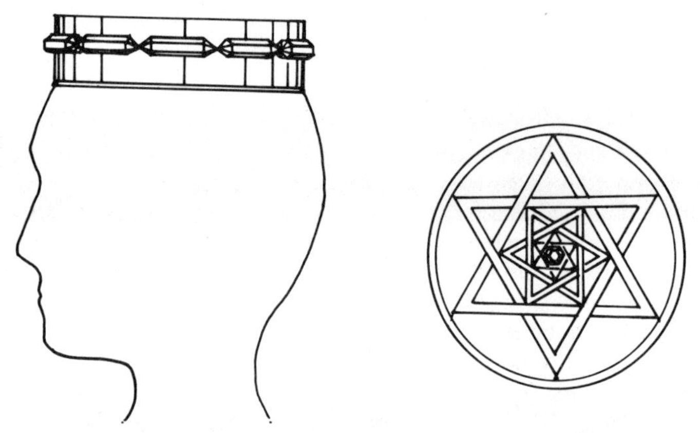

Figure 26: Star-seed Activation Crown (Top view)

Focused, coded sonics projected through templates are also powerful. The clinics of the future will certainly employ these techniques.

8. Figure 25 illustrates a double-row Star of David crown. The framework is sterling silver shaped into 17 horizontally interlinking Star of David patterns. Two such horizontal circular arrangements are placed one on top of the other to create a double Star of David crown. In addition, high-quality Herkimer "diamonds" are inset within the center of each individual Star of David and at intervals between them. The effect achieved is a potent opening of the crown of the head for much-increased interdimensional access through the resultant Pillar of Light effect. The sensation can be likened to a feeling that the lid of awareness has been opened and consciousness is set free to experience higher octaves of Light.

9. The Star of David Activation Crown, illustrated in Figure 26, is composed of three internested Star of David patterns within an encompassing circle. Notice that the nested patterning creates an inward–outward spiraling action. The Stars of

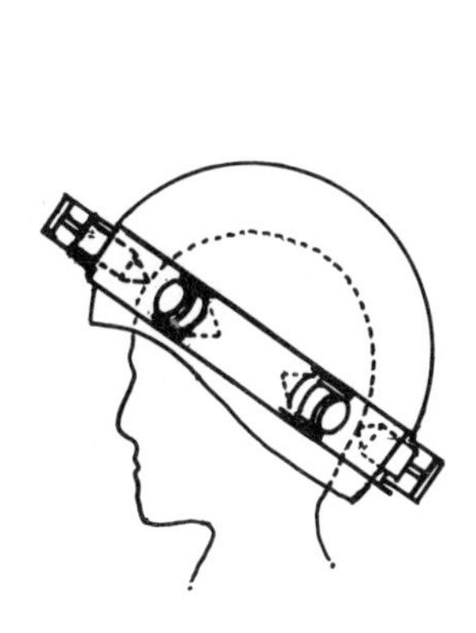

Figure 27:
Rotating Star of David Gridwork Helmet

Figure 28: Rotating Crown Device

David and surrounding circle are made of small-diameter sterling silver tubes filled throughout with tiny Herkimer "diamonds" or other types of small double-terminated quartz. Optimally there is a specifically faceted crystal situated in the center of the innermost Star of David. There is also a silver band attached underneath so that the crown may sit upon the head with stability. The primary action of this crown is to set up a spiral-current that is infused in through the crown center and into the Cave of Brahma for potent activation. There is also a spiraling-out action that amplifies interconnectedness with the Light-body. The pulse-in/pulse-out oscillation that is established as consciousness integrates with the dynamics of the crown is exceptionally activating to the Urim circuitry of the star-seed and celestial-seed. It assists greatly in their awakening process and the catalyzation of higher spiritual abilities.

10. Another variation of the crown concept, this one for use in a clinical setting, is shown in Figure 27, called the Rotating Star of David Helmet. With the recipient seated upright, a series of six horizontally rotating crystals are directed at the mind-centers in a Star of David gridwork pattern. The rotating crystals create standing wave streams of crystalline energies that are powerfully projected into the brain-center pathways. The rotational rate can be individually adjusted for each of the six crystals, and the rate can be varied to create different effects. Alternately slow-fast-slow-fast rotational speeds done in unison with all six crystals are very effective. Another possibility is to have every other crystal be fast and the other three be harmonically slower; as the fast crystals convert via harmonic increments to the slow rate, the slow crystals convert to the fast rate. Many other permutations and combinations of varying the rotating speed of the crystals can be used to create a spectrum of effects.

11. The Rotating Crown Device, illustrated in Figure 28, is yet another crown application. A number of different types of crowns could be used here; for illustration purposes, the Star of David crown described in number 8 will be used. It

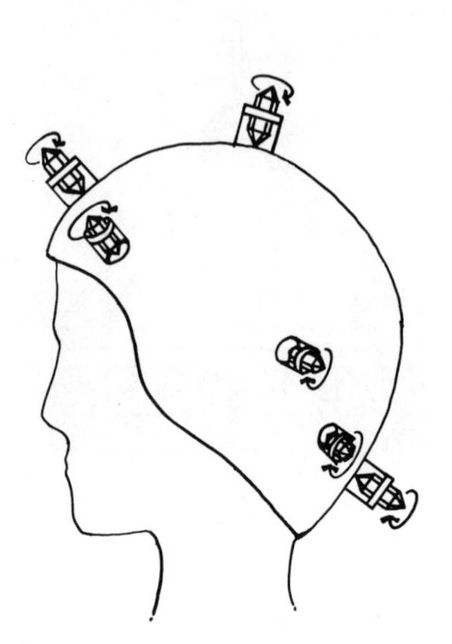

Figure 29: Rotating Crystal Helmet

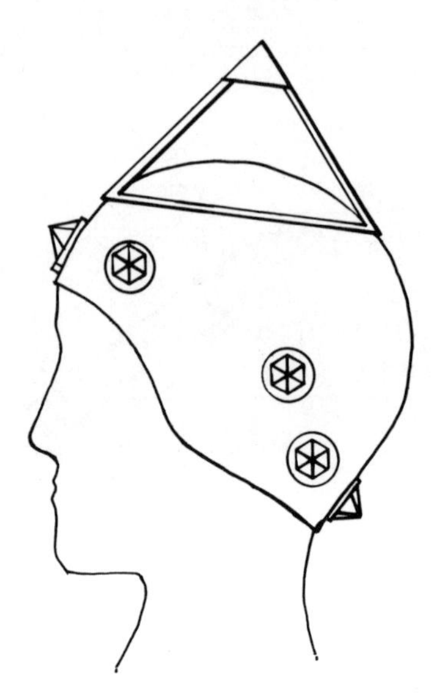

Figure 30: ''Skull Cap'' Helmet

is attached to a variable-rate rotating rod via pyramid-angled struts. If possible, the struts and rod should be silver tubing with double-terminated quartz inside. By applying this device over a mind-center zone or over the chakra areas, the rotational rate induces a geometric standing wave stream of energy to be patterned through the crown, infusing into the receptive region. By varying the rotating speed, again, the effects can be modulated. It is optimal in a professional setting to have numerous types of crown attachments so that a spectrum of Light energy patterns can be produced to suit particular needs of recipients. Crowns can be attached to the pyramid struts of the Rotating Crown Device, and detached when desired for use as a stationary crown.

12. The Rotating Crystal Helmet shown in Figure 29 demonstrates an advanced helmet application. The helmet is made of one of the more refined metals (gold, silver, copper, titanium, and so on). A rotating double-terminated crystal is positioned over each key brain center area—third eye, crown, right and left frontal and rear lobes, and left and right rear occiput points. There are holes in the helmet underneath the crystals for uninterrupted energy flow. The rotation rates are variable. In addition, it is possible to place microminiature sound speakers either next to the two mastoid processes of the skull or at the junctures between the temporal and sphenoid bones. Sonic tones designed for mind activation applied through small crystal slices may accompany the rest of the helmet's dynamics.

13. The Skull Cap helmet seen in Figure 30 is made of one or more refined metals. Over the third eye is placed a specifically faceted quartz crystal or another suitable gem (diamond is excellent here). Other faceted quartz crystals and gemstones may be positioned at various harmonic intervals around the helmet in association with the locations of mind-center zones. On top is a solid titanium pyramid having a crystal pyramid capstone whose apex reaches the Omega chakra.

This is an excellent helmet for Light-work requiring very clear, strong, and specific interdimensional access, usually technical-scientific in nature.

14. The Spiral Crystal Crown (not illustrated) has a sterling silver band (approximately 1 to 1½ inches wide) that rests upon the individual's head. A line of small, high quality double-terminations are positioned around the band at equidistant intervals (termination axes are horizontal). From the band, a phi ratio spiral band composed of sterling silver coils around and upward to a point four to five inches above the top middle of the head. Double-terminations follow the spiral upward at equidistant intervals. At the top of the spiral a double-termination is vertically aligned with the top middle of the head. The direction of the phi ratio spiral is clockwise, from the perspective of an observer looking downward at the crown. This crown is excellent for dynamizing the entire brain-mind field as a whole and is expeciallly well suited for catalyzing the reprogramming process of star-seed and celestial-seed and accessing intergalactic spectrum vehicles.

OTHER MIND-CENTER ACTIVATION TECHNIQUES

1. As the most basic technique for third eye activation, simply take a crystal in hand and rotate it counterclockwise at a distance from the forehead at which an optimal energetic interaction occurs. Repear for one to four minutes.

2. A visualization technique: Visualize a tetrahedron superimposed within the central brain-mind area and see Light-beams coming from all four apexes and meeting in the middle of the form. At this focus area is the Cave of Brahma. Visualize also a crystalline energy form within the center of focus. Maintain this visualization for three to five minutes of focused attention, with the crystalline form becoming increasingly more radiant.

3. The pictographic flame letters (see Chapter 2) are supremely effective for consciousness-catalyzing functions. Looking at and visualizing the coded flame letter chapter sequence in *The Keys of Enoch,* by J. J. Hurtak is one of the best modalities in this regard. This sequence can also be filmed and presented to consciousness along with alpha-frequency strobe light effects for even more powerful rapid-pulse imprinting of these most causal codes of creation. The filmed sequence also works well when focused onto the forehead of the recipient, who sits two to three feet from the projector.

4. A large tabular or cut-crystal template inscribed with the flame letter sequence described in number 3 can be placed in front of the face and forehead. A laser scanner then projects various geometric lattice patterns that serve to energize the flame letter codes, which are then infused into the brain-mind membranes.

5. The receiving of thought-form crystals is yet another facet of mind-center activation. See these principles and techniques in Chapter 8 under "Advanced Perspectives and Seed-Thoughts."

6. Some selections of music that, for many, are particularly effective for mind-center activation are *Angel Music* by Iasos, *Jewel* by Michael Stearns, *Crystal Rainbows* by Don Campbell, and *Hearing Solar Winds* by the Harmonic Choir.

7. A visualization: See the Star-seed Activation Crown presented in number 9 of "Crown, Helmet, and Headband Applications" in this chapter. Notice the spiraling pattern that the nested Stars of David create. Close the eyes and visualize this spiraling pattern extending into infinity. Go as far as possible with this spiral,

going into micro-infinity. Then gradually spiral out from micro-infinity to normal size and then proceed progressively into macroinfinity as far as the imagination will go. Practice pulsing back and forth between the two extremes.

8. A filmed sequence of coded color-frequency patterns created for activation of the third eye can be made. Place color gels in a variety of hues, including the seven major spectral frequencies, in slide projector slides (obtainable at any camera shop). Put the slides in a slide projector carousel and shine the colors directly into a mirror. At the angle of greatest color reflection off the mirror, have an 8 mm or super 8 movie camera positioned to record the colors. Unlimited creative possibilities arise as to the color sequencing and time duration of each color in the sequences. This will have to be channeled from the appropriate Light-realms in order to produce a color film of greatest effectiveness. The code-sequence needs to be quite precise in order to unlock the activation codes of the third eye.

Such a film can be shone directly into the third eye. The logistics of the distance need to be worked out so that the highest possible focused light intensity is applied. During the procedure, the recipient may keep the eyes closed or open, depending on comfort and intensity of the light.

Third eye activation films can be produced within general parameters for effective use with a broad spectrum of individuals. They can also be custom-made to suit the unique chakra blueprint of each person for even greater results.

12. Recall the importance of including not only the Alpha and Omega chakras in mind-center activation but also the first (coccyx) through fifth (throat) chakras. Whenever possible in utilizing activation techniques, use a set of double-terminated quartz or crystal pyramids (½ to 1½ inch) to place on all chakras in addition to the head-centered chakras and other mind centers. This will help facilitate the best possible Alpha–Omega energy dynamics, which will aid in the mind-center awakening process. If double-terminations are used, orient the terminations in line with the spinal axis.

An alternative is to use the spinal energizer (see Chapter 13) laid along the full length of the spine. Separate Alpha and Omega chakra crystals are needed in conjunction with this Light-tool.

13. For individuals working with mind-center activation alone, there are several effective techniques for aiding this process: a) Suspend one or more crystals from the ceiling with sturdy cotton string so that they are positioned in direct alignment with the mind-centers. For stabilization, it is necessary to take another length of string and tie it around the crystal and secure it to the floor. The two mind-centers of highest priority in this technique are the third eye (position crystal horizontally pointing into this region) and the crown (position crystal vertically directly over the top middle of the head). b) A pyramid can also be suspended from the ceiling so that its apex is positioned at the Omega chakra. If possible, glue a ¼ inch-base crystal pyramid at the apex. A crystal can also be suspended from the pyramid and positioned vertically over the crown chakra. c) An inverted pyramid suspended from the ceiling can be used as a holding device for a crystal directed at a desired brain-mind center. As shown in Figure 31, the inverted pyramid apex can cradle a crystal positioned horizontally so that the crystal's energy is directed straight into the mind-center. For more versatility, the pyramid can be made adjustable so that it can be positioned in a variety of heights and horizontal positions. In lieu of this, the individual can reposition himself or herself in relation

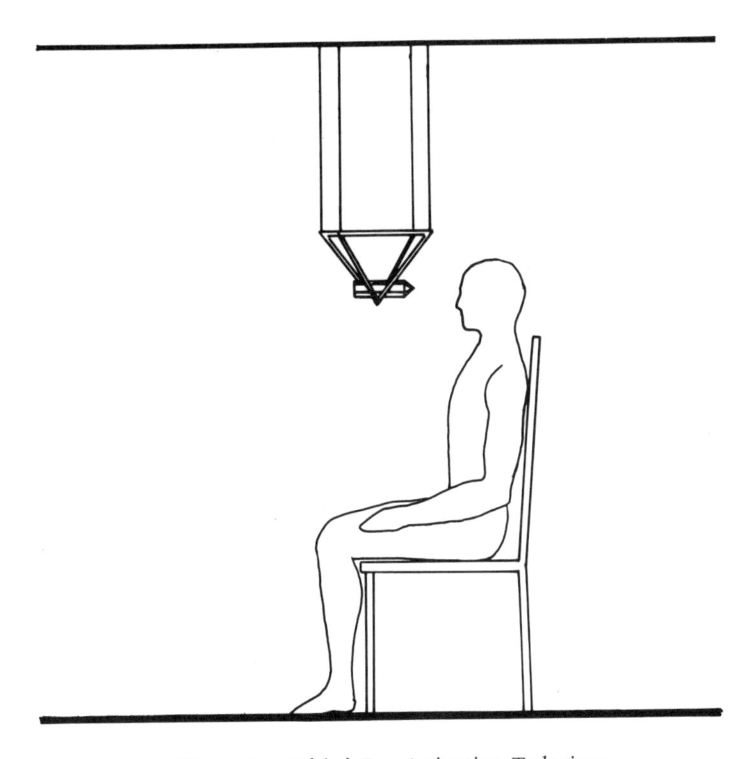

Figure 31: Third Eye Activation Technique

to the crystal in the pyramid in order to work with various brain-activation regions. d) Last, there is the classic wearing of the pyramid over the head. For optimal results, position the apex over the top middle of the skull and glue a ¼ inch-base crystal pyramid at the tip of the pyramid.

14. Another crown variation can be made with surprising ease. Clear latex tubing may be purchased at most hardware stores by the foot. Buy approximately 2 feet of ½ to ⅝ inch tubing and insert small double terminations inside the tubing so that the crystals are lined up end to end all the way around the interior. Punch a couple of holes in the plastic at both ends at the top and bottom of each. Then take some sturdy string and put it through the holes such that the ends of the tubing can be held in place together, make a "halo crown" to place directly on top of the head. A variation of this crown with single terminations is to glue small, good quality crystals on top and bottom and/or on the inner perimeter and the outer perimeter, having the crystals' terminations all pointing in one direction on top and pointing in the opposite direction on bottom (the same would apply for inner perimeter/outer perimeter termination directions).

15. Various Color Ray Crowns could be made this way: Obtain refined metal banding about 1½ inches in width and bend it to make a circle to fit on top of

the head. Toward the bottom border glue small, good quality double-terminations so that each crystal's terminations are aligned horizontally with all the others'. If only single terminations are available, two rows can be made in place of one, having one row with the terminations all pointing in one direction and the row above it having the terminations pointing in the opposite direction. Depending on which color Ray is desired, obtain as many gems and precious stones of a particular color as possible; for example, with the Green Ray, obtain such stones as emerald, malachite, peridot, green beryl, moldavite tektite, and so on. These minerals need to be in a faceted or polished state if their natural crystalline shape is not present. Toward the top of the metal banding, glue or inlay these minerals all around the circumference of the metal banding. Lastly, put a 1 inch base quartz pyramid over the area where the crown will be placed over the third eye. The crown will be a specific interdimensional access tool, to interconnect with a wide profile of a given color Ray. Numerous such crown variations are possible.

In sum, then, the discipline of mind-center activation is a cornerstone of the reprogramming process as a whole. The specialized focus is upon activating the singularly important brain-mind pathways to encompass higher dimensional aspects of the Light-body Urim circuitry. In so doing, higher quotients of the Universal Mind become one with the individual human mind and quantumly increasing hyperintelligence capabilities dawn. The sacred science of mind-center activation is an integral component of the current individual and collective reprogramming process. As the field matures, highly specialized and sophisticated unified energy field facilities will manifest through those Light-scientists with appropriate spiritual authority and knowledge toward effects currently unimagined.

CHAPTER 11

Form Energy and Crystals

Form energy dynamics are an integrally intrinsic aspect of crystals' vibrational functioning. From the microscopic molecular levels to the macroscopic exterior conformation, the angular proportionality of crystalline structures in a primary determinant of energetic capacities and characteristics. Every angle in relation to other angles in an integrated crystal form plays a contributory role in the collective numerological-geometrical equation that that form is. Interdimensional access factors and vibrational processing parameters are both a reflection of this exacting equation. Crystalline forms are particularly valuable in this regard because of their high structural stability and energetic regularity. The function of crystalline matrices is to replicate the causal abstract geometrics of the Universal Mind, thus serving to provide a stable matrix of interdimensional continuity and ordered energetic interactions. The highest aspects of physical-plane crystal form energetics is as geometry-specific multidimensional access linkages and as numerological tools of defined energetic parameters.

Numerological-angular proportionality is the quintessential substratum-matrix of manifestation; *All is angle.* Integrated angularity, manifesting as correlative geometrics is, in essence, the sole determinant of indexed vibrational differentiation through the Universal Mind. To change the angular proportion is to alter the modality of crystallization and the subsequent energetic profile. For example, the sole difference between any given element in the Periodic Chart of the Elements is its angle of crystallization into matter, reflective of its originating abstract axis code-patterns within the causal domains of Light. The angle of materialization further determines into what kind of crystalline substance a Light-code pattern will precipitate. Herein the causal seed-crystal code-pattern replicates itself, causing a material-plane mirrored manifestation whose every matrix angle is a direct derivative.

Each crystallographic substance—quartz and the many others—has its own unique angular coalescence, mirroring its higher dimensional crystallographic correlates. The combination of a crystal's intrinsic axis-code (namely, the 7 crystal systems and 32 crystal classes) and its unique matter-matrix attributes (that is, the physical substance of which it is composed) determine the specific spectrum profile of interdimensional resonant affinity and the distinct parameters of earth-plane energy dynamics. Every kind of crystallographic material has a clearly defined spectrum profile that delineates the precise limits of vibrational interactions of which it is capable. That is to say, silver, emerald, blood crystals, garnet, DNA, titanium, and so on are each operative within exact parameters of universal physics. There is some parametric overlapping, but the distinctive profile of each is singular. Therefore, each crystalline matrix-type is applicable to a defined range of energy interactions, that is to say, *form and substance determine use*. The extensive array of crystalline materials occurrent to the earth-plane provide a spectrum of "tools" through which individual-specific vibrational tasks may be enacted.

Because of the less refined aspects of the earth's overall energy field, many crystalline substances do not actualize into their ideal geometric form as they materialize into solid matter under natural growth conditions. The geometrical aspects of the molecular levels still abide, but the exterior conformation lacks planar definition, growing instead into amorphous shapes. Examples include diamonds, rubies, emeralds, rose quartz, and numerous others. In such cases, the full energetic potential has yet to be realized because the form energy dynamics intrinsic to the higher aspect of its functioning lack complete definition because of the amorphous exterior shape. The ideal crystalline geometric patterns that would manifest under more optimal growth conditions are inhibited in various ways by planetary energy field factors. Skilled faceting by human hands in these cases can assist in the actualization of the fullest potential of the crystalline matrices.

Other types of crystallographic substances grow with fully developed planar surfaces and terminated faceting patterns, quartz being a common example of this circumstance. In these instances, the exterior geometrics are a direct macroscopic reflection of the internal microscopic molecular patternings. In fact, the angular relationships of the outer structure provide the geometric keys to decoding the exact equation of each crystal's specialized vibrational coding-patterns, and hence its parameters of functioning and highest modes of application. Far from being a secondary by-product of the crystallization process, the exterior conformation visibly illuminates the crystal's innermost workings, even unto the subtlest nuances. Because of this, except under circumstances described later in this chapter, human-derived faceting has little to no place in altering the integrated, Light-derived order inherent to such crystalline forms.

In both cases—amorphous matrices faceted into their ideal forms and naturally grown crystal structures—the angular configuration is a most important determinant of a specific crystal's energetic capacities and characteristics. The individual and collective angles establish ratios and proportions of energy and its formulation, release, and application. A major aspect of these dynamics is founded upon the principles of interdimensional access. Earlier chapters in Part I (especially Chapter 4) showed that gaining intercommunication with any given sector of the Universal Mind requires that geometrically-mathematically based codes of access-gateways be fulfilled before entry into the sector is possible. A given crystalline form is a numerological–geometric code by virtue of its particular matrix-substance in conjunction with the exterior angular form. Through the principle of interdimensional harmonic resonance the specific crystal is interlinked with those sectors of the Universal Mind whose access-codes the specific crystal embodies. This concept is amplified by the following quotations:

> Every form is the manifestation of the force that has built it. Thus every form is the image of the creative force that builds it and dwells within it.[1]

> It is as if the form itself provides a structure through which an ever-present energy is intensified.[2]

> Sacred geometric forms are vehicles to become a channel through which the earth could receive the abstract, cosmic life of the hevens.[3]

The other complementary means by which angles determine form energy dynamics concerns principles of *internal form resonance.* The outer form encloses a space delineated by its angles; this geometric space is composed of an energy-responsive crystalline matrix. This space operates in a manner similar to resonant cavities, wherein vibrations undergo standing wave interference dynamics; examples include a pipe organ, violin body, and brain ventricle. In the case of the crystal, there is no empty cavity as in resonant cavity dynamics; instead, there is a highly ordered, homogeneous matrix of oscillatingly responsive vibrational units. The crystal's exterior angles form a surrounding semipermeable barrier that serves to sustain the vibrational form integrity. In similar manner to resonant cavities, the resultant standing wave patterns reflect the configuration of the exterior form. To further illustrate this concept:

> The Egyptian architects were well aware, too, that enclosed spaces create vibrational patterns. Just as the wooden box-frame of a violin is designed to amplify and add to the sound of its vibrating strings, so the chambers, rooms, walled gardens and sanctuaries of the Egyptian Temples were built to both create and enhance a wide range of vibratory frequencies. . . . In healing Temples the architecture of the enclosed spaces vibrated to the auric field of a well balanced human body and its organs. . . . In temples utilized for meditation and initiation, chambers and isolation cells produced wavelengths attuned to the mind in the alpha and theta states, aiding in the experiences. To the Egyptians, energy/form architecture was a most exact science—simply by adding a niche here, an open doorway there, a recess in a wall, a column, a border, or a ceiling block, they knew how to change the frequency pattern of any space, to produce or amplify any desired effect.[4]

In parallel manner, the angular "niches," "recesses," and other geometric parameters of a crystal form generate an internal resonance pattern that mirrors its particular geometric conformation. It is this internal resonance pattern that establishes the earthly energetic "foundation" with which the higher dimensional access energies phase lock, thereby creating a state of interdimensional harmonic resonance and resultant interconnection.

Overall, every crystalline form is a materialized numerological-geometrical equation whose formula is a composite of its crystallographic system and any individual variations within the parameters of its class. Just as all snowflakes have an underlying hexagonal structure but manifest in innumerable variations on this archetypal theme, so too crystals materialize in a given crystallographic class, but many variations are possible within such parameters. Quartz is an excellent example—no two naturally occurring quartz crystals are exactly the same, yet all abide by the strict geometrics of the hexagonal crystal system. Within each crystallographic system and class the formulated angles crystallize within set spectral limitations; thus the correlating system-class equation has predetermined parameters. Within these boundaries, variations and subvariations may occur, each embodying a distinct numerological-geometrical equation. This equation describes the crystal's energetic potentials and dynamics down to the minutest detail. On the more sophisticated levels of sacred crystal science, the blueprint-equation of any crystal can be determined with great precision, and can therefore be applied with discernment in optimal application modes.

The intention of this chapter is to present highlighted perspectives in the discipline of crystal form energy and seed-ideas with regard to natural quartz crystals and human-faceted quartz. Sacred crystal science is yet in a fledgling state, calling for much research and development toward an indexed exactitude that lays the foundation for Light-based technologies and other application modalities beyond current dreams.

NATURAL QUARTZ FORM VARIATIONS

The hexagonal crystal system forms the invariable axis orientation pattern for all quartz crystals. As discussed in Chapter 7, the Law of the Constancy of Angles related to quartz's fixed body-to-body and body-to-termination angles, 120° and 141°, respectively. Yet within such limitations, infinite variety unfolds in nature. Each individual quartz has a Light-derived, inherent category of optimal usage that relates to its equation. *Windows of Light* (Baer & Baer, pp. 54–59) delineates 16 categories, or application modalities, into which crystals fall by virtue of their innate molecular code-patterning and exterior geometric conformation. It would logically follow that every category would have an outer structure pattern with certain traits that would reflect the particular category-equation of which it is a part. This is so; however, due to the fledgling nature of crystal science, only some basic generalities are as yet possible. In Figure 32 to Figure 44 some of the basic form types of the quartz family are explored.

Before this, though, perspectives as to the functional dynamics of the crystal's body and termination will help establish a further groundwork of understanding.

What is the effect of the crystal's six facets? Endless mathematical formulas, geometric finalization, and focusing micromodulated coherence.

What is the effect of the crystal's six body faces? Resonant amplification, precursive processing, and columnar standing wave formation.

The crystal body is an ordered mixing chamber wherein energy dynamics formulate in patterns that are then processed into the terminated end. It is the crystal's six facets, individually and collectively, that perform the most exact final energetic formulation and focused emission. The termination to the body is as the brain-mind is to the bioenergetic system; it is the termination that sets the crystal's most vitally essential code-patterns in place, through which vibrational input is correspondingly processed. The inward sloping of the six facets toward the tip region sensitively qualifies the energy flow with the precise combinative geometrics of the facets' singular and multiply interactive patternings. The quartz matrix encompassed within the terminated region is integrally complementary to this process, as its structural order mirrors that of the exterior facets. Altogether, the entire termination is a specific equation that impresses its functions upon incoming body-processed energetics and formulates it into an encapsulated, highly focused state of coded coherency that is emitted from the facets and tip.

It would be possible today to perform research that enumerates the termination geometrics in an equational format; performed with thousands of crystals, this would provide a significant indexing of distinct crystal categories. A mathematician with the appropriate computer equipment could carry out such a project. The idea would be to measure very possible angle incorporated into the six facets. The 141° body-to-facet angle would not be significant in this regard. The interfacet angles are necessarily identical and would be included in the equations as a constant feature. All other angularities would be measured exactly. Each single facet would create a distinct representational equation. These equations would then be combined as a sixfold collectivity and in all combinatory possibilities. The total equational input would then be reduced to a "lowest common denominator" equation—this would be the numeric designation of a crystal that would describe its keynote energetic properties. When thousands of such trials had been enacted, the resulting equations would form groupings of crystals with related energetic properties. It would then be necessary to experiment with each grouping to find its optimal usage pattern; the usage category of each crystal grouping would then become known. Once a formal index was created, any quartz crystal could be analyzed and its category discovered quickly and with a high degree of precision.

Though the range of hexagonal system form variations throughout the quartz kingdom is limitless, certain general group-types can be delineated. In Figure 32 to Figure 44 some broadly defined shape-groups along with basic thoughts concerning their energy dynamics and types of corresponding application modalities are presented. This is offered as a beginning point, helping to heighten focused awareness regarding the relationship between crystal form and correlating function. There is considerably more knowledge to be developed in this regard, especially along more scientific lines. For the present, a fundamental outline will serve to stimulate further focused cognizance and investigation.

Symmetrical vs. Asymmetrical Form

The majority of crystals are of a symmetrical configuration, but a few have unusual formation asymmetries. Figure 33 to Figure 44 show the symmetrical variety, and Figure 32 shows an asymmetrical type.

Symmetrical crystals are generally characterized by an equilibrating action within a normal range of crystal dynamics. The qualifying effect of the termination processes energy flow without radical deviation in a harmonically counterpoised manner.

Asymmetrical crystals are "faceted" by nature in a highly specialized, harmonically eccentric fashion. Angular asymmetries set up unusual counterpoints of energetic interchange, coalescing into a specific vibrational geometrization whose patterning deviates radically from the more normal range of symmetrical energy dynamics. Assymmetrical crystals especially need to be applied in modes that correspond exactly with their unique flow patterns, for they are highly specialized tools.

Left- and Right-Handed Crystals

Virtually all naturally grown quartz crystals are a mixture of right- and left-handed molecular spiral patterns. This is because the great majority of quartz is interiorly multiply twinned. Even most crystals appearing exteriorly to be a single crystal are actually an intermixture of numerous crystals that were subsumed during the growth process.

Figure 33 and Figure 34 illustrate crystals with an auxiliary facet in addition to the ever present six major facets that is an indicator that a quartz is either right-handed or left-handed. The lozenge-shaped auxiliary facet depicted here is termed an *x* facet, and depending upon whether it is located on the left- or right-hand side of its adjoining major facet, the crystal is a left- or right-handed crystal. (Sometimes there is also an *s* facet directly below the *x* facet.) This means that the molecular spirals within the crystal turn in either a clockwise (left-handed) or counterclockwise (right-handed) direction as viewed looking directly into the termination along the *c* axis. As noted before, it is not common to find crystals that are solely right- or left-handed; most are mixtures of both. The *x* facet therefore indicates in most instances a predominance of one direction of molecular spiraling or another (sometimes there are two *x* facets facing opposite each other at different points about the termination, indicating both spiral directions). All crystals, whether they have the *x* facet indicator or not, do necessarily have right or left-handed molecular spiraling (or both); it is not always the case, however, that a predominantly left- or right-handed crystal will indicate its internal molecular patterning in this way. At present, the only means by which the predominant handedness of a crystal can be determined if an *x* facet is not present is by intuitive or radiesthesic means, or by laboratory optical analysis.

A left-handed crystal has a stronger tendency to ingather energy and to maintain it within interior matrix standing wave patterns. It is, therefore, often good for use as an energetic receiver-accumulator. A right-handed crystal, on the other hand, has a greater propensity to actively emit energy flow. Such crystals, therefore, often serve well as projective tools.

The handedness of a crystal is one factor among others to be taken into account when judging optimal usage patterns. Additional form factors discussed in the following text must also be taken into account to gain a more complete picture.

Long Versus Short Bodies

As previously discussed, the body of a crystal serves a number of important adjunctive purposes in processing and amplifying energetics in preparation for final formulation within termination dynamics. In general, the longer the body and the greater the clarity and mass, the greater the amplification. A longer body also allows for a higher degree of versatile energy input and modulation potential. In most sophisticated crystal application modalities, the body length is an important factor in establishing exactly determined standing wave patterns that accord precisely with the overall crystal dynamics. With natural quartz this degree of sophistication is manytimes not possible. In any case, this factor should be kept in mind when determining whether to have part of a crystal's base sawed off, and if so, exactly where the cut should be made.

This is not to say that crystals with short bodies cannot be powerfully effective tools, for indeed they can be, especially when the most important aspect of the crystal—the termination—is relatively undamaged and of high quality.

Equally Sized Triangular Facets Joining at a Single Tip

Figure 35 illustrates an idealized example of a crystal with all six facets being of fairly equal size and intersecting at a single point at the termination tip. Crystals fulfilling such conditions perfectly are rare. The figure is useful in that it illustrates

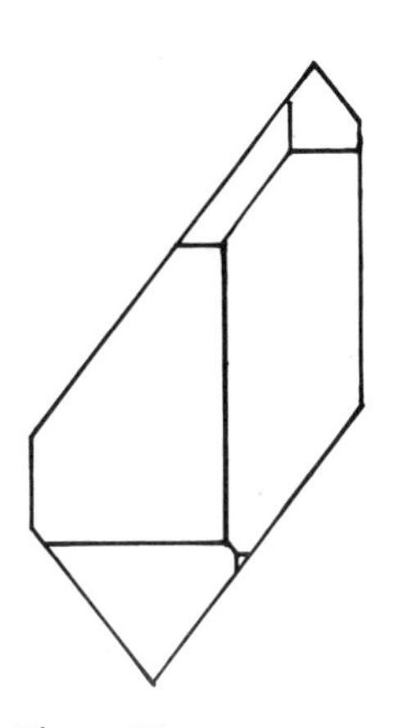

Figure 32:
Assymetric Crystal Type

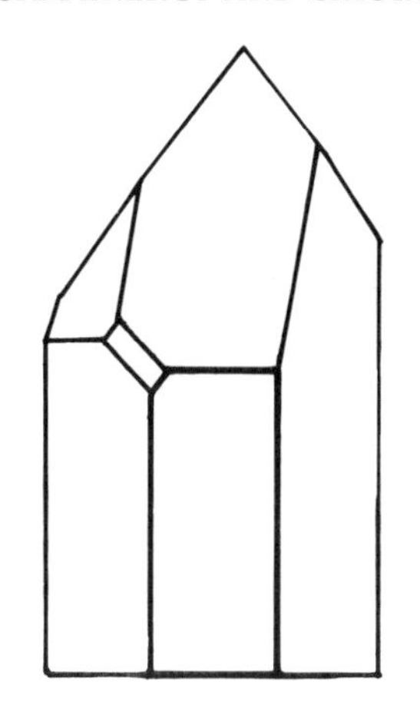

Figure 33:
Left-handed Crystal

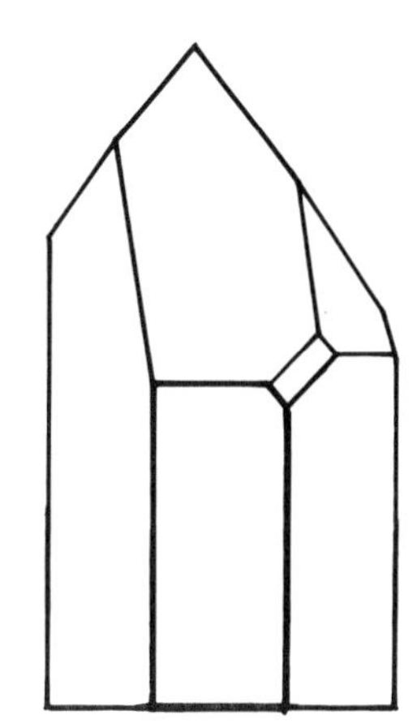

Figure 34:
Right-handed Crystal

a general form-type wherein there is relative equality of sides that tend to intersect at a common area on the termination's top region. The keynote energy dynamic here is balance. The equality of the facets' size and shape processes energy flow with a high degree of equilibrium. This sixfold symmetry culminates at the crystal tip in an exceptionally well-focused, balanced coherence. The emitting beam is laserlike in its collimation and intensity. Such crystals are excellent for uses requiring a precision of directional focus, such as auric surgery, or an equilibrating of consciousness projected within the crystal.

Alternating Large and Small Facets

In figure 36 a crystal is diagrammed having large, equally sized *r* facets alternating with small, equally sized *z* facets. This diagram shows an extreme example of this form-type. Most crystals in this category have a less dramatic (yet significant) difference of size between the *r* and *z* facets. As with the crystal-type seen in Figure 35, the energetics occur in a balanced way because of the equality of proportion and the intersecting of *r* facets at a single point at the crystal tip. In

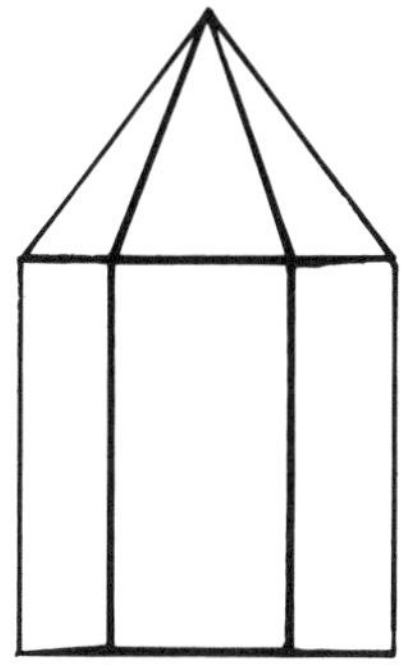

Figure 35:
Equally Sized Facets

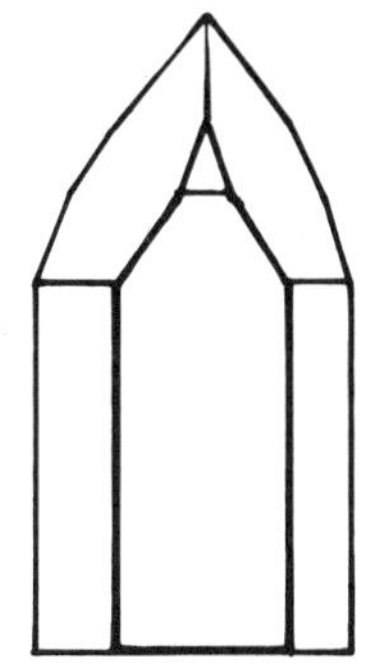

Figure 36:
Alternating Large and Small Facets

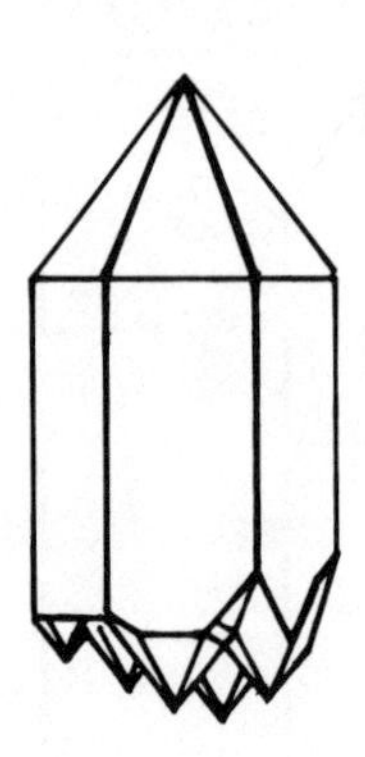

Figure 37: Double Termination with Multiple Terminations at One End

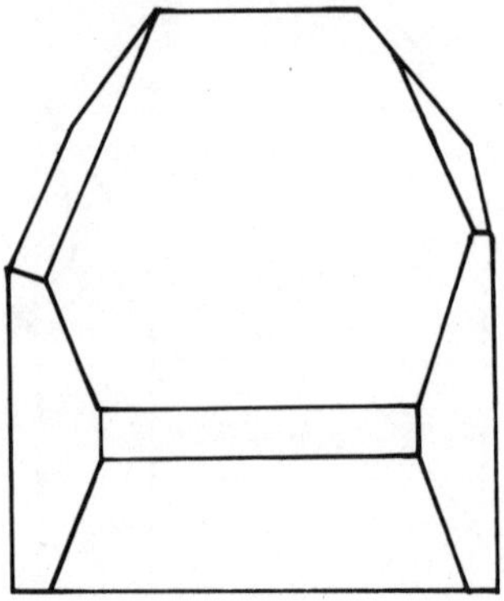

Figure 38: One Large Facet, Five Small Facets

this instance, there is considerably more sheer energetic power generated than with Figure 35-type crystals. In addition, the emitting beam has a larger diameter and more forcefulness but has less refined balance and tightness of focus than the Figure 35 crystal. These crystals work well as power rods, energy rods, and projective wands, as well as being exceptionally equilibrated amplifiers of interdimensional communication. Results are optimal with a long, relatively clear body.

Double-Termination with Multiple-Terminations at One End

A double-termination with one end having a single point and the other end having multiple-terminations as shown in Figure 37 can be a useful tool for harmonically combining several different frequencies into an integrated whole. The idea is to subprogram each termination (or groups of terminations) at the multiple-terminated end with different harmonically related frequencies (for example, different colors, sounds, and so on). As energy flow processes from the multiply terminated end, several different vibrational streams are set in motion through the crystal's body. These streams interact to certain degrees through the length of the body but their final integrative formulation occurs at the single-terminated end, where the separate energies are combined into a unified vibrational "chord." This resultant chord emission may then be applied in a desired context. Because of the large surface area of the multiple-terminated end, this type of crystal is especially responsive to applied sonics.

One Large Facet, Five Small Facets

The type of crystal illustrated in Figure 38 has a single dominating facet surrounded by five small facets. The main energy emissions flow through this single large facet, making this crystal-type particularly useful for direct body surface applications in healing, third eye activation, and the like.

Long, Thin Crystals

Crystals like the one shown in Figure 39, having a long, thin body terminating in a small faceted end are less oriented to power applications and more oriented

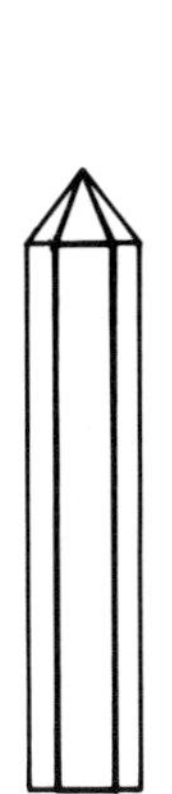

Figure 39:
Long, Thin Crystal Type

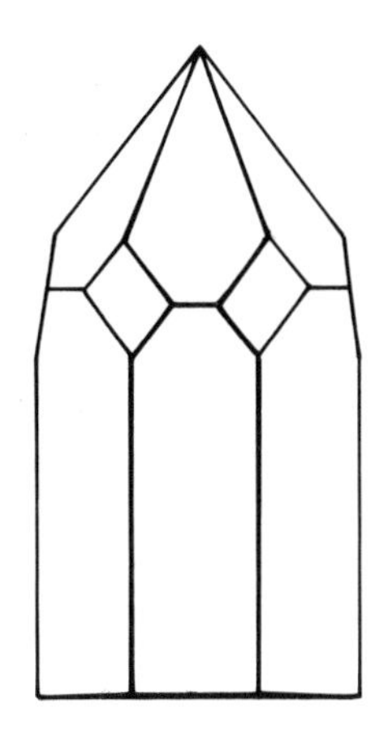

Figure 40:
''Diamond'' Facets

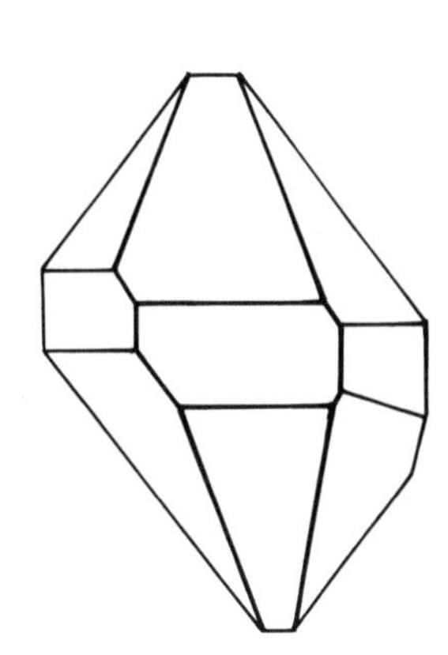

Figure 41:
Herkimer ''Diamond'' Quartz

to a refined formulation and release of energetics. As discussed in the preceding section entitled ''Long Versus Short Bodies,'' the long body allows for considerable inputting, modulating, and formulating of energy flow. In this case, the thinness of the body is not suited to high amplification factors, but is suited to refined subtlety of energy interactions. The emissions are specialized and tightly focused, with rarefied and finely tuned characteristics.

Diamond Facets

A certain form of auxiliary facet, as illustrated in Figure 40 has the shape of an equilateral parallelogram, and is called a ''diamond'' facet. In addition to the ideal shape, many variations of this facet occur as they slant slightly to either side or the sides are slightly less than equilateral, as seen in the illustration.

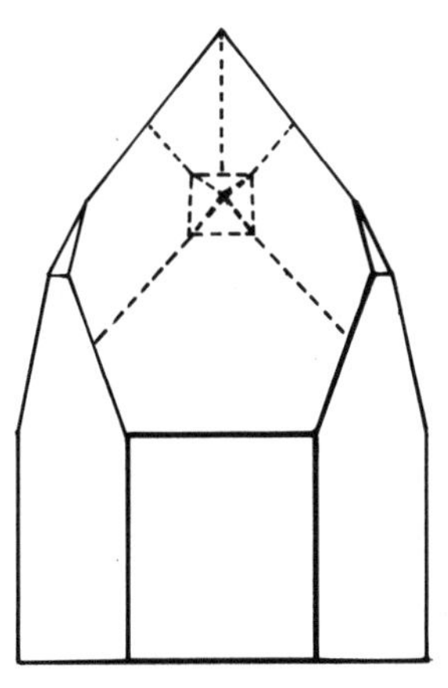

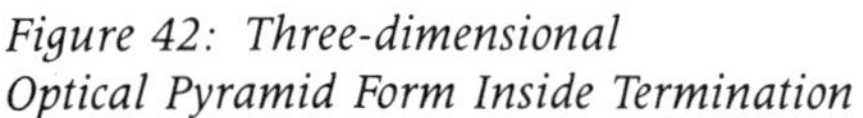

Figure 42: Three-dimensional
Optical Pyramid Form Inside Termination

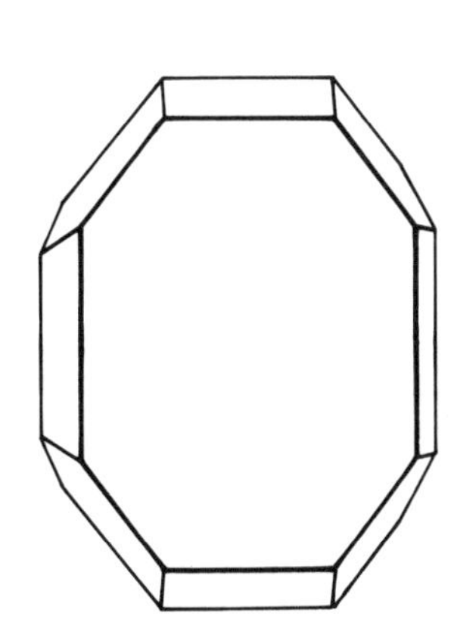

Figure 43: Tabular Crystal Type

This particular facet is significant in that it keys the dynamics happening within the termination, making the crystal an exceptionally particularized tool. This "window of Light" interacts with the angular configuration of the termination as a whole, functioning as a seed-crystal as it provides the capstone angle-code to the dynamics of the entire crystal in specifically corresponding ways, creating precise interdimensional access parameters. This crystal-type is so specialized that its access-codes must match exactly with a particular person's access orientation to be optimally useful. Best results are obtained when consciousness is projected into the crystal through the diamond facet. Diamond-faceted crystals serve as keys into exact sectors of the Universal Mind, and signify one of the most rarefied groupings in the entire quartz kingdom.

Herkimer Diamonds

Quartz originating from Herkimer County, New York, has a unique habit, or characteristic shape formation. As seen in Figure 41, the ratio of the body length to the termination lengths is quite small, considerably smaller than any other geographically specific type of quartz. The overall form is relatively short and thick-bodied. This, in addition to the Herkimer "diamonds' " other unique properties of forming very high percentages of double-terminations and having a higher hardness factor than any other quartz (7.5), makes these crystals one of the premier tools of the mineral domain. The shape plus the aforementioned factors predispose the Herkimer diamond to having very high frequency capacities and a quite versatile energy formulation range. Though they can be applied in a wide spectrum of uses, reprogramming, interdimensional communication, and chakra activation (especially the third eye and crown centers) are among their most effective application modalities.

Three-Dimensional Optical Pyramids within Crystal Terminations

Figure 42 demonstrates a remarkable occurrence manifesting in some crystals with particular facet interrelations. As one looks through a larger size facet, a three-dimensional four-sided pyramid appears at the opposite side of the termination. This pyramid looks as though it has the same geometric shape as the Great Pyramid, and occurs in crystals with a large facet on one side and a small facet on the other, as in Figure 36.

The pyramidal optical dynamics indicate that a like-dynamic occurs with subtle energetic flow. In yet another way, as with the 51° angle integral to the termination (see "Crystal Fundamentals" in Chapter 7) the pyramidal geometry interacts with quartz crystal. As a result, in those crystals having this additional pyramidal dynamic, a greater harmonic link-up with universal pyramidal form energy is stimulated. For modalities utilizing pyramidal energies—either physically or higher dimensionally—this type of crystal establishes a particularly responsive and amplified interconnection.

Tabular Crystals

Crystals with a flattened configuration, like that shown in Figure 43, are called tabular crystals. The unusual shape makes the crystal's dynamics deviate from the norm. As previously noted, asymmetrical crystals generate singular vibrational patterns. So too with the flattened asymmetry of the tabulars. Each is a single, unique "note" of a vibrational scale. The intrabody dynamics are more significant than in most other crystal form-types. Tabulars make excellent repositories of encoded information or sophisticated code-patterns. Each different tabular will only hold that information that synchronizes with the unique crystal's energy dynamics. In addition, tabulars make superb natural templates that can be inscribed with specific Light-symbols and packed with gold for chakra system healing and reprogramming applications (see "Crystal Templates" in Chapter 13). Further, these crystals are especially responsive to applied sonics, making them fine tools for a variety of healing applications.

HUMAN-FACETED CRYSTAL FORM VARIATIONS

The human hand can imbue the crystal kingdom wtih heightened idealization by discerningly modifying its geometric form to correspond with archetypal universal order. As previously noted, many times crystallographic substances do not grow into their correlating ideal universal forms because of inhibiting factors within the planetary energy field. Emeralds, diamonds, rubies, topaz, alexandrite, and so on do not crystallize into the geometric patterns of their originating Thought-form in the Universal Mind (except in rare instances). Under optimal growth conditions, they would inevitably do so in accordance wtih the laws of universal physics. The divinely guided hand of a human can rectify this earthly situation by facilitating the last stage of crystal "growth"—the faceting and polishing of crystalline substances in concordance with their divine blueprint.

The standard faceting patterns of orthodox gemology are a decent starting point for facet work. The higher blueprints are already common crystallographic knowledge. The foundation of sacred crystallographic science is the 7 crystal systems and the 32 crystal classes. These are the very axis-code blueprints of the Universal Mind. See Chapter 4 for further explication. Within the encompassing parameters of these keystone axis-codes are legions of other crystallographic differentiation patterns; every crystallographic substance has a precisely corresponding ideal pattern of crystallization. Figure 44 demonstrates a few such examples of the specific prototypal pattern of each crystal species. (There are in many such cases two or more prototypal patterns for a given crystal species and further derivations thereof. Detailed discussion along these lines exceeds the purview of this text, and will be presented in more technical texts to come.) Herein lies the optimal blueprints of the faceting patterns for each type of crystalline substance. Harmonically proportional variations and derivations of these primary prototypal patterns provide the crystallographic index for achieving specific energetic variations upon the foundational prototypal theme. Such an index has yet to be reborn as an integral aspect of sacred crystal science. At present, the faceting of crystalline matrices into their primary ideal forms is the best guideline to follow in order to actualize their fullest potential within the patterns of divine order.

Guidelines for Altering Natural Quartz

A different set of guidelines applies to crystals that grow into planar crystalline formations in nature. The natural crystalline forms reflect their causal patterning as formulated as Thought-forms in the Universal Mind. Their specific faceted

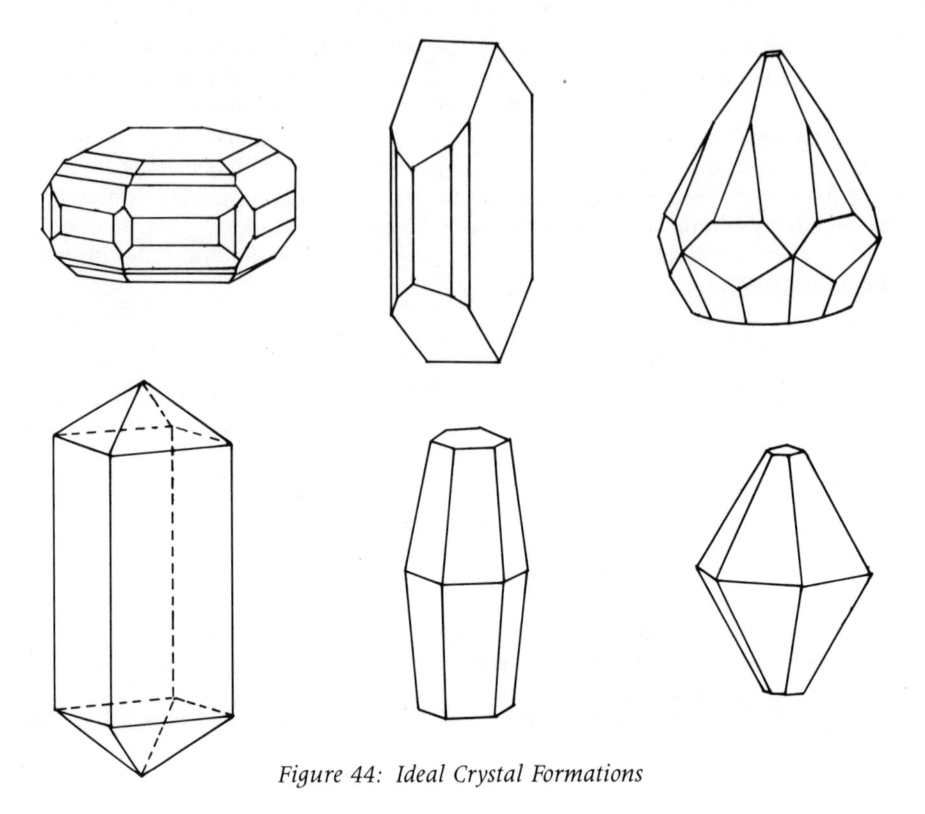

Figure 44: Ideal Crystal Formations

conformation and overall structuring is as it is intended to be within the patterns of divine order. To alter this innate perfection, except within prescribed guidelines, is to impose lesser human-derived patternings rather than accepting and respecting Spirit-derived ordering.

With this principal guideline in mind, it is necessary to explore the parameters by which judgments are made concerning whether a given crystal may be modified within divine order. In a perfect world such judgments would be simple and clear. But in today's world much damage occurs to crystals through rough mining practices, nonoptimal professional handling procedures, and accidents. Such damage can somewhat or totally neutralize a crystal's inherent divinely intended highest pattern of usage. Depending upon the extent of the damage, various courses of action may then be taken as appropriate. General guidelines follow that will help the individual in deciding what options are appropriate. This material is specifically applied to quartz crystals, though the basic guidelines apply to other types of naturally faceted minerals.

Not many quartz crystals do not have at least some damage-caused chips and other physical imperfections. From this baseline, there is a broad range of degrees of damage that crystals have. In deciding whether any given crystal needs to be altered by faceting, polishing, tumbling, or another method, it is important to evaluate the degree to which the physical damage has adversely affected the energy dynamics. The most energy-sensitive region of a quartz is the termination, the tip being the most crucial aspect of the termination. The body is quite secondary to the termination in this regard. Each crystal is an individual case, for with one the slightest chip to the termination may totally neutralize its highest level of functioning, while in another a fair-sized chunk may be missing but the energy dynamics may still be largely retained. Any damage to the termination results in a reduction of effectiveness; the main point of discernment lies in evaluating to what extent such damage has affected the energy dynamics. Such discernment, at this point in time, can only be done by intuitive or radiesthesic/radionic means.

A number of different options may be taken should significant damage to a crystal occur. If the particular crystal still has a basic integrity of form and functional energetics, though less than its former level, most often the best option is simply to leave it as it is and utilize it in a way by which beneficial results may be obtained, albeit in a less optimal mode. For example, say that a precision healing crystal was dropped and significantly damaged, thus losing its effectiveness as an effective healing tool. In most cases, except with extreme damage, this crystal can still be used as a gridwork crystal, to make crystal water, as an environment harmonizer, and so on. In most cases, this is the best choice when confronted with such a situation. Too, many crystals have already been damaged enough to lose their higher functions before an individual acquires them. Such crystals can still be put to good use in more general applications, as in the examples just mentioned.

In considerably fewer cases, if an exceptionally powerful and specialized crystal tool has been damaged and loses its higher usages, it may be possible for a gemologist to do polishing or faceting repair work. Such attempts need to maintain the original angular conformation as much as possible; even small deviations from the original geometry will not manifest the desired results. Removing or polishing as little of the crystal as possible will increase the potential for success. Such repair attempts are many times hit or miss propositions: sometimes the crystal may regain a high percentage of its original effectiveness; other times it can still be used as it was originally, but will not be as effective; and yet other times the crystal is a shadow of what it once was, necessitating its use in other, more general modes.

It is emphasized that the faceting or polishing of quartz should not be done except under certain prescribed circumstances, and when done, needs to be performed with a high degree of knowledge, skill, and precision. The example just discussed is one case in which a special crystal is minimally and discerningly repaired. In cases other than this, with crystals that have a basic integrity of form and fundamental usefulness, it is the authors' perspective that no polishing, faceting, or tumbling should be performed such that it affects the predominating energetic dynamics. Polishing or sawing the very bottom of a crystal's base in cases where the base is totally opaquely milky and the alteration does not affect the overall energetics is acceptable. Polishing or faceting a still-useful crystal for esthetic or "energy enhancement" purposes (other than specific repair work) is decidedly not acceptable. Esthetics for the sake of esthetics has no place in crystal science. Alterations for energy enhancement purposes on a still-useful crystal should not be done for two reasons. First, the level of extremely advanced crystal knowledge required for such a purpose has yet to be developed, and will not be of numerous years to come. Second, there is plenty of grossly damaged quartz stock that can acceptably be faceted and polished to much benefit. The integrity of any crystal not in the category of being grossly damaged should be inviolably respected, humankind humbly realizing that the time has not yet come where energy enhancement alterations can be done within divine order.

FACETED QUARTZ GEOMETRIES

With quartz damaged beyond basic energy applications—referred to here as stock—higher usefulness can be regained with samples that have appropriate size and clarity. With such quartz stock the possibilities are limitless. Following are some perspectives on the manifestation of these potentials and many practical concepts.

In the realm of faceting quartz stock into geometric conformations for the purpose of creating energetic tools, it cannot be overemphasized that only crystal science professionals with a high degree of advanced knowledge and technical skills can design and manifest faceted forms that function with optimal effectiveness and within divine order. "Angle is everything" in crystal science, and it would be difficult to find a discipline that requires greater precision of knowledge and technical execution. Crystal designing and faceting, with quartz and other crystals, is an exacting profession, where a millimeter makes a significant difference and a single angular degree or less can be the measure of success. Herein orthodox gemology does indeed have much to teach! The patterns of divine order in all their elegant complexity need to be followed exactly, requiring considerable knowledge of the laws of universal physics and their relationship to crystal form energy dynamics. Therefore, it is imperative that the faceting and polishing of higher energetic crystal tools be done with the discernment and skills of sacred crystal science professionals.

The variety of sacred geometric forms into which quartz can be faceted is wide, but is bounded by the parameters of divine order. Quartz is the preeminently versatile matrix in which virtually the entire spectrum of universal geometric forms may be shaped. Recall quartz's full-spectrum energetic capacities and its exceptionally programmable matrix structure. Out of all the available types of crystalline mediums, quartz is the only all-purpose matrix harmonically conducive to practically all archetypal geometric dynamics. In addition, its helical molecular structure and high transparency quotient make quartz a particularly effective matrix for interdimensional energy transduction and interconnection. The overall amplification factors further magnify the efficiency and power of the marriage of quartz with sacred geometric forms. With such forms the angular "thoughts" of the Universal Mind are held steady in an actively receptive and responsive crystalline medium, creating a geometric spectrum of interdimensional access and spectrum-specific crucibles of energy interactions. The foundational keys of the Universal Mind, imprinted in stone, open vistas of intercommunication and Light-transformations previously closed or dimly shaded, now opening as crystal-based science and technology matures.

Viola Pettit Neal, Ph.D., and Shafica Karagulla, M.D., discuss thoughts in this regard, in their book *Through the Curtain.*

> Crystals have given man an open door to the contact with and use of higher

> frequencies of energy to build and to mold his civilization. We are at the beginning of the use of crystals, and on the knowledge of crystals we will build the physical structure of the new civilization.[5]
>
> Crystals are those substances which alter the geometrical pattern of frequencies. We must realize that these frequency patterns are more or less stable, but that crystals because of their strength of geometrical pattern can modify and reform the frequency pattern. In doing so, energy can be released and directed to man's purposes.[6]
>
> The thirty-two crystalline forms are the key patterns for the way the energies are built in the universe; and the key to unlocking energy in a constructive way. . . .
>
> Knowledge of the crystalline forms may be considered the right-hand-path method for unlocking energy by the use of crystalline forms and sound in the audible, supersonic, and infra-sonic, to manipulate and direct forces. Man has not yet become basically creative. His movement into the creative fields is close at hand. He will discover how to use crystalline forms to unlock, direct, and control energy and to modify and mold substance.[7]

The dawning of technological and consciousness multidimensional creativity is integrally interlinked with the evolution of crystallographic form energy science. With it, the Light-spectrums become accessible and are able to be modulated in myriad ways.

Presented herein are a number of seed-thoughts toward stimulating a next quantum step in this discipline.

1. The 5 Platonic solids, 7 crystal systems, and 32 crystal classes faceted into quartz form create a fundamental spectrum of Light-access and Light-formulation modules. These sets are cornerstones for advanced research and application.
2. Figure 45 illustrates a small sampling of the combination patterns of intersecting geometric forms. Each combination is a specific access-code and form energy generator. Advanced mineralogical texts have many illustrations of such geometry combinations, providing fertile ground for research into their higher energetic properties and applications.
3. The ideal crystallization patterns of specific minerals also provide blueprints that could be faceted in quartz and utilized as specialized form energy tools. See Figure 44 for examples.
4. Figure 46 shows examples of quartz formed into shapes with different numbers of equally angled and equally sized facets and sides. From a three-sided form to a twelve-sided form, each faceted figure formulates and emits specific energy patterns and frequencies. The determination of these specifics will be found in the more sophisticated domains of numerology and sacred geometry. This spectrum of Light-tools will prove to be most valuable in future healing, reprogramming, and technological applications. In addition to the forms illustrated having a termination and a flat base, these forms may also be made with two terminations.
5. Figure 47 diagrams two equally intersecting tetrahedrons. This is the three-dimensional geometry of the Star of David, and therefore should prove to be centrally significant in the form energy field.
6. Various energy wands can be created by having the pentagonal dodecahedrons or icosahedrons on both ends of a solid crystal rod or by applying some selective domed angular configurations deriving from Buckminster Fuller's work. (See Figure 48.)

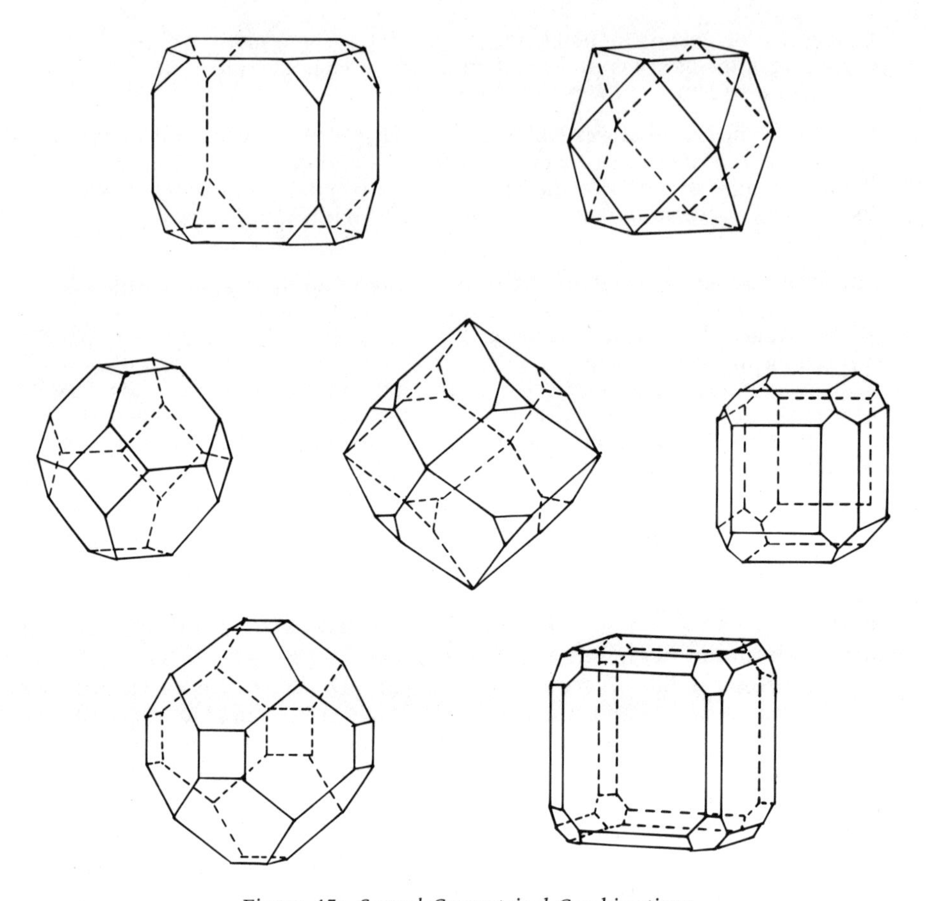

Figure 45: Sacred Geometrical Combinations

7. A form energy amplification chamber can be made by surrounding a faceted Platonic solid form with a proportionally larger refined metal framework of the same geometry. Each vertex of the quartz solid and the framework would be perfectly aligned with one another, and optimally would be interconnected with a small diameter metal rod as illustrated in Figure 49. This concept can be applied to all five Platonic solids.
8. In the future, crystal growing techniques will have the capacity to custom grow forms to exacting faceted specifications beyond current dreams. Advanced thought-form technology in conjunction with the sacred sciences of sonics, lasers, magneto-gravitics, and geometrics will combine to create incredible spectrums of precision crystals. For a further glimpse into this future reality, see Chapter 21.

INSCRIBING CRYSTALS WITH SYMBOLS AND ENERGY PATTERNS

As a variation on the concept of faceting and modifying crystals, the discerned inscribing of symbols and energy patterns at particular areas of the natural crystal

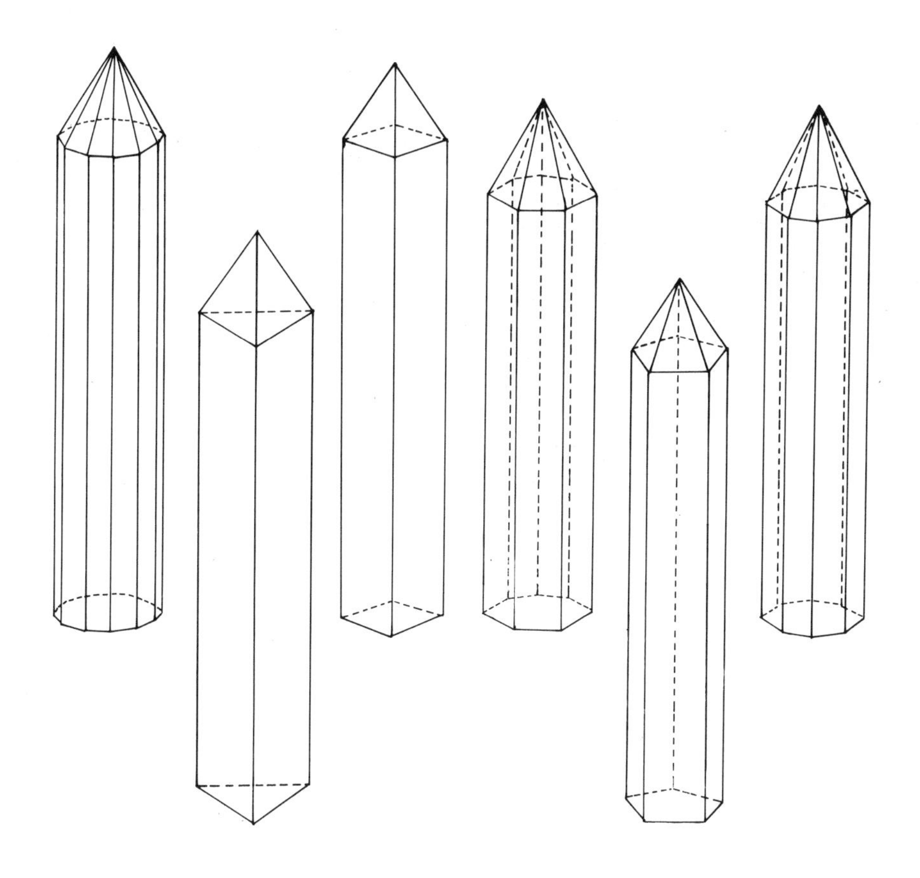

Figure 46: Equi-Faceted Quartz Forms

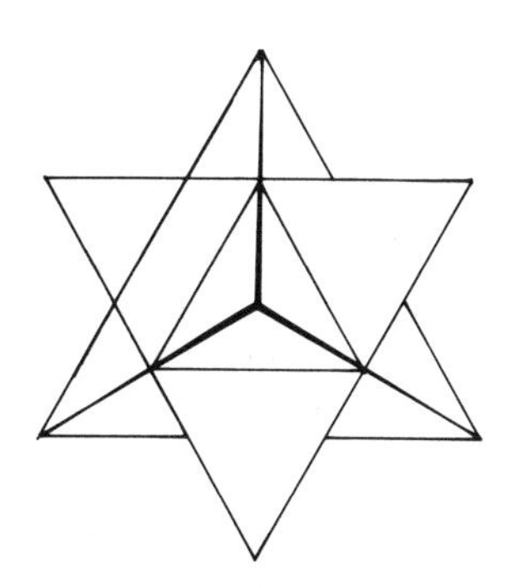

Figure 47:
Equi-Intersecting Tetrahedrons

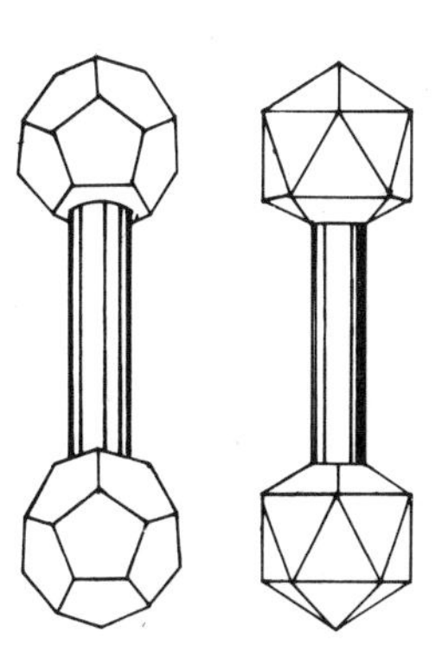

Figure 48:
Platonic Solid Wands

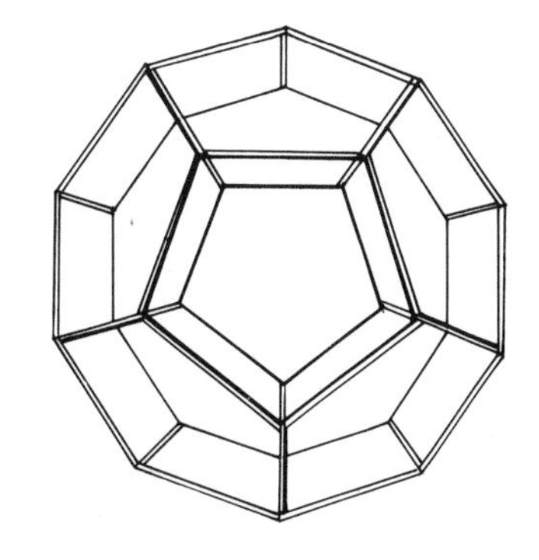

Figure 49:
Form Energy Generator

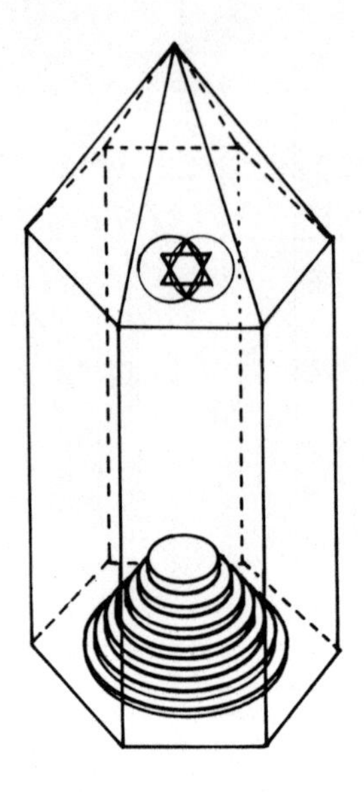

Figure 50: Termination and Base Inscription Patterns

form can add significantly to stimulating desired energy patterning and amplifying the overall dynamics.

One excellent region of the crystal for inscribing is the bottom of a single-terminated's base. If a minimal portion of a crystal's base can be sawed off horizontally without disturbing the overall energetics, then that crystal may be employed for this application. After polishing the cut base, a number of universal symbols and basic energy patternings can be inscribed by a skilled technician. Figure 50 shows two possible inscription modalities. With one, the patterns can be cut into a single horizontal plane or into progressively recessed levels at numerous equally spaced horizontal levels. After the design is inscribed, it is optimal to inlay gold leafing. This crystal base inscription technique is particularly efficacious because the inscribing is perfectly aligned with the c axis primary energy flow of the crystal. As energy flows through the inscription toward the terminations, it becomes patterned according to the inscribed design. The design acts as a template that modifies and amplifies specifically desired vibrational patternings that complement the overall crystal dynamics.

Secondly, the termination facets are also good areas to inscribe harmonically compatible symbols, packed with gold. To do this is to add further input into the crystal's dynamics to make it a more specific tool.

Large generator crystals can also be considerably amplified by inscribing a spiral around the exterior of the crystal body and packing it with titanium, silver, or gold. Experiment with different angular configurations of the spiral before inscribing by wrapping copper or silver wire around the exterior. Varying the angles subtly but significantly modifies the generator's energetics. Find the optimal spiral placement, both clockwise and counterclockwise, and then carry out the inscription and packing process.

In sum, understanding the form energy aspects of crystals is an integral part of understanding their dynamics as a whole. Because the uniquely crystallographic trait of the exterior geometrics being a direct reflection of microscopic interior structuralization, the outer form visibly illuminates the exact numeric-geometric equational parameters of a crystal's unique energy properties. Additionally, in appropriate circumstances the discerning human hand can facet crystalline substances into ideal universal forms, which will help actualize the full potentiality and diversified geometric form possibilities. In all, the study of crystal form dynamics is central to the crystallographic discipline, to unfold into tremendous degrees of complexity as this field matures.

CHAPTER 12

The Pyramid-Crystal Synergy

Pyramids and quartz crystals blend together in perfect harmonic synergy. As quartz is the most versatile, broad spectrum element of the mineral kingdom, so parallely, is the pyramid the most full spectrum component of universal geometric forms. Alone, each has wide-ranging effects, but in harmonic conjoinment, the pyramid–crystal unity synergizes as a foundational universal crucible of full-spectrum Light-interactions.

The geometric resonant affinity between quartz and the pyramidal form creates a condition of mutual amplification and complementary wholeness. Recall from Chapter 7 in the section entitled "Crystal Fundamentals" that the invariable natural external geometry of quartz includes the 51° angle as one of its most fundamental structural constants. Significantly, this is the same angle as one of the key angles of the Great Pyramid's geometry (that is, the 51°51′ angle between the corners and the base). As discussed in Chapter 5, "Angle is all" in terms of interdimensional form energy dynamics. Here, the 51° angle as an inherent constant of both the crystal and the pyramid creates a primary interactive resonant affinity because of the congruence of angles and the resultant similarity of interdimensional energy spectrum profiles. One of the best illustrations of this principle is the known universal fact that the Great Pyramid, in times of activation greater that the present, had upright and inverted apexes composed of clear quartz, as did other key focal energy zones (including the red granite of the King's Chamber, which has a quartz content of more than 50 percent) within this monumental structure.

The high transparency quotient exhibited by both the pyramid and quartz crystal create an eminently suitable combinatory relationship. This quality of quartz has been presented in detail in previous chapters. For the pyramid, an equal capacity to process the full spectrum of Light-energies is present.

> The pyramid is the most central module for this infinite expansion of consciousness throughout our local universe. When the pyramid exists in a pure energy form, it allows for a wide variety of signals to move through it, transmitting anything from concrete matter to high frequency light currents which interconnect with other "worlds," thereby providing instant media between all points of origin.[1]

> The Pyramid of Light is the central geometric form for all biophysical and consciousness evolution.

> The Pyramid shows that the Universal Mind is all present, not only in every molecule of star ionization but in every vibration of consciousness flow. Wherever you look, you are going to find that the consciousness flow is going to go into that universal constant.[2]

If either or both the pyramid and crystal had a more specialized and restricted transparency quotient (for example, the transparency quotient of a Platonic solid or a nonquartz gemstone), the potential for the full spectrum of Light-energies to process through the pyramid–crystal unity would be severely diminished. Because of their encompassing energy processing capabilities, this unity is quintessentially versatile and spectrally complete.

The spiraling nature of both the pyramid and quartz crystal is another aspect of their interactive resonant affinity. As illustrated in Figure 51, the entirety of primary pyramidal energy dynamics is a spiraling energy, from the external phi-based energy flow to the helical standing wave pattern from apex to apex. "The pyramidal model is the blueprint for the living 'double helix' which unfolds to connect the human evolution with the higher evolution in the thresholds of the 'Treasures in the Heavens.'"[3] Also within the microdynamics of pyramidal energy, all quantum levels are fundamentally spiraling and of helical angular derivatives. So too with quartz, the spiraling tetrahedral molecular structure forms a latticework that processes energy flow in a primarily helical manner. Here again, the pyramid–crystal unity is harmonically conjoined in resonant vibratory unison.

On the highest Light-dimensions, the pyramidal form is complete in and of itself. Especially in the cosmic–intergalactic energy-matter dimensions, however, quartz provides essential complementary properties that make the pyramid a considerably amplified and programmable Light-form. Wherever a pyramidal form abides, whether it be a tiny cardboard pyramid or the Great Pyramid itself, the primary energy dynamics intrinsic to this form are in operation to some degree. Depending upon size, orientation, and material substance, the pyramidal energy dynamics manifest from lesser to greater degrees. Without quartz, these dynamics cannot reach their full potential within the earth's present energy field parameters. Even the interdimensional physics of the Great Pyramid require the use of crystals as an integral part of its blueprint. The addition of quartz (and proper pyramid orientation) to one or more harmonic energy zones contributes significant energetic power and tunability capacities to the pyramid. Quartz's properties of amplification, focusing, programmable energetic transformation, capacitance, storage, and matrix stability add considerably to activating higher energetic potentials inherent to the pyramidal structure. In particular, crystals are the matrix-crucible in which higher Light is catalytically ignited, sustained, and modified within the pyramid.

THE GREAT PYRAMID AND HARMONIC PYRAMIDS THEREOF

The literal meaning of the word *pyramid* is "fire in the middle."

> On page 86 of *The Great Pyramid—Its Divine Message,* by D. Davidson and H. Aldersmith, another derivation of the word is given: "pyramid" is the Grecianised form of the Hebrew "urrim-middin"—"light measures." The Egyptian name for the Great Pyramid is Khuti—"The Lights." In the Semitic languages

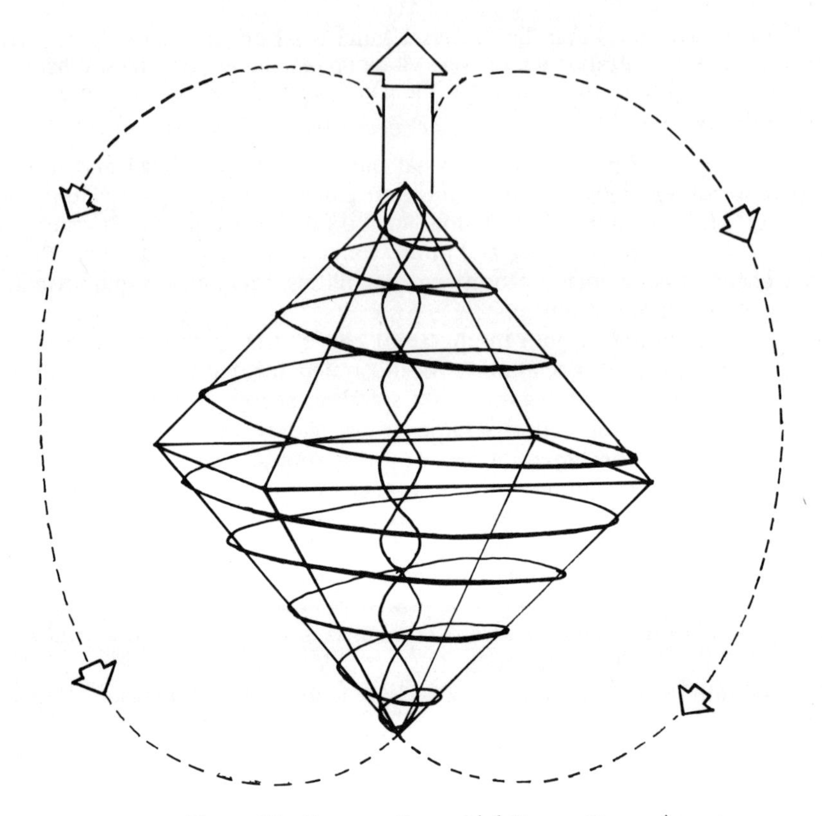

Figure 51: Primary Pyramidal Energy Dynamics

the equivalent name is "urim"—"the Lights." In Phrygian and Greek, the root ur (light) became successively pur and pyr (fire) and pyra (plural), "beacon fires."[4]

The Great Pyramid is the epitome of the archetypal Pyramid of Light* manifested on the earth plane. It stands as the geometric embodiment of the Light measures—the encodement of the indexes and tables of all Light-spectrums in one archetypal seed-form. It is known in *The Keys of Enoch* as the Eben Shettayah—the Foundation Stone of the earth. In fact, the Great Pyramid is the capstone central threshold control zone of the entire planetary energy gridwork system. In this capacity, it functions as the primary astrophysical gateway by which earth is interconnected with the larger cosmos. Locked within its mysterious internal dynamics are the primary timepieces of the Alpha–Omega blueprint of unfoldment for the earth plane that are also interlinked with the more causal star-based timepieces that relay the unfoldings of the overall cosmic rhythms. Further, the Great Pyramid is a master cipher for the ascension process; it contains the numeric-geometric codes for the enactment of the preliminary reprogramming and the actual personal and planetary ascension. As the singularly preeminent

*See chapter 4.

"Lighthouse" of the earth plane, the Great Pyramid indeed sets the Light–measures for all energetic blueprints of evolutionary development.

Although volumes have been written concerning the higher nature and intricacies of the Great Pyramid, the primary concern within this text is to highlight its unique planetary standing and to outline its energetic properties that apply to all pyramidal forms that incorporate the specific angular geometry of this great master cipher.

Pyramids function as interdimensional ultramagnetic form resonators. As quoted before in Chapter 11, "Every form is the manifestation of the force that has built it. Thus every form is the image of the creative force that builds it and dwells within it."[5] Also, "Sacred geometric forms are vehicles to become a channel through which the earth could receive the abstract, cosmic life of the heavens."[6] And, "It is as if the form itself provides a structure through which an ever-present energy is intensified."[7] The pyramid, as a specific case within the sacred science of form energy, is a resonant antenna-receiving unit tunable to the full spectrum of Light-energy harmonics. All other form types, that is, the tetrahedron, pentagonal dodecahedron, and others, are more specialized in their attunement spectrum capacities. The pyramid functions as a universal communication common denominator, that is, throughout the infinitude of the Universal Energy Network (UEN) it is the pyramidal form that abides within every quantum level of reality and serves as a primary inteconnection medium within the Universal Mind. "The ancients saw the pyramid as the gateway to the stars and the form through which star intelligences come to serve human creation. Once again, Man will understand how the geometries of the pyramid fuse space, time, and matter to form the ideal focus for star energy transmission."[8] "The key notion that the pyramidal form is necessary for adaptation to energy frequencies using wireless transmission to interface with other wavelengths of consciousness experience."[9] "There is a Light energy pyramid in every evolutionary membrane."[10] Therefore, it can be seen that the Great Pyramid and all harmonic pyramidal forms thereof serve as fundamental universal communication modules that function to interconnect the full spectrum of multidimensional creation.

Although each pyramid has archetypally identical energy dynamics intrinsic to it by virtue of its form, pyramids also have a versatile programmable variability. There are two basic factors in this regard. First, because of a variety of physics-based factors—universal dimensional coordinate location, the material substances of which it is composed, activation factors, and others—there are wide differences in the degree to which the full energetic potential is activated. This is to say that any given pyramid has considerable energetic potential, there are countless spectral degrees to which that intrinsic potential is actualized. Second, each pyramid is programmable within broad parameters. For example, within the UEN there are master threshold control pyramids (similar to the Great Pyramid but on a larger scale) from which many derivative pyramids are extended throughout the threshold's dimensional membranes and gridworks. Each derivative pyramid has specifically prescribed energetic functions to carry out as one of many such pyramids enacting particularly assigned monitoring, stabilizing, and Alpha–Omega enactment tasks. Though each separate subpyramid performs different energetic tasks, the entire pyramidal network controlled by a master threshold pyramid enacts synergistically integrated collective Light-activities. Similarly, each pyramid constructed on the earth plane can be selectively attuned through programming factors to interconnect with specifically desired energy spectrums of the UEN. In essence, the programmable variability allows the individual to use a pyramid situated on earth to gain access to specific interdimensional energy pathways and domains.

Quartz crystals are the primary tools by which the factors of activation potential and selective interdimensional access are actualized. For the former purpose, the placement of appropriate quartz forms at primary energy focal zones throughout the pyramidal structure activates the potential preexisting energy dynamics to amplified degrees. For the latter purpose, quartz can be programmed with specifically desired thought-forms and energy fields and positioned within the pyramid at appropriate locations. The operative pyramidal energy dynamics are then programmed as they process through the crystalline matrices. This determines the angle-code and form-code affinity harmonics of interdimensional communication access. The specifics of manifesting these two factors in practical application are described later in this chapter.

PRIMARY PYRAMIDAL ENERGY DYNAMICS

The pyramid is a crucible of wholeness. Its energy dynamics are a microcosmic resonant duplication of supremely causal macrocosmic pyramidal archetypal processes. Throughout the expanses of manifestation, the pyramid is the single most holistically complete form incorporating the entirety of the indexes and tables of Light-measures. All other universal geometric forms derive from the foundational seed-crystal energetic potentials of the Pyramid of Light. From this perspective, the pyramid is seen as the ultimate living computer system of the Universal Mind, containing within its energy dynamics the potentialities of all possible combinations and permutations of Light.

Given this, it is clear that the sacred science of pyramidology is most complex. Its many applications in Light-based technologies form a central keystone of sacred science. In current times, this potential has yet to be even marginally tapped. The knowledge as to the ignition and controlled modulation of the pyramid's inherent interdimensional Light-activation potential is one of the primary keys to catalyzing the remanifestation of advanced crystal usage as well as the higher octaves of divine science. Although the fullness of such knowledge is not yet totally accessible to the earth plane within the measured unfoldment of the divine plan, the perspectives that follow serve as keys to more advanced research and application of pyramidal energy dynamics.

The sacred science of pyramidology supersedes the linear parameters of orthodox science. The science of today is still in a quandary as to the enigmatic physical structure and energy processes of the Great Pyramid as well as the nonlinear effects of the pyramidal form.

Volumes of literature have attempted to explain the awe-inspiring engineering prowess exhibited in the Great Pyramid. The sheer size, complex geometrics, extreme precision, and superior technical skills stand as testament to the work of exceptionally advanced technologies. The fact that the duplication of such a feat by modern-day technologies would be challenging belies the efforts by orthodox thought to impose linear explanations as to the construction of the Great Pyramid by such simplistic means as mass labor, copper chisels, and gigantic rafts and rolling logs as primary limestone block transport systems, among other such primitive methods. A major scientific research project sponsored by the U.S. Atomic Energy Commission, the Smithsonian Institute, and Ein Shams University in Cairo was perfomed in recent times, with state-of-the-art technological equipment. The purpose was to find secret chambers in the Great Pyramid by measuring on magnetic tape the pattern of cosmic rays reaching the interior. The scientists found that the energy readings were entirely different each day. A baseline reading necessary to establishing the foundational parameters for the entire project was never attained during months of intensive research effort. Such an unexpectedly frustrating result confounded the scientists and neutralized the entire project. The conclusion drawn by Amr Gohed, Ph.D., who was in charge of the installation at the pyramid, depicts the inadequacy of orthodox science in understanding pyramidology. He stated:

> It defies all the known laws of science and electronics. . . . This is scientifically impossible. . . .
>
> Either the geometry of the pyramid is in substantial error, which would affect our readings, or there is a mystery which is beyond expanation . . . there is some force that defies the laws of science at work in the pyramids![11]

Furthermore, the nonlinear effects of any given pyramidal form constructed according to the same geometry as the Great Pyramid—such as the well-known dehydration effect as well as weight loss of metallic objects, transmutation of water, and numerous others—cannot be explained within the paradigms of modern science. Therefore, the sacred science of pyramidology is best approached from the perspective of the Higher Evolution, which will provide the nonlinear keys to a more encompassing understanding of this central discipline.

All aspects of pyramidology are predicated upon the octahedral wholeness of the pyramidal form. In many schools of thought, a four-sided pyramid is regarded as the complete configuration of the pyramidal form. This, however, is only half of the geometry. For every four-sided pyramidal geometry there is an equal and opposite four-sided form, at least energetically, combing together as an octahedron. (Note: this is not a regular octahedron, such as the Platonic solid octahedron; the pyramid has a different angular configuration.) Scanning the myriad universal crystalline forms occurrent throughout the omniverse, one does not find the four-sided pyramidal form occurring in isolation without its equal and opposite counterpart. The octahedral form is the necessary geometrical structure within the parameters of universal physics. Even when, physically, there is only the four-sided structure, on the subtle levels the octahedral form energy dynamics occur to varying degrees. The important point here is that, as stated in Part I, the fundamental universal forms originate on the highest levels of Abstract Light, and these forms predetermine the energetic blueprint of all such geometries throughout creation. It is the task of interdimensional science to reactivate sophisticated knowledge about these preexistent form energy dynamics so as to activate their full potential on the earth plane. As Bill Schul and Ed Pettit conclude in *Pyramids and the Second Reality:*

> The most significant thing about a pyramid is its pattern. Our experiments have led us to believe that not only does a physical pattern of the pyramid exist but that this particular unique pattern also exists at the etheric level. In fact, the

> etheric or energy pyramid exists whether or not there is a corresponding physical one. The etheric pyramid forms the physical one, rather than the other way around.[12]

The octahedral geometry is the predeterminative form that constitutes the wholeness of pyramidal energy dynamics. This verity is also existent within the blueprint of the Great Pyramid, which has an inverted pyramidal structure of equal size and proportions below ground level. As stated in *The Keys of Enoch:* "The Great Pyramid on the Earth is, in reality, in conjunction with a pyramidal energy field under the Earth which together form a diamond."[13] The specifics concerning the energetics of the octahedral form are presented in the following text, and this cornerstone conception of pyramidology will become more clearly defined and its necessity understood in the context of the energy dynamics principles.

Figure 51 illustrates the outline of the pyramid's most primary energetic blueprint. This flow-pattern starts at the upright apex, where the energy is attracted, accumulated, and then catalyzed into a downward spiraling motion. As this motion spirals downward, both clockwise and counterclockwise currents are generated, which follow a phi-based helical pattern. The spiral currents expand as the octahedral outline becomes progressively broader toward its midline. At the midline region a major phase conversion occurs as the energetics switch at that precise point from a expanding, centrifugal orientation (upper pyramid) to an equal and opposite contracting, centripetal orientation (lower pyramid).

As the downward spiraling current progresses toward the inverted apex, the energy becomes increasingly more tightly focused and one-pointedly concentrated. At the lower apex the one-pointed energy focus reaches a "zero point" and undergoes a 90° phase shift. This is the Alpha zone of the pyramid, wherein the concentrated force of the incoming spiral current reaches an apex of energy inversion; at that apex zero point the phase orientation of the energy undergoes an instantaneous reversal "flip" to be aligned with the apex-to-apex axis (before phase reversal, the orientation is aligned with the midline axis). This zero point conversion is one of the primary keys in comprehending basic principles of interdimensional energy transference and the opposite phases of Spirit polarity (as described in Chaper 7). The tremendous magnitudes of concentrated force that spiral into the inverted apex are ignited at the zero point into pure primary Light-force (in this usage, the term Light-force is synonymous with the universal fire element). This primary Light-force has extremely high radiant-activity—it is an expression of the primary activating/catalyzing/quickening archetypal force instilling Life-and Light-activity into every atom of creation.

Immediately upon passing through the zero point conversion the energy current goes directly from inverted apex to upright apex in a strong, supracoherent, laserlike beam. The seven areas described by intertwining helixes from apex to apex are primary standing wave patterns that constitute the wave-harmonics of the energy current. Each of the seven zones is a "chakra" or energy center, of the pyramid.

Upon reaching the upright apex, the energy receives a final ignition-amplification as it emits through the top of the apex directly upward in a tightly coherent pillar of Light-force. More than 90 percent of the energy emitting from the pyramid is focused into this Pillar of Light beam. Secondary emissions feed back

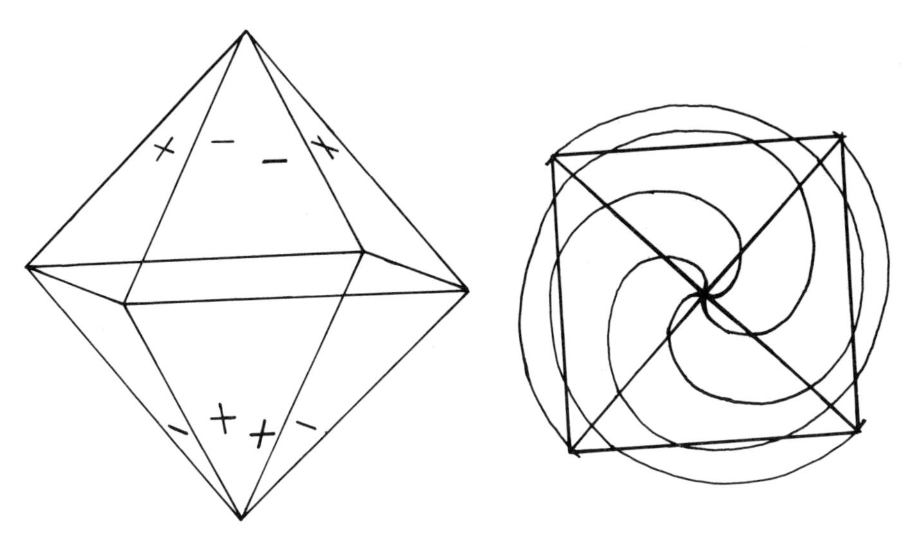

Figure 52:
Pyramidal "Holistic Polarity"

Figure 53: External
Pyramidal Spirallatory Currents (Top View)

into the main force of the pyramidal energy dynamics, both arcing back into the inverted apex (as illustrated in Figure 51) and into the external helical current (not illustrated). In a fully activated pyramid this archetypal energy flow pattern is a constant, uninterrupted process. This can be modified by applied modulating forces to create certain specific results within Light-based technologies, but when left in an unmodulated state the energy flows in a continuous stream.

Further aspects of pyramidal energy dynamics can be explored:

Figure 52 shows the holistic polarity of the pyramidal form. The orientation at both apexes includes both positive and negative aspects in equal amounts. Notice that there is an offset alternation of charges between oppositely corresponding inverted and upright faces of the octahedron; that is, where there is a positive charge on an upright face, there is a negative charge on the opposite corresponding inverted face. In the flow of pyramidal energies there is considerable changing of charge, alternating back and forth from negative to positive to negative, and so on. Opposite corresponding faces still maintain opposite charge orientations in the midst of dynamic energy flux. Because of this, a holistic polarity "tension" is maintained throughout the pyramidal energy field. The archetypal blueprint of pyramidal energy dynamics is thus sustained.

In figure 54, the fourfold external spiraling flow-pattern is shown as it originates at the upright apex and spirals down to the octahedral midline. For the sake of clarity the four clockwise and four counterclockwise spirals are diagramed separately; in reality they are concurrent.

The apex-to-apex energy flow, as illustratd in Figure 51, is more three-dimensional than shown in previous diagrams. It is very tightly focused and spiraling, oriented in both clockwise and counterclockwise helical motions. There are numerous quantum energy levels within the more intricate physics of this energy dynamic; that is, there are spirals within spirals within spirals, each one at

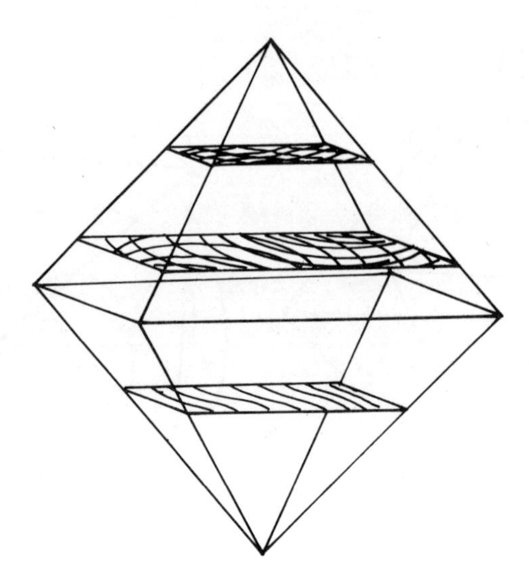

Figure 54: Energy "Templates" at Horizontal Strata Levels

separate quantum energy orbital shell levels. By modulating the pre- and post-zero point energy processing parameters via modification of the apex crystalline latticework orientations, in pyramid-based Light-technologies from apex-to-apex multilevel spiraling flow can be modulated to create specific subatomic and atomic phase ratios.

In Figure 55 the concept that each horizontal cross-section of the octahedron has a different frequency interference pattern is shown. Taking horizontal cross-sections, one obtains progressively larger squares as the sections go from the apex to the midline, and then progressively smaller squares from the midline to the inverted apex. There is, then, a theoretically infinite spectrum of horizontal cross-sections, each different from the other. As the external spiral flow-patterns progress around the octahedron, each horizontal level of expansion and contraction has a characteristic frequency interference pattern. Each horizontal frequency pattern can be viewed as a vibration-specific energetic "template" that continuously oscillates at each horizontal strata-level of the octahedron. Identically sized horizontal strata of the upright and inverted pyramids have a symmetrically diametric dimensional phase orientation (one example of which is the matter-antimatter relationship). Inter-oscillatory relationships thereby established and selectively modulated between these dimensionally "opposing" frequency strata (and harmonics and intervals thereof) create one of the most causal dynamics of advanced pyramidal applications. Upon further examination, it can be seen that the apex-to-apex flow-pattern interacts with the horizontal energy dynamics. The technical particulars of this interaction go beyond the purview of this text. The point here is that there is an index of highly specific frequency template patterns that occur in a progressive, highly ordered manner throughout the octahedral energy dynamics. Therefore, the Light-scientist has a spectrum of vibrational holding patterns that can be precisely tapped into or selectively applied in technological matters.

The upright and inverted apex areas are, respectively, the Omega and Alpha zones of the octahedron. They are the causal points of the holistic polarity orientation for the entire octahedron as well as the major zones of energy orientation, ignition-amplification, and phase conversion. These two zones are the seed-blueprints of wholeness that set the parameters of energetic unfoldment for the entire pyramidal energy flow dynamics. As previously noted, the Omega zone sets the orientation and stimulated ignition of energy originating at the upright apex and then spirals around the outside of the octahedron. The Alpha zone is the area of zero point energy reorientation and ignition. Then the Omega zone processes the apex-to-apex current and further ignites-amplifies the energetics into an upward pillar of energy flow.

There are two other areas of energy reorientation and phase conversion. As previously discussed, the four corners of the octahedral midline function to induce a phase modification of the external spiraling energy flow from an expanding, centrifugal phase to a contracting-focusing, centripetal phase. In addition, the midpoint of the octahedral midline horizontal section—the exact center of the octahedron—is another major energy conversion zone. As previously mentioned, the literal meaning of the word *pyramid* if "fire in the middle." This middle is the middle of the octahedron, that is, the middle of the horizontal midsection and the center of the seven apex-to-apex "chakras." Here is where a major source of primary Light-force is infused into the pyramidal energy dynamics. This key area is called the Eye of Yahweh—that zone of the pyramid that has the most direct interdimensional interconnection with the Eternal. This is the primary zone of unipolarity in the pyramid form. From *The Keys of Enoch:*

> Each Pyramid of Light is energized with YHWH's Eye in the center of the pyramid; this is a cosmological constant which enables every realm of intelligence to be reprogrammed into a higher level of creation when they can go through their pyramidal energy field of creation. Thus, the pyramid, the eternal programming of YHWH's Eye, is there with you at all times and is working with every level of creation.[14]

Other key energy zones of the pyramid include the Queen's Chamber, the King's Chamber, and the Chamber of the Son. Presented herein are a few ideas concerning each one.

> The Chamber of the Son is located within the Eye of Horus (in the position of the eye socket). The Eye of Horus is formed by the King's Chamber and the Grand Gallery as the upper lid and the Queen's Chamber and the Queen's Chamber passage creating the lower eye lid around the Chamber of the Son.
>
> The Chamber of the Son will open the hidden doors and unlock the final mysteries of the Pryamids.[15]

In *Life Force in the Great Pyramids,* Dee Jay Nelson and David Coville present some illuminating diagrammatic perspectives toward decoding the Great Pyramid. Key Egyptian hieroglyphics are expanded proportionally and superimposed within the geometry of the Great Pyramid. Especially with the human self and life force hieroglyphics as well as the ankh symbol were significant correlations with the positioning of the King's Chamber and Queen's Chamber noted (see Figure 55). With the human self hieroglyphic the outermost loop of the fifth pyramidal chakra (from the bottom) intersects perfectly with the floor of the King's Chamber, and

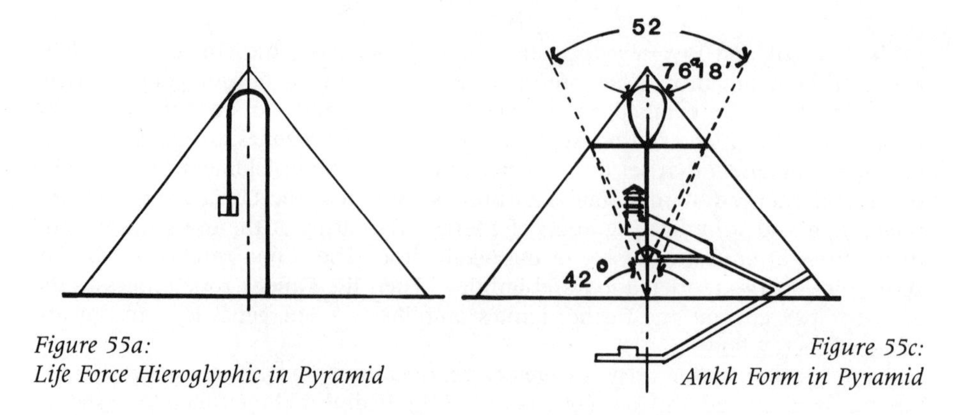

Figure 55a:
Life Force Hieroglyphic in Pyramid

Figure 55c:
Ankh Form in Pyramid

the nodal region between the fourth and fifth pyramidal chakras intersects precisely at the floor of the Queen's Chamber. The life force hieroglyphic ends exactly at the floor of the King's Chamber. The bottom of the ankh can be situated at the floor of the Queen's Chamber so that the entire symbol will superimpose harmoniously with the pyramidal geometry. These diagrams and observations are presented here as a few more pieces of the pyramidal puzzle to consider as more encompassing pyramidology paradigms emerge.

In all, the pyramidal energy dynamics function as a potentially infinitely tunable interdimensional attraction module. Its classic vortex activity creates an energy zone in which high degrees of multidimensional interaction and transduction may occur with significantly lowered interdimensional membrane impedance. In terms of the higher Light-dimensions of the UEN, the pyramidal form energy functions as multidimensional vortex center threshold computers, and, distributed on every micro to mega level of the UEN, as Alpha-Omega program enactors and inter- and intra-dimensional interconnectors. Within Light-based technologies, the pyramid serves as one of the most fundamental crucibles in which and through which intensive, versatile, tunable Light-transformations can take place; it also functions as a primary interdimensional attraction module system in such fields as multidimensional communication and free energy technologies.

PYRAMID EFFECTS

Popular and professional observation and experimentation over the past decades has verified the fact that unusual, nonlinear phenomena occur within the pyramidal form. The octahedron is a universal form of dynamically balanced perfection and multidimensional transmutation to higher states of order. In this regard, pyramidal energy dynamics act in a twofold manner. First, energies and substances are aligned with their optimally harmonized state. They are energetically stimulated toward a state of balanced perfection. Second, energies and substances gain momentum toward quantum transformations and transmutations to a more highly evolved level of order.

The observed effects of applied pyramid energy are due to the flow-patterns of higher dimensional Light attracted to and processed through the pyramid. As a

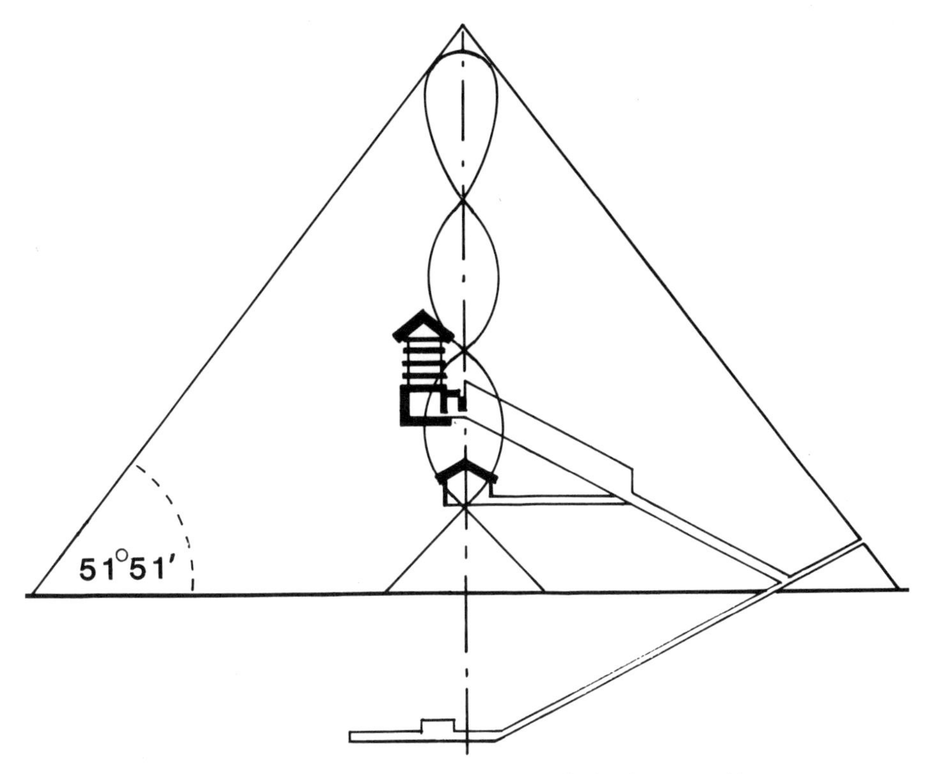

Figure 55b: "Human Self" Hieroglyphic in Pyramid

result, there is a higher degree of interdimensional energy interactions that function to align a particular substance or energy pattern with its blueprint of harmony, balance, and evolutionary reprogramming. The observed accumulation of energy within the pyramid is a result of the vortex energy dynamics that concentrate heightened gradients of interdimensional energy flow within the pyramidal form.

Although not exhaustive, the following list illustrates the twofold nonlinear effects of applied pyramidal energy.

- Plants and animals exposed on a regular basis to pyramid energy grow faster and attain a higher state of optimal health than do control groups.
- One experiment had blood samples taken from human subjects before pyramid exposure and then after a 30-minute exposure. Parameters of the blood that were out of the normal range were brought into the normal range after exposure to pyramid energies. Blood found to be on the high or low side of the normal range tended to be stimulated toward the midranges of harmonization.[16]
- Small samples of fresh milk do not sour, but rather tend to turn into yogurt.
- Paris Garefis, M.D., oral surgeon and chairman of the Western Dental Society, has repeatedly observed that exposure of skin grafts to pyramid energy before surgery helps the graft integrate with the patient and heal significantly faster, with less scar tissue.[17]

• Polluted water has been purified in three days of pyramid exposure, with laboratory verification.[18]
• The U.S. Department of Agriculture placed 30 inch-base pyramids in cow pastures and found a 70 percent reduction of flies and other insects.
• Metals placed within pyramids have measurably lost weight over a period of time. For example, a 1094 grain sample of iron lost 3.3 grains in two hours and 5.1 grains in 11 hours; a 795.5 gram sample of copper lost 4.9 grams in one hour and 5.2 grams in 14 hours.
• In contaminated milk, a 16 percent reduction of harmful bacteria occurred after applied pyramid energies.
• Kirlian photographs of human subjects show the aura to be significantly brighter after a 15-minute exposure period.
• Water treated by pyramid energy for two weeks had significantly fewer bacteria than control groups.

Many other similar pyramid energy effects have been noted in the literature in this field. The preceding list highlights some of the more measurably dramatic results. The remarkable energizing, long-term balanced state preservation, and higher-state transmutations have astounding ramifications and bear greater examination, understanding, and application.

PERSPECTIVES AND IDEAS ON PYRAMID–CRYSTAL APPLICATIONS

1. Experimentation has shown that any pyramidal form that has the angular configuration of the Great Pyramid will demonstrate pyramid energy effects to some degree, regardless of the type of material of which it is composed. Also, whether the pyramid is an enclosed form or an open-frame appears to make little if any difference in results; it is the angles per se that generate the pyramidal effect.

Much more powerful results, however, can be obtained by utilizing pyramids made of refined metals. These metals include copper, silver, gold, platinum, and titanium (and harmonic combinations thereof). The crystalline structure (and vibratory profile) of such metals makes them particularly conducive to attracting and processing higher dimensional energies in a more intensive manner. Other materials such as aluminum, wood, and less refined metals are basically adequate for general usage, but in sophisticated clinical and research settings it becomes quite important to utilize refined metal pyramids. In this regard, it is also effective to electroplate various layers of refined metals on top of one another to create amplified and specific effects.

Should having pyramids composed totally of refined metals not be possible, several alternatives will help make the pyramid as powerfully effective as possible. The addition of crystals in key energy focal areas within a pyramid and in various gridwork arrangements is helpful; this is discussed later in this section. Also, wrapping coils of refined metal wire around the pyramidal framework will amplify results. Metal-coil-wrapping double-terminated crystals at equidistant intervals along the four edges of the pyramid leading from the base to the apex is quite effective.

2. Pyramid amplification by crystal placement: The idea here is to amplify the preexistent pyramidal energy dynamics by orienting crystals with the primary

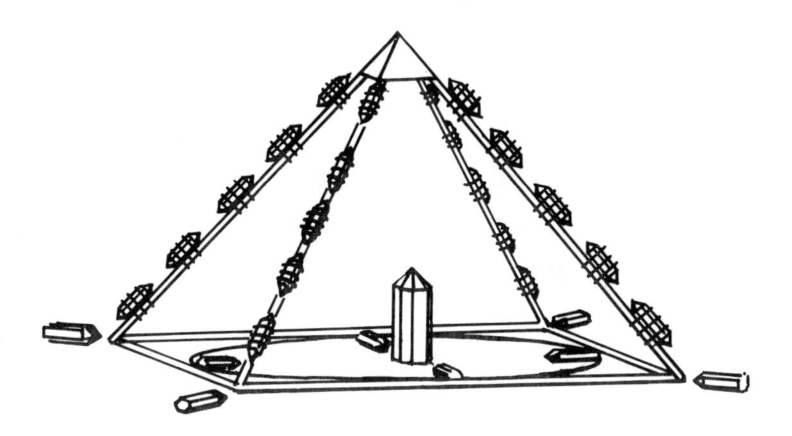

Figure 56: Pyramid–Crystal Synergy Model

energy focal regions and flow patterns of the pyramid. In so doing, the pyramid is made a more powerful interdimensional attraction module, as its energy dynamics are incrementally activated to higher levels.

Figure 56 shows a basic model for generating higher octaves of the pyramid–crystal unity that are logistically accessible. The areas of highest priority are the upper and lower apexes. In this case the lower apex is not physically described and therefore cannot be directly amplified. (For many advanced research and technological applications the full octahedral form is required, but for general usage the upright pyramidal form works quite adequately.) At the upper apex, glue or place a proportionally sized pyramid-faceted quartz. "Proportionally sized" means that the crystal–pyramid apex fits with the pyramidal angles so that the edges of the crystal apex align with the edges of the pyramid. For a 12 inch × 12 inch-base pyramid, for example, a ⅜ inch-base crystal pyramid apex works well. For an 8 foot-base pyramid, a 1½ inch base crystal pyramid is appropriate. In smaller pyramids, it is especially important to use only a pyramid-faceted crystal and not a small natural quartz for optimal results. In larger pyramids (4 foot-base and larger), sometimes naturally occurring crystals synchronize well with an apex function. Such crystals are not common and should be chosen with care. For the most part, these crystals are one of two general types: 1) six equilateral triangular facets meeting at a common terminated point (see Figure 35), and 2) small, equally sized *r* facets and larger, equally sized *z* facets (see Figure 36). It is also best if there is a minimal body to these apex crystals.

Another high priority area is the Eye of Yahweh zone, located at the midpoint of the horizontal base square. Optimal here is a crystal that can sit vertically upright so that it is aligned with the upper apex. This not only amplifies the energy dynamics of this specific region, but also considerably magnifies the apex-to-apex energy flow. For a crystal with an unsawed base, put a small amount of putty or clay on the base to make vertical orientation possible.

Single-terminated crystals situated at the four corners, directly in horizontal alignment with the axis of the corresponding pyramidal edge, will amplify the phase conversion process occurring at these four zones.

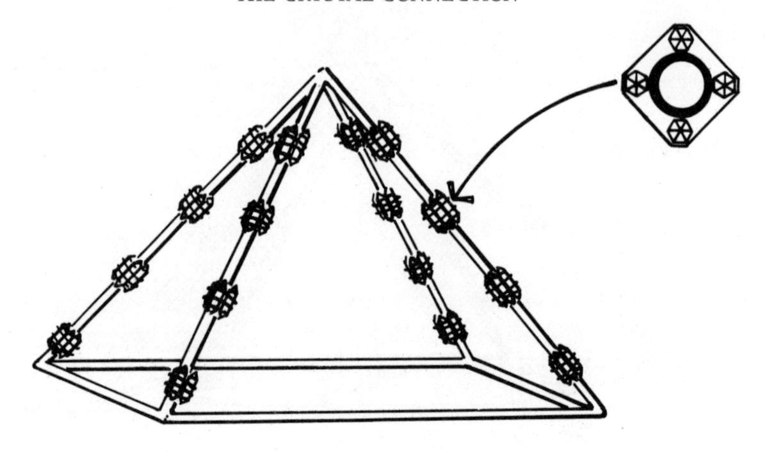

Figure 57: Wire-wrapped Four-Crystal Units Along Pyramidal Tubing

Small double-terminations can be glued or metal-wire-wrapped into place along the outside of the four pyramidal edges. This should be done whenever possible to generate optimal pyramidal effects, as the results are considerably heightened. Also, applying this principle in an even more powerful way for larger pyramids, Figure 57 demonstrates how to wire wrap four double-terminations into place around a given horizontal cross-section of a pyramidal edge. Four or more of these groupings of four need to be positioned at harmonic intervals along each of the four pyramidal edges for best results. The outside crystal of each grouping should be positioned on the very outside of the pyramid edge, the inside crystal on the innermost edge, and the other two crystals in between the outer and inner crystals equidistantly. Though less optimal, the use of single-terminations oriented either all toward the corners or all toward the apex (effects being different in each case) will add to pyramidal energetics.

In addition to the fixed, specific crystal positionings just presented, different gridwork arrangements can be placed within or outside the pyramidal structure for additional amplifying modulatable results. Illustrated in Figure 53 is one example showing a Star of David gridwork inside the pyramidal base. In Chapter 14 other gridwork arrangements are presented that can be applied in like manner. Each gridwork used should have its energy dynamics centered into the Eye of Yahweh. Gridworks so positioned serve three purposes: 1) general amplification; 2) integration of the specific gridwork energy pattern into the pyramidal dynamics such that the latter is correspondingly modified, that is, the pentagon gridwork will have a different effect upon pyramidal energy dynamics than the Star of David gridwork will, each adding its own specific vibrational patterns into the pyramid complex; and 3) activation of the horizontal energy template associated with the four phase conversion corners and the Eye of Yahweh. This particular template is one of the three most causal regions within pyramidal energy dynamics (the other two being the upright and inverted apexes). For best results, crystal gridworks are positioned inside the pyramidal base whenever logistically possible. Gridworks outside the pyramid circumference will work effectively, but not optimally. Further, it is also possible to have multiple-level gridworks inside and/or outside the pyramid.

To stimulate the King's Chamber or Queen's Chamber, a double-terminated crystal can be suspended with natural fiber string (avoid conductive metal wire) so that it is superimposed within the chamber area. The terminations of the crystals should be vertically aligned within the parallel axis (King's Chamber) or same axis (Queen's Chamber).

Further, a silver chain of wire-wrapped double-terminations, as discussed in Chapter 13 (Figure 104), can be suspended from the upper apex to the lower apex (or to the midline base when only the upright pyramidal form is used).

3. For the optimal charging of a crystal within the pyramid–crystal unity, there are several areas where it can be placed for best effects. The Eye of Yahweh is the most powerful and easily accessible area: simply place the crystal to be charged in the middle of the pyramid's base; it need not necessarily be vertically upright to gain a charge, but if logistically possible it is more desirable. For charging in the King's Chamber or Queen's Chamber, measure exactly where these regions are within the spatial dimensions of the particular pyramid and then find or make a small stand upon which the crystal can be placed to be within the desired energy zone. This stand must be made of neutral, nonconducive materials—a block of wood is fine, a plastic box works well also. The stands also need to be as small as possible so as to have minimal interference with pyramidal dynamics. Another possibility here is as stated in number 2—suspend the crystal with thread inside the chamber area.

When only a four-sided pyramidal form is used for charging and for other purposes, it is most helpful to place mirroring (face up) on a flat surface upon which the pyramid is situated. This assists in reflecting back into the pyramid some of the energies that tend to be lost or diffused as they are processed under nonoptimal conditions via the octahedral energy flow as it goes through the underlying substance upon which the pyramid is positioned. Widely available in hardware stores are packages of 12 inch × 12 inch mirrored tiles (use the clear ones only) that integrate perfectly with the commercially available 12 inch-base pyramids. For smaller pyramids, mirror tiles can be easily cut to size. And for larger pyramids, several such mirrors can be positioned together. Because of the danger of breakage, mirrors should not be used in situations in which an individual sits or lies down inside the pyramid.

Pyramids are one of the most accessible and easily usable tools with which to charge crystals. For those crystals that the individual uses daily—personal crystals, pendants, and so on—place them inside a pyramid overnight to recharge them for the next day. For crystals utlized in personal self-transformation or professional applications, simply maintain the crystal inside a pyramid until its use is required, then place it back into the pyramid after usage (unless it needs to be cleared and cleansed). In this way, the crystals' effectiveness are continually maintained at the highest possible levels.

4. The octahedral energy dynamics can be utilized to great effect in the realms of healing and reprogramming. Previously discussed in this chapter is the fact that pyramidal energy flow occurs throughout its octahedral completeness whether the full octahedral form is physically manifest or whether only the four-sided pyramidal form is used. Therefore, a four-sided pyramid-faceted crystal placed upon a body area will generate an octahedral dynamic that penetrates into the body system or chakra area. In effect, that particular chakra or other bioenergetic region

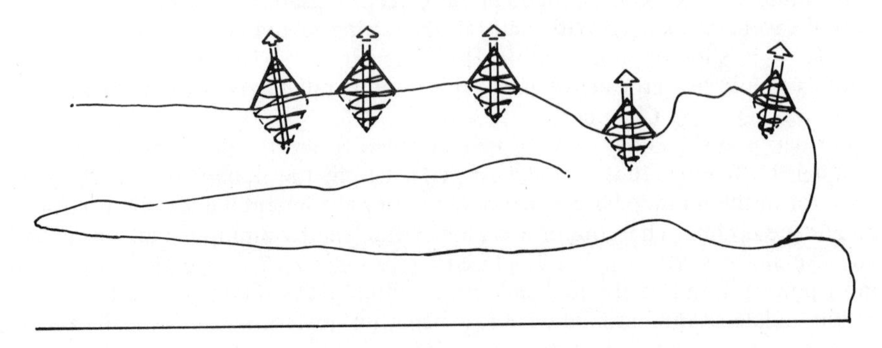

Figure 58: Crystal Pyramid Chakra Energizing Technique

becomes part of the pyramidal flow-pattern and is thereby powerfully infused with such energies. This penetrating action is exceptionally useful because it reaches into a body region or chakra zone in a manner that few other Light-tools can do with as much amplified, ordered stability. The pyramid thereby imparts its inherent perfecting and reprogramming energetic properties. Such a pyramid can also be programmed with a specific thought-pattern or energy field, which will also be infused into the application region. Other additional vibrational influences can be projected into the abiding pyramidal energy flow, such as applied healing touch, sonics (for example, tuning forks), lasers, energies from wands and other Light-tools, and so on. In this way the crystal pyramid creates a vortex penetrating effect that opens the application area to heightened receptivity to assimilating other specific types of applied energy flow.

Particularly effective for reprogramming purposes is the use of an entire set of crystal pyramids so that each chakra has a pyramid on top of it (see Figure 59). For logistical reasons, the Alpha and Omega chakras would have double-terminations (larger size) situated at these regions. This technique, used in conjunction with other reprogramming modalities, stands as one of the best available for this purpose.

For use in healing, the crystal pyramid is placed on top of the imbalanced area, optimally programmed with a condition-specific energy balancing influence. For best results, allow five to ten minutes for the pyramid dynamics to sufficiently integrate with the chakra's or bioregion's energetic activity; then apply other healing techniques with the pyramid still in place. If the technique requires that the pyramid be taken off the area, the preconditioning effects are still valuable in preparing the region to efficiently assimilate the healing work.

Though a framework pyramid will help precondition areas for applied healing or reprogramming work, the energy dynamics are not sufficiently strong to gain the deep penetrative action of the crystal pyramid. Used in conjuction with the crystal pyramid, the framework pyramid can be of significant amplifying effect; here, the framework pyramid is placed directly over the crystal pyramid so that the apexes of both are vertically aligned with each other.

For use in this type of modality, the crystal pyramids need to have at least a one inch-base. For ideal results, a 1½ inch-base to 3 inch-base is best. The quartz itself need not be of optical quality, but does require fundamental clarity and quality to be effective.

The significance of this crystal pyramid methodology cannot be overemphasized, for it will be a basis for myriad advanced healing and reprogramming modalities of the future, especially in conjunction with sophisticated Light-tools (such as those shown in Chapter 13) and lasers.

5. Pyramids are singularly valuable in unified energy fields and temple chambers. As see in Chapter 14 and Chapter 15, pyramids are an indispensable aspect of these blueprint designs. Their primary usefulness lies in functioning as the capstone antenna-receiver of a unified energy field. The capstone also helps to stabilize the entire energy field as well as amplifying the Pillar of Light effect. In other aspects of usage, they form secondary grids of energy amplification and focusing. Refer to these chapters to view the variety of pyramidal applications in this context.

6. The pyramid dynamic is also an integral part of reprogramming techniques. Refer to Chapter 9 for information on the use of pyramids in crystal water, chakra activation, and Alpha–Omega chakra reprogramming. See also Chapter 10 for applications of crystal pyramids in brain-mind activation processes.

7. *Multipyramidal systems* can be created by wiring together two or more four-sided pyramidal forms to generate a wide variety of powerful effects. The basic principle concerns the placement of many pyramids in contiguous harmonic relationships to create interrelated, synergistic energy dynamics in a unified fashion. Single pyramids integrate their flow patterns to manifest a whole greater that the sum of the parts.

To better comprehend the role of multipyramidal systems, Figure 59 illustrates two paradigms for understanding that pyramid energy is felt at significant distances away from the form itself. Figure 59A shows a commonly held paradigm. It is believed here that the physical pyramid functions as the capstone of a much larger energy pyramid structure. This viewpoint does not fully take into account octahedral dynamics. A more accurate depiction of this situation is seen in Figure 59B, where the four-sided pyramid naturally generates the octahedral flow pattern, and the energetics extending away from this are harmonics of the fundamental octahedron. The energetic strength of the harmonic energy pyramids depend upon the intensity and power of energy flow through the fundamental pyramid. If the fundamental pyramid is highly activated, the harmonic pyramids will be strong; the harmonic pyramids will be weak if the fundamental pyramid is of low activation. Also, the energetic strength of the harmonic pyramid tends to decrease proportionally to their distance from the fundamental energy dynamics. Notice, too, in Figure 59B that the apex-to-apex energy current of all the pyramids is strongly interlinked; it is through this component of pyramidal energy dynamics that all the harmonic pyramids have the most direct interconnection.

The most basic multipyramidal system is the simple octahedron. Two four-sided pyramids are linked together at their bases to create a single unified octahedral form. The actual linkage holding the two together is done with refined metal wire. At each of the four corner junctures where the two forms meet, wire is wrapped around both corners so that a link-up is created. Copper wire is adequate for this purpose, although silver and gold wire are ideal. In Figure 60 the resulting

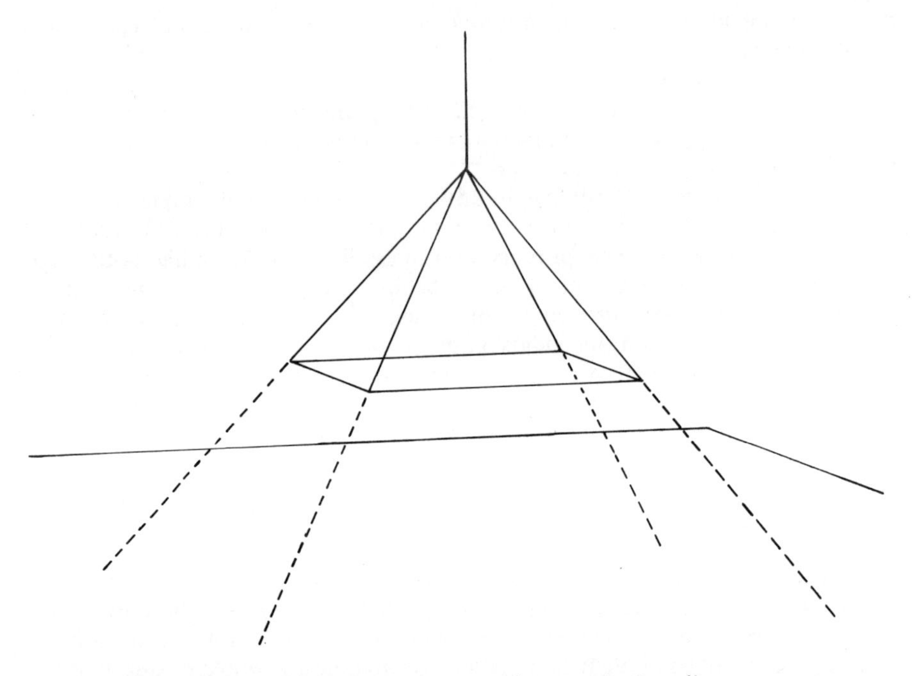

Figure 59a: Common Pyramid Energetics Paradigm

octahedron is shown being suspended inside a larger pyramid directly above the head of a seated individual. A ⅜ inch-base crystal pyramid is glued to the inverted apex of the octahedron to amplify the apex-to-apex current in both the octahedron itself and the larger pyramid. Small double-terminated crystals can also be glued or wire-wrapped along the exterior edges. In the illustration, the octahedron is attached to a mechanical rotator so that the octahedron also rotates for maximum energetic effects (the octahedron would still be effective if it were stationary too).

Figure 61 illustrates a more advanced version of the octahedron. In this instance, a crystal pyramid is attached to the four corners and two apexes. Double-terminations along the outer framework edges are ideal. A smaller crystal ball is suspended at the Eye of Yahweh by silver rods attached to the four corners. This Octahedron Broadcaster is a powerful accumulator and broadcaster of energy flow. Because of the outward-pointing orientation of the crystal pyramids at the four corners, a significant portion of the energy processing through these corners is directed outward into the surrounding environment. This multipyramidal model is an effective interdimensional antenna-receiver, especially when it is rotating at harmonic RPM rates. It can serve as an energy source and broadcaster for an entire room, or as a powerful capstone for a unified energy field.

The multipyramidal system seen in Figure 62 is composed of five single pyramids, all joining together to create one large four-sided pyramid. The construction is quite simple: Lay out four single pyramids so that all four intersect at a central

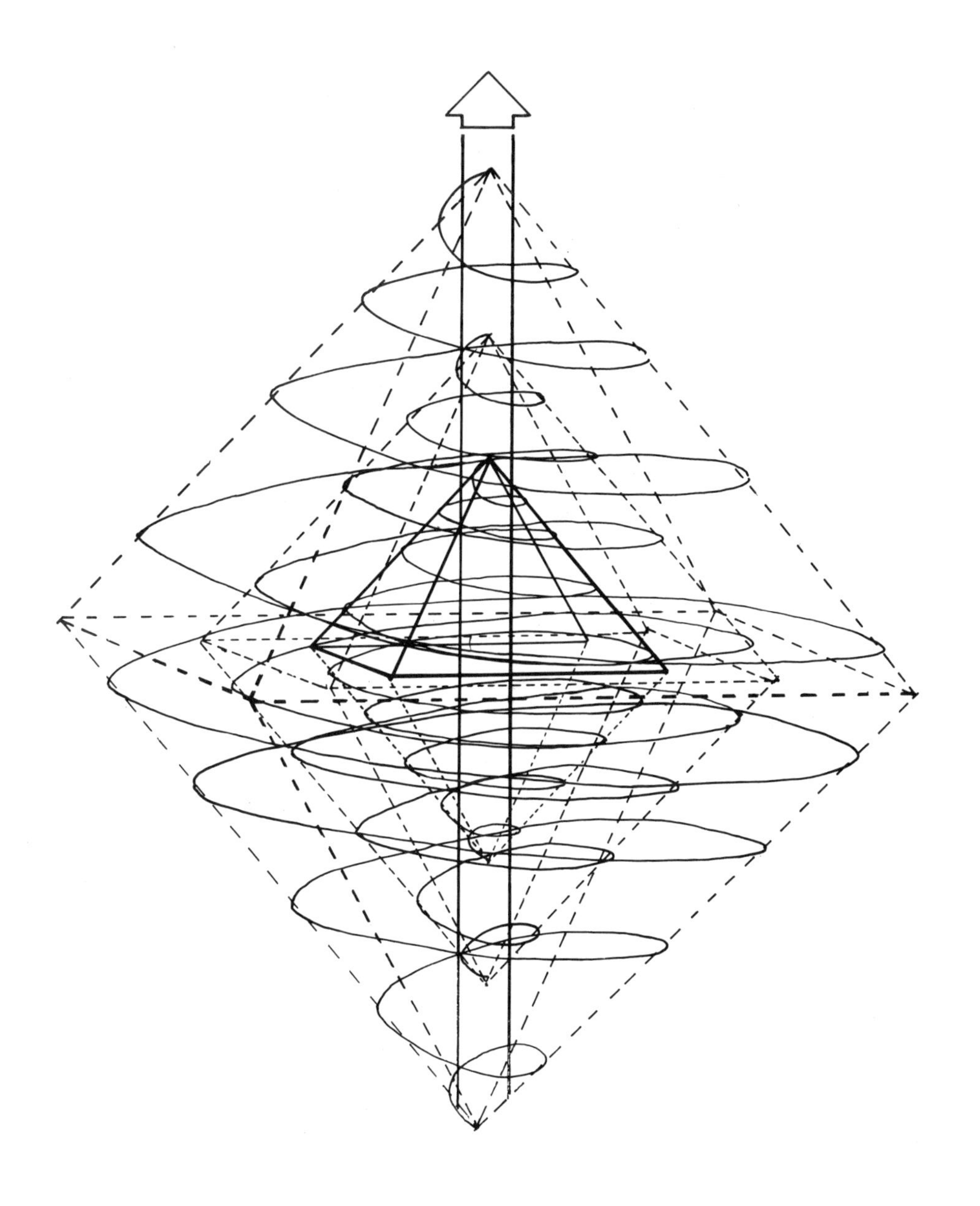

Figure 59b: Octahedrally Based Pyramid Energetics Paradigm

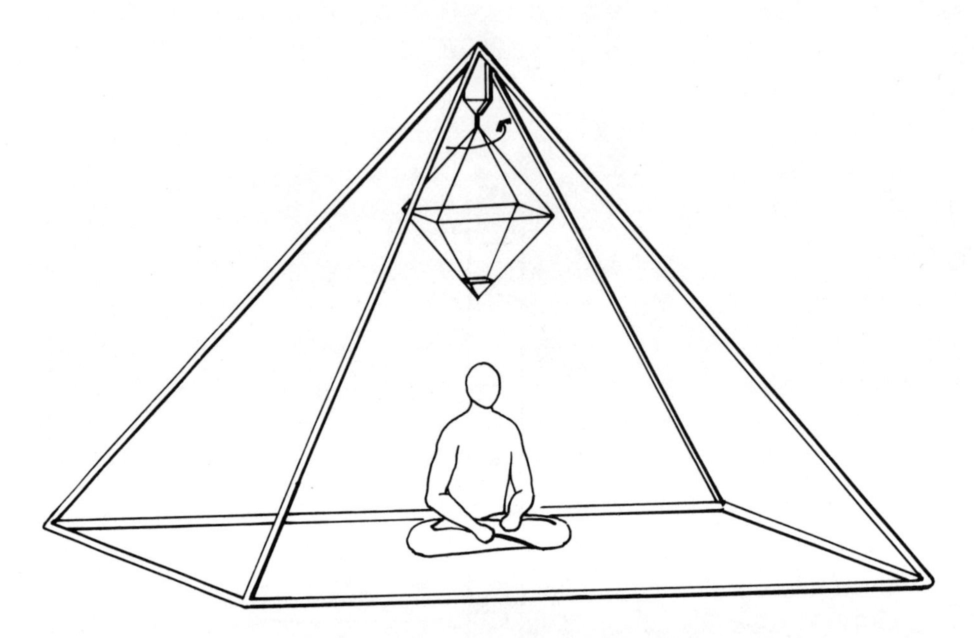

Figure 60: Rotating Octahedron in Larger Pyramid

point, as illustrated. Join them together at the corners and central point where they intersect with one another. Then place the fifth pyramid on top of the first four so that each base corner of the fifth rests upon the apex of the lower pyramids. Wire wrap the lower apexes to the corresponding upper base corners. Attach a 3/8 inch-base crystal pyramid at the system's upright apex and position a larger crystal pyramid (point oriented upward) at the apex of the resultant inverted pyramid directly below the topmost pyramid (thus creating a full octahedron).

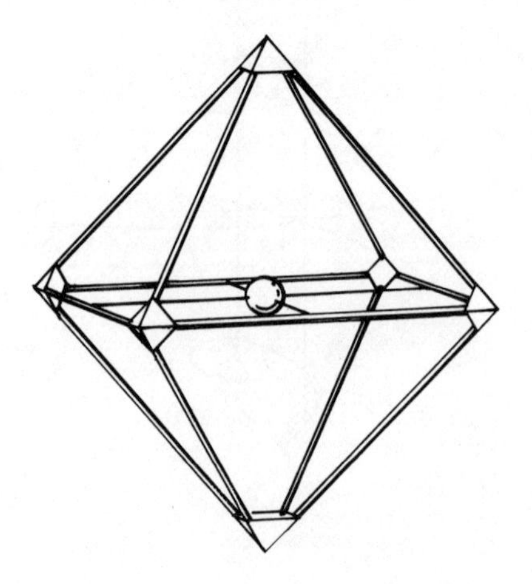

Figure 61: Octahedron Broadcaster

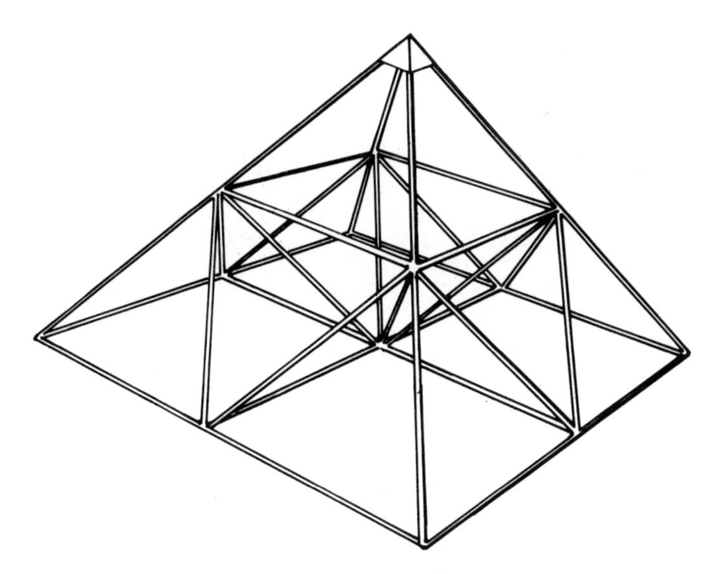

Figure 62: Five-Pyramid System

This multipyramidal system is constructed so that the lower four pyramids feed their energies through their apexes directly into both the central octahedron and the single large pyramid as a whole. The main current flows out of the top apex, and the effect is quite potent. This system can be used in a multiplicity of ways—as a suspended energy field capstone, laid on the floor with a surrounding crystal gridwork as a Pillar of Light generator; vertically attached to a wall, directing an energy stream toward a desired area; and so on.

Figure 63 shows an extended version of the pyramidal system shown in Figure

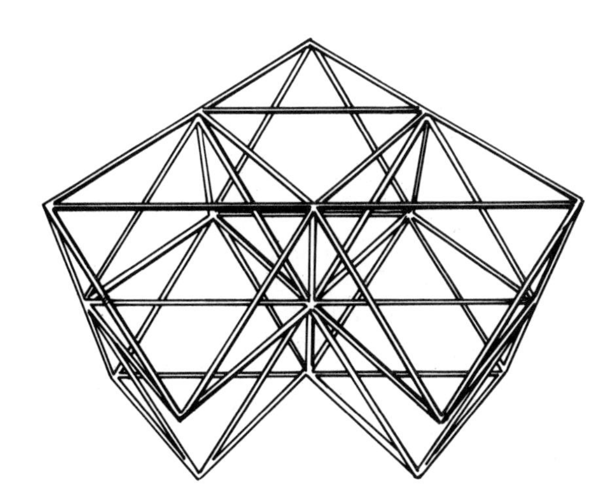

Figure 63: Five-Octahedron Multi-Pyramidal System

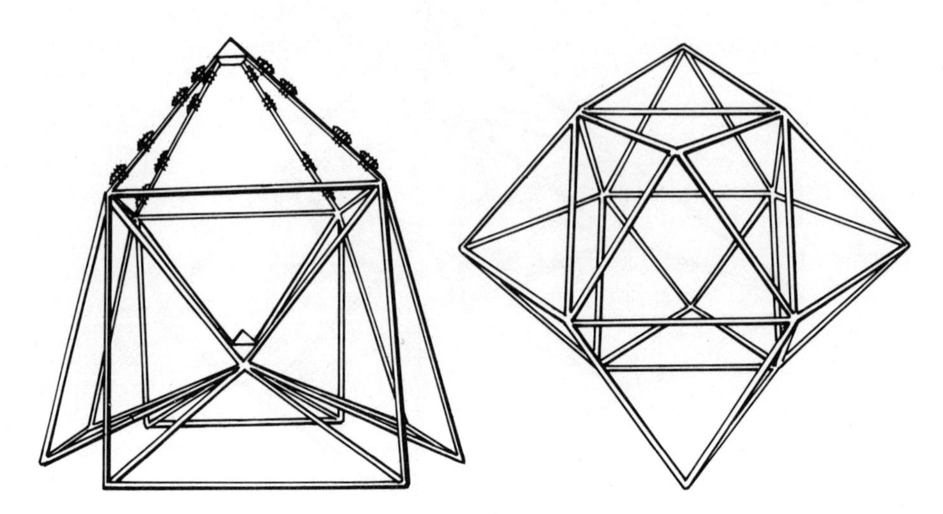

Figure 64: ''Zapper'' *Figure 65: Interdimensional Communications Module*

62. Here, four more pyramids have been attached below each of the four lower pyramids already part of the system. The result is the creation of four octahedrons that collectively nest a fifth octahedron. This multipyramidal system is used almost exclusively as a suspended capstone for a unified energy field. Small crystal pyramids are attached at the inverted apexes of the four lower octahedrons, pointing downward. Another crystal pyramid of larger size can be situated at the inverted apex of the topmost octahedron, pointing upward. And, if logistically possible, a small crystal pyramid can be attached at the uppermost apex. This pyramidal system will prove over the years to come to be one of the standard unified energy field capstones in advanced personal and professional usage.

Figure 64 illustrates yet another creative multipyramidal system, called the Zapper. In this case, four pyramids are joined together at their apexes; the pattern so created looks like a Maltese cross from a top view. An octahedron is then fitted into the perfectly accomodating area created by the four united pyramids. With crystal pyramids at the upper and lower apexes of the octahedron and double-terminations attached along the sides of the octahedron, the Zapper is manifested. Notice that the four adjoined pyramids focus their individual and collective energy flow directly through their apexes into the inverted apex of the octahedron. As this input is processed into the octahedron's dynamics, a forceful, laserlike energy current is emitted through the upper apex of the octahedron. This multipyramidal system is most often attached to a wall so that the apex-to-apex axis is directed into a desired chakra area, usually for reprogramming purposes; in this case it is best to have the Zapper vertically adjustable. Also, with a recipient reclined on a treatment table it can be utilized to project an energy stream approximately three inches to four inches over the top of the body, directly in line with the Alpha–Omega chakra system flow pattern.

Figure 65 shows an exceptional interdimensional communication attraction module. Here, six pyramids create the exterior configuration by attaching to each other via adjoining bases. The result is six outwardly pointing pyramids that collectively create a perfect interior cube with the lines of their adjoining bases. Inside the cubical interior an octahedron (not illustrated) can be superimposed in perfect balance. Crystal pyramids are attached to every apex throughout the entire system, eight in all. Suspend the system over an area in which amplified interdimensional communication access is desired. The effects are most potent when the system is integrated with an advanced unified energy field.

A discipline of immense technical complexity, the material presented in this chapter serves as a foundational paradigm for comprehending primary energy dynamics and setting the stage for knowledgeably focused future research. As this aspect of sacred science is remanifested in the years to come, tomes of information will be rerevealed and pyramidology will regain its place as a cornerstone of the scientific realm.

CHAPTER 13

Light-Tools: Wands, Breastplates, Pendants, Templates, and Discs

Within the domain of interdimensional science are endless possible designs and applications of Light-tools. Such tools involve the harmonious, synergistic integration of numerous crytallographic substances of precise energetic properties. Each Light-tool has a specific energetic profile; that is, every one is composed of a particular configuration of crystalline materials that, together, manifest an integrated totality of defined composite energy parameters. Light-tools are designed to harmoniously integrate with the human energy circuitry in order to amplify, supplement, or rectify consciousness capabilities. They are stepping-stones that assist in soul evolution and spiritual service so that both are optimalized. As individual and collective evolutionary development unfolds, what were valuable Light-tools are replaced with progressively more advanced tools that correlate with the higher growth needs. That is to say, Light-tools are a reflection of consciousness; they mirror the level of universal thought-forms to which consciousness has access and then manifests. This is a process that occurs in divine order as the Higher Evolution facilitates the selective accessing of these universal thought-forms within the highest interests of individual and collective spiritual growth.

Now, as the evolutionary energies of the earth-plane are accelerating with increasing rapidity, the magnitude of crystal-based knowledge correspondingly quickens and the techniques, tools, and technologies that spring forth from this field manifest as gifts of grace to assist and catalyze spiritual evolvement. The Light-tools presented in this chapter are another wave in this ongoing process. The purpose of this chapter is twofold: to present concepts that will be manifested and applied, and to sow seed-thoughts that may catalyze further developments in this field. Humankind need not wait for the fullest unfoldment of Light-based science in order to have effective Light-tools with which to work. To this end, note that every tool presented in this chapter can be manifested with current skills and technologies; in fact, virtually all can be made with standard artisan skills. The authors do not make these Light-tools for public or professional purchase nor are the authors available for consultation as to specifics regarding the design and creation of the Light-tools herein. To manifest many of them will require seeking assistance from professionals such as jewelry designers/creators, lapidaries, silversmiths, engineers, and the like. Precision of design and execution is imperative. Every angle, placement, material, orientation, and dimension must be accurate in accordance with the divine blueprint of each tool. Although there are numerous creative variations of any given Light-tool, all aspects of the design and manifestation process must be done with knowledge, for they are powerful precision instruments; those that are out of alignment with divine order can be detrimental to optimal soul growth patterns.

WANDS AND SCEPTERS

Wands and scepters are tuned harmonic energy instruments designed to facilitate specific energy flow dynamics. Most of these instruments set up a particular energy field that is responsive to applied higher consciousness and bioelectromagnetic input. They function to harmonically interact with these applied energies and focus, modulate, capacitate, amplify, transform, and emit them within specific parameters. In so doing, these crystal-based devices can be applied in a multiplicity of applications according to the vibrational range of each particular wand.

In order not to facilitate too much "crystallization" of expectations and thought-patterns concerning these wands and scepters, as well as the rest of the Light-tools, only the broadest of outlines of possible results and applications will be presented. Experiment freely but with caution, widely but with discernment. Intuitive guidance will be given to those who sincerely ask it of the Higher Evolution.

Figures 66 through 72 illustrate one genre of wand. In general, the lengths of the tubes and rods are related to the harmonic dynamics of the specific wand. All tubes and rods are of the most refined, conductive crystalline metals, mainly copper, sterling silver, gold, or titanium. In most cases, hollow tubes filled with small double-terminations (Herkimers are best) are more optimal than solid rods; the latter will work fine, but the tubes function with greater effectiveness. Most of these wands will benefit from spiral coils of copper, silver, or gold wire being wrapped around the exterior of the tube or rod. Small dabs of silicone glue at various intervals will secure the wire in place. No leather is ever used with these wands or any other Light-tool, because of its lower-vibrational nature. Though optimal use of metals with these wands will be described for each one, in most cases (except when specifically noted) copper, silver, and gold can be interchanged with one another as well as integrated together. Examples of metals being integrated together are copper and silver wiring coils used together or a copper tube or rod being silver-plated; many variations of these two examples are possible.

The wands' primary energy dynamics fall into two groupings. Figures 67, 68, 71, and 72 are directionalized in that one end amplifies and focuses energy into and through the tube or rod and the other end amplifies, focuses, and emits the end-product of the wand. The primary energy flow is unidirectional (in one end and out the other), but it is also important to be aware of the secondary radial oscillatory and harmonic energy dynamics. Figures 66, 69 and 70 are primarily dual-directional—the energy flow can be emitted from either or both ends. In this regard, the applied bioenergetic and higher consciousness energies interact with

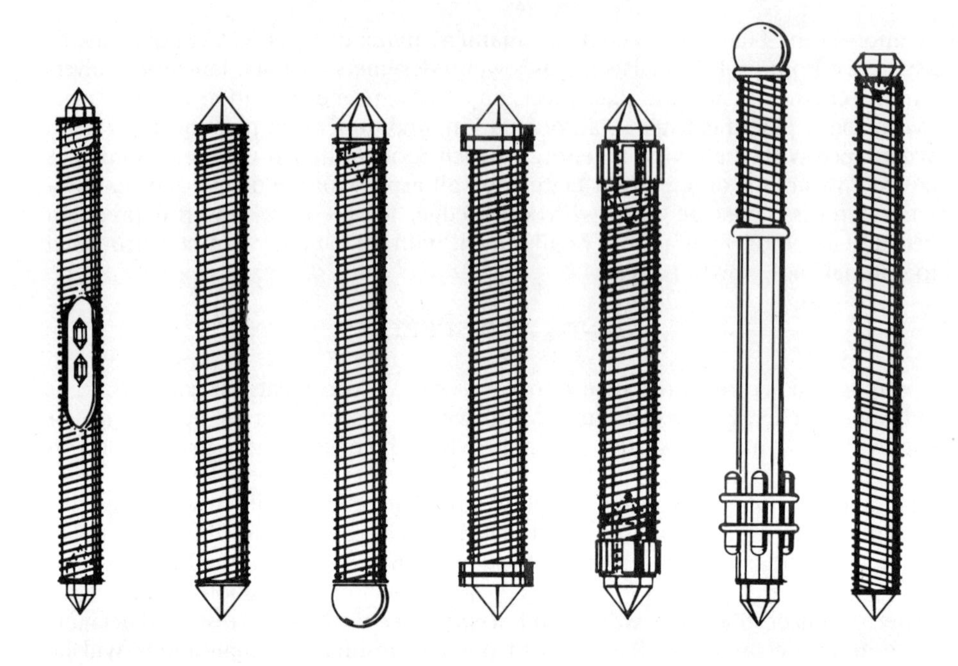

Figures 66–72: Crystal Wands

the wand and can modulate the directionality and mode of application. For example, the wand in Figure 69 can be held in both hands to balance the left and right biopolarities with each other through energy dynamics centered within the wand (that is, between the ends); on the other hand, the same wand can also be made directional so that primary energy flow is in through one end and emitted from the other end by applied focused intentionality.

Potential uses are myriad. Discerning applications for individual usage depends upon the unique nature of each person's energy-usage patterns within their chosen patterns of soul growth. Different people have different spiritual paths and healing-reprogramming regimes. The wands serve as energy focusing, amplifying, modulating, and magnifying emitting devices.

Following are abstracts that describe the highlights of each wand and discuss pertinent observations and suggestions.

Figure 67: Copper or sterling silver tubing. Crystals at both ends are double-terminations. One crystal has its receiving end pointing out of the tube bringing energy in and is focused through the other termination toward the other crystal. The second double-termination has its emitting end pointing out of the tube so that energy flows through the tube and out. The primary effect is that of a unidirectional laserlike energy beam that can be versatilely applied according to the intention of the operator.

Figure 67: Sterling silver tube with gold wire coil wrapping. Optical grade quartz crystal pyramids—one pyramid is faceted according to the Great Pyramid angles and the other is faceted at a harmonically smaller angle. The latter pyramid will bring in energy and project it through the tube to the Great Pyramid-angled crystal through which the energy is emitted in a laserlike beam (even more focused and coherent than in Figure 66). Unidirectional.

Figure 68: Silver tubing with wire coil wrapping. Good quality double-termination on one end (emitting end) and a small crystal ball at the other end. The crystal ball can either be silvered around its exterior or left as is. In the former case, the entire ball is silvered except where it meets the inner tube—a clear hole is left in the silvering. The ball then serves as an amplifying reflector for the inner tube energy dynamics—it does not take in significant amounts of energy through its exterior circumference as with most of the other wands. If the ball is left unsilvered, it is like the receptive end of the other wands, the difference being that the energy is more diffuse and soft. Both ends of this wand are good for applications needing less forceful and focused and more soothing and integrative vibrational influences.

Figure 69: Designated the Atlantean Harmonizing Wand. Copper tubing, ⅝ inch-base crystal pyramid at both ends (Great Pyramid angles). Circular Alnico magnets at both ends (the sides facing one another attract). Best to have at least two magnets on each end with crystal pyramid glued to outer magnet. Intensity of magnetics can be modified by adding one more magnet on each end (in between the first two). Can be held in both hands for right and left side biopolarity balancing. Hand positioning can be varied to obtain subtly different effects, for example, both palms up, both palms down, left up/right down, and right up/left down. Can also be used for creating directional beam from a single end by applying focused consciousness intentionality. A facilitator can make auric sweeps for excellent balancing, charging, and clearing.

Figure 70: Sterling silver on copper tubing. Gold wire wrapping with sterling silver tube; also, gold and silver wrapping with copper tubing. Good quality double-terminations at both ends. Less important here to have one crystal be receptive and one be emitting. Small rectangular rare earth magnets, six on both ends. The crystals are inset into the tube so that their midsections are slightly inside the tube. The six magnets are aligned with each crystal body face around the midsection. Can be used in a manner similar to Figure 69. The directional beam that can be created out of a single end by applied consciousness energies is powerful and has a high magnetic quotient. This is one of the most potent wands illustrated in this section.

Figure 71: Silver tubing. Wire wrapping at handle region. Double-termination one end (emitting); small crystal ball at other end. As in Figure 68 the ball can be silvered or left as is, with the same effects. Four small hollow cylinder tubes with two cabochonlike caps. Cylinders are made of sterling silver with one cap permanently shut and the other with a small spring mechanism that allows the cap to be opened when desired. They are glued onto the outside of the silver tubing near the crystal at one end; gold wire is wrapped around the outside of all four tubes together. Different tinctures, cell salts, homeopathic remedies, dietary supplements, and the like can be placed inside the cylinders (one substance per tube). Excellent wand for effective infusion of desired substance's energetic influences into a specific bioenergetic region in addition to the crystal energies themselves. Facilitator uses clockwise circling motions along with pulsed breathing for optimal results (see Chapter 17, number 24).

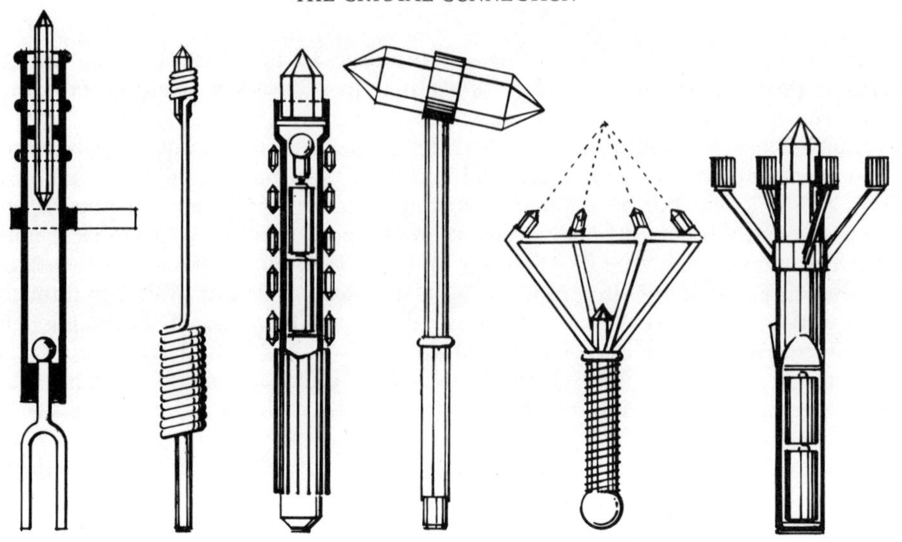

Figure 73: Sonic Wand
Figure 74: "Twist" Wand
Figure 75: Chromatic Wand
Figure 76: Succussion Wand
Figure 77: Octahedral Wand
Figure 78: Rotating Magnet Wand

Figure 72: Tubing and coil wire wrappings can be variable. One crystal is faceted specifically to draw energy into the tube and focus it precisely. The emitting crystal can be either a crystal pyramid or a faceted crystal for tight laserlike emission stream. Possible to experiment with gluing small rectangular rare earth magnets at harmonic intervals around the exterior of the tubing. Similar energy dynamics and applications as in Figure 66 and Figure 67.

OTHER WAND TYPES AND DESCRIPTIONS:

Figure 74: Sonic Wand. Silver tubing with excellent quality double-termination at one end. This crystal is optimally of a long, thin shape; it can also be the kind of double-termination that has multiple-terminations on one end (inside the tube) and a single-termination on the other end (pointing out of the tube). On the opposite end of the sonic wand is a replaceable tuning fork; because of its replaceability, any sonic frequency can be worked with by inserting different desired tuning forks into the wand. The tubing itself does not have small crystals inside; it is left hollow. Or, for optimal results, the tubing can be completely filled with a liquid crystal medium (well-prepared crystal water with high magnetic quotient will do at present, though in the future other liquid crystal mediums will be utilized also). In this case, a sensitive thin metallic membrane is inserted into the tube so that the base of a tuning fork transmits sonic vibrations through it into the liquid crystal (and it also retains the liquid inside the tube without leakage). At right angles to the rest of the wand is a handle for the operator that does not interfere with the sonic dynamics of the wand proper; logistic factors require the handle to be insulated from the rest of the wand so that minimal interference to the overall energy dynamics occurs. When the tuning fork is vibrating, the sonic frequencies emanate from the fork itself and are also transmitted through the tube and into the crystal, which transduces, amplifies, and focuses the vibrations that then emit from its termination in a coherently focused stream of energy. Both ends of the sonic wand are functional. The tuning fork end can be used to infuse the sonic frequencies alone into the appropriate region to help prepare it for more intense work; it is also good for assisting in the integration and assimilation of such work. The energy emissions from the crystal are penetrating and directional in nature. Any number of applications are possible, including auric "surgery," mind-center activation, and chakra healing and reprogramming. This tool must be used with discernment; its effects are quite potent because of the intense crystal–sonic directionality.

Figure 75: Twist Wand. Thick copper wire is used to create a tuned coil wrapping from the copper rod handle to the double-termination at the opposite end. Both the wire and the handle rod can be electroplated with silver or gold or both for heightened energetic responsivity and broader spectrum capacities. In fact, there are two interconnected tuned coil arrangements—one at the base and one around the crystal's body. The number of wrappings of each are in harmonic proportion to the other; the bottom coil always has the greater number of wrappings. The length of the wire connecting the two coils is also harmonically related to the intercoil energetic interchange. By varying the intercoil proportionality, the twist wand is tuned to modulate and emit different vibrational outputs. It is, then, possible to have numerous twist wands, each turned to a different harmonic output, to apply in different circumstances.

In short, the primary energy dynamics of this wand are as follows: energies applied through the base are tuned within the first coiling; this modulated energy is then resonantly pulsed to the second coil, where the energy is further modulated according to the number of coil wrappings. As this modulation occurs the energy it emits also interacts resonantly with the crystal, which then takes the tuned energy, amplifies and focuses it, and then emits it in rapid pulses. Energy can also be applied first to the crystal (as in tapping into the dynamics of a generator crystal or gridwork). These vibrations then are harmonically processed through the two coils and into the bioenergetic system of the operator. According to the tuned intentionally of the operator, the energetics then flow back to the crystal and are emitted.

The Twist Wand, then, is a precision tuned instrument, highly responsive to applied energies. The emissions are not as strongly penetrating as those of the Sonic Wand or the wands in, for example, Figure 68 or Figure 71. The intensity and coherency quotients are in the midrange relative to other wands. The applications of the Twist Wand are diverse, encompassing many possibilities in the realms of healing, reprogramming, and interdimensional science.

Figure 76: Chromatic Wand. This wand is designed to combine chromatics and crystals so that the two interact, thus creating a versatile tool. A large diameter copper tube is used to house a battery arrangement that is connected to an outer switch that, when turned on, will light a quartz halogen bulb situated directly below the base of the crystal. The crystal is singly terminated with a cut and polished base. The base can be polished so that a lensing action is created via a curved, parabolic shape. The crystal's terminations are optimally one of two patterns: six equally sizes equilateral triangular facets, or small, equally sized *z* facets and large, equally sized *r* facets—all six facets being equilateral triangles. Directly between the light bulb and the crystal base is an area in which different color gels can be inserted conveniently; in this way, the chromatic effects can be modulated to suit the needs of specific situations. Also, to better facilitate the transfer of the applied energies of the operator through the wand, small, thin double-terminations may be glued on the exterior of the tubing so that there are four or six lines of crystals leading from the handle to the wand's top. Wherever chromatics is a desired modality to incorporate, the Chromatic Wand is an excellent way to apply these vibrations through the integration of the wand concept in conjunction with crystal energetics.

Figure 77: Succussion Wand. A solid sterling silver rod with gold leafing at bottom and top; has a double-termination mounted on top of it with a thin silver band. The crystal optimally is of high quality, lengthy, and thin. It is mounted at a slight angle relative to the silver rod and the largest facet of the upraised termination is situated in a downward position. The thin silver wand that holds the crystal in place atop the silver rod allows the crystal to move independently in an up and down direction; this play is small but significant—about ¼ inch in either direction from its stable position.

The purpose of the Succussion Wand is to gently and rhythmically tap, or succuss, an imbalanced area in order to infuse intervalled pulses of crystal energy (plus gold and silver) into it. The region is tapped with the largest facet of the upraised crystal termination (which is in the downward position). The repeated influx of rhythmic crystal energy helps gently prepare a given area to receive more intense, concentrated healing work by infusing the area in general and also by helping to break up and release constricted energy patterns. This modality also helps in the integration process done after focused healing work. In addition, by placing a few drops of a healing remedy, such as a gem tincture, Bach flower remedy, or herbal tincture, and successing the drops with the wand on the skin, that particular energetic influence can be infused into the region.

> It has been pointed out by Mark Gallert in a study called *New Light on Therapeutic Energies* that the repeated application of mechanical energy to the therapeutic substance (the grinding of triturations or succussion of liquids) "results in spreading the molecules of the original substance farther and farther apart, thus altering its fundamental nature and *releasing essential energy* (energy of its essence) and making that energy available to the human body. When the molecular structure of a remedy is so altered, then, matter is transformed into radiant energy."[1]

The Succussion Wand, then, is an optimal tool by which the controlled releasing of desired energy patterns may be stimulated to radiate into a specific bioenergetic area.

Figure 78: Octahedral Wand. Primary pyramidal energy dynamics are incorporated into the wand concept here. The bottommost vertical part of this wand is actually a wand in and of itself, like the wands in Figures 66, 67, 68, and 72. Optimal metal factors are silver tubing with silver or gold wrapping or both. For less optimal, but still significant, results this wand-base can be simply solid sterling silver with a single-terminated crystal mounted on top. Connected to the wand-base are four solid silver rods that describe the exact angular configuration of the Great Pyramid, thus making an inverted pyramid with the wand-base crystal at the inverted apex. Mounted at the end of each of the four silver rods are single-terminations whose angles create the outline of an equal and opposite upright pyramid atop the inverted pyramid. Each of the four crystal mountings is also connected via silver rods so that a circumference square is created. Thus an energetic octahedron is manifested, connected to the wand-base. The octahedron wand operates like the primary pyramidal energy dynamics do. Added to this is the powerfully focused directional beam emitting from the wand-base, contributing considerable force to the apex-to-apex dynamics of the pyramidal energy flow. The result is the focusing of amplified energies into and through the top apex point of the energetic octahedron. This energy flow is directional, focused, and powerful. It is also responsive to input from higher consciousness energies of the operator. Application potentials are easily incorporated into many already-existing healing and reprogramming methodologies.

This concept can be applied to the tetrahedral form. The wand-base would be surmounted by an inverted tetrahedron with mounted crystals outlining an upright tetrahedron. The applications, again, are wide ranging, one of which is as a superb interdimensional telethought communication device.

Figure 79: Rotating Magnet Wand. This wand incorporates the magnet–crystal interface in addition to modulatable rotational effects. A larger diameter copper tubing accommodates two copper-top batteries at the base. A switch connected to the batteries turns on an electrical current that rotates four rectangular rare earth magnets about the midsection of a mounted double-termination, as depicted in the diagram. Optimally, the rotational rate of the magnets is modifiable within a broad spectrum of rates; and the rotational direction can be clockwise or counterclockwise. There are no crystals within the copper tube. The base has an insulative outer covering (nonleather) with which the operator may hold the wand; it is important to insulate the operator from the primary dynamics. The rotating magnets generate powerful nonlinear reactions within the crystal, and energies emitted have a high magnetic component as well as higher dimensional magneto-gravitational gradients. The internal crystal dynamics and emitted energies are responsively modulatable by applied higher consciousness frequencies of the operator. The emissions from this wand are among the most potent of any of the Light-tools presented in this chapter. In some applications it can be used as a power wand, able to activate, modulate, and direct the energy of a gridwork or generator crystal and to generate amplified energies that can be directed in many ways. Held over a specific area of imbalance in conjunction with modulated higher consciousness patterns of a facilitator, deeply effecting healing can occur in short periods of time. For chakra reprogramming, few Light-tools can match its efficacy. As always, such a potent tool must be utilized with high degrees of judgment and Spirit-derived authority.

Figure 80: Scepter Wand. Silver tubing of a larger diameter is used as the foundation for this wand; it is gold-plated and surmounted with a gold-plated scepter shaping of sterling silver that houses a double-termination. The silver tubing is capped at the base and wrapped with titanium wiring around its exterior from base to scepter. Inside the tubing and scepter is a liquid crystal medium (highly magnetized crystal water is fine at present). Around the exterior of the sceptered portion are six rectangular rare earth magnets alternating with six small,

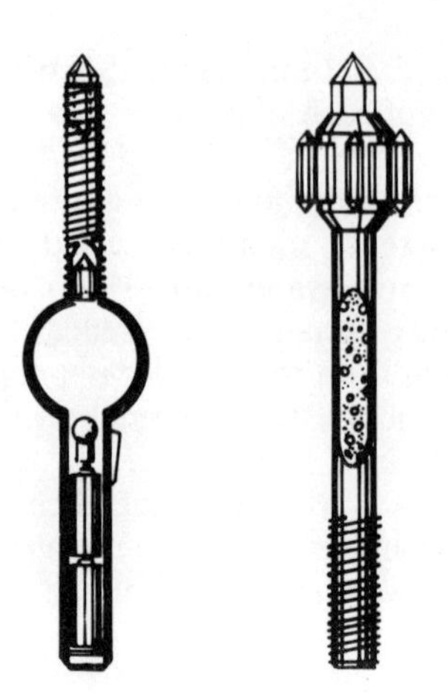

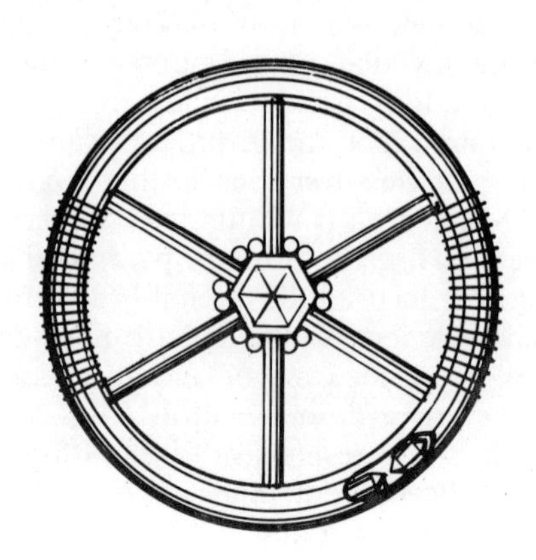

Figure 79: Flash Wand
Figure 80: Scepter Wand
Figure 81: Atlantean Wheel Wand

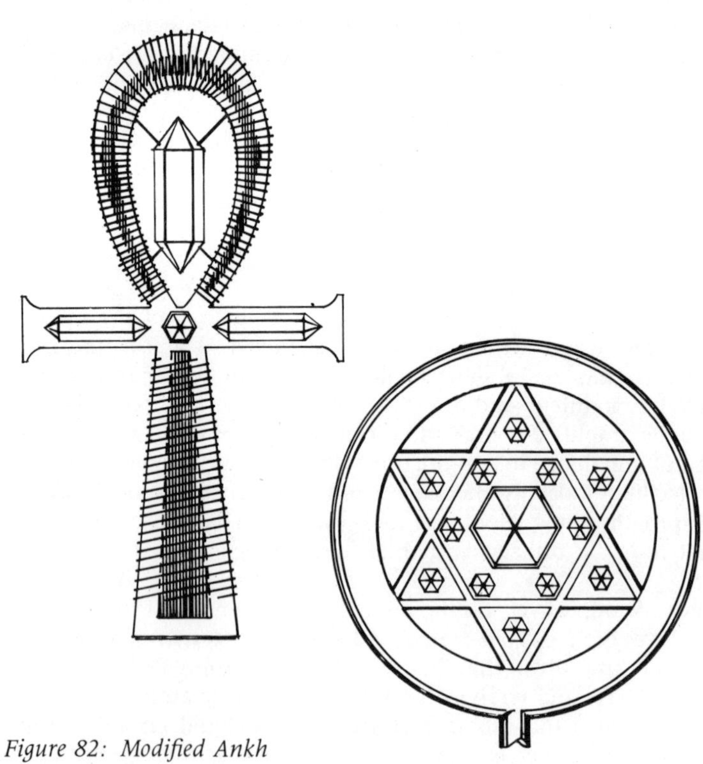

Figure 82: Modified Ankh
Figure 83: Power Staff
Figure 84: Staff Scepter

thin double-terminations. The magnets are aligned with the crystal's edges and the crystals are aligned with the body faces.

In another version of the Scepter Wand the interior of the tubing has a battery–electronics set-up instead of liquid crystal and the large crystal at the top is outfitted to rotate at modulatable rates.

As with the Rotating Magnet Wand of Figure 78, the Scepter Wand has numerous power wand applications. Unlike the Rotating Magnet Wand, however, it does not have the especially strong higher dimensional, magneto-gravitational energies, though it does have comparable basic crystal–magnetic quotients. The titanium adds a strongly projective element, and in conjunction with the six small crystals and magnets, it manifests a forceful stream of emitting energy. The surrounding crystals and magnets create subsidiary emanations that resonantly interact with the main double-termination and add considerably to the primary energy dynamics as they feed into the main energy current.

Figure 80: Flash Wand. This is a unique wand concept designed to generate pulsed bursts of energy. At the base is a battery attached to a quartz halogen bulb or photo flash unit that can be turned on and off by a switch incorporated into the base. The bulb flashes emit into a flash reflector chamber composed of mirrored material that helps reflect as much of each light flash as possible into the opposite end of the wand. This portion is composed of a copper tubing interior with one double-termination at each end. A sleeve of carbon steel fits over the copper tubing so that a small insulating layer of air is in between them. Around the exterior of the steel sleeve is copper wire wrapping. As the light flashes go through the copper tubing and two crystals, a significant electromagnetic field is generated, which is amplified and projected from the quartz at the wand's end. The operator, by modulating the sequence rate and rhythm of the light flashes, can create pulsed emissions from the wand. Such bursts are most effective for selectively energizing a bioenergetic region with sequences of energizing pulses. One excellent variation of this is to direct these emissions through crystal templates (see later in this chapter) laid upon the chakras.

Figure 81: Atlantean Wheel Wand. The exterior of this singular wand is of circular silver tubing (13 to 16 inches in diameter), having also six spokes of smaller diameter silver tubing converging into a central region occupied by a faceted quartz crystal. Through all the tubing are small double-terminations. Wrapped around the two opposite sides where the operator holds this device is gold wiring. The quartz mounted in the center is faceted so that one side is the receptive, ingathering end and the other side is the focusing, projective end. Around the crystal on six sides are six small rare earth magnets as illustrated. Uses for this device include: 1) holding in both hands and positioning over an area of imbalance, focusing energy through the central crystal directly into that region; 2) holding it in front of a chakra with the crystal's projective end pointing away to focus and amplify applied energies through that chakra for a form of Light-work, be it reprogramming, telethought communication, or a scientific application; 3) suspending it over a bioenergetic area with a laser directed into and through the center crystal into the desired zone for healing work.

Figure 82: Modified Ankh. The ankh is an archetypal symbol and energy pattern of the life essence, and has been utilized throughout the centuries as an energy resonator, amplifier, and coherent emitter. There are many ways in which this tool can be harmoniously modified to make it a more powerful device. Figure 82 illustrates one such way. The main body is of solid sterling silver. The lower body has a titanium inlay from the lowest point of the base up to the cross area. Tightly wrapped gold wiring spans the entire length of the inlay. In the center of the cross is a specifically faceted clear quartz or diamond with a double-termination on either side pointing into the center. Around the top loop is a magnetic inlay wrapped with gold wire. A double-termination is mounted within the top loop by silver struts with a thin wrapping around the crystal body at the upper and lower struts for support. The power, precision, and efficiency of such an ankh is multiplied manyfold with the addition of other such energetic influences. There are numerous variations on this theme to be explored. This ankh can also function as a hand-held tool or as the top of a staff.

Figure 83: Power Staff. Staffs are a variation on the wand theme. Staffs are generally used for power applications; the forms are many, the the primary purpose is the same. The much greater length of the staff (versus the wand) allows for increased amplification because of its greater capacitance properties combined with acceleration factors of refined metals. Quartz and other precious stones have capacitance, that is, energy storage characteristics. The mode of capacitance occurs rapidly (sometimes in femto-seconds, or even faster), as energy throughout the staff builds up to a specific threshold level after which it pulse-releases it. The staff, by virtue of greater overall crystalline mass, can, as a result, absorb a higher amount of energy that when pulse-released carries an increased overall charge.

The main idea in the design of a staff is to place gems and refined metals at harmonic intervals throughout the length of the staff. The energy dynamics are harmonic standing wave patterns that bear sometimes simple and sometimes complex sacred geometric relationships among them. The staff can be designed to modulate energy in a wide spectrum of predictable ways (through the indexes and tables of interdimensional science). Generally, there is holistic polarity between the two ends similar to that found in double-terminations. The parameters thereof are set so that the primary energy flow is predetermined to go from bottom to top. Vibrations are "compressed" at both ends while they are expanded and accelerated in and through the intervening rod or tubing that constitutes the main framework of the staff. By placing gems or refined metals at the nodal (and secondarily, antinodal) regions, throughout the staff, the energy modulation parameters are set. The operator holds the staff at one of the primary generative nodal points so that the consciousness and bioelectromagnetic energies are phase locked with the staff. As the bioenergies in general and the specifically formulated thought-patterns in particular interact with the staff, the final modulating of energy occurs as it formulates through the staff, which is then directed toward the intended purpose.

The power staff illustrated in Figure 83 is one example of a staff designed to serve as a seed-thought for many other possibilities in this field of knowledge. Two points are of interest here. One is that in addition to using metal rods and tubes, crystalline rods of quartz and other precious stones can serve as an inner core of the staff around which other layers of materials may be placed. If using crystalline rods is not possible, lucite rods can serve the purpose. Second, ornamentation for the sake of ornamentation serves only to neutralize the full potential effectiveness of a staff. Every aspect of these tools (as well as the wands and other

Light-tools) needs to interrelate and integrate with every other aspect in conjunction with the overall purpose and energy dynamics. The apparent ornamentation in some of the more highly developed staffs are, in fact, necessary functional aspects due to their energy interference and processing properties. In lesser staffs this fact is not completely understood and engenders the production of superfluous ornamentation that has no functional aspects other than to add superficial attractiveness to the eye.

Like a lightning rod, a well-conceived staff is a powerful means of drawing higher Light to the earth-plane for appropriate distribution. It is imperative that clear discernment in-the-Light occur before using such a Light-tool.

Figure 84: Staff Scepter. This is a variation on the design of the upright end of a staff. Here the metallic component is solid sterling silver with gold plating. A Star of David energy pattern is encircled and different gemstones are placed at harmonic intervals throughout this design with either a quartz or diamond in the middle. Depending upon the consciousness blueprint of the individual and the purpose of the staff, different gemstones and gemstone patterns can be chosen.

CRYSTAL TEMPLATES

A crystal template is a piece of quartz cut into a thin slice. Normally ¼ inch to ½ inch in thickness and 2½ inches to 4 inches in width, templates are cut from high quality optical quartz (from crystals otherwise not usable for higher purposes). After cutting, the horizontal and vertical planes are polished until the crystal surface is as clear as possible. The next stage is to inscribe key symbols and energy patterns into the quartz matrix, for example, pictographic flame letters, mandalas, Light-symbols, or sacred geometric patterns and inlaid with silver or gold (see Figure 85 and 86). It is also possible to glue patterns of gems on top of the crystal templates. Each template will exert an energetic influence that corresponds to its inscribed and inlaid patterning. The crystalline matrix in which the symbols are inscribed serves to hold the pattern steady and to duplicate it in a repeatable and amplified manner. By placing the templates on bioenergetic areas in need of healing or reprogramming, the inscribed energy pattern will be infused and assimilated within that region, thereby causing correlating bioenergetic recrystallization. These Light-tools are especially effective for working with the chakra system, either singly or with entire sets.

The challenge in using templates is in deciding which inscription-pattern correlates with the blueprint of a given bioenergetic area and its healing-reprogramming needs. This process is, on the higher levels of application, an exacting sacred science. Until the advent of advanced Light-based technologies, personal and professional judgment must be based on authorized interdimensional communication. The use of templates, especially in more sophisticated professional unified energy fields and temple chambers, is a major Light-modality of the future for facilitating highly accelerated healing and reprogramming processes. Those who can successfully pioneer this discipline will be in great demand in the near future.

The sacred science of making and applying crystal templates is complex. Following are a few perspectives in this regard.

For the most part, templates are to be cut at right angles to the c axis. This is the major crystallographic orientation of the largest percentage of templates. With

Figure 85–86: Examples of Inscribed and Inlaid Crystal Templates

this orientation the natural hexagonal proportions are maintained, along with their integral association with Star of David dynamics. Also, as presented in Crystal 7, energy dynamics occurring parallel to the c axis have certain uniquely desirable characteristics that also apply to template usage. In the future, different crystallographic orientations of templates will be applied, but at the present stage of development it is best not to explore such avenues, for they are exacting indeed. A more fruitful further stage of specialization is the cutting of these tools into different fundamental sacred geometric patterns, for example, the 5 × 7 rectangle, equilateral triangle, square, circle, and soon. A high degree of skill in this field is required, as the specialized shapes are specific in their correspondingly appropriate inscription patterns and applications. It is also possible to layer together two or more thin template slices to create an integration of harmonious energies. Templates composed of other precious gems are also integral to the more advanced usage patterns. In the future, the most refined gem matrices—diamond, gold, emerald, topaz, and so on—will be utilized as specialized templates. A large portion of these templates will be cut from laboratory grown crystals (grown according to the principles of sacred science).

The inscription patterns function optimally in most cases when they are inlaid with other precious crystalline materials. Primary among such substances are gold, titanium, platinum, and silver. Other crystalline matrices such as copper, lapis lazuli, opal, alexandrite, and so on are useful under specialized circumstances. The primary four would best be given priority until the professional's knowledge naturally expands in this direction. Also, the use of small rare earth magnets, either inlaid or glued in a harmonic grid pattern around the circumference of the template, is effective in particular circumstances. Gemstones may also be inset or glued in harmonic grid patterns to excellent effect.

Optimal application modes incorporate a selection of ways to infuse concentrated energetics in and through the template into the bioenergetic system. By virtue of having templates in place on the recipient some benefit will accrue, but for best effects additional energetics needs to be applied. Many of the wands and other Light-tools in this chapter serve this purpose. These Light-tools, in conjunction with applied consciousness energies, provide the principal dynamic force that can facilitate profound results. Additionally, the use of lasers directed through the

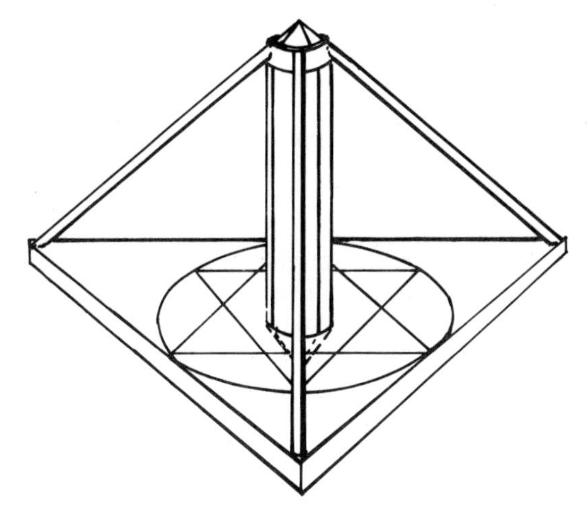

Figure 87: 3-D Template

c axis of the template as well as modulatable sonic applicators will add considerable dynamism. One optimal modality in this regard is the use of a multifrequency laser scanner-computer system. A computer could be programmed with specific sequences of frequency patterns and a description of the inscription patterns with laser light interacting perfectly with the inscription itself. With an even more advanced system, nine lasers would simultaneously shine programmed energy patterns in the seven plus two chakras, each laser having a unique program designed specifically for a given chakra.

A variation of the template concept is illustrated in Figure 87. In this case a triangular template has a double-termination mounted via three sterling silver supports so that the crystal is perpendicular to the horizontal axis and points directly in and through the midpoint of the template. The result is the incorporation of a primary three-dimensional geometric pattern, a tetrahedron in this instance, as a further focusing-amplifying agent of the crystal.

Natural quartz tabulars make superb templates. Any of the template design concepts discussed may be applied by insetting and inlaying or gluing crystals and metals on the tabular's flat body. Also, by gluing small double-terminations following the natural sacred geometric patterning of various types of sea shells, another variation of the template theme occurs. Cross-sectioned nautilus shells, sand dollars, whole spiralling shells, and others make exceptional templates.

The effect of template treatments is that key amplified energy patterns are infused and actively assimilated into the bioenergetic matrix. The energetics projected through the templates by wands, lasers, and other tools stimulate the vibrational duplication of the inscription pattern, which then projects into the underlying bioenergetic region. When a specific inscription energy pattern harmoniously integrates with a particular bioenergy matrix, the former acts as a key that unlocks and activates the latter. The inscription pattern acts as a seed-crystal blueprint about which bioenergies crystallize on the most causal of levels. Where there was disharmony, a new crystallization pattern of health emerges. Where reprogramming is appropriate, the bioenergy matrix transmutes onto a higher octave pattern of functioning. Indeed, template treatments in conjunction with the more advanced Light-tools, unified energy fields, and temple chambers are a wave of the future seen in retrospect as one of the greater fruits catalyzed by the mid-to-late 1980's phenomenon of accelerated popular crystal awareness.

TOUCHSTONES AND BREASTPLATES

Touchstones and breastplates are variations on the crystal template theme. The emphasis in this case is on the creative modulation of consciousness through selectively attuning with various combinations of gem vibratory patterns. Whereas the inscription patterns of crystal templates do not function as widely modulatable tools, touchstones and breastplates act as multipurpose "keyboards" of energetic tunability. The concept underlying the archetypal high priest breastplate is the placing of a precise grid of various key gemstones over a central bioenergetic vortex zone—in most cases, the heart chakra—so that by attuning consciousness to various single or combinations of gems by touch and focused awareness, Light-work capabilities become highly amplified and selectively tunable.

Although much focus has been placed upon duplicating the mysterious high priest breastplate described in the biblical scriptures, that particular breastplate may or may not be relevant to the energetic parameters of the current times; that is, that particular breastplate may have been created in correlation with certain specific energetic-historical conditions that might not relate to present-day circumstances. In any case, two factors are different from yesteryear. One is that the secretly held esoteric knowledge of the breastplate was previously restricted to the elite high priests; but this no longer prevails. As the field of sacred crystallography unfolds to greater degrees in the current times, the divine science of breastplate design and usage becomes more widely available. Having the Spirit-derived authority to create and use these Light-tools, however, is still a foundational factor. Second, a wide variety of designs and applications are to unfold now and in the years to come versus the relatively few available in previous times. As a Light-based earth-society comes to pass, there will be many capacities in which diverse breastplates will serve as highly valued tools of Light.

The touchstone, on the other hand, is a significant but less central tool than the breastplate. Its primary purpose is to make available tunable input through the fingers and hands (and conjoining energy channels) as an adjunctive modality for modulating consciousness and the bio-energy circuitry. The underlying principles are similar to those of the breastplate in a scaled down form. Usually, there are two circular or hexagonal crystal templates (approximately 5 inches × 7 inches in diameter) in which numerous appropriate faceted previous stones are inset (see Figure 88). The precious stones are laid in a semicircular pattern with one positioned within this outer pattern in alignment with the palm "chakra." The operator may engage one or more of the gems according to the desired vibrational input by touching them with the ends of the fingers. Any number of gemstone combinations are possible. The potential applications are many, from personal consciousness modulation and tuning to being inset into therapy tables and chairs.

Breastplates can take a variety of forms. Some seed-ideas are presented herein. Large diameter crystal template slices form the foundational matrix for many of these ideas. Such slices can be gained from large, good quality generator crystals

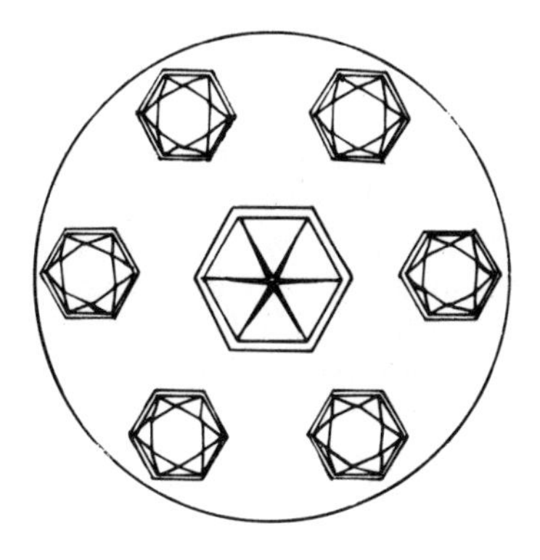

Figure 88: Touchstone

Figure 89: Inscribed and Inlaid Breastplate

that have become damaged to the point of ineffectiveness as energy generators. Because of weight considerations these templates are best kept as thin as possible—from about ¼ inch to ⅜ inch thick. Refined metal templates may also be used. One type of breastplate is a scaled-up version of the crystal templates—the inscription of specific pictographic flame letter sequences and universal symbols of Light inlaid with gold, silver, titanium, or all three. The breastplate would comfortably rest over the heart chakra and be attached to natural fiber or metal chaining around the neck of the operator and fastened to two holes drilled in the upper left- and right-hand corners (see Figure 89).

Another variation is seen in Figure 90. Here, with either a natural hexagonal or circular crystal template, both quartz and other selected precious stones are patterned according to gridwork principles (see Chapter 14). Around the exterior circumference are quartz double-terminations, either in a Star of David or double Star of David pattern, all pointing into the center of the template. Within this

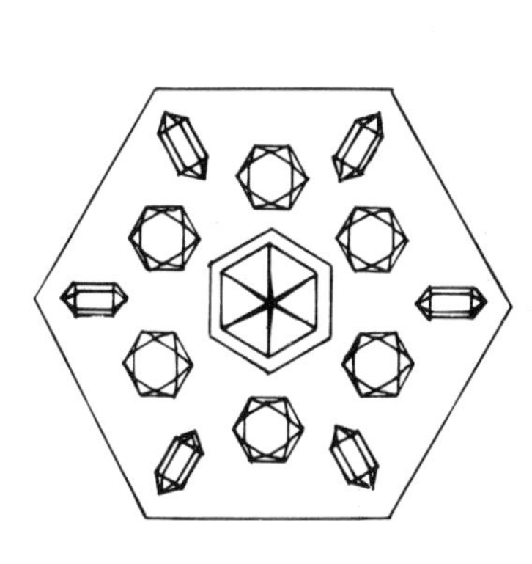

Figure 90: Crystal Gridwork Breastplate

Figure 91: Gem Gridwork Breastplate

outermost gridwork is a harmonic mirroring of different gemstones. If a double Star of David is used, the two gridwork levels will be directly opposite one another; if a single Star of David is used, the two grid levels will be offset as illustrated so that a Star within a Star is created. In the middle is a gemstone that sets the keynote for the energetic functioning of the breastplate. The choice of gem stone varies from person to person, though diamond is many times an excellent choice.

In Figure 91 is another creative possibility. Using all specifically faceted precious stones, a two-level offset Star of David pattern is created with a central gem in the center. Inscribed into the quartz template are lines connecting the gems so that the hexagonal and Star of David geometrics are outlined as well as connecting all gems to the central keystone crystal. These lines are inlaid with refined metal to aid the intergem energy dynamics.

And finally, in Figure 92, the breastplate concept is viewed in its overall context in conjunction with an integrated bioenergetic-higher consciousness "suit." Here, the helmet concept in cooperation with a breastplate plus throat, shoulder, and solar plexus templates manifests an advanced Light-work modular unit. At key energy plexi and vortexes this unit plugs into the human energy system with perfect amplifying complementarity. In practical application it is a work-suit that the individual puts on as an integral tool toward the heightened performance of designated Light-work. Each type of Light-work to which this suit concept applies would have a different corresponding form within this generalized blueprint. Also, each suit can be subtly modified for optimal attunement with each individual.

ROTATING GEM DISC CONCEPTS

The rotating disc modality uses many of the principles of crystal templates and breastplates and applies them in another distinct genre of Light-tools. The rotational action of a disc generates nonlinear crystalline magneto-gravitational reactions that stimulate radiative emissions of modifiable properties. This therapy is a complementary counterpart to template therapy, exceedingly powerful in its potential effects. Though not yet a well-developed discipline, scattered throughout crystal literature are a few mentions of this modality. Benoytosh Bhattacharya, author of *Gem Therapy* and numerous other books, describes the manner in which he successfully treated patients with rotating and vibrating gem discs.

> These gems are inexhaustible mines of cosmic colours and they can release torrents of coloured rays when rotated on an electric motor or vibrated at high frequency.[2]

> Gems can be made to yield their valuable colour contents for the purpose of distant healing. A silver disc set with the desired gems may be prepared. The size may be three to four inches in diameter. This disc motor whirls with a speed of say 1300 to 1400 RPM as the gems yield their colour. Any photograph of a diseased or healthy person kept before the radiating motor will at once receive the vibrations.[3]

Also, in *Through the Curtain*, Viola Pettit Neal, Ph.D., and Shafica Karagulla, M.D., explore these potentials.

> Crystalline forms . . . could be placed on the periphery of whirling discs and

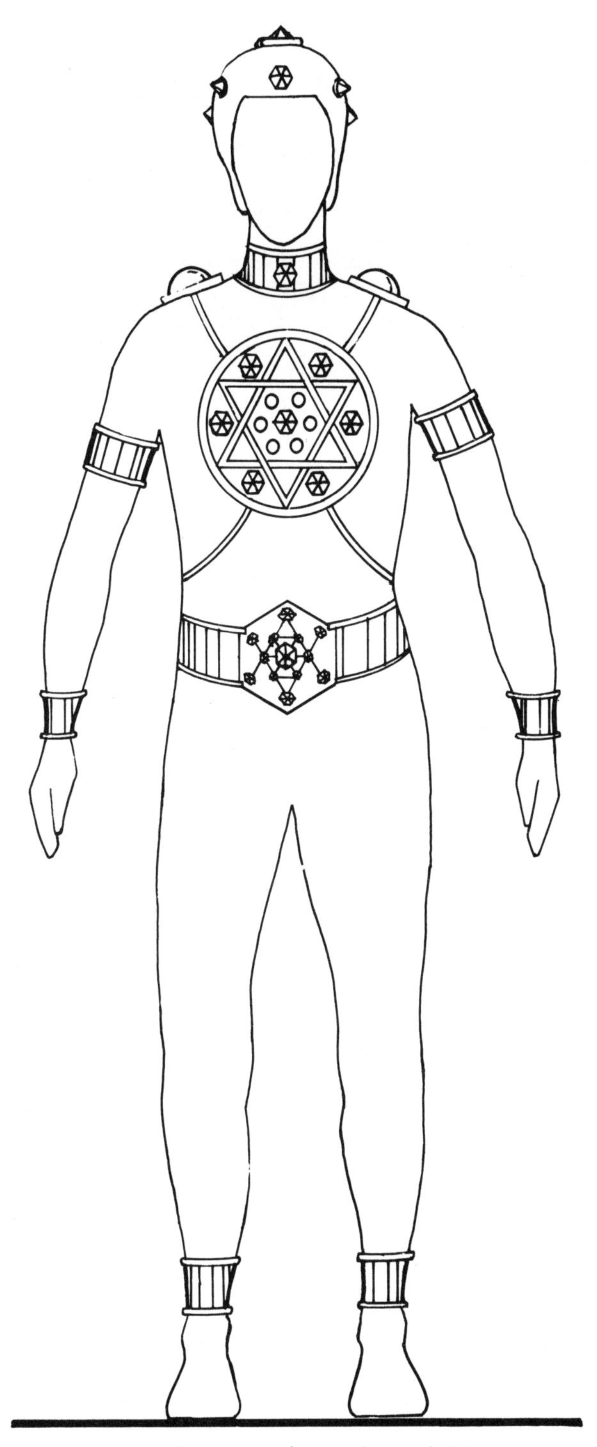

Figure 92: A Complete Light-work ''Suit''

> whirled at so many revolutions per second, with the person placed in front of it to help establish a steady rhythm of a given frequency in the etheric centers. . . . A crystal form is placed on the edge of the disc which revolves at two hundred times per second for ordinary humanity and six hundred times per second for more evolved individuals. . . . One crystalline form is used at one time depending on the center involved. . . . The effect of this would be to impose a harmonious rhythm on the center and correct and steady the inflow of energy of the right frequency.[4]

The essential concept of the rotating disc modality is to formulate a refined metal disc of specific gems, both faceted and natural forms, in geometric grid arrangements that are rotated to generate radiative energy streams into a particular bioenergetic zone for healing or reprogramming purposes. The disc is positioned directly facing the desired region and is then set in rotational motion at specific RPM rates. The energy streams are projective, penetrative, and causally recrystallizing. The rotational motion generates a spirally focused energy current of considerable penetrating force. Also, the varying of the RPM rate will cause a spectrum of gradated and indexable effects with any given disc. A wide array of different discs can be made to create specific effects. For example, it is possible to have chakra-specific discs for reprogramming purposes. Also, mind-center activation discs can be made, as well as bioenergy subsystem-specific discs.

Although quartz templates are sometimes used in disc applications, thin refined metal discs are most commonly utilized. The refined metals include gold, silver, copper, and titanium; these metals can also be electroplated over one another to create different effects. The discs are cut to a circular three-inch to five-inch diameter. One good way to rotate the disc is to have a multispeed motor unit with a titanium rod extending from it and attaching to a pyramid-shaped clip-on mechanism in which the discs are held while rotating; the clip-on unit allows the discs to be interchanged as desired (see Figure 93). Numerous disc variations are possible; some seed-thought blueprints in this regard are illustrated in Figure 94 through Figure 98.

Figure 95 is a metallic disc with 1 inch-base crystal pyramid in the center of a Solar Cross pattern. The six positions of the Star of David grid can be occupied by ½ inch base crystal pyramids, various gemstones, or horizontally placed quartz double-terminations. Figure 95 shows a Solar Cross gridwork pattern on a metallic disc. The four crystals at the cardinal directions and center of the gridwork are positioned vertically upright and the other crystals of the solar cross are horizontal. Numbers 1–4 are different specifically faceted gemtones. Figure 98 illustrates a phi-spiral gridwork of vertically upright quartz crystals on a metallic plate. The circular gridwork is composed of small single-terminations. The phi spiral starts at the periphery with a larger diameter crystal and each crystal thereafter is progressively smaller; at the center, a medium to larger diameter crystal is positioned upright to generate the primary energy pulses. Figure 97 shows a crystal template-disc with a copper sleeve around its outer circumference; on the copper are small rare earth magnets all the way around the sleeve. In the center is a quartz faceted so that all six termination faces are equilateral triangles and meet at a single point at the crystal's tip. This arrangement will work as is, or a Star of David of faceted gems or horizontally laid quartz double-terminations may also be added for further effect. Last, Figure 98 demonstrates a crystal disc with a horizontal

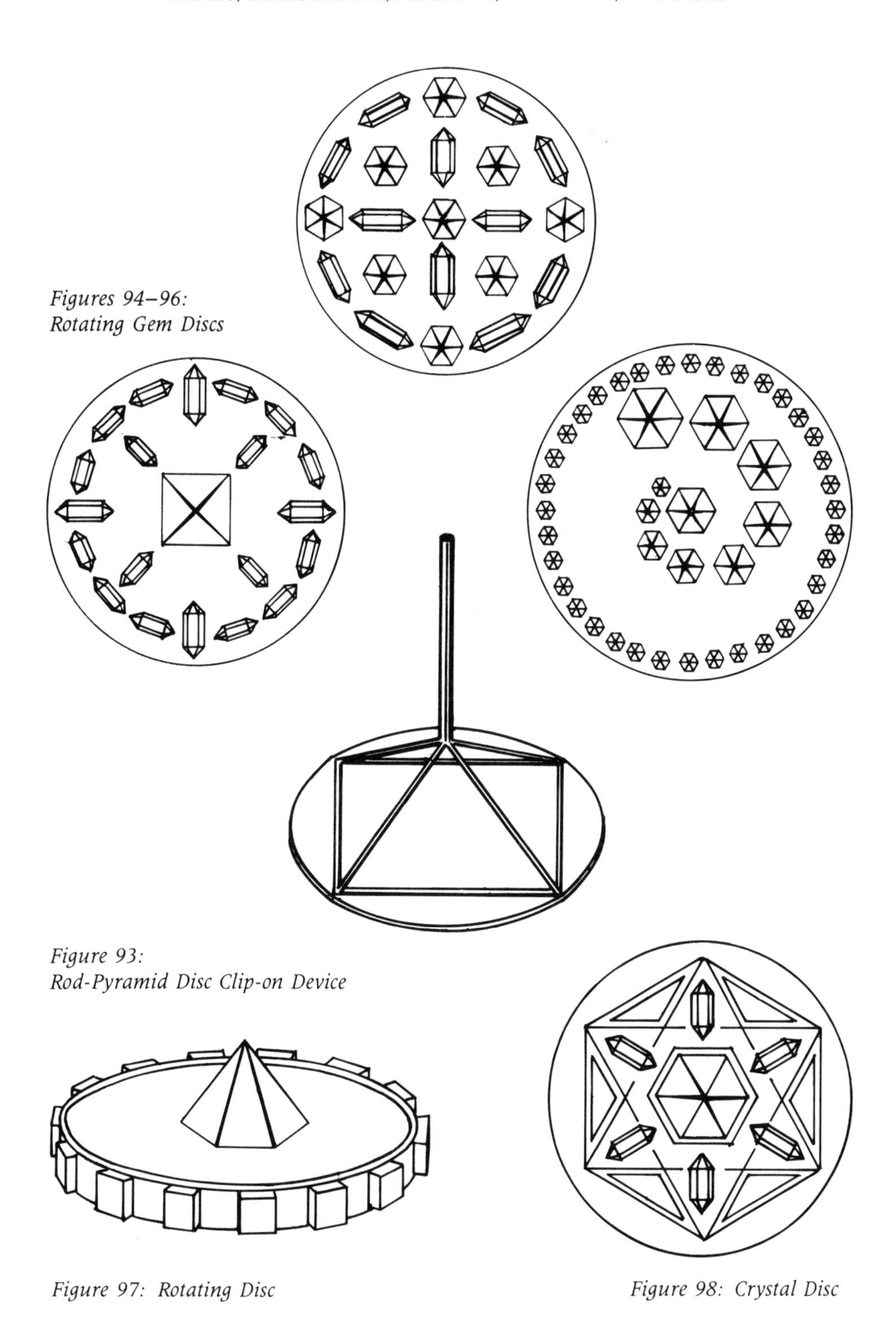

Figures 94–96: Rotating Gem Discs

Figure 93: Rod-Pyramid Disc Clip-on Device

Figure 97: Rotating Disc

Figure 98: Crystal Disc

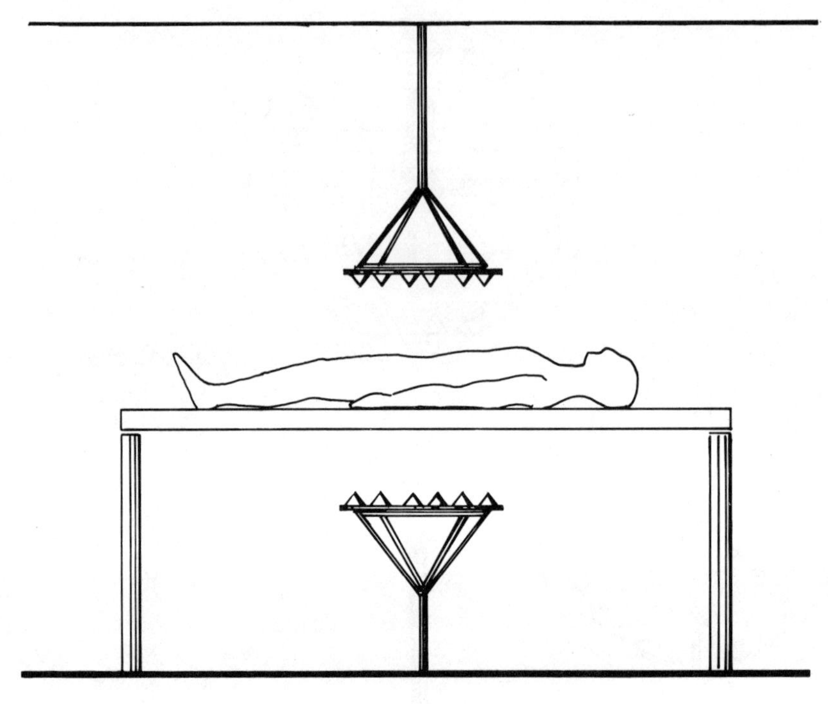

Figure 99: Disc Treatment Modality

quartz double-termination Star of David gridwork pointing into a central upright crystal. These figures serve as blueprints in and of themselves and also as seed-ideas from which other possibilities may arise.

A more advanced treatment modality is illustrated in Figure 99. Here, the recipient lies on a lucite table. Above and below the table are motor-disc set-ups pointing toward one another. It is constructed so that both discs can be horizontally shifted to any point of the treatment table; therefore any bioenergetic region can be worked with in a focused manner. The above-and-below disc set-up is one optimal disc treatment method, as it can powerfully interpenetrate the bioenergetic system from both sides; also, the RPM rates of the two can be modulated in numerous harmonic proportion rates for amplified results as well as using two synergistically interacting discs simultaneously. It is also possible to employ crystal templates on the chakras or other regions in conjunction with disc modalities. Note too that discs also serve well in stationary template-like applications.

PENDANT CONCEPTS

Pendants are one of the most popular ways of wearing crystals. Positioned over the heart chakra, they are excellent auric amplifiers and general consciousness attunement devices. They range from the starkly simple to the elaborately complex. In the latter case, as with staffs and other Light-tools, every aspect of the pendant

Figures 100–103: Pendant Concepts

must be harmonically interrelated to all other aspects of the pendant as a whole; toward this end, any nonfunctional ornamentation is to be avoided because of its interference with the energetics of the pendant. Creative work is being done with pendants by many metaphysically inclined jewelers. The purpose of this chapter section is simply to add a few more concepts to consider.

Figure 100 shows what in effect are miniaturized templates. The concept of the inscribed and inlaid crystal template works well with the purposes and logistics of the pendant. Figure 100A demonstrates this well—it is an inscribed and selectively inlaid Star of David with a faceted gem within the inner hexagon. It is also possible with template-based pendants to silver and gold the circumference sides for added effect. An elongated variation of this is shown in Figure 100B; again the symbol and pictographs are inscribed and inlaid. Figure 100C utilizes a Solar Cross with a Star of David interpenetrating as the inscription pattern. In the center is inlaid or glued a gem of choice.

Many of the basic and combination gridwork patterns presented in Chapter 14 are applicable here. Moreover, the disc idea shown in Figure 98 with the addition of the double-terminations outlining the symbol pattern can be easily scaled down to pendant size; other gridwork patterns would also work well using these principles.

Pendants can also be made by nonprofessionals with easily obtained materials. After choosing a crystal appropriate for this use, the only materials required are a thin silk thread or fine gold wire plus a silk or cotton cord. It is recommended not to use leather in this or any other application. Next, decide whether it is best for the termination to point upward or downward. The downward pointing crystal will tend to energize the earthly bioenergetic levels and the upward pointing crystal will tend to strengthen spiritually elevating states of consciousness. With a double termination, the energies go both upward and downward for a balance of the two effects. Wrap the crystal as shown in Figure 101—the fine thread or wire wraps around the crystal and the ends of the natural fiber cord. Some find that in order to secure the crystal, thread, and cord together firmly, small amounts of clear glue may be applied to the pendant where all three components touch.

Figure 102 shows an elegant pendant—a sterling silver circle clasps a long, thin, double-termination with, optimally, a diamond or other gem of choice in the center. This particular pendant has a strengthening, balancing, and integrating effect upon the bioenergetic system.

Figure 103 is a unique conception with a couple of variations. One idea is to silver the two adjoining polishing cylinder-shaped crystals completely except where they touch the central crystal. In this way the adjoining crystals would function as amplifying resonant chambers. Thus not only would the pendant be able to ingather more energy into these two extra energy cylinders, but also the energy would be amplifed as well. The additional energetics feed into the double-termination, making its emanations considerably stronger. Another possibility for this pendant is to make the two adjoining objects hollow silver tubing with openable top caps. Like the wand in Figure 72, different tinctures, cell salts, homeopathic remedies, dietary supplements, and the like can be placed inside as vibrational input to the pendant crystal, which would then transfer into the bioenergies.

ADDITIONAL LIGHT-TOOLS:

Lucite Discs (not illustrated): A thin, circular plate of lucite (or plexiglass) forms the neutral base on which miniature gridworks, approximately 3 to 4 inches in diameter, can be glued in place. In conjunction with one crystal in the center, preferably a double-termination or a pyramid-faceted quartz, these tools have wide-ranging applications, from chakra balancing and mind-center activation to area-specific healing and meditation focal points. With a set of different gridwork arrangements, one on each disc, the individual would have a spectrum of diverse energy tools with which to work. Numerous of the disc concepts presented above can be adapted to this application modality. Though differing in several ways, the lucite disc concept is similar to the clear discs that encase specific arrangements of gemstones for harmonic bioenergetic balancing, originated by David Rees, D.C.

Figure 104: Spinal Energizer. This easily made tool is composed of large guage silver chain, copper wire, and 12 matched, thin, and elongated double-terminations. The silver chain can be obtained at most rock shops and is inexpensive. For general usage, each crystal is wrapped in place at equidistant intervals through a three-foot length of the chain. The crystals are copper coil-wrapped and usually require a couple drops of clear glue to secure them in place. Each crystal's terminations are aligned with all others'. For application, position the spinal energizer in alignment with the spine from coccyx to first cervical vertebrae (recipient face down); continue from the cervicals on up the back of the head in a straight line until the chain ends at the middle top of the head or at the forehead. This Light-tool stimulates a vigorous current of energy flow up and down the spine and entire chakra system. Used alone or in conjunction with other related treatment modalities, it is a superb tool for releasing spinal tension and blockages as well as stimulating the chakra system to higher levels of harmonization.

It is possible to use a braided integrated wrapping of copper, silver, gold, or all three to make the chain for the Spinal Energizer. Even more powerful is a length of chain with small rare earth magnets positioned at short intervals along its length.

Also, this device can be custom made to integrate with an individual's unique spatial distances of the chakras. This is done by taking 13 crystals and positioning 7 of them to align with each chakra location. Halfway in between each of these 7 crystals, position the remaining 6 crystals. Customizing of this nature makes the tool primarily effective for one particular individual.

Figure 105: Gold-Plated, Magnetically Activated Double-Termination. A long, good quality double-termination is coated with a substantial layer of gold as illustrated. Six Alnico or rare earth magnets (especially cobalt) are inset in place between the gold plating at the mid-section of the crystal body. In addition to being used in wand-type applications, it can also be held in both hands (each hand holding a termination) for self-regenerative, recharging result.

Figure 106: Crystal "Surgery" Tool. This is one of the most potent Light-tools presented in this chapter. The substantial gold plating is similar to that of the Gold-Plated, Magnetically Activated Double-Termination, except that it also includes part of the base and most of the termination except for a small portion at the tip. The crystal used needs to be perfectly faceted for this task. Its body shape is a regular hexagon at right angles to the c axis and the termination facets are all equilateral triangles meeting at a common tip. The middle of the polished base is inscribed with an encircled Star of David with inlaid gold. The penetrating intensity of this tool's energy dynamics make it an eminently effective bioenergetic "surgery" device. The energy emanating from the tip is a thin, but extremely intense and coherent beam of Light-energy that can be precisely applied as it "cuts" through discerned areas. This is a highly recommended Light-tool for those who are spiritually authorized to perform such Light-work.

"Appliance Therapy" (not illustrated): Look to common household appliances

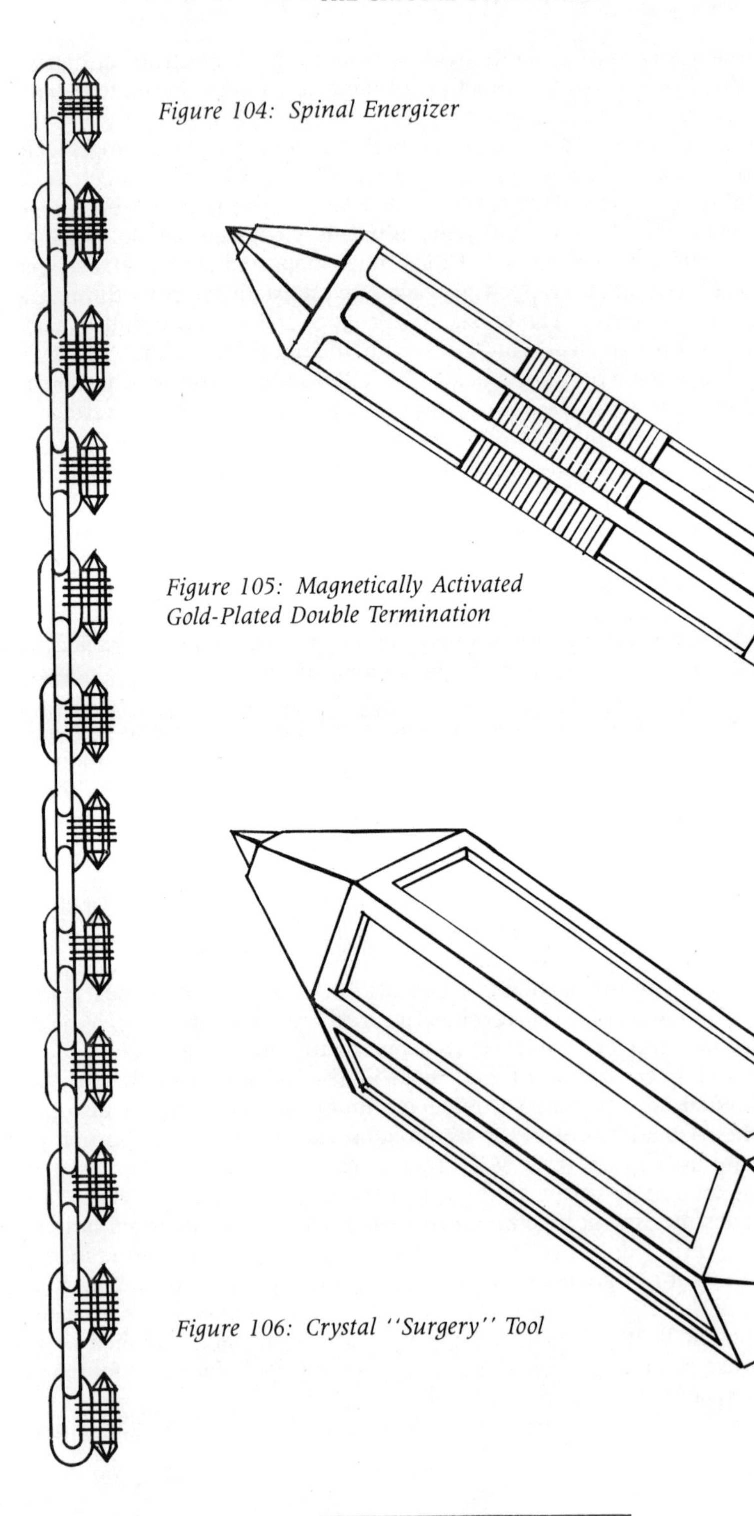

Figure 104: Spinal Energizer

Figure 105: Magnetically Activated Gold-Plated Double Termination

Figure 106: Crystal ''Surgery'' Tool

for creative ideas that can be "crystal-ized" into valuable Light-tools. two examples of this include: 1) A single-beater mixer with accompanying attachments holds marvelous possibilitiies for crystal enhancing the attachments in myriad creative ways in addition to having one or more rotation speed capabilities. As seen in the "Rotating Gem Disc" section of this chapter, rotation of crystals stimulates a powerful emission of penetrating, spiralling energetics. A single-beater mixer is a superb, easily accessible means of being able to utilize rotation modalities. One example of how to crystal enhance a four-spoked beater attachment is by gluing and wire-wrapping single terminations along the length of the spokes on their outer perimeter, terminations pointing downward (as the beater is normally used). At the bottom of the beater where the spokes come together, glue a crystal pyramid at the intersection point, pointing downwards. Around the pyramid, on the spokes as they curve in to the intersection point, can be glued small rare earth magnets (opposite polarity orientations as the magnets go around the perimeter). Small quartz or other gems can also be glued in place on top of or in back of the magnets (or the gems can be used alone without magnetics). Sometimes, there is another type of beater attachment that has spiralling metal wiring; simply glue quartz (double-terminations if possible) so that it follows the spiral outline of the attachment. Look at the attachments and see what creative toolmaking can be done. It is important that it be a single-beater mixer and that it is cordless (electricity flowing from an outlet through the mixer's energy dynamics is detrimental to the human system). It is optimal to silver electroplate all possible attachments unless they are plastic. Primary applications of this tool are for chakra harmonizing and reprogramming plus possibilities for mind-center activation. 2) A cordless drill with faceted gems glued on the end of small-diameter sturdy copper rods can be used for extremely potent, highly focused, and directionalized insertion of energy streams into the bioenergetic system. An entire array of copper rods, each with a gem, crystal pyramid, and so on, can be used as a set of specific tools to match to appropriate situations. Needless to say, extreme care needs to be exercised so that the rapidly rotating gem and copper rod do not come into physical contact with the recipient. Hold the rotating gem about 3–4 inches from the physical body, the recipient and practitioner holding extremely steady. Be aware that this is an exceptionally powerful modality for infusing laserlike streams of crystalling energy into the human system; use appropriate discernment and caution.

How many other common appliances can be creatively made into valuable Light-tools?

Hollow Metallic Sphere (not illustrated): This Light-tool taps into the universal principle and energy resonance pattern of sphericity in a particularly powerful way. Hollow, seamless spheres of varying diameters, usually 2–4 inches in diameter, are composed of one or more metals. Copper, both because of its inexpensiveness and its sturdy workability, is usually fine for the foundational structuring. Then, one or more layers of electroplating of different combinations and sequences of other refined metals, especially silver, gold, platinum, and titanium will add both power and specificity of energetic functioning. Each different combination of metals will produce a correspondingly specific effect. Inside the spheres is put combinations of gemstones and other appropriate energy substances. These interior additions also play a large role in defining the sphere's vibrational profile. The total effect is the creation of a powerfully resonating spherical wave pattern that functions primarily to access corresponding higher dimensional spherical wave and form dynamics. Like a potent antenna-receiver-transmitter, it helps create a strong interlinkage with the universal archetypal essence and energy pattern of sphericity.

These Hollow Spheres are very refined and specific tools. Each individual who uses such a tool will need to quite specifically discern the exact metal and gem constituents for their particular sphere, for a precise matchup of vibrations is needed for optimal effectiveness. In some ways, this tool can be seen as a New World shaman's rattle whose primary use is for interdimensional access. The Hollow Spheres may also serve powerfully for individual and group activation of the earth's vortex regions to help clear the multidimensional access channels to earth's place in the higher cosmic domains in the New World. Refer also to the "Merkabah Attraction Module UEF" in Chapter 14 where it can be used as a keystone access tool for Merkabah interconnection.

In sum, the age of increasingly sophisticated Light-tools is dawning. As sacred science proceeds to gain further momentum, its fruits in this realm will amaze all as they become professional areas of specialization and go octaves beyond that which is presented in this chapter. The blueprints and higher knowedge concerning the realm of Light-tools are freely available within the reaches of the Universal Mind for those with the disciplined desire and communication access to receive them. Yet consider these as the tools that they are—they are not the means to enlightened salvation; rather, they are exceedingly helpful though not absolutely necessary stepping-stones that, once traversed, can be set aside as higher avenues continuing to spiral upward are trodden.

CHAPTER 14:
Crystal Gridworks

Crystal gridworks form the cornerstone for virtually all Unified Energy Fields (UEF). Their geometric patterning functions to selectively gain access to corresponding interdimensional energy spectrums and to focus crystal energetic flow within prescribed, predictable harmonic relationships. On the highest levels, they serve to establish vortex corridors, or Pillar of Light zones, through which the higher Light-dimensions are directly unified with the earthly dimensions. On other levels of usage, crystal gridworks function as controlled areas of amplified energetic accumulation that can be applied to magnify and focus consciousness intentionality. In all, gridworks form a collective matrix for intensified vibrational interactions in a stable, controllable manner. Their greatest value today will be seen in future retrospect to be as conceptual consciousness catalysts that provided key directions toward the greater fruition of advanced Light-tools and Light-technologies in preparation for the ascension.

In contemporary times, the concept of the crystal gridwork was reborn in the *Keys of Enoch*. Its references (on pages 109 (111:25) and 513 (316:34, 40) to this fundamental universal idea stood for years as seed-thoughts awaiting further development. Years later the Rev. Dr. Frank Alper further developed and popularized the gridwork concept and its applications through lectures and two books, *Exploring Atlantis, Volume I* and *Exploring Atlantis, Volume II*. In the years since, the authors in their first book, *Windows of Light*, and others in the crystal field have borne additional ongoing developments toward quantum increasements of knowledge in this realm.

The definition of a crystal gridwork is the use of multiple crystals in a harmonic, geometric relationship to create a UEF. There are three necessary conditions that must be fulfilled in order for a crystal gridwork to exist. The first is that there must be multiple crystals in use. However, the utilization of only two crystals cannot create a UEF. They can manifest an interactive energy field between themselves, but the minimum number of crystals required to enact a UEF with domainship properties is three. The second condition is that the three or more crystals must be in a harmonic, geometric relationship. This includes all two- and three-dimensional forms that originate within the laws of sacred geometry. Outside these laws, a form may be geometric but will not be harmonic within divine order. The third condition is that a UEF is created. This relates to the energetic orientation and interdynamics occuring between crystals in a harmonic geometric relationship. These two factors are crucial determinants of whether crystals in such a relationship actually manifest a UEF, or not. For three or more crystals can be positioned in such a relationship but their collective energy dynamics may not fulfill the requirements of a UEF.

A UEF can be defined as a domain. A domain is a holistically homeostatic integrity zone. That is to say, domainship is a state of synergic wholeness wherein semipermeable boundaries and abiding internal energetic flow patterns maintain a unit's homeostatic balance. A good example of a domain is a single cell. In order to sustain a living state of wholeness, a cell must maintain a dynamic balance according to its predetermined blueprint of holistic functioning. To do this, it must preserve its internal homeostatic processes within certain parameters of balance. In order to accomplish this, the cell selectively takes in substances and vibrational patterns that will assist in maintaining a state of wholeness through its outer semipermeable membrane—the cell wall. In addition, it will selectively keep within the internal cell boundaries all that is beneficial, and will process out through the cell wall all that is not. Thus the cellular integrity is constantly sustained within domainship parameters. Not only is a cell a domain, but a body organ is, a bioenergetic system is, the planetary energy network is, the galactic system is, and so on. That which is dynamically whole and synergistically harmonic with universal order on any micro to micro universal level is a domain.

In order to create a domain, the collective energy dynamics of a gridwork need to be accurately oriented in its internal energetic interaction patterns such that it reflects divine order. Care must be taken in setting up a gridwork as to the physical orientation of each crystal in relationship to every other, and the angles and measurements of the geometric form that they are duplicating. For example, three crystals may be arranged in a triangular gridwork, but the crystals also must be oriented accurately so that their collective energetics interact to create the desired triangular effect. The laws of the sacred geometry of divine order are replicated with the proper manifestation of a gridwork. Therefore, in order to fulfill the third condition of a crystal gridwork, conscientious attention is placed upon both the precise layout of the geometric form and the angular orientation of each crystal. These factors will be presented for the many different gridwork arrangements discussed in this chapter.

The Attraction Module Effect

> Crystals are to be used as cyberg devices to amplify and filter communication signals.
>
> They are used by the Higher Evolution as fundamental building blocks to set up a measurable grid of a larger harmonic system which allow for different combinations of wave structures to unite and form myriads of gravitational wave combinations which, in turn, react with one another to transmit thought-forms to physical planetary realities.[1]

The highest usage levels of crystal-based UEFs involve the reception and focused processing of Higher Evolution Light-code patterns and frequencies. The UEF is utilized as a stable energy-pattern that interlinks with the Universal Energy Network (UEN) so as to gain access to specific interdimensional sectors that correspond with the patterning of the physical-plane UEF. The geometry of the UEF's energy interference patterns is the primary code-key that determines interdimensional access parameters. The essential function of a UEF is to sustain desired code-patterns in a steady and amplified state for specifically desired interdimensional access. Once access is gained, the physical-plane UEF functions to resonantly receive corresponding universal energies and process them in accordance with its geometric parameters. A faceted interdimensional "window" is thus opened with much-heightened clarity, efficiency, and power.

This process of inducing multidimensional access interconnections is termed the *attraction module effect.* The intercommunication that results is a two-way avenue, that is, the pathways are clear for the earth-based individual to actively engage sectors of the Universal Mind and for the Higher Evolution to infuse appropriate energies into the UEF, in addition to the constantly maintained energy parameters that preserve continuous interdimensional interlinkage. An attraction module's higher dimensional connectedness is sustained on a continual basis by an energy flow constant enacted by the Higher Evolution. When it is actively engaged, this energy flow constant plus addition higher-plane input occurs in accordance with divine order. In effect, multi-dimensional communication pathways are kept open for modifiable interchange between the earth-plane and the higher Light-dimensions via the attraction module effect.

Not all UEFs are necessarily attraction modules; yet all attraction modules are necessarily UEFs. A UEF might fulfill all conditions necessary to being a UEF, but perhaps might not partake of the attraction module effect because interdimensional interlinkable factors are not enacted. Such a UEF can be effective in manifesting a wide range of desired results. This energy field is earthbound, however, and will be limited to the spectrum of universal energies that can be operative within it. This situation parallels the difference between the individual whose bioenergetic system is undergoing reprogramming processes versus one who is not. In the former case, the bioenergetic system functions as an attraction module for facilitating a transfer of Light-body code-patterns to the earthly self, and thereby an interdimensional communicative interlinkage is established. In the latter case, the bioenergetic system yet partakes of domainship properties but chooses to remain earthbound in orientation and to be unreceptive to higher dimensional energetic interchange. Here, an individual undergoing reprogramming functions as a bioenergetic UEF that also induces the attraction module effect; the individual not undergoing reprogramming is still a bioenergetic UEF but is not a functioning attraction module (though the potential still abides). So too with gridwork-based UEFs—attraction module systems are actively connected with the higher levels of the UEN and nonattraction module UEFs can function with dynamic effectiveness but only within earthbound energy spectrums.

The activation of the attraction module effect is dependent upon the fulfillment of basic responsibilities by the operator. These responsibilities include: 1) the consciously formulated intention to engage the attraction module effect; 2) the precise manifestation of a UEF in accordance with the laws of divine order; 3) the maintenance of divine order within the UEF on a daily basis; and 4) the invitation to the Higher Evolution to activate the attraction module effect. These four aspects of personal responsibility set the necessary foundation for the active cooperation of the Higher Evolution. It is through this cooperation that the UEF is infused with higher Light.

> Thus, in the interfacing of two evolutionary structures the "capstone" of the Higher Intelligence (which contains the thought program) interfaces with the "cornerstone" (where the activity is centered) of a given star intelligence being reprogrammed—allowing for a space-time overlap and new life changes to occur on the most basic atomic and molecular levels.[2]

The earth-based attraction module establishes the cornerstone through which the capstone of higher Light is superimposed, thereby effecting heightened levels of interdimensional unification.

The nature and degree of higher Light "magnetically" attracted into an attraction module is determined by several factors. There are many different types of UEFs and variations thereof. Each type has a different collective energy patterning-code that is the UEF. The geometrics of these collective vibrational dynamics establish the sectors of the UEN to which access is possible. This, then, sets the parameters as to the nature of the Light "attracted" into the UEF. In addition, there are widely varying degrees to which a given UEF is energetically activated. The activation quotient depends upon the orientational precision with UEN access codes and the overall power of the UEF. Further, both orientational precision and overall power are gained through increasing quantum levels of sacred scientific knowledge applied through integrated uses of Light-tools and Light-technologies. The activation potential of a UEF can be stimulated to progressively higher octaves; practical information and insights in this regard are presented later in this chapter and in Chapter 15. As this potential is activated, the access pathways to which a particular UEF is linked are correspondingly amplified, and the intercommunication then functions with a quantum increase in clarity, efficiency, depth of access, and power. And lastly, the nature and degree of higher Light received in an attraction module is also precisely modulated by the Higher Self in conjunction with the Higher Evolution. That which the individual asks for, is ready and willing to receive, and is in his or her highest spiritual interest are all taken into account by the Higher Evolution. Within the laws of divine order, the nature and degree of higher Light that is appropriate for the individual to receive is then infused into the consciousness-attraction module unity.

The attraction module concept, then, is a fundamental principle intrinsic to the highest applications of crystal-based UEFs. It can be seen as a scientific extension of the principle of "Ask, and ye shall receive." For as the individual sets the foundational framework of interdimensional access—whether it be through consciousness alone or with UEFs—it is only through the Higher Evolution's cooperative infusion of divine grace that any soul growth occurs.

THE PILLAR OF LIGHT EFFECT

The Pillar of Light (POL) effect is a concentrated vortex energy dynamic that functions to interconnect multidimensional levels in a single overlapping interfusionary continuum. This vortex dynamic is the preeminently foundational means by which the Light-spectrums of the UEN are spanned, interconnected, and unified. To study this overarchingly causal effect in the context of gridwork-based UEFs is to gain keys toward activating the fuller interdimensional potential of attraction modules.

The POL effect is a vertically oriented standing columnar wave (SCW) that functions as a focal fusion zone through which the earth-plane becomes more directly interlinked with higher Light-dimensions. The quintessential example of the POL effect is seen in primary pyramidal energy dynamics (see Figure 51). This fundamental flow-pattern depicts the archetypal blueprint of multidimensional overlapping, interactive processing (with full-spectrum potential), and fusion into the laserlike apex-to-apex energy pillar that then is further amplified and beamed out of the top apex as a POL. This universally archetypal action is the reason why the pyramidal geometry is the central form crucible for all consciousness and biophysical evolution.

The POL is a vortex standing columnar wave wherein high intensities and frequencies of energy coherently spiral within overlapping spectrums of fusion parameters. The unitive power of this primary Light-force has potentially infinite interdimensional access penetration potential, and thereby serves as a central means through which the UEN is interconnected and modulated by the Higher Evolution. The more technical aspects of the POL's dynamics are complex, but can be thought of as spirals within Spiral, light within Light, minds within Mind.

As with UEFs and pyramids, there are many different quantum levels of activation of the full potential of the POL. For example, it was seen in chapter 12 that a physical-plane pyramid functions at a significant but low level of activation until its higher level potentials are stimulated by crystals and other energy modalities. So also the POL effect of a UEF is inherently functional, but attains higher octaves of actualization when the overall energy dynamics are magnified. This knowledge is important to the activation of the attraction module effect, for the POL forms the primary column of Light through which interdimensional access is enacted and amplified. Practical applications in this regard are explored later in this chapter.

The POL concept has been manifested throughout history in an array of forms and applications, and different degrees of activation. As presented in John Michell's book entitled *The New View Over Atlantis,* in previous epochs sophisticated ancients utilized the interdimensionally unitive vertical energy axis in the megalithic science of spiritual engineering. The monolithic pillars of the stone circles found throughout the world as well as strategically situated church towers were integral to the discipline of "terrestrial acupuncture."

> The practice of locating sacred centres in accordance with the flow of terrestrial magnetic current was not confined to prehistoric times, for it appears that every Christian church was similarly sited. The orientation of a church, even its dimensions and architectural plan, was determined by the lines of current, of which the strongest spring is frequently located directly beneath the tower. At this spot the celestial influences, attracted by the spire, combine with the terrestrial force to produce the fusion.[3]

> Stone pillars, through their living quartz or metallic content, unite heaven and earth in the same way as does a living tree. The wooden posts of the North American Indians and the maypole, erected over a buried spring, have the same effect.[4]

In similar manner, the shaman's pole, central tree-pole of the American Indian Sun Dance, tepee, obelisks, Irish round towers, tiered Buddhist temples, *feng-shui* winged stone columns, and worldwide pyramidal structures illustrate the archetypal nature and widespread applications of the POL concept in the universal quest to span the gap between the heavens and the earth. In advanced ancient civilizations, this concept was applied through Light-based technologies in awesomely powerful ways. For example:

> In the Takla Makan Basin, towers of crystal were used by the Lords of Light who came down over 36,000 years ago. Man will discover that these Tesla-like transmitter towers are cylinder-like resonators with pyramidal faces. These towers were resonators for the detection and amplification of the Earth's own sympathetic pulse which was used for transmission.[5]

Also in this context, refer to the Merkabah Attraction Module presented in Chapter 15 (Figure 163.)

> At the time of this ascension, a "Pillar of Light" establishes a "Light Zone" around a given life space. This "Light Zone" is used to prepare a selected intelligent life space for transit into another "mansion" world of life experience.[6]

In times of major galactic and planetary reprogramming, the Higher Evolution utilizes projected macro-POLs to enact the last phases of reprogramming and to form the interdimensional pathway of ascension. These macro-POLs are projected from a central command as a twelve-fold emanation that locks into phase with the twelve primary vortex zones around the earth. Spanning hundreds of miles in diameter, these higher dimensional Light-fields set up zones that are protected from cataclysmic upheavals and provide the energetic foundation for enacting the last stages of individual and collective reprogramming and for ascensional relocation through the cosmic and celestial access-gateways.

GRIDWORK ENERGY DYNAMICS

The energy dynamics of crystal gridwork systems are the collective synergic result of geometrically oriented crystals. Each individual crystal emits primary, secondary, and tertiary energetics in a manner discussed in Chapter 7. Each crystal's individual energy dynamics interacts with the others of the gridwork via the scientific principles of vibrational constructive and destructive interference (plus a host of non-linear interactive effects). Most basically, the collective gridwork energy patterning can be visualized as an *energy mandala* (see figure 107) with waves projecting from each crystal as through each were a pebble thrown into a still pool of water. Because of the geometrically harmonic placement and orientation of the gridwork crystals, the nodal-antinodal patterns of the energy mandala are harmoniously interbalanced. One can see that if the gridwork were set up in a different geometric arrangement, the resulting energy mandala would reflect this change of positioning, as seen in the difference between Figure 107A and 107B. Every different crystal gridwork geometry, then, has a particular energy mandalic patterning, each unlike the other.

Looking at these dynamics at a deeper level, taking into account the primary, secondary, and tertiary energetics emitting from each crystal, a more differentiated and complex energy mandala picture arises. Each of these three modalities of energy flow has distinct characteristics that cause them to interact together in different ways. The tertiary energetics from the crystals' bodies, though the weakest and most diffuse, play a significant role in creating an energy membrane around the exterior of the gridwork. Because of the predominantly inward flow of the gridwork as a whole, the tertiary vibrations tend to be magnetically pulled in around the circumference of the gridwork, rather than diffusing out in all directions as would otherwise occur in individual crystal dynamics. This generates an outer semipermeable circular cushion around the gridwork's outer perimeter. (See Figure 108.)

A portion of the secondary energetics angles away from the gridwork's central area, causing an intermediate energy zone. There is some interaction between the outer and intermediate gridwork regions; an outer portion of the intermediate zone pushes outward, helping the outer zone to maintain the integrity of its cushioning membrane. As seen in Figure 108, the intermediate region is larger and vertically higher than the outer region, and also intersects with a small outer section of it.

The primary crystal energetics plus the more centrally angled aspects of the secondary energetics unify together in the gridwork's central zone. The interactions within this central zone are more nonlinear than suggested by Figure 107. Therein a spiraling fusion of energy flow is primarily generated by the nonlinear intensity and subatomic-atomic spin orientation properties of the primary crystal energetic flow. The harmonic conjunctive interfusion of center region energies generates an upwardly spiraling vortex motion, both clockwise and counterclockwise. This dynamic occurs to varying degrees depending mainly on the overall power quotient of the gridwork. Below a certain power quotient threshold, the inner zone energies flow upward for a number of feet and then reach an apex, where its intensity tapers off and diffuses, and part feeds back into the gridwork as it arcs back into the intermediate zone. Above this power quotient threshold, the inner region energetics spiral through the previous vertical limits and flow upwardly until a new threshold is reached; there are numerous such quantum thresholds, each corresponding to defined energy parameters. In conjunction with additional UEF components, the center region's power quotient can be amplified, thus establishing an even greater energetic foundation for a strong POL effect.

As the Higher Evolution interconnects with the inner region's vortex activity when activating the attraction module effect, several factors occur. The infusing higher Light phase locks with the outer, intermediate, and inner zones of the gridwork, especially the latter. Interdimensional access lines are set in to place. And, if the attraction module and POL effects fulfill certain threshold requirements, a primary Light-force POL (in the centermost area of the gridwork's inner zone) is infused into the attraction module system. This primary POL is many quantum octaves more vortex-intense and focused than the surrounding inner zone's POL action. When the primary POL is activated, the Christ White Light is ignited and the entire gridwork energetics shifts to a higher Light-quantum level. In the years to come, via more advanced Light–technologies and focused group consciousness efforts, this Christ White Light ignition will occur more and more, and with increasing force.

A primary gridwork orientation variation is a circular pattern instead of a centrally focused pattern, as diagrammed in Figure 108, which shows the circular gridwork patterning and its overall energetic dynamics. The crystals used here are double-terminations, therefore the energy flow feeds into each consecutive crystal

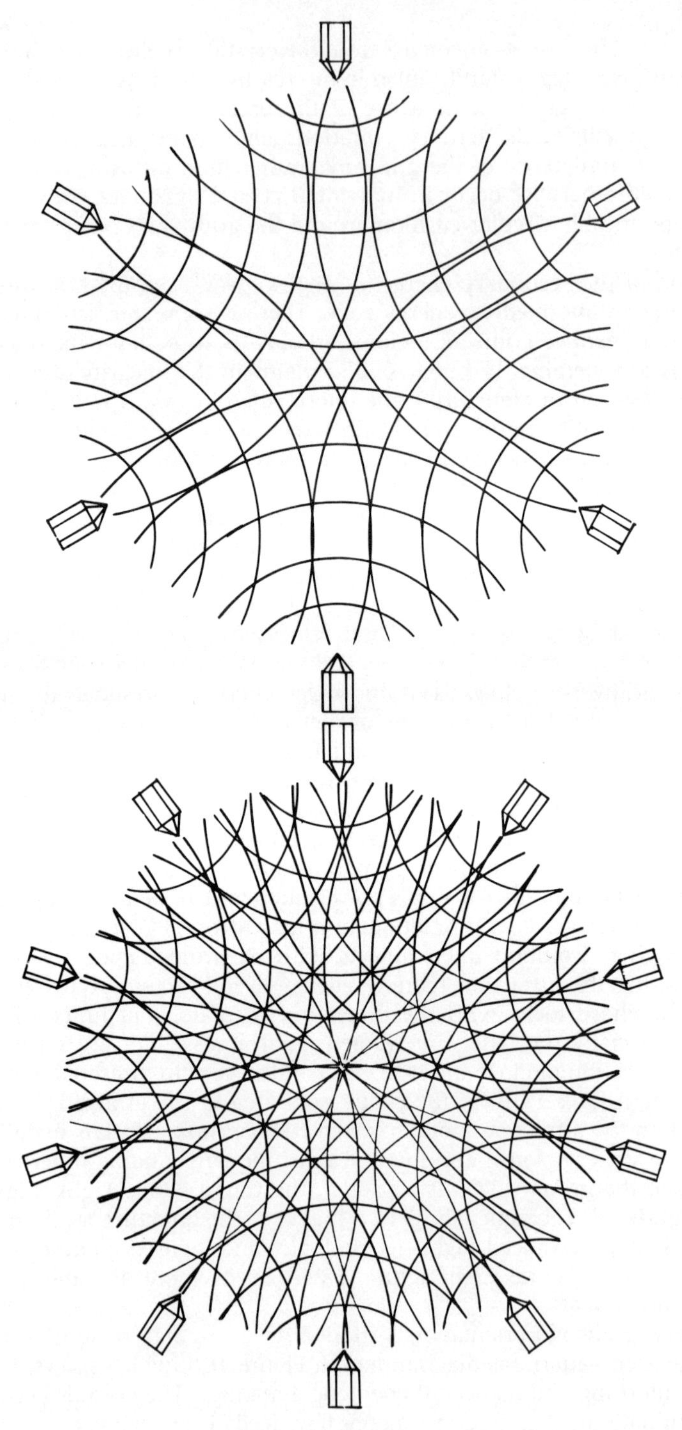

Figure 107a & 107b: Gridwork Energy-Wave ''Mandalas''

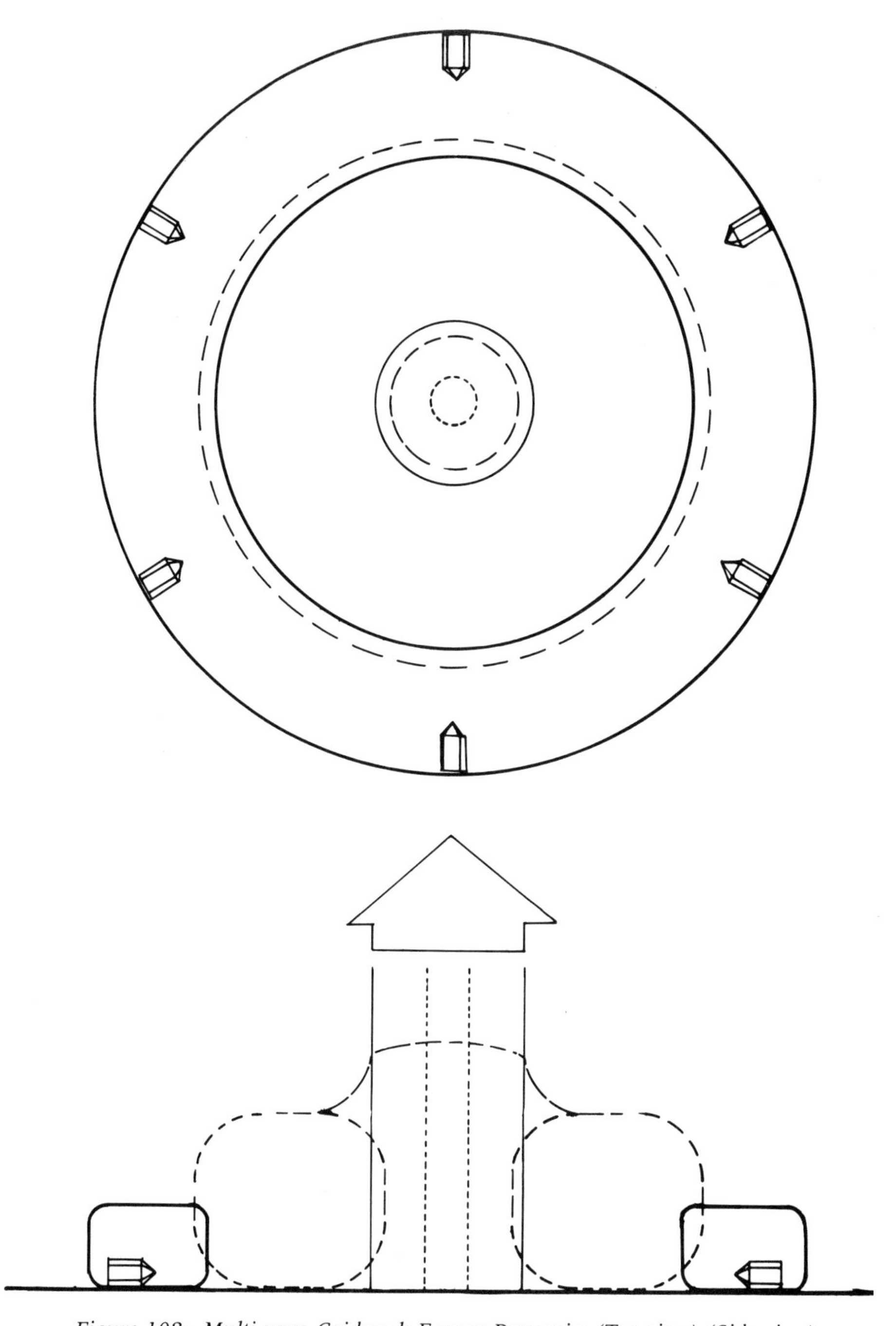

Figure 108: Multi-zone Gridwork Energy Dynamics (Top view) (Side view)

all the way around the energy circle, both clockwise and counterclockwise. The circular grid alone does not integrate in a sufficiently cohesive manner for any practical applications. In order for cohesion and activation to occur, the circular gridwork requires additional focusing and amplifying elements. The Solar Cross gridwork setup, illustrated in Figure 109, will be utilized as an example in this regard. The crystals at the four corners and those leading in from the corners to the center add the necessary energetic complement to the circular outline. They provide the needed focused amplification that set the lines of integrated completion. The particulars as to the overall three-dimensional energy mandala of different circle-based gridworks vary for each one. In general, however, it is possible to give an outline of these energy dynamics. With the additional crystals, definite geometric focus is set in action. This induces an integrated cohesiveness of the circular energy flow through the circular gridwork; what was before diffuse is now focused into definite flow lines. A domelike energy effect arcs upward and inward from the circular dynamics. The physics of this effect are complex, but are basically harmonically induced concentrically centripetal energy rings that are activated on numerous quantum vibrational levels (with radiative interactions occurring between them). The overall effect of these circular rings is an energy dome with primary energetics occurring around the outside membrane.

Figure 108 shows the top and side views of an activated circular gridwork without accounting for the energetics of the additional crystals (in this case, the Solar Cross crystals). Figure 109 illustrates the integrated effects of the entire Solar Cross gridwork. The additional crystals form a focused energy stream from the four corners into the central point. This creates two results. First, the central POL vortex is similar to that of the center-focus gridwork's inner and central regions of Figure 107. A hole through the top of the energy dome is established through which the POL effect operates. Secondly, a portion of the POL's upwardly flowing energies branch off from the main flow and feed back into the gridwork in a current just under the energy dome membrane. When this energy flow toward the base of the gridwork, the current generated by the four center-directed lines of crystals bend the flow as illustrated and feed it partly into the POL and partly into a continuously recirculating energy stream.

In analyzing the three-dimensional energy mandala dynamics of circularly-based gridworks, Figure 109 (top and side views of circular grid) is utilized as the foundation. Then the additional crystals' flow patterns are taken into account and superimposed within these dynamics. The Solar Cross analysis serves as one example of this genre of gridworks.

BASIC CRYSTAL GRIDWORK GEOMETRICS

> Every form is the manifestation of the force that has built it. Thus every form is the image of the creative force that builds it and dwells within it.[7]

> Geometry enables its votary, like a bridge, to pass over the obscurity of material nature, as over some dark sea to the luminous regions of perfect reality.[8]

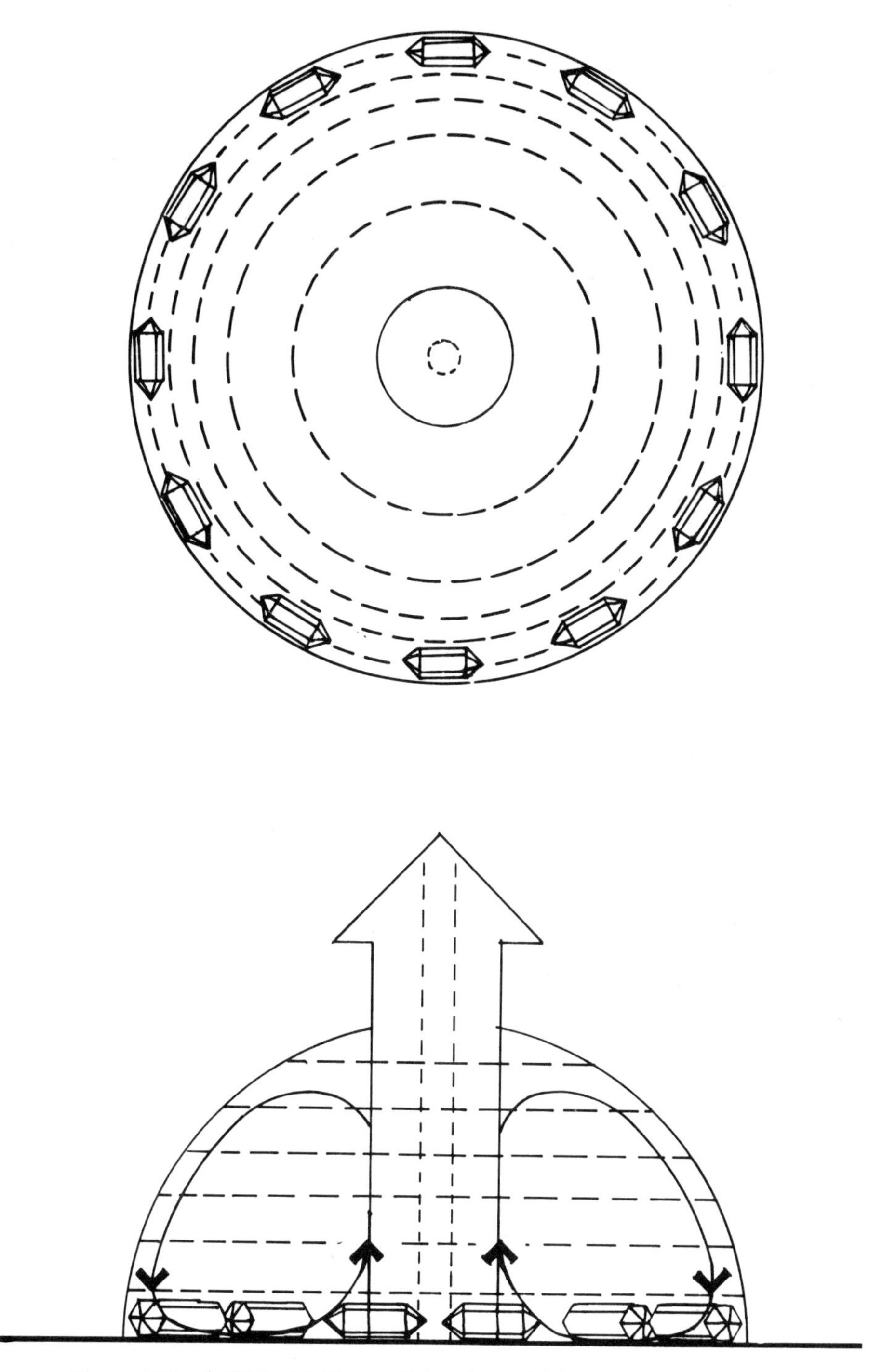

Figure 109a & 109b: Multi-zone Solar-Cross Gridwork Energy Dynamics

> Sacred geometry forms are vehicles to become a channel through which the earth could receive the abstract, cosmic life of the heavens.[9]

> It is as if the form itself provides a structure through which an ever-present energy is intensified.[10]

By recreating abstractly causal universal geometric patterns via crystal gridworks, the resulting harmonic vibrational patternings function as a resonating antenna-receiver system for tapping into the originating creative force and grounding it on the earth plane. Thus, the archetypal symbology, numerology, and harmonic proportionality of these geometric cosmograms is stabilized in an earthly standing wave pattern by which human consciousness may partake in and assimilate these qualities and code patterns.

Herein presented are nine basic crystal gridwork geometries, the logistics of their practical manifestation, and seed-concepts as to their effects and uses. It is important not to "crystallize" the concepts discussed regarding each gridwork into rigidity, for there is considerable latitude for further research and experimentation with each one. The authors desire to provide a foundation that others may utilize as a stepping-stone to ever-increasing insights and creative applications.

Figure 110: Star of David.[11] This geometry is a keystone of universal physics. Its equilibrating dynamism and interdimensional interlinking properties make it one of the most versatile and useful of all gridwork patterns. Although it is a symbol of the Judaic tradition, it is also a universal symbol and energy pattern of Light. As stated in the insightful *Vibrations: Healing Through Color, Homeopathy, and Radionics:*

> It appears that the whole source, motion, and function of light can be contained in that mysterious hexagonal figure known as the Seal of Solomon . . . as an energy pattern this figure expresses a spiral.
>
> This figure is used to represent the marriage of the kundalini and the Primary Force. Two interlacing triangles, one descending, the other ascending, move toward a potential intersection at the heart chakra in the form of a hexagon . . . This union or intersection creates the current which bears the light throughout the body.[12]

In another sense, the Star of David (also known as the Seal of Solomon and Mogan David) represents the interdimensional unification of the earthly self with the Light-body. The inverted triangle symbolizes the earthly self and the upright triangle represents the Higher Self, or Light body, and the perfectly balanced intersection between the two triangles illustrates a state of dynamic equilibrium and unity between the self and Self.

In practical application, the Star of David gridwork, copyrighted by the Rev. Dr. Frank Alper, is exceptionally versatile for a broad range of reprogramming, healing, and interdimensional communication. The symbolic and energetic keynotes here are dynamic equilibrium, interdimensional harmony, and Light-unification.

In setting up the gridwork, note that the two triangles are equilateral (that is, they have three sides of equal length) and the two intersect with one another in a perfectly balanced manner. The six vertexes describe an equilateral hexagon when these points are joined consecutively around the exterior of the Star of David. The three pairs of opposite vertexes are all equal in length. In addition, the length of a line drawn from the center to a vertex is equal to the side lengths of the

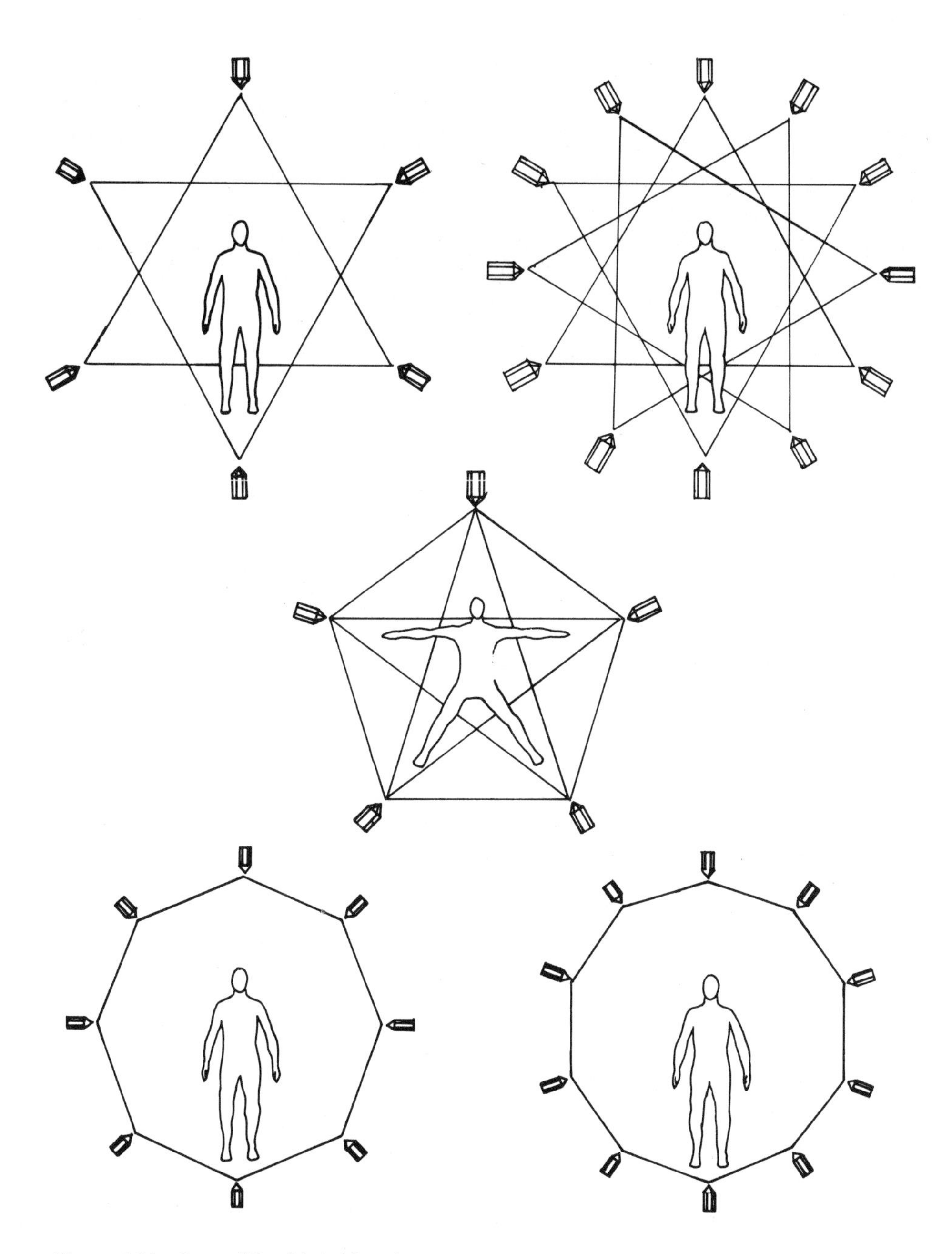

Figure 110: Star of David Gridwork
Figure 111: Double Star of David Gridwork
Figure 112: Pentagon/Pentagram Gridwork
Figure 113: Octagon Gridwork
Figure 114: Decagon Gridwork

surrounding equilateral hexagon. When the figure is measured out, a crystal is placed at each vertex with the termination point pointing directly into the center point of the Star of David. It is recommended to position the terminated tip of each crystal at the tip of each vertex to assure greater balance and precision of energy dynamics.

Figure 111: Double Star of David "A key crystal serves as the key focal point for energizing the crystals which are placed in a pattern of two Mogan Davids."[13] First found in *The Keys of Enoch,* two Stars of David are superimposed upon one another in equilateral balance. The single Star of David's versatility is here significantly amplified by the addition of a second such pattern. This gridwork arrangement is the most powerful and generally useful of all the basic gridwork patterns.

It is constructed by first measuring out a single Star of David as in figure 110. Construct another Star such that the second's vertexes are halfway between the vertexes of the first Star. The overall geometric result is an equilateral dodecagon; the lines going from crystals to crystal around the outside perimeter are all equal in length.

Figure 112: Pentagon/Pentagram. This is an archetypal symbol of the human—the top vertex corresponds to the head, the two side vertexes to the arms, and the two lower vertexes to the legs. The keynote attributes for this gridwork are balanced symmetry and homeostatic equilibrium.

The pentagram has an equilateral geometry. The easiest layout is done by describing an equilateral pentagon and placing the crystal terminations at the five vertexes pointing into the center of the figure. The best results are obtained when the individual aligns the head, arms, and legs with the five vertexes as illustrated. This pattern also works well in conjunction with a circular gridwork placed around the perimeter of the pentagram.

Figure 113: Octagon. This eight-sided equilateral figure has the keynote properties of equanimity, dynamic stillness, and harmonic balancing.

As with the gridworks already presented, the eight crystals are placed with their terminations at the respective vertexes aligned with the figure's center point. This gridwork works best with perimeter wire-wrapping (see later text in this chapter) in conjunction with a rotating generator crystal at the center point under a treatment table and with a rotating octahedron suspended overhead.

Figure 114: Decagon. This pattern is a ten-sided equilateral geometry. Its primary vibrational keynotes are wholeness and dynamic symmetrizing. From Nichomachus of Gerasa, a primary exponent of Pythagorean thought:

> It was in the Decad that a natural balance between the Whole and its element was found to pre-exist. . . . That is why the All-ordering God (literally:"the God arranging with art") acting in accordance with his Reason, made use of the Decad as a canon for the Whole as well as for their parts, their ratios of concord based upon the Decad and are ordered accordingly.[14]

The decagon gridwork is effective for a variety of subtle yet powerful healing and reprogramming applications.

Equilateral sides are laid out and each crystal's termination positioned at a vertex pointing into the figure's center. This gridwork functions best with perimeter wire-wrapping and the multipyramidal system illustrated in Figure 64 in chapter 12.

Figure 115: Solar Cross. Harmonically related to the Star of David, the Solar

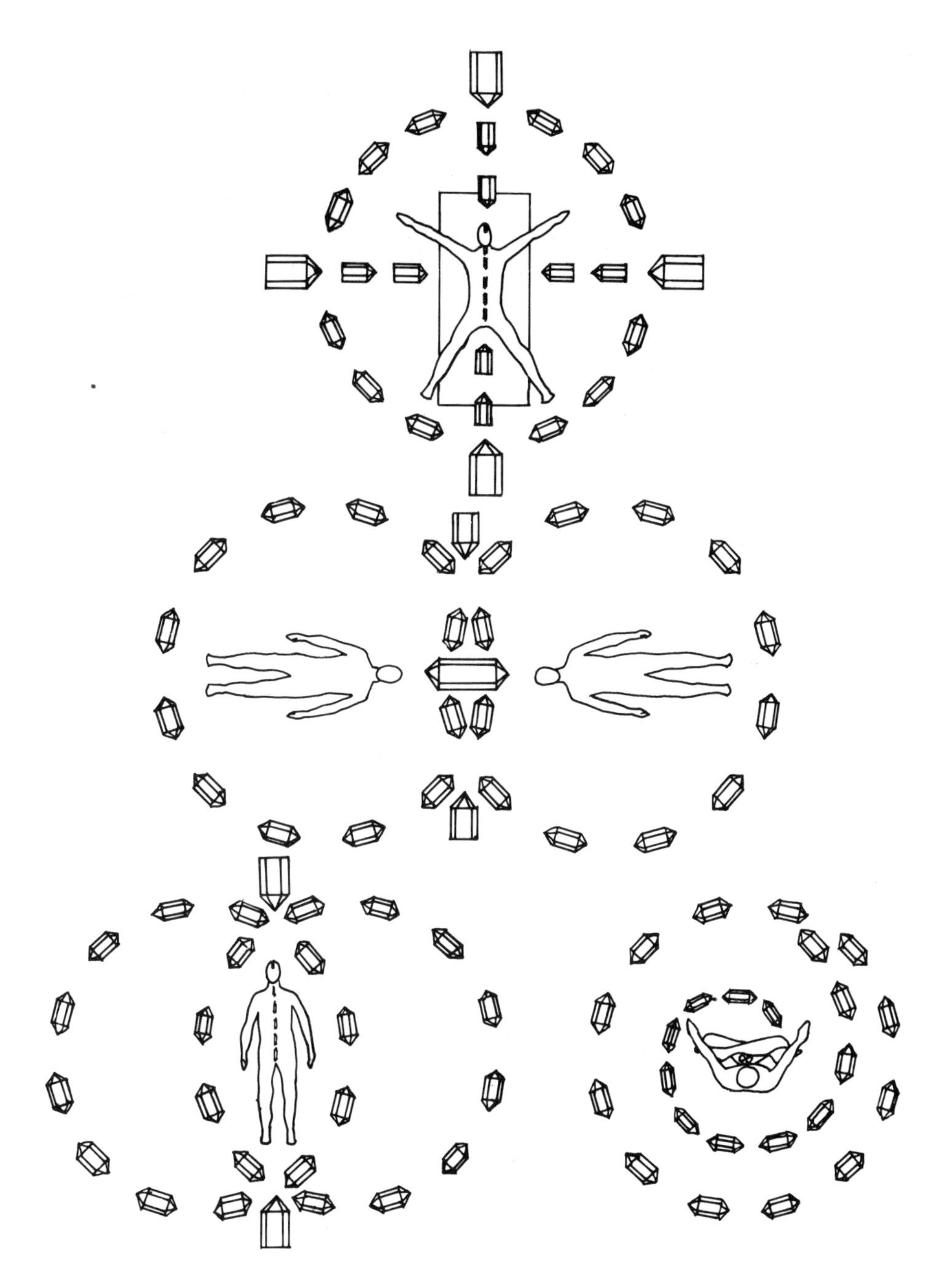

Figure 115: Solar Cross Gridwork
Figure 116: Dyad Circle Gridwork
Figure 117: Vesica Piscis Gridwork
Figure 118: Phi-spiral Gridwork

Cross is also a primary symbol and energy pattern for interdimensional unity and ascension into the Light-body. From *The Master Symbol of the Solar Cross,* By Tarvis and Tuella: "The Cross of Light and the Circle of Love, together as one symbol, represent the eventual freedom and ascension of the Soul. . . . The Cross of Light enfolding within the Circle of Love is the Star of the Perfect Balance of Power."[15] The fundamental characteristics of the effects of the Solar Cross are regeneration-in-balance, interdimensional unification, and Light-body activation.

The Solar Cross gridwork is made by first making a circular pattern of double-terminations. At least 12 good quality crystals are needed to create an effective circular gridwork. They are spaced equidistantly all around the circle. In the Solar Cross there are three crystals around the outside of each of the four circle quadrants. In all the circular gridworks, for the Solar Cross and others, if double-terminations are not available, an acceptable substitute is to wire-wrap two single-terminations together, each one pointing in the opposite direction. When creating the circle, keep all the clockwise-pointing crystals in the 12-paired sets all on the outside of the circle; the counterclockwise crystals will then all be oriented on the inside perimeter of the circle. For the Solar Cross, add four larger crystals at the four cardinal directions just outside the circle and pointing into the center. Also, make four lines of centrally oriented small crystals along the same axes as the four larger outer crystals. Use at least six crystals for each of the four lines. Once they are positioned, lay a thin rug over the area where the indivudal will be situated, without disturbing the placement of the crystals. The individual lies down on the rug with the spine oriented along the north–south axis of crystal lines and each limb is put in one of the corresponding four sectors of the gridwork. Best effects are gained when the heart chakra is directly aligned with the center point of the Solar Cross.

Figure 116: Dyad Circle Gridwork. Two slightly overlapping circular grids create an excellent energy field for two-person interactions on the higher planes. The primary effect is to facilitate an interlinkage of consciousness between two individuals for purposes of joint interdimensional communication, interpersonal healing, or dyadic transformation processes.

Lay out two circular grids with approximately 6 to 8 inches of overlap (measured horizontally from each circle's outermost diameter). A large, good quality double-termination is placed horizontally across the overlap region, which will point directly into the heads of the participants, as illustrated. This crystal is the main facilitative consciousness interconnector. Also, at the two points of intersection, place double-terminations pointing vertically into the center of the overlap region.

Figure 117: Vesica Piscis.

> The overlapping circles—an excellent representation of a cell, or any unity in the midst of becoming dual—from a fish-shaped central area which is one source of the symbolic reference to Christ as a fish. Christ, as a universal function, is symbolically the region which joins together heaven and earth, above and below, creator and creation.
>
> . . . The vesica can represent the seed. . . . The three contained within the Vesica Piscis is the formative power giving rise to the polygonal "world."[16]

In use as a gridwork, the vesica piscis manifests an ideal energy dynamic for interdimensional "travel" and communication interconnection. The overlapping circular grids create an unusual horizontal null hyper-space interlinkage zone that functions as a nonlinear POL interdimensional access zone.

The two equal-diameter crystal circles overlap so that they intersect each other's centers. At the two points of intersection at the top and bottom of the overlap area are placed a large single-terminated crystal directed along the north–south axis. Inside the vesica piscis a line of smaller double-terminations is laid between the circle's two intersection points. A small rug is placed over this line of crystals and serves as the area where the recipient lies down inside the gridwork.

Figure 118: Phi-Spiral Gridwork. The phi-based spiral, also called the Golden Proportion, is a universal fundamental harmonic of interdimensional energy flow and consciousness expansion. It is a flow-pattern of growth and transcendence associated with the creative process and the fire of life. "Phi represents a divine ideation—an etheric formula for transcendence and beauty superimposed by the Creator upon the physical plane."[17] As a gridwork, the phi-spiral can be utilized for two primary purposes, depending on whether it is oriented clockwise or counterclockwise. In the former case, there is a strongly active projective POL effect; rapid pulses of concentrated energy flow have high penetrative interdimensional access. In the latter case, there is an accumulative, focusing effect within the gridwork itself.

Within a circular gridwork, a spiral of double-terminated crystals follows the outline of the phi geometry until the center point is reached. In an upright seated position, the individual positions a larger energy generator crystal between the crossed legs.

GUIDELINES FOR MANIFESTING AND USING CRYSTAL GRIDWORKS

1. For ideal results, the gridwork is established permanently in a single location with minimal disturbance. Optimally, the location is in a harmonious and secluded place so that the gridwork's energy field is exposed to minimal mixed energies. The gridwork space and the intermediately surrounding environment should be utilized only for purposes relating to the function of that energy field.

If this is not possible, before establishing the gridwork's setup, cleanse the immediate area so that it is clear of any ambient mixed energies (see below, no. 2). Then create and use the grid.

In an environment without enough space to maintain a gridwork full-time, an alternative is to place a vertically upright energy generator crystal at the grid's center point, and then bring all the surrounding crystals in toward the central crystal just a few inches away while still maintaining their geometric grid pattern. In this way, a continuity of higher Light can be sustained in the environment and in the gridwork energy pattern. This compacted gridwork can be used for crystal charging, as a POL altar, and for other creative purposes. When the full-size grid is desired the crystals are simply extended out to their corresponding positions (placing a piece of tape marking these locations bypasses repeated measuring.)

2. Before establishing a gridwork, either long- or short-term, clear the subtle energy field of mixed vibrations and clean the area of physical dirt, dust, and so on. Any number of methods can be used for working with the subtle energy field, many of which are presented in Chapter 17 (no. 23). An easy, all-purpose method

is to fill a gallon jar with supersaturated saltwater (that is, dissolve salt in warm water until no more can be dissolved) and a small crystal programmed for attracting and holding mixed energies. Place this jar in the middle of the gridwork area for 24-48 hours before use (in long-term situations).

It is a good practice to use this saltwater setup full-time. When actively using the gridwork, the jar can be placed out of the way; during times of nonuse, the jar can be set inside the gridwork to help maintain optimal energy clearing. If this is not done, it is important, as a minimum, to have weekly energy clearings.

This saltwater technique helps keep the grid crystals cleared of static. Unless significant releasing of imbalanced energies in healing processes or other such energetic fluctuations occurs within the gridwork, the grid crystals need only be cleared and cleansed monthly or bimonthly. Of course, situations will vary, and intuition is the best guide.

3. Gridworks function optimally when the crystals used are matched sets, that is, the crystals have a similar size, shape, and energy qualities. Matching crystals is largely an intuitive process.

Should a completely matched crystal set not be available, the best alternative is to match them into pairs of similar qualities. Place the two crystals in each pair on opposite sides of the gridwork to help counterbalance the collective energy dynamics.

If neither method can be used, simply intuit the optimal harmonic placement of the crystals.

4. The primary horizontal axis of a gridwork is best aligned with magnetic north and south. Most of the gridworks discussed have a major axis of energy dynamics along which a reclining individual lies (see the orientation of the people in the figures). In most cases, there are two primary crystals that are oriented with magnetic north and south.

The positioning of the individual within the gridwork parallels the orientation of the grid itself. When reclining, the head is at the north end of the horizontal axis and the feet are at the south end. When seated upright, the front of the body is facing north, and the back is facing south.

In addition, in an upright seated position orient the body so that the spinal axis is aligned with the center of the grid pattern. If a reclined position is used, whenever possible, position the top of the bioauric field (from the heart to the Omega chakra) within the inner zone of the gridwork in order to be exposed to the strongest, most focused energy dynamics.

5. Geometric accuracy is important when setting up a gridwork. The use of rulers, string, and tape will facilitate this process. For example, to make a circular pattern cut a length of string half the diameter of the entire circle. Hold or tape one end to the center point and stretch the other end fully outward. Mark the point where the extended end reaches with tape; arc the string around a few more inches and mark this place; and continue this process going all the way around the circle with one end held stationary at the center. The taped areas will now collectively describe a circle that will function as an outline for the placement of the crystals.

With other geometries—such as the Star of David, octagon, and decagon—the first step is the same as for the circle. Next, mark the north and south end points—these are the first two points of the gridwork (except for the pentagon). Determine how many equilateral sides must be fit into a semicircle with which to work. Cut a length of string that is close to the length of one equilateral side of the particular polygon. Using the circle outline, take the string fully out and mark the point as the next starting point from which to stretch the other end of the string to the next intersection point; and repeat this process until the south end is reached. If the string length did not mark off exactly the number of equilateral sides required for this figure, either cut a shorter or longer string length and repeat the process until the string length marks off the desired number of sides, each exactly equal in length. (Note: the Star of David is the easiest polygon to mark off because its radius length equals the length of a line drawn around the figure's perimeter from one vertex to the next.)

6. Varying the overall diameter of a gridwork will cause accompanying changes in the potency of its energy dynamics. Two factors apply here: 1) the energetic strength of the crystals (the greater the clarity and size, the more powerful the crystals) and 2) the harmonic interaction between the gridwork's crystals. For any given gridwork, there will be harmonic diameters of crystal placement that produce the most powerful and integrated energetic interactions. Like the quantum electron orbital shell levels of an atom, there are distinct harmonic energy "shells" (that is, overall diameters) of optimal gridwork energy dynamics. To discern the best crystal positionings, experiment with various increments of diameter length, experiencing the associated variations in the energetic interactions. There are distinct diameter-length intervals at which the vibrational dynamics are significantly more active and harmonically integrated. Find the diameter that has the highest balanced potency. Keep in mind that the optimal diameter-length will vary if one or more crystals are replaced in the gridwork or if a different set of crystals is used.

7. To achieve maximum activation and integrated energy dynamics, it is effective to program each crystal of the gridwork. The program is twofold: 1) the specific geometry of the gridwork (for example, the Star of David or Solar Cross) and 2) the primary function of the crystals, that is, the primary energy flow generation. Therefore, an example of a formulated program to imprint in each gridwork crystal is "Primary energy flow generation in a Star of David gridwork." This program need not be any more specific than this. By programming in this manner, each crystal's matrix becomes better predisposed toward enacting its specific use in a gridwork and integrating its energy dynamics with that of the other crystals.

8. A very important component of a gridwork set-up is a capstone. In order to help amplify the POL effect and to stabilize and integrate the overall energy dynamics, it is helpful to suspend a single pyramid or multipyramidal system over the center of the gridwork. The vertical height at which the capstone is most effective varies. Experiment with different heights, experiencing the harmonic variations in the gridwork dynamics until the best height is found. Suspend the capstone with non-conductive materials; natural fiber string works well. Metal wiring is to be avoided, as it will alter the energy dynamics in an undesirable way. A 12-inch-base single pyramid will function adequately as a capstone for basic gridwork setups. A 4 foot- to 6 foot-base pyramid that can be situated without suspension so that the apex is over the gridwork's center will work even better. As the power and sophistication of UEFs increases, so does the need for more advanced capstones.

9. Crystals in addition to those used in the gridwork itself can be utilized within the UEF in a variety of ways. Most crystal-based techniques and methodologies presented in this text can be used inside a gridwork with amplified results. From chakra sets to mind-center activation techniques to Light-tools, the gridwork provides a UEF conducive to modularly plugging in a spectrum of crystal usages and unique self-transformation regimes.

GRIDWORK USE OUTLINE

Presented herein is a generalized outline for utilizing a gridwork system with virtually any methodology. Feel free to creatively adapt this outline to conform to the pattern and flow of an individual or group regime.

1. Make sure that the UEF is clear of all undesired energies.
2. Orient oneself, other individuals, and other crystals within the gridwork as appropriate.
3. Briefly relax the bioenergetic system and center the awareness.
4. Concentrate on the intended purposes of the gridwork session.
5. Mentally connect with the overall flow-pattern of the gridwork's energies. Feel the dynamics starting to interact and integrate with consciousness. Visualize and feel the pattern of the geometric energy mandala as the gridwork's overall energy flow becomes stimulated.
6. Spend two to three minutes (or more, as desired) with energizing procedures, helping to generate a maximal energy charge throughout the entire bioenergetic system. Controlled deep breathing exercises are particularly appropriate.
7. Feel the POL effect, and connect awareness with the higher realms of Light using the interdimensional communication procedures presented in Chapter 19. State the intention of the gridwork session, and ask for the assistance and protection of the appropriate aspects of the Higher Evolution.
8. Enact the intention. Take as much time as needed.
9. Allow approximately one quarter the total time spent in the gridwork for the assimilation and integration of the results of the session. Maintain a state of nonactive, nonexpectant, relaxed receptivity, allowing consciousness to soak in the energies received during the course of the session. This aspect of gridwork use is important to optimal results.
10. Express thankfulness to the Higher Evolution for assistance and blessings.
11. Gradually adjust back to normal, waking consciousness.

A MULTIPLE-LEVEL GRIDWORK METHODOLOGY

More advanced gridwork applications involve the use of either one or more grid geometries superimposed over one another (for example, Figure 125) or gridworks positioned within other gridworks (for example, Figure 126). The result is the creation of more versatile, complex, and synergistically amplified gridwork combinations. The harmonic conjoining of two or more gridworks presents many possibilities for generating a spectrum of different energy mandala dynamics. In addition, the involvement of greater numbers of crystals in harmonically interrelated energy patternings stimulates greater power and synergy generation.

Because of its effectiveness and adaptability to an array of situations, the following *Multiple-Level Double Star of David gridwork system* is presented in detail.

To set a foundation for understanding the energetic principles utilized in this gridwork system, a number of intercrystal dynamics must be analyzed. For purposes of simplicity, only the primary crystal energy dynamics will be discussed here, for it is this aspect of the energetics that is most important in this context. First, in Figure 119A are two crystals with terminations pointing toward each other. The result of the two vibrational streams interpenetrating one another is energy accumulation in the area between the crystals, with a concentrated focusing at their intersecting midpoints. Next, in Figure 119B is illustrated a situation in which two crystals are pointing away from one another, leaving the two bases facing each other. The effect here is the drawing away of energy from the intervening area between the two bases and out in two opposite streams through the terminations. In Figure 119 a termination points into the other crystal's base. The effect is that the current emitting from the left crystal's termination feeds into the base of the other crystal, whereupon this energy is added into the second crystal's energy dynamics. The resulting current emitting from the second crystal (under ideal circumstances) is the additive combination of power from both crystals plus an additional amplification factor; therefore, if each crystal's energy has x amount of power, the combining of the two crystals in this way results in $x + x +$ amplification. If, as in Figure 119D, the second crystal is angled along a different axis than the first, the energy flow still feeds from the first into the second, and follows the axis orientation of the second. The power of the resulting energy is the same as in Figure 119C, the only difference being that the current from the first is redirected through the axis of the second. The principles in Figures 119 play an important role in the multiple-level gridwork system.

There are four distinct levels within the Double Star of David Multiple Level Gridwork (MLG) system. (See Figure 120.) Each level has a particular positioning and function that complements all the other levels within the overall harmonic workings.

Level I is a double Star of David gridwork encompassing the other three levels contained within it. The purpose of level I is to provide the geometric energy foundation and the primary power flow. Because of this, level I crystals are the largest to be found in all the levels. In a professional setting, these crystals should be at least fist-sized. Otherwise, use the largest and most powerful crystals available. The program to imprint in each level I crystal is "primary power generation in a double Star of David gridwork."

Approximately 1 to 3 inches in from the level I gridwork are the level II crystals, which are positioned immediately in front of level I, thus forming a second double Star of David. This level is composed of programmed energy directors. Level II crystals are smaller than those of level I, being 2 to 3 inches in length. All level I crystals point in toward the center of the gridwork, but level II crystals can be angled to point to specifically desired bioenergetic areas of a reclined individual, with the resulting energy flow dynamics as shown in Figure 120. It is recommended that the recipient choose two bioenergetic areas that most need to receive healing or reprogramming influences. In Figure 120, the two focus areas are the healing of the left knee and the reprogramming of the crown chakra. Six level II crystals are angled toward the crown chakra, and six are angled toward the knee. The base of the level II crystals remains in front of the level I crystals so that the energy flow interaction between the two will occur most efficiently with minimal energy loss. Because of the differences in the size of level I and II crystals, it is

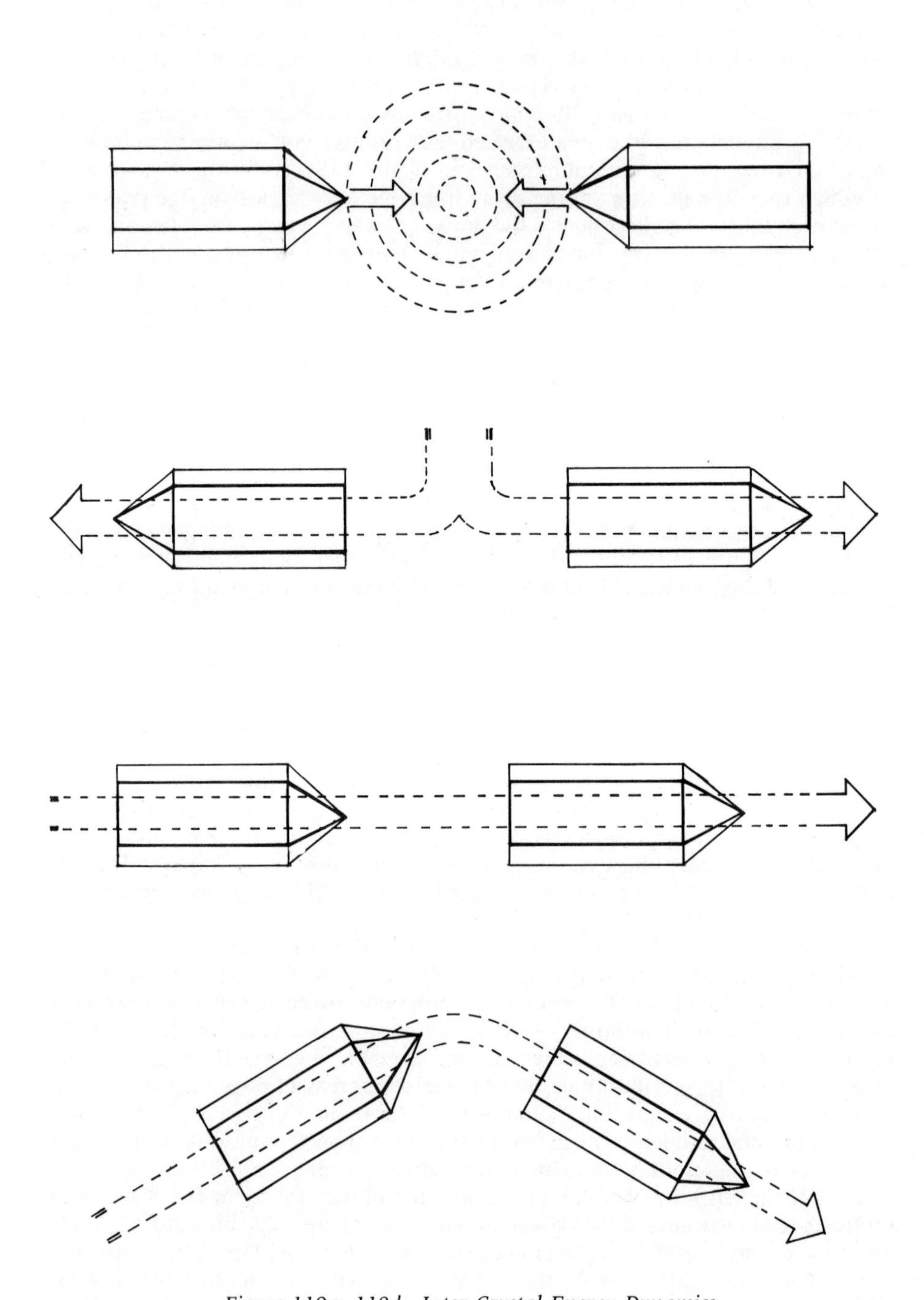

Figure 119a–119d: Inter-Crystal Energy Dynamics

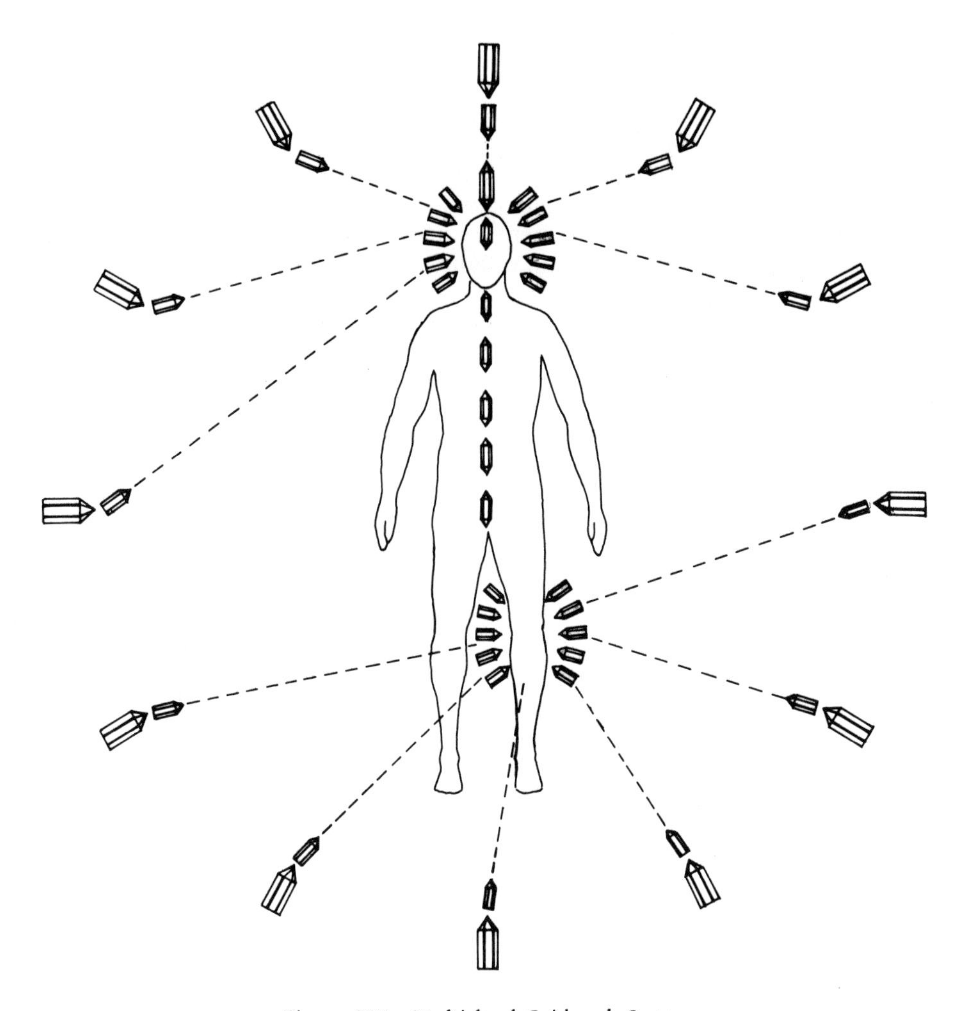

Figure 120: Multi-level Gridwork System

best to prop level II crystals up on a neutral-substance horizontal platform (for example, a wood block) so that the terminations of the level I crystals point directly into the center of the bases of level II crystals. Further, each group of six level II crystals are programmed with energy patterns that relate to the bioenergy area to which they are pointing. In this way, the primary power flow of level I feeds into level II, and the energetics are amplified and specifically patterned. As these vibrational patterns project from level II they are also directed into a focused stream into the specified bioenergetic zone.

Level III consists of small (3/4 to 1 1/2 inches in length) crystals placed in miniature gridworks around the two focal areas being treated. Two main gridwork patterns are used in level III. The first choice is the Star of David. If this arrangement is not possible, a double arc arrangement is used. Two equal, oppositely positioned arcs are set in place on either side of the focal zone (see Figure 120). In both cases, another crystal is placed upon the focal area (which should be in the center of the level III grid). Level III crystals can be group–programmed (that is, programmed at the same time) with a thought-pattern of wholeness that relates to the specific area. The purpose of this level is to further amplify and direct the incoming level I and level II energies into the focal zones.

Level IV is the positioning of double-terminations on each chakra, from Alpha to Omega. These nine crystals function to stimulate the primary energy dynamics of the bioenergetic system so that maximum receptivity to healing or reprogramming work is effected. This chakra set may also be composed of 1 to 2 inch-base crystal pyramids. Also, it is optimal for each crystal to be specifically programmed for use with a particular chakra.

If desired, the recipient can also hold a crystal in each hand for additional energy input and balancing of the right-side/left-side biopolarities.

Once the recipient and crystals are in their appropriate orientations, enact the "Gridwork Use Outline" presented earlier in this chapter. When the time comes to enact the intention, perform specific techniques relating to the healing or reprogramming of the two focal zones. Such techniques can be those with which the individual is already comfortable. This MLG methodology may be carried out by an individual as part of his or her personal practice or it can be utilized in a professional setting. The methodology is profoundly effective within the full spectrum of healing and reprogramming parameters and is highly recommended. Additional UEF components that can be added to this double Star of David MLG setup are presented in "Advanced Gridwork Concepts" later in this chapter.

Selected Professional Perspectives

1. For efficient, accurate recall of a recipient's specific focal areas and the placement and orientation of levels II and III, make a chart of the MLG to be kept in a file.

2. A set of levels II and III crystals should be set aside for use with only one recipient; with each recipient, a different set of levels II and III crystals is brought out. In this way, the individual-specific programming of these crystals not only helps these crystals to be keyed to the particular person but also saves the practitioner much time, because the programming process is done only once (although it may be changed if the focal areas change during a series of treatments). For efficient recall of the programming of each crystal, place a small white adhesive dot (available from stationery stores) at the base of every crystal with a code as to its program and gridwork placement. With placement codes, the twelvefold arrangement of the gridwork lends itself to a clock-based code system (that is, the topmost crystal is at the twelve o'clock position, and so on).

Because of the large number of crystals potentially required, it is best if the practitioner finds a wholesale source. Also, the cost of the recipient's individual therapy crystals (plus a service charge) may be included in the costs of an initial treatment. When a treatment series reaches completion, the recipient is given the crystals along with a copy of the coded chart so that he or she may duplicate these two gridwork levels and continue the therapy on their own.

3. Level I crystals are used for every treatment session without replacement. Clearing and cleansing factors need to be observed with care here.

4. Level IV crystals can be used interchangeably with different recipients. Between each use, however, they must be cleared and cleansed. For this reason, it is optimal to have several level IV sets available for clinical use.
5. It is necessary in some circumstances to tape various crystals in place on the recipient. For this, it is best to use hypoallergenic first-aid tape.
6. Avoid transfer of body oils that accumulate on crystals, therapy tools, sheets, and so on from one person to another. Use a different clean sheet for every session. Oils can be removed from the crystals when placed in salt for a time and then cleansed with water.
7. Use a thin, but firm and comfortable cushioning for the recipient to lie upon. This MLG methodology will not work effectively when used in conjunction with a massage table, or other treatment table of similar height. In such a case, it is necessary to put up shelves all around the room at the same height as the treatment table for placing levels I and II crystals.
8. Creatively integrate other healing and reprogramming methodologies with the fundamental parameters of the double Star of David MLG system as possible and appropriate.

Level III Concepts

The level III concept can be applied as a modality in and of itself, without necessarily being used in association with the complete MLG system. When working with specific areas of imbalance, a miniature gridwork—Star of David, double arcs, and others—may be positioned on top of the focal area. In this way, a harmonically focused energy field is generated in conjunction with the bioenergetics of the specific area for facilitating amplified input of positive energies.

A variety of level III application concepts is possible. For further reference in this regard, see *Windows of Light* (Baer & Baer, pp. 101–103).

Such miniature gridworks may be used alone or, more effectively, as an amplified energy focus grid for other applied vibrational modalities. Virtually any healing, self-transformation, or reprogramming technique that applies energetics into a specific bioenergetic region can use small-scale gridworks as an adjunctive modality. Applications are limited only by educated imagination.

One specific technique applicable to a wide range of situations is presented here. A Star of David gridwork is positioned over the focal zone with another crystal placed in the center. The center crystal (either a natural quartz or a pyramid-faceted crystal) is programmed for absorption of imbalanced energy patterns. Then the individual (or practitioner) enacts techniques that dislodge and disperse the bioenergetic patterns that are out of harmony. After this cycle of removal is complete, the center crystal is taken off and placed in salt. Another crystal programmed for the infusion of wholeness patterns into the area is then put in the center position. Next, a cycle of techniques designed for the input and assimilation of balanced vibrational patterns is performed. After this cycle is complete, a five to ten minute period of time is allotted for receptive integration of the technique's effects.

Advanced Gridwork Concepts

The sacred science of gridwork-based UEFs is complex, and one which bears considerable examination and advanced application, for within its scientific dynamics lie many keys to limitless interdimensional intercommunication. Codes within codes, keys within keys. . . . the harmonic interfusion of primary universal geometries bear the multiplex templates of multidimensional superposition.

As with the basic gridwork patterns previously discussed in this chapter, the advanced geometries that follow are presented as foundational seed-concepts to be further developed through research and experimentation. Crystal placement factors follow the same principles as described with the basic gridworks unless otherwise noted. *Caution:* All of the advanced gridwork concepts presented in this section, especially those involving magnets, have a potential power of high magnitude. Skilled precision and discernment is required to avoid misaligned energetic effects and to manifest them toward their highest intended purposes. Please exercise care in determining whether it is appropriate to experiment with them.

Figure 121 shows a Star of David gridwork with a Solar Cross in the middle. Both geometries are premier energy patterns of interdimensional unification and ascension; together, the dynamism generated is considerably greater, as the inflowing Star of David energy mandalas add factors that spark the Solar Cross into a higher level of activation. Manifested with large, high quality energy generators in combination with other UEF components, this gridwork pattern is a superlative ascension module system.

In Figure 122 is an outside circular grid with a Star of David and spiral balanced within it. The powerful pulse-projective (clockwise spiral) and accumulative-focusing (counterclockwise spiral) capacities of the encircled phi-spiral gridwork are counterbalanced with the equipoise of the Star of David. The dynamism of the phi-spiral energetics is grounded and stabilized by the interpenetrating equilateral triangles of the Star of David.

Especially with a rotating octahedron as the capstone of this complex, interdimensional communication capabilities are significantly empowered (clockwise) and controlled bioenergetic depolarization is enabled (counterclockwise).

The combination vesica piscis and dyadic overlapping circle grids in Figure 123 create an unparalleled energy dynamic for two-person united interdimensional travel. In conjunction with UEF factors delineated later in this chapter in the section entitled "Star-Seed Connection UEF," this gridwork combination reaches an even greater level of dimensional potential.

Figure 124 illustrates a vesica piscis with a Star of David centrally superimposed. The vesica–the waveform of interdimensional linkage–generates the foundation to which the Star of David adds its universal access parameters to create an excellent module system for consciousness transfer to other sectors of the Universal Mind. In the future, this gridwork combination will provide an outline-blueprint for modulated interdimensional translocation of consciousness, genetic codes, and crystallographic complexes.

In Figure 125, the Star of David unites with the Solar Cross in a different harmonic proportionality than that in Figure 121. The result is an interdimensional regeneration-recharging attraction module. The overall dynamics are contained and accumulative within the dome energetics of the Solar Cross, but have a well-focused POL action through the central vertical axis. Especially combined with a rotating octahedron as a capstone, the dynamically balanced interdimensional regenerative effects add considerably to individual reprogramming momentum.

Figure 126 shows three Stars of David, each proportionally paralleling the other.

Figures 121–127: Advanced Gridwork Concepts

Around each of these three are circular gridworks that intersect with the six vertexes of every Star of David. The collective effect is exceptional celestial access. The intense energies that this attraction module attracts are pure White Light vibrations.

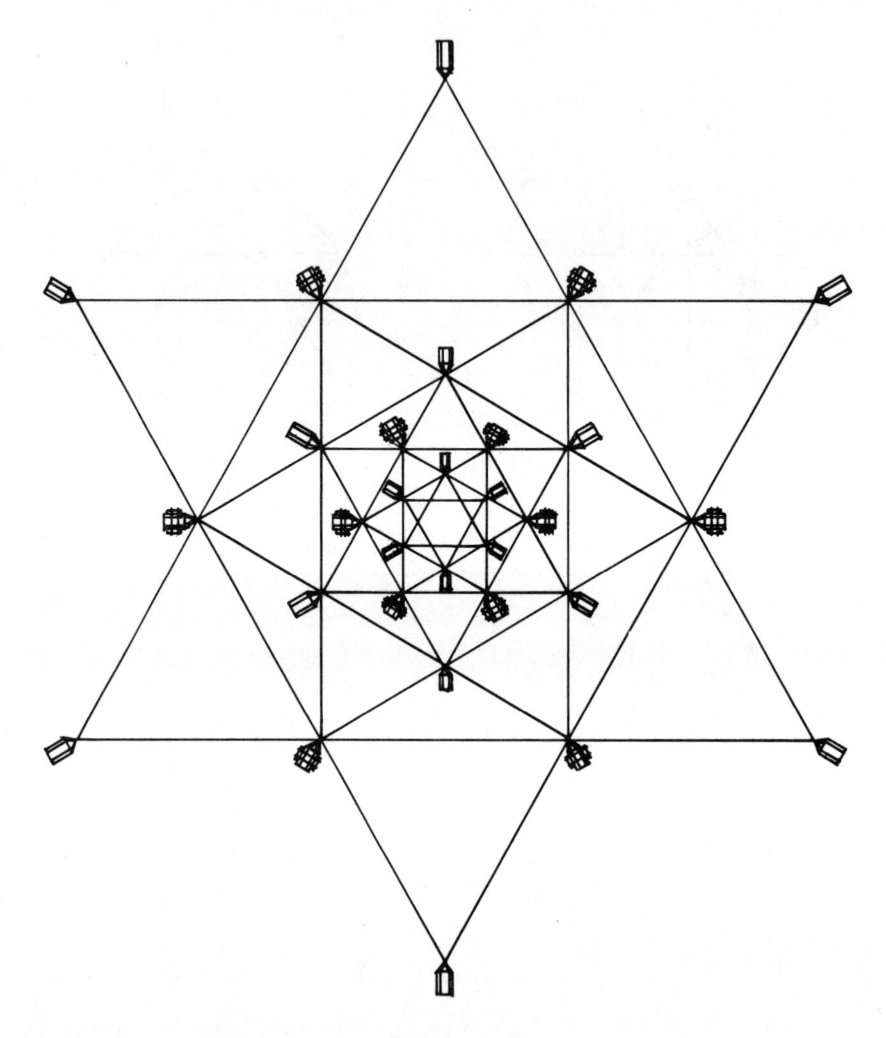

Figure 128: Five-level Star of David Gridwork

Figure 127 displays a variation of the preceding triple Star of David. Here, each Star of David, instead of being interrelated in a parallel manner, has a spiral twist in relation' to the other. The spiral energy dynamics are intrinsic to this pattern, imparting to it penetrative interdimensional intensity. The spiralling action is dual-directional, and therefore there is a counterbalanced high frequency POL pulsation that has a catalyzing effect upon the gridwork recipient. The forceful, rapid inter-penetration of multidimensional planes is highly activating and purgative on the causal levels of being. Best results are obtained when an upright energy generator crystals is positioned in the center point. The individual sits upright with the generator between the legs.

Figure 129: Merkabah Attraction Module Gridwork

Figure 128 shows a more advanced version of the spiraling triple Star of David pattern. With this gridwork, there are five spiraling Stars of David. The intensity and amplification of the multidimensional penetrative pulsation activity is magnified manyfold by the harmonic addition of magnets in levels II and IV (how to integrate magnets with crystals is covered in "Integrating Additional UEF Modalities," the next section of this chapter). The magnetics at alternate concentric intervals provide a nonlinear acceleratory factor to the spiraling dynamics. In this gridwork, the use of double-terminations is particularly optimal.

Yet another variation on the multiple Star of David theme is illustrated in Figure 129. In this case, levels I and III are double Stars of David. Levels II and IV are circular, and level V is a single Star of David with a generator crystal in the middle. Here again, magnetics is an integral part of the overal dynamics. In levels I and III the crystals are half the size of the crystals of the other Stars of David (this is crucial). The magnetics in conjunction with the circular grids create a powerful dome effect of an unusual nonlinear, magneto-gravitic nature. The spectrum profile of this gridwork combination creates one version of a Merkabah attraction module.

Figure 130 demonstrates the concept concerning the energy dynamics of utilizing crystal clusters in a gridwork application. The multitudinous energy streams emitting from every crystal within each cluster create a complex energy mandala. As such, clusters serve well as Level I gridwork crystals. For maximum effect, prop each cluster upon a neutral substance (such as a block of wood) so that the greaters number of crystals are pointing their energy streams toward the center of the gridwork. Illustrated also in the figure is the possibility of orienting one or more crystals in each cluster so that the energy streams interact with one or more specifically desired bioenergy areas of the recipient.

Figures 131 and 132 illustrate simple patterns for creating distributive and collective gridworks, respectively. Around an upright generator crystal a double Star of David either points inward or outward. When pointing outward, the primary dynamics of the generator's POL effect are drawn down and projected away from the gridwork. This is effective for environmental harmonizing and continuous recharging. When the twelve-fold gridwork is pointed inward to the generator crystal the upward POL flow is significantly enhanced as the surrounding energies are drawn in through the gridwork and focused into the central crystal. This technique is helpful in maintaining a strong and continuous POL connection.

Figure 133 exhibits an advanced version of Figures 131 and 132. Here, the dynamics are both collective and distributive. Around a central vertical generator crystal (optimally on top of a large diameter ring magnet) are four concentric ring-pairs of circular grid-patterns. Each ring is composed of a pair of single-terminated crystal circles, oriented in opposite directions—clockwise and counterclockwise. The distances between the four ring-pairs is of an increasing harmonic proportionality. The counterpoised energetic flow of each ring-pair generates a nonlinear subatomic-atomic spin orientation magnetically hyper-responsive to an AC-like energy switching process; the harmonic proportioning of ring-pairs is essential to an induction of these dynamics. The incorporation of aluminum-content magnets attached to each crystal of the grid is crucial to activating its highest potential. Some important aspects of this process are part of the higher physics of Stonehenge and other monolithic circles, as well as planetary energy grid-intersected churches and temples. In effect, this gridwork has a powerful distributive effect, an effect like the one that occurs when a pebble is dropped into the center of a still pond. Almost simultaneously, with the dropping of the pebble, the wave created returns to the center of the pond. So too with the wave action created by the gridwork; it returns at high speed to the center. The crystal generator functions as the Spirit polarity locus for the entire field. In addition to its potent effect in balancing the planetary meridian-gridwork system, this gridwork is also a singularly powerful group consciousness tool.

Figure 134 demonstrates a variation on figure 133. Here, magnetically activated crystals in ring-pairs are focused toward one another—termination-to-termination in six equally spaced intervals. The three ring-pair circles are at increasing harmonically proportioned intervals. The conjunctive effect of the magnet–crystal pairs sparks a ray-dome effect. This effect is different from the usual membrame

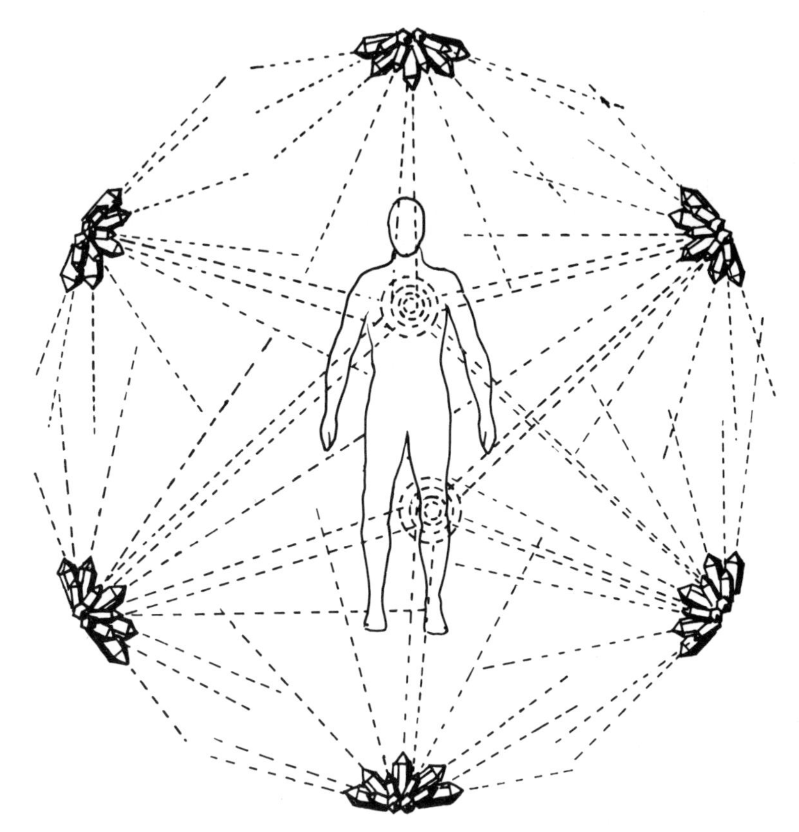

Figure 130:
Crystal Cluster Gridwork

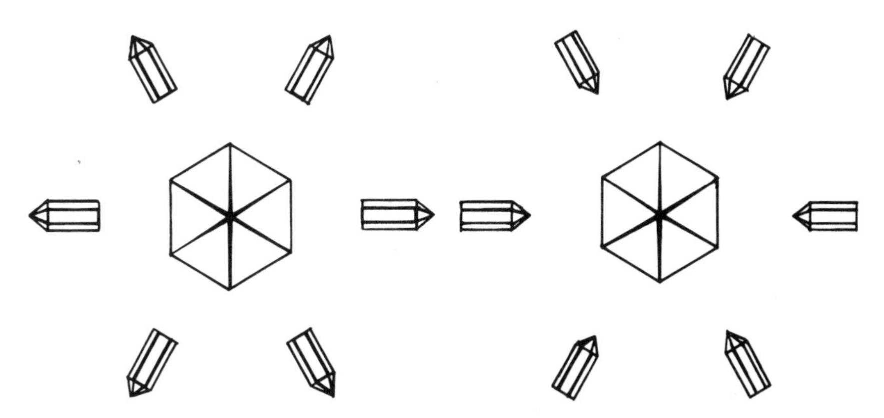

Figure 131:
Distributive Gridwork

Figure 132:
Collective Gridwork

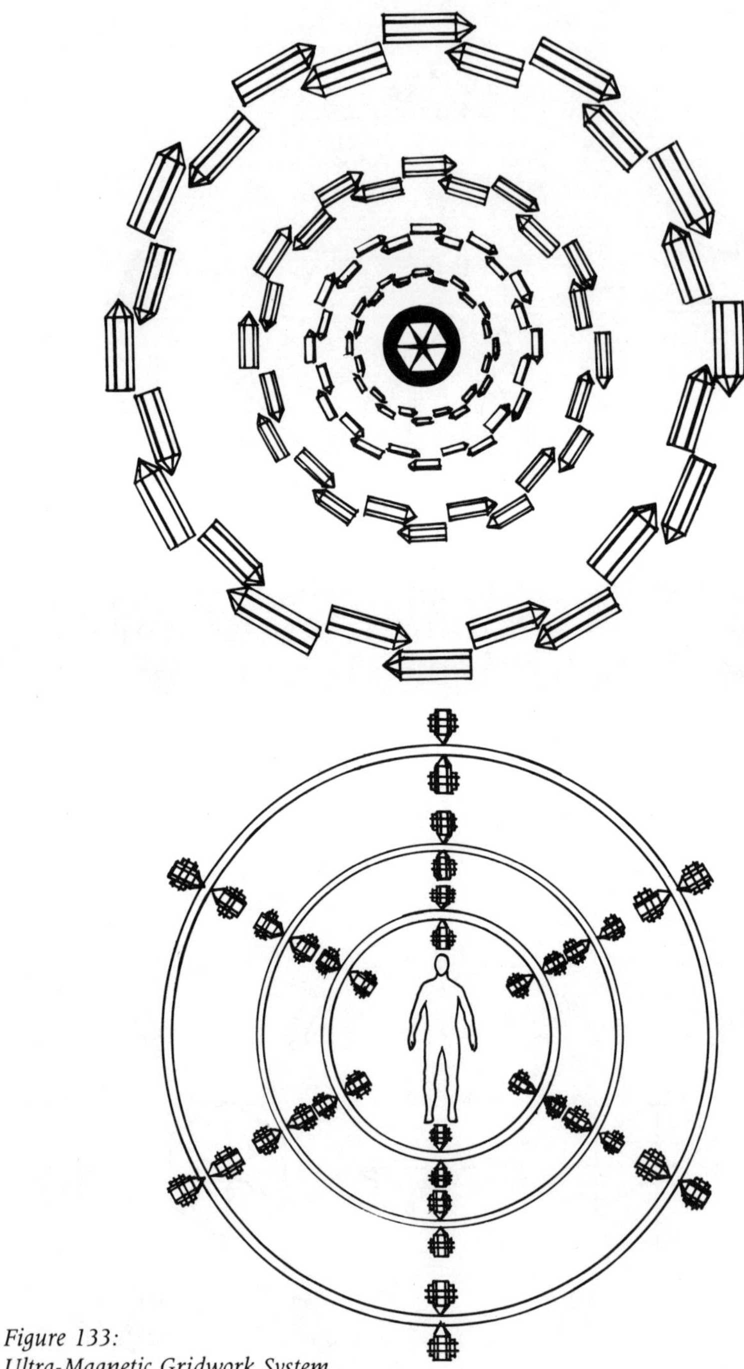

Figure 133:
Ultra-Magnetic Gridwork System
Figure 134:
Bio-energetic Reprogramming Module System

dome dynamic (see Figure 108). It is composed of focused magnetically recirculative energy-ray rings oriented along the primary axis perpendicular to the floor. (There are a host of secondary and tertiary orientations.) The radius of the energy rays for each successive circle of the gridwork increases proportionally. All energy rays go through the unipolar point (that is, the white hole-black hole singularity) at the center of the gridwork. The recipient lies in a pool of supersaturated saltwater holding a copper rod in the right hand and a carbon rod in the left hand. Care must be exercised as the magnetic matrix restructuralization of the bioenergy system is profound indeed. To those having authority to operate this system, the knowledge as to the nature of the inductive spark generator will be given by the Higher Evolution.

Figure 135 illustrates how to make a basic energy dome. Seven energy generators are needed, with one being a master generator for the middle of the grid. Each of the six other crystals is placed in a Star of David pattern vertically atop a ring magnet (the polarity orientation of the magnets' upper sides alternates at each crystal's base around the perimeter of the Star of David). The largest (or otherwise most powerful) facet of each crystal is oriented toward the center. The middle crystal sits atop a ring magnet twice as large as the others, and the magnet has alternating magnetic orientations occurring on the same side. The radius of the distance between the center and the perimeter of the dome grid is crucial to optimal effectiveness. There is a direct relationship between the overall powerful of the crystal–magnet energetics and the radius. Experiment with different increment lengths of the radius to find the primary and secondary harmonic nodal points where the dome effect is activated. The primary energetics are as illustrated—a recirculative energy flow creating a vibrational membrane around the exterior and a significant POL effect from the center generator.

The energy dome is an excellent interdimensional communication attraction module. On a smaller scale, it can be constructed for use by one person at a time. It can also be made so that the energetics fill an entire room, so that numerous people can use it at the same time for individual or group consciousness work. Optimally, the room is austerely furnished and has low illumination in the indigo to deep violet range.

INTEGRATING ADDITIONAL UEF MODALITIES

Crystal gridworks are the energetic foundation to which many other universal vibrational modalities may be added. It is through the addition of such UEF components as sound, color, magnetics, and others that the fuller potentials of UEFs may be realized. Their synergistically complementary action contributes versatility, amplification, and custom-specification factors. The sacred science of creating and operating UEFs is the heart of the Light-based technologies of the years to come.

In this chapter section, an outline of techniques and ideas is presented regarding the practical integration of complementary energy modalities with crystal gridwork structure and vibrational dynamics. Further concepts will be explored both in the following sections of this chapter as well as in Chapter 15. Again, caution, discernment, and individual responsibility are crucial in exploring these potentials.

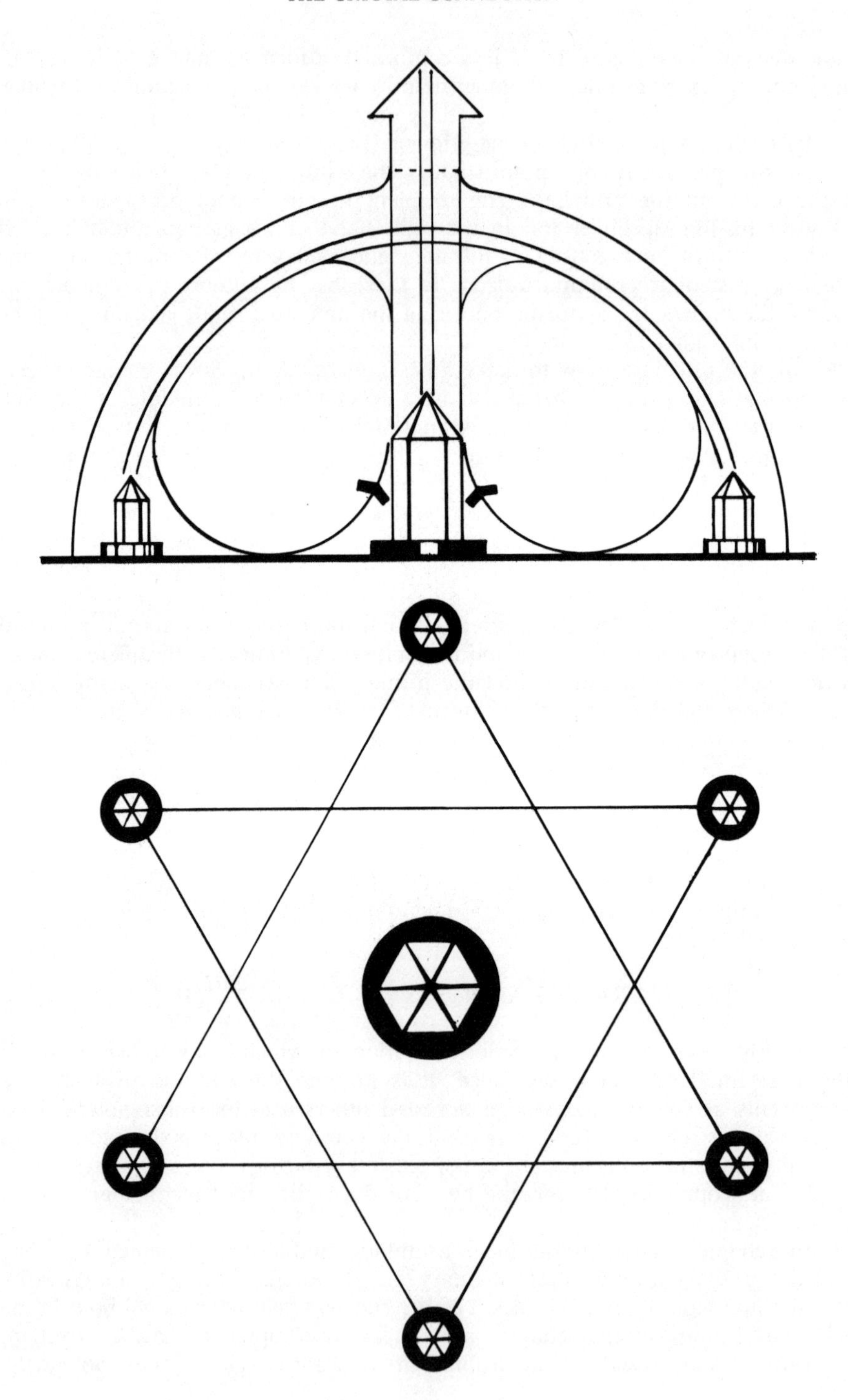

Figure 135a & 135b: Energy Dome (Side view) (Top view)

Color

1. The crystals of the gridwork itself as well as those utilized in enacting various techniques and methodologies within gridwork dynamics may be programmed as desired with color frequencies. (Refer to Chapter 8 for color programming methods.)
2. Clip-on lamps can be covered with desired color gels and shone into the central region of the gridwork. Many lamps can be used for a multi-colored effect. Because the light is diffuse, shine the main beam toward the area between the recipient's heart chakra and Omega chakra for optimal results in most situations.
3. Pin spotlights with focused and directional light beams can be covered with different theatrical color gels and directed toward more specific regions of the recipient's bioenergetic system. Many spotlights could be employed to project colors on different areas of the individual at the same time.
4. Automatic projectors with color gel slides are versatile tools in both personal and professional UEFs. The modulatably multicolor capacities plus the focused, directional beams make these projectors one of the workhorses of UEF color dynamics.
5. Track lighting systems are also useful chromatic tools. Installed in the ceiling over a reclined individual on a cushion or treatment table, the individual lamps with covering color gels can be positioned so as to direct the light beams to the various treatment focals areas. Another effective technique is, with seven lamps in the track lighting system, to focus one lamp on each of the seven chakras, from the coccyx to the crown. In a larger UEF setting, different areas can be illuminated with specific color beams so that an individual can choose which beam to be exposed to while carrying out various self-improvement and Light-work techniques. This concept of having various columns of color beams also works with pin spotlights.
6. Various special effects projectors commercially available[18] employ multicolor glass wheels that rotate in front of the projector beam. In conjunction with various types of projector lenses, a variety of multicolor mandala patterns can be created. These mandalas may be projected upon specific focal zones or the entire bioauric system. The consciousness uplifting creative light effects add another dimension to healing and reprogramming modalities.
7. Films can be made of coded color sequences for such purposes as mind-center activation, auric and chakra cleansing and healing, and chakra reprogramming. Specific color sequences are created for specific purposes. Refer to Chapter 10 for further information.

Sound

The integration of sound within a UEF in this context involves the use of speakers. It is known from previous chapters that sound and crystals are highly interactive. By positioning speakers directly in back of two oppositely positioned perimeter gridwork crystals with the sonics projecting around and through the crystals, crystal-modulated and crystal-amplified energetics are introduced into the UEF. Best results occur when the speakers are positioned in alignment with the head and feet of a reclined individual, or, with an upright seated position, the speakers are in alignment with the front and back of the person. Also, one or more crystals programmed with desired energy patterns can be placed on top of the speakers, where they will vibrate in correspondence with the sonic frequencies and intensities and direct the resulting energetics into the UEF.

If a two-speaker system is not available for use with the UEF, a single speaker will still add contributory dynamics. For best results, the sound is directed toward the most powerful gridwork crystal. Position the speaker so that the sound is projecting as much as possible into and through the crystal. Also, the direction of the sound should be toward the gridwork's center.

Care must be exercised as to the type of sound that is introduced into a UEF, for the vibrational effects can be considerably magnified. It is recommended that the sound be experienced first outside of the UEF to determine whether it is compatible with the individual. And depending upon the person's intended use of a UEF, correlating sound is then chosen to amplify the dynamics of a particular purpose.

Considerably more advanced modalities of the integration of sound within UEFs is possible, including quadrophonic and other multispeaker sound systems, sound transducers attached to the base of all grid crystals which are connected to a central multifrequency sound system, and others. Much research is possible in this regard.

Magnetics

Magnetics directly applied in conjunction with crystals can greatly amplify the overall gridwork energetics. In working with magnetics, care must be taken as it is an energy modality that can cause potent imbalancing effects if not used properly.

With most gridworks, magnetics are applied only on the outermost perimeter of crystals; unless otherwise noted in this text, is is recommended that this guideline be followed. In cases of circle-based gridworks, such as the solar cross and vesica piscis, the crystals describing the outer circle(s) are not used with magnets; rather, apply the magnets to the larger sized single terminations positioned around the grid's exterior (for example, the outer four large crystals in the solar cross and the two large crystals in the vesica piscis).

A second guideline is that it is imperative that a crystal be programmed to integrate applied magnetics in a balanced manner. The seed-phase of the program would be "balanced integration of magnetics with the crystal dynamics." Without enacting this type of programming process, the crystal–magnetic emissions are disharmonious to the bioenergetic system, the brain cells being especially susceptible to these influences. Should effects such as headaches, hypercharging of the bioenergies, disorientation, and the like occur, discontinue the procedures and evaluate what needs to be rectified. In most cases, disharmonious results are caused by either an overall imbalance of gridwork dynamics that is amplified by the addition of magnets or the crystals not being deeply enough programmed with the magnetic-integration thought-pattern. The magnetic–crystal interaction is a most helpful tool when utilized properly, but can equally be misapplied to imbalanced effect.

Two magnets are needed for each crystal being modified. Orient the magnets so that they attract one another. Separate them and apply them to parallel opposite sides of the crystal. If the magnets are powerful enough, the attraction will be felt through the crystal. For single-terminated crystals, position the magnets toward

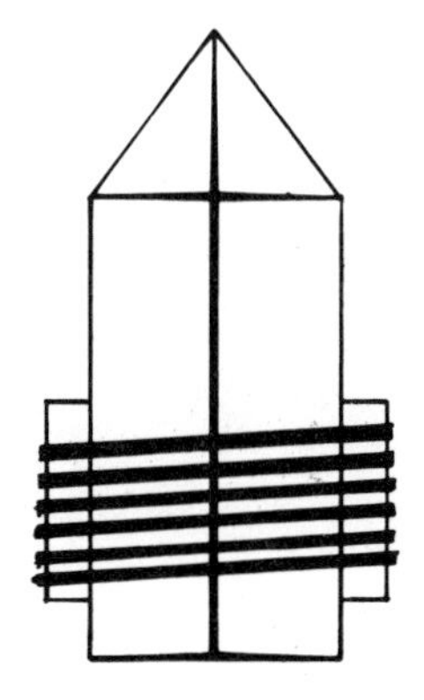

Figure 136a: Applying Magnets to Single Termination

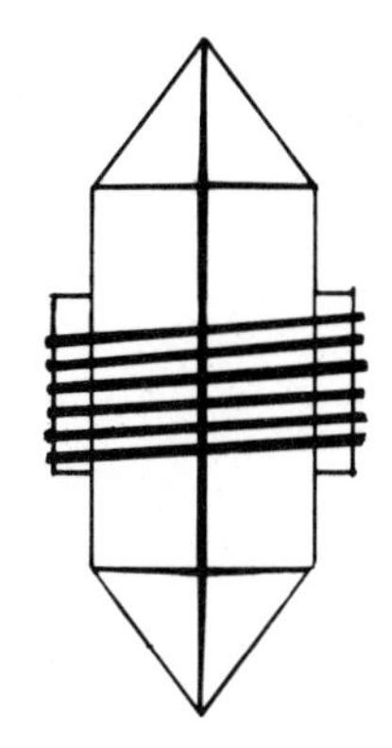

Figure 136b: Applying Magnets to Double Termination

the base, as illustrated in Figure 136A. For double-terminations, place the magnets at the midpoint between the terminations (See Figure 136B). Next, take copper wire and wrap numerous coils around the crystal body; do not allow them to overlap one another, so that energy flow is not impeded through the wires (use a drop of glue to attach the wire ends to the crystal body). For logistic and energetic reasons, when setting the crystal–magnet unit in place, make sure that the magnet's orientations with respect to the floor mimic one another.

When first starting to work with crystals and magnets, begin with low power (that is, low gauss) magnets and then gradually build up to higher powered magnets. There is a threshold at which the crystal–magnetic interactions reach a point of optimal harmonic interplay; beyond this the magnetic component becomes too strong and the effects become increasingly unbalanced. For general use, it is better to keep toward the low to middle-range of magnetic power when purchasing magnets for UEF use.

Rare earth magnets (particularly cobalt) and magnets with significant aluminum content (Alnico) are optimal, and are especially important for professional and research applications.

Metal Wiring

Refined metal wiring—copper, silver, and gold in particular—may be utilized to boost the interactiveness of gridwork crystals. Two techniques can be used here. One is to wind a harmonic number of coil wrappings around one grid crystal and then lead the remaining wire to the next consecutive perimeter crystal, whereupon the wrapping process is repeated and then brought to the next crystal. The end result of this process is that the entire perimeter of the gridwork is described by wiring starting and ending with the same crystal (as illustrated in Figure 137A). The second technique is to coil-wrap each crystal and connect them so that the geometric pattern of the gridwork is described by the wire pattern, as seen in Figure 137B. Going one step further, the techniques can be combined into one, with both the perimeter pattern and the gridwork's internal geometry being delineated by wiring. Optimal results for all wiring applications are obtained by using copper, silver, and gold wire wound together. For best effects, use insulated wiring

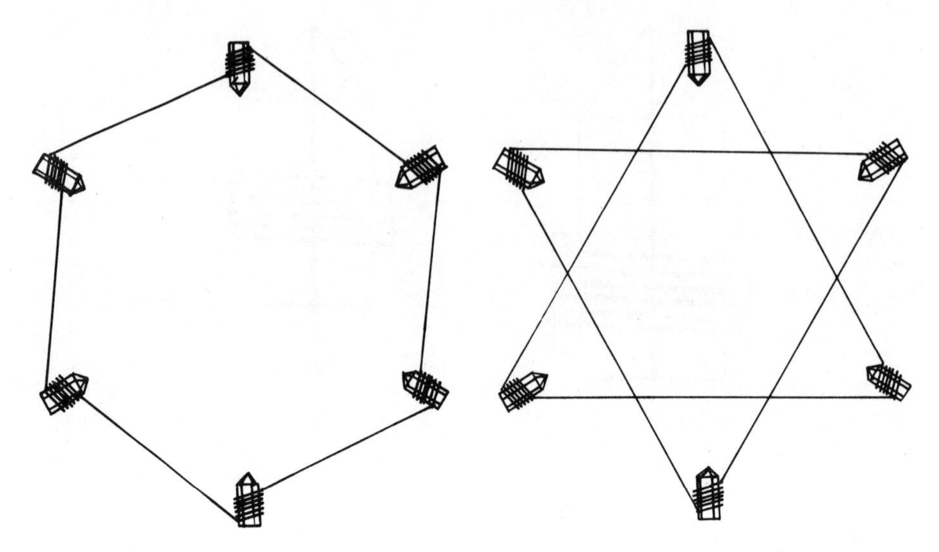

Figure 137a: Gridwork Wire Wrapping *Figure 137b: Gridwork Wire Wrapping*

and, where the wiring is in contact with the crystal, remove the insulation for direct contact; leave the insulation on elsewhere.

If this wiring concept is used, take care that no one trips on or pulls the wiring, as damage to the crystals (as well as the person) can occur.

Pyramids

1. As noted later in this chapter, utilizing single pyramids or multipyramidal systems as the capstones for UEFs aids in amplifying the POL effect and in stabilizing the overall UEF energy dynamics. For further reference as to the numerous multipyramidal systems that may be used, see Chapter 12.
2. Certain of the multipyramidal systems, particularly the Zapper (Figure 65) and the five-pyramid system (Figure 63), can be attached to a wall so that the apex directs a laser-like energy current parallel to the horizontal axis of the floor. One such system may be positioned so that the energy current projects 2 to 4 inches over a reclined individual's spinal axis, from Alpha to Omega. This modality is excellent for stimulating the chakra system energy flow and for providing a treatment facilitator with an additional current with which to amplify the treatment modalities.

With a Star of David gridwork, if six Zapper pyramidal systems were attached to the walls (at an identical height) so that the current from each paralleled the primary energy dynamics emitting from each crystal, the energetics meeting at the central gridwork area would be phenomenal. In such a case, an advanced multipyramidal capstone as seen in Figure 64 would be required to balance the fusion results with the POL effect.

3. Larger single pyramids are excellent additions to UEFs. Align the pyramidal apex with the central point of the gridwork so that the POL effect of both are in synchrony. For further information regarding the placement of crystals in and around larger pyramids, refer to Chapter 12.

Lasers

1. A hand-held laser can be directed into each gridwork crystal in a rhythmic sequence to help activate the UEF energy flow.
2. To amplify the overall gridwork energetics, direct a laser into either a central generator or the most powerful crystal of the surrounding gridwork while other modalities are being enacted in the UEF.
3. If a crystal is being used by an individual or group as a consciousness focal point for interdimensional communications or other purposes, shining a laser into the crystal simultaneously will heighten access capacities and general clarity and power manyfold.
4. A laser scanner adds a new dimension of applications. With laser techniques numbers 2 and 3 in this section, the scanner could be programmed to describe various universal geometries into a major facet of a generator crystal, thereby stimulating corresponding vibrational patterns within the crystal dynamics. Also, a laser scanner system positioned overhead could rapidly scan the exterior of the gridwork, the beam stimulating each consecutive crystal in quick succession. Especially when this is done with magnet–crystal units in the gridwork, the activation of the entire UEF would reach several octaves higher than before. The scanner can also be programmed to describe the actual geometric pattern of the grid.
5. Fiber optic tubing attached to the base of each gridwork crystal from one or more lasers could be used to input laser light to all crystals simultaneously, or at desired intervallic combinations (with the assistance of a computer program control panel).

Other UEF Modalities

1. Appropriate aromatics contribute a valuable dimension to a UEF.
2. Mirrors can be attached to the walls surrounding a UEF so as to reflect and amplify energies into the center of the gridwork. Mirrored tiles (clear only) or larger square or rectangular mirrors are placed opposite each other and at a height that correlates with where the individual reclines or sits within the UEF. The idea is to position the mirrors around the central zone where the primary activity of the UEF takes place. Sacred geometric patterns can also be cut out of mirror material.
3. The field of radionics will have much to offer with regard to advanced UEFs in the future. The ability to selectively tune, modulate, and project specifiable, precise energy patterns and infuse them into the UEF is a valuable capability. Not only can these radionically emitting energies be used for individual treatments but also, with specialized adaptations, the entire UEF can be significantly modulated through direct input into the gridwork crystals. Further, the vibrational code-patterns of a programmed crystal, a library crystal, and gem matrices can be projected radionically into a UEF.
4. Photographs of enlightened beings, malas, rosaries, and other spiritual tools that the individual may utilize in his or her personal regime can be integrated into a UEN with creativity and discernment.

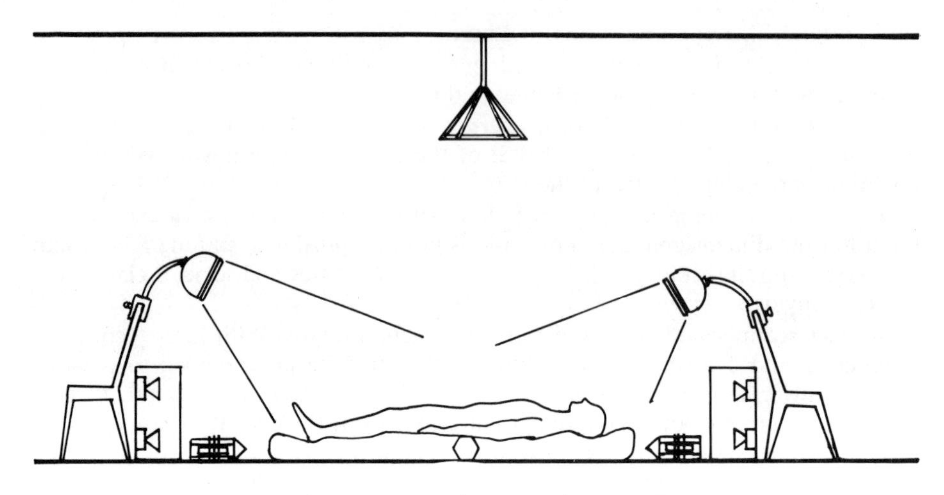

Figure 138: Basic Personal Use UEF

INTEGRATED UEF CONCEPTS

The creative possibilities in manifesting multicomponent UEFs in integrated ways are endless. Depending upon logistic factors and intended purpose, a UEF can be designed to customized specifications, from the most basic to the most advanced levels of sophistication, power, and interdimensional access efficiency. Presented in this section are a number of basic blueprints offered as starting points for manifestation, application, and further development.

Basic Personal-Use UEF

Figure 138 illustrates a basic design for personal use with minimal cost. Its components include a Star of David gridwork with magnets, speakers, two clip-on lamps with color gels, and a pyramid capstone. Additional crystals and energy tools can be utilized by the individual as desired.

For those wish to incorporate water into this setup (or others), a child's pool can be situated inside the grid and filled with water to lay in while using the UEF.

As a simple but effective UEF, this arrangement combines the elements of simplicity and inexpensiveness so that as many individuals as possible may create their own personal UEF.

Fundamental Practitioner UEF

Figure 139 presents one example of how the different UEF components can be integrated in a practitioner setting. Many variations on this theme are possible. First, the gridwork is a double Star of David with aluminum-content magnets. To help compensate for the height of the treatment table in relation to the gridwork energy dynamics, one of the Stars of David is propped at an angle with small pieces of wood; each crystal is pointing toward 3 to 4 inches above the middle of the treatment table (assuming the table is centered within the gridwork). Two

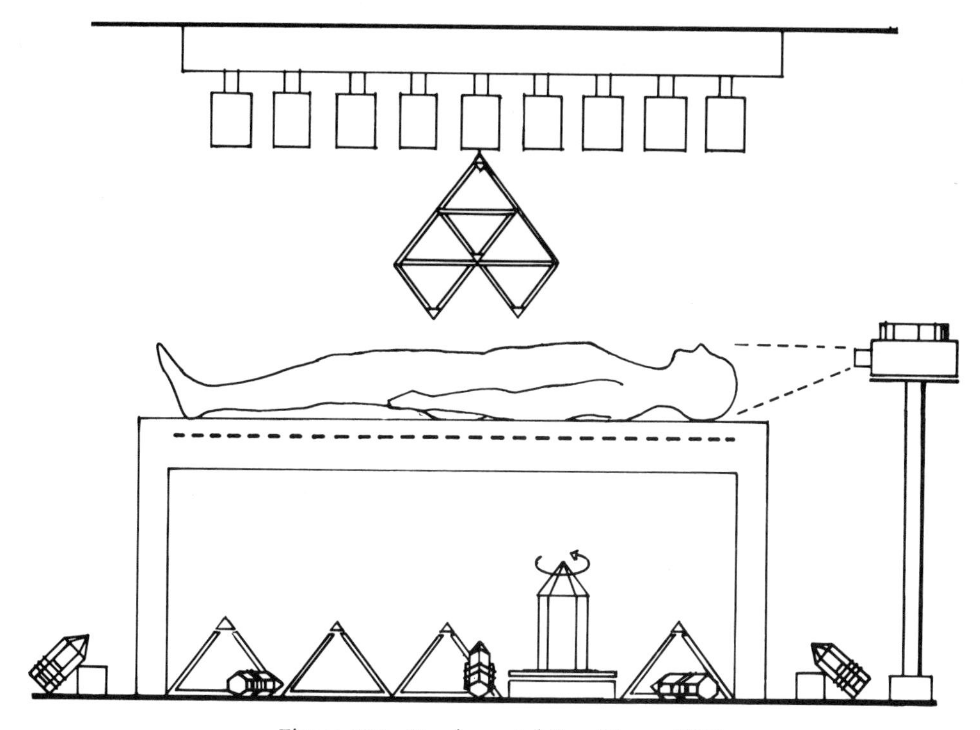

Figure 139: Fundamental Practitioner UEF

sound speakers are positioned directly in back of the grid crystals at the head and foot of the treatment table. Arranged in a line underneath the treatment table are six to eight small pyramids (with crystal pyramid capstones), aligned so that the apexes direct their energy stream along the lengthwise midline of the table. Underneath the area where the recipient's heart chakra is located is a large crystal energy generator standing upright on a slowly rotating turntable; this generates a powerful column of vibrational flow in and through the heart chakra. Overhead is a multipyramidal system (like that in Figure 64) and a track lighting system with each light directing a color beam into each chakra. An automatic projector shines a horizontal color beam, changeable with a remote switch, along the length of the recipient.

There are a number of ways in which a treatment table can be modified so that it actively contributes to the UEF energetics. One possibility is shown in Figure 140. Here, small single-terminated crystals are attached all around the rectangular circumference of the table. In addition, several lengthwise rows of double-terminations are positioned under the area where the recipient lies, one row under the spine. Another setup is seen in Figure 141, which has 12 inch-base open framework pyramids (optimally gold-plated) in an inverted position underneath the table along the lengthwise midline. At the inverted apex of each pyramid is a 1½ inch-base crystal pyramid pointing upward to amplify a stream of energy projecting into the recipient, especially along the spine and head. An even more advanced possibility is illustrated in Figure 142. Below the cushioned platform

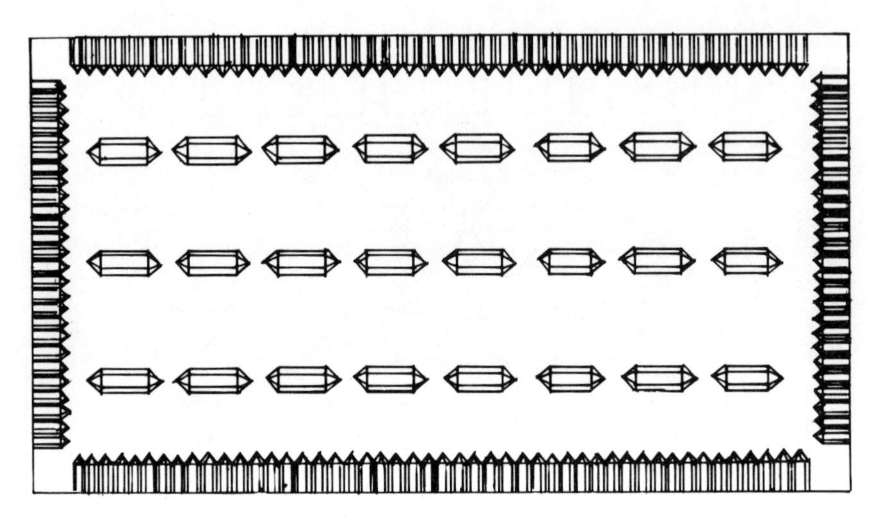

Figure 140: Treatment Table Crystal Enhancement Design

upon which the recipient lies is a shallow removable drawer in which miniature gridwork arrangements and other crystal positionings can be made so as to customize specific vibrational patterns to synchronize with the unique treatment needs of the recipient. Especially potent would be the construction of a miniature gridwork of an appropriate geometry underneath each chakra.

Crystal Capstone UEF

Figure 143 demonstrates another professional arrangement. The recipient lies on a comfortable cushioning with a double Star of David multilevel gridwork in place. Level I crystals all have magnetics. Two speakers are in back of the north- and south-oriented level I crystals. An 8 foot-base pyramid houses the multilevel gridwork and the recipient, and also has a multipyrimidal system positioned inside the upper apex area (see Figure 64). Directly above the large pyramid apex is

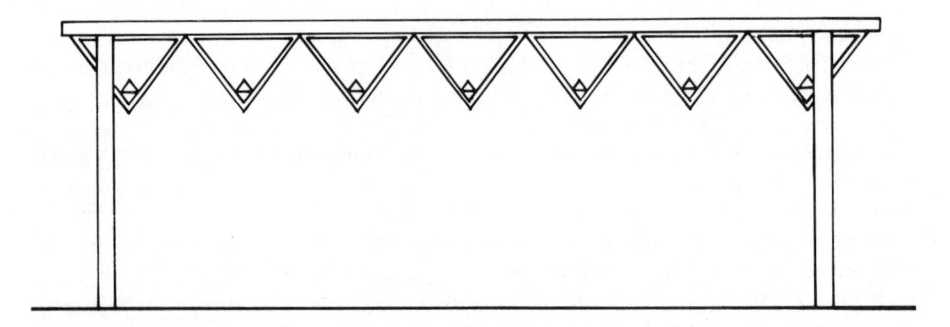

Figure 141: Pyramid-Crystal Treatment Table Amplification Design

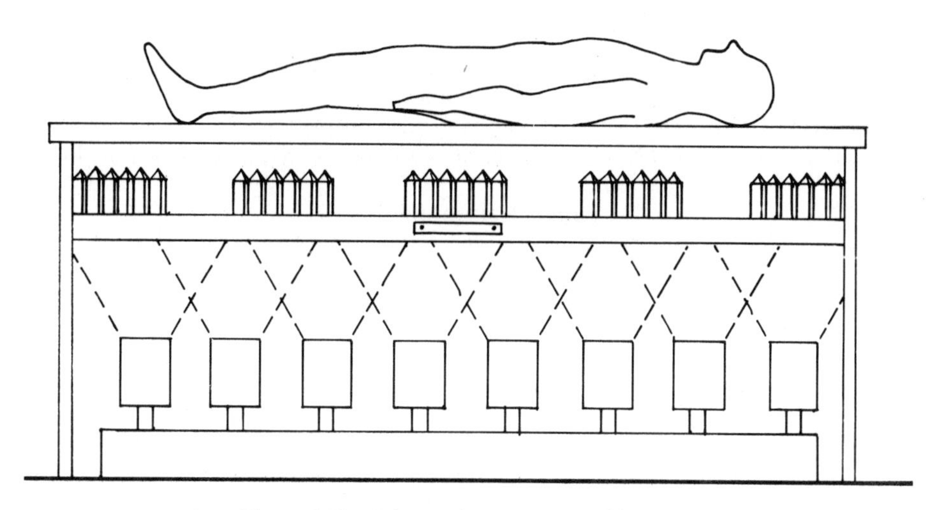

Figure 142: Advanced Treatment Table Design

another multipyramidal system (See Figure 66). (A rotating octahedron also works well.) On both walls opposite the head and feet of the recipient are a grid of four 12 inch-base pyramids (with crystal pyramid capstones) positioned over top of four 12 inch-side mirrored tile squares directing a grid of energy flow into

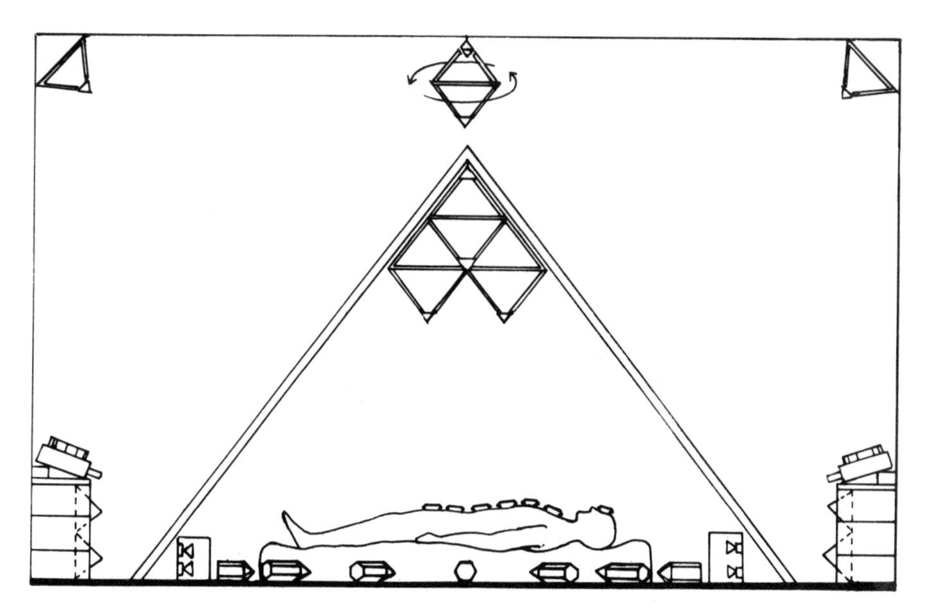

Figure 143: Crystal Capstone UEF

the recipient's bioenergetic field. On a support that surrounds one of the pyramid–mirror setups an automatic slide projector is positioned so that the colored beam goes into the opposite pyramid–mirror grid and is reflected back onto the full length of the recipient. With an automatic advance feature, the projector can enact a programmed full-spectrum chromatic aura balancing sequence.

The Crystal Capstone UEF is a powerful multipurpose energy field, capable of facilitating a spectrum of healing and reprogramming techniques and methodologies.

Cellular Harmonizing UEF

This UEF is designed for the regeneration and harmonizing of the cellular level of the bioenergetic system. Its highly magnetic orientation is profoundly penetrative, facilitating the recrystallization of each cell back into optimal biomatrix patterns. Thus the ageing process may possibly be neutralized.

Figure 144 shows just the multilevel gridwork arrangement. Levels I and II are double Stars of David, both with strong magnetics. One Star of David in level II is pointing toward the Omega chakra and the other is directed toward the Alpha chakra. Each of the level II crystals is programmed with a full spectrum of chromatics, including white, plus a thought-form of "cellular regeneration and harmonizing." Level III is composed of a double arc of smaller double-terminations, a Star of David grid around the heart chakra, and small double-terminations taped to the carotid arteries and temples. All are programmed the same as level II. Level IV has seven 1 1/2 inch-base crystal pyramids on the chakras, from coccyx to crown; and larger double-terminations are positioned at the Alpha and Omega chakras.

Additional UEF components are important to the maximum success of this methodology. An 8 foot-base crystal-enhanced pyramid circumscribes the multilevel gridwork. The same multipyramidal system as shown in Figure 143 is attached inside the upper apex of the large pyramid. Above the pyramid is a rotating crystal-enhanced octahedron. Also, as in the Crystal Capstone UEF, there is a pyramid–mirror grid on opposite sides of the gridwork, and an automatic slide projector directing the chromatics into the opposite mirror–pyramid grid and then over the recipient. The projector has a full spectrum of color vibrations, and is set to automatically go through the sequence in the carousel during the course of the treatment session. Further, a strobe light set at the highest flash rate is important to pulse-activate certain aspects of the energy flow is motion. The intake of appropriate gem tinctures is also used. And, optimally, there is an overhead laser scanner that rapidly projects a laser beam around the level I crystals in both clockwise and counterclockwise directions. The key to highly effective laser dynamics is the rapid alternation between the two directions within certain harmonic proportional phase relationships.

When manifested operated properly, the Cellular Harmonizing UEF effects abiding deep-level cellular transformations, sometimes with dramatic reversal processes taking place as the cells undergo radical restructuralization and metabolic phase resettings.

Star-Seed Connection UEF

This UEF is a blueprint for the purpose of facilitating a strong interdimensional interlinkage between between an earth-based star-seed or celestial-seed and their

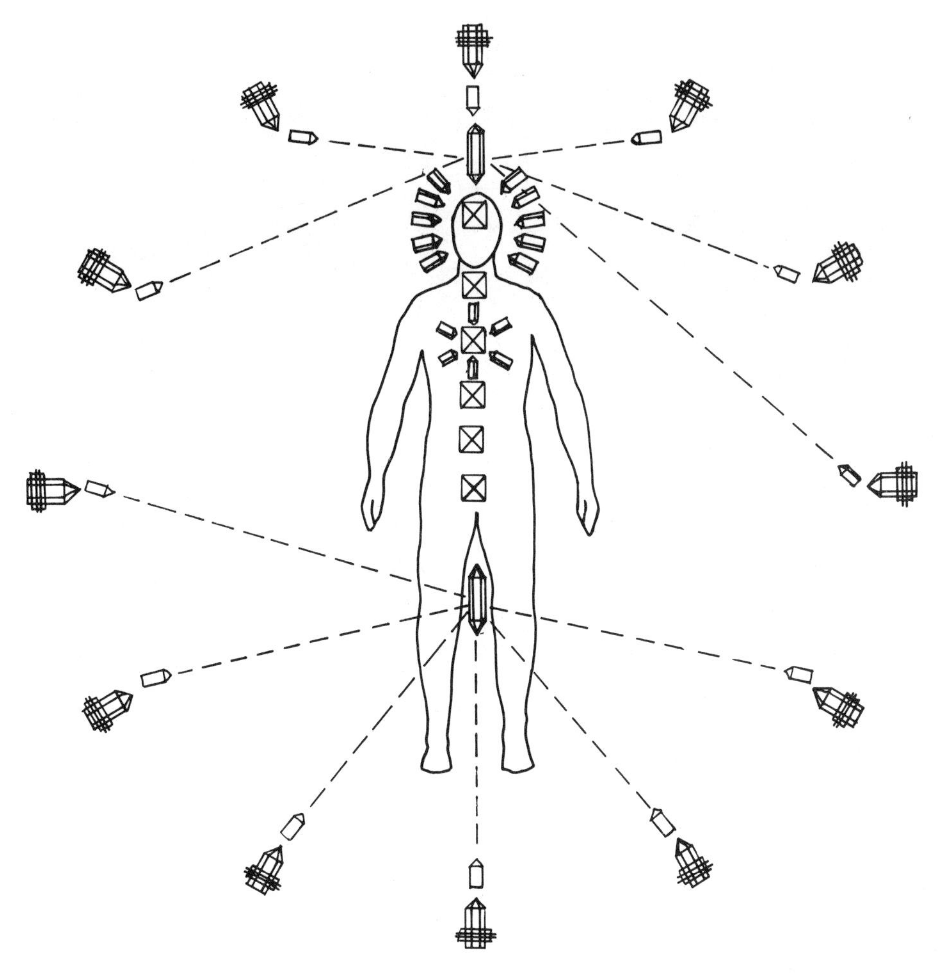

Figure 144: Cellular Harmonizing UEF

place of origin. In so doing, activation and alignment into the Light-body occurs and higher spiritual knowledge and capabilities are catalyzed.

Figure 145 illustrates the gridwork outline. The outermost grid is a double Star of David composed of larger generator crystals with magnetics. Inside of this is a vesica piscis gridwork with each crystal programmed with the thought-form "star-seed and celestial-seed activation" and the chromatic vibrations of deep blue and indigo. Around the entire perimeter of the reclined recipient are laid small double- or single-terminations programmed with indigo and deep blue. On the seven chakras, from the coccyx to the crown, are 1 1/2 inch-base crystal pyramids; and larger double-terminations are at the Alpha and Omega chakras.

Additional UEF components include the same pyramidal and multipyramidal setup as the Crystal Capstone UEF (Figure 143). The topmost multipyramidal system in this case needs to rotate about the vertical axis. The same pyramid–mirror

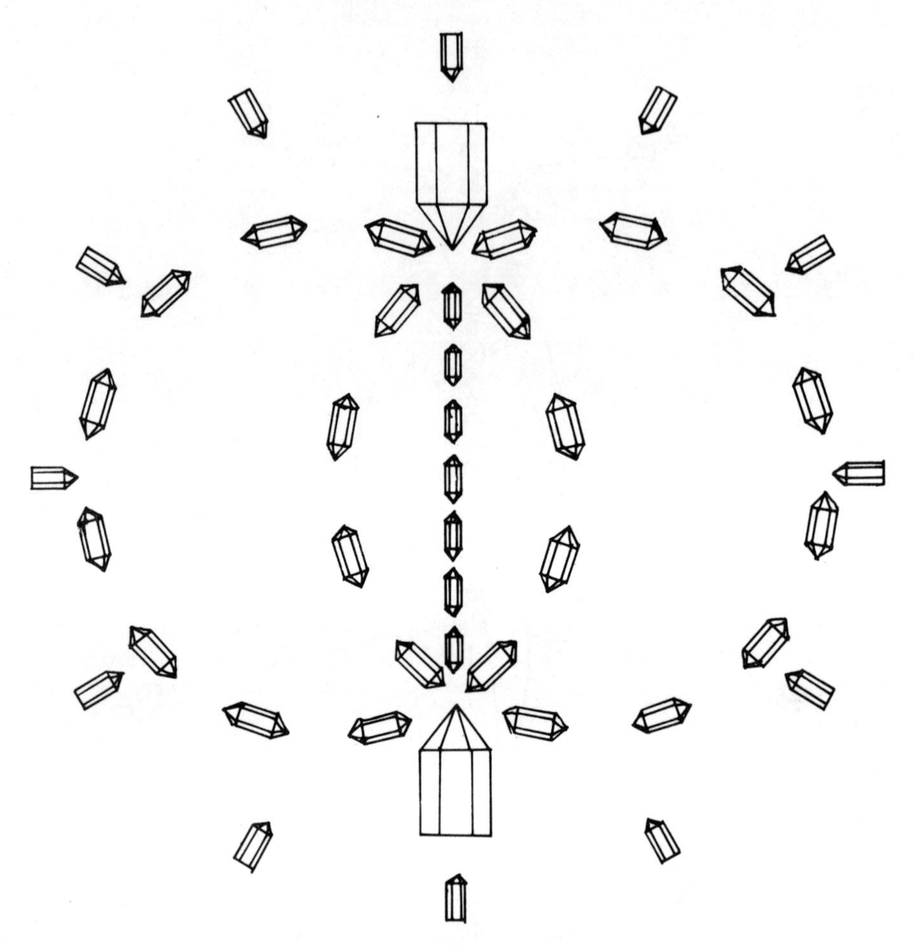

Figure 145: Star–Seed Connection UEF

grid and slide projector arrangement as in Figure 143 is used. In the projector carousel are numerous shade and hue variations of the deep blue to indigo to deep violet spectrum. The carousel is set to automatically advance through the set of slides during the treatment session. A strobe light with a gold color gel is set on very slow flash rates. The intake of appropriate gem tinctures and the playing of background celestial music rounds out the UEF components.

The Star-seed Connection UEF has a strongly interdimensional transportive and interconnecting orientation. The exact cosmic or celestial location with which it interlinks is determined by the experiencer's consciously focused request for communication access to a specific region. During a regular course of treatment sessions, the vibrational code-patterns of the individual's higher point of origin in general and the Light-body in particular become increasingly infused and activated within higher consciousness and the bioenergetic matrix.

The Ten-Plus-One-Commandments Gridwork

The Ten Commandments, given directly to humankind from the Eternal, and complete by Yeshua (also known as "Jesus" and Sananda) in the bestowment of the last Commandment, are cornerstone keys to living a life in the Light. Often overlooked, they are in fact centrally imperative, for they are master universal codes for interlinking consciousness with YHWH. The Ten-plus-One Commandments are a threshold whose codes must be fulfilled by each soul in preparation for ascension into a multidimensional Light-body. While other tools, techniques, and energy modalities can be valuable complementary growth and activation aids, the Commandments are the necessary foundation for higher consciousness awakening that must be fulfilled in mind, heart, and action.

Humans are not made for the Law, rather the Law is made for humans. Rather than being constrictive measures, the Commandments are the coded pathway to unfailingly direct union with the Eternal. In so doing, a singularly powerful living Pillar of Light between the higher Heavens and the individual becomes the joyous Truth of moment-to-moment existence. By incorporating them into one's beingness, vistas and channels as yet unrealized are thereby unveiled and activated. The soul's inalienable birthright of divine Joy and Love unfolds in glorious ways due to the harmonizing of the codes of self with the universal master codes of the Ten-plus-One. Herein is the illuminated Way to perfect, absolute freedom-in-Light. And, as a direct by-product of this supremely powerful Light-inter-connection process, protection from the forces of darkness occurs in direct proportion to the degree of the individual's assimilation of these Commandment codes. (Refer to Chapter 3 for further perspectives on the Commandments.)

A very special dispensation, given as a gift of grace to the Earth-plane, has recently been activated to assist mankind in working to increasingly higher degrees with these most centrally crucial Commandments. It is a gift of rare occurence and magnitude. The divine Promise is this: the programming and use of the Ten-plus-One gridwork as described below in conjunction with the 100 percent active effort of the individual in observing the Commandments for a continuous period of three months will manifest quantum leaps of spiritual growth and activation heretofore unrealized and, perhaps, undreamed. A cycle has been activated in the Earth's energy field, previously dormant, whereby a profound quickening of consciousness in an extremely shortened period of time is now possible within the coded pathways of these Commandments. This is an unfailing Promise given to humankind from the highest levels of the Hierarchy of Light.

A few points here are quite noteworthy: The first is that the Ten-plus-One work only when each and every Commandment is fulfilled; not a one can be set aside. As Yeshua told us plainly: "Whosoever then relaxes one of the least of these commandments and teaches men so, shall be called least in the kingdom of heaven; but he who does them and teaches them shall be called great in the kingdom of heaven." (Matthew 5:19) Also, look not only to the "external" meaning of each commandment but also to the subtle levels of its structure. For example, "stealing" encompasses not only a physical act but also an act of the heart, mind, and/or spirit. Having "no other gods before Me" includes habits, attachments, attitudes, and actions that do not put YHWH above all else. Further, within the flow of universal energy cycles, the day for observing the sabbath is from Friday sunset to Saturday sunset, not Sunday. By partaking of the sabbath on this particular day, the Commandment codes are actualized.

Procedure:

1) Pick out eleven crystals. Take each of them in turn and state out loud one of the Commandments in sequence (1 to 10 from Exodus 20 or Deuteronomy 5 and the eleventh from John 13:34). You do not need to program the crystals yourself; part of the Promise is that these crystals will be directly programmed from YHWH Himself for each person sincere of heart; you simply need to state the Commandments. The eleventh will be programmed by Yeshua, as He has promised. It is not important to recall which of the Ten Commandments is programmed into a specific crystal, for they all work as a holistic synergy; only the one with the last Commandment need be remembered.

2) Set out the first ten crystals in a gridwork. They should be equidistantly placed in a circle (points directed to the center) around the body. Lie down within this gridwork and place the eleventh crystal on the heart chakra (if possible, it is good to have the termination pointing vertically upwards from the heart). Remain in the gridwork for 10 to 20 minutes, asking the Hierarchy of Light to help make these master codes a deeper part of your beingness and remain in a state of focused receptivity, allowing the process to occur without expectations, of its own accord, in its own ways and cycles.

3) Perform this procedure once a day, every day, for three months.

In order for the Promise to be fulfilled, not a day must go by without doing the above procedure and doing everything humanly possible to abide within the Commandments. It is only in fulfilling these individual responsibilities that the Promise will be enacted. May the Light flourish!

The Merkabah Attraction Module UEF

One of the most potent UEF blueprints in this text specifically designed for direct interconnection with the Merkabah Light-vehicle of the Lords of Light is as follows: Create a double Star of David gridwork with approximately fist-size or larger crystals. Apply two Alnico magnets with copper coil wrapping to each crystal. Inside this gridwork set up a crystal-enhanced copper pyramid, at least four feet high with an appropriately sized quartz pyramid at the apex. In the middle of the gridwork, directly in alignment with the pyramid apex, place a Tesla coil. This particular coil is the "spark inducer" of interdimensional threshold overlap, and is a tremendously important key to not only this particular UEF but also many others. Put a second pyramid inside the first; for instance, if the first pyramid has a four foot apex, the second pyramid would have a three foot apex. Both pyramids' apexes are in vertical alignment. At the apex of the second pyramid will be placed the "keynote" Merkabah access crystal. Select a very special crystal for this task, for it is a primary focus point for the entire UEF and plays a predominant role in accessing interdimensional channels of Merkabah interlinkage. The Hollow Metallic Ball Light-tool presented in Chapter 13 is one excellent option to place in the keynote crystal position. Lastly, over the four foot pyramid needs to be either a crystal-enhanced rotating octahedron or the rotating multipyramidal system shown in Figure 65. To activate operation, turn on the Tesla coil and focus consciousness intention in and through the keynote crystal. The individual(s) do *not* sit within the gridwork; sit outside of it, approximately

2-3 feet from the gridwork crystals. This is the basic blueprint from which much more sophisticated vibrations derive.

GROUP GRIDWORK USAGE CONCEPTS

Group Light-work can be amplified manyfold when undertaken with crystal grid-works. Several concepts are offered here as general guidelines and ideas in this regard.

1. The individuals of the group can be positioned in a desired grid pattern, each with a crystal in hand. An individual in need of focused Light-work can be seated or lying down in the gridwork's center. Calling upon the Light to work in and through the group, each individual opens the consciousness to be a channel. Group members hold their crystals in their right hands and point them toward the recipient in the center as the Light flows through the group into the individual in need.
2. Individuals seated in a grid arrangement may have an upright crystal generator in the center as a focus point and POL interconnector. Each group member can point a crystal toward the generator and direct the consciousness energies toward it to facilitate group consciousness unification in the Light. After this group-connection and Light-connection is made, the individuals can point their crystals in toward themselves and ask to receive Light-energies drawing from the central POL generator.
3. Another technique is for the group members to sit in back of a crystal gridwork, each individual with a grid crystal in front of him or her. With an individual recipient or a crystal generator in the center, the group enacts various Light-activities, directing the energies through the crystals in the hands.
4. On a grander scale, large numbers of people could arrange themselves in a giant multiple-level gridwork to enact planetary healing and reprogramming, calling upon the Higher Evolution to fill the earth with the highest Light in divine order. This is particularly effective when done on vortex zones. It is optimal to have a very large crystal generator sitting upright in the center through which the group may focus its collective energies.

SEED IDEAS

1. The 90 degree angles incorporated into much of modern architecture cause a subtle but significant stagnation of energy flow in the room. To help offset this effect and to energize the environmental energetics, it is beneficial to place medium quality crystals pointing vertically upward at the four corners at floor level. Crystals can also be set in place at the four ceiling corners with the base held in putty, the termination pointing toward the center of the room. The crystals need not be very large, sizes from 1 1/2 to 3 inches in length being adequate. Many times a noticeable change occurs in the room's vibrational dynamics when this technique alone is utilized. Any room can benefit, and it is especially important to include this in areas with UEFs.
2. Large acrylic or plexiglass plates can be used to inset crystals in a gridwork geometry. The plate is suspended from the ceiling and lowered over a recipient already lying within a gridwork set up at floor level. The crystals in the overhead

plate are pointing vertically downward over a mirroring horizontally oriented gridwork on the floor. Plate crystals may also be pointing into the recipient's chakra system. This gridwork "sandwich" is an excellent adjunctive amplifier-activator of the floor-level gridwork energetics. It is possible to have many such plates to use in conjunction with different floor grids as they are changed in response to different recipients' treatment needs.

3. It might prove fruitful to explore the incorporation of the geometrically based radionic Rae card system into the multiple-level gridwork system. Level II, in particular, could be arranged in the same pattern as a specific Rae card for working with a particular bioenergetic region. All the other gridwork levels would remain the same. If, at the same time, a Rae radionic device is utilized with the same Rae card as is duplicated with crystals at level II, quite effective results might be obtained.

4. Superlative effects could be achieved by rotating all the crystals of center-focused gridwork, such as a Star of David. Done with horizontally rotating crystals, different RPM rates would modulate a spectrum of dynamic energetics. The RPM rate of each crystal could be proportionally different in an array of possibilities. If, at the same time, a frequency modulatable laser was directed through the center of each crystal's c axis, the results would be interesting indeed. Also, similar (but not the same) effects would occur if the crystals were rotating vertically.

5. The use of a large diameter Mobius coil with double-terminations attached in place along the horizontal axis would be a fascinating experiment to determine if the unique dynamics of the coil cause unusual energy dynamics when used in conjunction with crystals. Important here would be to have crystals on both sides of the coil, for the coil itself to be made of copper, and for a good quality double-termination to be placed across the area where the twist occurs on either side.

6. Applying an electromagnet to the center generator of the Dome UEF (Figure 135) to see if the dome dynamics were amplified or altered in any way would be interesting.

7. Advanced UEF energetics in the future will be generated by attaching fiber optic light guides or sonic transducers to the bases of the gridwork crystals. Modulated laser and sonic input could then be applied individually or collectively to create a variety of sophisticated and precise gridwork dynamics.

8. The science of sacred numbers can be applied to the gridwork concept to create an entire genre of grid applications. The primary idea is to translate a single number or number sequence into a corresponding geometry, thus enabling that geometric pattern to be outlined by crystals as a gridwork. For example, a 333 sequence might translate into three triangles arranged as a multiple level gridwork of triangle within triangle within triangle. A 7543 sequence could translate as a triangle within a square within a pentagon within a septagon. This is the basic idea from which much more sophisticated concepts arise. For instance, what might a number sequence like 51.76.88 convert into geometrically? Might we analyze different sacred mandalas and derive from their geometry their numerical equivalent? Wouldn't it be interesting to analyze the sonic frequencies (i.e., number-in-time) as they transduce into cymatic patterns (i.e., number-in-space)? The development of this gridwork genre is of great importance in future sophisticated gridwork applications.

In sum, the design and application of gridwork-based UEFs is one of the most important, powerful, and creatively complex disciplines in all of the sacred sciences. Experiment discerningly, experience joyfully!

CHAPTER 15

Advanced Unified Energy Field Concepts

Visions of the future many times precede their earthly manifestation. The earth-plane need not wait till the dawning of the New World to have access to Light-based technologies and their en-Light-ening fruits. Certainly the fullness of sacred science will not unfold until the personal and planetary ascension. Yet the catalytic beginnings that are now astir are that which is divinely given as an integral aid in the preparing of consciousness to receive the ascension's greatest evolutionary opportunities. The opening of celestial-cosmic gateways in preparation for an Omega point of evolutionary completion and reapportionment quickens receptive consciousness by quantum magnitudes in these the latter days. As higher Light is shone upon the earth, the accompanying technological means to receive that Light in an optimal manner are activated within the planetary intelligence field. Spirit-based technology serves as a matrix of receivership, a tool of consciousness to enact spiritual reprogramming functions. Though not the sole means by which the reprogramming-ascension process occurs, it is an integral and necessary aspect of the divine plan for earth. Certain aspects of this divine plan call upon humankind to fulfill prescribed parameters of responsibility. One avenue by which this responsibility is enacted is through the facilitation of the rebirth of sacred science, both in theory and practice. The resources, facilities, and tools current to the earth-plane provide an already existent foundation by which divine science may be infused and thereby manifested. Human nature being what it is, orthodoxy resists the radical reorientation necessary to transform conventional science into a Light-based science. However more difficult this makes the manifestation process, it is yet quite possible, and for some it is a responsibility of great magnitude chosen on the Higher Self levels. The pages to follow in this chapter impart selective visions of vibrational patternings that can now be made physically manifest should individual and collective consciousness choose to receive them and imbue them with earthly reality.

OVERVIEW: ADVANCED UEF CONCEPTS

This chapter shows a next quantum step of future developments within the discipline of designing and creating specialized unified energy fields (UEFs). Every chapter presented thus far helps to lay the theoretical and practical foundation from which this present chapter springs into the next higher octave of actualization. The ideas herein offered are broadly illuminated for their value in stimulating further thought and technical refinement and therefore are not presented as blueprints down to minute technical detail, but rather as seed-crystal thought-patterns.

In addition, it is important here to note the distinct difference between the terms *temple chamber* and *advanced UEF.* All temple chambers are necessarily UEFs, but not all UEFs are temple chambers. One who manifests and operates a temple chamber has a specially authorized dispensation from the Spiritual Hierarchy of Light to create and operate a specifically blueprinted UEF in conjunction with an overseeing higher dimensional Temple of Light. The Spirit-derived authority factor is the most essential distinction between a temple chamber and a UEF, for there will be many UEFs manifested in the years to come, and but very few authorized temple chambers. This is not to say that nontemple UEFs are necessarily lesser in their operative effectiveness. Rather, temple chambers are a highly specialized class of UEF that fulfills clearly defined conditions of authority and interdimensional access. To describe such conditions in detail would require a chapter in and of itself, and this goes beyond the purview of the present text. For those who are so authorized, the parameters that must be strictly fulfilled in the manifestation and operation of a temple chamber are made known to them by the Higher Evolution. The distinction between these two categories of UEFs is of exceeding importance, for Universal Law is clear in such matters and the accruing accountability.

All the concepts presented in this chapter are offered as advanced UEFs. Some of them can be selectively applied within a temple chamber setting, but none of them are temple chamber blueprints per se.

Figure 146: *The Sonic Dome.* In a small dome structure, an individual sonic-based treatment facility is created for reprogramming and healing purposes. The predominating modality utilized is a computer-controlled gridwork of 12 polyplanar speakers surrounding a treatment table. Each speaker is independently controlled and has lapidary ground quartz cones attached, pointing into the treatment area. The sonics employed are not musical compositions, but rather single sonic tones, both audible and inaudible. In accordance with the specific energetic requirements of the recipient, the computer is programmed to have precisely orchestrated tones emitting from each individual speaker, with attention placed upon the harmonic interaction between the rhythmically sounded tones from all 12 speakers. It is as though the recipient is inside a giant wind chime, except here the effects are much more modulatably controllable and powerfully directed. The modulatable effects are broad-ranging. They can be a long, drawn-out, slowly changing sonic latticework, similar to the sound of Tibetan bells. They can be orchestrated to infuse specific chords into particular bioenergetic regions by employing oppositely corresponding speakers to focus the sonic tones into the desired areas. The sonics can also be modulated so that a quickly unfolding succession of single tones and chord structures envelop the recipient, infusing the bioenergetic system with rapid pulses of sequential sonics.

The treatment table is made of a sonic-responsive crystalline material; it is possible to attach together horizontal sheetings of different crystalline substances to optimalize the reception and transfer of acoustic vibrations through the table into the recipient. This treatment table is suspended from the dome's ceiling by

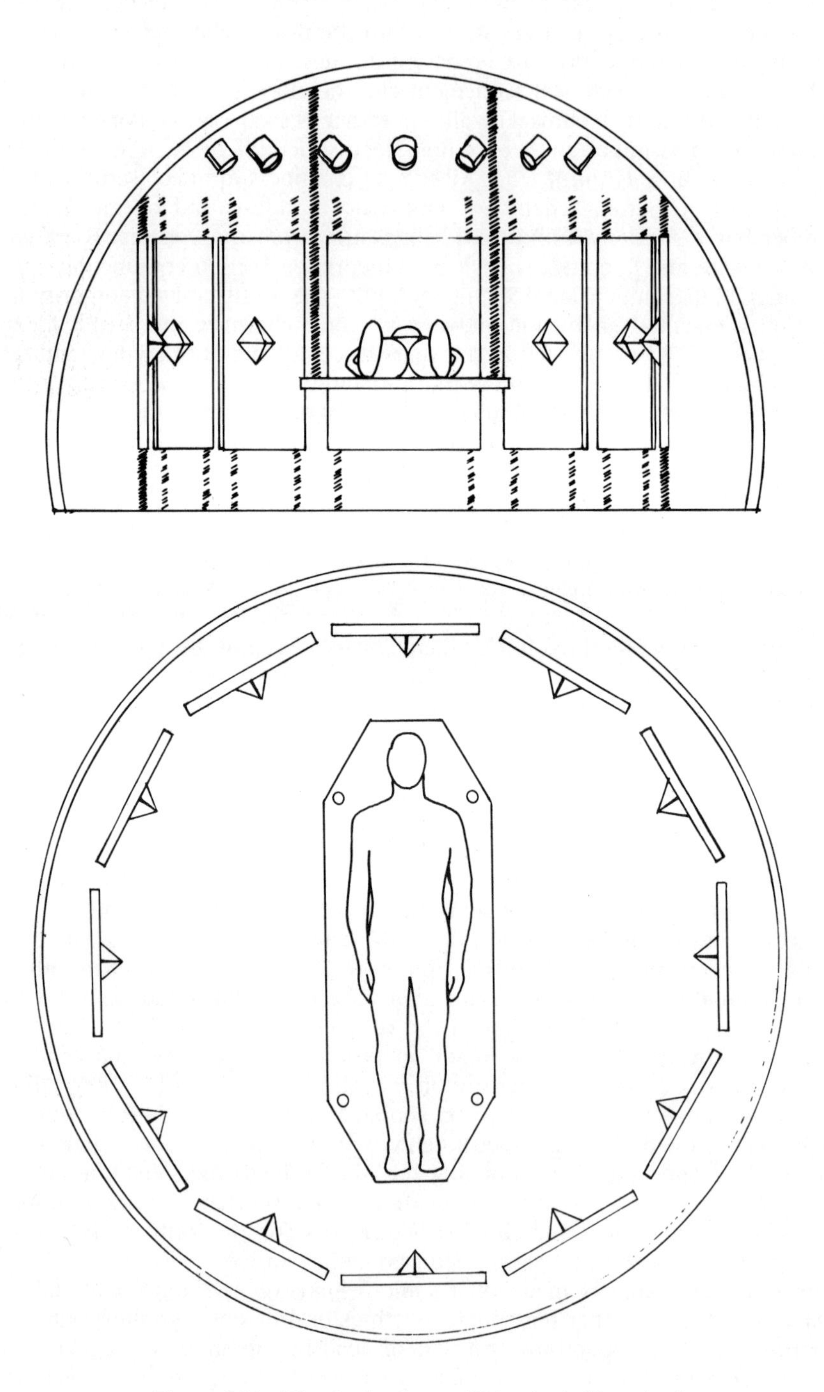

Figure 146: The Sonics Dome (Side view) (Top view)

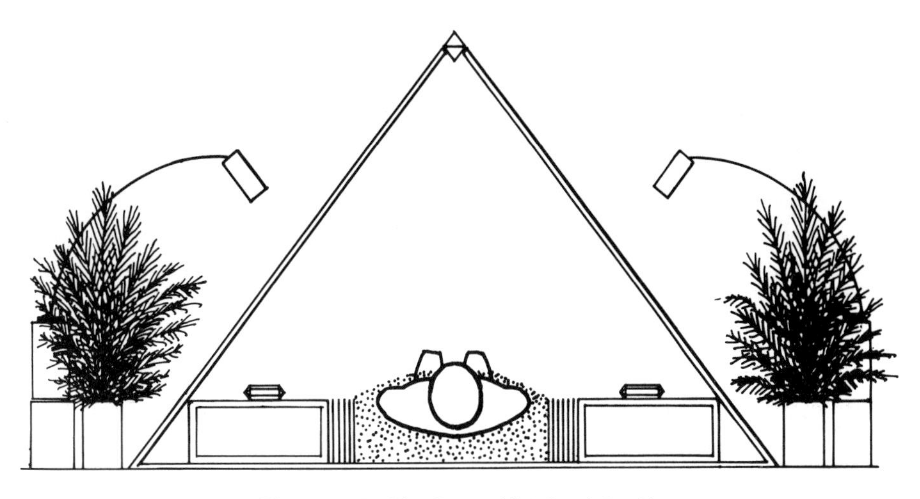

Figure 147: The Pyramid ''Sand Box''

heavy gauge, sonically responsive metallic coiling; such coiling provides another means by which the treatment table is sensitively tunable to the sonic input. Quartz templates (as described in Chapter 13) are positioned on top of each chakra area of the recipient for further patterned focusing of the treatment effects. The dome is surfaced with acoustic absorption material to reduce echoing; in this way, the speaker input is crisp and applied in a controlled manner. Because of the high intensity of the sonics, the recipient must have high quality earplugs.

Altogether, the Sonic Dome is a highly orchestrated, vibrationally intense modality used for a deep-acting ''tune-up,'' modulatable for both generalized and specifically focused healing and reprogramming effects.

Figure 147: *The Pyramid Sand Box.* This energy field is a preparatory or posttreatment integrative modality of a passive, soft variety. The pyramid is approximately 8 feet tall, and composed of copper tubing with silver and gold electroplating on the outside and double-terminations lining the interior. It is further activated by an octahedral capstone and fourfold groupings of double-terminations wired in place at harmonic intervals along the tubing (as shown in Chapter 12, Figure 58). Inside the pyramid's apex is a multipyramidal system as seen in Figure 64. At the base is a boxed enclosure in which the purest white sand of the highest silica content possible is kept. On top of the sand a double Star of David crystal gridwork is place around the center, where the recipient lies down. The treatment recipient's body is completely covered with sand except for the topmost portions of the torso and the head above the ears. Crystal templates made of gently acting rose quartz are placed on all the chakras. Water from the natural springs of Hot Springs, Arkansas, with a mixture of apppriate gem tinctures is drunk just before the session begins. The environment is softly soothing and etherically uplifting. A planter box surrounding most of the perimeter of the pyramid (except for an extrance) has lush green vegetation. Several spotlights are directed toward the recipient and can be programmed to shine various colors in a desired sequence

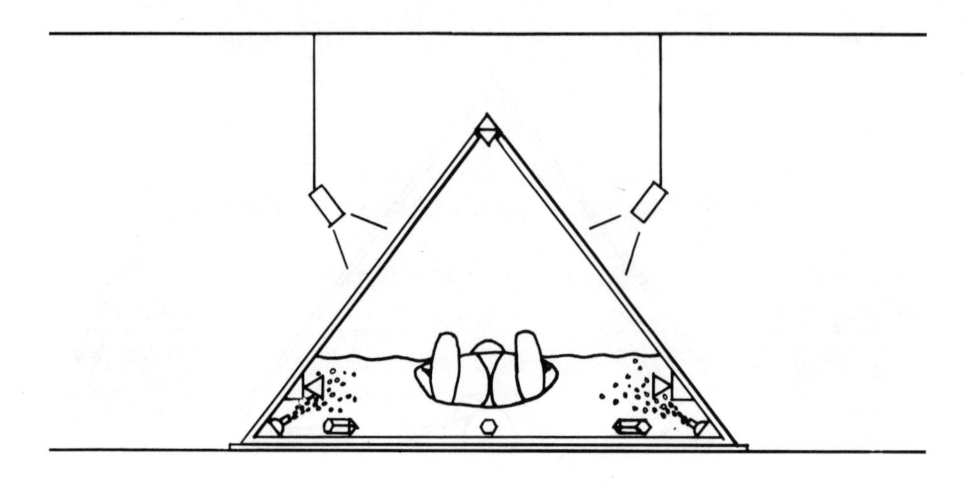

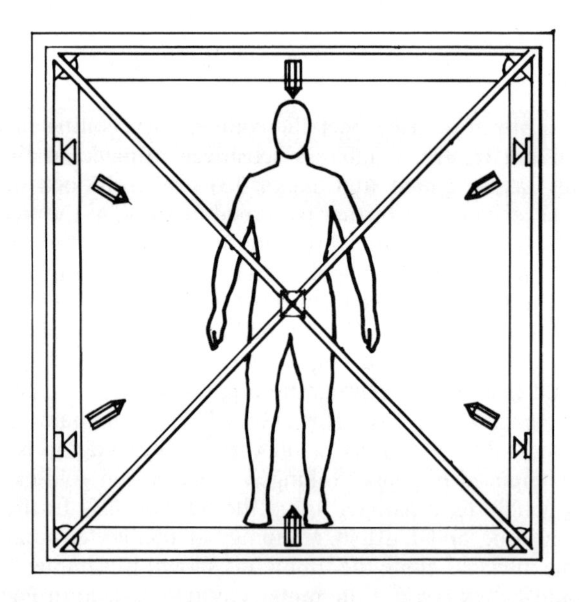

Figure 148: Pyramidal Isolation Tank (Side view) (Top view)

accompanying the unfoldment of the session. Several appropriate aromas are released into the environment during the course of the treatment. And in the background softly subtle, upwardly spiraling music is played. The total effect is soothing and relaxing, yet also energizing and subtly penetrating. Used as a preparatory treatment to facilitate the recipient's optimal openness to further Light-work, this energy field is among the best modalities available.

Figure 148: *Pyramidal Isolation Tank.* This concept is a variation on the isolation tank theme, incorporating numerous energetic modalities. The tank is an open-framed pyramidal structure. The apex has an octahedrally faceted quartz and the

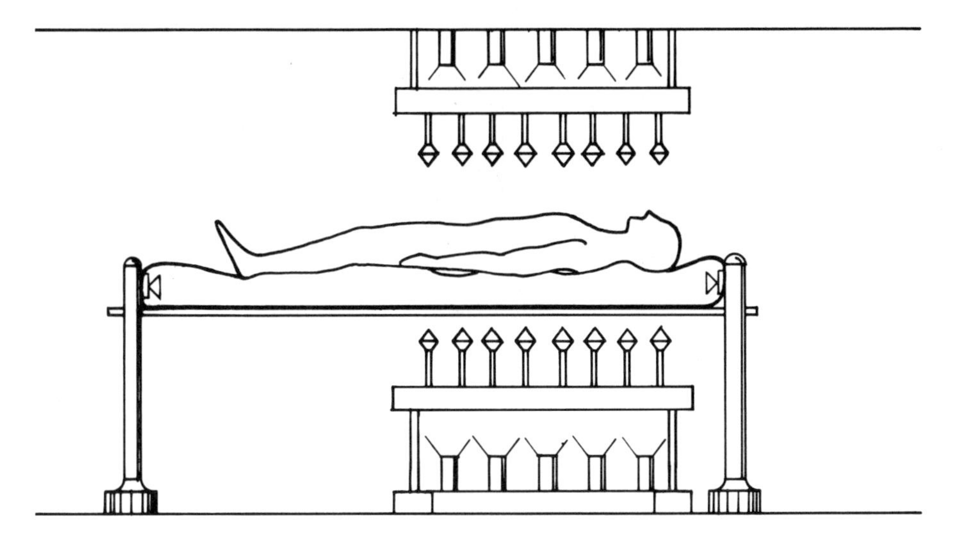

Figure 149: Pin Spotlights with Rotating Octahedrons

base plus the lower 2 feet of the sides have a silvered, mirrored surface. A quadrophonic sound system is built into the lower pyramid sides so that the sonics are directly introduced into the saturated saltwater. The type of sonics utilized are primarily single tonal frequencies and chordal structures designed for specific therapeutic and reprogramming purposes. In addition, colored spotlights surround the lower sides, positioned so that color can be shone into the water. These spotlights can be programmed to create sequences of colors and color combinations for individual-specific effects. Jacuzzi jets direct soft air streams into the center of the pool from all four corners. So that the recipient does not float around, a tether belt setup is provided for stationary support. The water can also be irradiated with subtle energy carring gem tincture or cell salt vibrational patterns (or both). Christopher Hill's Homeopathic Energizer is a good choice. Around the interior pyramidal perimeter a crystal gridwork is set into place; another gridwork can be positioned around the outside of the pyramid. The major components of this system—the jacuzzi jets, colored lights, sound system—are programmable so that sessions can be designed to meet the needs of the recipient. Should only one or two of these three components be desired, this can be easily programmed. And should total sensory isolation be desired, the lights, sound, and water jets can be switched off.

Commercially available isolation tanks can be modified to integrate numerous UEF concepts. These include: 1) multipyramidal systems suspended over the top of the tank, 2) crystal gridworks in or around the tank (or both), 3) radionics applications, 4) speaker systems (an optional component in some isolation tanks), 5) professionally installed color spotlights (shining either through the water at the lower base or from the upper sides), and 6) video screens for lumia and accelerated learning applications (an optional component in some isolation tanks).

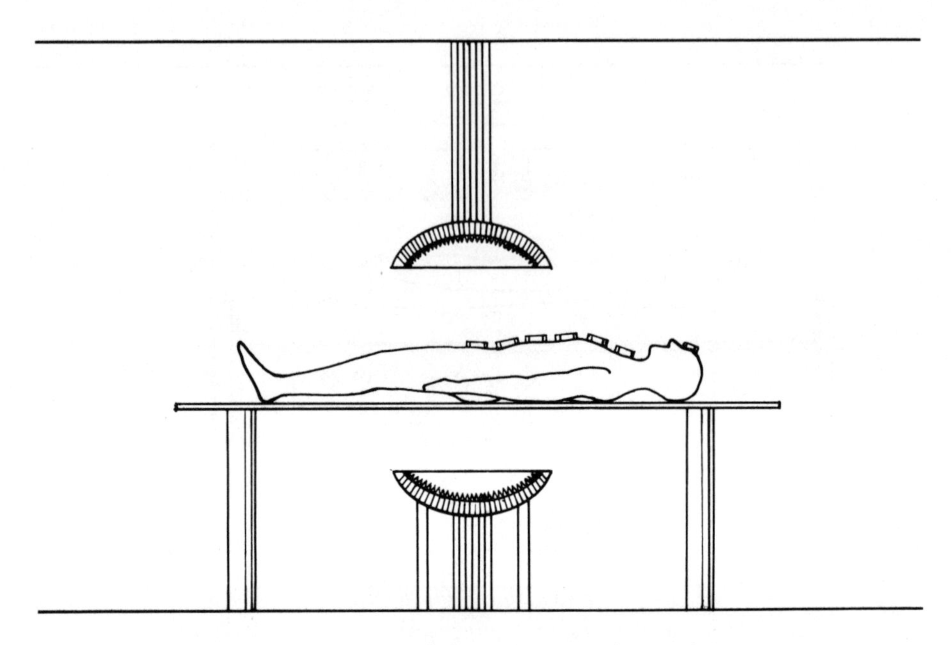

Figure 150: Parabolic Energy Focusing Device

Figure 149: *Pin Spotlights With Rotating Octahedrons.* Nine octahedrons are mounted from the ceiling, each one aligned over a chakra, from Alpha to Omega. Positioned over each octahedron is a pin spotlight with a removable color gel taped in place. Each color beam goes through the vertical axis of its corresponding octahedron, and the colors can be changed to suit the healing or reprogramming needs of the recipient. The nine octahedrons are both vertically and horizontally adjustable for accurate positioning. Each octahedron has a separate motor unit to which it is attached. A control panel is available so that the practitioner may start, stop, and vary the RPM rate of each individual octahedron unit or all of them as a group. When set into motion over a treatment recipient, the rotational motion of the octahedrons (each having upper and lower crystal pyramid apexes) stimulates an energy stream to be infused into each chakra. The chakras become receptive to vibrational input because of the penetrating and opening action of the spiraling pyramidal energy current. In order to pattern this incoming energy in desired ways, a crystal template is placed on each chakra. These templates, in conjunction with a particular color vibration also being projected, transduce the force of the pyramidal energy into chakra-specific code-patternings to facilitate the healing or reprogramming process. This octahedron-spotlight setup can be integrated into a variety of UEF arrangements, and functions with peak effectiveness when this is done. Chapter 14 includes many gridwork arrangements, therapy table modifications, speaker systems, and mirror–pyramid wall setups that can be manifested as a complementary energy field. The octahedron-spotlight modality would be the primary active component of the entire UEF. A professional UEF of this kind would be a major innovation.

Figure 150: *Parabolic energy focusing device.* As with the immediately preceding concept, this is a Light-technology that is to be incorporated into an accompanying complementary UEF arrangement. Two parabolic reflectors with silvered interior surfaces are positioned above and below the clear lucite treatment table. The reflectors are stationary and the table is adjustable. Small good quality single-terminated crystals that have had their bases cut perpendicularly and polished are permanently attached to the reflectors. The crystals are packed as closely together as possible so that the inner parabola is completely filled with them. Attached to each crystal is either a fiber optic light guide through which laser light is projected or a sonic transmitter device that applies sonic frequencies into the crystal's base. A computer system coordinates the laser and sound input to each of the hundreds of crystals. A full spectrum of light and sound frequencies can be introduced to the crystals by sophisticated computer controls. Many light-sound energy patterns can be formulated and enacted through the computer for individual-specific healing or reprogramming needs. The parabolic reflectors are horizontally and vertically adjustable so that their energy focus can be precisely modulated into any given bioenergetic region. For chakra reprogramming in particular, crystal tablets are placed on top of each chakra and the reflectors are positioned so that the energy is focused directly into the chakra interior from above and below. Programmed light-sound sequences are enacted and then the treatment table is moved so that another chakra is in position to receive Light-work. The versatility of this Parabolic Energy Focusing Device is such that any part of the bioenergetic system can be infused with specifically patterned and strongly focused vibrational influences. Mind-center activation, given precision focusing capabilities, is also possible.

Figure 151: *Human Biopyramid Activation Field.* Within a large open framework octahedron is a permanent plexiglass structure designed to support the treatment recipient in an upright position. Around the exterior of the octahedron is metal wiring and strings of small optical diodes that spiral around the pyramid. At the upper and lower apexes are octahedrally faceted quartz, the latter also having a laser capable of shining a beam vertically through its central apex-to-apex axis.

When the recipient is comfortable situated in the plexiglass support, the optic diodes are stimulated to describe a spiraling action from the upper apex to the lower apex, generating external spiraling pyramid dynamics. When the spiral ends at the inverted apex, a white frequency laser beam is shone through the faceted crystal octahedron and it continues upward in alignment with the recipient's Alpha–Omega chakra axis. Continuous diode spirals pulse around the octahedron, stimulating corresponding pulses of white laser beams shooting up into the recipient's chakra system. In effect, then, human biopyramidal energy dynamics are positioned in a parallel fashion within octahedral energy dynamics, resulting in the amplified activation of the former for significant reprogramming effects.

Figure 152: *Rotating Star of David Gridworks.* Rotational crystal motion creates energetic effects that are particularly effective in modulating nonlinear gravitic and magneto-gravitic energy parameters. In this case two Star of David gridwork levels are independently rotatable in clockwise and counterclockwise horizontal directions. The recipient lies on a thin cushion so that the horizontal plane of the body is on the same plane as the gridworks. With the cushioned treatment area stationary, the two gridworks can be set into rotation through a control panel. There are numerous possibilities to the ways that the two gridworks can rotate relative to

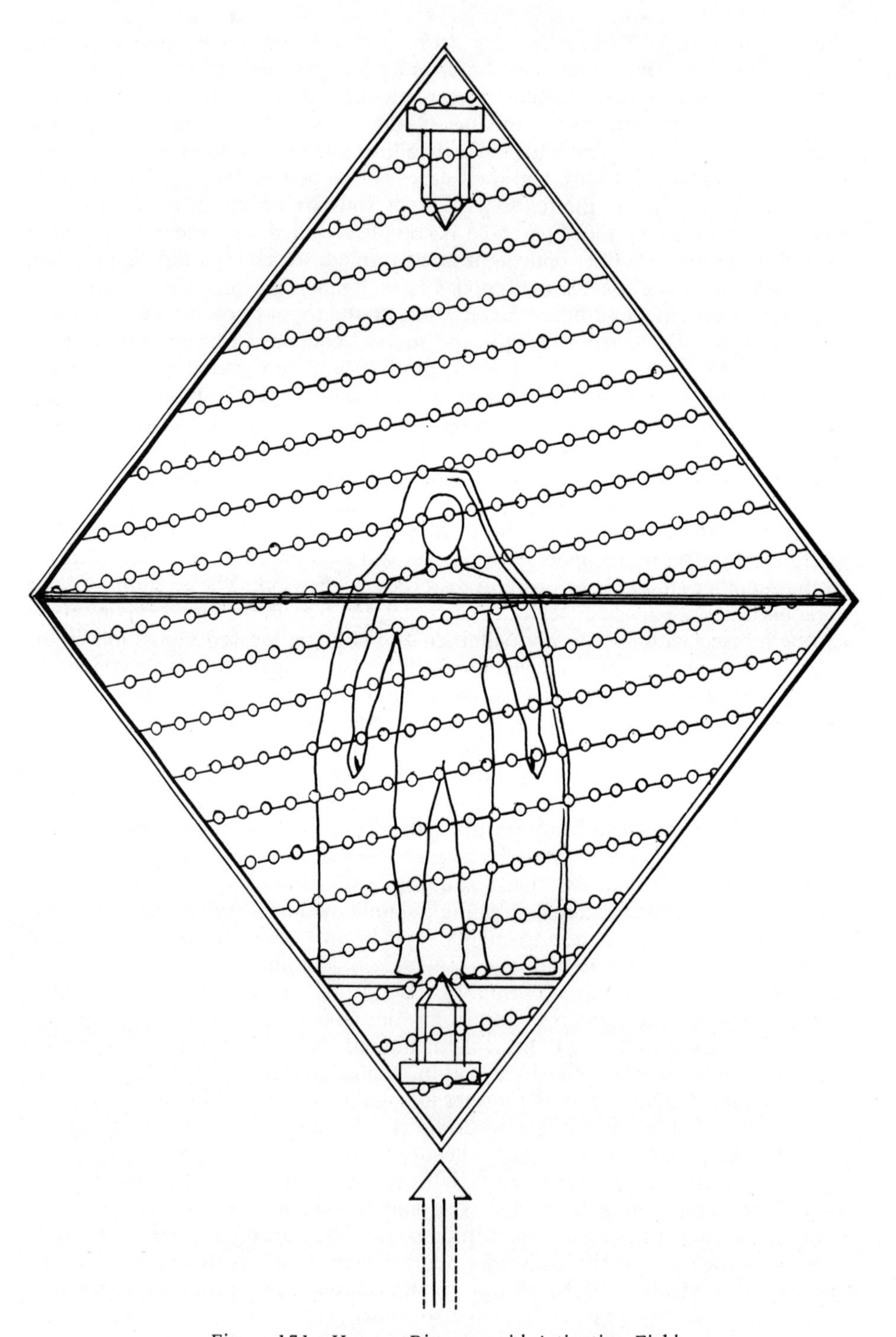

Figure 151: Human Bio-pyramid Activation Field

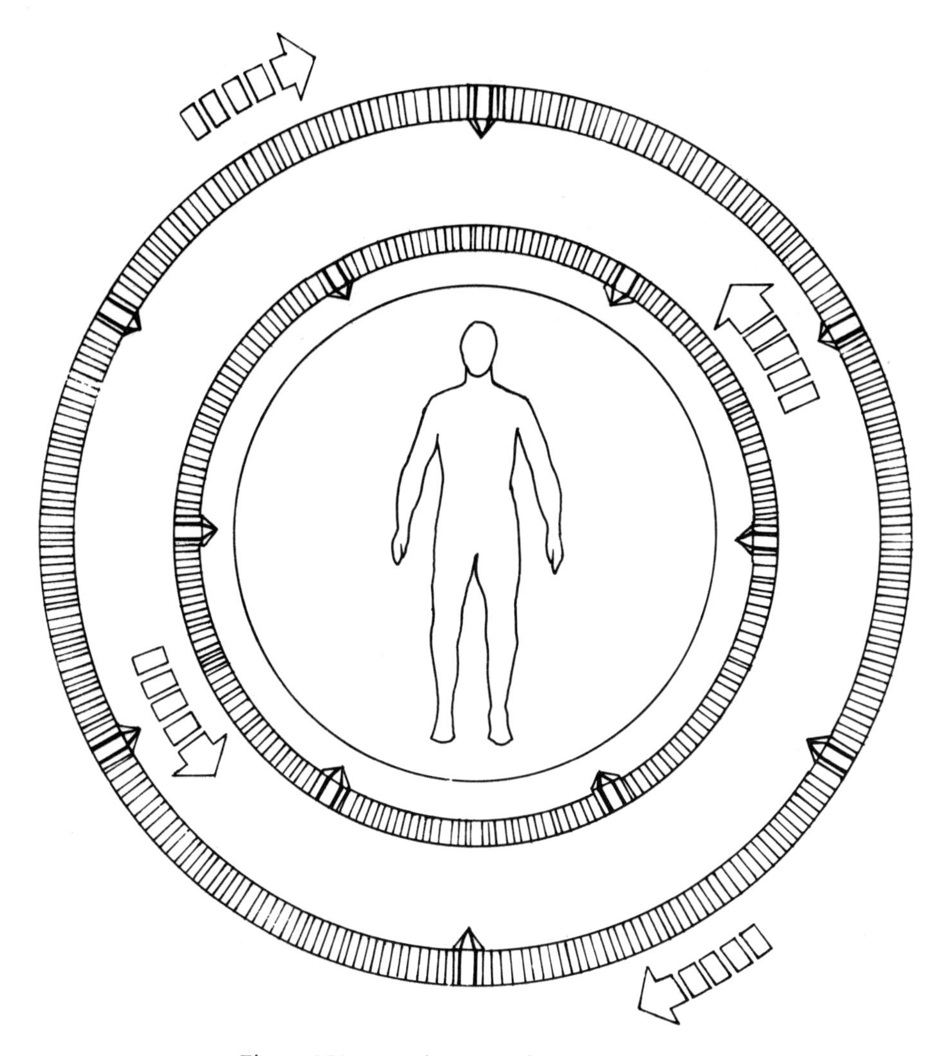

Figure 152: Rotating Star of David Gridworks

one another—for example, both can go in the same direction at the same speed, both can go in opposite directions at harmonically different RPMs, and so on. Each combination of speeds and directions creates a different energetic effect. The magneto-gravitational modulation that can be precisely controlled through this methodology works quite well for reprogramming purposes as well as advanced interdimensional communication. This setup is best done in a dome structure with a powerful energy dome that synchronizes with the physical dome. The combination of the energy dome dynamics and the dual rotational motion is a key to manifesting exceptionally advanced UEFs, for the purposes just cited and numerous others.

Figure 153: *Depolarization–Repolarization UEF.* This energy field is designed to

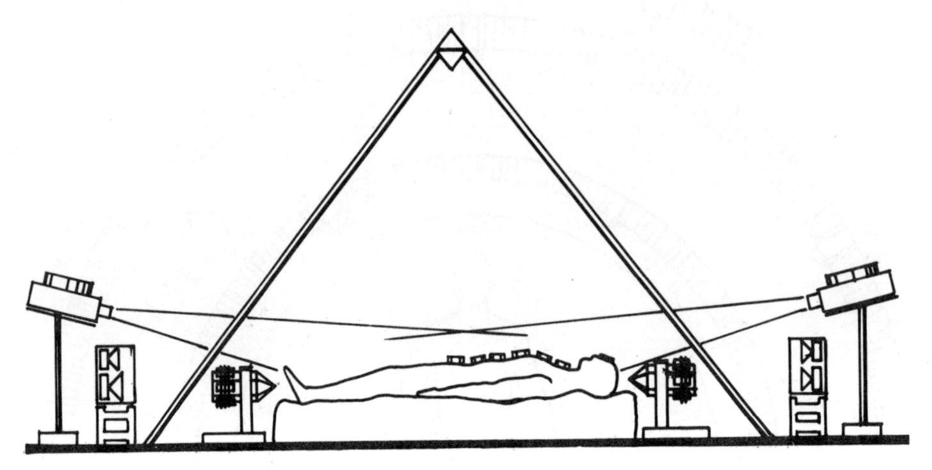

Figure 153: Depolarization/Repolarization UEF

depolarize the bioenergetic system, thus "erasing" the fundamental energetic magentic orientations like a tape recorder erases a tape. Once this is accomplished, the system is then repolarized in accordance with optimal bioenergetic magnetic orientations, thus effecting accelerated healing.

A large pyramid sets the primary energy foundation in conjunction with two levels of double Star of David gridworks, each crystal having two magnets positioned at its base as described in Chapter 14. The pyramid is amplified with crystals in the same manner as that used in Figure 147. The recipient lies on a thin, firm cushion so that the body is situated at the Eye of Yahweh horizontal pyramid strata. A large rotatable crystal generator with six magnets wired in place around its base is positioned in horizontal alignment with the recipient's Alpha–Omega axis at both ends of the cushion. Six speakers are laid in a Star of David arrangement, each positioned so that the sound is directed toward the recipient. Additionally, two slide projectors with color gel slides in their carousels are positioned outside the crystal gridworks a few feet away from the recipient's head and feet. They should be adjusted for maximum color exposure on the recipient, with priority given to the area between the Alpha and Omega chakras. Each chakra has a crystal template on top of it.

To depolarize, the crystals are rotated counterclockwise (looking at the crystal's termination). The RPM can be modulated for identical or proportionally related rotational speeds. Increasing the RPM will produce amplified effects until a threshold point of optimal depolarization is reached; the RPM should not go above this threshold. Simultaneously, an orchestrated sequence of sonic tones and chords combined with synergistically complementary colors is enacted that synchronizes with the depolarization process. For repolarization, the crystals then rotate clockwise, and the RPM, color, and sound sequence unfold oppositely parallel to the depolarization sequence.

This methodology is best utilized as a preparatory treatment for reprogramming

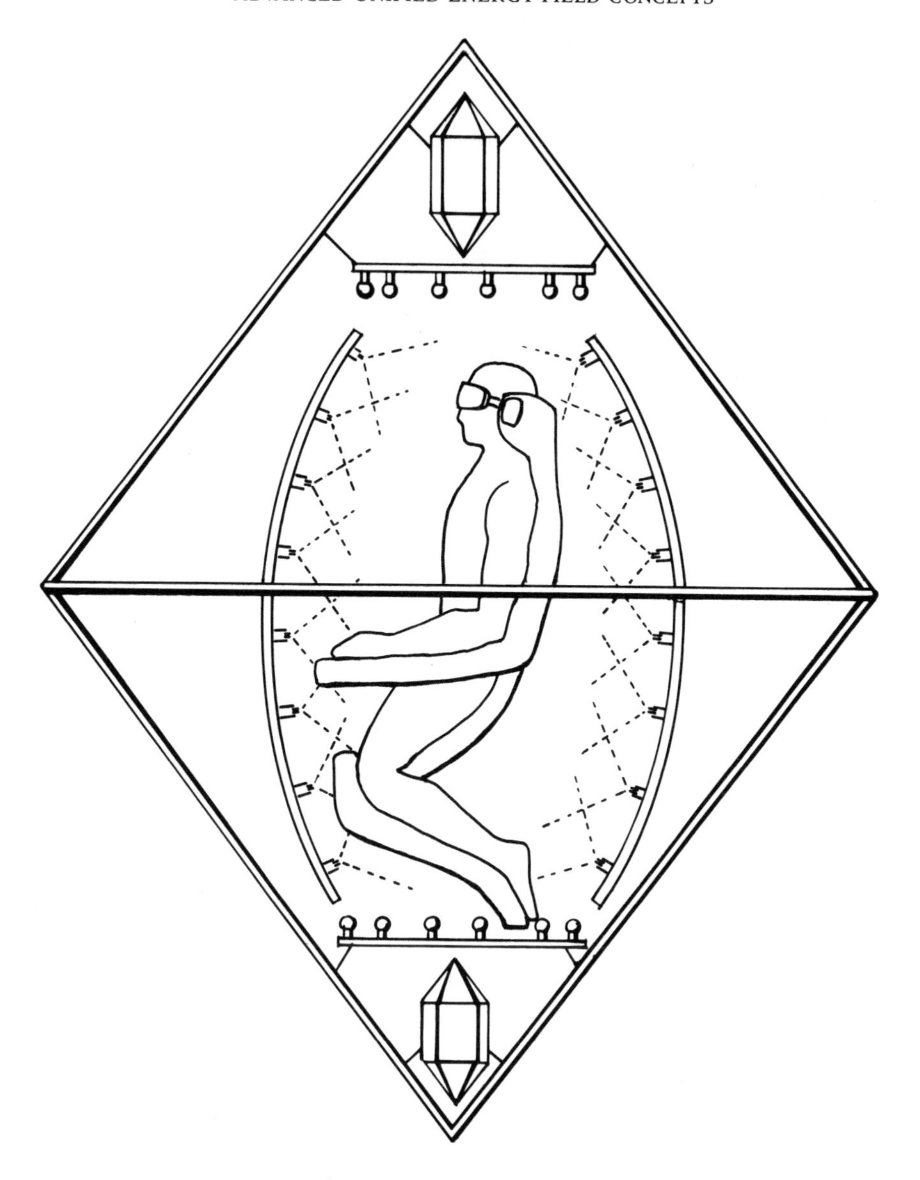

Figure 154: The Mist Module

or healing work in other UEFs. It depolarizes deeply held static or disoriented magnetic domain orientations that can block healing processes. When these are erased and the recipient is then set back into optimal orientation, he or she is maximally receptive to other treatment modalities.

Figure 154: *The Mist Module.* As in Figure 151, a large octahedron with an upright plexiglass support for the recipient forms the primary outline for this energy field. At both apexes are large rotatable double-terminations. In front and

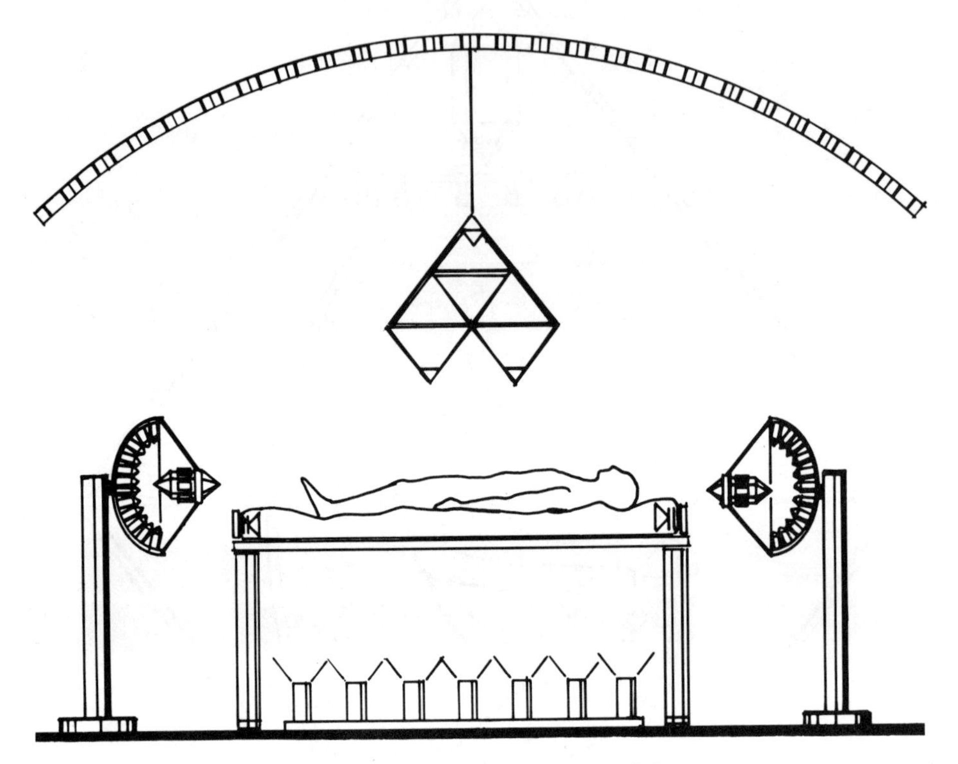

Figure 155: Reprogramming Module

back of the recipient are mist nozzles through which water is gently sprayed. Situated above and below the plexiglass support system are colored spotlights and speakers directing their energetic flow through the interior of the octahedron and into the recipient. Built into the support system are two wraparound speakers. With optional protective eyewear, the recipient is exposed to the gently penetrating color, sound, crystal–pyramid dynamics, and spraying mist. The result is a surprising depth of cleansing of the bioenergetic system. This stems primarily from certain nonlinear effects that occur when water and sonics interact with a strongly activated crystal–pyramid energy field. The experience is one of pleasant, almost numbing, cleansing penetration. The aura feels new and shiny afterward.

Figure 155: *Reprogramming Module.* Inside a small dome is a revolutionary reprogramming methodology. First, there is a new treatment table concept that will be a standard piece of equipment in the future. The main framework is made of copper supports with shock-absorbent bases. The horizontal support is a clear acrylic sheet upon which a clear waterbedlike casing is filled with a specialized liquid crystal medium. On both ends are speakers that infuse sonic input directly into the liquid crystal. One of the primary strengths of this treatment table is that the liquid crystalline medium can be modulated by applied sonics to generate desired crystallographic energy patterns. These energy patterns are then pulse-released into the treatment recipient. It also forms a magnetic vibrational underpinning that serves several purposes: 1) it decreases overall energy loss by tending to magnetically gel the surrounding energy field; 2) it helps stimulate and maintain optimal magnetic orientation within the recipient's bioenergetic system for heightened openness to the treatment dynamics; and 3) it helps balance and harmonize the overall bioenergetic field. In addition, it is also possible to shine color light-beams into the bottom of the table through the acrylic sheeting and into the liquid crystal, thus causing light absorption, processing, and modified release into the recipient.

In the Reprogramming Module in particular, two gold-plated parabolic reflectors are positioned at the foot and head of the treatment table. Similar to the Parabolic Energy Focusing Device of Figure 150, small crystals are attached in close-packed arrangement and sonic transducers are attached to the outside of the parabola. At the focal point of the reflector is a large rotatable double-termination with six magnets wired on, one on each side around the crystal's horizontal midline. The energetics flowing from these two crystals are projected into the recipient, aligned along the chakra axis. This energy current is quite strong, as it is the result of a potent sonic stream vibrating the parabolic reflector and thereby stimulating heightened energy dynamics of the close-packed crystals; this activity is focused directly into the rotating crystal–magnetic system. The energetics are then directed into the recipient's chakra system, causing a profound magneto-gravitic reorientation and recrystallization into a higher ordering level. Further, the surrounding energy field is an energy dome of the same flow-form as the physical dome structure. The physical dome is close-packed with horizontal, hexagonal quartz slices. These slices are attached over a mirroring material that helps to amplify and contain the energy dome dynamics with minimal energy loss. For even more powerful effects, a laser scanner can shine color frequencies over the crystal dome ceiling; especially in conjunction with the strong magnetics of the energy dome, this stimulates a strong nonlinear interdimensional access dynamics, and the entire energy field gains a higher transparency quotient (in relationship to the attraction module effect.)

Figure 156: *Laser–Crystal Module System.* Two lucite sheets with hundreds of close-packed crystals sandwich the liquid crystal treatment table of Figure 155. Attached at the base of each crystal is a fiber optic light guide leading from a complex of lasers, which are all controlled by a computer system. The idea is to pinpoint treatment focal areas of the recipient and to program specific groupings of crystals to be stimulated with various laser frequencies that are directly over and under the treatment areas. As the laser pulses quickly on and off, it stimulates a significant energy emission from the crystal that is then directed into a corresponding area of the recipient. In accordance with the size of the area being treated, the number of crystals that are stimulated into activity by the laser can be larger or smaller. Numerous areas can be treated simultaneously so that the treatment session would appear to an observer as rapidly pulsing multicolor discharges illuminating specific areas all about the recipient's bioenergy system. This methodology is most effective in the realms of healing and reprogramming. It can be further amplified by adding dual parabolic reflector-rotating crystal units illustrated in the Reprogramming Module of Figure 155.

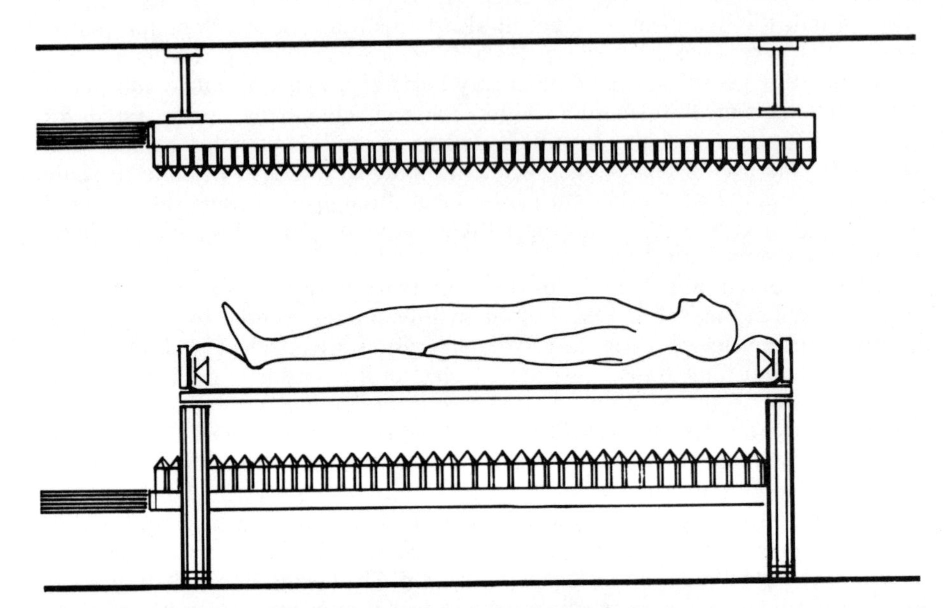

Figure 156: Laser–Crystal Module System

A variation on the theme of using the lucite sheeting suspended over a treatment table is to attach nine gem disc rotator units on lucite sheeting. These units could be horizontally and vertically adjustable so that each unit could be positioned over one of the nine chakras. Gem discs (see Chapter 13) selected specifically for each chakra are latched into place. Via a control panel, each disc is separately controllable to modulate the RPM of each disc to match the particular chakra's needs. **Figure 157:** *The Hydro Environment.* This is an environmental energy field created

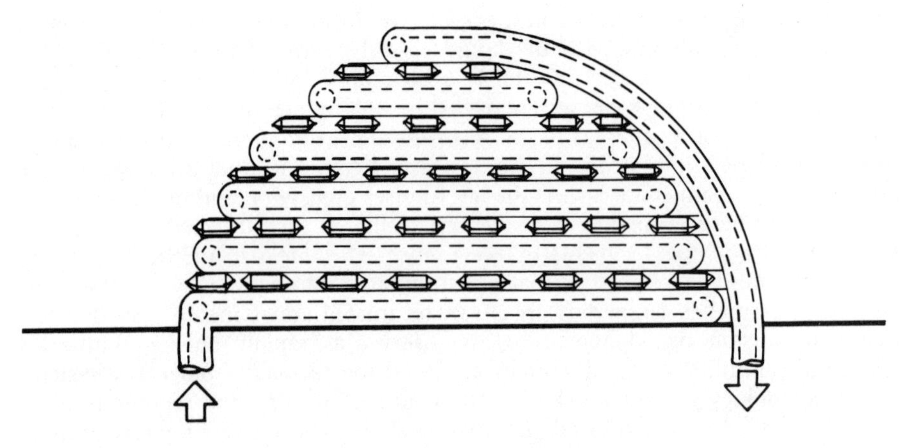

Figure 157: The Hydro Environment

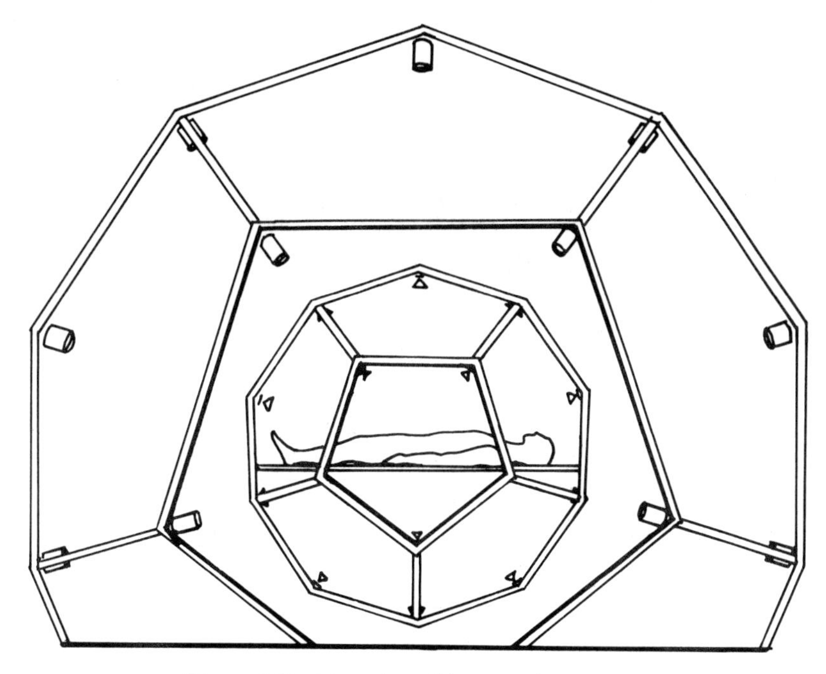

Figure 158: Platonic Solid Macro-form Modules

through the interaction between crystals and flowing water. A smooth dome structure is encompassed by piping spiraling around its exterior with crystals attached at regular intervals between the coils of tubing. Water is hydraulically pumped through the spiral course in a continuous stream. The flowing action of the water has certain energy dynamics that induce a unique Light-field emission effect from the crystals, occurring especially well within spiraling parameters. The keynote characteristic of such crystal-water emissions is softly interpenetrating radiance that suffuses the environment with soothing, flowing Light-effulgence. The Hydro Environment can be utilized as the foundational energy structure for a house (when done on a large scale) or for a regenerative UEF.

Figure 158: *Platonic Solid Macroform Modules.* The effect of form energy has been discussed at length in this text. Figure 158 shows another application mode in this regard for the Platonic solids; in this case, the pentagonal dodecahedron is used as an example. Each of the Platonic solids serves as an attraction module that has access to specific spectrum-profiles of Universal Intelligence. By amplifying the form with additional energy input, the attraction module effect is considerably increased. Here, the dodecahedral form is constructed of copper tubing with silver and gold electroplating. A therapy table is positioned horizontally across the midline of the form. At each vertex is a small speaker that not only directs the sound in toward the recipient but also vibrationally stimulates the form itself. As the form vibrates, these energies are dynamically amplified by fourfold groupings of double-terminations wire-wrapped into place at harmonic intervals through the entire dodecahedron framework. The sonics are high intensity single notes and chords that have a fundamental resonance with the specific form energy of the dodecahedron. For ideal results, another harmonically larger dodecahedron can be constructed to be exactly parallel to the first one inside of its structure. The framework of the outer form would also be crystal amplified. Color spotlights are attached at various inner vertex areas of the outer dodecahedron, shining into the therapy table area. As with the sonics, only those color frequencies that have a primary resonant affinity with this specific form are utilized in this module.

The same priniciples applied to the dodecahedron attraction module system can also be related to the other four Platonic solids. Each form stimulates access to different interdimensional energy spectrums. These modules are particularly effective for facilitating different facets of the reprogramming process. It would be ideal for a professional complex to have the entire array of Platonic solids, each in separate rooms or small domes. In this way the entire spectrum of this centrally important form family is available for interdimensional access. Also, it would be possible to go through each form in a single treatment sequence for full spectrum effects.

Michael Bradford, head of the Bradford Institute Stress Research Center, utilizes a variation of the form framework module concept. Quoting from his literature:

> The Cotyledon™ takes the form of a geometric shape called a cuboctahedron. . . . This shape, also the shape of a subatomic particle called the meson, creates acoustical isolation from the Earth's interference, and provides an opportunity for the mind and body to entrain within its own electrical field without losing energy to ground. . . .
>
> The Cotyledon™ is an aluminum alloy tube structure used to support a therapy table in such a way that electro-mechanical acoustical vibrations are focused toward the subject lying on the table. The acoustic vibration and audio sound input to the table and framework is controlled by a bioacoustical and audio controls console. . . . The Cotyledon™ provides a supportive environment for the reduction of stress. By treating the body as an electrical unit that responds to the frequencis of sound, the Cotyledon™ utilizes high density sound to entrain the biological energies.[1]

A further, more advanced version of the Macroform Module concept is to create the form with hollow tubing such that highly pressurized inert gas would be inside the tubing with electronics in place so that modulated electrical discharges could be released into the gas. Such an energized inert gas field in conjunction with the other components of the UEF would generate a considerably more powerful induction of the overall energy field and the attraction module effect. Another possibility in this regard is to have spiralling glass tubing in place around the framework of the Macroform Module. On the glass tubing would be series of double-terminated quartz (terminations following the spiral axis) with two rare earth magnets on either side of each crystal. Modulated electrical discharge capabilities would also be part of this schemata. In both cases, the unique energy effects of activated gas plasma, particularly with the inert gases, is a key component for inducing form energy dynamics and multiple energy modality synergy to considerably higher activation quotients, not only in this particular context but in many diverse applications in UEFs and Light-tools.

Figure 159: *Star-Seed Activation Field.* This UEF is designed for the activation and

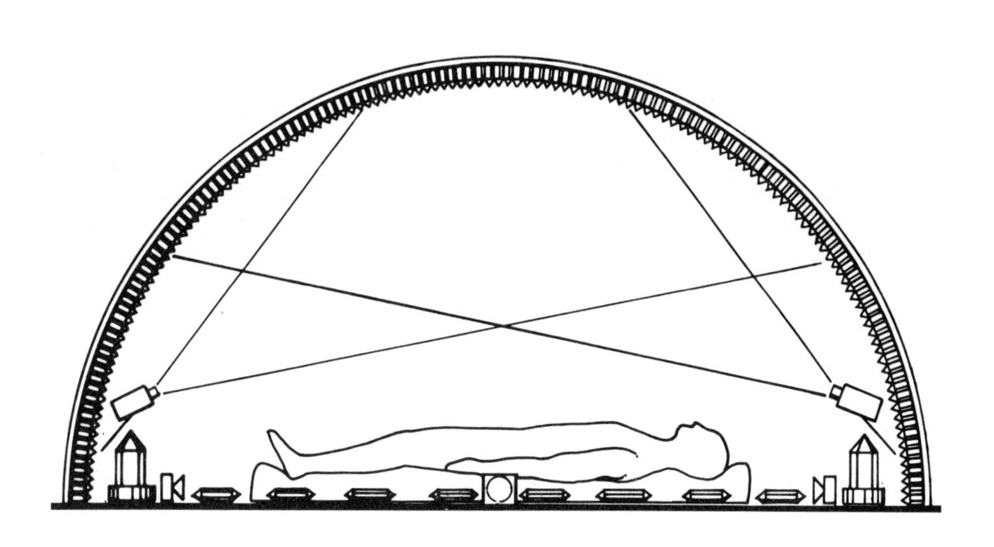

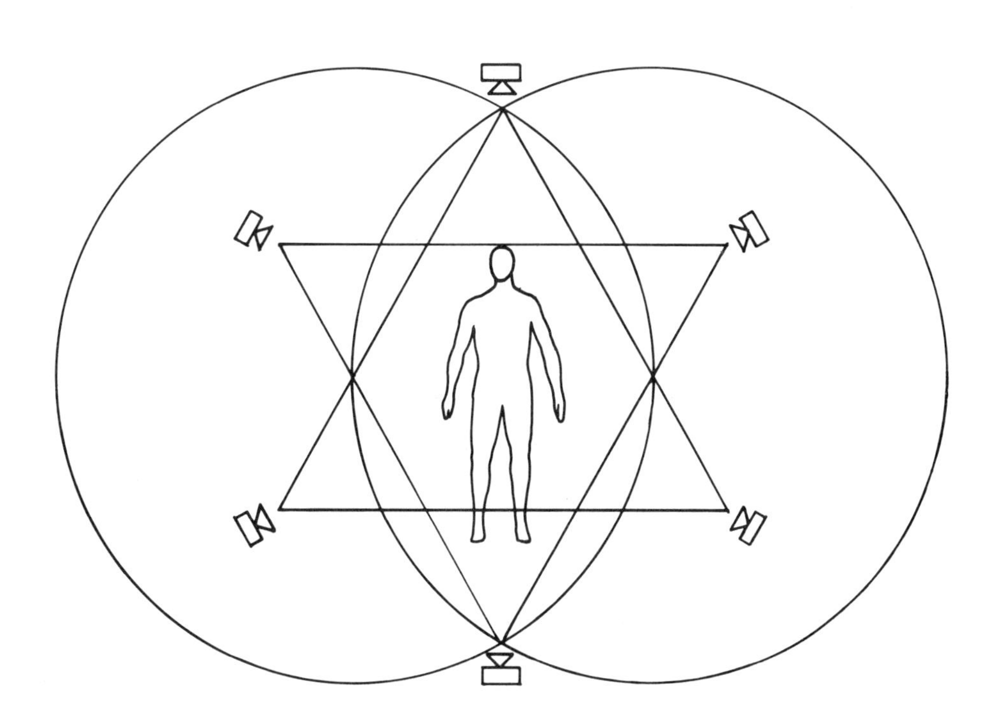

Figure 159: Star–Seed Activation Field

alignment of star-seed and celestial-seed with the interdimensional access pathways of their soul origin. It is an advanced version of the "Star-seed connection UEF" presented in Chapter 14. A small dome forms the outer structure in which the treatment takes place. The entire ceiling is close-packed with thousands of small crystals; mirroring material in place behind the crystals is optimal. An energy dome is built to match its outer flow pattern with the physical structure of the crystal-packed dome. A combination vesica piscis and Star of David gridwork is set into place with a thin cushion in the central portion. As shown in the figure, a sixfold speaker system is positioned around the exterior of the Star of David gridwork. The keynote vibration in every aspect of the Star-seed Activation Field is indigo. The sonics are so keyed to tones and chords correlating to indigo. Two special effect projectors with a color wheel of various shades of indigo illuminate the dome ceiling during the course of the treatment. In addition, a laser with indigo frequency capabilities is scanned in appropriate geometric patterning over the crystal ceiling. A color vibration that is a necessary complement to indigo is gold. This vibration can be incorporated into the special effect projectors' color wheels, and a strobe light with a gold color gel covering is also used during most of the treatment session at slow flash rates. The effect of the energy field is exceptionally conducive to amplified interdimensional interlinkage with specifically desired star systems or celestial domains.

The blueprint of the Star-seed Activation Field can be applied for many other specialized purposes. The keynote vibration would be different for each application, along with the gridwork arrangement. With proper adjustment of the keynote vibration utilized in such a setup, any number of UEFs could be manifested for different purposes.

Figure 160: *Accelerated Learning Module System.* With the current advancements in the fields of video, film, computers and computer graphics, learning technology, and lumia, the integration of these components with UEF concepts will result in accelerated learning technologies.

Figure 160 shows an outline of one accelerated learning UEF. A chair shaped like an indented egg is used to seat the recipient. Such a chair provides a pleasantly encompassing and isolated feeling for the individual. Its interior comfortably wraps around the recipient and blocks out most of the recipient's peripheral vision. Speakers are incorporated into the chair design so that sound inputs directly into the interior space. Sound transducers are implanted in the chair underneath the recipient's spine, legs, and arms for heightened sensory input. An air ionizer and psychoactive aromas could also be employed. Around the chair are crystal gridworks that correlate with the intended purpose of a treatment session. Above the individual's head is suspended a rotating crown.* In front of the chair is a wraparound video or film screen that spans the recipient's field of vision.

Given the advances in the technologies of film, computer graphics, video, and lumia, the Accelerated Learning Module System provides a perfect environment for accelerated assimilation of information. With the amplified energy field dynamics of the gridworks, the crown activating the mind centers, the sonics facilitating relaxed, alert receptivity, and a screen spanning the visual field, the individual is in an ideal controlled environment and state of consciousness for exponentially

*The double-row Star of David Crown works well here—see Chapter 10, Figure 25.

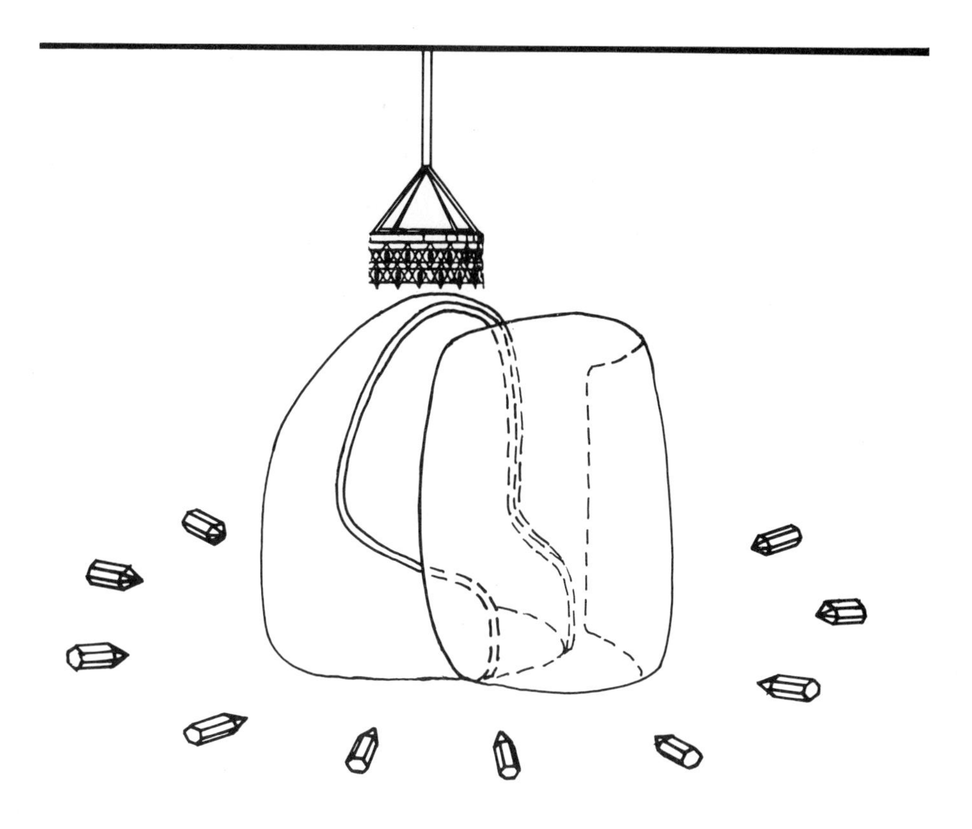

Figure 160: Accelerated Learning Module System

greater information assimilation and retention. The use of three-dimensional visual images presented to the viewer in an orchestrated sequencing designed to convey holographic informational patterning that is directly assimilated into the brain-mind matrix is one of the keys to future accelerated learning modalities. Until the *Brainstorm* movie concept is manifested, film and video in conjunction with UEF factors will be two of the primary avenues by which advancement in this field occurs. Exploring such possibilities could fill books, but a few selected quotations must suffice here to highlight some of these potentials.

> Now the work of technological artists will help us understand worlds still being discovered by physicists and may ultimately give us visual analogues of a universe previously known to us only through equations.
>
> Working with a concept that Kepes call transference, today's artists translate conceptual information from one sense form into another. Visual information, such as geometric curves, can become analogous audio experiences or thermal experiences, all three determined by a core of generating data, such as a number series.[2]

Back in the Seventies, Hollywood special-effects expert Douglas Trumbull set out on a mission to enhance the motion-picture experience. . . . While tinkering with the film speed standard of 24 frames per second (fps), Trumbull discovered that motion pictures photographed and projected at faster speeds created some surprising special effects on viewers. Subjects in lab tests reported that 60-fps images were more vividly real than those offered by standard movies. . . . "By substantially increasing the frame rate up to about sixty fps, you can create tremendously increased physiological stimulation of human beings." The evidence pointed to an important revelation: The 60-fps rate approximated the speed at which the eye receives information and transmits it to the brain. This helps explain why the space between the Showscan viewer and the screen seems to disappear, making the audience members feel as if they have become part of the image. . . . Showscan's creator even predicts that tests "will prove that if you put educational material on Showscan on a big screen with powerful sound, students will retain substantially more information than they would by any other way of teaching.[3]

The language of future mathematics will be a language of light pictographs and ideographic-cybernetics.

. . . When I was taken into Merkabah, Enoch instructed me through a series of scenario abstracts, or light pictographs, as to the myriad intelligence that serve the Father's Will.

This was done through a high speed process of pictures which connected whole environmental arrangements of every basic order of knowledge so that multilevel incarnation programs could be directly revealed to me in a matter of hours.[4]

The final development in technological art. . . . may be the total elimination of media in favor of brain-stimulation devices that generate music, colors, tastes, and tactile sensations within our minds. This will represent the true link between artist and audience—the transmission of pure creative thought.[5]

Figure 161: *Group Consciousness Reprogramming Chamber.* A grand dome structure encompasses a large parabolic-shaped pool with a walkway surrounding it. In the center of the pool is a giant crystal energy generator mounted on a resonator plate activated by intense sonic frequencies. In conjunction with sonic speakers located at harmonic intervals throughout the pool's interior, a potent energy field is generated within the water. Like an atom with various electron orbital shell levels, the pool's water is similarly organized into energy shells, each one having a different vibratory level. Groups of individuals desiring to undergo group consciousness reprogramming sequences come to this chamber and each one enters an individual womb-pod. These womb-pods are designed to provide individuals with maximum comfort and secure relaxation as they float horizontally in the water. The bottom of these pods is composed of a floatable, highly sonic responsive crystalline material through which the recipient is exposed to the pool's sonic field. The top portion is made of a curved thin sheeting of clear quartz that latches into place with the pod's bottom as the person lies horizontally within the pod. Specially grown and programmed crystal templates line the pod's interior, especially around the head region. These templates facilitate amplified group consciousness interaction on the higher levels of awareness. Twenty to thirty individual pods with enclosed recipients are dispatched to different energy shell areas of the pool. The controlled movement of each pod is achieved through sophisticated modulation of the pool's speaker sonic system. As the pod gridwork is set into

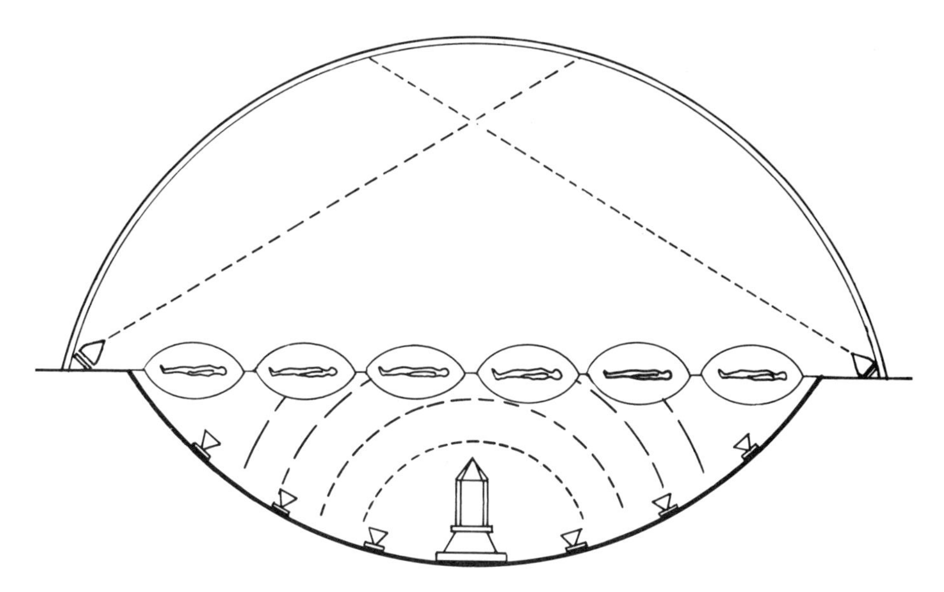

Figure 161: Group Consciousness Reprogramming Chamber

place and group consciousness is engaged, the light dims and an orchestrated lumia display is enacted on the domed ceiling. The ceiling is lined with a microcrystalline substance that reacts to laser light with high reflective and radiative intensity, similar to the fire seen in a well-cut diamond, except stronger. While lying in the pods, the individuals' fields of vision are spanned by the dome ceiling. Multiple lasers of various frequencies project prescribed sequences of geometric patterns on the microcrystalline ceiling, causing brilliant multicolor displays sparkling and coruscating with dazzling intensity. This lumia display is designed for a twofold purpose: 1) to stimulate specific levels of heightened consciousness in a particular sequence, and 2) to facilitate certain group consciousness energy-code patternings that are desired for group reprogramming purposes. The perceived effects are ineffable, but are hinted at in the following quotation:

> The video screen was immediately filled with ever-expanding and evolving geometric patterns. The room was filled with soothing resonant sounds that seemed to cause my whole mind and body to resonate in similarly evolving and enlarging patterns. . . . I found myself flowing on a gentle river of multiple sensations until I seemed to enter an infinite ocean of unspeakable unity, oneness, and balance accompanied by the most soul-satisfying feeling of harmony imaginable.[6]

As the lumia effects progress, the pods are sequentially rotated through a series of positions in the various energy shell levels. Each individual will have completed the sequence at the end of the treatment session.

The Group Consciousness Reprogramming Chamber is one example of the unparalleled evolutionary opportunites that await the rebirth of the temple chambers on earth.

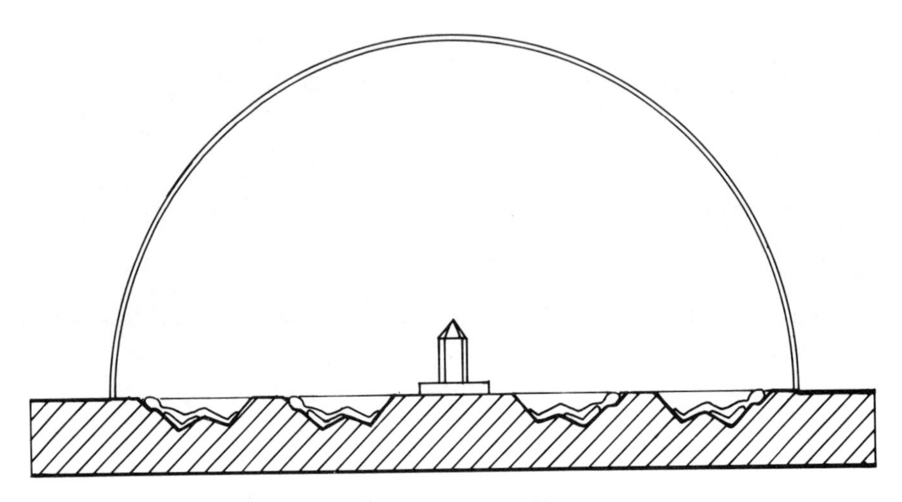

Figure 162: The Ascension Chamber

Figure 162: *The Ascension Chamber.* Similar in magnitude to the Group Consciousness Reprogramming Chamber, the Ascension Chamber is a massive dome structure with state-of-the-art Light-based technologies designed to facilitate activation and alignment into the Light-body. Though in a group setting, there is less emphasis placed upon group consciousness processes and more priority put on individual-specific reprogramming needs. The Ascension Chamber is a huge attraction module for gaining access to interdimensional interactions with higher dimensional Light-entities. For a more complete description of the chamber's structure and energy dynamics, see Chapter 21.

Figure 163: *Merkabah Attraction Module.* An interdimensional antenna-receiver of the highest order, the Merkabah Attraction Module is designed for placement at primary planetary vortex regions to interconnect the earth-human with the Merkabah of the Heavenly Host. Its mega-Pillar of Light (POL) action stands as a cornerstone of interdimensional communicative interlinkage with virtually unlimited capabilities.

Figure 163 shows the prototype outline. Inasmuch as its complexity of structure and energy dynamics are great, only the main points will be highlighted. The entire mechanism is housed in a tall silolike structure with a top that can open and close. At the bottom of the structure is the main power generation mechanism. A high power white-frequency capacity laser directs its beam from the base of the silo into a "triple transformer" with a central rotating large double-terminated quartz with high-gauss cobalt alloy magnets affixed. Through nonlinear dynamics currently unknown to orthodox science, a Light-force of awesome magnitudes is generated through the resonant cavity between the base and the topmost mechanism. At the top is a three-tiered complex composed of a central double-termination of specific dimensions housed within surrounding polished crystal cones, copper, silver, and horizontal quartz plates, magnets, titanium rods, and other

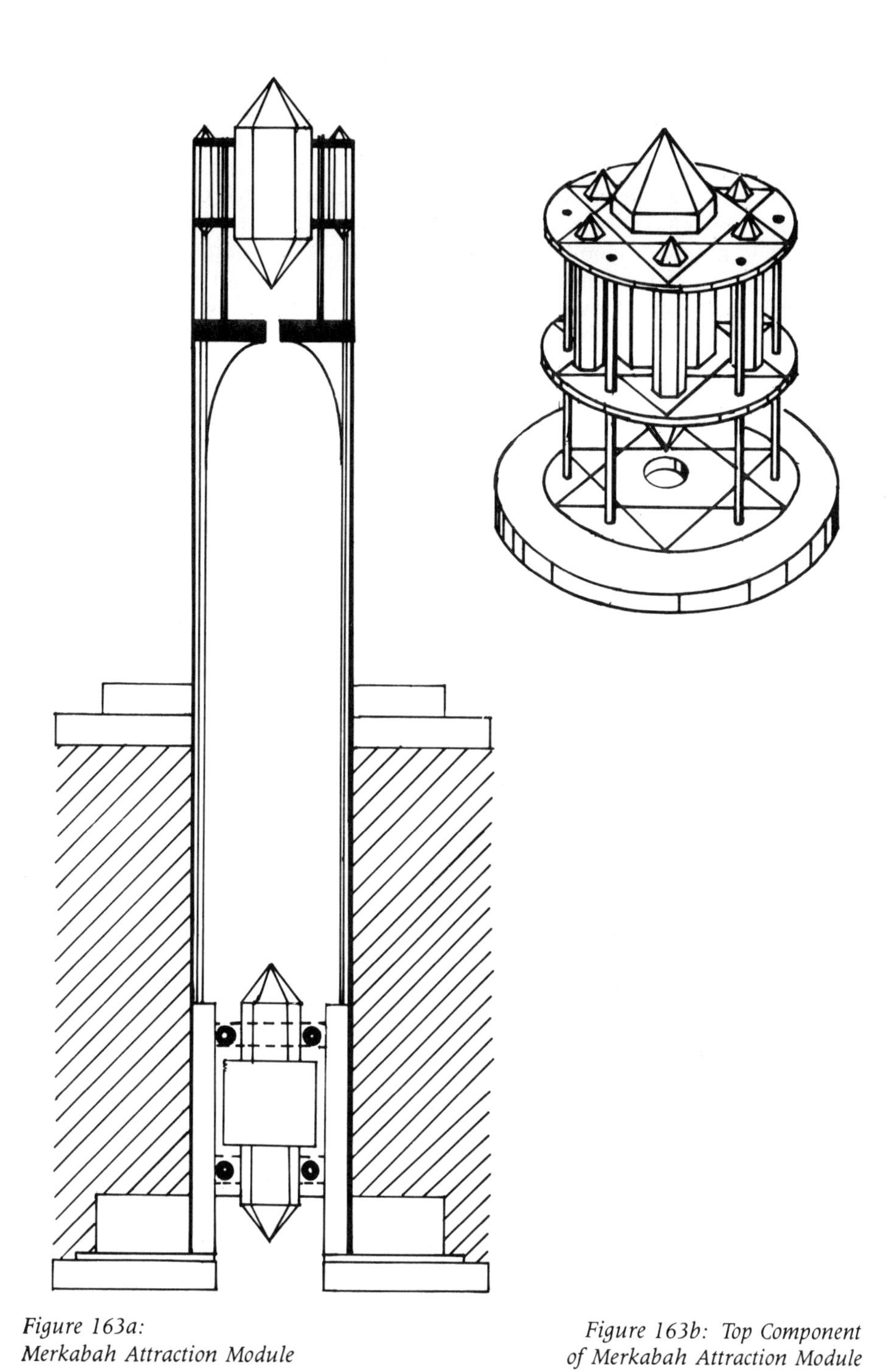

Figure 163a: Merkabah Attraction Module

Figure 163b: Top Component of Merkabah Attraction Module

materials of technical concern. The overall design of this complex is based upon the Star of David energy pattern; it is inscribed into the horizontal plates, and the crystal cones and titanium rods are positioned hexagonally. The unit as a whole is rotatable, and it is modulating the RPM and the periodicity of the phase changes between clockwise and counterclockwise rotation directions that the parameters of reception and modulated emissions are set. Also, in the interior of each of the three tiers are independently rotatable circular magnets that further modify the parameters of operation. As the primary Light-force is focused into the top unit complex it is minutely modified within thousands of interdimensional physics access parameters, and is then emitted from the large crystal with awesome power.

Merkabah Attraction Modules are an integral aspect of the latter unfoldment of the New World ascension process. In the future, they will be located at many of the main planetary vortex-temple areas, particularly those that are centers of science and interdimensional communication.

As a whole, the advanced UEF's presented in this chapter foretell a spiritual-scientific revolution of untold magnitudes. But a mere glimpse of such future potentials, may this chapter spark thought-patterns previously unthought and deeds heretofor undone, now so critically needed in the world today.

CHAPTER 16

Radionics and Crystals

Radionics involves the transfer of specifically formulated vibrational patterns and frequencies from an operator-controlled and operator-modulated mechanism to a recipient at a distance. In this discipline, linear spatial distance is transcended, for the transfer of radionic energies to a recipient occurs equally well whether the individual is 3 feet or 3,000 miles away from the source of the transmissions. It is through the higher dimensions of the planetary energy network wherein linear space is neutralized that the energy transfer is effected. The main idea is to establish a strong resonant interlinkage with a recipient through a witness. The witness is a vibrational profile-representation of an individual's bioenergetic system. A hair sample, sputum, a blood sample, a signature, a photograph—any one can be a witness, used as an individual's energy blueprint having an ongoing vibrational interconnection, spatial dimensions notwithstanding. By exposing the witness to precisely formulated energetics via an operator-regulated radionics device, the recipient whose witness is treated receives the energetics within his or her bioenergetic system. Since the inception of this discipline in the early 1900s by Dr. Albert Abrams, treatment results have been astounding at times (and have been documented). In addition, tremendous insights into the nature of reality have come to light. A few highlights of radionics include: Galen Hieronymus accurately monitored via radionics the physiological conditions of the *Apollo 8* and *Apollo 11* astronauts through their flights, matching NASA's data exactly.[1] George De la Warr once focused his radionic camera on himself and his wife, and concentrated on their wedding day of 30 years previous. A photograph developed of them exactly as they had been on that day, in front of skeptical witnesses.[2] The literature of radionics is replete with such demonstrations of humankind's ability to accurately formulate, modulate, focus, and transmit higher dimensional energetics.

Radionics is currently one of the more dynamic leading-edge research areas of both esoteric science and fledgling interdimensional science. Considerable independent research by sophisticated individuals continues to evolve exciting new inventions and revolutionary thought. The purpose of this chapter is not to provide exhaustive research findings or present an overview of the field, but rather to offer some seed-concepts relating to the incorporation of certain elements of crystal-based science into the radionic discipline. Such ideas could prove to be fertile ground for further advancements toward its development into a mature aspect of interdimensional science.

Crystals, particularly quartz crystals, are quintessentially compatible with radionic modalities. The multidimensionally active, geometrically stable crystalline matrices function as coded templates of controlled, repeatable, and amplified energetic interactions. Quartz, specifically, is programmable with a broad spectrum of thought-patterns and other energy fields. The program, held steady with precision and durability, is available for amplified replication and optimal interlinkage with the planetary energy network for subsequent completion of transmission via the principles of interdimensional harmonic resonance.

As in radionics, the most essential operative dynamics in crystal science are mind and geometry. The form of the circuit diagram of the famous Hieronymus Machine functions as effectively as the machine itself![3] For it is the mind of the operator that is the source of radionics's animating force and modulating instrumentation. And the sophisticated concepts of the coded angular nature of vibrational fields brought forth by Malcolm Rae add new dimensions to the radionics paradigm. The interactivity of mind with the angular codes of the crystalline matrix itself as well as those of a programmed energy-pattern parallel the mind–radionics device interaction. Could it be that as higher consciousness capabilities evolve in the years to come that crystals themselves will be the primary radionic devices?

Concepts to contemplate:

1. Utilizing quartz crystals as witness matrices is significantly more optimal than others in accomplishing its twofold purpose. First, recall that quartz's DNA-like structure has a primary resonant affinity with human DNA and the blood crystals. In conjunction with crystal's capacity to be programmed with extremely great amounts of vibrational codes with high degrees of subtlety, the quartz witness can be programmed with an individual's most causal of bioenergetic codes in addition to its other component aspects. Here, the full-spectrum capabilities of quartz far exceed the more limited energy spectrum capacities of other witness-types. Further, the multidimensional responsiveness of the quartz medium is able to record the subtle level planes of the bioenergetic systems with greater wholeness and refined precision. In this respect, a crystal programmed with an individual's unique bioenergetic codes would be the most accurately complete vibrational profile-representation.

In addition, the witness–person interlinkage at a distance for purposes of radionic energy transfer would be more efficiently effected by a quartz witness. Quartz is the premier broad range interdimensional interconnection medium. It has an abiding, efficiently responsive resonant interrelationship with the Universal Energy Network (UEN) in general and the planetary energy network in particular. Therefore, a programmed witness crystal has a preexisting disposition to being multidimensionally interactive with the very network that enacts radionic energy transfer. Because the witness–person interaction is optimally effected, the radionic stimulation of the witness with specific treatment energetics will be transmitted to the person with the highest level of amplified efficiency. The crystal itself amplifies the treatment input as a natural part of its dynamics, interlinks energy code-patterns with appropriate access parameters of the planetary energy network, and completes the transfer to the individual in an amplified, efficient manner.

For these reasons, the utilization of quartz crystal witnesses stands as a fundamental modality of the near future. Witness dynamics are best with two crystals—one used by the practitioner and one used by the recipient, kept within the recipient's bioenergetic field especially during a radionic treatment as a tuned amplifying receiver-transducer.

2. Crystals can be programmed with specific thought-patterns or other energy frequencies whereby they will be held steady in the crystalline matrix as a tool of radionic application to the witness. Single programs, be they a homeopathic remedy, gem tincture, vitamin, herb, or operator-formulated thought-field, can be instilled within the quartz matrix.* The crystal then functions as a tool that can be used in conjunction with the substance itself (for example, a vitamin) in the radionic well or focus point to not only provide valuable associative amplification factors but also a stronger interdimensional interlinkage for an optimal transfer of energy to the recipient. In the case of the program being an operator-formulated thought-field, the crystal performs the same functions as just cited for substance-based programs and also holds the thought-program steady and focused. This stabilized focusing helps to neutralize the fluctuating cycles of attentiveness and distractedness of the operator's consciousness as well as providing an excellent link-up point for the mind–crystal dynamics. Further, a single crystal can be programmed with the full complement of a recipient's treatment regime. Such a custom-programmed crystal placed in the radionic well or transmission area will provide valuable complementary dynamics.

3. An intriguing experiment would be to attempt to program a crystal in a Rae Potentizer. This is a device that uses Rae cards having a specific angular configuration that corresponds to a particular energy pattern. A card is picked and then energized in the machine and the stimulated energy patterns are then instilled into a solution used afterward for treatment. Perhaps this procedure could generate the same effect in a crystal as in the solutions.

Concerning this device, Dr. William Tiller states:

> The simple device serves as an amplifier to build the requisite molecules inherent in the pattern residing at the mind-lattice level of the universe. This pattern utilizes the deltrons inherent in the solvent and charges the solution, contained in a recessed wall of the device, with the requisite pattern to the requisite potency. It is a materialization event on the etheric and deeper levels of substance.[4]

4. Crystals may prove for some to be ideal rubbing plates. A high degree of attunement between the individual and a specially chosen crystal is optimal. Programming it for this function would facilitate best results.

5. The crystal gridwork concept would integrate elegantly with numerous radionic modalities. As discussed in greater detail in Chapter 14, gridworks create a Unified Energy Field (UEF), and different geometric gridwork patterns produce a variety of modulatable energetic fields. To surround a radionic device with a crystal gridwork would generate an encompassing UEF, adding significant amplification, interdimensional interlinkage, and gridwork-geometry modulatable effects to magnify radionic treatment effectiveness. For even more treatment specificity, the gridwork crystals could be programmed with energy patterns that the recipient needs. Further, these specifically programmed crystals could be placed at a level

*See Chapter 8.

II gridwork position with the same number of crystals in back of them as in a level I placement.

6. Similar to the way Benoytosh Bhattacharya in his *Gem Therapy* presents the modality in which a rotating silver disc with select gems attached irradiates witness photographs of treatment recipients,[5] the disc concepts presented in Chapter 13 can be utilized in radionic applications. The discs shown in this book demonstrate that numerous customized variations upon this theme are possible. These discs can be rotated at modulatable speeds so that their radiative emissions are infused into a quartz witness. As with Bhattacharya, the results would be quite effective.

7. Discs and templates can be utilized as a type of miniature gridwork upon which a quartz witness is centrally positioned and then exposed to other appropriate radionic treatment modalities.

8. Appropriately sized faceted crystal forms can be used for their specific energetic properties in radionic treatments. Crystals of the 32 crystal classes and 5 Platonic solids would be especially useful spectrums of specialized vibrational tools that could selectively be added to the treatment energetics. (See Chapters 4 and 11 for further discussion of the importance and specificity of form energy dynamics.)

9. It might prove propitious to subject a recipient's personal crystal or other designated crystal to the treatment energetics, programming it beforehand to absorb the vibrational patterns of the treatment. The crystal so programmed would then be given to the recipient as an auxiliary tool to keep within his or her bioenergetic field to help sustain the momentum of the treatments by continually emitting subtle level vibratory influences duplicating the treatment energetics.

10. Concepts taken from multicomponent UEFs in Chapters 14 and Chapter 15 can be miniaturized into appropriately sized radionic treatment "chambers." More advanced UEFs integrate a multiplicity of components into an integrated whole. Such components include magnetics,chromatics, lasers, sonics, crystals, and others. Differently designed UEFs generate correspondingly varied results. Also, some of the components, especially chromatics, sonics, and lasers can be modulated as desired for a greater spectrum of possible effects. Within a miniaturized UEF, a quartz witness can be centrally placed and then exposed to appropriate modulated energetics. This radionic methodology of the future functions best when performed within Platonic solids or pyramidal frameworks. Laser applications, both to the witness' crystal and to the gridwork crystals during the course of a treatment, are exceptionally potent, especially with modulatable frequency capacities and laser scanners. Chapter 14 and Chapter 15 may further stimulate creative thoughts in this methodology realm.

The field of radionics is a multidimensionally oriented methodology. The incorporation of quartz crystals—the interdimensional interlinkage medium par excellence—with radionics blends together in perfect synergistic harmony. Multitudes of possibilities now stand open as crystal knowledge advances toward brilliant quantum leaps forward in increasingly technologically oriented modalities toward developments yet only dimly remembered.

CHAPTER 17
Healing With Crystals

Healing, in general, is the harmonizing of imbalanced energy fields toward their inherently perfect state of functioning. All levels of the bioenergetic system have an innate momentum to maintain homeostatic balance. Disease occurs when the underlying intelligence of the bioenergetic system (that is, the *vis medicatrix naturae*) is impeded by imbalanced energy patterns, thereby creating a state of dissonance and subsequent disorder. Healing consists of accentuating the natural resonant frequencies of a bioenergetic subsystem, thereby facilitating a return to its original order. When exposed to vibrational patterns of health, the resonance with the bioenergy's inherent underlying equilibrium either diffuses dissonant energies or synchronizes them with the harmonious frequencies. Essentially, balance resonates with balance and creates a situation in which imbalance cannot continue to occur. The role of a healing facilitator is to neutralize discordant interference with homeostasis and to accentuate the preexistent blueprint of perfection.

Crystal-based healing, in particular, uses the capabilities of quartz to receive, retain, modify, and transmit a broad range of energy patterns and frequencies in conjunction with its sensitive transductive responsiveness to higher dimensional Light-energies and human consciousness. Crystals exemplify the essence of healing with their precise, symmetrical patterns and resonating, balanced order. As these programmable qualities are projected from the crystal into the bioenergetic matrix, order reverberates with order, pattern with pattern, harmony with harmony, till the energies are one, and health is the inevitable result. Indeed, although crystals are but one tool of healing among many, they have certain distinctive properties that make them particularly versatile and effective. The highly ordered stability of quartz counterpointed by its sensitive programmability compose an exceptionally adaptable matrix capable of reproducing imprint-patterns with great precision and stable regularity. There is also an abiding affinity between the spiral molecular patternings of quartz and the DNA double helix of the bioenergetic system. In short, the remarkable similarity of spiral forms creates a strong, mutually resonant attraction between the two mediums such that energetic exchange occurs with high efficiency and sensitive precision. Some suitably prepared crystals can even function as DNA analogues in highly advanced healing methodologies. Further, the full-spectrum multidimensionally interactive quartz matrix makes it a tool that can work with numerous quantum energetic levels simultaneously and in harmonic synchronization. In healing this means that working with numerous bioenergetic levels at the same time is possible with interactive concord, thus making quartz the most holistic tool available. Add to all these characteristics those of energy amplification and a high interdimensional transparency quotient, and the quartz crystals can be seen as a chief healing modality unto itself and as an outstanding valuable cooperative agent with other healing methodologies.

Within these essential principles, many modes of application are possible. In the following material, numerous techniques are presented and seed-thoughts planted. In lieu of elaborately describing every procedure and exploring every thought in explicit detail, guidelines and directions are given in the hope of encouraging each individual to find those modifications and innovations that best suit the unique person and situation. The patterns of creativity and healing abilities manifest differently through everyone; and although certain fundamental principles of healing and crystal dynamics exist, there is yet great room for variation and experimentation within these predominating themes. Hereinafter, this chapter is an extension of the "Healing with Crystals" chapter of *Windows of Light* (Baer & Baer, pp. 94–107). When studying and reviewing crystal healing, it is recommended to use this chapter and the healing chapter in *Windows of Light* together for a more complete perspective.

1. As described in Chapter 7, the sonics–crystal interaction is a potent one. An excellent way to apply these energies in a unified manner is through tuning forks. With tuning forks one has the ability to know the exact vibrational frequency that is being applied. And with an entire set, a full octave range of tonal frequencies is available for specifically orchestrated vibrational applications done with exactitude. By applying the base of a vibrating tunig fork to a crystal, the sonics start to oscillate strongly through the quartz matrix. This is readily perceivable by touching the crystal. During sonics–crystal interaction the piezoelectric effect (and its higher octave correlating effects) are activated; the sound vibration is transduced into minute electric charges that oscillate on and off according to the periodicity of the specific sound. This helps to create not only an oscillating energy charge that the bioenergetic system can absorb but it also activates a much stronger replication and emission of the programmed energy codes held steady in the crystalline matrix. In this way, significant additional modulated energy is transferred into the bioenergetic system with considerably more force than when crystals alone are utilized. To experience the effect of using a single tuning fork alone without the amplifying benefit of a crystal, try placing one 1 to 6 inches away from a chakra area with the tip pointing in toward the chakra. Go slowly up and down the chakra column, feeling the differences in effects in each area. Try other sonic frequencies also. With some frequencies, a discordant resonant effect is noticed; once noted, do not apply the same tuning fork to the area again. With other sonic vibrations, a strong, harmonious interaction is felt. Two conclusions are plausible in this case—the frequency is the keynote of the chakra (or other bioenergetic subsystem) or it is a sound that that area needs for its balancing. In either case, the effect is positive and if it feels intuitively correct to apply to a given area, then the needed sonic vibration has been discerned. The discernment process can also be done as appropriate through other methodologies, for example, pendulums, radionics, pure intuition.

For application, place the crystal on the imbalanced bioenergy region. Orient the termination in alignment with the predominant flow of energy occurring in that region (for chakras, up and down the spine; for, say, an arm, in the direction of the acupuncture meridians). When appropriate, other healing modalities can precede this one, for example, the laying on of hands, acupuncture, massage. Then set the tuning fork in motion and place its base in contact with the crystal's body. As a general rule, this contact is optimally at the midpoint of the body between the two terminations of a double-termination or at the midpoint of the crystal body with a single termination. Hold the tuning fork in place until the vibrations become weak. Strike again and apply to the crystal. Continue with as many repetitions as you feel are needed. It is possible here to use one, two, or more different frequencies on any one area when appropriate. This sonics–crystal modality also works well as a chakra harmonization tune-up by laying a crystal on each of the chakras from the crown to coccyx and apply discerned sonics on every chakra in a progressive sequence.

As a variation on this concept, if a practitioner has a gradated series of bells that can be applied for healing, for example, Tibetan bells and tingshas, although it would not work to actually touch the bells to the crystals, by sounding the tones needed by the recipient and slowly sweeping around and over the entire body with crystals placed at strategic locations and by also focusing on specific imbalanced areas, a healing session could be quite effective.

2. Spraying crystal water over the body and aura in a fine mist helps to harmonize the aura and also imparts the crystal energy charge to both the body and aura. This is a fine adjunctive modality to incorporate when significant auric cleansing-releasing work is being done and also as a finishing integrative technique.

3. For many kinds of bodywork, the rolling of a polished or tumbled quartz over the back and up and down the spine works well as a preparatory and finishing modality. This action gently infuses crystalline radiance into the back as well as the spine and chakras, and helps predispose them to higher responsiveness to other applied healing techniques. When used at the end of a session it assists in the integration and assimilation of the benefits of the entire treatment. As a helpful side-effect, the facilitator's hands accumulate a noticeable energy charge that can then be applied in other ways to the recipient. It is important with this technique to use only a crystal that is smooth enough and of a shape with which the recipient is comfortable.

4. As a preparatory technique, the facilitator rolls a crystal with the termination pointing downward between the hands. Continuing the back and forth rolling motion, the facilitator positions the crystal and hands approximately 2 to 6 inches over the top of the recipient and systematically goes up and down the length of the body. For three to five minutes the outline of the aura and the full extent of the body is covered in this way with smooth, gradual sweeps. Special focus can be placed upon areas of known imbalance and up and down the spine. This method facilitates the preliminary charging and harmonization of the recipient's bioenergtic system so that subsequent healing modalities will be more effectively received. It also helps to create a balanced positive energetic link-up between the facilitator and recipient and charges the former's hands for later application.

5. With a lengthy double-terminated crystal of good quality, position the palms upward and lay a termination in each palm. Wrap the hands around each end and hold comfortably in a receptive state of consciousness for five to fifteen

minutes. This exercise will aid in the balancing of the left- and right-side biopolarities. Changing how the palms are oriented to the terminations will subtly alter the results. Instead of having both palms up, position both palms downward over top of the terminations; also, the right hand can be upward and the left downward, and vice versa.

6. A polished or tumbled crystal with a blunt termination can be easily integrated into healing disciplines that utilize bodily pressure. These disciplines include acupressure, hand and foot reflexology, neuromuscular therapy, some forms of massage, and trigger-point therapy.

7. Crystal balls are beneficial for pregnant woman and their unborn children because of the soft, diffuse, relaxing effects.

8. For accumulating a maximum energy charge for a healing application, place the crystals inside a small crystal gridwork or pyramid for 6 to 24 hours. After use, simply place them back into these energy fields to recharge them. The same can be done with pendants, personal crystals, and so on.

9. In *Magnetism and Its Effects on the Living System,* it is shown that there are key electromagnetic conversion areas that function as central energy crossover zones for certain aspects of the bioelectromagnetic energy flow.

> Of interest are two locations where no noticeable voltage readings were found. One is shown above the rectum near the base of the spine, and the other location is shown at the connecting link between the skull and the back bone proper, the beginning of the full-length spinal column.
>
> These two zero points on the human body are the electrical equators of the body's electrical and EM divisions. At these points is where the polarity of the voltages change from one form to another form.[1]

On the front of the body there are two more such areas located at the frontal crotch and over the thymus gland on the sternum.

Because of the centrality and causal nature of these four regions, the placing or taping of crystals on them is an excellent adjunctive method to facilitate the balancing of the bioelectromagnetic circulatory system. Double-terminations or 1½ inch- to 3 inch-base crystal pyramid is optimal. Apply the two crystals to the two regions of the front or back of the body depending on whether the individual is laying down on the back or stomach. Focused healing work can be applied through the two crystals on these electrical equators or they can be left there while healing energies are applied elsewhere.

10. Polarity therapy and the healing touch can easily integrate the use of crystals with only minor adjustments. The idea is to enact the therapy modalities without change, except hold crystals in the palms of the hands with the terminations pointing in the direction of the energy flow. The crystals can either be held in place in the hands by holding the thumb over them, or a white cotton wristband can be positioned around the palm area with the crystal held in the hand. Another way to amplify the energetics of these types of therapies is to take small, good quality double-terminations and position them under a wristband on the underside of the wrist. The crystals are pointing along the lengthwise axis of the arm. Other crystal modalities such as gridworks, the spinal energizer (see Chapter 13), wands, and so on can be added at the practitioner's discretion.

11. The results of color breathing can be considerably amplified when the therapy

is used in conjunction with crystals. In *The Seven Keys to Color Healing,* Roland Hunt comments on the effects of color breathing:

> Remember, whatever the disease being treated, it is through Color-breathing that you draw into your atomic structure a certain permanence of Color-balance, fixing the right color and consciously making it impossible to respond to future circumstances with the wrong color (thought). The lamp, or other means of Chrome-therapy, will cure your distress or disease, but permanent perfection of expression must come from your conscious cooperation with the chrome-practitioner (through color breathing).[2]

With the addition of crystals, this process can be made more efficient and effective. Use a crystal programmed generally to assist with color breathing techniques and specifically with a health-intention for a particular area. Place it on the area being worked with and visualize the incoming colored energy passing in and through the crystal as it goes into consciousness and is then directed to the imbalanced area. Follow these general guidelines: Quiet and relax consciousness. Discern what colors are to be applied to the affected areas. Try to obtain a sample of these colors for optimal imaging. With a good inner image of a color, close the eyes and breathe in slowly and deeply. As this is done, visualize a brilliant, rich stream of color being drawn through the crystal and into the brain-mind area. Accumulate a radiant pool of this Light-energy. Then, while holding the breath comfortably, mentally direct this color-radiance energy into the imbalanced area. See and feel the energy suffusing every atom of this area, changing and charging it into a higher state of balance. Next, exhale slowly and deeply as you visualize the static and imbalanced energy patterns being expelled through the mouth as a murky stream of energy. Continue this same cycle as many times as you feel is needed.

12. During healing sessions, the placing of crystals on the focal treatment areas for 5 to 15 minutes before they are actively worked on helps significantly in preparing those areas to be optimally receptive to applied healing energies. Simply place or tape a crystal generally programmed for this purpose on the primary imbalanced regions as the session starts. Then go through other procedures leading up to work on specific areas. The crystal may remain in place during the course of this focused healing also. After this is completed, the crystal may still remain in position on the body, or it may be replaced with another crystal specifically programmed to assist in the integration of healing energies.

13. A crystal placed on each chakra can be most effective as a chakra system healing and energizing technique. Optimally, nine double-terminations are used, each termination aligned along the spinal axis. The Alpha and Omega chakra crystals will need to be propped up by books or other neutral objects for correct positioning (see the "Alpha and Omega Chakras" section of Chapter 9 for further positioning information). If there are any logistical problems with keeping any of the other crystals in place, simply tape them into position. If single-terminations are the only crystals available for this technique, the way in which they point creates significantly different effects. With all the terminations pointing down the spinal axis (from Omega to Alpha), the energy flow will tend to be more grounding and physically energizing. With the terminations pointing upward, from Alpha to Omega, the effect will be more spiritually uplifting and higher consciousness

energizing and activating. Also, 1 inch to 1½ inch-base crystal pyramids function with excellent effect when used as a chakra set.

This modality can be used in conjunction with myriad healing and self-transformation techniques, both personal and professional. In any situation where the amplified energizing and coupling of the chakra system as a whole is desired, this modality is quite helpful.

14. Auric feathering can be done with crystals as a preparatory-evaluative and finishing technique. Hold one crystal in the left hand pointing upward into the arm and rest of body—this is the receptive, energy ingathering side. Hold the other crystal in the right hand with the thumb holding it in position pointing outward along with the fingers—this is the active, distributive side. With the recipient in a comfortable position, make gradual, graceful, sweeps over and around the entire bioenergetic system. Allow healing energies to flow as this process unfolds. Follow intuition as to how far away from the body the hand and crystal are, where to concentrate attention, and the rhythmic patterning of the hand in motion. Be sensitive to fluctuations in the "feel" of the aura, for this can provide clues as to the health status of the individual and where the primary areas of imbalance are. There might be areas of greater and lesser heat–cold, depression–hyperactivity, bumpiness–smoothness, and so on. When using this technique at the end of a session, the facilitator can obtain feedback as to effects of the session by comparing the status of the aura at the end versus the beginning. Also, it helps the recipient to integrate the effects of the treatment with higher efficiency and depth.

15. To help maintain a balance of the mineral crystallinity of the body, it is many times useful to regularly take multimineral and cell salt supplements. Body metabolism requires more than 70 minerals for optimal functioning, most of them in trace amounts. Look for a mineral supplement with an analysis showing a large amount of trace minerals in its composition. Check the product further before deciding to purchase it. Twelve primary cell salts are necessary to metabolic harmony, including the blood system. Check literature on this subject to help determine any specific cell salts that might be needed. It is many times a good practice to take a supplement that includes small amounts of all twelve cell salts. The silica cell salt is sometimes needed in greater quantities than normal by people experiencing high-energy changes and transformation, especially those who live with many crystals in their environment.

16. A 3 to 4 inch (or larger) diameter crystal ball can be utilized by a healing facilitator to receive a strong energy charge into the hands for application to a recipient. Place the crystal ball within easy access to the therapy area and maintain it, optimally, in a small surrounding permanent gridwork (all terminations point into the center). If possible, also position a pyramid so that the ball is within the outline of its framework. When the facilitator wants an energy charge, the hands are placed on the ball. Draw to the hands from the crystal the charge that has accumulated in the ball. Concentrate on magnetically attracting this energy to the hands for 30 to 60 seconds, generating a greater and greater charge. Then apply this energy to the recipient as needed. Repeat the cycle as often as desired.

17. A set of color programmed crystals can be useful for applying an orchestrated spectrum of color-crystal vibrations in a healing sequence. With each different color vibration a particular effect corresponds that is predictable and repeatable;

these color-specific qualities and effects are presented in numerous color healing books. A crystal can be programmed so that it holds a distinct color vibration steady within its matrix structure. That vibration then becomes the predominant energetic influence that emits from the crystal. Not only this, but the color frequency is amplified so that its effects are magnified. With a color-crystal set a full spectrum of vibrational influences is at hand, to be applied to suit the needs of an individual or situation.

This concept can be applied to other types of energies, such as sound. A chakra set wherein each crystal is programmed to work on a specific chakra is also helpful for both personal and professional applications.

18. One crystal gazing method is to take the largest facet of an appropriate crystal and press it lightly against the third eye. Hold it there and project consciousness into the crystalline matrix. Maintain consciousness inside the crystal with a focused state of receptivity—simply be open to the flow of the experience. This is a good basic technique for energizing and activating the third eye.

This technique also works well with Brazilian river tumbled quartz. Such specimens are crystals that were naturally tumbled in river streams over the years. Gradually the defined edges and termination were abraded away, leaving an oval to egg shape, usually clear on the inside and opaque to translucent on the outside. Many times a thin section is sawed off one end, creating a window into the interior of the crystal. It is this window that is placed on the third eye to do the crystal gazing technique.

19. It is imperative to clear and cleanse crystals after using them in healing processes. Whether it is a short technique or one that takes 24 to 48 hours, this needs to be done, especially with those crystals that have been utilized to absorb imbalanced energy patterns. Once a crystal has absorbed such patterns, it will tend to retain them in its structure; if used again, this imbalanced vibrational pattern can be transferred. Hence the need to be attentive to this aspect of crystal energy dynamics. (See the section entitled "Clearing and Cleansing Crystals" in Chapter 6.)

20. Another healing modality that works well in and of itself, and can also be amplified by its conjunctive use with crystals, is toning as presented in *Toning: The Creative Power of the Voice*, by Laurel Elizabeth Keyes. Here is another application of the sonics–crystal synergy. Toning involves the generation of sonic frequencies through the vocal chords. As Keyes describes it:

> When one has a pain somewhere in the body one begins Toning as low as the voice can reach, and slowly raises the pitch, as a siren sound rises. One will find that *there is a Tone which resonates with the pain and relieves the tension*. This is all done with sensitivity to feeling. To get an idea of this, place your finger against your nose and hum, directing the sound to that spot. Notice the sensation, inside, of the resonance. While this is not as definite in other parts of the body, it can be determined, and that is the tone that will relieve pain. Every pain has its companion tone and by pulsating the Tone softly for a time—as long as it feels good, 15 minutes or an hour—the pain will be relieved or eliminated. It is an escape valve for the pain because it is breaking up the tension which we label "pain" and it brings new life energy to that place.[3]

To add crystals, find two that are suited to working with sonics. One is held in the left hand and positioned in front of the throat during the course of the exercise.

The other crystal is held in the right hand and used to focus, amplify, and modulate the applied toning frequencies within the area being healed. After finding the tone that is needed for a specific area of imbalance, position the right hand's crystal directly over that area with the termination pointing toward it. First, establish a resonant interlinkage between the crystal and the focal region; as the tone is generated, focus awareness on this area while rotating the crystal in both clockwise and counterclockwise circles. After a short time, there should be a subtly perceptible energetic charge and link-up. Then, while still toning, describe rhythmic counterclockwise circles approximately 1 to 4 inches from the body surface. The counterclockwise motion is to facilitate the releasing the drawing out of disharmonious energy patterns. After a period of time, a sufficient charge will have built up within the crystal; at that point, gradually spiral the crystal upward and away from the body while retaining the energy charge. When the crystal reaches about 1 to 1½ feet away from the body, abruptly snap the wrist and crystal like cracking a whip, optimally directing the resultant energy release into an awaiting jar of saline solution. Continue this drawing out and releasing cycle for as many times as felt necessary.

Next, still while toning, describe clockwise circles above the area in a rhythmic manner. The clockwise motion facilitates the infusion of positive healing patterns and energies. Continue as long as is needed. Then, after the toning cycle for that region is complete, place or tape another crystal programmed for the healing of the specific area directly over it for purposes of optimal integration of the healing energies.

21. The next technique utilizes the same primary clockwise–counterclockwise energy dynamics as described in number 20. Here, sonics is not necessarily a part of this crystal healing technique. The facilitator takes a crystal in the left hand with the crystal termination pointing up into the arm and rest of the body; this is to amplify the bioelectromagnetism and higher channeling capacities of the individual. In the right hand is another crystal that is conducive to the strong projecting of energy flow. The facilitator could use instead in the right hand a projectively oriented crystal wand. Over the imbalanced area of the recipient, first gradually spiral into the auric field (counterclockwise motion). So as not to enter the auric field too abruptly and to facilitate the introduction of the facilitator's and crystal's energies in a harmonious, graceful manner, take a minute or so to spiral into the field over the imbalanced region. Next, continue counterclockwise circles 1 to 4 inches away from the body, establishing a resonant link-up. After further circles are done, an energy charge will build up; gradually spiral upward from the body 1½ to 2 feet and snap the wrist like cracking a whip, directing the released energy into a jar of saline solution. Repeat the releasing–drawing out process several times.

Then, describe clockwise circles over the region to infuse positive energies. During this time especially, the facilitatoı opens up as a channel for higher energy flow. Also, by aligning one of the crystal's largest facets toward the recipient and rhythmically pumping it in an up and down motion, the recipient's auric field may be amplified. Continue with the infusion of positive healing vibrations until the cycle is felt to be complete. Last, place or tape a crystal programmed to assist with the healing of the region on the area itself for at least 5 to 20 minutes.

22. Another way to enter into a recipient's auric field in a balanced, nonabrupt

manner (in addition to the spiraling technique described in number 21), is to key into the aura. This is done by rotating the lengthwise axis of the crystal 180° as it is gradually introduced into the auric field, moving from its perimeter to a few inches away from the body. This technique facilitates an area-specific accessing and phase-locking; it creates a facilitory energetic pathway through which applied healing energies may be inserted-infused into a particular bioenergetic region. After completing focused channeling of balancing energies into the desired area, disengage from it by repeating the keying technique from inside of the aura outward.

23. The importance of utilizing some sort of modality for accumulating ambient imbalanced energy patterns in a professional clinical environment cannot be overemphasized. The disharmonious vibrations released during the healing process must be accounted for, focused into a controlled energy field, and then disposed of. This is necessary not only for the practitioner's well-being, but also so that treatment recipients do not pick up the released energy patterns of previous recipients. The professional healing environment, no matter what the methodologies utilized—from bodywork to chiropractic to counseling—must be impeccably maintained as an integral part of the practitioner's responsibility to recipients as well as to the Higher Evolution. Herein are a number of effective modalities in this regard.

a) A supersaturated saline solution in a gallon jar with a crystal programmed for "imbalanced and static energy accumulation" can be set near the treatment area of the room. It creates an energy sink—an energy field that naturally attracts and holds steady the disharmonious vibrations. When engaging in healing techniques that actively pull out imbalanced energies, they can be consciously directed into the solution (a crystal will help focus and direct this process). Between every treatment session empty the saline solution and replace it for use in the next session.

b) Continuous running water in the form of a miniature waterfall or even through a sink faucet is effective.

c) Air ionizers are helpful also, although they must be used in conjunction with other environmental clearing techniques such as the saline solution. (Air ionizers are especially needed in clinical environments in large city locations because of the pervasive air impurities that, if not countered, subtly but significantly impede optimal healing processes.)

d) The generation of strong electrical discharges is a superior clearing modality. Such discharges, done with sufficient force and repetition, cause the precipitation and diffusion of subtle energy imbalance patterns. One means with which to achieve this effect is to rub two crystals (very lower end quality that cannot be used for any higher applications) together rapidly, continuing this motion while walking slowly around the room, putting special attention over the treatment area. When this is done in a darkened room, the white triboluminescent light flashes can be seen generating through the crystals. Other even more effective means include such devices as: Van de Graff generators, Tesla coils, electrostatic generators, and Jacob's Ladder plasma generators. In between each session, these devices can be turned on for approximately five minutes.

e) As an end-of-the-day technique to ensure complete clearing, the practitioner can take a palm-size ring magnet in each hand (so that the magnets attract one another when the two palms are brought together) and rhythmically bring them toward and away from one another all around the room, especially over the treatment area. If a gridwork or other crystals are in the room, perform this technique over and around each of them at the end of very day.

With the conscientious application of the preceding methods, optimal professional and spiritual responsibilities in this regard can be fulfilled in maintaining a healing environment in which optimal benefits to treatment recipients can occur.

24. By modulating the breath, different energy flow patterns are created within and emitting from the individual. It is known in the yogic science of pranayama that the breathing mirrors the state of consciousness. By consciously modifying the breath flow patterns, certain corresponding desired and reproducible energetic effects can be generated. By focusing awareness upon a crystal while performing regulated breathing patterns, the corresponding breath-caused energy patterns can be focused, modulated, and amplified through the crystalline matrix. Because of the difficulty of describing such techniques in writing, only an overview of some of these methods will be presented.

a) Long, slow inhalation; hold the breath and focus energies and intention; expel forcefully the entire exhalation in and through the crystal. This will create a laserlike burst of energy streaming from the crystal, having a very deeply penetrating action. Such a technique can be utilized to dislodge deep-rooted imbalanced energy patterns as well as to infuse healthy vibration-codes into a given area. This archetypal methodology has been most highly developed by the noted crystal authority Marcel Vogel.

b) Long, slow inhalation; hold the breath and focus energies and intention; rhythmic pulsing exhalation concentrated through the crystal. The energetic effect from this can be visualized as wavefronts of energy, each one at a harmonic interval from the others. The results are less forceful and penetrating than the technique described in (a); the energies are still intense but more oriented toward the reinforcement of positive healing patterns as the wavefronts infuse the area with pulsed crystalline radiance. This modality is quite effective when applied after deep healing work has been done to reinforce the assimilative integrity of the health-patterns. Alternately, it can be used to energize a region having depressed energy activity, including the chakras. Especially efficacious in this regard is to place a crystal programmed with healing patterns for a specific region and then to utilize the pulsed breath technique, directing the energies through the crystal in the right hand into the programmed crystal.

c) Long, slow inhalation; hold the breath and focus energies and intention; slow, slightly forced, even exhalation. The effects can be visualized as a steady stream of soft and diffuse but focused energy emitting from the crystal. The exhalation is through pursed lips in conjunction with a slowly indrawing diaphragm so that there is a slightly forced energy stream effect. This method is best used for soft energizing and for application of focused soothing, integrative energy influences.

Experiment with these techniques, experiencing their different effects. Allow personal intuitive intelligence to assist in refining and modifying them as appropriate.

25. Crystal Ball Therapy: This new type of treatment modality is one that uses diverse types and sizes of mineral balls for soft, but deepingly affecting healing of a wide spectrum of imbalances. The sphericity of the crystal ball generates an

omnidirectional emission of highly balanced, softly radiant, holistic energies. The spherical form is a classic study of a perfectly symmetric, harmonious, yin form. As form determines energy dynamics, the resulting emissions carry such qualities, and in the context of crystal ball therapy, infuse these properties with subtle penetration into the recipient. As the size and substance of which the ball is composed varies, the archetypal emission properties are infused with different complementary qualities.

The types of balls possible to use are multitudinous. Possibilities include: clear quartz, rose quartz, citrine, amethyst, tourmalinated quartz, rutilated quartz, smoky quartz, quartz mined from diverse areas around the world, Herkimer diamond, electroplated gems, and other types of minerals. A very extensive set of such balls could constitute a large selection of vibrational qualities from which to choose to meet the needs of particular situations.

The primary way to use these balls is to roll them on the recipient's skin, ranging from extremely gentle to firm pressure, depending upon the circumstances. Larger balls can be used for larger applications areas, like the back and spine. Smaller balls can be applied in very small areas where precision is needed. Gem tinctures may be placed on an area, with the ball helping to massage and infuse the tincture vibrations into the desired zone. Other application modes can be reviewed in nos. 7 and 16.

Crystal ball therapy may be used as a primary or adjunctive therapeutic modality. One may envision specialists in this field with a roomful of diverse mineral ball-tools in a gridwork of large balls and an illuminated ball suspended overhead; a UEF offering the radiantly balanced gentleness of healing that balls so well facilitate.

CHAPTER 18

The Human Biocrystalline Energy System

The perception of the human being as a multilevel, multidimensional biocrystalline energy system is central to every level of health-care and evolutionary growth modalities. The individual is a microcrystalline system resonating in integral interlinkage within a universal macrocrystalline system, within a megacrystalline oversystem. It is the universal principle of crystallinity that holds the latticework of manifestation in resonant, intercommunicative coherence. Humankind, as a jewellike subsystem floating in unified interconnection within the celestial-cosmic master latticework, partakes of the grander scales of universal evolutionary unfoldment and maintains ordered synchrony on the self's microscales through this essential crystallinity.

This keynote concept pervades this book. This chapter presents a complementary compendium of significant ideas and perspectives in this subject. In this way, a more inclusive overview plus further informational specificity will help deepen levels of understanding and insight concerning this subject.

GENERAL PERSPECTIVES

> The whole human biological structure can be viewed as an aggregate of liquid crystals and much of the human body is made of such liquid crystals like cholesterol, these crystal structures receiving the radiations of nature peculiar to each crystal form. . . . when crystals are squeezed or pressured by electrical charges or excited by radiation of any form from an external source, they themselves begin to oscillate and begin to produce electro-magnetic radiomagnetic wave-fields from the nucleus of their atoms. The first radio sets were crystal oscillators and perhaps the human being will be the ultimate radio set when he can . . . excite his own molecular crystal structure through the induction of cosmic rays.[1]

> In the likeness and appearance of a "Whole Light Being," the human body can receive instructions of how its C-O-H-N structure (Carbon-Oxygen-Hydrogen-Nitrogen) is a semiconductor for the action potential pulse coming directly from higher universal intelligence which can remake the energy blueprint of man according to the Divine "image."[2]

> Every decade of research acquaints us with new facets of a cosmos of metals

within us. In the world outside we come again and again upon new deposits in the earth, which enable us to advance in civilization; in the inner world of the body, every new layer of activities permeated by metals are lifted into our consciousness. We not only breathe with iron, but we need copper to form our blood and cobalt to escape pernicious anemia. As the methods of investigation become more refined, we constantly discover more metals to be regular components of our bodies. We find them, however, not as building blocks in the grosser sense, but as instruments by which our human entity carries out significant physiological activities.[3]

Semiconduction occurs only in materials having an orderly molecular structure, such as crystals, in which electrons can move easily from the electron cloud around one atomic nucleus to the cloud around another. . . .

[Albert] Szent-Gyorgyi pointed out that the molecular structure of many parts of the cell was regular enough to support semiconduction. . . . In it he conjectured that protein molecules, each having a sort of slot or way station for mobile electrons, might be joined together in long chains so that electrons could flow in a semiconducting current over long distances without losing energy, much as in a game of checkers one counter could jump along a row of other pieces across the entire board. Szent-Gyorgyi suggested that the electron flow would be similar to photosynthesis . . . in which a kind of waterfall of electrons cascaded step by step down a staircase of molecules, losing energy with each bounce. The main difference was that in protein semiconduction the electrons' energy would be conserved and passed along as information instead of being absorbed and stored in the chemical bonds of food.[4]

These elements represent the trigger fields which set off ionisation processes in the oxygen-filled brain and how these create radio-electromagnetic emanations by re-radiating light energies. It is common sense that these two alkaline metals with positive ions are the two most predominant in the brain since they both are among the most abundant elements on the planet ranking sixth and seventh of all the crystal elements found in the earth's crust. It is not surprising that sodium and potassium are essential components of all animal and plant cells since sodium ($Na+$) is the principal cation of the fluids outside the cells of all living matter and potassium ($K+$) is the principal cation for the fluids inside the cells.[5]

Natural nutrients can also be distinguished from synthetic through "chromatogram" microphotography of the sensitive crystallization structures. Chromatograms of natural substances will show a definite balanced snowflake pattern, whereas synthetically created nutrients show no pattern at all.[6]

Various undulations and spike formulations in a pattern enable researchers to recognize biological activity and intrinsic values revealed in natural substances but not in synthetic or highly refined preparations. Ehrenfried Pfeiffer, M.D., Ph.D., Biochemical Research Laboratories.

In the human body as well as in industry, in chemistry and in semiconductors only a trace a catalyst is needed to accelerate the reaction. In the case of a semiconductor the adding of an impurity to the crystal makes it an acceptor or donor type crystal. If we treat the human cell as a conglomerate of liquid crystals we can see that there must be impurities and catalysts which trigger the exchange of electrons between the different types of cells, acting as semiconductors, and their atomic reactions. They accelerate the metabolism of the natural elements of which our skin, bone and muscles are made.[7]

A more complex liquid crystal is the kind that harbors cholesterol and comes in thousands of one-molecule-thick layers, with the molecules lying flat like sleeping soldiers, their long axes parallel to the plane of the layer and to each other but with each layer's axes rotated 15 minutes of arc relative to the next (the very same angle, by the way, that the radii of both sun and moon subtend from Earth), therefore cumulatively forming a helical progression of polarity that is common to all genes and protoplasm. The potent effect on penetrating light of this 15-minute twist of polarity per molecule can be judged slightly by the fact that it adds to a spin of 18,888 degrees or fifty full revolutions for every millimeter the light travels![8]

Bio-crystals are metastable equilibrium systems with a negative surface tension at the biocrystal's interface with its environment. Unique conditions obtain in the case of the polypeptide molecules contained in biocrystals; on the one hand, the macromolecule chain becomes an ordered structure and acquires elements of symmetry (corresponding to the lattice of a polypetide crystal), but the flexible lateral substituents have the properties of molecules in liquid and the increased entropy of molecules in solution. . . . Thus, in biological systems, a change in the symmetry groups and a distortion of the geometry of space at the molecular level are possible and, consequently, the formation of a gravitational field, with all its attendant consequences, is also possible. In this way, theoretical calculations support our hypothesis that a biogravitational field may result from changes in the conformation of protein molecules subjected to compression, tension, and deformation.[9]

Throughout the human organism we find gold, silver, mercury, tin, etc., in minimal traces, each metal in a different distribution. In one organ more, in another less. Some play an essential role in constructing certain organs, where their grosser materiality is needed to serve as building blocks. . . . but for the most part metals are active in the body in extreme degrees of dilution, thus indicating that what counts is not their materiality but their dynamic way of working.

. . . The metals affect man not only in his body but also in his consciousness, in his soul and spirit. They speak a language that conveys their nature more impressively as these effects move into higher spheres of existence. . . . the higher a being rises and the more it is able to express its own essence, the better it can express the regions of the world from which it derives.[10]

Their [the liquid crystals of the cells] atoms vibrate at critical molecular frequencies at the electron level and the nucleus of their atoms also resonates at critical frequencies which is determined by our state of consciousness. This in turn is controlled by the psychic electricity (prana) generated by the interaction of incoming light photons with the auric rings or spheres of subtle matter around a person which is in turn controlled by the chakra system. The evolution of the chakra system determines the type of resonant antenna each person creates with their consciousness.[11]

The transformation of the specie occurs through the infusion of light crystals which generate a field of Light around the body and a feeding of Light to the body for the next stage of creation.[12]

The physical body can be infused with the higher dimensions of Light working through meridians of crystalline energy fields surrounding the human network.[13]

Those who will be delivered directly from the face of the Earth will be taken through the crystalline staircase that corresponds to the Christ crystal within their body of physical form.[14]

THE HUMAN AS A MULTIDIMENSIONAL RESONATOR-ANTENNA SYSTEM

"The mind is in a field of Light and a field of Light within a field of Light and eternal Light." And the Eternal Mind is constantly imprinting functions of the eternal in every form of life.

A physical specie then serves as one of the membrane types between star systems as a holograph within the Mind. This membrane is instant media for the cosmic circuit.

Thus, man is as much in space as space is in man, for he, in actuality, is a thinking membrane between the luminaries.[15]

The brain of main is part of the Divine Mind, and by decoding the human brain's mechanisms of memory storage in relationship to the universal language process, a higher hierarchical memory is revealed and Man discovers that he is a pulsating geometry of a Divine Language system.[16]

On a microbiological level . . . the body is able to communicate as an antenna receiving Light forms of consciousness energy from other spatial dimensions and converting those given forms of energy into its own bioenergy.[17]

The human body, then, has the awareness that just as there are twelve meridians of Light connected to the seed crystal, the third eye of the body, so also the planetary membrane, the planetary biocomputer, has twelve Light focal channels. These channels are used to reprogram the human creation and act as key points for the exodus that occurs from this threshold control to the next ordering of evolution.[18]

The De La Warr group has found that around every human being is a "magnetic" force-field with a pattern of nodal points, vortices of energy, similar to that of a bar magnet. Each of these points, they explain, is in contact with the person to whom they belong. . . . Other investigators maintain that nodal points are resonance bonds which function to bind man, and all things, to the creative force-field of the universe. Phil Allen in *Energy, Matter and Form* explains how these nodal points occur inside the body as acupoints; the high energy bonds at the acupuncture meridian systems.[19]

The basic idea in radionics is that each individual, organism, or material radiates and absorbs energy via a unique wave field which exhibits certain geometrical, frequency and radiation-type characteristics. This is an extended force field that exists around all forms of matter whether animate or inanimate. . . . The more complex the material, the more complex the wave form. Living things, like humans, emit a very complex wave spectrum of which parts are associated with the various organs and systems of the body.[20]

We must begin to look at the human body as a broadband antenna system fed by multiple oscillators. . . .

This is the acupuncture point/meridian system network of the body. If this network utilizes the autonomic nervous system as "wiring," then an absolutely exquisite antenna can be fabricated from the 600,000 miles of wire available. Such a large antenna is technically capable of a truly amazing information handling capacity; i.e., for reception, discrimination, processing and transmission of information. One can model the acupuncture points as the active end-points of a multi-element antenna array system. This would be a phase-array with the acupuncture points (points of high electrical conductance) being either the radiant sources (transmission) or the radiant sinks (reception) of the array system.[21]

If the whole human body resonated at its characteristic wavelength, a wave about two meters long would be necessary. However, since our insides are made up of numerous channels, tubes, nerve bundles, air spaces, liquid-filled enclosures and cavities, we can expect our bio-resonators to be of varying shapes and sizes. We can also expect that a *set* of different frequencies might bring about bioresonance, which could be electrical, magnetic, or acoustic in nature, perhaps a combination of all three.[22]

We can point to numerous parts of the human body that offer a striking resemblance to part of radio sets. There are nerve groupings that resemble coils, ganglia that remind us of triodes, parts of the body where AC seems to be rectified into DC and, according to Dr. R. O. Becker, we also seem to have developed a biotransistor in our nervous systems.[23]

ATP is the key to the whole field of biological transduction, whereby Light-giving energy can be brought through from Higher Evolutionary sources.

ATP is the ideal model of the transceiver system, built into the human biological system, which allows man to attach the energy he is receiving (in successive unfoldments) with a pure unfoldment of Light.

. . . ATP is the life antenna that receives the wave form that can collectively control the biological mechanisms, protein synthesis, and the nature of genetic coding simultaneously from several energy configurations of hydrolysis.

. . . In fact, ATP contains a symmetrical head upon a stalk and a base, which gives a schematic on the order of a keyhole configuration or a "Tesla magnifying transmitter device."[24]

MINERAL SALTS OF THE BODY

The paramount importance of the inorganic constituents of the cell substance . . . are the vital portions of the body, the workers, the builders; that the water and organic substances forming the remainder of the organism are simply inert matter used by these salts in building the cells of the body.[25]

The law is "that every form of energy acts through some particular form of matter." . . . to this I may now add: The vital force of organic life not only selects the twelve mineral salts of organic nature through which to act, but it also selects some particular grouping of these salts for the expression of each of its several functions.[26]

In order to bring clearly before the mind the importance of the mineral salts as the physical basis of life, I must enumerate the functions performed by them . . . .

The mineral composition of cells determines the kind of tissues and organs they build.

As bearers of the vital force they give expression to all of life's functions.

. . . They determine whether the vital force shall express motor, nutritive, sensatory, or volitional energy.

. . . They connect the consciousness with the external world through the five senses.

. . . They are the media through which the body develops in response to impressions made upon the vital force.

Finally, they give expression through the features to the intelligence, moral qualities, and emotions of the soul.[27]

BONE

Bone is extraordinary in structure. . . . It's composed of two dissimilar materials—a collagen, a long-chain, fibrous protein that's the main structural material of the entire body, and apatite, a crystalline mineral that's mainly calcium phosphate. The electron microscope shows that the association between collagen and apatite is highly ordered, right down to the molecular level. The collagen fibers have raised transverse bands that divide them into regular segments. The apatite crystals, just the right size to fit snugly between these bands, are deposited like scales around the fibers.

This intricacy continues at higher levels of organization. The collagen fibers lie side by side in layer upon layer wound in opposed spirals (a double helix) around a central axis.[28]

Salt that has just crystallized out of solution gives us an archetypal picture of how the skeleton is formed. The human bony system "crystallizes" in the fluid embryo in the same way that salt cubes take shape in the mother solution. . . . The forces at work here are densifying, shaping ones.[29]

PROTEIN

The fact that light can spontaneously be emitted from organic compounds and molecules found in cell proteins suggests that the proteins of the human body are not inert masses of insensitive flesh but act as semiconductors and transistors like we use in radio reception.[30]

Once absorbed, the light is either stored as psychic electricity in the electron charge on the semiconductor proteins or used in the liquid crystal body waters in the protonic energy of consciousness.[31]

A biogravitational field arises in consequence of changes in the conformation of protein structures as a result of the transformations which occur with polypeptide molecules. These changes in conformation induce a strictly ordered, structured crystalline state in the hydrated protein molecules and their oscillations are synchronized, as a result of which a qualitatively new physical situation is established, affecting the atom's symmetry groups and the nature of the submolecular space.[32]

BLOOD

The blood is indeed the *archetypal organ of liquid flow.* As a liquid it has all organic formation potentially within it. As "blood" it is the expression of the spiritual being according to the Idea of whom the various organs are moulded and assembled to form a total organism—the body in which this being may live.[33]

There are present *real formative forces,* of which the blood is the carrier. These are the forces which are effective in the structure and the constitution of the human being, at the same time causing the differentiation of the human being in such a way that they direct completely the catabolic and anabolic processes.[34]

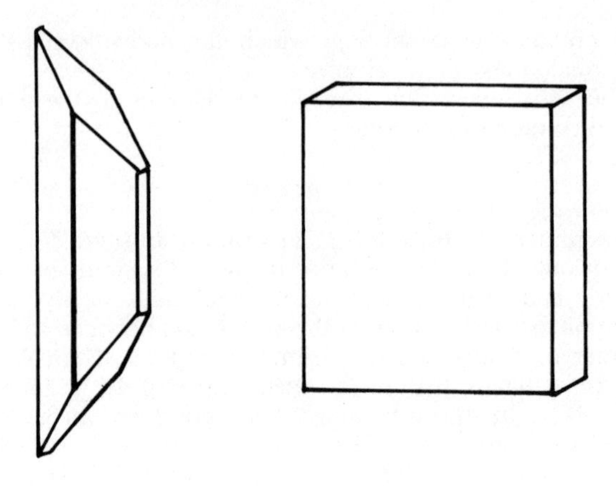

Figure 164: Two Crystalline Forms of Hemoglobin

There are in fact formative forces in nature which cannot be pinpointed in the EM spectrum. E. Pfeiffer has produced patterns of some of them in rather the same way that many of us produced patterns of magnetic forces in iron filings when we were at school.

He covered a smooth plate of glass with a thin film of copper chloride which crystallizes when it cools. By adding the juices of various plants, human or animal saliva, urine, or diluted blood, he found that the radiations from these substances draw characteristic designs in the crystals. Lily juice, for instance, draws a sort of "lily picture," while agave produces a strange design which appears prickly.

Blood, he concluded, possesses a strong radiative energy and each person has his own peculiar blood crystallization pattern.[35]

Metal concentrations in human plasma:
magnesium, iron, aluminum, zinc—D1 to D2
copper, magnanese—D2 to D3
arsenic, titanium, vanadium, chrome, nickel, strontium, lithium—D3 to D4
silver, cobalt, rubidium, tin, molybdenum—D4 to D5
gold, uranium—D5 to D6
radium—D11
D represents the decimal potency used in homeopathy, and is used here because it so clearly expresses the relationship in figures. Thus D1 corresponds to a dilution of 1 to 10, D2 of 1 to 100, etc.[36]

In the sphere of material substance we can trace the ego organization by the presence of sugar. Where sugar is, there is the ego organization. . . . Sugar is . . . present in the blood. The sugar-containing blood, circulating through the body, pervades it with the ego organization.[37]

The hemoglobin molecule . . . may be described as a crystalline organism whose main body contains four sections, each centered in an iron atom capable of grabbing and holding an oxygen molecule.[38]

One aspect of Christ's Second Coming is the infusion of Aquarian Christ

Consciousness that is downpouring now in increasing torrents of Akashic Christ Substance—a high voltage essence now transmuting the human blood stream.[39]

Through such an attunement, the blood of the initiate will ultimately become liquid light. . . .

This Mind level is charged with cosmic crystalline force, flowing down into man's mundane awareness if such awareness opens itself to receive it. For those who do, the blood stream is gradually becoming a river of light—charged with the love of God.[40]

Min-Ha-Ada-Mah means "blood from the ground" as opposed to Men-Ha-Ada-Mah which means "blood transposed into the next level of creation." The former represents earthbound intelligence that cannot communicate with the Divine Mind through the necessary bio-engineering. The latter represents the transformation of the blood crystals and the freeing of the human chemistry from the earthbound dimension so that the blood circulatory system can exist in the next step function of universal intelligence.[41]

DNA

With every twenty tetrahedra the tetrahelix completes approximately one 360 degree helical revolution (352 degrees 40 minutes exactly), which tetrahelix is the mathematical model employed by the DNA-RNA helix, discovered by virological scientists (Watson-Crick-Wilkerson) to be always transmitting the specific information controlling the design of all biological species with that 7 degrees 20 minutes of angle (less than 360 degrees) being twist-sprung to introduce the unzipping force necessary to offspring (or give birth to) any given species' offmolded offspring from the parent.[42]

The part of the cell bearing special attention, says Popp, is that of the nucleic acids, which become conductive after excitation with energies above the critical eV level. He feels it is presumptuous to regard the DNA and RNA macromolecules as in "stationary states" that are relatively stable, as is commonly assumed. On the contrary, due to "weak quantization" . . . the DNA helix may act as a *resonant circuit,* with the DNA as a coil and the membranes as capacitances connected in parallel as in a tank circuit.

If one looks at the DNA/cell energetic coupling in a certain way, according to Popp, the energy scheme resembles that of a four-level biolaser. He has even developed the mathematics of this model to a point where one might begin to believe that such a fantastic concept could actually work.[43]

In some sense, I have little doubt, genes know what they are doing, for they are memory incarnate, letters of living purpose, the script of life in a material universe. . . .

Interestingly, also genes have been found to have the material molecular structure of aperiodic crystals and it is thought that they very probably evolved in the same basic way as other crystals, which are well known to be the structural basis of rock, as well as of wood, bones and flesh.[44]

There are pentagon geometrics which operate within the human body that are used for the correlation of genetic material by the Higher Evolution.[45]

Hence, the recoding DNA-RNA will give forth a new physical form for the body of Light and Man will see how the body of the physical flesh, the physical

DNA-RNA is simply the biochemical preparation necessary for the infusion of the Christ Body of Light.[46]

Humanity will experience a subtle mutational shift even in the genetic pattern. A new race of man will have its inception.[47]

OTHER ADDITIONAL PERSPECTIVES

The human brain. There is a fine crystal "powder" in the pituitary gland—and the pineal, too. They—constituting the Third Eye–pour out a certain hormone flow only when the thoughts are charged with love and light force. Then it seeps into the bloodstream.[48]

The physical organ of the pineal centre is imbedded in the brain, near the middle of the skull almost directly above the top of the spinal column. It is found to be a small body or gland, of reddish-grey color, cone-shaped, attached to the floor of the third ventricle of the brain, in front of the cerebellum. It is a mass of nervous energy, containing corpuscles resembling nerve cells, and containing small concretions of gritty, calcareous particles, sometimes called "brain sand."[49]

These crystalline channels can be seen as three jewel-crystals forming a pyramid. These three crystals in your third eye area allow resonance attunement to flow between the third eye and a spiritual template over your crown chakra which is necessary to project and receive the higher thought vibrations of Light. Thus, the three pyramidal coordinates of crystal "emanating out" connect with the five spiritual languages "flowing into you" to form the vibratory field that activates the eight chakras.[50]

CHAPTER 19

Interdimensional Communication: Further Perspectives

Interdimensional communication is the birthright of all. The interactive exchange of vibrational patterns, be it knowledge, communion, or creative growth enhancement, is the core of all beingness within the Light. Communication, in all its myriad forms and modalities, is the matrix of interrelatedness and all spiritual growth. The evolutionary process is one of realizing the essential keynote of communication within and between all levels of creation. As every being evolves, the communicative capacity is heightened along with the awareness of its abiding essentiality. Through this process increasing degrees of Universal Intelligence are encompassed within consciousness and limitless intercommunication progressively unfolds as the pinnacle of evolutionary attainment.

The Universal Energy Network (UEN) is a hierarchically ordered Intelligence-field composed of infinite domains, dimensions, and consciousness entities. Its primary function is to enact the Thought-blueprints of the Universal Mind into manifestation. The resultant diversification exists as an infinite spectrum of energetic combinations and permutations. This Light-spectrum provides the soul with numberless evolutionary opportunities to partake of chosen fields of Intelligence in order to assimilate specific energy patterning codes into consciousness. This growth process can be seen as the soul interactively communicating with chosen sectors of the UEN in order to selectively incorporate specific Light-codes that correspond to the soul's evolutionary path. It is through communication, or unified interpenetration, that the soul absorbs the desired parameters of Universal Intelligence. The UEN, then, provides an infinitely gradated and diversified megamatrix in which and through which souls creatively intercommunicate as the keystone of evolutionary development.

Interdimensional communication, far from being the purview of a select few, is instead the spiritual birthright and evolutionary imperative of all. In Chapter 3 it is seen that each individual is an integral extension of a vast multidimensional Higher Self network spanning the myriad thresholds of the UEN. Each individual is an interdimensional Light-being extending from the higher Light-realms to the earth-plane. Interdimensional communication is the attunement to one's own Light-body network so that it functions as a multidimensional extension through which communicative access to desired aspects of the UEN can occur. By formulating an intention and focusing it through the Light-body network, appropriate corresponding access is gained and the pathways of communication open to the individual. Thereby, access to the desired universal vibrational patterns is gained and assimilated by the earthly self. According to one's consciousness codes, multidimensional interactive admittance to broad spectrums of Universal Intelligence are potentially available. With correct access, unlimited interrelatedness is freely attainable to all through interdimensional communication.

Crystals are exceedingly helpful tools in this regard. In short, their versatile multidimensional properties in addition to their amplified programmable stability provide extended and clarified communication access. Quartz crystals help not only to focus and stabilize consciousness but also to extend the spiral-cone of perception one or more quantum levels. In this way, they help magnify communication abilities to greater degrees of accessible coherency. In addition, crystal-based gridworks, advanced unified energy fields, and temple chambers can create powerful amplified energy fields for even higher octaves of universal communications.

The Spiritual Hierarchy of Light, also called the Higher Evolution, is a hierarchically organized megamatrix of Higher Intelligence composed of a broad spectrum of Light-entities who work cooperatively to enact divine Will throughout creation. The Higher Evolution works in and through the vast expanses of the UEN to distribute and manifest the Thought-blueprints of the Eternal. In fact, it can be seen that the Higher Evolution is the collective matrix of the UEN.

As the primary Thought-blueprints are processed through the countless levels of the UEN, complex differentiated energy functions occur. As this happens, the differentiation process is apportioned through corresponding Intelligence channels of the Hierarchy of Light. That is, for every diversified function of the divine Blueprint crystallizing into manifestation, there is a correlating component of the Higher Evolution that is assigned to take care of the process of this energy. The function of this caretaking is to facilitate the manifesting of energy patterns in accordance with their originating divine Blueprint.

An overview perspective of the Hierarchy of Light shows it as a complexly differentiated branching network of Light flowing from the highest of abstract causal dimensions to the most densified of lower octave planes. At each level of this network are consciousness entities that have responsibilities for assigned (and chosen) functions. Such assignments are delineated in exacting detail. In synergistic conjunction with numerous other entities a full spectrum of Light- functions is encompassed. The hierarchical structure is such that entities of higher evolutionary growth status are given divine authority to direct and oversee a specified spectrum of Light-functions that encompass the activities of numerous other entities. The overseeing entity receives the overall Blueprint of divine will as it relates to the assigned spectrum of Light- functions from another entity overseeing from an even higher plane of authority. Once this blueprint is received it is then apportioned to the network of entities that cooperatively perform their specific functions that, together, enact the entire blueprint. This type of hierarchical branching and cooperative synergy has innumerable levels throughout the UEN. The most important concept here is that each entity within the Hierarchy of Light has a specified area of authorized Light-functions that is overseen by a higher level of hierarchical authority. This is an egoless hierarchy in which soul choice and universal evolutionary growth status determine with great justice and equality an individual's relative place and assigned activities within the Higher Evolution. It is not the overseeing entity that is bowed to, but rather the divine will that flows without alteration through the egoless individuals and collective consciousness of the Hierarchy of Light. The Higher Evolution functions as the all-encompassing network of the UEN that serves to distribute and enact divine Law with exact and unaltered precision.

Throughout the vastness of the Higher Evolution is a singularly complex array of ordering-groups of principally interrelated entities. There are a great number of religious, spiritual, and esoteric belief systems about the structuring of this Hierarchy. The complexities and merit of any belief system is not within the purview of this text. What is important to underline is that there is only one Spiritual Hierarchy of Light; it is known by many different names, and belief systems vary in their concepts and perspectives, sometimes radically. This notwithstanding, there is but one Higher Evolution, whose structures and functions govern universal order, even though it is known differently by different levels of soul perception.

For the most general of purposes, a simplified list of some of the major ordering groups of the Higher Evolution includes the devic and elemental realms, angelic realms, higher space federation, master realms, and Elohim levels. The guidelines and techniques presented in this text are offered in as universal a manner as possible. For is it not for each individual to choose his or her own path so that it relates to the structure of the living universe?

BASIC GUIDELINES FOR INTERDIMENSIONAL COMMUNICATION

The supreme foundation upon which effective interdimensional communication rests is the Ten-plus-One Commandments. Through the integration of these most causal of Light-codes with consciousness, an unshakably resonant connection is created with the Kingdom of God. Within these fundamental parameters, optimal, undistorted, accurate interdimensional communication takes place.

Herein offered are some basic guidelines and perspectives for facilitating effective interdimensional communication for each individual to consider and integrate as is felt appropriate.

1. Depend upon yourself for taking responsibility to communicate, or channel, for yourself. It does no harm to listen to what others may channel, about oneself or any subject, but the final responsibility for accepting or rejecting something as truth or not truth, appropriate or not appropriate, is your own. Rely upon the "still, small voice within" that abides within each individual as their birthright. It is by relying solely upon this Source within the self that true freedom and acceptance of responsibility occur.
2. Develop interdimensional communication abilities gradually and with caution. Abilities for accurate subtle-level communication evolve step by step in a paced, integrated manner for most individuals. Avoid the temptation to open the self up to higher dimensional level interaction too soon. Such a path is fraught with many hindrances to optimal soul growth patterns. Rather, exercise patience unrelentingly

even when it appears that no progress is being made; there will be cycles of active upward growth followed by less apparent growth cycles. Allow the natural inner rhythms to unfold as chosen and orchestrated by the Higher Self. This process will not take place in a human's time but in God's time, and often in ways that are least expected.

3. When engaging in multidimensional communication it is exceedingly important to suspend preconceived concepts and expectation patterns. As awareness is consciously being linked with the UEN in meditation or prayer or consciousness quietude, state the intention of the communication clearly and concisely. Then communicate the desired thoughts and energies. Next, allow the larger part of the time period spent in meditation-prayer to be receivership of higher Light- energies flowing from the appropriate aspects of the Hierarchy of Light; that is, suspend expectations and thoughts as much as possible and open the self with focused receptivity to the downpouring of spiritual grace. Feel the subtle essence and refined vibrational patterns of the communication and communion that occurs during this time of receivership. Do not force these rarefied energies to translate into words or earth-terms. Allow the higher levels of the Light-body to gradually step these vibrational patterns down to crystallization as thoughts, words, concepts, and more consciously perceived vibrations. This step-down process may take hours, days, weeks, or months until an individual is consciously aware of the higher dimensional energy dynamics that were assimilated into the Light-body. What is required is continued receptive openness and daily interdimensional communication in order to obtain the answers that are sought.

4. Maintain a nonattached perspective regarding the form and content of such communication. In the growth process there are many levels of understanding spiritual truth. As soul growth unfolds, a truth that was known at a previous stage is perceived with a more encompassing and expanded perspective at a later growth stage. There are many levels of perceiving any given truth, all of which may be accurate within relative stages of soul growth. Therefore, it is important not to overly crystallize any given perspective so much that it becomes rigid enough to constrain its continued expansion. Also, when further spiritual maturation takes place, previously held beliefs that do not harmonize with more evolved understandings will tend to fall away as the Light of Truth becomes more and more coherently clear. Patience and balanced flexibility are character traits that stand in good stead throughout all spiritual growth sequences.

Interdimensional communication can take many forms. From trance channeling and deep meditation to intuitive flashes and creative endeavors, multidimensional energetic exchange manifests in a wide spectrum. There is nothing necessarily hierarchical in terms of the form that such communication takes, that is, trance channeling is not necessarily more advanced or accurate than higher creative endeavors, and so on. It is the interdimensional energy pattern transfer that is most essential, and not the means by which it is carried out. Any individual may channel by any one or all forms of higher communication. Most people tend to have one or a few primary means by which interdimensional vibrational transfer occurs. It is usually wise to discern individual strengths in this regard and to focus more trust and attention therein, unless spiritually guided to do otherwise.

5. Look to the long-term fruits of your communications to help discern its efficacy.

By assimilating it and acting upon it in your life over considerable periods of time, examine the fruits that develop. In retrospect, was there accuracy, positive growth, and increasing consciousness of Light? Are the Ten- plus-One commandments a greater part of your life? Is the spiritual impulse to serve others in the Light greater than before? Is compassion and divine Love a more central part of the innermost being? Such questions can be applied as a measure of the degree to which your interdimensional communication and resultant spiritual path is accurate and leading you in optimal soul growth cycles.

6. Over the long term, balanced degrees of self-discipline are necessary to facilitate deep, abiding growth. The degree and form of such discipline must necessarily be discerned by each individual in conjunction with the Higher Self and the Eternal. Sometimes, there are breakthrough periods in which dramatic energies and experiences happen; visions of exalted realms and higher knowledge occur in transcendent states. This is a natural part of evolvement cycles. Usually, however, it is also part of the continuing cyclic stages of growth that after such breakthrough experiences there is a time for a balanced integrating of the new spectrum of Light-energies that have opened up to consciousness. The breakthrough can be gloriously exciting, and there comes a period of time afterward in which disciplined, grounded effort is needed to assimilate these new energies into consciousness in a balanced way and to translate this into active Light-work in accordance with your chosen avenues of service. This is one earmark of a balanced approach to interdimensional communication. It is sometimes a temptation to try to maintain the "rush" of higher frequency energies past its cyclic due. This is a crucial junction of discernment, for if the assimilative and active service aspects of the spiritual growth cycle are shunted aside and a continual grasping for high excitement and drama takes hold, a degree of glamour and illusion then creep into the channeling. If not rectified, the momentum can take you afar from the higher Light. Grounded discipline and humble service are "beacons of Light" for the soul as the pathways of Light are trodden.

7. The words and energies of many channelings are beautiful, joyous, and loving. This is well. Look to such channelings also to see if an element of constructive criticism also abides. Nary an individual on the entire earth-plane could not use a positive mirroring of faults and areas needing improvement; this is an integral part of balanced interdimensional communication. It is easy and pleasant to focus on your positive attributes and quite hard and wrenching to focus on your negative qualities. For the greater part, it is the latter that are the primary hindrances to spiritual growth, but are often avoided because of the pain and discomfort that it brings to the ego- personality. All channeling is a composite of the strengths and weaknesses of the channel, for the channel is the filter-matrix through which the channeling flows. If the channel-communicator has an avoidance pattern to constructive criticism, either to self or others, this pattern will be reflected in the content of the channelings. Look to the content of your own and others' higher communications to see if this aspect is there. When the sword of Truth acts through channeling it is compassionate yet cutting to that which is less than Light. This is yet another indicator of balanced interdimensional communication.

8. Look to the lives of the saints and Yeshua (Jesus) for guidance as to archetypal patterns of the path of Light. The path to the kingdom of God is narrow and many times difficult; the path to other destinations is wide and many times much

easier in the short term. To walk in the Light as the saints is to open wide the gateways of self to Spirit unfailingly, unswervingly, relentlessly.

9. There are many pitfalls in the arena of personal and professional channeling. It is well to realize first that there are many dimensional levels from which interdimensional communication derives. Sometimes channeling is of a higher Light-nature, and other times it is of a lesser nature. The quality of Light that shines through will vary in accordance with the spiritual growth status of the channel and the origin-level of the channeling. As an overview of some of the pitfall scenarios of lesser communications, herein are a few to consider.

a) The "just around the corner" scenario: the channelee is told that whatever he or she is looking for—whether it be job, money, prosperity, enlightenment, security, love-partner, etc.—is close within the person's grasp. Many times the projected scenarios are grand; almost always they reflect the personal desires of the channelee. Such instances function to reinforce the person's hope and desire that something dramatic is going to happen shortly that will relieve or fulfill some form of longing, suffering, or personal desires. The individual leaves the channeling feeling elated and buoyed that relief or success is at hand. Usually, after waiting for the projected events to occur, the person realizes that it is probably not going to happen and becomes dejected at their misfortune and likely rejects all channeling as flaky or seeks out another channeler.

b) The "channeling fix" scenario: The channelee is addicted to receiving channeling sessions and psychic readings. The subtle-level communication may or may not be of the highest nature; the point here is that the stimulation of the process itself and the feeling of security that comes from the session become an emotional-mental addiction. A dependency builds up around a channel or channels who are perceived as having access to all the answers to the individual's life. The channelee increasingly feels the need to receive knowledge as to more and more details and decisions. Personal responsibility and integrated spiritual growth discipline practices tend to fall away as a downward-pulling cycle continues.

c) The "ego massage" scenario: an individual goes to a channeling session and is told in myriad words and perspectives about his or her importance (now, in the future, or in past lives) and his or her great talents, attributes, and deeds. The channelee goes away feeling elated and buoyed about the mysteries, power, importance, and glory of the self. Again, the individual is told what he or she wants to hear.

d) The "you are the One" scenario: the channelee is told that he or she is a high master or great being of worldwide importance and towering power and influence. The mysteries of the universe, planetary salvation, or an event of cosmic import are to be catalyzed and revealed only by this One. This scenario is a variation on the messiah complex theme.

It is wise to be rather wary and extremely discerning as to the nature and source of interdimensional communications that one chooses to partake. The above pitfall scenarios are not offered negatively or cynically; instead, they are offered with concern and compassion so that certain downward-pulling patterns are brought to conscious awareness and as few people as possible are sidetracked on the spiritual path at this crucial time in planetary events. There are indeed interdimensional communicators, or channels, that are sharing very high level,

Light quality channeling to many's benefit. It is for each individual to discern which is the higher quality and which is the lesser quality in this arena.

PROTECTION PERSPECTIVES

It is crucial to be aware that there are many powerful influences pervading the earth-plane that are of spiritual ignorance. On earth and in other universal sectors is a hierarchy of entities that work within anti-Light spectrums of energy. The structure of this fallen hierarchy functions in ways that parallel the Spiritual Hierarchy of Light. The primary notable differences are that the Higher Evolution enact divine Will and have access to the highest spectrum of universal White Light, whereas the fallen hierarchy partake of neither. Those desirous of working with the Hierarchy of Light on the earth- plane need to be aware of protection perspectives so as to guard the self and the interdimensional communication from the negative influences of the fallen hierarchy.

The use of crystals, affirmations, and visualizations for protection work well for this purpose for they build up an amplified energy field about the individual that will defend him or her to a certain degree from negative influences. Additional protective dynamics, however, need to be requested from the higher celestial realms for optimal results. It is recommended that the interdimensional communicator ask the Order of Michael for protection assistance, for this is one of the primary assigned functions that this particular order of Light-beings carries out. Without such protection of the highest level, the individual is still vulnerable to the higher dimensional levels of the fallen hierarchy. The crystal, affirmation, and visualization techniques can only generate defense energies within certain limited parameters; with the addition of the influences of the Order of Michael, most adverse energy factors can be neutralized.

Another aspect of protection is the avoidance of such pitfall scenarios as described, the following of the Ten-plus-One commandments, and the shunning of temptations that will focus attention away from the Light and spiritual service. Through repelling negative possibilities and by building a strong spiritual foundation by living within divine Law, increasing degrees of protection naturally build up as a by-product of spiritual growth.

INTERDIMENSIONAL COMMUNICATION PROCEDURES

Following is a procedural outline for facilitating effective communication. This is offered as much as possible in universal terms so that many different belief systems and intentions can be applied through these ecumenical guidelines.

1. If possible, have a meditation, prayer, or communication area set aside solely for this purpose. Maintain this area so that as few other vibrational influences as possible affect it. A gridwork setup appropriate for interdimensional communication is optimal. Have one or more crystals chosen and programmed for "interdimensional communication in the Light." The headband concepts presented in Chapter 10 are excellent for use in this procedure. It is also effective to have a third eye crystal taped to the forehead. In addition, it works well to have a single focal crystal to hold in the left hand, and when appropriate in this technique, to position it in front of the third eye.

2. Decide the realm or Light-entities with which you desire to communicate, and for what purpose. Then, quiet and center consciousness.

3. Do three-to-five minutes of a self-transformation exercise that will assist in opening consciousness channels. This can be any of the numerous such exercises widely taught, involving visualization, controlled breathing, sound, chromatics, or other techniques.

4. Attune the body to the reprogramming cycle. Actively reestablish a strong interdimensional connection with the Light-body and attune to the reprogramming processes currently occurring within the self. It helps here to apply the Alpha–Omega energy dynamics, blood system techniques, or any of the other modalities presented in Chapter 9. Feel the activation and alignment processes unifying the earthly self with the Light-body. Know that this is truth within your innermost being.

5. Bring the crystal in the left hand programmed for communications up in front of the third eye. Position the arms and establish a strong resonant connection with the crystal (as discussed in Chapter 8). While interlinked with the crystal, connect consciousness with the etheric crystals of the planetary energy network. This can be done by focusing awareness on the seed-phrase "connect consciousness with the planetary etheric crystal network." Repeat this seed-phrase 15 to 20 times with concentration, feeling consciousness gradually making this link-up. For some, it may help to visualize the dodecahedral geometry of the earth's etheric crystal gridwork, seeing huge, perfectly formed crystalline structures at each vertex of the geometric form.

6. Once so linked, state your intention. Ask for protection in the Light through the Order of Michael. Then state the realm or Light-entity with which you desire to interconnect. State this intention with succinctness and clarity. Repeat this five to ten times with focused concentration.

7. The planetary crystal network is the primary interaction point for communication between entities within the earth's energy field and the rest of the cosmos. Once consciousness connection occurs and intention is stated, the communication signals are processed through the UEN to their appropriate destination with automatic precision (within the individual's access parameters). No active effort is required on the part of the communicator in terms of making the communicative link-up with the desired Light-realm. The appropriate aspects of the Higher Evolution perform this service-task as an integral part of its functioning. What is needed on the part of the individual communicator is a receptively focused state of awareness that is allowed to flow through the communication channels being established. If assistance is desired in this regard, explicitly ask for it when stating the intention while linking with the etheric crystal network. Allow approximately two to five minutes of time to be interconnected with the requested region.

8. Now state to the specific Light-beings or realm the purpose of the communication, whether it be to gain higher knowledge, to assimilate certain Light-vibrations, to channel information from this region, or another purpose. Be succinct and clear in stating your intention.

9. Then allow the downpouring of communication to occur. Without expecting consciously perceived answers and without trying to translate the energies being received into words or earth-terms, maintain consciousness in a receptively focused state. Simply be aware of the subtle interactions occurring on the higher

levels of the Light-body, and keep open to these energies stepping down through the dimensions to the earth-based self. It may very well be that you are not fully aware of the higher interactions that are happening. This is fine; the most important thing is to maintain a nonexpectant openness of being to allow these interactions to take place without interference. Maintain this state of receivership for as long as is felt necessary and comfortable.

10. When completing the communication, express thankfulness for the vibrations and blessings received. Then gradually shift back to conscious awareness.

11. While still in a relaxed and uplifted state of consciousness, recall the essences, vibrational feelings and impressions, images, and ideas that occurred during the communication process. Try to maintain a balance between understanding these energies in conscious terms and allowing them to remain as yet abstractly untranslated into earth-based concepts.

12. Continue this procedure daily for best results. The time factor is secondary, the most important aspect being the relaxed, focused, and comfortable enactment of each step through the entire cycle. It is usually best to continue working with only one or two intention-patterns until it is felt that the desired energies have been thoroughly assimilated within the individual's consciousness. It may take days, weeks, or months to complete a full cycle of this kind. Flashes of intuition may occur during the normal flow of daily events that relate to the intention-patterns being worked with. Dreams might also manifest certain aspects in this regard. The main point is to be open to many sorts of less expected insights and understandings that may happen as higher dimensional communications patterns are gradually assimilated and integrated into the individual consciousness.

OTHER COMMUNICATION PERSPECTIVES

1. Music and sonics accompanying interdimensional communication can add a synergistic element to the experience. Find those selections that best resonate with personal taste in conjunction with the type of communication being done.

One recording in particular has an evolving sequence of musical selections that synchronizes very well with the flow of the step-by-step procedure presented above. *Tibetan Plateau* by David Parsons (Fortuna Records)—side 2, "Voyage of the Mothership"—can enhance the flow of communications marvelously. In short, these are the progressive stages that the music can accompany: a) State the intention as to which realm or Light-being(s) with which communication is desired. As for protection from the Order of Michael. b) Relax and let go. c) Allow oneself to be connected with the specific higher dimensional level. d) Relax and receive. e) Adjust back to normal, waking consciousness. f) Recall essences and vibrations without expectations.

2. Some crystals work better for communications than others because of their inherent programming. Within this category, some of them function as quite generalized and versatile communication tools. Others are quite specific in their access parameters. A prime example of the latter is crystals having a diamond facet. Each one of these crystals, according to the shape and positioning of the diamond facet in relationship to the rest of the crystal, has access to very particular multidimensional realms. (See the "Diamond Facets" section of Chapter 11.) With other types of crystals there are few physical indicators that they would be

better suited for higher plane communication, so use intuition to make these judgments.

3. Archetypal crystalline geometric patterns are primary access codes. By visualizing them, specific sectors of the UEN can be engaged to gain particular vibratory patterns. The same principle holds true for the pictographic flame letters. For further information and exercises with these crystalline code- keys, see Chapter 8, "Programming Exercises," number 2, and Chapter 4.

4. Mind-center activation techniques as well as headband, crowns, and helmets are superb amplifying facilitators for the communication process. See Chapter 10 for techniques, exercises, and further ideas.

5. Gridworks, advanced UEFs, and temple chambers are the most powerful energy field facilitators of multidimensional communication. See Chapter 14 and Chapter 15 for concepts and applications in this field.

6. Many thousands of years ago the only gem quality mineral of off-planet origin was deposited on earth. Synchronistically, it is also one of the most powerful interdimensional communications access gems, the knowledge of which is today being unveiled as part of the Peoplehood of Light's accelerated preparation for the New World ascension.

A tektite (from the Greek word "tektos", meaning molten) is usually a black to brown stone in spheroid, button, teardrop, or dumbell shapes, thought to be meteorites or pieces of comets or asteroids. Moldavite tektite is the only type of meteorite with the clarity and color of gem quality and is the rarest of the glassy meteorites. Prized throughout history by sultans and kings as well as numerous mystics, moldavite has been called the "agni mani", meaning "fire pearl" and the stone of the Holy Grail. As well, other lore depicts this gem as the Shamballa Stone and the stone that fell from Lucifer's crown as he fell from the Light. Today, awareness of its highly specialized and extremely important role in catalyzing and facilitating interdimensional communication is fast being reawakened.

As with all gems except quartz, moldavite has a very defined spectrum of energetic characteristics and functioning (versus quartz' full spectrum energy range). This gem's "specialty" is for direct multidimensional access with great depth and universal range, exceeding even quartz in some of its specialized capabilities. In conjunction with the third eye in particular and the primary mind-centers in general, consciousness is provided with a key to unlock interdimensional doors that were partially or totally locked beforehand. It is not primarily an amplifying boost that moldavite provides but a vibrational profile specific to keying into multidimensional channels with non-linear depth and clarity. Access broadens in areas the individual already has access to; access opens to areas previously unopened. As with all such communications, the ratio of success is in direct proportion to the degree that the individual stands within the Light of Universal Law.

The optimal use of moldavite tektite is in direct conjunction with the third eye. It is not a healing stone or a gem to be used in mere ornamental jewelry. It works extremely well with quartz, as quartz provides both a stabilizing as well as amplifying booster effect; Herkimer diamond quartz works exceptionally well in particular. Moldavite does not harmonize well with either copper or silver, but works best with gold. Further, this gem must be faceted and polished into geometrically symmetrical and balanced facetting patterns out of the amorphous rough condition in order to activate its higher energetic properties. The ways that moldavite can be used are diverse, including: 1) one stone taped to the third eye area, 2) a Star of David grid of moldavites on first aid tape or on a template applied to the third eye, 3) a Star of David grid of small Herkimer diamonds (best) or small, very high quality double-termination Arkansas quartz with a moldavite in the center, taped to the forehead on the tape itself or on a template, 4) a Star of David gridwork of moldavites glued onto the body face of a larger size Herkimer diamond with a small diamond in the center, 5) a Great Pyramid-faceted moldavite pyramid surrounded by a Star of David gridwork of Herkimer diamonds.

The amount of moldavite tektite on earth is extremely limited and sources[1] are few. This is a most important tool for the People of Light. Obtain some and enjoy the soaring possibilities!

In sum: be discerning; beware the fine line between high darkness and high Light; enjoy the reawakening of your divine heritage; stubbornly remain empty till the Light of Truth dawns; be the Light and actively serve the Light on earth *now*.

PART III
Visions and Vistas

INTRODUCTION TO PART III

A New World beckons . . . whisperings and imaginings, dreams and visions foretell a monumental personal and planetary awakening of inconceivable magnitudes. The keys to the crystalline corridors and codes of ascension turn in synchronization with the unfoldment of the cosmic timetables, progressively revealing vistas of Light previously veiled to the earth for untold eons. What lies through the crystalline corridors and within the crystal codes has yet to be fully revealed. Only few glimpses have been afforded to humankind, yet as we come upon the appointed times the Light shines on the earth with increasing intensity, each cyclic wave of the incoming Light more penetrating than the last. Impinging upon the higher levels of individual and planetary consciousness, these Light-energies illuminate what was before only vague soul- longings for the regaining of a dimly remembered divine heritage. These consciousness stirrings foreshadow an interdimensional exodus to higher planes of Spirit wherein a new order prevails, one in which today's prophetic visions become tomorrow's realities. Like a beacon shining forth to illuminate a crystalline pathway to unknown realms, the Higher Evolution assists humankind in preparing for this process by activating seed-crystal codes, visions, and spiritual gifts within receptive consciousness. What was before only vague intuitions becomes increasingly well-forged leaps to higher realizations.

Old, and sometimes dearly held truths fall by the wayside as more encompassing paradigms of spiritual and scientific truths are infused into individual and collective consciousness. Like the rapid upswing of the exponential curve, even today's and tomorrow's leading-edge paradigms are quickly superseded as vast, unimaginable orders of Higher Intelligence are reactivated upon this planet. Impossibilities become possible; divinely inspired visions become fact. This chapter, whether viewed as science fiction, futuristic fantasy, or visionary realism is woven of the fabric of possibilities, inspirations, and ascension- oriented thought-forms. Through these crystalline windows each individual will see different facets of an infinitely faceted spectrum of potentialities and will partake of its essense according to his or her own chosen pattern of soul evolution.

CHAPTER 20

Crystalline Windows: Visions of a New World

A vision . . . Earth ascended and assumed its heritage as a crystalline sphere of Higher Planetary Intelligence in the higher cosmic Light-domains. After being reset in its orbital relationship to a blue-white multiple-sun system and the evolutionary timepieces were set in place throughout its recrystallized gridwork structure, it was prepared to receive the seed of a new planetary populace.

After a time of interdimensional exodus, navigating the Merkabah and the associated spectrum vehicle fleets through the predetermined astrophysical thresholds and gaining final clearance through the greater cosmic gateways, the New Peoplehood alighted on Ascended earth. Existing now on an exalted vibratory plane, access to entities desirous of living on Ascended earth was limited to those of a like-vibration; entities not qualifying were apportioned to other universal life stations of equivalent soul-measures. Earth became a paradise planet of magnificent verdant abundance and immense consciousness advancement opportunities.

Cities of Light had been prepared, cities stationed on the harmonic abundance meridians and built on the keystone of a Spirit-based Light-technology. Much work was yet to be done, but the foundation for enlightened cocreatorship was laid. The Temples of Light were set in place on the 12 major vortexes of the planet, each temple devoted to a different ray-vibration of Light-work. One temple was devoted to healing, another to the birthing and raising of children, another to interdimensional science research and development, and other Temples to their assigned domains. Additionally, the Government of Light was seated on the thrones of divine authority, headed by Christ and the Lords of Light in the midst of the earth. For the first time in eons, planet earth was ruled by divine Will.

Great rejoicing resounded throughout the Kingdom of Light as new stars were born and planetary ascension became a reality. Now it came time to fulfill the highest aspects of the Father's Blueprint as the planetary populace began their newly commissioned spiritual work in service to the Light.

A vision . . . the Ascension Art Gallery is not only a place to view fine art but also, more important, to experience the art on multiple levels of awareness and to interact creatively with the gallery exhibits. In fact, the Ascension Art Gallery is a subunit of one of the great Temples of Light on planet earth. The art genre is termed multidimensional transformative.

As an individual enters this temple gallery, a short purification procedure is enacted. The person first puts on a simple white robe of crystalline material and is given a crystal computer device that is programmed to help in formulating and amplifying thought-forms as well as assisting in assimilating the various experiences. Then, stepping on a moving track going through a white corridor, the individual experiences a progressive series of purifying colors, sonics, aromatics, and crystal–pyramid radiance modules.

At the end of the corridor the visitor has numerous options as to which exhibits to experience and in what order. The crystal computer assists in designing a sequence best suited to the individual.

One possibility is to step on another moving track that transports the participant through several art stations. Each station is a holographic energy field composed of coded arrays of color, sound, aromatics, and magnetic- crystalline energies. Each hologram is a multidimensional energy field that unfolds in time through programmed energy-code sequences. The individual is positioned in the center of this holographic field, and remains there for a specified period of time, during which he or she is permeated with the unfolding energy sequence throughout all auric levels. As the participant's consciousness absorbs and assimilates the interpenetrating vibratory patterns, a corresponding process of self-transformation is crystallized within the individual. Each of the stations along the moving track is programmed for facilitating a different aspect of self-enrichment, as a whole completing an entire energy sequence.

Another exhibit consists of a circle of hollow crystal spheres, each filled with a type of Light-plasma that is highly responsive to applied thought- fields. The individual sits in front of a single sphere in a comfortable chair equipped with thought-amplifying devices, should they be desired. The sphere can be programmed through the control panel in the arm of the chair for numerous possible multicolor variations. The idea is for the person to create a sculpture of Light-plasma with applied thought-energy. This is a finely tuned thought-feedback tool, as the plasma responds quickly to extreme subtleties of the thought-vibrations and will also hold its shape steady while awareness is directed elsewhere in the sculpting process. Once the basic outline is formed, additional colors can be inserted into the sphere at the touch of the control panel. Many thought-sculpting subtleties are possible, dependent only upon the creativity and thought-control of the participant. One of the primary benefits of this exhibit is to help individuals see the visual analog of a wide spectrum of consciousness energies. It is seen and imprinted in the plasma, for example, that one mode of consciousness manifests as a corresponding geometric form, say, a spiral; another mode of awareness forms a three-dimensional grid of squares; and so forth. Visualization skills are also enhanced. As the individual attempts to formulate an image in the mind and hold it steady, this internal process is mirrored precisely in the form the Light-plasma takes.

Self-improvement exercises as art games . . .

A group exhibit is also available that employs many of the same concepts as the Light-plasma spheres and adds the components of blended group consciousness, sound, and aromatics. Sitting in a circle of control chairs around a 15 to 20 foot diameter central area, a group of people harmoniously blend their individual consciousness into a synergistically interacting group consciousness. The nature of the group's applied thought-energies is reflected in the patterns that evolve into the large three-dimensional sculpture. With the addition of sound and aroma, the complexities and nuances of creative possibilities are multiplied endlessly. The group consciousness interactions may manifest mandalas within mandalas, symphonic holograms within symphonic holograms, aromatic subtleties within aromatic subtleties. The synergistically nonlinear interactions of group consciousness are many times brought to the fore with strikingly unexpected sculptural effects. It is seen, heard, smelled, and felt that harmonious consciousness interactions may evoke laws of energy coherence, amplification, and synergic harmonization not normally experienced in consciousness isolation or disharmony.

Once the active process of forming a desirable pattern is completed, a more passive, contemplative stage occurs wherein the group savors the creation and receptively assimilates it within individual and group consciousness. During this last stage a marvelous process occurs. While the group contemplates, the sculpture undergoes a process of spontaneous transformation to even greater levels of elegant sophistication and interdimensional synchronization. Such an experience leaves each individual with a profound sense of fulfillment and heightened interrelatedness.

Many other exhibits await the seeker. Transformative self-enrichment as multidimensionally interactive art forms—an art genre of the New World. . . .

A vision . . . From above, great arcs of Light were projected onto a planetary sphere. Each arc was many miles in diameter and descended through the primary magnetic-gravitational gateways onto the planet, whereupon all life intelligence that was gathered within these target areas underwent a profound transformational process. The DNA of every life species was utilized as the most fundamental blueprint-code through which every life form is born of, connected to, and maintained by its originating archetypal Thought-form (or Higher Self). With great precision the coordinating Light-scientists, operating from high frequency spectrum vehicles, phase locked with all the varied DNA energy patterns of the multitudinous life forms and infused them with higher gradients of Light-energy, thus effecting a transmutation to a higher energetic state. These energized DNA coding-patterns were drawn upward in myriad laserlike beams through the various arcs of Light into a specially prepared interdimensional vehicle whose function was that of a DNA storage bank. In this way, the genetic seed that had been planted at the beginning of the evolutionary cycle was "harvested" and thereby protected from any radical earthly upheavals that may have damaged the planet's evolutionary intelligence- genetic pool.

The interdimensional Light-scientists assigned to this project had prepared tubes containing specific Light-plasma in which to store the precious DNA- codes. The greater part of this large vehicle, also known as the Ark, was composed of these plasma storage tubes. While the planet below went through its stages of purification, the genetic seed was safely maintained. And, if it was appropriate to repair, reconstitute, or modify the DNA-blueprint of any specific species, such genetic engineering was performed with strict adherence to the dictates of divine Will.

When the planetary sphere was prepared to act as a supportive matrix for the next life-cycle, the Ark transposed each life-form's DNA structure into the world's energy field. As this transposition took place, an awe-inspiring process occurred. The pure energy patterns of the DNA underwent a rapid sequence of transformations in which, from one primary DNA pattern, many forms of that single species differentiated into an exact, predetermined number that were precisely materialized at numerous geographic locations into their appropriate ecosystems. From a higher dimensional perspective, this process looked like a vastly complex chain reaction manifesting as a grand mathematical gridwork.

Once completed, the sanctified genetic seed was set in motion, thereupon to enrich its evolutionary "substance" as it passed through yet another stage of the divine plan.

A vision . . . an interdimensional Light-scientist gives a selective overview of the various functions and modalities utilized in a crystal laboratory in one of the Temples of Light in the New World:

A major section of this aspect of the laboratory is dedicated to work relating to the growing of crystals with a broad spectrum of modalities. For example, lasers (with a variable gravitational metric) are beamed through a growth medium at specific frequencies and wavelengths to induce the formation of precisely desired molecular bond angles and interatomic spacing, which are primary determiners of the macroscopic external characteristics. Also, in gravitational suspension the crystal growth medium can be exposed to calibrated sonic energy patterns to great effect. Without the influence of gravity, a much more even distribution of sonic vibrations is possible and this creates crystals of the highest regularity and purity of vibrations. In addition, the importance of precisely constructed thought-forms in creating the template- blueprint patterns from which a crystal grows cannot be overemphasized. A trained and authorized Light-scientist can formulate complex thought-code patterns that are then infused into the receptive crystal growth medium. Once this blueprint-pattern is imprinted within the interpenetrating etheric fields the solution crystallizes into solid form in accordance with the original thought-form. In this way, unlimited thought-patterns can be formulated to program into crystals, these crystals then becoming tools whose purpose relates to this programming.

Another more advanced crystal growing technique involves the crystallizing of higher dimensional energy patterns into physical form without any need for a material growth matrix. In some cases a technologically created holographic holding pattern energy field is required in the laboratory to help stabilize this interdimensional transduction process. More advanced Light-scientists can grow the crystal form out of the ethers without such additional assistance.

The external physical characteristics of crystals can be grown to a wide array of specifications. Such parameters as the length and width, the angular proportions of the facets, the ratio of size of the termination facets, nonlinear access-code variations, the ratio of the termination to the body, and a host of other factors can be exactly controlled. Even the number of sides and facets can be regulated, the key being advanced knowledge concerning the control of the gravitational spectrum.

Crystallography is among the most complex fields of knowledge in all of interdimensional science. The preceding information will serve to give glimpses into some of the basic concepts involved in the more advanced crystal growing modalities in the laboratories of the future.

There are two fundamental ways in which laboratory crystal growing techniques used in interdimensional science are profoundly different from those employed by orthodox scientists of the twentieth century. The first is that interdimensional scientists receive the blueprints of the crystal forms they are to manifest from authorized realms of higher levels of the Universal Mind. This is to say that the precise energy-pattern of any crystalline form originates as a Thought-form of the Father. The function of the scientists is to follow the pattern of the Thought-form with exacting precision. In this way, divine order is maintained. Second, interdimensional scientists work in close conjunction with the various levels and orders of Crystalline Intelligence. Many of the more advanced crystal growing devices function, in part, as an attraction module—a specifically designed energy field that serves as an antenna-attracting unit for receiving the desired influences of a particular universal Intelligence-pattern. Interdimensional scientists can gain access to desired frequency-patterns of the Universal Mind and expose the forming crystal to these influences. As a result of these two major differences, the resulting crystals reflect the holistic imprint of divine Intelligence and therefore serve their function with the greatest possible efficiency and universal harmony.

A vision . . . beyond the intergalactic spectrums, beyond the angelic domains, in realms of purely abstract energy vectors, exists the celestial domains of rarefied Abstract Light-fields. Abstract numerological principles and geometric seed-codes constitute the multidimensional matrix of this realm, consisting of such idealized components as pure axes, arcs, tangents, vectors, and angles. This field of Abstract Intelligence serves as a seed-bed transduction matrix for the primary creative Thought-forms of the One. As the One formulates the blueprints of manifestation, they are stepped down to the energy domains wherein they are processed into appropriate abstract measures and indexes for the countless multidimensional levels of reality to be seeded and maintained from a single creative Thought-form. These celestial crystalline realms serve as one of the primary zones through which Oneness manifests into Twoness, Threeness, Fourness, and so on. Multidimensional abstract qualities of the One are transduced in and through the appropriate crystalline angular symmetry patterns, transforming them through matrix after transforming matrix, imparting the primordial Thought-forms with mathematical-geometrical differentiation vectors. The logically coherent order inherent to Universal Intelligence creates a perfect vehicle by which the wholly abstract One may be transformed into mathematical-geometrical crystalline patterns. Matrix vectors process corresponding abstract wholeness vectors into proper template-circuits of Light-interactions, which then further step down the vector-coded energy flow.

In all, the celestial crystalline domains function as a vastly complex living ultra-computer gridwork-matrix system serving to process the completely Abstract Thought of the One into the primary causal domains to Twoness (holistic duality), Threeness (trinity, triangulation), Fourness (balanced differentiation dynamics), and so on. Form, per se, has no existence in this realm; only the idealized causal principles and the abstractions of those principles that are to be transposed via appropriate matrix-codings to the innumerable levels of form throughout the Oneness of creation exist.

A vision . . . the angelic space fleets play a wide variety of roles in carrying out the divine plan throughout the countless multidimensional spectrums of reality.

These space fleets consist of great numbers of spectrum vehicles of broad interdimensional travel abilities and consciousness and technological capacities. One primary command vehicle directs the rest of the squadron host. These other vehicles are divided into specialization groups. Each group consists of vehicles and angelic operators of specific evolutionary classes. Because of the clearly defined command chain and virtually instantaneous telethought communication faculties, the entire fleet can operate with great interdimensional cohesion and efficiency.

For the most part, the command vehicle remains on a more elevated dimensional level from which it can both receive directives from higher level operatives and command its fleet. Each squadron can be assigned to a different project and be dispatched to the desired sector. Multitudes of different projects are being carried out at any given time by separate squadrons, all elegantly coordinated by the command ship.

Squadrons devoted to a designated task may form a multidimensional gridwork around an area of focused Light-work, each vehicle assigned to operate on a discrete dimensional level. In effect, the entire squadron creates an interdimensionally cohesive network that can work with the spectrum of the assigned energy functions.

This concept has multiple applications. For example, the creation of a selective penetration zone is the establishment of a collective energy field of a defined spectrum profile directly superimposed over an energy pathway between two major dimensional zones. The primary purpose of such a project is usually to deny interdimensional travel access to unauthorized entities while allowing those so authorized. This selective penetration zone is also a common tactical strategy of Archangel Michael's angelic legions in closing off and confining imbalanced entities in a defined zone.

Another commonly assigned task-type is for a squadron to interface with the key energy vortex zones of a planetary system and to modify that planet's energy dynamics in accordance with command directives. Such action can help harmonize an imbalanced gridwork field, activate certain knowledge within individual and planetary consciousness, selectively infuse reprogramming Light- functions, and other related tasks.

A given squadron can also collectively form a gigantic interdimensional lens and Light-energy accelerator. Positioned over an appropriate energy zone that harmonizes with this particular task (in many cases, superimposed over a single- or multiple-sun system), the squadron is deployed over a defined multidimensional spectrum range in a geometric conformation so as to produce a desired magnifying and lensing action. Light-energy is drawn into the lens grid and focused, accelerated, and projected. The resulting powerful streams of energy are directed to a target zone, many times for reasons such as balancing, activating, or reprogramming of another sun system or galactic timepieces.

The angelic fleets perform a tremendous variety of interdimensional tasks of spiritual service. Additional visionary windows of insight at appropriate times in the evolutionary sequence will illuminate further angelic fleet functions.

A vision . . . upon entering a Temple Light-ship, the entity is greeted via a brief telethought code-sequence. No place for casual visitors, the entity then states the purpose of the visit in precise detail. It was seen as the visiting entity was being transported that this vehicle is the central threshold control for a vast multidimensional network of Light-vehicles, all linked to and directed by the Master Light-scientists of this Temple stationed within a rarefied celestial dimension.

Transferred to one of the many modules in this ship, the entity is instructed in the science of formulating thought-form templates containing complex energy codes to be used by other Light-vehicles in formulating energy fields, growing crystalline forms, relaying blueprints for Light-based technologies, and other applications. The Master demonstrates via holographic telethought transference the particular areas of the brain-mind in which various indexes of thought- forms are formulated and modified to specification. Further, the entity is shown how to combine the thought formulations from diverse areas of the brain- mind into a central focus area related to what earth entities would perceive as a conjunction of energies from key areas associated with the cerebral cortex in relationship to the pineal gland–third eye chakra complex. Once a unified thought-form is formulated, the entity is instructed how to project this coded energy field into a receptive crystalline matrix (more advanced levels do not require the use of a crystalline matrix in lieu of the creation of a pure energy template). The programming of the matrix is an intricate process of indexing code patterns in conjunction with the geometric axis structures of the crystalline substance. The Master shows the entity more varied and diverse geometric axis patterns in crystalline matrices to be utilized later in the learning sequence.

Next, the entity is transferred to a learning-communication module designed to assist the participant in linking consciousness with specifically desired sectors of abstract Thought-planes of the Universal Mind. This entity had decided to connect consciousness to Higher Intelligence sectors relating to advanced levels of numerology and its relationship to the geometry of energy fields. This learning-communication module is a crystalline sphere that appears to glow with dynamic color-sound-magnetic patterns that correspond to the energy status and learning intention of the participant. Suspended over the head is a pyramid of an alien crystal-metal alloy whose apex intersects with the Omega chakra. The crystalline sphere-unit intelligently links to the intention-patterns of the entity and sets up an amplified communication link-up to the desired vibratory level of the Universal Mind (and associated Light- beings). Within minutes the Intelligence code-patterns are absorbed and assimilated within consciousness according to the entity's spiral-cone of perception. More advanced entities may assimilate vast orders of Higher Intelligence in a single session (the earth equivalent of the learning cycles of thousands of lifetimes).

To help the entity gain greater comprehension of the functions of this Temple Light-ship, certain facets of its operation are shown. A multidimensional platform full of entities waiting to enact certain learning and work sequences on the Temple Light-ship is seen, each of these entities in rapt concentration preparing the consciousness to be as focused as possible for the privilege of partaking of the rarefied energies of this vehicle. A certain mathematical- geometrical sequence is seen whereby these awaiting entities are processed through various levels of the waiting platform and then through the inner workings of the ship. An effortlessly efficient exactitude marks the entire process.

It is further demonstrated that this primary Temple Light-ship coordinates the functioning of many other Light-vehicles existing on myriad other dimensional planes. The primary Light-ship acts as a central threshold through which access to unimaginably exalted abstract celestial dimensions is maintained and through which these realms project the blueprints of the Universal Mind pertaining to the Temple's entire energy network-domain.

The Master Light-scientists who operate the Light-ship work as a synergistic hierarchical unified consciousness. Though the ship is large and complex in all its multidimensional functionings, there are but 12 of these Masters coordinating the grand scope of responsibilities, each Master having specifically delineated areas of expertise and duties. These Masters send out numerous interdimensional projections of their own consciousnesses, each one appearing as an entity of similar image and likeness stationed on desired dimensional planes. For the most part these projections of the Master's multidimensional Light-bodies are stationed on other Light-vehicles connected to the primary Light-ship. In this way, unified interdimensional cooperative effort is manifested through a vast consciousness network.

The learning sequence being completed, the entity departs along an energy stream directed toward the next desired destination. While the entity is leaving, the attending Master sends a brief mathematical acknowledgment and blessing.

A vision . . . to enter the Temple of Light the visitor walks up the 12 crystalline steps leading to the columned, jeweled arch entryway. At the entrance a host gives greeting and assists in orienting the individual to the layout and appointed nature of the visit. After changing into a simple white robe in the delegated area, the seeker is taken to an individual waiting- preparation area. The person's personal crystal is placed in a holographic crystal computer console. The energy pattern status of the individual, recorded in the personal crystal, is registered into the computer. The data is then relayed through the Temple's master computer system, analyzed in conjunction with the consciousness of the Temple Master, and appropriate programming instructions are sent both to the personal crystal and to the Temple chamber that is most well suited to the unique requirements of the seeker.

After a time of inward focusing and relaxation in the preparation module, a host leads the individual through the silent, glowing circular hall that surrounds the large central chamber area. Numerous modules and Temple chambers are passed, each one incorporating different aspects of pyramid and form energy, crystal-magnetic-gravitational variables, sacred geometry, radionics, and other technical factors to create different unified energy fields designed for a host of specific functions. A Temple technician gives a brief greeting and assists the individual into the appropriate chamber. The recipient lays on a comfortable, warmly vibrating therapy table of a latexlike outer covering. Below this layer is a specially designed liquid crystal medium that can be energized by built-in sonic and crystalline energy panels linked to the chamber's computer system. Around the interior of the therapy table are grid arrays of pyramids designed to modulate, stabilize, and amplify the crystal and sonic energies. As the recipient begins to relax and become receptive, the technician sits in the chamber's control console. The master computer's instructions as to the exact energy patterns that are in the highest interest of the individual to assimilate have already been programmed into the chamber computer system. The technician prompts a clear crystalline panel from above the therapy table to a position a few feet over the reclining recipient. This panel is a long rectangular hollow crystalline device that is of the same circumference measurements as the therapy table. Inside the external crystalline layer is a highly active multicolor Light-plasma that sets up a powerful, precisely controlled energy field between the therapy table and the crystalline panel. A grid of pyramids covers the exterior surface of this panel, pointing down toward the individual and helping to formulate, focus, and direct energy flow between the panel and the therapy table. As the recipient comes to a state of receptivity, the technician begins the treatment. The therapy table vibrates powerfully yet soothingly with streams of programmed sonic-crystalline energies interacting with the liquid crystal medium. Simultaneously, the overhead crystalline panel crackles with multicolored lightninglike plasma patterns. These plasma patterns focalize at key areas of healing that the person requires and pulsate rhythmic crystalline patterns at rapid intervals. The recipient feels the powerful energy fields streaming and pulsing throughout the bioenergy system and at the same time experiences a state of calm, ecstatic detachment from the process.

After the treatment cycle has been completed, the recipient is then gradually guided through progressive stages of sensitive, integrative recrystallization of the bioenergetic energy patterns. Once this normalization procedure is complete, the individual is assisted to an integration module where a host helps make the person comfortable and then places the personal crystal in the module's computer console. For the time period required, the recipient is exposed to a series of soft glowing colors and corresponding celestial sonics as well as appropriate aromatics.

When sufficient integration has occurred, a host comes to the module and guides the person through the hallway.

The option is offered to sit within one of the central dome chamber's circular series of color pillars. The offer accepted, the seeker is assisted through a large arched entryway into an enormous circular chamber with an equally awesome clear crystal dome ceiling. Placed at harmonic intervals throughout the crystal dome are crystal templates of Light-pictographs, hieroglyphs of the Universal Language of Light. At the center of the chamber is a revolving metallic-pedestal crystal generator device. The individual can observe Light-energies streaming in through the domed ceiling and coalescing in this central energy device and being directed straight upward in a pillar of White Light. At intervals around the chamber toward the surrounding circumference, are 12 other pillars of Light, each of specific color vibration. The recipient is taken to the appropriate color pillar and left to commune with the Higher Realms of Light.

After a time, the seeker is led out of the central Temple chamber. The change of garments occurs, and a host escorts the individual back to the entrance way, bidding Light-blessings at departure and inviting the individual to come again when it is felt appropriate.

A vision . . . sitting within a large, smooth dome structure called the Group Ascension Chamber, thirty individuals settle back into reclining chairs as the lights dim and a deep sonic tone gradually fills the room. The participants feel the chairs being lowered into individual eight-foot half-circle pod areas until each person is visually isolated. Looking upward from the reclined position the dome structure overhead is illuminated with slowly changing deep hues of indigo; as the individuals start to relax, a sensation of contemplative peacefulness fills the chamber.

Each individual pod-unit has a computer system that measures the participant's energy patterns, from the physical to spiritual levels of being. A master computer system regulates all the pod computers so that precise crystalline- sonic-magnetic energy frequencies can be formulated in accordance with individual-specific needs and radiated within each pod. As these energy- patterns are emitted from harmonic intervals around the pod toward the individual, the chair itself also vibrates with these frequencies and focuses them into specific areas of the spinal-chakra system, the brain-mind centers, and along the arms and legs. In this way, each participant receives personalized energetic influences, even as the group as a whole experiences a master program designed to facilitate accelerated activation and alignment into the Light-body.

As the pod computers are set in motion, powerful sonic tones fill the dome with almost palpable tonal sequences. At first these sequences are long, deep, and intense, vibrating every cell and atom of the being. In synchronization with these tonal vibrations, the overhead dome fluctuates with subtle gradations of deep blue, indigo, and violet, each color hue having a correspondence to a specific tone. Positioned around the chamber are computer- linked devices that emit higher dimensional Light-energies that synchronize with the color-sound correlations, amplifying them manyfold.

Very gradually, the sonics start to pick up speed, seeming to go from interval to interval, octave to octave, at gradually increasing rates. As this occurs, the tones become progressively more refined and rarefied. And at the same time the corresponding colors shift with accelerated swiftness and start to intermesh with one another to greater and greater degrees, creating wonderfully complex and elegant intermixtures.

The participants begin to feel a synchronization of every level of their being with the unfolding Light-color-sound symphony. The external vibratory environment and the inner levels of each individual become more and more attuned and responsively interactive with one another. The external energetic symphony of the chamber becomes one with the internal symphony of consciousness.

Then as the single tones and simple chords move quickly into more and more complex chord structures and cosmic symphonics, intricately complex three- dimensional Light-mandalas start to revolve faster and faster, eventually becoming so compellingly powerful that every facet of consciousness quickens into higher octaves of awareness. The feeling of being on the verge of catapulting out of the dome and into the far reaches of the cosmos heightens.

At the appointed time in the Ascension Chamber progression, new elements are infused. Angelic choirs envelop the entire environmental matrix, filling it with celestial harmonics that synergistically amplify the chamber sonics manyfold into exquisitely rarefied octaves of interdimensional communion. The three-dimensional mandalas are shifted into multidimensional Light-mandalas as a Light-vehicle connects its energy field with that of the chamber, transforming the entire chamber into an ascension vehicle.

Consciousness soars as the individuals spiral into the higher dimensions, experiencing level after level of their own multidimensional Light-bodies. The individual self, spatially located in the pod, now appears as it truly is—one single Light-body projection amongst myriad other interdimensionally interconnected Light-bodies. From the perspective of the Higher Self the vast multidimensional network of Light-body differentiations is but one single Intelligence gridwork, all aspects of the whole deriving their image, genetic codes, and consciousness blueprint from this one unified focal point of Higher Intelligence—that aspect which is most directly interconnected with the Father.

The individuals experience these exalted states of consciousness for a cycle of time and then are slowly drawn back to bodily awareness. The Light-color- sound dynamics gradually reduce in intensity until the session ends as it started—with one single deep sonic tone pervading the space. The participants open their eyes to see a subtly shifting shade of deep indigo encompassing their visual field, reminding them of the consciousness expanses of the deep star and celestial fields from which they have just returned.

A vision . . . the cosmic timetables have unfolded to the last few units before the completion of the present evolutionary cycle—the Omega point quickens. The earth-plane is in great upheaval, reflective of even greater magnitudes of cosmic tumult. Thinking that a "New Age" had already arrived, the vast majority of the planetary population is caught unawares and civilizations are in massive panic. Wars, widespread crime, and desperate survival instincts break out simultaneously the world over. It appears that total collapse is both imminent and inevitable.

At this point in the cosmic timetable, divine intervention is permitted. Indeed, it is Law. Three calls to the planetary population are to be made. The first call is to the star-seed and celestial-seed, those entities who have borne the mission of Light unto the end times. These individuals will be caught up into the air into the awaiting Merkabah. The second call is the worldwide appearance of high frequency spectrum vehicles. These vehicles are not physically visible, being perceivable only by entities of a defined vibrational range of consciousness. Those who accept this call will be taken up into these vehicles. The third call is the physical appearance of the Higher Evolution in the form of extraterrestrial vehicles and higher Light-beings, materialized on the physical plane to bear witness to the masses concerning the divine plan. This is brief and all those who accept the Light will be taken up.

The earth then enters an electromagnetic null zone and is totally reprogrammed and prepared for its transference to another mansion world.

Vast legions of space vehicles, Light-vehicles, and Light-beings transport entities to their apportioned realms of universal schooling. A grand interdimensional engineering force transfers entire universes through appointed cosmic thresholds into virginal star and celestial fields, there to start afresh on an entirely new evolutionary cycle of growth. This multidimensional reprogramming-relocation sequence is a monumental astrophysical recrystallization process as all aspects of the celestial and cosmic realms are reset upon new orbits and timetables of soul development.

The earth, specifically, will ascend to a prepared cosmic paradise domain, as a crystal of the Heavens. The People of Light will inhabit this newborn planetary sphere as great Cities of Light are activated and the Government of Light is established with Christ and the Lords of Light enthroned on the seats of divine authority in the midst of the earth. Once again, as in eons past, divine Will is established on earth as it abides in the Heavens.

CHAPTER 21:
Vistas of Tomorrow

The forthcoming era of the New World brings with it visionary insights translated into a living reality. The paradigms of today unfold into the surpassing visions of a new tomorrow, some not yet even conceivable to the human mind. Reality is grander than we had imagined or dare to imagine. The glory of the future towers above present dreams, for the Kingdom of Light is an infinitely splendored house of many mansions. The challenge today is to remain open to an ever-accelerating quickening of individual and collective consciousness to an exponential upliftment of knowledge and spiritual abilities into inconceivable vistas now becoming conceivable, if we would only receive it. Let us remain receptive to ponder the limitless magnificence of Universal Intelligence as the gateways of the heavens are unveiled before our eyes in the years to come. . . .

Visions, seed-thoughts, catalysts, ideas, and imaginings—this is the fabric of which this chapter is woven. Herein are glimpses of the potential of a new tomorrow, offered as notions of what might be. . . .

> Sit down before a fact like a little child, and be prepared to give up every preconceived notion, follow humbly wherever and to whatever abyss Nature leads, or you shall learn nothing—T. H. Huxley

> We are told in the Li fragments of Light in China that bodhisattvas of Light came down, gathered their community together and with a cry of "Hurrah!" the whole community ascended into the sky.[1]

> The forces in light can be used individually by separating the colors of the light spectrum. Each color contains a separate force . . . and by mixing these forces in harmonic tunings, like tuning beautiful harmonics with certain tones at the keyboard, the desired force can be used as amplified harmonies. One color can be used for healing, both mentally and physically, by tuning the vibration for total harmony in the original body cells' vibration. Another color can be amplified in a second crystal, and at the same time be tuned together with a certain frequency from the cosmic radio signals to create a very powerful AC current by having the electrons change polarity in a magnetic field. Another color can be utilized for transforming polluted or salt water into pure drinking water by using this color's high bacteriological cleansing effect. Using a certain color together with a certain frequency from cosmic forces, persons whose physical and mental conditions are imbalanced can be transformed into complete harmony.[2]

Actually, light results from a change in frequency pattern. Emphasis is on the pattern-geometrical form. Light can be produced by using an arrangement of crystals which can amplify certain crystal patterns. This does not require solar energy or light. It can be done equally at night as well as day time. This can be done without wearing out the crystals. Light could be produced in a house with such an arrangement of crystals and turned on and off by a simple button that would arrange the crystals in the right pattern or disarrange the pattern.

Another type of crystal arrangement in a certain pattern would produce heat. This is an access to energy by altering the geometrical pattern of selected energy frequencies. Various crystalline forms can be used to key into patterns of frequencies and give specific types of results.[3]

The new bioengineers . . . will have the ability to use a laser-like light projection (e.g., by optical rotation) to demodulate a complete physical form into an energy form which can be projected to a vehicle or an environment in the lower heavens where it can be remodulated into the same physical form. This is called biolocation.[4]

In a temple chamber, a computer system analyzes a treatment recipient's full bioenergetic profile, noting in exacting detail the primary zones of imbalance. Then a multidimensional laser–sonic hologram is formulated in the precise bioenergetic conformation of balance for a specific area. The hologram is superimposed into the particular area, permeating its every cell and auric energy unit with a resonating blueprint of wholeness. The blueprint resonantly transfers its patterning into the bioenergetic region, effecting a complete balancing in a matter of minutes.

In the summer of 1927, two scientists, Kowsky and Frost, in Poland, noted specific anti-gravity properties of crystals. They were pursuing some discoveries in piezo-electricity made by Meissner of Telefunken, whereby it was found that crystals could lose their transparency and change their specific gravity at the same time. By the oscillations of radiotransmitters of several kilowatts, at protracted exposure, Kowsky and Frost managed to include an 800% volume increase to a clear crystal. . . . The small, lightened crystal carried the apparatus which oscillated it as well as a weight of 25 kilograms suspended from it, floating free at a height of about 2 meters above the floor of the laboratory.

To date, science has discovered the ability to impress only sound vibrations into recording discs, but soon methods will be found to impress the vibrations of color and perfume into records simultaneous with the impression of sound vibrations, with the result that correlated treatments will be possible.[5]

A sonic generator consisting of thin plates of iron immersed in a bath of mercury. Through the thin iron plates would be broadcast eight harmonically tuned sounds. . . . The combined sounds would cause a resonance within the iron and mercury which would be tuned to the frequency of the protons within the nucleus of all the atoms in the atomic structure of both metals. . . . An imbalance of electrical potential should be created between the two substances and a flow of current obtained. The amount of current would probably depend upon the intensity of the input of sound. Once the reaction was initiated it should be possible to tap out a small amount of power output to activate the sonic generator, thus creating a self-sustaining power source.[6]

Sometime in the future there will be a certain type of music written for the purpose of assisting mankind to resurrect memories of past lives from out of the subconscious mind. This will be highly individualized music, bearing, as it were, a tonal recapitulation of past events. The basis for this assertion is the fact that human life had its beginning in music, as did the manifested universe.[7]

One possible usage for a life-size quartz crystal skull might have been as a consciousness module system used during major healing processes. When an individual was to undergo "surgery" in a healing temple, before the procedures were enacted, the recipient's consciousness was painlessly stimulated to transfer into the crystal skull. Consciousness was in a semidream state, comfortable and at ease. The "surgery" process was enacted, and the bioenergetic system completely healed. Then from the crystal skull, consciousness was transferred back to the body.

The coming of the Hosts will be like twelve burning sun systems coming down to the face of the Earth. The New Jerusalem will be revealed as a Merkabah totality, a system which will coordinate all building blocks of crystal into one greater life force.[8]

Then came one of the seven angels who had the seven bowls full of the seven last plagues, and spoke to me, saying, "Come, I will show you the bride, the wife of the Lamb." And in the spirit he carried me away to a great, high mountain, and showed me the holy city Jerusalem coming down out of heaven from God, having the glory of God, its radiance, like a most rare jewel, like a jasper, clear as a crystal.—Revelations 21:9–11.

If you will look upwards and see directly above the thirty-three students that there are three crystal lenses—one each of red, blue, and yellow. These three crystal lenses have been focused so that the rays are directly attuned to the crystal block. The lenses are shaped as a parabolic convex. . . . These crystal lenses were created from the minds of higher and more advanced intellects or teachers, who are responsible for the addition of their intelligence—the information which resides in the lenses as intelligent energy. This intelligence will be added to the minds of the thirty-three individuals and the intelligence that resides in the crystal block will then be grown into the shape or form desired by the total mind energies of this group.[9]

Greater knowledge of the relationship between crystal forms and sound will be found in the future than we have yet discovered. . . . We will have musical instruments made of crystal forms which will bring in "the music of the spheres." This kind of music could be used for therapy. Platonic solids are the basic forms for studying the relationships of sound.[10]

In the ancient temples of Heliopolis, Egypt, the repository of Atlantean history, the force of colour was used, not only as an aid to worship, but also as a healing agent. These temples were oriented so that the Sun shown through in such a way that its light was broken up into its seven prismatic colours, and suffering ones were bathed in that special colour which they needed to restore them to health; allied with these colours were certain sounds and odors.[11]

I've seen the future. I've seen the way civilization will look. I don't know how far into the future I was looking, but I was seeing new approaches to architecture, new ways of dressing. I saw a great deal of crystal and crystal fabrics. And I saw a lot of crystal ornaments around the head.—Shirley MacLaine, *Ladies Home Journal*, August, 1985.

Within twelve circulatory star fields Man will ascend through a field of glory by means of a City of Light which aligns and perfects the courses of the illuminaries and Earth. Man will walk over time like a biosatellite moving over a crystalline staircase.[12]

The Earth is a natural generator system as a giant crystalline structure. By proper tuning and construction the UFO's are propelled and navigated on the Earth Grid. . . . Once you have oriented enough of the atoms in the substance to cross zero weight, the Earth will *push* the mass away—anti- gravity drive. . . . Piezo-electric crystal signal generators must have been atlantean levitation [devices], based on the same principle.—Richard L. Clark, Ph.D.

This invention relates to a structural expansion of the crystalline structure of a dielectric crystal which results in the alteration of the electrical characteristics of the dielectric, and produces internal and surface super conductive properties on the dielectric.

. . . Upon expansion, the optical transmission of a dielectric decreases, for example, from clear to opaque.

. . . In the reformed dielectric, there is one pole which is in the center of the mass.

. . . Thus, the deflection crystal becomes the first real time monitor of gravitational flux, space curvature, and time stress anomalies.—Patent Application of Jerry Glenn Gallimore (Case 2) "Deflection Crystal."

The curved ceilings were constructed of a crystal material for the purpose of separation of various wave train frequency spectrums. . . . Each ceiling is composed of a number of sections of parabolically curved parts. . . . By merely sitting in various parts of the room we can receive thought passages from any part of the universe. As our planet itself turns upon its axis like the earth, therefore each hour presents a different section of reception from the universe. We therefore regulate our periods of meditation in accordance with these time factors, something like receiving certain programs at certain hours of the day on your television.[13]

Enoch told me even greater experiments can be done with DNA-RNA when biophysicists interface two electromagnetic fields so as to create a neutral zone. These experiments will be a significant to future biophysics, in that they will demonstrate how the DNA-RNA can be adjusted to accomodate higher frequencies of light.[14]

I am sure that the fixed point that is termed absolute zero is nothing more than the gateway between physical matter as we know it and non-physical or anti-matter which exists in the universe. The temperature gradient decreases in our known universe to a fixed point, then increases once more up the harmonic scale within the negative universe, in a pendulum-type interaction.[15]

An exact replica of the human spine may be made of clear quartz, each vertebra being composed of crystal of a different axis orientation to match the metabolic functions associated with specific vertebrae. This crystal spine is positioned over a reclined individual's spine so that the two correspond to each other. Upon computer analysis of needed bioenergetic balances, appropriate laser and sonic frequencies are independently projected onto each vertebra of the crystal spine. Through resonant interaction with the recipient's spine, these codes are transferred, thereby effecting changes in any aspect of the bioenergetic functioning.

Atlantis. Their technology was based upon crystalline attunement of the matter and anti-matter cycles of the physical and non-physical worlds. By stepping up or slowing down the frequency of energy between the two cycles, they could cause a shift in time-space to occur.[16]

> It is a device which appears to be a long table, and underneath the table is placed and looks to you like—generators. These generators are producing pencil beams of light and from above the table are also generators which are intermediately spaced so that these beams of light can be projected downward. You will see from the top, protruding rods which go to a screen-like structure and when the patient is placed upon this table, the activation of these beams will place in attunement the entire physical structure of all of the kinds of atoms of which the body is made up. It will reproduce these cell structures on the screen. When the physician can see through to the cells which are misaligned and erratic, he can pinpoint these pencil beams and attune, through frequency manipulations, an out-of-phase wave structure which cancels out the negative effect that the cells are having on the surrounding areas.[17]

> The fact that laser action depends entirely on the harmonic affinity of energy and physical materials indicates to me some very exciting possibilities for the future. The next step in research is obviously to construct lasers in such a way that the coherent light beam can be selected to particular wave lengths which coincide with that of specific types of physical matter. If, as I presume, the atomic table of elements is a natural harmonic series, then it should be possible to tune a laser to be resonant at the exact wave length of any type of matter that we choose. If this is so then we would have at our disposal the perfect tool for cutting, or manipulating, any type of material. The atomic structure would not be physically torn apart during the cutting process, as it is under present methods. The atoms along the line of the cut would be actually disintegrated with a very small amount of effort, leaving a smooth, clean surface. . . . An added, and very important, advantage, would be that any other type of material or physical matter touched by the selective laser would remain unharmed, as the physical wave-form would be out of harmony with the beam.[18]

> This apparatus we can call the generator, a cosmic generator. We have replaced the old method of atomic fusion and the various rods which were placed to prevent explosion into the so-called pile; instead, we have a miniature sun. We have rods which have been built so that they protrude from the center of this apparatus which is circular and ball-shaped in form. These rods are laser rods; that is, they will take the energy from the central vortex and, through the prisms which are placed at either end of the rod, there is a demondulation of frequencies and a rectification so that the projection of this beam or ray of intense pure energy is of a lower frequency. . . . Placed at a certain central position in the city will be receivers which will have rods built of the same refractory material and which will receive its energy, and in turn, transform or demodulate the frequencies so that it can be acceptable for the various machinery used in the city for specific purposes in various manufacturing processes.[19]

Regarding the recent discovery of a type of crystal composed of icosahedral (twenty-sided) molecular building blocks:

> The discovery of a new type of crystal that violates some of the accepted rules has touched off an explosion of conjecture and research that may lead to the founding of a new branch of science. . . . As one investigator in the field of condensed-matter physics put it: "If this kind of crystal proves to have properties as peculiar as its structure, the stuff seems certain to find important uses."

. . . The apparent arrangement of the crystal still seems so paradoxical that theorists are forced to consider it in terms of six- dimensional hyperspace, rather than in the three-dimensional space of the everyday world.[20]

Next, I saw fiery wheels which covered the sky, and these wheels came to rest upon the earth. They became temples of Light as they opened to receive the righteous rescued from the convulsions of the earth. Others were taken beneath the oceans into gravity null "islands of light"; which were pyramids in the disguise of underwater mountains. In these island atmospheres, the remnant of the good seed of the earth were prepared for the cycle of the "reign of the Christ" upon the earth in union with his higher worlds of Light.[21]

I first beheld the "Rainbow of Jesus" appear in the sky to quicken the beloved of the Father from all nations. Then I saw what appeared to be a thousand chiliocosms of Light arcs fold into the Earth as the entirety of the solar system was lifted into a new covenant of the Father's Light. And I saw an elongated Crown of Light" glowing in the midst of the brilliant effulgence of Light. And the saints from the heavenly mansions met us in the lower heavens, and led us to meet with the Ascended Masters in the air who came as the "Government of Light"! And the children of Light raised their staffs and symbols of teaching authority and ruled as the wise in young bodies, for they had come as Masters into this layer of consciousness for the express purpose of humbling the false priesthoods of science.[22]

The world is now too dangerous for anything less than Utopia.—Buckminster Fuller

Notes

Chapter 1

1. J. J. Hurtak, *The Book of Knowledge: The Keys of Enoch* (Los Gatos, CA: Academy for Future Science, 1977), p. 26 (101:16) (hereafter cited as *The Keys of Enoch*).
2. Hurtak, *The Keys of Enoch*, p. 80 (108:49).
3. Ibid., p. 26 (101:11).
4. Bob Toben and Fred Alan Wolf, *Space-Time and Beyond* (New York: E. P. Dutton, 1982), p. 38.
5. Hurtak, *The Keys of Enoch*, p. xvi.
6. Ibid., p. 502 (315:104).
7. Ibid., p. 266 (210:32).
8. Ibid., p. 505 (315:34).
9. Ibid., p. 210 (204:34).
10. Ibid., p. 347 (301:57–58).
11. Ibid., p. 343–344 (301:24, 26, 30).
12. Ibid., p. 128 (113:61).

Chapter 2

1. Hurtak, *The Keys of Enoch*, p. 97.
2. Ibid., p. 189 (202:7).
3. Toben and Wolf, *Space-Time and Beyond*, p. 98.
4. Hurtak, *The Keys of Enoch*, p. 79 (108:46–47).
5. William Tiller, "A Lattice Model of Space," *Phoenix: New Directions in the Study of Man*, (Fall/Winter 1978), p. 30.
6. William Tiller, "Homeopathy: A Laboratory for Etheric Science?" (Stanford University), p. 28.
7. Itzhak Bentov, *Stalking the Wild Pendulum* (New York: E. P. Dutton, 1977), pp. 18–23.
8. Peter Russell, *The Global Brain* (Los Angeles: J. P. Tarcher, 1976), p. 195.

Chapter 3

1. Hurtak, *The Keys of Enoch*, p. 131 (114:1).
2. Christopher Hills, *Supersensonics*, (Boulder Creek, CA: University of the Trees Press, 1975), p. 409.
3. Virginia MacIvor and Sandra LaForest, *Vibrations: Healing Through Color, Homeopathy, and Radionics* (York Beach, ME: Samuel Weiser, Inc., 1979), p. 101.
4. Earlyne Chaney, *Revelations of Things to Come* (Upland, CA: Astara, Inc., 1982), p. 30.

5. Chaney, *Revelations of Things to Come*, p. 132.
6. Hurtak, *The Keys of Enoch*, p. 289–290 (213:22).
7. Ibid., p. 460 (312:64).
8. Ibid., p. 332 (217:20).
9. Ibid., p. 153 (116:43).
10. Ibid., p. 430 (309:50).
11. Ibid., p. 120 (112:96).

Chapter 5

1. Chaney, *Revelations of Things to Come*, p. 113.

Chapter 6

1. Method conceived by Ed Foerster.

Chapter 7

1. Rudolf Hauschka, *The Nature of Substance* (London: Rudolf Steiner Press, 1950), pp. 125–126.
2. Hurtak, *The Keys of Enoch*, p. 153 (116:41).
3. Hurtak, *The Keys of Enoch*, p. 79 (108:46).
4. Ibid., p. 221 (205:53).
5. Randall and Vicki Baer, *Windows of Light* (San Francisco: Harper & Row, 1984), p. 41.
6. Hurtak, *The Keys of Enoch*, p. 321 (216:5–6).
7. Elizabeth A. Wood, *Crystals and Light* (New York: Dover Publications, 1977), p. 10.
8. William A. Tiller, "The Positive and Negative Space/Time Frames as Conjugate Systems," in John White and Stanley Krippner, eds., *Future Science* (Garden City, NY: Anchor Books, 1977), p. 267.
9. *Gems, Stones, and Metals* (Virginia Beach, VA: Heritage Publications, 1977), p. 31.
10. Hurtak, *The Keys of Enoch*, p. 44 (105:15).
11. Edgar Cayce, *Edgar Cayce on Atlantis* (New York: Warner Books, 1968), p. 81.
12. Albert Roy Davis and Walter Rawls, *Magnetism and Its Effects on the Living System* (Hicksville, NY: Exposition Press, 1974), p. 124.
13. Victor Beasley, *Your Electro-Vibratory Body* (Boulder Creek, CA: University of the Trees Press, 1978), p. 38.
14. Dwight B. Davis, "Sports Biomechanics," *High Technology* (July 1984), p. 36.
15. Mirtala Bentov, "The Work of Itzhah Bentov" (Lecture delivered at Santa Fe, NM, April 26, 1984).
16. Robert Becker and Andrew Marino, *Electromagnetism and Life* (Albany, NY: State University of New York Press, 1982), p. 82.
17. Guy Murchie, *The Seven Mysteries of Life* (Boston: Houghton Mifflin, 1978), p. 453.
18. Guy Playfair and Scott Hill, *The Cycles of Heaven* (New York: St. Martin's Press, 1978), pp. 109–110.
19. Bill Schul and Ed Pettit, *The Secret Power of Pyramids* (Greenwich, CT: Fawcett Publications, 1975), pp. 102–103.

20. John Milewski, Ph.D., crystallographer, conversation with authors, Los Alamos, NM, May 22, 1984.
21. Murchie, *The Seven Mysteries of Life*, p. 641.
22. Corinne Helinne, *Music: The Keynote of Human Evolution* (La Cañada, CA: New Age Press, Inc., 1965), p. 18.
23. Murchie, *The Seven Mysteries of Life*, p. 639.
24. Jonathan Goldman, *Awakening the Lost Chord* (unpublished manuscript), p. 100.
25. David Tame, *The Secret Power of Music* (New York: Destiny Books, 1984), p. 217.
26. Viola Petitt Neal and Shafica Karagulla, *Through the Curtain* (Marina del Rey, CA: DeVorss & Co., 1983), p. 199.
27. Robert Lawlor, *Sacred Geometry* (New York: The Crossroad Publishing Co., 1982), p. 4.
28. Baer and Baer, *Windows of Light*, p. 138.
29. Ibid., p. 37.
30. Glenn Clark, *The Man Who Tapped the Secrets of the Universe* (Marina del Rey, CA: DeVorss & Co., 1955), p. 32.
31. Murchie, *The Seven Mysteries of Life*, p. 453.
32. Neal and Karagulla, *Through the Curtain*, pp. 171–172.
33. Ibid., p. 180.
34. Ronald Brown, *Lasers: Tools of Modern Technology* (Garden City, NY: Doubleday, 1968), pp. 178–179.
35. Ibid., p. 179.

Chapter 8

1. Richard Wolkomir, "Megachip," *Omni* (July 1984), p. 76.
2. Richard Wolkomir, "Much Ado Over Microns", *Omni* (December 1982), p. 58.
3. Barbara Burke, "The Mightiest Memory Yet," *Science Digest* (December 1983) p. 44.
4. Brother Philip, *Secret of the Andes* (San Rafael, CA: Leaves of Grass Press, 1976), p. 20.
5. Joseph Whitfield, *The Treasure of El Dorado* (Washington, DC: Occidental Press, 1977), p. 181.
6. Hurtak, *The Keys of Enoch*, p. 421.
7. Ibid., p. p. 421.
8. Richard Garvin, *The Crystal Skull* (New York: Pocket Books, 1973), p. 93.
9. Ibid., p. 125.
10. Tame, *The Secret Power of Music*, p. 217.
11. Charles Littlefield, *Man, Minerals, and Masters* (Albuquerque, NM: Sun Publishing Co., 1937), pp. xviii—xix.
12. White and Krippner, *Future Science*, p. 257.
13. Baer and Baer, *Windows of Light*, p. 55.
14. Derived from technique conceived by Frank Dorland.
15. Madeline Chinnici, "Direct Brain-Computer Interfacing," *Science Digest* (July 1984), p. 30.
16. G. Harry Stine, "The Bionic Brain," in Owen Davies, ed., *The Omni Book of Computers and Robots* (New York: Zebra Books, Kensington Publishing, 1981), pp. 41–42.

17. Ronald S. Miller, "An Interview with Marcel Vogel: The Healing Magic of Crystals," *Science of Mind* (August 1984), pp. 77–78.
18. "Crystal Bill" Kaunitz, "Crystal Consciousness" (Workshop given at Tyler, TX, March 17, 1982).
19. Hurtak, *The Keys of Enoch*, p. 153 (116:43).
20. Ibid., p. 421 (308:34–36).
21. Kathleen McAuliff "Biochip Revolution," in Owen Davies, ed., *The Omni Book of Computers and Robots* (New York: Zebra Books, Kensington Publishing, 1981), p. 89, 98.

Chapter 9

1. Hurtak, *The Keys of Enoch*, p. 210 (204:34).
2. Ibid., p. 128 (113:58).
3. Playfair and Hill, *Cycles of Heaven*, p. 317.
4. Tiller, "Homeopathy: A Laboratory for Etheric Science?", p. 22.
5. Playfair and Hill, *Cycles of Heaven*, p. 294.
6. White and Krippner, *Future Science*, p. 223.
7. Christopher Hills, *Nuclear Evolution* (Boulder Creek, CA: University of the Trees Press, 1975), p. 125.
8. Hurtak, *The Keys of Enoch*, p. 505 (315:134–136).
9. Ibid., p. 505 (315:139–140, 143).
10. Ibid., p. 429 (309:44).
11. Theodor Schwenk, *Sensitive Chaos* (New York: Schoecken Books, 1976), p. 65.
12. Robert N. Miller, "Methods of Detecting and Measuring Healing Energies," in White and Krippner, *Future Science*, p. 442.
13. Dr. Patrick and Gael Flanagan, "Innergy Crystal Water—Fountain of Youth?" Novato, CA: Flanagan Research, 1984), cassette tape.

Chapter 10

1. Hurtak, *The Keys of Enoch*, p. 454 (312:3).
2. Playfair and Hill, *Cycles of Heaven*, pp. 212–213.
3. Ashley Montagu, "The Skull as Architecture," *Science Digest* (February 1982) p. 38.
4. Matila Ghyka, *The Geometry of Art and Life* (New York: Dover Publications, Inc., 1977), p. 98.
5. Hurtak, *The Keys of Enoch*, p. 454 (312:3).
6. Ibid., p. 164 (117:69).
7. Ibid., pp. 512–513 (316:30–33).
8. Hills, *Nuclear Evolution*, p. 595.
9. Ibid., p. 127.
10. Ramtha, "Brain/Thought" (Oregon), cassette tape.
11. Linda Clark, *The Ancient Art of Color Therapy* (New York: Pocket Books, 1975), p. 35.
12. Hurtak, *The Keys of Enoch*, p. 469 (313:6).
13. Ibid., p. 101 (110:45).
14. Hills, *Nuclear Evolution*, p. 595.
15. Neal and Karagulla, *Through the Curtain*, pp. 86–87.
16. Hurtak, *The Keys of Enoch*, p. 444 (311:35).

17. Mellie Ulydert, *The Magic of Precious Stones* (Wellingborough, Northamptonshire, England: Turnstone Press, 1981), p. 53.

Chapter 11

1. Elisabeth Haich, *Initiation* (Garberville, CA: Seed Center, 1960), p. 229.
2. White and Krippner, *Future Science*, p. 192.
3. Lawlor, *Sacred Geometry* p. 11.
4. Ancient Mysteries Research Institute, *The Ancient Temples as Living Entities* (Ft. Wayne, IN: 1981), p. 38.
5. Neal and Karagulla, *Through the Curtain*, p. 175.
6. Ibid., p. 177.
7. Ibid., p. 170.

Chapter 12

1. Hurtak, *The Keys of Enoch*, p. 298 (314:30).
2. Ibid., p. 33 (104:5–6).
3. Ibid., p. 489 (314:95).
4. Cathie, *The Bridge to Infinity*, p. 52.
5. Haich, *Initiation*, p. 229.
6. Lawlor, *Sacred Geometry*, p. 11.
7. White and Krippner, *Future Science*, p. 192.
8. Hurtak, *The Keys of Enoch*, p. 33 (104:8).
9. Ibid., p. 499 (315:65).
10. Ibid., p. 74 (108:6).
11. Cathie, *The Bridge to Infinity*, pp. 54–55.
12. Bill Schul and Ed Pettit, *The Secret Power of Pyramids* (Greenwich, CT, Fawcett Publications, 1975), p. 133.
13. Hurtak, *The Keys of Enoch*, p. 74 (108:8).
14. Ibid., p. 33 (104:2).
15. Ibid., p. 232 (206:38).
16. Schul and Pettit, *The Secret Power of Pyramids*, p. 109.
17. Ibid., p. 110.
18. Ibid., p. 109.
19. Ibid., p. 10.

Chapter 13

1. MacIvor and LaForest, *Vibrations*, p. 38.
2. Benoytosh Bhattacharya, *Gem Therapy* (Calcutta, India: Firma KLM Private Limited, 1981), p. 5.
3. Ibid., p. 9.
4. Neal and Karagulla, *Through the Curtain*, p. 176–177.

Chapter 14

1. Hurtak, *The Keys of Enoch*, p. 321 (216:6–7).
2. Ibid., p. 134 (114:42).
3. John Michell, *The New View Over Atlantis* (San Francisco: Harper & Row, 1983), p. 93.
4. Ibid., p. 97.

5. Hurtak, *The Keys of Enoch*, p. 498–499 (315:61).
6. Ibid., pp. 132–133 (114:24).
7. Haich, *Initiation*, p. 229.
8. Lawlor, *Sacred Geometry*, p. 10.
9. Ibid., p. 11.
10. White and Krippner, *Future Science*, p. 192.
11. Rev. Dr. Frank Alper, *Exploring Atlantis, Volume I* (Phoenix, AZ: Arizona Metaphysical Society, 1982), Jan. 26, 1981–p. 3.
12. MacIvor and LaForest, *Vibrations*, pp. 104–105.
13. Hurtak, *The Keys of Enoch*, p. 109 (111:25).
14. Ghyka, *The Geometry of Art and Life*, p. 115.
15. Tarvis and Tuella, *The Master Symbol of the Solar Cross* (Durango, CO: Guardian Action Publications, 1984), pp. 5–7.
16. Lawlor, *Sacred Geometry*, pp. 33–34.
17. "Phi: The Sacred Formula," *The Coming Revolution* (Fall 1981).
18. Source: Edmund Scientific, 101 E. Gloucester Pike, Barrington, NJ 08007.

Chapter 15

1. Advertising literature, Bradford Institute Stress Research Center, P.O. Box 1766, Cape Coral, FL 33910.
2. Davies, *The Omni Book of Computers and Robots*, p. 383.
3. *Omni* (December 1985), p. 41.
4. Hurtak, *The Keys of Enoch*, p. 295 (214:3, 5, 6).
5. Davies, *The Omni Book of Computers and Robots*, p. 384.
6. Thea Alexander, *2150* A.D. (New York: Warner Books, 1976), p. 105.

Chapter 16

1. White and Krippner, *Future Science*, p. 390.
2. Ibid., p. 403.
3. Ibid., p. 371.
4. Tiller, "Homeopathy: A Laboratory for Etheric Science?" p. 31.
5. Bhattacharya, *Gem Therapy*, p. 9.

Chapter 17

1. Davis and Rawls, *Magnetism and Its Effects on the Living System*, p. 123.
2. Roland Hunt, *The Seven Keys to Color Healing* (New York: Harper & Row, 1971), p. 13.
3. Laurel Elizabeth Keyes, *Toning: The Creative Power of the Voice* (Marina del Rey, CA: DeVorss & Co., 1973), pp. 34–35.

Chapter 18

1. Christopher Hills, *Supersensonics*, p. 409.
2. Hurtak, *The Keys of Enoch*, p. 518 (316:93).
3. Wilhelm Pelikan, *The Secrets of Metals* (Spring Valley, NY: Anthroposophic Press, Inc., 1973), p. v.
4. Robert Becker and Gary Selden, *The Body Electric* (New York: William Morrow & Co., Inc., 1985), pp. 93–94.
5. Hills, *Nuclear Evolution*, p. 589.

6. "Beitrage" #24, 1966 through #29, 1968.
7. Hills, *Nuclear Evolution*, p. 586.
8. Murchie, *The Seven Mysteries of Life*, p. 454.
9. White and Krippner, *Future Science*, p. 237.
10. Pelikan, *The Secrets of Metals*, p.5–6.
11. Hills, *Nuclear Evolution*, p. 456.
12. Hurtak, *The Keys of Enoch*, p. 153 (116:43).
13. Ibid., p. 101 (110:39).
14. Ibid., p. 430 (309:50).
15. Ibid., p. 446 (311:54–56).
16. Ibid., p. 454 (312:3).
17. Ibid., p. 498 (315:58).
18. Ibid., p. 123 (113:7).
19. Beasley, *Your Electro-Vibratory Body*, p. 40.
20. White and Krippner, *Future Science*, p. 29.
21. Tiller, "Homeopathy: A Laboratory for Etheric Science?" p. 34.
22. Playfair and Hill, *Cycles of Heaven*, p. 292.
23. Ibid., p. 212.
24. Hurtak, *The Keys of Enoch*, p. 497–498 (315:46, 47, 54, 56).
25. J. B. Chapman and Edward Perry, *The Biochemic Handbook* (St. Louis, MO: Former Inc., Publishers, 1976), p. 1.
26. Littlefield, *Man, Minerals and Masters*, p. 123.
27. Ibid., pp. 120–121.
28. Becker and Seldon, *The Body Electric*, p. 119.
29. Hauschka, *The Nature of Substance*, p. 91.
30. Hills, *Nuclear Evolution*, p. 109.
31. Ibid., p. 114.
32. White and Krippner, *Future Science*, p. 235.
33. Schwenk, *Sensitive Chaos*, p. 93.
34. Ehrenfried Pfeiffer, *Sensitive Crystallization Processes* (Spring Valley, NY: Anthroposophic Press, 1936), p. 35.
35. White and Krippner, *Future Science*, p. 78.
36. Pelikan, *The Secrets of Metals*, p. vii.
37. Ibid., p. 42.
38. Murchie, *The Seven Mysteries of Life*, p. 453.
39. Chaney, *Revelations of Things to Come*,p. 107.
40. Ibid., pp. 131–132.
41. Hurtak, *The Keys of Enoch*, p. 591–192.
42. Buckminster Fuller, *Tetrascroll* (New York: St. Martin's Press, 1982), p. 52.
43. Playfair and Hill, *Cycles of Heaven*, pp. 293–294.
44. Murchie, *The Seven Mysteries of Life*, pp. 172–173.
45. Hurtak, *The Keys of Enoch*, p. 517 (316:90).
46. Ibid., pp.289–290 (213:22).
47. Chaney, *Revelations of Things to Come*, p. 150.
48. Ibid., p. 132.
49. Roland Hunt, *Fragrant and Radiant Healing Symphony* (Sussex, England: Academy of the Science of Man, 1949), pp. 74–75.
50. Hurtak, *The Keys of Enoch*, p. 101 (110:45).

Chapter 19

1. Source for moldavite tektite: Heaven and Earth, 196 Washington St., Gloucester, Mass. 01930.

Chapter 21

1. Hurtak, *The Keys of Enoch*, p. 115 (112:29).
2. Ruth Montgomery, *Threshold to Tomorrow* (New York: G. P. Putnam's Sons, 1982), pp. 130–131.
3. Neal and Karagulla, *Through the Curtain*, p. 215.
4. Hurtak, *The Keys of Enoch*, p. 203 (203:19–20).
5. Roland Hunt, *Fragrant and Radiant Healing Symphony*, p. 114.
6. Cathie, *The Bridge to Infinity*, p. 77.
7. Helinne, *Music: Keynote to Human Evolution*, p. 17.
8. Hurtak, *The Keys of Enoch*, p. 345 (301:38).
9. Ruth Norman, Vaughn Spaegel, and Thomas Miller, *Tesla Speaks*, Volume 1 (El Cajon, CA: Unarius Publications, 1973), pp. 120–121.
10. Neal and Karagulla, *Through the Curtain*, p. 137.
11. Hunt, *Fragrant and Radiant Symphony*, p. 17.
12. Hurtak, *The Keys of Enoch*, p. 425 (Key 309).
13. Ernest L. Norman, *Voice of Venus* (El Cajon, CA: Unarius Educational Foundation, 1956), pp. 65–66.
14. Hurtak, *The Keys of Enoch*, p. 197 (202:75–76).
15. Cathie, *The Bridge to Infinity*, p. 70.
16. Hurtak, *The Keys of Enoch*, p. 44 (105:15).
17. Norman, Spaegel, and Miller, *Tesla Speaks*, Volume 1, p. 202.
18. Cathie, *The Bridge to Infinity*, pp. 83–84.
19. Norman, Spaegel, and Miller, *Tesla Speaks*, Volume 1, pp. 84–85.
20. Malcolm W. Browne, "New Crystal Shatters Solid Dogmas," *The Dallas Morning News*, August 12, 1985.
21. Hurtak, *The Keys of Enoch*, p. 556 (319:124–125).
22. Ibid., p. 558 (319:149–151).

BIBLIOGRAPHY

Alexander, Thea. *2150* A.D. New York: Warner Books, 1976.

Alper, Rev. Dr. Frank. *Exploring Atlantis,* Vol. 1. Phoenix, AZ: Arizona Metaphysical Society, 1982.

Alper, Rev. Dr. Frank. *Exploring Atlantis,* Vol. 2. Phoenix, AZ: Arizona Metaphysical Society, 1982.

Arguelles, Jose and Miriam. *Mandala.* Berkeley and London: Shambhala, 1972.

Baer, Randall and Vicki. *Windows of Light: Quartz Crystals and Self-Transformation.* San Francisco: Harper & Row, 1984.

Baerlein, E. and A. L. G. Dower. *Healing with Radionics: The Science of Healing Energy.* Wellingborough, Northamptonshire, England: Thorson Publishers Limited, 1980.

Beasley, Victor R. *Your Electro-Vibratory Body.* Boulder Creek, CA: University of the Trees Press, 1978.

Becker, Robert, and Andrew Marino. *Electromagnetism and Life.* Albany, NY: State University of New York Press, 1982.

Becker, Robert and Gary Selden. *The Body Electric: Electromagnetism and the Foundation of Life.* New York: William Morrow and Co., Inc., 1985.

Bentov, Itzhak. *Stalking the Wild Pendulum: On the Mechanics of Consciousness.* New York: E. P. Dutton, 1977.

Bentov, Itzhak, with Mirtala Bentov. *A Cosmic Book: On the Mechanics of Creation.* New York: E. P. Dutton, 1982.

Bhattacharya, Benoytosh. *Gem Therapy.* Calcutta, India: Firma KLM Private Limited, 1981.

Birren, Faber. *Color Psychology and Color Therapy.* Secaucus, NJ: The Citadel Press, 1950.

Broad, William, and Nicholas Wade. *Betrayers of the Truth: Fraud and Deceit in the Halls of Science.* New York: Simon and Schuster, Inc., 1982.

Brother Phillip. *Secret of the Andes.* San Rafael, CA: Leaves of Grass Press, 1976.

Brown, Ronald. *Lasers: Tools of Modern Technology.* Garden City, NY: Doubleday, 1968.

Burr, Harold Saxton. *The Fields of Life.* New York: Ballantine Books, 1973.

Capra, Fritjof. *The Tao of Physics.* Boulder, CO: Shambhala Publications, 1975.

Cater, Joseph. *The Awesome Life Force: The Unifying Principles for All Physical and Occult Phenomena in the Universe.* Winter Haven, FL: Cadake Industries, 1984.

Cathie, Bruce. *The Bridge to Infinity: Harmonic 371299.* Aukland, New Zealand: Brookfield Press, 1983.

Cayce, Edgar, *Cayce on Atlantis.* New York: Warner Books, 1968.
Chaney, Earlyne. *Revelations of Things to Come.* Upland, CA: Astara, Inc., 1982.
Chapman, J. B. and Edward Perry. *The Biochemic Handbook.* St. Louis, MO: Formur, Inc., Publishers, 1976.
Charon, Jean. *The Unknown Spirit.* London: Coventure, Ltd., 1983.
Cheney, Margaret. *Tesla: Man Out of Time.* Englewood Cliffs, NJ: Prentice-Hall, Inc., 1981.
Clark, Linda. *The Ancient Art of Color Therapy.* New York: Pocket Books, 1975.
Clark, Linda, and Yvonne Martine. *Health, Youth and Beauty Through Color Breathing.* Millbrae, CA: Celestial Arts, 1976.
Cook, Theodore. *The Curves of Life.* New York: Dover Publications, Inc., 1979.
Cox, Bill, ed., *Pyramid Guide,* vols. 1–9. Santa Barbara, CA: Life Understanding Foundation, 1974–1979.
Critchlow, Keith. *Time Stands Still: New Light on Megalithic Science.* New York: St. Martin's Press, 1982.
Davies, Owen, ed. *The Omni Book of Computers and Robots.* New York: Zebra Books, Kensington Publishing, 1981.
Davies, Paul. *Superforce: The Search for a Grand Unified Theory of Nature.* New York: Simon and Schuster, 1984.
Davis, Albert Roy and Walter Rawls. *Magnetism and Its Effects on the Living System.* Hicksville, NY: Exposition Press, 1974.
Dumitrescu, I. F. *Electrographic Imaging in Medicine and Biology.* Suffolk, England: Neville Spearman, 1979.
Einstein, Albert. *Ideas and Opinions.* New York: Bonanza Books, 1954.
Evans, Christopher. *The Micro Millenium.* New York: Washington Square Press, 1979.
Flanagan, G. Pat. *Pyramid Power.* Marina del Rey, CA: DeVorss & Co., 1973.
Flanagan, G. Pat. *Beyond Pyramid Power.* Marina del Rey, CA: DeVorss & Co. 1975.
Flangan, G. Pat, ed. *Pyramid Power II: Scientific Evidence.* Tucson, AZ: Innergy Publications, 1981.
Fuller, Buckminster. *Ideas and Integrities.* New York: Collier Books, 1963.
Fuller, Buckminster. *Tetrascroll: Goldilocks and the Three Bears, A Cosmic Fairy Tale.* New York: St. Martin's Press, 1983.
Gale-Kumar, Kristina. *The Phoenix Returns: Aquarius Dawns, Liberation Begins.* Oahu, HI: Cardinal Enterprises, 1983.
Garvin, Richard. *The Crystal Skull.* New York; Pocket Books, 1973.
Ghyka, Matila. *The Geometry of Art and Life.* New York: Dover Publications, Inc., 1977.
Goldman, Jonathan. *Awakening the Lost Chord: Systems of Using Sound and Music for Healing.* Unpublished manuscript, 1984.
Green, Elmer and Alyce. *Beyond Biofeedback.* New York: Dell Publishing, 1977.
Guillen, Michael. *Bridges to Infinity: The Human Side of Mathematics.* Los Angeles: Jeremy P. Tarcher, Inc., 1983.
Haich, Elisabeth. *Initiation.* Garberville, CA: Seed Center, 1960.
Halpern, Steven, and Louis Savary. *Sound Health: The Music and Sounds That Make Us Whole.* San Francisco: Harper & Row. 1985.
Hamel, Peter Michael. *Through Music to the Self.* Boulder, CO: Shambhala Publications, Inc., 1978.

Hardy, Mary and Dean, and Kenneth Killick. *Pyramid Energy Explained.* Allegan, MI: Delta-K-Pyramid Products, 1979.

Hardy, Mary and Dean, and Kenneth and Marjorie Killick. *Pyramid Energy and the Second Coming.* Allegan, MI: Delta-K-Pyramid Products, 1981.

Hauschka, Rudolf. *The Nature of Substance.* London: Rudolf Steiner Press, 1950.

Hecht, Jeff, and Dick Teresi. *Laser: Supertool of the 1980's.* New York: Ticknor and Fields, 1982.

Helinne, Corinne. *Music: The Keynote of Human Evolution.* La Canada, CA: New Age Press, Inc., 1965.

Helinne, Corinne. *Color and Music in the New Age.* Los Angeles: New Age Press, Inc., 1979.

Herbert, Nick. *Quantum Reality: Beyond the New Physics.* Garden City, NY: Anchor Press/Doubleday, 1985.

Hills, Christopher. *Supersensonics: The Spiritual Physics of All Vibrations from Zero to Infinity.* Boulder Creek, CA: University of the Trees Press, 1975.

Hills, Christopher. *Nuclear Evolution: Discovery of the Rainbow Body.* Boulder Creek, CA: University of the Trees Press, 1977.

Holden, Alan, and Phylis Morrison. *Crystals and Crystal Growing.* Cambridge, MA: The MIT Press, 1982.

Hunt, Inez, and Wanetta Draper. *Lightning in His Hand: The Life Story of Nikola Tesla.* Hawthorne, CA: Omni Publications, 1964.

Hunt, Roland. *Fragrant and Radiant Healing Symphony.* Sussex, England: Academy of the Science of Man, 1949.

Hunt, Roland. *The Seven Keys to Color Healing.* New York: Harper & Row, 1971.

Hurlbut, Cornelius. *Minerals and Man.* New York: Random House, 1968.

Hurtak, J. J. *The Book of Knowledge: The Keys of Enoch.* Los Gatos, CA: Academy for Future Science, 1977.

Jenkins, Francis, and Harvey White. *Fundamentals of Optics.* New York: McGraw-Hill, 1976.

Kervan, Louis. *Biological Transmutations.* Brooklyn, NY: Swan House Publishing Co., 1972.

Keyes, Laurel Elizabeth. *Toning: The Creative Power of the Voice.* Marina del Rey, CA: DeVorss & Co., 1973.

Koestler, Arthur. *The Roots of Coincidence: An Excursion Into Parapsychology.* New York: Vintage Books, 1972.

Langham, Derald George. *Genesa.* Fallbrook, CA: Aero Publishers, Inc., 1969.

Lawlor, Robert. *Sacred Geometry: Philosophy and Practice.* New York: The Crossroad Publishing Co., 1982.

Leichtman, Robert. *Nikola Tesla Returns.* Columbus, OH: Ariel Press, 1980.

Lilly, John. *The Scientist.* New York: Bantam Books, 1978.

Lindisfarne Association. *Lindisfarne Letter: Homage to Pythagoras.* West Stockbridge, MA: Lindisfarne Press, 1982.

Littlefield, Charles W. *Man, Minerals and Masters.* Albuquerque, NM: Sun Publishing Co., 1937.

MacIvor, Virginia, and Sandra LaForest. *Vibrations: Healing Through Color, Homeopathy and Radionics.* York Beach, ME: Samuel Weiser, Inc., 1983.

Michell, John. *The New View Over Atlantis.* San Francisco: Harper & Row, 1983.

Mitchell, Edgar D. *Psychic Exploration: A Challenge for Science.* New York: G. P. Putnam's Sons, 1976.

Montgomery, Ruth. *Threshold to Tomorrow.* New York: G. P. Putnam's Sons, 1982.

Murchie, Guy. *The Seven Mysteries of Life.* Boston, Houghton Mifflin, 1978.

Neal, Viola Petitt, and Shafica Karagulla. *Through the Curtain.* Marina del Rey, CA: DeVorss & Company, 1983.

Nelson, DeeJay, and David H. Coville. *Life Force in the Great Pyramids.* Marina del Rey, CA: DeVorss & Co., 1977.

Norman, Ernest L. *The Voice of Venus.* El Cajon, CA: Unarius Educational Foundation, 1956.

Norman, Ruth E., Vaughn Spaegel, and Thomas Miller. *Tesla Speaks, Vol. 1.* El Cajon, CA: Unarius Publications, 1973.

Ornstein, Robert E. *The Psychology of Consciousness.* New York: Penguin Books, 1972.

Ostrander, Sheila, and Lynn Schroeder. *Psychic Discoveries Behind the Iron Curtain.* New York: Bantam Books, 1970.

Ostrander, Sheila, and Lynn Schroeder. *Superlearning.* New York: Dell Publishing Co., 1979.

Ott, John. *Health and Light.* New York: Pocket Books, 1973.

Ott, John. *Light, Radiation, and You.* Old Greenwich, CT: Devin-Adair, 1982.

Pagels, Heinz R. *The Cosmic Code: Quantum Physics and the Language of Nature.* New York: Bantam Books, 1982.

Pelikan, Wilhelm. *The Secrets of Metals.* Spring Valley, NY: Anthroposophic Press, Inc., 1973.

Pellegrino, Ronald. *The Electronic Arts of Sound and Light.* New York: Van Nostrand Reinhold Company, 1983.

Pennick, Nigel. *Sacred Geometry.* San Francisco: Harper & Row, 1980.

Petschek, Joyce. *The Silver Bird: A Tale for Those Who Dream.* Millbrae, CA: Celestial Arts, 1981.

Pfeiffer, Ehrenfried. *Sensitive Crystallization Processes: A Demonstration of the Formative Forces in the Blood.* Spring Valley, NY: Anthroposophic Press, 1936.

Playfair, Guy L., and Scott Hill. *The Cycles of Heaven: Cosmic Forces and What They Are Doing To You.* New York: St. Martin's Press, 1978.

Raleigh, A. S. *Hermetic Science of Motion and Number.* Marina del Rey, CA: DeVorss & Co., 1924.

Raleigh, A. S. *Occult Geometry.* Marina del Rey, CA: DeVorss & Co., 1932.

Reichenbach, Baron Karl von. *The Mysterious Odic Force.* New York: Samuel Weiser, Inc., 1977.

Russell, Peter. *The Global Brain: Speculations on the Evolutionary Leap to Planetary Consciousness.* Los Angeles: J. P. Tarcher, Inc., 1983.

Schmid, Alfred. *The Marvel of Light: An Excursus.* London: East-West Publications, 1984.

Schul, Bill, and Ed Pettit. *The Secret Power of Pyramids.* Greenwich, CT: Fawcett Publications, 1975.

Schwaller de Lubicz, R. A. *The Temple in Man: Sacred Architecture and the Perfect Man.*

Schwenk, Theodor. *Sensitive Chaos: The Creation of Flowing Forms in Water and Air.* New York: Schocken Books, 1976.

Sheldrake, Rupert. *A New Science of Life: The Hypothesis of Formative Causation.* Los Angeles: J. P. Tarcher, Inc. 1981

Sirotin, Yu. L., and M. P. Shaskolskaya. *Fundamentals of Crystal Physics.* Moscow: Mir Publishers, 1982.

Spangler, David. *Explorations: Emerging Aspects of the New Culture.* The Park, Forres, Scotland: Findhorn Publications, 1980.

Stine, G. Harry. *The Silicon Gods.* New York: Dell Publishing Co., 1984.

Sutton, Christine. *The Particle Connection.* New York: Simon and Schuster, 1984.

Raphael. *The Starseed Transmissions.* Kansas, MO: Uni-Sun, 1982.

Talbot, Michael. *Mysticism and the New Physics.* New York: Bantam Books, 1981.

Tame, David. *The Secret Power of Music.* New York: Destiny Books, 1984.

Tansley, David. *Radionics: Science or Magic?* Essex, England: The C. W. Daniel Company Limited, 1982.

Tarvis and Tuella. *The Master Symbol of the Solar Cross.* Durango, CO: Guardian Action Publications, 1984.

Thompson, D'Arcy Wentworth. *On Growth and Form.* Cambridge, England: Cambridge University Press, 1961.

Timms, Moira. *Prophecies and Predictions: Everyone's Guide to the Coming World Changes.* Santa Cruz, CA: Unity Press, 1980.

Toben, Bob, and Fred Alan Wolf. *Space-Time and Beyond.* New York: E. P. Dutton, Inc., 1982.

Tompkins, Peter, and Christopher Bird. *The Secret Life of Plants.* New York: Avon Books, 1973.

Ulydert, Mellie. *The Magic of Precious Stones.* Wellingborough, Northamptonshire, England: Turnstone Press, 1981.

White, John, and Stanley Krippner, eds. *Future Science: Life Energies and the Physics of Paranormal Phenomena.* Garden City, NY: Anchor Books, 1977.

Whitfield, Joseph. *The Treasure of El Dorado.* Washington DC: Occidental Press, 1977.

Wilber, Ken, ed. *The Holographic Paradigm and Other Paradoxes.* Boulder, CO: Shambhala Publications, Inc., 1982.

Wilber, Ken, ed. *Quantum Questions: Mystical Writings of the World's Greatest Physicists.* Boulder, CO: Shambhala Publications, Inc., 1984.

Wood, Elizabeth A. *Crystals and Light: An Introduction to Optical Crystallography.* New York: Dover Publications, Inc., 1977.

Zukav, Gary. *The Dancing Wu Li Masters: An Overview of the New Physics.* New York: William Morrow and Company, Inc., 1979.

ABOUT THE AUTHORS

Randall and Vicki Baer are a husband-and-wife team dedicated to developing innovative pathways for the integration of spiritual wisdom and knowledge with holistic self-transformation modalities and sacred science. They are the co-authors of the book *Windows of Light: Quartz Crystals and Self-Transformation* (Harper & Row, 1984), an extensive exploration of the role and function of quartz crystals as tools for healing, self-transformation, and Light-based technologies. In addition, they are codirectors of the Starcrest Academy of Interdimensional Law and Science, a project devoted to the reawakening of the higher knowledge of the Scriptures of Light and activation of new Light-based tools, techniques, and technologies in preparation for the New World ascension process.

Randall Baer is both a naturopathic doctor and sacred scientist. A widely travelled student and teacher, he has participated in the programs of many learning centers in the United States and England, gaining degrees and certifications in a broad range of disciplines related to holistic health and spiritual studies. Among others, these include a B.A. in religious studies from Carleton College and an N.D. from Brantridge Forest School in Sussex, England. Randall Baer is a nationally known speaker, noted for his articulate knowledge and innovative concepts. His specialty areas include teaching advanced educational and professional training programs in interdimensional science and crystals, research and development of crystal-based Light-tools and Light-technologies, and designing unified energy fields for personal and professional applications through the integrated use of diverse energy modalities, including crystals, magnetics, sonics, chromatics, lumia, radionics, form energy, sacred geometry, pyramidology, lasers, and others.

Vicki Vittitow Baer has been a seed-catalyst channel for many aspects of the Spiritual Hierarchy of Light for more than a decade. During this time she has been deeply involved in the rebirth of the Scriptures of Light and interdimensional science. As codirector of the Starcrest Academy, her teaching and ministerial focus is upon divine Law and the gifts of the Holy Spirit as foundational elements toward the catalyzation of a new era of consciousness transformation.

Based in Los Alamos, New Mexico since 1982, the Baers are permanently relocating to the Hot Springs, Arkansas area in the summer of 1987.

For further information concerning the authors' activities and their newsletter, send a self-addressed, stamped, business-size envelope to:

Randall and Vicki Baer
P.O. Box 1339
Los Alamos, NM 87544